TH

RICHARD STRAUSS

AND

HUGO VON HOFMANNSTHAL

Richard Strauss and Hugo von Hofmannsthal at Garmisch

THE CORRESPONDENCE

BETWEEN

RICHARD STRAUSS

AND

HUGO von HOFMANNSTHAL

TRANSLATED BY

HANNS HAMMELMANN AND

EWALD OSERS

INTRODUCTION BY

EDWARD SACKVILLE-WEST

CAMBRIDGE UNIVERSITY PRESS

CAMBRIDGE

LONDON   NEW YORK   NEW ROCHELLE

MELBOURNE   SYDNEY

Published by the Press Syndicate of the University of Cambridge
The Pitt Building, Trumpington Street, Cambridge CB2 1RP
32 East 57th Street, New York, NY 10022, USA
296 Beaconsfield Parade, Middle Park, Melbourne 3206, Australia

Complete edition originally published in German as
Richard Strauss und Hugo von Hofmannsthal: Briefwechsel
by Atlantis Verlag A.G., Zürich, 1952
Edited by Franz and Alice Strauss. Arranged by Willi Schuh
Copyright 1952 Atlantis Verlag A.G., Zürich

First published in English by William Collins 1961
© 1961 in English translation, William Collins Sons and Co. Ltd, London
First published by the Cambridge University Press 1980

First printed in Great Britain at the Curwen Press, Plaistow, London E. 13
Reprinted in Great Britain at the University Press, Cambridge

British Library Cataloguing in Publication Data
Strauss, Richard
The correspondence between Richard
Strauss and Hugo von Hofmannsthal.
1. Strauss, Richard
2. Hofmannsthal, Hugo von – Correspondence
3. Composers – Germany – Correspondence
4. Authors, Austrian – 20th century –
Correspondence
I. Title   II. Hofmannsthal, Hugo von
780'.92'4   ML410.S93   80-40072

ISBN 0 521 23476 X hard covers
ISBN 0 521 29911 X paperback

CONTENTS

ILLUSTRATIONS

TRANSLATORS' FOREWORD

FOR this English edition of the Strauss-Hofmannsthal correspondence the translation has been made from the German text published by Atlantis Verlag, Zurich, in 1955 (second complete edition, edited by Franz and Alice Strauss with the assistance of Dr. Willy Schuh). Certain textual errors and misdatings which have since come to light have been corrected, but for a number of reasons, principally of time and money, it was found impossible to check the entire text against the original letters. There remain, as in the German text, a number of excisions, the more substantial of which are indicated by dots.

For the purposes of this edition the Strauss letters have been translated by Ewald Osers and Hofmannsthal's letters by Hanns A. Hammelmann.

★　　★　　★

The unique interest and value of this correspondence lies in the fact that it accompanies, step by step over a period of nearly twenty-five years, the making of six operas which have become classics of the operatic stage: it leads us into the 'workshop' where the composer and the poet endeavoured to forge works of art from heterogeneous material. To be able to follow the process of creation with its shifts of aim and emphasis, and to possess, so to speak, a running commentary by these two great artists on their own work, is of most immediate practical significance to all concerned with the performance of the Strauss-Hofmannsthal operas, to producers, artists, musicians and audiences alike. The problems and possibilities of collaboration between poet and composer, of fusion between word and music, have rarely, if ever, been discussed with such serious and searching intensity as they are in these letters, and much of what is said here, in the discussion of specific points, has wider application to all collaboration between two artists.

It is this wider aspect which gives the whole correspondence its remarkable human interest; it follows, over the years, the ups and downs of an important and in many ways difficult relationship between two very different men, through situations which have frequently an almost dramatic quality. In background, personality and inclination, Strauss and Hofmannsthal were poles apart; what brought and kept them together, despite everything, was their common purpose and their respect for each other as artists in different spheres.

It seemed to us essential that this contrast of personalities, which expresses itself in many ways and is reflected in the manner and style of the letters, should be fully preserved in the translation. The most promising way of achieving this end appeared to be for each of us to handle one side of the correspondence. Of the two men, Strauss was undoubtedly the more robust and impulsive: in the translation of the Strauss letters an attempt was made therefore to convey something of the composer's rough-and-ready approach, his careless phrasing which often leads him to plump for the first word that happens to come into his mind, his condensed telegraphic style, his hurried abbreviations, and, above all, his directness. Hofmannsthal was a very different letter writer: invariably highly conscious of his position as poet (and indeed his responsibility as he saw it), he tended to write elaborately, often with over-elaboration, and at times in a manner both stylized and laborious. In many of Hofmannsthal's letters every word seems carefully weighed, so as not to give away too much; but whereas in his published writings (which are far easier to translate) the poet was careful to simplify his sentences and to render them as lucid and concrete as possible, the absence of such revision makes some of the letters rather difficult reading in the original. It seemed desirable to preserve, as far as possible, his inversions, his circumlocutions and even, though only where this appeared to be of significance, his long, breathless sentences. An attempt was made to strike a fair balance between readability and Hofmannsthal's characteristic tone, and to resist the temptation, however great at times, to 'improve' on the original by a more straight-forward rendering.

We are of course aware that success in such an attempt as ours can only be relative. We should like to acknowledge here our debt to Michael Rose who has read the proofs and has given us the benefit of his advice on countless points, and to Harold Rosenthal for his work on the index.

H.A.H.
E.O.

EDITORS' PREFACE

From the introductory remarks to the (German)

complete edition of 1952

THE reasons which led Richard Strauss, in 1925, to propose to Hugo von Hofmannsthal the publication of their correspondence were summarized by the poet in a letter dated 4 May of that year: 'To make evident, on the one hand, the seriousness of our joint labours; to avail ourselves, on the other, of the casual commentary provided by the letters to remedy the lack of understanding still shown for some of our works. And finally to kindle that response which, among Germans, often has to be provoked by means other than the direct ones.' These aims, as well as deference to certain extrinsic considerations both factual and personal, dictated the manner in which the correspondence was first presented to the public.[1] Hofmannsthal and Strauss—who had been brought together by 'something higher than mere chance'—were still in the midst of their artistic collaboration. The letters they decided to publish represented a selection which was, moreover, limited at Hofmannsthal's suggestion to the period from 1907 to 1918. Both agreed that everything was to be expunged which could have 'served as ammunition' in the hands of spiteful critics or might have provided 'fuel for fresh misunderstanding'. Numerous passages, mostly of a personal nature, were deleted, names of individuals omitted or rendered unidentifiable; harsh expressions of opinion were toned down and so forth, as required by the particular circumstances, of the case, that is the publication of letters exchanged between two artists still living and exposed to the full blaze of publicity.

These considerations, still imperative a quarter of a century ago, could almost without exception be disregarded in the preparation of the present complete edition[2] which was undertaken at the express request of Richard Strauss and begun while he was still alive. Our purpose now

[1] *Richard Strauss, Briefwechsel mit Hugo von Hofmannsthal.* Herausgegeben von Dr. Franz Strauss: Berlin 1925. English translation by Paul England, London 1928.

[2] *Richard Strauss und Hugo von Hofmannsthal: Briefwechsel. Gesamtausgabe.* Herausgegeben von Franz und Alice Strauss. Bearbeitet von Willi Schuh. Zürich, 1952.

has been to present the full picture of this unique collaboration with all its vicissitudes, all the happy and the difficult phases through which it passed in the course of more than twenty years.

Hofmannsthal's letters have been preserved very nearly in their entirety, but there are unfortunate gaps on the Strauss side of the correspondence which explains the numerical preponderance of the poet's letters over those of the composer. Frau von Hofmannsthal, who has kindly placed at our disposal the Strauss letters in her possession, was unfortunately unable to discover the missing letters which must therefore be regarded as irretrievably lost.[1]

From this complete edition we have had to exclude, in addition to a few wholly irrelevant communications, all references to business matters, and a small number of other passages whose omission is in most cases due to Frau von Hofmannsthal's desire to respect the feelings of living persons. All these excisions are indicated by dots in brackets. Certain names given in full in the original letters have been replaced by initials only.

The task of preparing the correspondence for publication was seriously complicated by the fact that Hofmannsthal's handwriting is often extremely difficult to decipher and that a very large proportion of his letters carry only incomplete date-lines or none at all. The problem of establishing a reliable text can on the whole be regarded as solved, but some of the dates given remain doubtful. Since, unfortunately, the envelopes are no longer in existence, only the dates of a few postcards could be ascertained from the postmarks; in all other cases they had to be reconstructed from internal evidence which is frequently scanty. When Hofmannsthal went through the correspondence in 1925, he attempted to date a considerable number of the letters; numerous mistakes, alas, crept in on this occasion, and as a result the letters concerned appeared in the wrong order in the first (German) edition (sometimes misplaced by several years). In the present complete edition the sequence has now been corrected and rearranged; the dates established by the editor are added in brackets.

The fact that fairly numerous passages were slightly revised by Hofmannsthal for publication in the first edition presented another

---

[1] Since the first publication of the complete correspondence in 1952 altogether nine new letters (seven of Hofmannsthal's and two from Strauss) have come to light from various sources; they are incorporated in the second (German) complete edition, Zürich, 1955.

problem for the editor. Wherever this revision involved a change or attenuation of meaning, or the substitution of German expressions for words of foreign origin and suchlike, the original version has been restored in the present complete edition. The punctuation of Hofmannsthal's letters is often incomplete, hasty or capricious, particularly in the wholly arbitrary alternation between commas and dashes; cautious adjustment was required to ensure an unambiguous and readable text, but definite idiosyncrasies have been carefully preserved. For the sake of uniform appearance, the purely formal part of each letter has been standardized; thus the full signature of the writer is given, even where (especially on postcards) it is indicated by initials only in the original.

FRANZ AND ALICE STRAUSS

WILLI SCHUH

Garmisch and Zürich, October 1951

Hugo von Hofmannsthal at the age of thirty-two

Richard Strauss a few months before his death

INTRODUCTION

IT IS unusual for a poet of genius not to have some element of rebellion in him, at least when he is young. The hostility need not take a political form: it may concern only the kind of art prevalent at the time; but some impatience, some tendency to collide, there probably will be, unless the poet grow up in perfect harmony with his surroundings—in which case he is unlikely to become a real poet at all, since poetry is harmony born of discord. There would seem to have been very little discord in the formative years of Hugo von Hofmannsthal, who was born in Vienna in 1874 and published his first poems, with considerable success, when he was only seventeen. There is a dangerous perfection about these wistful poems and the series of brief verse dramas that followed them. They are the work, not of a man bursting with some 'message', but of a youth who has already had leisure to recollect in tranquillity, and who finds life agreeable enough to be able to face, not perhaps its tragedies, but its ineluctable sadness. Such poetry, when written by a young man, is often a flash in the pan, because there is no original drive behind it. But Hofmannsthal went quietly on, feeling his way forward in a series of Knight's moves, from verse to prose and back again, until he settled down into his career as a dramatist with the Oedipus plays, with *Elektra* and *Der Abenteurer und die Sängerin*, by which time Richard Strauss had planted himself determinedly in the Knight's path.

Good librettists have never been common at any period. The reason, I suppose, is that poets who take themselves seriously tend to regard the job as beneath them—a form, as it were, of domestic service. And of course it is true that the writer of an opera text must be prepared to give the composer precisely what he wants. But this submission does not rule out distinction of style: librettos are not necessarily worse literature than independent plays—they are merely different in form, texture and diction; and it is not a paradox to assert that it is harder to write a good —a really expert—libretto than a competent play. This remark was indeed made by Hofmannsthal to Strauss, and no doubt he intended it as a retort to those who deplored the fact that he had taken to spending so much time writing librettos rather than poetry and plays. There is no evidence that this choice involved sacrificing a poetic gift which might otherwise have been turned to better account. In the curious and moving *Letter of Lord Chandos to Francis Bacon* Hofmannsthal shows the natural bent of his mind in youth towards the all-embracing work of art, of which Wagnerian opera is the most highly evolved form. The drama based on E. T. A. Hoffmann's story, *The Mines of Falun*, the first act of which dates from Hofmannsthal's early years, could, with a little cutting, be set straight to music. His romantic imagination, which ranged easily from baroque pastiche to oriental fantasy; the regal simplicity of his images; the classical rhythm and euphony of his verse: all these bespeak the born librettist.

In general it might perhaps be said that the librettist must be a decent poet, but had better not be too good a one, for his task is an exercise in humility, and first-class poets are not usually remarkable for that virtue. In the last resort it is a matter of temperament. The unmusical Maeterlinck, for instance, wrote one of the best librettos in existence—*Pelléas et Mélisande*—without being aware that he was doing so; whereas the elaborate and self-conscious Gabriele d'Annunzio, who was always trying to gate-crash the operatic world, would have made a poor librettist, and those of his plays which have been set to music have not (with the possible exception of Pizzetti's *Fedra*) made very good operas. Usually, the most expert purveyors of operatic texts—men like Scribe, Meilhac, Halévy, and Louis Gallet—were content to write any kind of text for anybody who happened to want one. The more distinguished partnerships are fewer: Mozart and Da Ponte; Verdi and Boito; Puccini and the Giacosa-Illica combination; Gilbert and Sullivan; Bruneau and Zola; last, and in many ways the most fruitful of all, Strauss and Hofmannsthal.

Like many of the happiest conjunctions in life, this one began quite casually—as will be clear from a perusal of the earliest letters in this volume. But Strauss was in his way an exceedingly clever man, and once he had seen a performance of Hofmannsthal's play, *Elektra*, he realized immediately that here was the librettist he was looking for. Thus he ends a letter (11th March 1906) on the subject of *Elektra* with the following significant passage: 'I would ask you urgently to give me first refusal with anything composable that you write. Your manner has so much in common with mine; we were born for one another and are certain to do fine things together if you remain faithful to me. Have you got an entertaining renaissance subject for me? A really wild Cesare Borgia or Savonarola would be the answer to my prayers.'

Maybe it would have been, but Hofmannsthal was no Scribe: he had his own brand of integrity, a finer taste than Strauss's, and he passed over Cesare Borgia and Savonarola in silence—just as, many years later, he greeted with derisive laughter the composer's suggestion that he should concoct a libretto about the Congress of Vienna in the style of Sardou's famous melodrama, *Diplomacy*. Hofmannsthal was much too intelligent—and, where music was concerned, too modest—not to defer to Strauss's judgement in all matters affecting the dramatic composition of a given text; but he rightly mistrusted the composer's taste in literature and the visual arts, and to the end of their partnership he reserved the right to dictate the subjects of the operas, and to have the principal say in the matter of scenery and costumes. This was all to the good, on the whole, though on occasion—notably in *Josephslegende, Die Frau ohne Schatten* and to a lesser extent in *Die Ägyptische Helena*—the poet, in his enthusiasm for his own vision, expected of Strauss some kind of music that he was temperamentally unfitted to write.

It is clear from the whole correspondence that the partnership between these two men of genius was not altogether an easy one: they were by temperament too dissimilar, and their outlooks—their social worlds even—too incompatible, for either to understand the other *à demi-mot*. Strauss seems to have been a jolly, extravert, not over-sensitive character, whose genius depended to some extent on enjoying the good things of this world—a description that hardly fits Hofmannsthal secure in the spartan tranquillity of his tiny baroque palace at Rodaun, on the outskirts of Vienna. For all the evidence goes to show that the poet was an exceedingly complex, tortuous character—nervous, fastidious, evasive and irritable; and there was an element in him of contrariness which brought out an obstinate resistance to pressing demands. In a letter written by him in July 1918, during the creation of *Die Frau ohne Schatten*, there occurs this most revealing paragraph:

'Rest assured of my lasting goodwill in all our future joint concerns. Your personality, such as you are with all your energy—and still more your ideal personality as I distil it for myself from your music—has won my genuine friendship, that is all I can say to you, for that is the best I have to give. I am a much more bizarre kind of person than you can suspect; what you know is only a small part of me, the surface; the factors which govern me you cannot see. And so I am grateful to you for not prodding me, I am very grateful to you for that. Please do not do it, even indirectly, and do not remind me of things, for then I shall remind myself and as a result admonish myself. So bizarre is my constitution in such matters that, having once spoken to you of a certain possibility (a subject taken from late classical antiquity), your repeated allusions to this idea, your taking it up, your acquaintance with it, made the whole period distasteful to me and have driven it out of my thoughts and dreams, perhaps for good. So please take me as I am, and take me kindly.'

Now, one of the most striking features of the whole long correspondence is the tact shown by Strauss in his dealings with his librettist. He was a most good-natured man and, by and large, he did take Hofmannsthal as he was.

This cannot always have been easy to do. At first all went swimmingly, for the dropping of a Semiramis project (of which Strauss 'reminded' the poet too frequently) made way for the creation of *Der Rosenkavalier*. This was to prove the greatest and most lasting popular success its authors ever achieved, but—perhaps for this very reason—they came to think less well of it in later years. To judge by the letters they exchanged at the time, the composition, both of text and of music, went much more easily and smoothly than that of the later operas—especially *Ariadne auf Naxos*, of which the various versions gave both of them enormous trouble. Considering the relative slightness and simplicity of the work in its final form, it may seem surprising what a fuss they made over it. But we may be less surprised if we consider that *Ariadne* is the most nearly perfect work of art Strauss and Hofmannsthal achieved, and that the little opera must have taxed the ingenuity and imagination of its creators to their utmost. It was here too that a fundamental difference between the minds of the two men first came to light. Hofmannsthal had at all periods of his career a sense of the numinous (to put it no more strongly), and enjoyed toying with mystical ideas. Strauss, on the other hand, had no religious sense whatever and made no bones about it (see letter of 28th July 1916). He was exclusively interested in the relations between human beings, and one of the most attractive qualities in his letters is the frankness with which he confesses his earthy humanity, in all its strength and weakness. No doubt it was this discrepancy of outlook that led Strauss to set the text of *Ariadne* to music which blandly ignores the subtle metaphysics of the heroine's mental state and of her relationship to Theseus and Bacchus—points on which Hofmannsthal insisted in great detail and at enormous length in his letters of the time. That Strauss was right, from his own point of view, in setting the text as he did, we need not doubt; for in the case of *Ariadne* the superficial aspect of the plot was satisfying enough to inspire him with some of his most entrancing music. But *Die Frau ohne Schatten* is another matter: the elaborate legend is meaningless at a superficial level; but, even when we have puzzled out the metaphysical significance of the story (and this can be done), a certain confusion remains between the Christian and pagan elements in the characters and their relationships. The result, for Strauss, was a long and exhausting struggle to rise to what he obscurely felt to be a great occasion. The complex plot thrilled him in some respects and repelled him in others. The man of the theatre—the born opera composer—was naturally and genuinely inspired by the romantic atmosphere of the poem, with its scenes of magic, its dramatic contrasts, and its many opportunities for grand stage spectacle; and to these he rose magnificently. On the intellectual side, however, Strauss was clearly somewhat at a loss to understand—and therefore to enter sympathetically into—the strange spiritual conflict which excited Hofmannsthal's more rarefied imagination.

Die Frau ohne Schatten marks the end of a period in Strauss's career as a composer: the vast score sums up everything he had done before; it was natural that he should want to turn to something quite different. What this something was is stated in a letter written as early as 1916, while Strauss was still labouring over *Die Frau*.

'When you've heard the new Vorspiel (to *Ariadne*) . . . you'll understand what I mean and will realize that I have a definite talent for operetta. And since my tragic vein is more or less exhausted, and since tragedy in the theatre, after this war, strikes me at present as something rather idiotic and childish, I should like to apply this irrepressible talent of mine—after all, I'm the only composer nowadays with some real humour and a sense of fun and a marked gift for parody. Indeed, I feel downright called upon to become the Offenbach of the 20th century, and you will and must be my poet.'

A few months later he adds: 'I promise you that I have now definitely stripped off the Wagnerian musical armour' (September 1916). But it was not true and never would be; the next result of the collaboration, *Die Ägyptische Helena*, turned out to be as inspissatedly Wagnerian as anything Strauss ever wrote—and this in spite of Hofmannsthal's admonitions to be 'light'. For the poet could no more escape from his metaphysical speculations than Strauss could abjure Wagnerian orchestration. I don't feel we need regret this too much; when Strauss aimed at lightness (e.g. in *Intermezzo*, in the ballet *Schlagobers*, and in most of *Die Liebe der Danae*) he achieved only a distressing cheapness that plays into the hands of his detractors.

Readers of this fascinating correspondence cannot fail to be struck by the infrequency with which the collaborators actually met. This was not the fault of Strauss, who was always trying to lure Hofmannsthal to visit him, in order to discuss some point or other. The poet remained curiously evasive. He was a far more punctual and voluminous correspondent than the composer, but scarcely ever would he accept Strauss's invitations. The mere fact that he was being pressed to do something was, as we have seen, enough to make him wish to refuse; and, apart from this, it may, I think, be assumed that the personality of Frau Strauss, as we know it from other sources, offended his susceptibilities. Had Hofmannsthal been more often willing to discuss common problems by word of mouth, misunderstandings would surely have been fewer and the difficulties of collaboration lessened. But then, of course, we should have been deprived of one of the most detailed records ever preserved of the creative imagination at work on its material; and that is impossible to regret.

The translators' problem has, in this case, been more than usually formidable, for it was necessary to capture the tones of two very different voices. Strauss's letters are easy-going and conversational; his sentences are nearly always short and to the point; he knows exactly what he means and says it without beating about the bush. Hofmannsthal, on the other hand, wields a highly conscious, 'literary' style, full of long, involved sentences. He expresses himself beautifully, as we should expect, but the thought is often far from simple, while on occasion he gives way to astonishing outbursts of nervous ill-humour, and at others he unwarrantably assumes in Strauss a sensitiveness equal to his own—an assumption which involves much needless expenditure of words. We seem to be watching a Siamese cat working out a *modus vivendi* with a Labrador. The spectacle is humorous and touching, but extraordinarily hard to convey through the medium of a foreign language. Readers, it is to be hoped, may feel that the present translators have carried out their prodigious task with tact and adroitness.

EDWARD SACKVILLE-WEST

1900

Vienna III, Salesianergasse 12, 17.11.(1900)

Dear Sir,

I do not know whether you recollect a conversation in Paris when I mentioned to you the idea for a ballet. Most kindly you gave me to understand at the time that you might care to set it to music.

My ballet[1] is now done, or almost so. Two acts are available in fair copy and I could add a detailed scenario of the third, which is to be short in any case, a kind of apotheosis. I should very much like to be allowed to submit the whole manuscript to you. But since I do not know how you feel at present about such a project and would not care to give either you or myself wholly pointless trouble, I am writing to ask whether your interest in this my project is still alive at all and whether you would kindly undertake to let me have, within a fortnight of receipt, some reaction to this piece of work which is for the time being at your disposal.

In expectation of your reply I remain yours truly,

HUGO HOFMANNSTHAL

Vienna III, Salesianergasse 12, 30th November (1900)

Dear Sir,

In the belief that a letter sent some ten days ago to what I assumed to be your address (Knesebeckstrasse 30) might possibly not have reached you for some reason or other—since I can hardly find any other explanation for the absence of at least a negative reply from you—I take the liberty of repeating today what I then said. Prompted by the desire you expressed in Paris for a ballet libretto written by a poet, I have now produced such a text in three acts with some parts predominantly in the nature of a pantomime and others designed rather for the introduction of dances. I believe that the subject, or chain of original ideas, was a very happy one and that the character of the piece will accord well with your music whether it be accompanying or absolute. Since I would rather not send off the manuscript wholly in vain, I took the liberty of asking you in my first letter whether you are still at all interested in such

[1] *Der Triumph der Zeit.*

I

a piece of work of mine and would like to see it. I should be most grateful for an early reply, even if negative.

> Yours truly,
>
> HUGO HOFMANNSTHAL

Charlottenburg, 14th Dec. (1900) Knesebeckstr. 30

Dear Sir,

Enclosed herewith your beautiful ballet which I am returning to you with many thanks. After some consideration I have decided to tell you right away that I shall not set it to music, much as I like it. The second act, in particular, is excellent; but the first, too, contains so many moments of great poetic beauty that I find it difficult to part with the lovely thing. Nevertheless I owe it to you to do so straight away. My reasons are not hard to guess: my own ballet,[1] which I pieced together last summer, though probably inferior to your work, is nevertheless so much nearer to me that I shall certainly tackle it first, as soon as a little opera of mine[2] is finished. And *after* this ballet (i.e. in about three years' time) the symphonic composer who has lain entirely dormant for the past two years will no doubt break through violently and I shall presumably lack the strength and the inclination for another ballet.

I hope you aren't angry: I assure you most sincerely that your piece is the kind one does not like returning. But I must not keep you in uncertainty when I am bound to tell you right away that I probably shan't be able to 'make it'. Once again, very many thanks and kindest regards.

> Yours, most respectfully,
>
> RICHARD STRAUSS

1906

Rodaun near Vienna, 7.3.1906

My very dear Sir,

How goes it with you and *Elektra*? It is, I must say, the hope of no mean pleasure which you have so unexpectedly aroused in me. Will you let

[1] *Kythere*. Not set to music.   [2] *Feuersnot*.

2

me know in a very few lines whether this hope may remain alive or is to be buried?

The more I thought about the idea, the more possible it seemed to me—but your experience may have been just the opposite.

In any case I shall be most grateful for a line of news.

I am, sincerely yours

HOFMANNSTHAL

Berlin W.15, Joachimstalerstr., 11.3.1906

Dear Herr von Hofmannsthal,

I am as keen as ever on *Elektra* and have already cut it down a good deal for my own private use. The only question I have not finally decided in my mind (no doubt this will be settled in the summer, the only time when I can compose) is whether, immediately after *Salome*, I shall have the strength to handle a subject so similar to it in many respects with an entirely fresh mind, or whether I wouldn't do better to wait a few years before approaching *Elektra*, until I have myself moved much farther away from the *Salome* style.

That is why anyway I should be glad to know if you've got anything else in stock for me, and if I might perhaps have a go at some other subject from your pen, farther removed from *Salome*, before doing *Elektra*. Apart from *Semiramis*, which I am extremely anxious to see, you mentioned some other work that you had in hand: perhaps I could see something of it soon? I could give you till the end of May, since it is only after that date that I can get down to creative work again.

In any case, I would ask you urgently to give me first refusal with anything composable that you write. Your manner has so much in common with mine; we were born for one another and are certain to do fine things together if you remain faithful to me. Have you got an entertaining renaissance subject for me? A really wild Cesare Borgia or Savonarola would be the answer to my prayers.

With warmest regards, yours sincerely and respectfully,

RICHARD STRAUSS

Rodaun, 27.4.(1906)

Dear Sir,

I am really ashamed to be so late in thanking you for your kind letter which was forwarded to me in Rome. Unfortunately I lost it and as a result no longer had your address. Your postcard has now restored this to me and offers at the same time the pleasant prospect of seeing you here on a visit. For, much as I would like to go, I shall hardly be able to get to Graz,[1] since it is exactly in the latter half of May that my wife expects her confinement. (In August, on the other hand, I shall myself be no more than an hour from Salzburg.) It gave me deep pleasure to find in your letter words that express what has long been my own wish and idea; I mean that sooner or later we shall and must do something together.

But I must honestly say that, as I see things, I should be very glad if you could manage to stick to *Elektra* for a start; the 'similarities' with the *Salome* plot do seem to me, on closer consideration, to dwindle to nothing. (Both are one-act plays; each has a woman's name for a title; both take place in classical antiquity, and both parts were originally created in Berlin by Gertrud Eysoldt; that, I feel, is all the similarity adds up to.) The blend of colour in the two subjects strikes me as quite different in all essentials; in *Salome* much is so to speak purple and violet, the atmosphere is torrid; in *Elektra*, on the other hand, it is a mixture of night and light, or black and bright. What is more, the rapid rising sequence of events relating to Orestes and his deed which leads up to victory and purification—a sequence which I can imagine much more powerful in music than in the written word—is not matched by anything of a corresponding, or even faintly similar kind in *Salome*.

But it is not for me to coax you into taking on a piece of work which, much to my own surprise, occurred to you yourself and at one moment appealed to you. I cannot, on the other hand, discern within the foreseeable future (and anyone who wants to go on creating and constructing must after all be concerned with what is foreseeable) a chance of producing any other literary work which in subject and length would seem suitable to serve you as basis for composition. In the far distance the vision of a *Semiramis* theme emerges rather like a mirage, but it is not possible for me to drag it up by force, and even if it were to yield me success, this particular subject with its oriental tissue of colours might easily threaten to compete with *Salome* more than *Elektra* does.

You spoke of some plot to be taken from the renaissance. Allow me, my dear sir, to make you a frank reply. I do not believe there is any epoch in history which I and, like me, every creative poet among our

[1] The first Austrian performance of *Salome* took place in Graz.

4

contemporaries would bar from his work with feelings of such definite disinclination, indeed such unavoidable distaste, as this particular one. Subjects taken from the renaissance seem destined to transport the brushes of the most deplorable painters and the pens of the most hapless of poets. Notwithstanding current lip-service—which incidentally has begun to die down in the last few years—I believe there is no other period in history when life was so utterly alien to our generation as it was then, and even on the stage no costume (not forgetting the period of built-up wigs) possesses less attractive associations than this particular form of drapery favoured, and so horribly over-worked, during the sixties and eighties of the last century: I mean the renaissance!

When it comes to the next of my own subjects, the situation is not as favourable for your purpose as I—who have, alas, no control over myself in this—would wish it to be. It is a subject focused on the hour of death, reminiscent of that unsophisticated, mediaeval spectacle *Everyman*, and the shape it is irresistibly taking on in my mind is a sequence of scenes somewhat realistically developed; it insists on being ushered into the world in prose, indeed in the Viennese dialect, and even if, in spite of this, there might be some music to be got out of it, I have not yet written down a line, and by that time your precious working months would be gone. Thus everything seems to point once again to *Elektra* even more than I could foresee in Berlin.

Let me now express the hope that I may have the pleasure of hearing your opinion by word of mouth out here at my home on May 9th or 10th. My wife is still reasonably well; I, in any case, shall be here and exceedingly pleased to see you for a meal or at any time that suits you.

Please send me a line before you arrive in Vienna and let me know your hotel.

I am, sincerely yours,

HOFMANNSTHAL

Marquardtstein, 5th June 1906

Dear Herr von Hofmannsthal,

I read Rückert's *Saul and David* today (Vol. 9 of his Collected Works, Sauerländers Verlag 1869, Frankfurt a. M.): there's a lot in it that might be usable. And since the raving Saul has long interested me I'd be glad if you would have a look at it. It might be possible to carve two grand acts out of it, more or less concentrated.

Samuel turning away from Saul and crowning David.

David playing to Saul.

David slays Goliath; amidst jubilation the victor is led by Saul's daughter before Saul.

Saul casts his javelin.

Saul pursues David and encounters him. David, surprising Saul in his sleep, spares him.

Saul's end before the Witch of Endor.

David is crowned king.

There's some great stuff in the subject, and you more than anybody else could make something really grand out of that splendid figure of Saul. Do please read up old man Rückert: maybe he will inspire you.

Since I saw Rembrandt's *Saul and David* in the Hague the subject's been haunting me: only I can't shape it myself. But the creator of the dancing Electra could!

With best regards, yours sincerely,

RICHARD STRAUSS

Rodaun, 9.6.(*1906*)

Dear Sir,

Within the hour I have received a letter from Fischer which brings me the reassuring certainty that I shall in the end unquestionably be able to arrange this matter as I wish it, and since it is above all my wish to smooth all avoidable difficulties out of your way, I hope we shall be through with it in the next few days. (If only you had informed me at once!)

Now I would like to suggest to you the following proposal to which Fischer's consent seems to me implied in his letter or can, I hope, in any case be secured by me. I, as well as my publisher, will renounce in favour of your music publisher all our rights in the libretto for *Elektra* as shortened by you and thus distinguished from the play, in return for a royalty in the German as well as in all foreign editions of this libretto to be settled between the publishers. But since, in doing so, I am surrendering substantial immediate rights and opportunities, especially abroad, I am asking for an advance (or fixed minimum payment on account) of two thousand marks payable on signing of this contract and to be deducted later from my share in the receipts arising from the sale of foreign language libretti.

6

Perhaps you will be so kind, my dear sir, as to wire as soon as this letter reaches you that I have your consent in principle. I will then formulate my detailed demands to Fischer on the basis of this telegram, and this will enable the two publishers to reach rapid and final agreement. Perhaps I may ask you at the same time to send me a short draft contract concerning the 25 per cent share in the royalty which we agreed on when we talked it over, so that we can soon be done with all these business aspects, the significance of which we are neither of us likely to overestimate and need not therefore affect to underestimate.

I am, sincerely yours,

HOFMANNSTHAL

R. 16.6.(1906)

Dear Sir,

(. . .)

as soon as we have managed to straighten out these business arrangements I shall be pleased to write to you a different kind of a letter containing some golden dreams about the *Saul* and *Semiramis* subjects.

I am, sincerely yours,

HOFMANNSTHAL

Marquardtstein, 16th June 1906

Dear Herr von Hofmannsthal,

I am already busy on the first scene of *Elektra*, but I'm still making rather heavy weather of it. As soon as the thing's definitely under way I'll get my lawyer, Dr. Samter, to send you the (. . .) agreement.

Always avidly eager for any 'Golden dreams'.

With best regards, yours

RICHARD STRAUSS

How about a subject from the French Revolution for a change? Do you know Büchner's *Dantons Tod*? Sardou's (*horribile dictu*) *Ninth Thermidor* has been warmly recommended to me by a fairly authoritative party: I don't know it, but have always strongly distrusted any such *sujet à la grand opéra*.

Dear Sir,

I am truly delighted to hear that you have got well into your work, and consider your amendment quite excellent; however hard I might try, I would not wish or propose to change a single word of what you have jotted down on that slip of paper.

Looking ahead I would like to make a suggestion right away. During a walk recently I strove to get thoroughly into the spirit of *Elektra* from your point of view, imagining the effect of the music, and in doing so came to the conclusion that the brief interlude of the cook and the young servant (page 51 on top to page 54) is quite superfluous. If therefore you should want to cut it out, you have my consent in advance. For the mute (but important) scene on page 76, where the old servant prostrates himself before Orestes and kisses his feet, I have the following proposal. Would not this scene be more effective for the music (and at the same time for the poetic mood) if *many* old servants, all the old servants of the house, were to come on the stage? Three or four of them are bold enough to advance towards Orestes; the other fifteen or twenty old heads are huddled together at the gate to the courtyard; when these three or four fall at Orestes's feet, the others by the gateway also sink to the ground. Then the whole group scrambles to its worn-out feet again and shuffles tremulously off the stage without a sound. That (*if I mistake not*) would be an effective point for the music.[1] Of course I hazard all this as a mere suggestion.

For *Semiramis* I have had many telling ideas, but I cannot speak of them for the time being because I shall have to work like the devil for the next six or eight weeks and must be most careful not to allow other subjects to obtrude and confuse my imagination. This is also the difficulty which is likely to prevent a meeting between us, although it would give me so much pleasure. From the day after tomorrow until early September I am going to be at Lueg on the Wolfgangsee, about an hour and a half from Salzburg. The obvious thing would be to meet in that enchanting town. Perhaps during the second half of August?

I am, as you know, always ready to do anything I can to help with textual changes (even if more arduous than today's). Please send the contract in due course also to Lueg on the Wolfgangsee.

I am, sincerely yours,

HOFMANNSTHAL

[1] Score and printed libretto provide for three accompanying servants.

8

Dear Sir,

I meant to tell you what follows as early as the middle of September, but at that time I read in the papers that you were in Italy and so I held it over. It really was not my fault that the news of your being at work on *Elektra* suddenly went through the Austrian press, to be repeated everywhere else. I had mentioned it to no one, absolutely no one, and had even instructed Fischer not to speak of it. I imagine it leaked out from Graz; that is my personal impression.

Towards December 10th I shall come to Berlin for a few days. I should like to look you up there and talk a little about future plans. What I feel is more than mere belief in a possibility: I *know* we are destined to create together one, or several, truly beautiful and memorable works. I should like at the same time to explain to you my notions (fairly liberal as they are) of what I consider possible opera subjects and what, on the other hand, I consider absolutely out of the question nowadays ('*Thermidor*'!).

Only one more thing. You wrote in July that I was to receive the contract covering the points we settled by letter, as soon as your legal adviser had returned from his summer holidays. There has obviously been some hold-up. But now the summer is long passed; might it be due to a little dawdling on the part of Fischer that I have not yet heard anything at all? May I ask you for a very brief, bare line on this matter? We both have to rid ourselves of a lot of these things, in many directions; this one, too, I should like to put aside as done with.

I am, sincerely yours,

HOFMANNSTHAL

(*October, 1906*)

My Dear Herr Strauss,

You can imagine how much I desire to hear *Salome* at long last, and how essential it is for me to learn from your dramatic music and to absorb as much of it as possible for the sake of our future plans. It so happens that I shall be in Dresden this month. I am to give a reading there on the 29th, but will also be in the town on the evenings of the 27th, 28th, and 30th, and possibly even on the 31st. Could you induce

Seebach to put on *Salome* one of these nights? Not of course on the 29th. I should be very glad.

I am, sincerely yours,

HOFMANNSTHAL

We shall meet in Berlin on December 8th and 9th.

1907

Dear Herr von Hofmannsthal,

Your pleasant visit the other day took me by surprise in that I had not by then found time to re-read *The Daughter of the Air* as I had intended. I am now belatedly putting down the points that have sprung to my mind following a fresh perusal of Calderon's work.

If I remember your own draft correctly, Act I in your arrangement ended with the spectacular arrival of the king. To my mind this is not quite enough, dramatically, and I believe that you imagine the purely superficial effect of the music at this moment to be rather more powerful than it can in fact be in present-day circumstances when so many effects have palled. I have a feeling that some strong dramatic complication ought to be worked right into the first act, and I would therefore suggest to you to consider concentrating the whole of the Memnon tragedy into the conclusion of the first act. How does the following synopsis strike you?

Opening of the act: a sunny idyllic atmosphere, broken, by way of contrast, by the first gloomy prophecies of Tiresias. Memnon arrives, finds Semiramis, pledges his troth to her and, having received her vow of fidelity, departs to meet the king who is out hunting and to make him amenable to his plans. During Memnon's absence, arrival of the king who—perhaps as in Calderon—can be saved by Semiramis. The king falls in love with Semiramis. Return of Memnon who has missed the king; and now we get the first clash between Memnon and the king, ending with Memnon's blinding and exile following Semiramis's decision in favour of the king. Semiramis thereupon, as in Calderon, is proclaimed queen amidst thunder and lightning. Here the act might end, unless you prefer, following the exit of Semiramis and the entire Court, to give a grand solo scene to Memnon, reeling around blindly

10

in the storm. I would add here that in opera all mass scenes and big ensembles make bad curtains; on the other hand, solo scenes or love duets, either with a jubilant fortissimo or fading out with highly poetical pianissimo endings, are the most rewarding.

If therefore the line of the first act were to run from a sunlit-serious, spacious start to tragic catastrophe, storm and savage curses, Act II would have to begin with a very brilliant, serene picture, such as either: Semiramis engaged at her toilet, as I believe you yourself had in mind, or Semiramis in the midst of a love affair from which, roused by trumpets and the noise of fighting, she rushes out into battle. Whether you want to fit any festivities, ballet, etc. into this second act—perhaps at the beginning, or after Semiramis's victorious return—I must leave to you. Anyway, the second act, if I remember correctly, ends with the great love duet in which her lover senses the curse of Semiramis's death-bringing proximity and slowly dies. Semiramis's savage despair makes a good curtain—unless of course you want to work in, at this stage, the arrival of Ninias, cheered by the people, whereupon Semiramis, as in Calderon, withdraws to her darkened chamber and, under the impact of her lover's death, renounces her crown. But needless to say, I leave it entirely to you whether you want to bring this Ninias drama into it. Anyway, a third act could show Ninias as a bad ruler: he is over-powered in his sleep by Semiramis who then sits in judgement in his place. This act might possibly be set in the Hanging Gardens, which I should be most reluctant to do without; I would urge you to consider where those Hanging Gardens might be installed—in the décor, of course—since, after all, they are the only thing the general public knows about Semiramis, and so they will all want to see them on the stage. You've no idea how the public still falls for decorative art. We are just witnessing a further example over here with Verdi's *Aida*, which, merely because it is a new production, has been drawing a full house twice weekly and beating all Wagner's pieces, simply because we have this lovely new Egyptian set. Do therefore spare neither cost nor effort, please, on a lavish spectacle and on rich decorative contrasts in *Semiramis*. As it is, my productions have always been so cheap in the past that for once the theatrical managers can spend a little more on my décor.

I hope that when you come to Berlin again in February or March, or at any rate when I come to Vienna on 1st March, I shall have the pleasure of hearing from you something more precise about *Semiramis*, to the idea of which I am beginning to warm more and more. There is only one thing I would ask you: when composing your text don't think of the music at all—I'll see to that. You just write me a drama that's full of action and contrasts, with few mass scenes, but with two or three very good rich parts. As for our recent conversation about *Elektra*, I believe that we can't leave out Aegisthus altogether. He is definitely part of the plot and must be killed with the rest, preferably before the eyes of the audience. If it isn't possible to get him into the house earlier, so that he is slain immediately after Clytemnestra, then we'll leave the next scene as it now stands—but maybe you'll think it over. It's not a good plan to have all the women come running on-stage after the murder of Clytemnestra, then disappear again, and then, following the murder of Aegisthus, return once more with Chrysothemis. This breaks the line too much. Perhaps something or other will occur to you. Couldn't we let Aegisthus come home immediately after Orestes has entered the house? And perform the murders in quick succession one after the other, possibly in such a way that, the moment Aegisthus has stepped into the house and the door is shut behind him, the distant cry of Clytemnestra is heard and then, after a short pause, the murder of Aegisthus is done the way it stands now—and after that the final scene with all the women? I think it might work all right.

Please let me have your opinion at your leisure and, of course, as soon as you have any of *Semiramis* ready do send it to me, even if it's only sketches, because as you can well imagine, I am tremendously interested.

With best regards, yours respectfully and sincerely,

RICHARD STRAUSS

1908

Rodaun, 3rd January, 1908

Dear Sir,

The double curve in the murder scenes to which you take exception can, I think, easily be converted into a single one by a simple rearrangement as follows. Up to page 85, Electra's cry: 'Triff noch einmal!' (last line page 85) everything stands as at present. Then, instead of bringing the serving maids on to the stage, all is still, a deathly hush, while Electra

12

listens with breathless intensity. Now Aegisthus appears at the entrance (right), Electra runs towards him and performs her terrifying torch act. Thus the Aegisthus scene, from his entrance (page 88) to his murder (page 92: Electra: 'Agamemnon hört Dich!'—Aegisthus: 'Weh mir!') remains exactly as it stands. Then the women come running from the house (left), but without Chrysothemis, and now follows the brief scene where they flutter about like frightened bats, with this one modi-fication that the words of Chrysothemis are now to be given to the first female servant, those of the first servant to the second, and so on. Electra stands in the porch, her back pressed against the door.—This short scene ends with the line: Several voices: 'Elektra, lass uns in das Haus!' At that moment the door opens from the inside, the women shrink back horrified with cries of: 'Zurück! Zurück!' Electra steps aside, her eyes fixed on the door. And now Chrysothemis is seen standing in the doorway (the central door leading to the house) and screams her mes-sage into the audience exactly as on page 92, with one slight alteration: 'Elektra! Schwester, komm zu mir! So komm zu mir! Es ist der Bruder drin im Haus!'—The rest continues unchanged. I hope that suits you.

About *Semiramis* I would like to say merely this: I mean to keep in mind above all that I am writing for myself, with complete freedom, and not for you—a piece with as much action as possible and with a few strongly developed characters and not many crowd scenes. As for the rest, I doubt whether I shall be able to do much with the incidents in the Calderon play; it will be my point of departure only and not the foundation. The government of Semiramis and the whole political action offers me nothing at all; the whole thing must in fact first melt into dreams of my own, before these can crystallize into drama. But the first scene with the prophecies of death, with the strange episode of the murder of the young fisherman by the temple servants (don't look for this in Calderon, it isn't there), with the approach of the royal hunting party and Semiramis's doubt whether she is goddess or woman, whether what she feels near at hand is a husband, a flash of lightning, or death, and with the suicide, at the end, of the mysterious old priest who throws himself into the mountain lake, all this is wonderfully definite in my mind. I mean to make it into a short scenic prologue or merely into the first seven scenes, and for this it has ample, more than ample, action. Rest assured, my dear Dr. Strauss, that over the whole text I shall rely upon myself alone and not at all on the music; this is indeed the only way in which we can and must collaborate. But your music will then add something most beautiful, something far exceeding, of course, what the actors and the stage-designer can ever give me.

With all good wishes for 1908, for your health, your happiness and your work, I am sincerely yours,

HOFMANNSTHAL

P.S. I definitely expect to come to Berlin in February for some little time.

Warsaw, 20th February (1908)

Dear Herr von Hofmannsthal,

I shall be in Vienna from 6th to 8th March (Hotel Imperial) and am already anxious to know if, when and where I could see you there.

Would you be kind enough to do me those small additions to *Elektra* (chorus and final scene)? If you could let me have something tangible of *Semiramis* by 1st June I should be grateful. And don't forget plenty of ballet, martial music and victory marching: these, apart from the erotic elements, are my strong suit. In Rome I had a word with Dr. Schanzer, who has produced the best translation of *Elektra* and can't publish it. *Elektra* is making vigorous headway. I could play it to you in Vienna.

With best regards, ever yours,

RICHARD STRAUSS

When writing: Berlin address.

Rodaun, 4.6.1908

My dear Doctor,

Please send me the list of corrections as soon as possible, so that I can get it all done. I hope I may be able to make a flying visit to Garmisch in September, but do not yet know whether I can manage it, for I have an exceptionally heavy programme for the summer. At the end of May, I had to decide which of my fragmentary scenarios and sketches I should take in hand, and the decision was dictated exclusively by consideration for you, my dear Doctor. For supposing I had now set myself to work on some other piece and had left off occupying my imagination with that happily conceived Casanova comedy,[1] I might quite easily have found it impossible, even by next spring, to get into it again. My imagination is highly capricious, I have an abundance of plots in my head, and so you might have been left in the lurch next

[1] *Cristinas Heimreise.*

spring, disappointed, and justly vexed with me. Therefore I have begun working on this subject and have already reached the point where he leaps into the gondola after the girl, even if the text as I have it at present may not stand in the end as the final version, but merely as very detailed groundwork.

But now allow me to discuss at once your main point, and please set my mind at rest by an immediate reply. You understand, don't you—and have never counted on anything else—that I shall have the comedy, just as it comes from my pen, performed first on the ordinary stage. There is, I think, in any case no other alternative, for what attracts me as an artist to the subject and what I aim at (now that I have got this good, slim scenario) is to round out the characters as much as possible and to produce as natural and varied a dialogue as I can. Quite conceivably you may be able to make direct use of this dialogue, after extensive cuts, as you did in the case of *Salome*. If so, all the better. But it is equally possible that you may wish me to transpose the whole thing into a simpler and more lyrical key, while preserving the scenario entire, an operation such as Da Ponte carried out on the text of the comedy *Le Mariage de Figaro*. This I would willingly undertake, but never could I attempt to formulate the text from the outset in this lyrical manner which leaves most of the characterization to the composer. To do this would make me lose all certainty of touch and so produce something that falls between two stools. On the other hand, once the comedy is done and has succeeded on the stage, and once each character has gained, so to speak, something of an independent existence, then it is possible to summon up the necessary effrontery to treat it all, if need be, very much *en raccourci*. You are so decidedly an artist yourself and know so much even of my metier that you will surely not close your ears to these arguments. And why abandon a method which has succeeded so well with *Salome* and will succeed again, we hope, with *Elektra*?

I have explained this to you in all frankness and hope to receive from you shortly a few lines expressing your kind agreement. I need hardly say how glad I am to know that you have read the scenario with such lively pleasure and that your touch might make of it something truly unique among comic operas.

With best regards, I am yours sincerely,

HOFMANNSTHAL

15

Dear Herr von Hofmannsthal,

In *Elektra*, page 77, I need a great moment of repose after Electra's first shout: 'Orest!'

I shall fit in a delicately vibrant orchestral interlude while Electra gazes upon Orestes, now safely restored to her. I can make her repeat the stammered words: 'Orest, Orest, Orest!' several times; of the remainder only the words: 'Es rührt sich niemand!' and 'O lass Deine Augen mich sehen!' fit into this mood. Couldn't you insert here a few beautiful verses until (as Orestes is about to embrace her gently) I switch over to the sombre mood, starting with the words: 'Nein, Du sollst mich nicht berühren . . .' etc.?

Your first consignment of lines received with thanks: very beautiful, but rather few. I must have material here to work at will towards a climax. Eight, sixteen, twenty lines, as many as you can, and all in the same ecstatic mood, rising all the time towards a climax.

One more thing: I still don't understand the scenic action at the end. Surely, Orestes is *in* the house. Surely, the front door in the middle is shut. Chrysothemis and the serving maids hurried off on page 88 *into the house on the left*. On page 91 they are 'rushing out madly'. Out of where? The left or through the middle?

Page 93: Chrysothemis comes running out. Out which way? Through the courtyard gate on the right? What for? Surely, Orestes is in the centre of the house! Why is she at the end beating at the front door? Surely because it is barred? Do please answer these questions of mine in detail. I have never been quite clear about the scenario since reading it through.

The full score is finished as far as Orestes's entry. I made a start yesterday on composing from there onwards, and I think I am now in a very good mood for it.

How's Casanova going?

Best regards, yours,

RICHARD STRAUSS

Page 77: Electra:. . . . . 'Orest!'
(whispering) 'Es rührt sich niemand.' (Softly) 'O lass Deine Augen mich sehen. Traumbild, mir geschenktes! schöner als alle Träume! unbegreifliches,

entzückendes Gesicht, o bleib bei mir
lös nicht in Luft Dich auf, vergeh mir nicht—
es sei denn, dass ich jetzt gleich sterben muss
und Du Dich anzeigst und mich holen kommst:
dann sterb ich seliger als ich gelebt!'

Rodaun, 25.6.(1908)

My dear Doctor,

I hope this suits you. Please send by return my additions to page 93;
I shall expand them.

Now for the stage directions for Chrysothemis and the serving maids:
On page 91 the women come 'madly rushing out' from their servants'
quarters, harem, *left*. On page 93 Chrysothemis runs out through the
courtyard gate on the right, because the whole din of battle, the mur-
derous fighting between the slaves who are loyal to Orestes and the
household of Aegisthus (this outstanding opportunity for orchestral
back-cloth painting) has in the meantime spread to the inner courtyards
to which the right-hand gate leads.

Here is the layout:

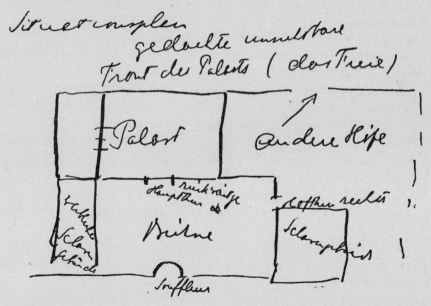

On page 94 Chrysothemis runs into the palace because she finds the
courtyard full of people and torches, of dead bodies and the wounded,

but cannot discover Orestes who has in the meantime presumably taken refuge at the domestic altar in the interior of the palace, and is perhaps already beset by the Furies. For this reason Chrysothemis, instead of taking once again the detour through the courtyard, in her excitement hammers at the central door to the house which may still be barred from inside as it was when Orestes committed the murder.

P.S. I shall write to you within the next few days about the Casanova comedy on which I am already hard at work.

Garmisch, 6.7.08

Dear Herr von Hofmannsthal,

Your kind letter of the 4th received with thanks. Enclosed herewith your final verses which I am asking you to extend as much as possible, as a *simultaneous* duet between Electra and Chrysothemis. Nothing new, just the same contents, repeated and working towards a climax.

Your verses when Electra recognizes Orestes are marvellous and already set to music. You are the born librettist—the greatest compliment to my mind, since I consider it much more difficult to write a good operatic text than a fine play. You will disagree, of course, and you'll be just as right as I am! As for your requests concerning Casanova, it is not quite easy to make an answer. In principle, of course, there's nothing to object to, and you know my opinion that every artist should derive all the advantage he possibly can from his work.

My misgivings about having Casanova run first as a comedy are of an artistic nature, in that I am not sure it would be a good thing for me if a comedy that hinges so much on its dénouement as your sketch does were to go stale as a stage play even before the première of my opera. At the moment I am merely raising this question in my own interest. Think it over, please.

Secondly, your draft seems to me so pure and so beautifully lyrical that I don't know whether, if spoken, it'll have anything like the effect that, as an opera, it is *bound* to have.

Thirdly, if you now want to get it ready for production as a recited comedy I fear that you will break up the dialogue too much for me and overload it with ideas.

Fourthly, I regard the subject matter as too meagre and too thin for a spoken play. It is the born operatic text. In other words, I am afraid of two things: If you now finish it entirely as a comedy play in the manner of your *Der Abenteurer und die Sängerin* I shall no longer be able to turn it into an opera. Moreover, if the comedy play—written by you in spite of everything with one eye casting sidelong glances at the opera—should not quite come off and should prove unsuccessful (which God forbid) it will then be more difficult for me to set to music than now.

Forgive me for bringing up all these misgivings, but I am so keen on the subject that I would rather make any sacrifice than not score a full and complete success with the opera later. My request, for the time being, is simply this: let's leave your question open for the moment, until you have finished the job, and let us then decide according to the impression the finished piece makes on me and other experts. I should be grateful to you if meanwhile you would say nothing about your work, until I have definitely made up my mind. Please do me this favour: you won't find me ungrateful.

Elektra is progressing and is going to be good. The scene between Electra and Orestes has, I think, come off very well. I hope to enforce the première by the end of January at the latest.

With kindest regards, yours

Enclosure:[1]
RICHARD STRAUSS

Page 93 Sheet A

Chrysothemis: Hörst Du denn nicht, sie tragen ihn,
                sie tragen ihn auf ihren Händen.
Electra (to herself, paying no attention to her):
                Wir
                sind bei den Göttern, wir Vollbringenden.
                Sie fahren wie die Schärfe eines Schwertes
                Durch uns dahin, die Götter, aber ihre
                Herrlichkeit ist nicht zu viel für uns!
Chrysothemis: Allen schimmern die Augen und die alten
                Wangen
                von Tränen! Alle weinen, hörst du's nicht?
                Ah!

[1] As requested by Hofmannsthal's letter of 25th June 1908, Strauss returned this sheet to the poet with the following notes (requests for additions): To Electra's 'Wir sind bei den Göttern' another 4 to 8 lines, and the same to Chrysothemis's 'Allen schimmern . . .' and the comment: 'always the same sense, only different words. Repetitions of meaning.' On sheet B. Hofmannsthal carried out Strauss's wishes.

Electra: 4 to 8 lines always to the same effect.
Chrysothemis: The same, only different words, same meaning.
Electra (to herself, ecstatically):
        Ai! Liebe tötet! Aber keiner fährt dahin
        und hat die Liebe nicht gekannt!
Chrysothemis: Elektra!
        Ich muss bei meinem Bruder stehn!
        (Runs out).
Electra has risen. She moves away from the threshold and so on, page 93 last paragraph.

Alternating or simultaneous, at the choice of the composer

(On verso of sheet A)

                                       Venice, May 19, (1908)

My dear Doctor,

I hope you are satisfied with what you find on the other side. It was not quite easy to do. Please acknowledge safe receipt to Rodaun. I am giving a great deal of thought to our *Figaro*!

                              Best wishes yours,

                              HOFMANNSTHAL

                                      Rodaun, 8.7.1908

My dear Doctor,

Many thanks for your good letter. I am quite certain that as long as we live we two shall reach rapid and easy agreement on every issue. As you put it in your letter, so it shall be. I have not seen Kainz since and he has no idea that I am working on this piece.

I accept every one of the arguments you put forward as perfectly just and to the point. Only, as usual in such unpredictable matters, the result looks entirely different from what in all probability you fondly imagine. It is in prose and contains not a single reflective line, scarcely a poetic image or simile; all is action, movement, pantomime, lively stage-play. It is miles apart from *Der Abenteurer* and resembles far more *Le Barbier de Seville* with which it shares, let us hope, the qualities which made first a good comedy and later a good opera. The final twist which winds it up emerges naturally out of the action and, pretty though it is, does not therefore overshadow everything in the finished play to the extent it does in the bare telling of the plot. The effect of such a twist is not in the least weakened but heightened rather by being known beforehand; this is an old and remarkable truth in the theatre. For if surprises on the stage were like those of real life, then the effects of every such twist would necessarily be quite spent after the première (at least for that particular town) and yet the opposite is what happens. So for the time being I continue to work most assiduously and with great joy and enthusiasm. In September we might meet somewhere and I dare say we shall both be content. To be called a good librettist is a compliment I value highly especially when it comes from you, and it makes me very happy.

The new additions I shall post tomorrow or the next day.

I am, yours sincerely,

HOFMANNSTHAL

To be inserted into sheet A.   (sheet) B

Ad libitum alternating or simultaneous

Electra:	Ich habe Finsternis gesät und ernte Lust über Lust. Ich war ein schwarzer Leichnam unter den Lebenden, und diese Stunde bin ich das Feu'r des Lebens und eine Flamme verbrennt die Finsternis der Welt!
Chrysothemis:	Gut sind die Götter! Gut! es fängt ein Leben für dich und mich und alle Menschen an. Die überschwenglich guten Götter sind's die das gegeben haben!
Electra:	Mein Gesicht muss weisser sein, als das weissglühende Gesicht des Mondes. Wenn einer auf mich sieht, muss er den Tod empfangen oder muss vergehn vor Lust. Seht ihr denn mein Gesicht? Seht ihr das Licht, das von mir ausgeht?
Chrysothemis:	Wer hat uns je geliebt? Wer hat uns je geliebt? Nun ist der Bruder da und Liebe fliesst über uns wie Öl und Myrrhen, Liebe ist Alles! Wer kann leben ohne Liebe?
Electra:	Ai! Liebe tötet, aber keiner fährt dahin . . . and so on.

21

My dear Doctor,

I hope this passage[1] now suits you; if not, please do not hesitate to return it again (address Bad Fusch near Salzburg). It is after all a passage of great importance to the opera. I have endeavoured to differentiate between the two also by what they say.

Best wishes, yours,

HOFMANNSTHAL

Work on my comedy progresses splendidly. I am *casting no sidelong glances*. (Quite the contrary; it is in the other event that I should have done so.) I believe this piece is destined to give us much pleasure in the end.

Trafoi, 16.8.1908

My permanent address will now be: Aussee, Obertressen 14

My dear Doctor,

I am sincerely delighted that you have made such happy progress with your work and are content with it; now I wish you all the energy and good spirits you may need for the conclusion which is bound to be far more impressive and important in the opera than in the play.

The French translation which I return herewith was already known to me. Verse translations from the German into French are among the most calamitous things; this one, despite a certain lack in precision and vigour, has nonetheless much to commend it and I doubt if it would be easy to obtain a better or even a more serviceable one. Perhaps Fürstner might get M. Strozzi to undertake a revision for our special purpose to achieve greater conciseness. Incidentally the translation has, as I happen to know, the approval of such competent judges as Maeterlinck and André Gide.

The situation concerning the comedy is this: I have reached the end of Act III and mean to complete the stage version in four acts; for the opera it would have to be reduced to three by running Acts I and II together with a musical interlude. (Act I the meeting and the leap into the gondola, Act II the night of love and the parting.) I hope to get it *finished* within the next three or four weeks, including the revision and completion of Act I. Had it not been for this need to revise Act I,

[1] The reference is to sheet B.

I should have sent it to you before (I did not catch the right tone in the beginning, of that I am now quite certain). Do tell me how long you will remain at Garmisch? Could you perhaps manage to come to Salzburg for twenty-four hours towards the 15th or 20th of September? Salzburg is halfway between Aussee and Garmisch; there I could read you the finished or almost finished comedy, and in talking it over we could no doubt easily reach agreement about the whole thing. Please send me *early* word to the above address whether this plan suits you.

Yours sincerely,

HOFMANNSTHAL

Rodaun, 7.10.1908

My dear Doctor,

Please don't be disappointed. It would distress me exceedingly to think that I could ever have given you cause to feel disappointed, and I trust I never shall. You say in your letter that the excellent opera plot you were looking forward to so much has now been turned into something quite different, and in this you are right and you are not right. But the evidence of your own eyes is more likely to convince you than any words of mine. I will send you several acts, if possible even the whole play, at the earliest moment—in any case while you are still well settled at Garmisch. This typescript copy will then remain your working copy. I ask you to read it pencil in hand and to mark with complete candour everything that in your opinion ought to be left out, while noting at the same time those points where the lyrical element will need to be more fully developed for the opera. What I have written is a spoken play, and where my text consists of twenty or thirty short speeches and replies, in the opera each of the characters concerned may perhaps give vent to his feelings in a single lyrical phrase. But the action, the framework which has delighted and convinced you, this remains entirely as it was. First meeting, seduction, rapture, and parting; unexpected return and introduction of the bridegroom; wedding and finale; all these are exactly where they were and form the cornerstones of the four acts. I say four acts, for the comedy has four, while the opera will only have three, since the whole psychological and conversational detail will disappear, and Acts I and II, that is the meeting and their joint departure by gondola, and later the seduction and parting will be connected by a musical interlude to form the first act of the opera. Once you have read the manuscript and have made yourself familiar with it at Garmisch, I count on our most necessary meeting in Vienna on December 10th. A prolonged talk after so much correspondence is quite essential to us both.

As for my possible intervention at the Dresden rehearsals, I shall try so to arrange things that I can get there in January, and I will intervene, provided you tell me that you still wish me to do so in the circumstances then prevailing; but I shall intervene only as a personal favour to you, since I do not in any way regard myself as a co-author and have no intention whatever of appearing as such.

Will you please accept in the same spirit a remark I would now like to make with reference to Vienna; I am speaking merely as a well-intentioned acquaintance of yours and am quite aware that I may be entirely wrong and that my whole warning may be irrelevant. It strikes me, however, quite distinctly that the preliminaries for the *Elektra* production in Vienna are being handled, if not with actual ill-will, at least with quite obvious lack of affection for the work. Of operas I know nothing, but with theatrical conditions in general I am fairly conversant and the upshot of my observations is this: the Vienna public is still just as impervious to everything that is new, as it was in the days when it scoffed at *Fidelio* and *Don Giovanni*. In Vienna, too, more than anywhere else, people (I mean those who come to first nights) care less about the work itself than the incidental to-do, a first-class cast and a conductor whom in their self-styled connoisseurship they can take for a great man. To my mind, what is hatching here is a première which, by these vulgar theatrical standards, *lacks lustre*, and is therefore somewhat hazardous. I am telling you this for two reasons: so that you may either intervene and do something about it, or, if you are not in a position to do anything, so that you may simply get your publisher to insist that the Vienna première must not take place too soon after Dresden, but only after Berlin is through, and perhaps also one of the foreign capitals. For once we have scored a whole series of successes, as I am sure we shall, the half-failure in Vienna which is, I think, equally certain as things stand, will naturally carry less weight. Given the availability of so exceptional a man as Roller, I would have been able—had you wished me to do so—to influence favourably and most extensively the Viennese mise-en-scène. But the essential prerequisite is that the musical and theatrical management at the highest level should be really well disposed towards the work. Otherwise it would be better for us both to keep right out of the whole thing and to disclaim the entire affair at least by staying away ourselves. But then you are far more familiar with all this than I am.

Yours very sincerely,

HOFMANNSTHAL

Rodaun, 18.10.1908

My dear Dr. Strauss,

I am grieved to think you may suppose that I am leading you a dance over this comedy of mine, or that I have a hidden ulterior purpose, or something of that kind. I sincerely hope you will accept, however, the explanation of the facts which is simply this: contrary to my expectations I have now been at work on this play for more than four months and I have not finished it yet. What is more, I feel I must tell you that I am now no longer in a position where I can possibly *withhold* it from the ordinary stage. Throughout the summer I believed—wrongly as it proved—that by the autumn I should be able to avoid this; I thought I could get the Casanova comedy done by the end of September at the latest, and then complete last year's half-finished comedy[1] in the Austrian dialect, in which case I would have been in a position to offer this to Reinhardt who, for the second time, is keeping his best date at the end of January open for me. This plan has now come to nothing, and I have absolutely no alternative whatsoever but to give him the comedy, and must of course give it at the same time to Kainz who has heard nothing at all from me so far.

To find myself unable to comply in all points with a wish you have expressed, and one which I should so dearly like to fulfil, would make me very unhappy were I not so utterly convinced that this piece of work, the way it has now turned out, could be of no immediate use to you to set to music without substantial changes (just as neither Mozart nor anyone else could have used the prose comedy *Le Mariage de Figaro* without alterations). I am equally convinced, on the other hand, that we should never have arrived at a useful opera libretto—which I trust we shall still get—had I not first worked out this plot in the form which is my own, namely as a psychological comedy in prose. It is only now that I possess the complete assurance and freedom, the courage and the desire to re-do the whole play—provided you, for your part, still

[1] *Silvia im 'Stern'.*

respond to the gist of plot and scenario as warmly as you did (and after the play has first had some success, great or small, as a comedy)—to re-do it with boldness and even with that touch of levity required to make it suitable for a comic opera, and to try and stress the lyrical element while keeping characterization in the background. The libretto will, moreover, benefit from the fact that more subtle psychological contours are now already latent in the characters, as they so evidently are in characters like Figaro, Susanna, Cherubino.

Before I tackle this new task which, as you will see, I shall do with the greatest joy and pleasure, we must get entirely clear between us the style in which you mean to write this opera. If I rightly understood the hints you threw out and which struck me as immensely promising, you intend to create something altogether novel in style, something which (since every development in the arts proceeds in cycles) will resemble more closely the older type of opera rather than *Meistersinger* or *Feuersnot*. You intend, unless I wholly misunderstood your hints, to alternate set numbers with passages which approximate to the old secco recitative. All this will require searching discussion and I very much hope that the result will earn me the proud title of librettist which I shall value most highly. However, as I have said, I am so much in awe of the difficulties of producing a really good libretto that to write one out of the blue would seem to me almost impossible; now with the comedy as a foundation I feel on the contrary full of confidence and in good heart.

Now tell me this: when shall I have the opportunity of showing you the comedy at last? You mentioned once that you were coming to Vienna towards the end of October. Does this still stand? If not, I intend to go to Berlin early in November and expect to have finished the play by then. Where do we meet at last? Please let me have a brief but immediate reply.

Yours sincerely,

HOFMANNSTHAL

1909

Weimar, 11.2.1909

My dear Doctor,

Hoftheatermaler Kautsky writes to me in a state of great excitement that you have told him I was 'unhappy' about his décor. This must be a complete mistake, for I consider his décor quite good; what (among ourselves) I did think absurd was only Herr von Hülsen's 'brain-wave' of turning the palace into a hen-yard. Had he done such a thing to me in one of my own plays, I should have forgotten all my manners and chased him off his own stage; never have I come across such arrant nonsense! But as things are and since I am concerned only with the opera's effect and with your wishes (in this case the wish for no trouble) I have never mentioned this particular detail except in that one remark I made to you during the rehearsal. I have not mentioned it to anyone nor against anyone, and in any case *I don't give a damn* for the whole thing. I have sent Kautsky a telegram to soothe his nerves with a non-committal compliment concerning his décor.

Now something which is (as I hope) of far greater importance to the two of us. I have spent three quiet afternoons here drafting the full and entirely original scenario for an opera,[1] full of burlesque situations and characters, with lively action, pellucid almost like a pantomime. There are opportunities in it for lyrical passages, for fun and humour, even for a small ballet. I find the scenario enchanting and Count Kessler with whom I discussed it is delighted with it. It contains two big parts, one for baritone and another for a graceful girl dressed up as a man, à la Farrar or Mary Garden. Period: the old Vienna under the Empress Maria Theresa.

After Sunday I shall be in Berlin, Schadowstrasse 4.

Shall we meet? (But not at a party, that is pointless.)

Yours sincerely,

HOFMANNSTHAL

Rodaun. 16.3.(1909)

My dear Doctor,

It was rather rash and silly of me to write that I would not care to read to you. On the contrary, I most decidedly wish to read to you, here, the beginning and the end of Act I (I have not got the middle yet) in order to clarify certain things in my own mind. The scenario is excellent, full of amusing and almost pantomimic details; I am aiming at the utmost conciseness and expect a duration of about two hours and a half, that means half of *Meistersinger*. Whether I am going *too far* in

[1] *Der Rosenkavalier.*

my disregard of operatic *convention* and whether, in the constant endeavour to maintain a characteristic tone, I accommodate myself too little to the needs of the singing voice—this is what I should like to hear from you and then I shall go on with all the more zest.

From six o'clock on Thursday onwards I shall be available any day wherever you wish, either out here or in town. It would be very nice of you if you could come out here for an evening, we could talk everything over at leisure and that would be a real gain. But if your wife were to come too, we could not do that, for she would of course be bored: and we have nothing whatever to offer her out here except melting snow. And since I am sure you prefer to play Skat in the evening, I should also willingly come to town one of these days between six and eight. So please let me know at once.

Yours sincerely,

HOFMANNSTHAL

Rodaun, 19.4.(1909)

My dear Doctor,

Here in haste is the first scene for you to go on with. More to follow as soon as possible. I have meanwhile been very industrious on Act II where transitions and so on have caused me a lot of trouble, and I did not wish to hold myself up by dictating Act I. I should very much like to send you Act II and perhaps even Act III reasonably soon, for you ought to see the MS. as far as possible as a whole to get an idea of contrasts, of the dynamic relations between the acts and so on. They will both be of approximately the same length, contain the essentials of the action and just as much characterization as is necessary to create sympathy with the various figures. Unless the music spreads itself very much at some point or other, each act ought to take three-quarters of an hour; that would be ideal.

(. . .)

Yours,

HOFMANNSTHAL

Garmisch, 21.4.09

My dear Herr von Hofmannsthal,

Your letters, as well as the first few scenes, received with thanks; am impatiently waiting for the next instalment. The opening scene is

28

delightful: it'll set itself to music like oil and melted butter: I'm hatching it out already. You're da Ponte and Scribe rolled into one. (. . .)

Elektra in Milan was a surprisingly good performance: Krucziniska as Electra first rate in every respect, the other parts vocally excellent— I've never heard the opera sung so beautifully. Orchestra very good, success colossal, the biggest takings of the season. I think we've now definitely turned the corner with *Elektra*. Congratulations to you and myself!

Best regards and thanks, yours,

RICHARD STRAUSS

Rodaun, 24.4.1909

My very dear Doctor,

Above all my warm thanks for your kind letter. I am altogether delighted to find that it gives you pleasure to work with me. How true this is of myself I hope I need not say. I am taking great pains over this comedy, especially over certain passages; and to build smooth transitions, to carve distinct characters out of a steadily moving action is no child's play. It seems to me that Scribe as well as da Ponte worked perhaps within a somewhat simpler convention. Yet the work gives me great satisfaction and I flatter myself that it will be good, excellent even let us hope. As *Elektra* has slain her thousands, I look forward to our slaying with this comedy tens of thousands, rather like Saul and David in the Bible, and they like us had to face the Philistines.

The job of dictating takes up more time than one would expect, on account of the many words in dialect, the punctuation and so on. I had hoped to dictate the first act at one go, but already I have twice dictated for two hours and am still not through, while the typing bureau in turn has not yet caught up copying the shorthand text. Even so, I count on sending you the major part of Act I by Monday at the latest. (. . .)

With best wishes, yours,

HOFMANNSTHAL

P.S. Not all passages, of course, will be as 'good' to set to music as this first, purely lyrical one. There are bound to be sticky patches, too, but none I hope where I have not explored with much thought the possibilities of musical interpretation . . . and the 'good' passages will,

I believe, outnumber the others. Do try and think of an old-fashioned Viennese waltz, sweet and yet saucy, which must pervade the whole of the last act.

Rodaun, 24.4.(1909)

My dear Doctor,

After the correct six-day interval, *Elektra* is now on the bill again for Thursday next; I assume this is a first result of your letter and so all is well for the time being. It would be an excellent idea if you were to write to Lucille Marcel (Hotel Sacher, Vienna 1)—that sort of thing always does a lot of good. When I heard her recently in performance I found her singing quite excellent, much better than at the première.

Finished today an important scene in Act II: Octavian-Sophie.

Sincerely yours,

HOFMANNSTHAL

Garmisch, 4th May 1909

My dear Herr von Hofmannsthal,

Received the first act yesterday: I'm simply delighted. It really is charming beyond all measure: so delicate, maybe a little too delicate for the general mob, but that doesn't matter. The middle part (antechamber) not easy to put into shape, but I'll manage it all right. Anyway, I've got the whole summer in front of me.

The final scene is magnificent: I've already done a bit of experimenting with it today. I wish I'd got there already. But since, for the sake of symphonic unity, I must compose the music from the beginning to the end I'll just have to be patient.

The curtain is delightful: brief and to the point. You're a splendid fellow. When do I get the rest?

All the characters are grand: drawn with clear outlines. Unfortunately I'll need very good actors again; the ordinary operatic singers won't do.

When you've finished Act II why don't you bring it here yourself and have a bit of a rest with us here? It's lovely here, you'll like it. Except that over Whitsun I shall be away at Aachen, I'm here all the time.

Once more, my very best thanks and warmest congratulations. Best regards, also from my wife, to yourself and your wife.

Yours sincerely,

RICHARD STRAUSS

Rodaun, 12.5.(1909)

My dear Doctor,

Let me thank you most warmly for the charming way in which you acknowledge the arrival of Act I and express your appreciation. It means a great deal to me to receive from you a letter such as this, and in reply I can only say that I work with you and for you with very real delight and with love for what we are doing. I use all my imagination to saturate myself with the possibilities, the demands and the laws of comic opera, expecting of course, and with confidence, that something will come of it which makes a real appeal to certain aspects of your individual qualities as an artist (that mixture of the burlesque with the lyrical), and which will keep its place in the repertory for many years, perhaps for decades. The third act will be the best of all, I hope; a little spiced to start with, then broadly comic, only to end on a note of tenderness.

Your apprehension lest the libretto be too 'delicate' does not make me nervous. Even the least sophisticated audience cannot help finding the action simple and intelligible: a pompous, fat, and elderly suitor favoured by the father has his nose put out of joint by a dashing young lover—could anything be plainer? The working out of this plot must be, I feel, as I have done it, that is free from anything trivial and conventional. True and lasting success depends upon the effect on the more sensitive *no less than* on the coarser sections of the public, for the former are needed to give a work of art its prestige which is just as essential as its popular appeal.

Strictly speaking only the title part[1] requires a singer who is also a truly gifted actor. Fugère, the famous Leporello, is said to be a real genius in such roles, and there is sure to be another singer at the Opéra Comique gifted in this genre. Even at the German theatres we shall manage somehow. In Vienna I can imagine quite a charming production. Roller is desperately keen on producing for us once and for all a

[1] The reference is to Ochs von Lerchenau after whom the opera was originally to be named.

31

prompt book with décor (stage sets and costumes) which Fürstner might distribute together with the score. (That is what Sonzogno does, for instance.) We shall have to discuss this in greater detail.

Cordially yours,

HOFMANNSTHAL

P.S. I was sorry to hear of that newspaper gossip and have no idea where it comes from. I never open my mouth and never see a soul who belongs to the world of journalism. It is a queer patch-work of lies; *Silvia im 'Stern'*, for instance, is actually the title of an earlier comedy of mine. N. can do nothing with the mere name of Semiramis, since *Semiramis* is no definite plot, no definite situation. My whole *Semiramis*, if it ever comes off, is pure invention. So never mind, the main thing is that the greater talent is on our side.

Garmisch, 16th May 1909

Dear Herr von Hofmannsthal,

Many thanks for your kind letter. My work is flowing along like the Loisach: I am composing everything—neck and crop. I am starting on the levee tomorrow. The Baron's scene is all ready; only you must write me some more lines. At the end of the Baron's aria, after the words: 'und eine Frau muss in der Nähe dabei sein' I need a great musical conclusion in the form of a trio. The Baron repeats in a very fast *parlando*:

> Dafür ist man kein Auerhahn und kein Hirsch,
> sondern ist man der Herr der Schöpfung,
> wollt, ich könnt sein wie Jupiter selig
> in tausend Gestalten,
> wär Verwendung für jede.

I now want him to go on bragging of all the things he can do, piling it on thicker and thicker all the time, preferably in a dactylic rhythm:

> 16 to 20 lines in buffo character

Overlaid by a duet of the Marschallin, continuing along the theme of

> Er agiert mir gar zu gut,
> lass er mir doch das Kind,
> er verdirbt mir das Mädchen,
> schweig er doch still, etc.

And on top of it Octavian, whom I want to let burst into loud laughter after the Baron's last words:

Nur eine Frau muss dabei sein

and who in his asides keeps mocking the Baron. This provides a first-class trio atmosphere up to the moment when the Baron remembers where he is and recovers himself with the words: 'Geb sie mir doch den Grasaff da,' etc. Would you add some more text here: the music is all ready and I only need the words for accompaniment and filling in?[1]

It would be very nice if for the second act you could write a contemplative ensemble passage, to follow the moment when some dramatic bomb has just gone off, when the action is suspended and everybody is lost in contemplation. Such moments of repose are most important.

Examples: Act II of *Lohengrin*, the great ensemble, known as the 'dark brooding'.

The *Meistersinger* quintet.

Also *Barber of Seville*, end of Act I, the A-flat ensemble 'Just look at Bartolo and Basilio'.

Every musician knows these pieces and could play them to you.

If things continue like this, Act I may well be ready in the draft by the beginning of June.

I should be very pleased if you could visit me here: apart from the Whitsun holidays, when I must go to Aachen for the music festival, I am here all the time. Best regards from us to you all.

Yours,

RICHARD STRAUSS

Garmisch, 22nd May, 1909

Dear Herr von Hofmannsthal,

The rough sketch of the first act is as good as finished: I am now impatiently waiting for Acts II and III.

I only need a few additions: Page 33, Octavian:

'Ja, ist sie da?
Dann will ich sie halten und sie
pressen'—another 3 or 4 lines
stammered words of love!!!
until 'dass sie mir nicht wieder entkommt'.

[1] Hofmannsthal complied with this request, but the additions are not included in the book edition of *Rosenkavalier*.

Further, page 35, Octavian: the following amplification:

> 'Wenn's *so* ein Tag *geben* wird, ich *denk* ihn *nicht*, now
> another 3 or 4 lines in the same form, e.g.
> Dass *diese* Zeit *kommen* soll, ich *will* es *nicht*, etc. etc.

Moreover, I have performed a transposition which I am sure you will approve. I think it's turned out well: that certain Viennese sentimentality of the parting scene has come off very well.

My wife likes it very much and sends her best regards.

In haste, with kind regards, yours

RICHARD STRAUSS

Garmisch, 26th May, 1909

Dear Herr von Hofmannsthal,

I shall be away from 1st to 5th June (in Aachen and Stuttgart). Any time after 6th June we shall be delighted if you would visit us. For this summer I shan't need more than Act II fully worked out. Of Act III only a detailed synopsis and the setting, as I don't intend to compose Act III till next summer.

Act I, set to music, takes an hour, although the dialogue is treated in a smooth flow throughout, and *prestissimo* in parts. It would be highly desirable to keep Act II much shorter.

With best regards, yours

RICHARD STRAUSS

Starnberg, 12.6.(1909) Villa Cantacuzene

My dear Doctor,

Everything you played to me from the first act of the opera is most beautiful and has given me great and lasting pleasure.

I have now re-read Act II and am absolutely determined to make drastic changes in the last five minutes of this act. Three 'quiet' curtains are impossible; they might even endanger the whole effect. I know already how to do it: Annina demands a tip for bringing her message, the miserly Ochs refuses her, Valzacchi comes to support her, the Baron calls in his retinue and makes them beat up and throw out the Italians, while he himself smugly watches and hums his little song. This gives us an energetic, grotesque, ballet-like curtain for the Act where your beautiful waltz theme can be introduced. I am glad to have hit on this idea before it is too late.

One more thing if you will allow me to speak quite frankly: a detail in the aria of Ochs distressed me profoundly when I heard it. The line 'Muss halt eine Frau in der Nähe dabei sein' can never conceivably be acted or sung in any but a sentimental manner. Ochs must whisper it to the Marschallin as a stupid and yet sly piece of coarse familiarity, with his hand half covering his mouth; he must whisper, not bawl it, for God's sake! It cut me to the quick to hear him shout the word 'hay' at *fortissimo*. Let me entreat you to alter this, not of course for my sake but for the good of the whole opera. Wagner differentiates such things in declamation with marvellous nicety. Tomorrow I shall send you the slight revision of this aria. When you enter once more into the detail of composition, further appropriate and characteristic shades may suggest themselves to you for this aria which is quite pointless unless it serves to characterize Ochs as definitely as, say, Beckmesser. Here the music must actually force the singers to act with unfailing authenticity, as Wagner's operas so happily contrive to do.

Many thanks once more for the happy time I have had.

Most sincerely yours,

HOFMANNSTHAL

Garmisch, 26th June, 1909

Dear Poet,

When do I get the additions to Act I:

Page 25, trio: Marschallin, Octavian, Baron.

Page 33, Octavian's declaration of love: from 'Ja, ist sie da?' 4 or 5
   lines.

And when do I get the end of Act II?

For the end of Act III, the softly-fading duet of Sophie and Octavian, I have a very pretty tune. Could you possibly write me some 12 to 16 lines in the following rhythm:

Süsse/ Eintracht, du/ holdes/ Band,
voll golden/ Liebe/ Hand in/ Hand
fest ver/ eint für/ alle/ Zeit
fest ver/ eint in/ Ewig/ keit

Can't think of anything better at the moment: it's the rhythm that matters. Some such popular vaudeville poem: about 3 verses, 12 lines. On the above pattern!

With best regards, yours

RICHARD STRAUSS

Rodaun, 26.6.(1909)

My dear Doctor,

Enclosed (1) the extra matter you wanted for page 6 (Sophie); (2) an *indispensable* short insertion for page 27. This is absolutely essential to avoid the danger of Quinquin's character becoming unattractive. The suggestion for the intrigue *must* therefore come from the Italians. (3), the end of the act, part Singspiel, part ballet which I hope will please you. I have intentionally avoided working up this finale to a choral climax as one could do at any time by bringing in Faninal's staff of male and female servants—intentionally, I mean, so as not to invite any comparison with *Meistersinger*, finale of Act II. It would be excellent if you could give *this* finale almost exclusively to the voices and were to rely on the strict rhythm of the lines given to the Italians, and on the Baron's waltz song, in contrast to the close of Acts I and III which are wholly orchestral.

I return by the same post the ballet *Kythere*[1] which I find a very pretty and picturesque idea.

Yours sincerely,

HOFMANNSTHAL

P.S. On page 9, line 4 from the top, Sophie's line about boxing the ears introduces into her character too highly coloured a trait, an unpleasant travesty, and must be cut, i.e. changed as follows:

... so will ich, meiner Seel', ihm schon beweisen, dass ich ...[2]

Mürren, 9th July, 1909

Dear Herr von Hofmannsthal,

Three days of snow, rain and fog have made me come to a decision today which I don't want to keep from you any longer. Please don't

---

[1] Ballet-scenario by Richard Strauss. Cf Strauss's letter of 14th December, 1900.

[2] Thus in the book edition. The libretto has: 'so will ich, wenn es sein muss, meiner Seel, ihm beweisen'; in the full score and in the piano score it remained: 'so will ich, wenn es sein muss, mit Ohrfeigen ihm beweisen,'—because the word 'Ohrfeigen' was already composed.

get angry, but think over calmly all I'm going to say to you. Even on my first reading of Act II[1] I felt that there was something wrong with it, that it lacked the right dramatic climaxes. Now today I know approximately what's wrong. The first act with its contemplative ending is excellent as an exposition. But Act II lacks the necessary clash and climax: these can't possibly all be left to Act III. Act III must over-trump the climax of Act II, but the audience can't wait as long as that: if Act II falls flat the opera is lost. Even a good third act can't save it then.

Now let me tell you how I picture the second act. If you can think of something better still, *tant mieux*.

Well then, up to the Baron's entrance everything is fine. But from there onwards it's got to be changed.

The Baron's two scenes with Sophie are wrongly disposed. Everything of importance in these two scenes must go straight into the first scene, when the Baron must at once become so distasteful to Sophie that she resolves never to marry him. Octavian must remain a witness to the *whole* scene, quietly getting more and more furious as the Baron, not in the least embarrassed by his presence but on the contrary treating him as a young buck and bragging to him about his successes with women, performs his capers with Sophie. Then the Baron's exit, to sign the marriage contract, and his parting words to Octavian, advising him to 'thaw Sophie out a bit'. Then the declaration of love between Octavian and Sophie, together with the highly dramatic effect of the couple being surprised by the two Italians.

But from here onwards: Attracted by the shouting of the Italians, the Baron himself enters, and the Italians tell him everything. The Baron, at first amused rather than angry, to Octavian: 'Well, my lad, it didn't take you long to learn from me.' The argument between Octavian and the Baron becomes increasingly heated; they fight a duel and Octavian wounds the Baron in the arm. At the Baron's scream: 'He has murdered me' everybody rushes in. Grand tableau. Scandal: 'the Rose Bearer has wounded the bridegroom!' Faninal horrified. The Baron's servants bandage their master. Sophie declares she will never marry the Baron. Here Faninal's part could be a little stronger: he shows Octavian the door, informs Sophie that the marriage contract has been signed, sealed and delivered, and that he'll send her to a convent if she won't have the

[1] The original version of Act II of *Rosenkavalier* was published (with an introduction by Willi Schuh) in *Neue Rundschau*, Vol. 64 (1953), No. 3, S. Fischer Verlag, Frankfurt a.M.

Baron. Exit Octavian, furious; to the Baron: 'We shall meet again.'
Sophie is carried off in a faint. The Baron remains alone, this time still
the victor. Short monologue, partly cursing Octavian, partly bemoan-
ing his wound, and partly rejoicing in the luck of the Lerchenau's. The
Italians creep in and hand him Mariandel's invitation to a *tête-à-tête*.
This can be left as an effective surprise for the audience. No leading up
to it. The end of the act remains as before, except that one might work
in the point that the Baron does not tip them. The later scene, which
you have sent me, is not necessary.[1]

The arrangement between Octavian and the Italians can be brought
up briefly at the beginning of Act III, just before Valzacchi hands the
lady's maid over to the Baron. As the Baron catches sight of Mariandel
he exclaims again: 'The resemblance!' and this pretty theme can then
recur repeatedly during the scenes between Mariandel and the Baron.
The Baron in *tête-à-tête* with his right arm bandaged is also a comical
situation.

What do you think of it? Don't be too anxious about motivating the
Italians' change of sides. Perhaps you'll even find an opportunity to
work in the little scene of Octavian outbidding the Baron with the
Italians, somewhere during the confusion of the scandal ensemble with
its choruses. The audience *does not need it*. They'll tumble to it all right.
The more mischievous Octavian is the better. At all events the clash
must come in Act II: the fade-out ending will then be most effective.
At present it isn't effective because the climax preceding it is too weak.
Have I made myself clear? Do please think it over. If you like I could
come to Aussee to consult with you. As it now stands I can't possibly
use the second act. It is not well planned and is flat. Believe me: my
instinct does not deceive me. The song: 'Mit dir, mit dir keine Nacht
mir zu lang' can be introduced in the first, and only, scene between the
Baron and Sophie. It'll then be most effective just before the curtain, as
a reminiscence. I can also see a lot of comedy in the third act when the
Baron, caressing Mariandel, is time and again reminded of that scoun-
drel of a Rose Bearer and works himself into a rage. That, as I see it,
should be great fun. He thus fluctuates between amorousness and fury
over the resemblance with those cursed features. A good comedy theme,
I think.

Well now, I hope you won't be angry with me. But I feel that, as it
now stands, I can't do anything with the second act. It's too much on

[1] See Hofmannsthal's letter of 12th June 1909.

one level. I must have a great dramatic construction if I want to keep myself interested for so long in a particular setting. Alternatively, Octavian might declare immediately after the duel that he too is willing to marry Sophie. Octavian could be a Baron and Lerchenau a Count; Faninal, a comical title-hunting character, wavers between the Baron and the Count, and eventually prefers the Count.

It's only an idea.

It is certainly right that in Act II Octavian should be defeated and Lerchenau, though winged, emerge victorious, until, in the third act, he is utterly and completely licked.

A possible good way of introducing the Marschallin into Act III would be if she had already, by way of gossip, learned of the events at Faninal's house. As you see, a wealth of themes: all that's wanted is the poet who could draw it all together and clothe it in graceful words, and that's you. Please don't let me down!

Shall I come to Aussee? Or do you get my point? Have I expressed myself clearly enough? No ill feelings. I've started on the draft of Act II and shall compose it, for the time being, as far as Lerchenau's entrance.

With best regards, yours

RICHARD STRAUSS

Rodaun, 10.7.(1909)

My dear Doctor,

You will not seriously believe that I could leave you in the lurch at such a juncture, or that I might create difficulties.

What you ask me to do is essential from your point of view, it contradicts neither the spirit of the chief characters nor the overall conception of the comedy. I will therefore make the alterations, and that as soon as possible. Only it may take me a little while to assimilate these ideas into my imagination since they are not my own, to feel and see once more the whole piece as a living organic conception.

In what is now to be the single scene between the Baron and Sophie (Lerchenau's entrance down to his exit with the notary) you must give me scope to establish the situation (as in *Meistersinger*) or else my characters will lack all substance; I don't mean I want more space for this, but not less than the scene now takes roughly down to the bottom of page 14 of my MS. Then I shall bring in the essential dramatic points from the final scene as it stands (his brazen impudence with her and the decidedly angry rebuff)—and so on according to your suggestions.

At Garmisch you will find requests and news from me (concerning the young Frenchman,[1] concerning Roller, and also addenda to Act I).

Please acknowledge to Aussee, Obertressen.

Yours sincerely,

HOFMANNSTHAL

Mürren, 10th July, 1909

Dear Herr von Hofmannsthal,

While I'm criticizing, and since you've now got over the first shock of my letter of yesterday, I will risk continuing to speak my mind. I keep thinking about that second act, and I'm more and more confirmed in my belief that, generally speaking, yesterday's letter has hit the mark in so far as the architecture and development of the act are concerned. No doubt it also happens to you, as it frequently does to me, that one is dissatisfied with something, but does not fully realize it until someone else puts his finger on the sore spot. You yourself felt that all was not right with Act II when you so emphatically urged me to consider Act III. But, as I said, Act III can't do the job by itself. The second act must be the success and the third must consolidate and reinforce it. I therefore implore you once again to condense the two duets in Act II between Octavian and Sophie, but even more so between the Baron and Sophie, into one scene each, or at least to transfer all the essentials of the second scene in each case into the first scene, so that of the second scene between Octavian and Sophie only the climax remains. In other words: throughout the whole scene between the Baron and Sophie (with Octavian as a progressively more and more infuriated listener) the psychological atmosphere must become so menacing, and Sophie's revulsion against the Baron so strong, that the moment the Baron leaves to append his signature (Sophie need not sign at all or else she can have signed beforehand) she bursts out: 'Save me from that monster' and falls into Octavian's arms. Now a short, passionate duet ending with their kiss and their discovery by the Italians. Please don't be angry with me for thus putting the spurs on your Pegasus, but

[1] Edgar Varèse.

40

this opera must be first-rate and, as I've said, the second act isn't up to what I expect of you or to what you're capable of.

One other thing: since you've got to re-write so drastically, will you please also revise once more the whole dialogue between the Baron and Sophie. Compared with the rest, I find it a little unimaginative and colourless, and I can't help feeling that your taste and talent could produce something much more witty and polished here. This dialogue is not up to Act I.

I hope I shall soon have good news from you and remain, with kindest regards, yours most sincerely,

RICHARD STRAUSS

Rodaun, 11.7.(1909)

My dear Doctor,

Only a line to set your mind at rest. I should not dream of making difficulties and shall recast the act the way you suggest (given our characters, the duel is the most obvious and effective device).

I have just written a long letter to Garmisch.

With best wishes,

HOFMANNSTHAL

Garmisch, 16th July, 1909

Dear Herr von Hofmannsthal,

Back here again, I am most grateful to you for your obliging co-operation concerning Act II. I am very glad that my suggestions appeal to you and I think it's going to turn out famously.

But one thing, please: after the duel and the wounding of the Baron an extensive indignant ensemble, with chorus: the domestic staff of Faninal, the Baron's servants as a comical extra group, and the rest of those present each according to their personal moods.

Another thing that I picture as very funny and boisterous is the Baron's scene, when everyone has left him and he is alone with his servants ministering to him, cursing Octavian and his wound and yet rejoicing in his Lerchenau luck. *After* this scene with its lively movement I believe that the final scene with the Italians will do in its original form, or at most slightly amplified, but without any dramatic emotional emphasis so that the descending line of the act can continue unbroken.

41

After this dramatic explosion the second act can now be allowed to run to a quiet and contemplative end. Only don't forget that the song 'Mit dir, mit dir' is now introduced in the first scene with Sophie so that it should serve only as a reminiscence at the close of the act.

As for the arrangement with Roller, I think this should be possible. I would only ask Roller to give me until the autumn for finalizing it, since I shan't be able to confer with my publisher till then. I'll write about Varèse next time.

I still haven't got the additions to Act I.

With best regards and many thanks, yours

RICHARD STRAUSS

Aussee, Obertressen 14., 18.7.(1909)

My dear Doctor,

Thank you very much for your letter of the 16th from Garmisch. The additions to Act I (trio etc.) were sent off to Garmisch early in July by *registered post*. Please look through the various big envelopes you have had from me. Otherwise let me know at once so that I can make inquiries. Perhaps the registered letter is still waiting at the post office. (. . .)

Your second letter of the 10th from Mürren contains a remark critical of the dialogue at Lerchenau's entrance and his courtship of Sophie which frankly I do consider unjustified. But I would rather not enlarge on this matter just now, since to do so might endanger the mood of good will and sanguine expectation with which I am embarking upon this revision. Anyway, once the two scenes between Lerchenau and Sophie have been run into one (with the little song at the end), the course of the whole action as well as quite a lot of the detail will change. At the moment I am concerned only with the broad sweep of the act, leading up to an excited ensemble as climax followed by a *diminuendo*.

Your criticism was definitely most helpful and beneficial. This act which brings Octavian and Ochs immediately into conflict now strikes me as a far better basis for the events in Act III.

Best wishes,

Yours, HOFMANNSTHAL

P.S. Please return manuscript once more to Edgar Varèse, Berlin-Wilmersdorf, Nassauische Strasse 61.

Dear Herr von Hofmannsthal,

Do not, I implore you, let my criticism discourage you. I can only judge from my own experience, but nothing does me so much good, nothing stimulates and fructifies my ambition and creative energy so much as adverse criticism from one to whose judgement I attach some importance. My criticism is intended to spur you on, not to discourage you. I want to draw the best out of you. (. . .)

In the proposal scene between the Baron and Sophie I feel sure that, during your revision, you'll hit on something even better, more comical and more striking. I know how it is: one feels annoyed when somebody else doesn't like a thing, but it goes on rankling all the same until one's hit on something better. Additions to Act I now all duly to hand. It's just that I always forget to acknowledge receipt straight away. So don't worry.

With best regards, yours

RICHARD STRAUSS

Don't forget that the audience should also laugh! *Laugh*, not just smile or grin!

I still miss in our work a genuinely comical situation: everything is merely amusing, but not *comic*!

Aussee, 26.7.(1909)

My dear Doctor,

I am already hard at work and with great pleasure. The sequence of the scenes has been recast; the second scene between Octavian and Sophie retains only its final emotional climax, all retarding elements have disappeared. It has gained instead a tender and youthful and, as I believe, very pretty love duet of twenty-one lines. The Baron is already wounded, the big ensemble is done and in a few days I hope to send you the complete manuscript. I hope you will be satisfied; I realize myself that for the stage at any rate the new version is very much more effective than the first one, and I am therefore very grateful for your energetic intervention.

Just a detail today with the request for an immediate reply by post-card. It concerns the line which the Baron, and others (aping him) are to repeat several times as a refrain. 'Das ist das Glück der Lerchenau' is how it sounds to you. But this particular turn of phrase occurs to you (and to everybody in the audience) merely because it recalls more or less automatically, but often quite consciously, a quotation: the refrain from Uhland's best-known ballad printed in every school reader where each stanza ends: 'Das ist das Glück von Edenhall!' So *that* is out of the question. The wording 'I hab' halt ja ein Lerchenauisch Glück!', on the other hand, strikes me as pleasant, rhythmical, lilting, complacent and therefore characteristic of Baron Ochs. (And no harm done if it suggests: 'ein sauisch Glück!' as a very coarse undertone.) The others can then sing 'Er hat halt ja ein Lerchenauisch Glück!' at the moment of his complete discomfiture.

Does this phrase suit you? If not I must think of some other. Reply, please!

Yours,

HOFMANNSTHAL

Garmisch, 29th July, 1909

Dear Herr von Hofmannsthal,

'Das ist das Glück von Lerchenau' is of course impossible. Do you know the popular hit:

> denn dort in Lindenau
> da ist der Himmel blau . . .

Nor am I particularly keen on the second version: 'Ich hab halt ja ein lerchen*au*isch Glück.'

Admittedly this is a little impersonal, and one would have to find a version that applies a little more directly to the Baron.

44

or: "Glück ham die von Lerchenau."

or: "Nein, so ein Glück wie (der Lerchenau..."
(ein

The last is perhaps the best. But maybe you'll hit on something even better and more striking.

"Nur ein Lerchenau hat a solches Glück"

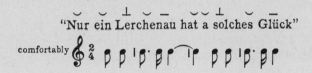

etc. etc.

With best regards, yours

RICHARD STRAUSS

Aussee, 3.8.(1909)

My dear Doctor,

I hope the second act gives you pleasure now, pleasure which you owe in the first place to yourself. From this one occasion I have learnt something fundamental about dramatic work for music which I shall not forget.

I have recast the wooing scene, too, to make it really funny with the Baron's irrepressible and pretty brazen sallies which culminate in that impertinent little song, with Faninal's (and the duenna's) grotesque enthusiasm and with Octavian's rising fury. I hope at the same time that I have so managed the scene which leads up to the duel that, given *reasonably* downright acting on the part of the bass buffo, it may raise a laugh or two rather than mere smiles. Actually I do not by any means deny that there is a great deal of difference between what is merely gay and what is broadly comic; only I tell myself that a general atmosphere of gaiety with animated, well-contrasted characters and without long-winded machinery or dull stretches must, *in the long run*, prove superior even in the eyes of the public to anything approaching the more obvious operetta. (See *Meistersinger* or *Figaro*, which contain little to make one laugh and much to smile at.)

If, what is more, we have a first act which is leisurely and full of sentiment, a second which is now very lively, and a third which will produce, in the police interrogation scene the height of forthright *quid pro quo* and confusion, then we are, I think, out of the wood. Given time I hope to make *a great deal* of this third act, both of its funny and of its emotional sections.

The words for our refrain song really trouble me. All the lines you suggest match Lerchenau's manner of speaking wretchedly, for he has his own most distinct individual idiom. (As Beckmesser, for instance, has his.) I have tried as hard as I can to introduce your lines (e.g. 'Nein so ein Glück wie ein Lerchenau') into the text, but they sound altogether alien, altogether superimposed, and are not particularly characteristic even when used to ape Ochs.

Do you insist on this small point? Would it not be possible to retain the various versions we now have so that he does not in fact use exactly the same words over and over again? Amateur as I am in matters of music I have noticed with consternation that you see *so many* alternatives for setting this passage to music (you even write 'etc.'). Had you tied me down to a given set metre I would have had to manage; as it is I am momentarily altogether at a loss.

Please send me a few lines to tell me what you think of the whole thing now.

With best wishes and regards, yours,

HOFMANNSTHAL

Garmisch, 9.8.1909

Dear Herr von Hofmannsthal,

Once more: *bravissimo* for Act II. Quite excellent. Only one question: how is the change of sides of the Italians motivated? Is there something at the beginning of Act III, showing how Octavian has won them over, or that the Baron has not paid them, etc.?

Of what I've read so far the only thing I still don't quite like is the chorus of the Lerchenau servants at the end of Act II: I should like

the Baron's monologue of triumph and curses to be a little more boisterous and expressive. Maybe you'll think of something on those lines.
Without chorus! Solo scene. I'm already at the Baron's entrance.

With best regards and congratulations, yours

RICHARD STRAUSS

Have you let Beer-Hofmann, Schnitzler, Bahr, etc., read the first two
acts yet?

Aussee, 11.8.1909

My dear Doctor,

There are several places in Act III where the volte-face of the Italians
can be briefly motivated; here in Act II it would have had a retarding
effect. Besides, as you yourself rightly pointed out in your letter from
Mürren, the public is very tolerant in such matters, especially where
professional intriguers are involved. In the short penultimate scene
between Faninal and Annina's entrance with the letter, the servants,
I imagine, ought to remain on the stage (to avoid too close an analogy
with the end of Act I), but they can keep their mouths shut. I feel you
have something quite definite in mind for the Baron here: a sort of
aria maybe? Corresponding, perhaps, to that in Act I, though with quite
different content? How many lines, roughly? Short lines or long?
Please drop me a card!

Yours,

HOFMANNSTHAL

Garmisch, 13th August, 1909

Dear Herr von Hofmannsthal,

In Verdi's *Falstaff* there is an amusing monologue at the beginning of
the last act; it starts with the words, 'Mondo ladro'. I picture the scene
of the Baron, after Faninal's exit, similarly: the Baron on the sofa, the
surgeon attending to him, the mute servants lined up behind the couch,
and the Baron talking in snatches, partly to himself and partly to the
others, in turn boastful and sorry for himself, always interrupted by
orchestral interludes

> Groaning with pain
> cursing Quinquin
> appraising his bride.

47

The plan is good, but it needs working out a little—some 8 lines or so.

But now something rather more important! From page 19 onwards, the scene between Sophie and Octavian doesn't quite suit me yet. What I need here is something much more passionate—after that preceding scene, and before the fatal scene when the Baron surprises the two.

As it now reads it is too tame, too mannered and timid, and too lyrical. For the time being I shan't be able to place the little duet since I've used up most of the lyricism at the beginning of Act II.

Couldn't you let me have this scene done anew?

Sophie much more horrified and desperate, almost throwing herself at Octavian's neck; from page 21 onwards intensification towards a climax and no more gentleness.

Can it be done? If not, I shall have to try and manage with what I've got. But I picture at this point something entirely different from the atmosphere of lovingly-gentle silence. First, Sophie's passionate outburst: 'Dear cousin, save me, rid me of that monster; I'd sooner go to a convent than marry this boor,' turning gradually into a full declaration of love up to the culminating point when the Italians start yelling.

With best regards, yours

RICHARD STRAUSS

Have got to page 18 with the composition.

Garmisch, 15.8.09

As a postscript to today's letter: up to the end of page 20 everything can stand, but change from page 21 onwards: outburst of despair, passionate heart-to-heart talk, and declaration of love.

Regards, in haste,

RICHARD STRAUSS

Aussee, (19.8.1909)

My dear Doctor,

I am very glad to learn from your postcard, which supplements your letter of the 13th, that you mean to keep at least the first few pages of the duet scene in its present form, since I would find it difficult to think of anything better for this beginning which *must* develop out of leisurely conversation; passages altered without inclination and without inspiration are apt to mar the characteristic style of a whole piece. Unfortunately, there is a discrepancy in pagination between my MS. and your copy, but I assume you mean to retain the text down to the kiss (Octavian—'Ich hab' sie recht von Herzen lieb') and all you require is some passionate, rising cross-talk of fifteen lines on the theme 'Ich hab' Dich lieb, Ich hab' Dich lieb' in place of the restrained duet. This is the solution I should prefer, please let it sink in and send me a definite reply.

Your word 'sofa' is a suggestive hint which helps me to realize exactly what you need. I had a mistaken notion that you might want something lively and full of action. I can, myself, see the scene much better on a quiet relaxed note and will get it on to paper without delay. I need from you only a line concerning the duet, to know whether I can proceed as suggested.

Yours,

HOFMANNSTHAL

P.S. Every time I read it, even in words alone, the duet scene Quinquin-Marschallin in Act I strikes me as *perilously* long.

I would suggest a cut on page 36 which sacrifices quite a pretty but not indispensable passage of the libretto, i.e. all the replies of the two characters which are on page 36. This leaves quite a tolerable transition. Dragging out the last quarter of an hour of a long act seems to me most risky.

Aussee, 2.9.(1909)

My dear Doctor,

Perhaps the enclosed words for the duet between Octavian and Sophie immediately after the duenna's exit will suit you now; I hope they may. Sophie's appeal: 'blieb' er nur bei mir!' (to be repeated ad lib.) might, so I imagine, provide the requisite occasion for swelling and poignant as well as tender music. What I would wish to avoid at all cost is to see these two young creatures, who have nothing of the Valkyries or Tristan about them, bursting into a Wagnerian kind of erotic screaming. If it isn't quite right yet, please let me have a line at once; we shall get it straight.

Yours sincerely,

HOFMANNSTHAL

Aussee, Obertressen, 9.9.1909

My dear Doctor,

I am very glad it is only a trifle which keeps you at this accursed place for a little while.

I, too, have suffered a tiresome interruption in the middle of my work, a slight but most deplorable nervous depression. As a result I have done practically nothing for the past three weeks, for I need to be light-hearted and cheerful to accomplish that gay ending and the alterations in the first act. Here in this lovely and familiar landscape I hope to get it done.

If, then, I were to come to Munich around the 10th October, or towards the 15th, would that suit you? We are bound to agree on something and so this piece, I feel sure, will in the end give pleasure to us both.

With all good wishes,

Yours sincerely,

HOFMANNSTHAL

Garmisch 15.9.09

Dear Herr von Hofmannsthal,

Am I getting a few more amusing lines for the final scene of Act II (the Baron alone): curses at Octavian, triumph over his victory, the pain in his arm—a kind of mixture of hangover and gaiety? Getting close to it now and hope to finish Act II by the end of this month. After 1st October: Berlin W, Joachimsthaler Strasse 17. Best regards!

RICHARD STRAUSS

Please reply by telegram!

Aussee, Obertressen 14,   16.9.(1909)

My dear Doctor,

I would like to think that your silence implies that the duet scene is now in order, but quite possibly you are not working at the moment, are unwell or something, and have not written for that reason. So will you please let me have a brief acknowledgement immediately upon receipt of this letter, for after the 22nd I shall disappear from the world for about six weeks, that is, hide away in Italy, Haute Savoie or somewhere, with my comedy, and neither letters nor telegrams are to be forwarded, not even yours. Before leaving I intend to send you, tomorrow or the next day, the slight alterations for the penultimate scene in Act II, the Baron's monologue on the sofa.

Yours sincerely,

HOFMANNSTHAL

Garmisch, 18th Sept. 1909

Many thanks for your letter: am impatiently awaiting the Baron's monologue, the more so as the final conclusion of Act II is now all composed and, I believe, has turned out a first-class hit. 'I am satisfied with myself.' I am feeling well and fit, and wish you likewise all the best for the successful conclusion of the comedy. Let me have your address just in case: I shan't worry you without weighty reason, especially as I shall embark on the orchestration of the first two acts in Berlin on 1st October. A tedious task! With best regards, yours very sincerely,

RICHARD STRAUSS

Aussee, 18.9.(1909)

My dear Doctor,

On the reverse of this sheet I present you with the Baron's monologue and interludes for orchestra, as follows:

(a) hangover,

(b) wrath against Octavian,

(c) gradual return of conceit,

(d) utter complacency and transition to the little refrain song.

Yours sincerely,

HOFMANNSTHAL

P.S. By tomorrow's post I shall send you the printed piano score of the one-act opera written by my old friend Franckenstein[1] which I have already mentioned to you several times. I send it with the earnest request to you to say a *telling* good word for it in Dresden unless you dislike it. I should feel, and prove myself, *particularly grateful* for your good offices.

[1] *Fortunatus* (?).

Aussee, 20.9.(1909)

My dear Doctor,

I could not ask for better news than that which is given in your recent card, and am sincerely grateful for what you say about the pleasure you take in our joint work.

As soon as I have got my comedy out of the way, I shall tackle Act III, and I know from the outset that these few months of rest will only have matured and enriched it. It must become the best of all, gay and full of feeling, and ought, in the character of the Marschallin, to touch once again the more sublime chords of tenderness.

Where I shall hide myself I do not yet know, but *every* letter in your handwriting will reach me through my wife at once if addressed to: Munich, Hotel Marienbad, from the 23rd to 28th September; (please send a note there to say when you are coming through); Aussee from 29.9. to 12.10., Schloss Neubeuern am Inn, Oberbayern, from 12.10. to 25.10.

Yours,

HOFMANNSTHAL

Schloss Neubeuern am Inn, Oberbayern, Tuesday (12. or 19. 10.1909)

My dear Doctor,

I am really quite flabbergasted to discover from the Vienna programme that *Elektra* has once again not been billed. I regret exceedingly that this should happen in Vienna of all places and that I should be so wholly unable to do anything about it. Indeed, given my considerable personal unpopularity and my lack of personal contacts (I have no means of approach whatever even to Obersthofmeister Prince Montenuovo, who might conceivably intervene), I am only too well aware that I would merely make matters worse by interfering. You, on the other hand, have Pötzl and Bahr, two men who should undoubtedly prove reliable at least in this particular matter.

Perhaps you have already done something about it. Or perhaps Weingartner has given you precise promises or assurances of some sort —and I agitate myself in vain. For this reason and not least because, at a moment when my work is progressing so strongly, I should like to rid myself of every tiresome distraction (or anyway would prefer to face definite and clear-cut trouble rather than this uncertainty), I beg of you to explain to me in two words, on a postcard, but as soon as possible, how matters stand.

Yours sincerely,

HOFMANNSTHAL

(*October 1909?*)

My dear Doctor,

Many thanks. Perhaps I too, have allowed myself to be worked upon! It may be so. In any case it was done with the best of intentions. Perhaps Mildenburg and Bahr are the kind of people who suffer a little from persecution mania. I shall certainly *not* refer the full details of Weingartner's letter back to Bahr, especially not the reference to Bella Paalen, since this would lead to interminable gossip.

Au revoir, I am working every day and with great pleasure.

Yours,

HOFMANNSTHAL

1910

Rodaun, 9.3.(*1910*)

My dear Doctor,

I hope the two registered letters with all the addenda to Acts I and II have reached you safely? Please acknowledge. The day before yesterday *I concluded the agreement* with Roller in your name and on the basis of what we discussed at Garmisch. He accepts a down payment of 5000 marks and a share in a *possible* surplus profit. He is getting down to work with great enthusiasm and wrote to me today that he has already settled the first outline of the décor.

Best wishes and regards,

Yours,

HOFMANNSTHAL

Garmisch, 23rd April, 1910

Dear Herr von Hofmannsthal,

I am in Garmisch and am in agonies waiting for Act III! The full score of Act II is already with the printer!

53

I shall be in Vienna in mid-June. Saturday *Elektra* has its Czech première in Prague.

All the best for the successful completion of our *Ochs* and kindest regards.

Yours very sincerely,

RICHARD STRAUSS

Roller's costume sketches are magnificent!

Rodaun, 27.4.(1910)

My dear Doctor,

Immediately upon receipt of your telegram, I dealt with the *Neue Freie Presse* matter, refusing. I am delighted you are so favourably predisposed towards Roller's collaboration. It is of the greatest value that we have at our disposal so able an assistant who in the end will help to put across the new *style* which is here involved. This is bound to be a tough job in any case, but a *conditio sine qua non* if the opera is to endure on the stage for some decades. Nothing can last except that which at first takes people aback on account of the novelty and unity of its style, and only gradually makes itself accepted.

I am really quite upset to learn you are 'waiting in agonies'. In the first place I did not expect you to be at home and at leisure, for I seem to read constantly of your flitting here, there and everywhere. What is more I hoped you might, as with Act I, be able to get on with the supper and interrogation scene which is complete in itself and already in your hands. Is that impossible? Please let me know by postcard. Tomorrow I shall dictate the continuation straight on to the typewriter and you will get it post-haste. Only the very end the trio-duet, which needs much subtlety and yet great sweetness, has had to be put off until now when I am feeling better and more in the mood. Alas, for each single day of spring weather we get a whole week of icy winter wind howling round the fruit-trees which are already in bloom. I did so want to write this last scene, a matter of only three or four pages, out in the garden.

Unfortunately I shall not be here when you come in June. I could not avoid booking rooms at the Lido from June 10th onwards.

Very sincerely yours,

HOFMANNSTHAL

54

Dear Herr von Hofmannsthal,

I am starting now on composing Act III. There's no hurry about the end. Only I like having everything a little while beforehand, so that I can work through the text and digest it before getting down to the music-making. By all means wait for your 'kindly hour'! Title? I'm still in favour of *Ochs*!

With best regards, yours,

RICHARD STRAUSS

Elektra last Friday in Frankfurt, before a full house, with Mildenburg a colossal success!

Rodaun, 4.5.(1910)

My dear Doctor,

Herewith the continuation, leading right up to the end, so that you will now get the idea of the over-all structure of the whole piece.

I would have found the end long ago, but for the appalling weather we have now been having here for weeks; it thoroughly depresses me. The end must be *very* good, or it will be no good at all. It must be psychologically convincing and at the same time tender, the words must be charming and easy to sing, it must be properly split up into conversation and again into numbers, it must provide a happy ending for the young people and yet not make one too uncomfortable about the Marschallin. In short, it must be done with zest and joy, and so I must sit in the garden and have sun, not icy rain-storms.

Tomorrow I am going to Budapest for a performance of *Cristina*[1] in a new shortened version.

Congratulations on *Salome* in Paris. Will the immense London success on which everyone congratulates you (it seems to have caused quite an exceptional sensation) really lead to no more than these eight performances? I should have thought it would have been good for a run of four hundred.

Very sincerely yours,

HOFMANNSTHAL

[1] The revised version without the fourth act.

Dear Herr von Hofmannsthal,

The death of my poor mother[1] has abruptly shaken me out of my work and it is only today that I can think of our plans again.

In brief: the disposition of the last bit that you sent me (enclosed!) is not at all to my liking.

Too broad, too scattered, everything in orderly succession instead of one thing bursting on top of another.

The Marschallin's entrance and the ensuing scene must be the focal point of the action and the suspense, and must be highly concentrated. When the Baron and the whole crowd are gone, then everything can gradually dissolve into a lyrical mood and return to soft outlines.

The focal point is the Baron's colossal embarrassment as he suddenly finds himself confronted by the fixed stare of three pairs of eyes: the Marschallin, Octavian and Sophie. His reeling about among the three must be exceedingly riotous. Perhaps you'll think of even apter tags for this situation than the ones I have jotted down on the enclosed, but on the whole I think the disposition I am sending you herewith is well planned.

Do please read it carefully, and with your great skill correct all the bits that are awkward in my version—but in general outline, I think, it must stand as it is.

The Police Inspector must be dealt with quickly: as a sideline. He's of no more interest once the main characters are facing one another threateningly.

Let me know soon what you think!

Kind regards, in haste, yours

RICHARD STRAUSS

Delighted to hear that *Cristina* has at last found in Vienna a public with taste and artistic sensibility.

23.5.(1910)

My dear Doctor,

I am very glad to have your constructive strictures. For some days I had felt there was something wrong with the whole passage, but without knowing quite what it was. You have hit the nail on the head: I have

---

[1] Josephine Strauss, *née* Pschorr, born in Munich on 10th April 1838, died there on 16th May 1910.

been dawdling over the minor figure of the Police Inspector. The rearrangement and telescoping you suggest is excellent; I am carrying it out faithfully, attempting merely to find a characteristic and comic turn of phrase for what is said by each person (especially by the Baron).

One thing only: the passage where Sophie describes Octavian prematurely as her betrothed is impossible. It is far too crude and sudden. Such an expression at this juncture, moreover, would have to lead, on the stage, to some far more forcible and definitive clash than the Marschallin's mere wincing. A few lines earlier, on the other hand, there is an opportunity for making Octavian and Sophie give themselves away to some extent (only not quite so crudely), and so to make the Marschallin wince. For Sophie and the Marschallin each to sink into a chair, one on the left, the other on the right, is thoroughly within the burlesque stage convention, but here it does not suit me since it blurs the difference in rank and character between the two women which is essential to the final situation. Sophie must stand, defiant, on the left, the Marschallin must be seated, sad, on the right, while Octavian oscillates between the two. Your rearrangement provides a better foundation for the final, lyrical scene and a better transition. Therefore many thanks.

Yours,

HOFMANNSTHAL

Rodaun, 6.6.(1910).   After Sunday: Venice-Lido, Excelsior

My dear Doctor,

I am expecting the typescript copy of Act III from Vienna any moment now, and will send it off to you at once. The middle section follows exactly the line you desired. I hope you will be pleased with the lyrical part at the end; it is above all short: only twelve minutes from the Baron's exit to the fall of the curtain. It could not be any shorter without taking away from the significance of the Marschallin's character. She is the central figure for the public, for the women above all, the figure with whom they feel and *move*. I have succeeded in getting the whole psychological content of the end into numbers, either trio or duet, with the exception of some very brief *parlando* passages. It is certainly an advantage if the last act is not only the gayest, but also the one *most full of song*. In the final duet between Quinquin and Sophie

I was obviously very much tied down by the metre scheme which you prescribed for me, but in the end I found it rather agreeable to be bound in this way to a given tune since I felt in this something Mozartian and a turning away from Wagner's intolerable erotic screaming—boundless in length as well as in degree; a repulsive, barbaric, almost bestial affair this shrieking of two creatures in heat as he practises it.

I pray you are content—for myself I must say I so enjoyed working on this piece that it almost saddens me to have to write 'Curtain'. (. . .)

'Your'

HOFMANNSTHAL

Rodaun, 10.6.(1910)

My dear Doctor,

Many thanks for your kind telegram. Yes, I too believe that the lyrical sentimental ending, and the big burlesque scene (the supper and the police interrogation) are good. But after reading the act aloud to two discerning friends I realize clearly that what is still, despite revision, *not good* is the connecting middle part, from the Marschallin's entrance to the exit of Ochs, roughly pages 27 to 33. This part flags and is tedious; it has the following faults:

(a) it is still too long,
(b) it is neither fish nor fowl, neither funny nor lyrical, too serious, too dry,
(c) the comic possibilities of the chief characters, of Ochs above all, are by no means exhaustively exploited,
(d) this business about the bewildering resemblance is flogged to death and in the end becomes boring,
(e) the fifth fault I cannot remember just now, but it will come back to me.

This passage must be newly written therefore, newly thought out and newly done. Though I should prefer to have a rest, I shall get down to it at once at the Lido (Excelsior Palace), for this is a matter of the greatest importance. In a work of this kind we must not tolerate a single weakness that we recognize or even merely suspect. In the meantime, I assume you are getting through your various *Elektras* and the *Strauss-Woche*.[1]

[1] In Munich.

Let me know whether the final words really do fit perfectly the closing tune you had in mind? And do let me have a brief postcard at the Lido some time.

Sincerely yours,

HOFMANNSTHAL

(Appended to a letter from Count Seebach)

Garmisch, 1st July, 1910

Dear Herr von Hofmannsthal,

Please read and consider this letter on official Court Theatre paper.

Received the conclusion of *Rosenkavalier*: seems perfect to me. Bahr, to whom I gave the third act to read in Munich, does not think Sophie naïve or attractive in the way she expresses herself. He's going to write to you about it himself. *Elektra* at the Prinzregententheater with Fassbender overwhelming!

Best regards, in haste, yours

RICHARD STRAUSS

Rodaun, 12.7.(1910)

My dear Doctor,

Please forgive the long delay; I have not been at all well.

It strikes me that Count Seebach's objections certainly deserve to be taken seriously. For what shocks him, will shock others too (and not in Court theatres only), and why should we needlessly put off any section of the public?

Therefore:

(1) That the Marschallin ought to be out of bed was already agreed with Roller (for prompt book and décor).

(2) The passage in Act II . . . had best, I suggest, be *left out*. I hope you can arrange this for the music also. Whatever I might put in its place would lack point, and would make a dreary, jejune passage, for there is nothing funny here except his saying just *that*. Therefore *please*, leave it out and establish some transition.

(3) For Ochs's rather downright words in the trio in Act I, I shall substitute something tamer in the same rhythm.

59

(4) I don't really agree that the passages in Ochs's big aria, especially 'that his wenching is not ruled by the calendar', are as gross as all that. Perhaps one could talk it over with Seebach—I mean you could, for I will deal only with you and you alone must represent us in all negotiations with outsiders.—

I am of course quite prepared to change such passages, if afterwards you should still wish me to do so, but by watering this 'aria' down one inevitably runs the risk of making it as dull as ditch-water.

Since we are now on the point of bringing our joint labours, so to speak, to a conclusion, I would like to tell you how *much* I have enjoyed working with you from the first discussion down to the last letter, not forgetting your occasional very valuable objections, and to thank you most sincerely. During the proceedings now impending I intend to keep myself altogether in the background, as I did in the case of *Elektra*, and I should obviously resent most strongly any attempt on the part of outsiders to exaggerate my share in the joint work; though of course I would gratefully accept any emphasis you yourself might be kind enough to bestow on it. (Like that Berlin interview which pleased me greatly.)

Bahr's remark about Sophie is of no relevance to me whatever, so long as he knows only Act III, for in that case he lacks the key to her personality which is characterized and realized through her manner of speaking. If he also knew Act II, he would surely have noticed that Sophie, whose character and speech are intrinsically naïve, is constantly voicing sentiments picked up at second hand either at her convent or even from her father's jargon. Sophie is a very pretty girl, but she is also a very ordinary girl like dozens of others—this is the whole point of the story; true charm of speech, indeed the stronger charm of personality is all with the Marschallin. Just the fact that, in this criss-cross double adventure, Quinquin falls for the *very first* little girl to turn up, that is the point, that is what unites the whole and holds together the two actions. The Marschallin remains the dominant female figure, between Ochs and Quinquin—Sophie always stands one step below these chief characters. A letter from Princess Lichnowsky, which I enclose and would ask you to return sometime, will show you how strongly women feel this—how they, who make up such an important section of our public, look upon the whole vivid unfolding of the action from the point of view of the Marschallin. I would like to impress this point upon you just at the present moment as you are presumably nearing the composition of this final scene which is so full of feeling. Even the musical, conceptual unity of the whole opera would suffer if the personality of the Marschallin were to be deprived of her full stature, and unless a definite allusion in the end of Act III to the end of Act I were to establish emotional continuity so to speak for the whole unfolding of the story. I shall be here until the 18th. Between the 23rd and 26th a letter would reach me at Konstanz, Insel Hotel.

Yours sincerely,

HOFMANNSTHAL

Aussee, Obertressen 14. (July 1910)

My dear Doctor,

Enclosed the three most important passages (the line with the cock pheasant, the passage referring to Paris and that concerning the hay) which I have toned down. But let us then accept these tamer versions uniformly for all theatres, for it would be a bore to have two different libretti, and why upset a section of the public needlessly with a handful of passages which are practically as good in the more restrained version! I have checked the copies made from the score and have sent them to Fürstner. A sheet containing a number of unavoidable comments on them is enclosed herewith. If, as I hope, you agree with these comments, please do not trouble to send me a reply (of course I see the points raised by Ottone Schanzer and have dealt with them). A number of small alterations from the Viennese diction of the characters must be restored again, if at all possible, in the text as sung, but in any case *certainly* in the libretto. They look casual and accidental, but to me they are really distressing (for Octavian, for instance, to say 'Therese' instead of 'Theres' sounds altogether *impossible*). You may well consider such changes of a syllable here or there, or even only a single letter quite trifling; I am as mortified by them as you would be if someone were to fiddle about with the notes in your score.

Sincerely yours,

HOFMANNSTHAL

Alterations Requested[1]

[1] Only some of these alterations were carried into effect, and even these only in the libretto, and not in the full score or the piano score.

61

Act I. 25 (cock pheasant passage)
Baron: Weiss mich im Heu und im Stroh zu bequemen,
　　　　Weiss im Alkoven mich zu benehmen,
　　　　Hätte Verwendung für tausend Gestalten
　　　　Tausend so Jungfern festzuhalten.
　　　　Wäre mir keine zu junge, zu herbe
　　　　Keine zu niedrige, keine zu derbe!
　　　　Tät mich für (=vor) keinem Versteck nicht
　　　　　　schämen,
　　　　Tät aufm Baum und im Korn mich bequemen—
　　　　seh ich was Liebs, ich muss mir's nehmen!
　　　　　　　　　　etc.

Act II. 15. (Paris passage)
　　　　Geniert sie sich leicht vor dem Vetter Taverl?
　　　　Da hat sie Unrecht. In der grossen Welt,
　　　　wo doch die hohe Schul' ist für Manieren,
　　　　da gibt's frei nichts,
　　　　was man nicht willig pardonnieren tät',
　　　　wenn's nur mit einer adligen Noblesse
　　　　und richtigen Galanterie vollführet wird.

I further suggest toning down the passage (before p. 25, Act I)
　　　　'Muss halt ein Heu in der Nähe dabei sein' to
　　　　'Darf halt kein Mensch in der Näh' nicht dabei sein!'
(to be sung in the same sly leering tone).

　　Last comments on final version of the text.

　　Act I, page 9, the red pencil has turned a 'Neapolitan' general into a 'Russian' one. This is impossible because in the first place a Russian is never, as a Neapolitan is, synonymous with running away (the word 'Russian' renders the whole passage quite meaningless); in the second place 'Russian' may give rise to political objections, while 'Neapolitan' is harmless, since the Kingdom of Naples has ceased to exist. (For Italian performances 'Neapolitan' might nonetheless be replaced by some other word.)

　　Page 43a should read: 'die schöner *oder* jünger ist' (not: 'schöner und jünger').

Act II, page 9: In the second version I have expressly cancelled the words 'mit *Ohrfeigen* ihm beweisen' since this coarsens Sophie's character. I have now replaced it by: 'meiner Seel' ihm beweisen', which can after all be sung in the same very emphatic manner. All this boxing of the ears must absolutely disappear from the libretto (and I sincerely pray from the score also!).[1]

Page 11 contains an unfortunate misunderstanding! 'Und da der Faninal' is meant to say: 'und *hier* der Faninal gehört ja sozusagen jetzo . . .'. You apparently mistook: 'und da der Faninal' as equivalent to 'und weil der Faninal': a complicated turn of phrase which is quite incompatible with Ochs's characteristic manner of speaking. Would it not be possible to restore my original words here without altering the music? What we now have is practically meaningless. If, after all, this unfortunate alteration (which arose out of a misreading) must *stand*, it should run at least (as I have inserted in black ink)

> und *weil* der Faninal sozusagen jetzo
> zu der Verwandschaft gehört,
> mach Dir doch kein dépit *darum*, Rofrano . . .

But, as I have said, there is absolutely no causal connection between these two sentences, and it would be most desirable to restore the original text.[2]

On page 31 you have made Octavian and Sophie address each other as 'Geliebter—Geliebte'; these high-flown terms run counter to the naïve idiom of both and are in this sense un-Viennese; occurring at so exposed a point they actually turn the character of these two people

[1] See footnote to Hofmannsthal's letter of 26th June 1909.

[2] In Hofmannsthal's libretto (book edition) the passage runs . . .

> Hab's aus der Fürstin eigenem Mund
> und da der Faninal gehört ja sozusagen jetzo
> zu der Verwandtschaft.
> Macht dir doch kein dépit, Cousin Rofrano
> dass dein Herr Vater ein Streichmacher war?

In the full score it reads:

> und weil der Faninal sozusagen jetzo
> zu der Verwandtschaft gehört,
> mach' dir kein dépit darum, Rofrano,
> dass dein Vater ein Streichmacher war, . . .

In the libretto the passage has been ruined by meaningless punctuation.

upside down. I have therefore replaced them by 'Liebster'—'Liebste' and *urge* you to accept this alteration.

Yours sincerely,

HOFMANNSTHAL

Garmisch, 22.8.10

Dear Herr von Hofmannsthal,

Shall settle all textual matters as far as possible in accordance with your wishes. In the cock pheasant passage Count Seebach still objects to:

Heu und Stroh, Baum und Korn

Can you tone this down a little further? Request *early* reply!

With best regards, yours

RICHARD STRAUSS

Aussee, 25.8.(1910)

My dear Doctor,

Then I propose: 'Weiss mich ins engste Versteck zu bequemen—weiss im Alkoven galant mich zu nehmen' etc.

And the same line once more where it comes again. Inevitably, the potion tastes increasingly insipid, the more water one pours into it in this fashion, and it is just this faunish aspect which gives the whole scene its *raison d'être*. But never mind. All good wishes for your work and cordial regards,

yours sincerely,

HOFMANNSTHAL

Garmisch, 29.8.10

Dear Herr von Hofmannsthal,

The amendments in deference to prudishness and hypocrisy continue to annoy me.

I've now done the following and am asking your approval of it. Cock pheasant passage altered in the libretto and piano score, but allowed to stand in the full score!

'Muss halt eine Frau' altered in the libretto, but allowed to stand in the piano score *and* the full score. The passage would have been too colourless musically, and surely our purpose is not to weaken our comedy but simply to bluff those people who read the libretto *in advance* with malicious intent! The Paris passage altered *in the libretto*, but allowed to stand in *the piano score and the full score*!

The remainder of *your* textual requests corrected and amended.

Do you agree with this? With best regards, yours

RICHARD STRAUSS

Unterach am Attersee, 30.8.(1910) (tomorrow Aussee again)

My dear Doctor,

Please take the following to heart and don't dismiss it lightly, even if it is troublesome to you at first sight. It is of extreme, vital importance to our opera.

Yesterday I read the opera aloud to four or six friends here in one sitting. Both the lyrical and the gay aspects of the whole work made a very considerable impression. A *definite falling off* in interest became apparent in the third act after the Baron's exit, a *longueur* which is wearying. The curtain is almost ready to fall, everything hastens towards the end. Any weariness at this point (and three minutes too much can produce fatal weariness and impatience) would be fatal to the overall success. I then and there made the necessary cuts with some assistance from Felix Salten; they refer to pages 34 to 38. I shall write out these pages in their shortened form and enclose them with this letter, and I beseech you to base your composition on this final version; otherwise I would have to wash my hands of all responsibility for any falling off in the last act—the most unfortunate thing that can happen at a première and one which might reduce by 75 per cent the great and far-reaching success it could have.

Sincerely yours,

HOFMANNSTHAL

Act III. I begin at page 34 at the bottom,

Marschallin: Geh Er doch schnell und tu Er, was sein Herz ihm sagt.

Octavian: Theres, ich weiss gar nicht—

Marschallin (laughs angrily): Er ist ein rechtes Mannsbild, geh Er hin!

Octavian: Wie Sie befiehlt (crosses over).

Sophie: speechless.

Octavian (close to her): Hat Sie kein freundlichs Wort für mich, nicht einen Blick? nicht einen lieben Gruss?

Sophie (nearly in tears): Verkriech mich in ein Kloster, lieber heut als morgen, so jung ich bin. Lass Er mich gehen.

Octavian: Ich lasse Sie nicht (takes her hand).

Sophie: Das sagt sich leicht.

Octavian: Ich hab Sie übermässig lieb.

Sophie: Er hat mich nicht so lieb als wie Er spricht. Vergess' Er mich, vergess' Er mich. Er hat mich nicht so lieb als wie Er spricht. Vergess' Er mich.

Octavian: Ist mir um Sie, und nur um Sie. Mag alles drunter oder drüber gehn. Seh allweil Ihr Gesicht, hab allzu lieb Ihr lieb Gesicht.

Marschallin (to herself): Heut oder morgen oder den übernächsten Tag.

And so on as on page 38.

Aussee, 10.9.(1910)

My dear Doctor,

I am sincerely sorry you are having so much trouble and annoyance over these contracts; today I read of another and, as it seems to me, *mistakenly* piqued letter of Seebach's—I must say I do hope all this will sort itself out. Dresden strikes me *so very much* as the place predestined for this première—a change on this point, any abandoning of the tradition which you yourself have created, would appear to me a bad omen. Maybe the matter has already been settled, in which case I should be most grateful to you for a line giving me news to this effect—news which would be very welcome.

I must not omit to send you now my carefully considered suggestion for the sub-title. I called my libretto provisionally 'Comedy for Music'. Obviously we cannot give that title to the finished comic opera. It is *linguistically* impossible, since Comedy for Music means a comedy destined to be set to music. This impossible title would invite the standing joke that your music is no music, and that the opera is still waiting to be set to music.

I am also very much against titles of the precious and pretentious kind like *musikalisches Lustspiel* (or *musikalische Komödie*). It is invariably only the third raters like (. . .) who choose to deck themselves out with such pretentious descriptions and try to avoid the straightforward title. The higher one's standing, the more imperative is simplicity and traditional correctness. I see, therefore, three possible sub-titles:

1. Opera in three Acts (see *Meistersinger*)
2. Comic Opera and
3. Burlesque Opera.

For weighty reasons I am much inclined to favour this last description. The point is this: the unusually forthright passages of broad comedy might quite conceivably cause frowns and bewilderment, if the title promises something tame in genre. If, on the other hand, any astonishment over the riotous scenes (especially in the third act) is eliminated in advance by the words 'Burlesque Opera', then we get double the credit for the tender, lyrical passages, for the psychological subtlety and the abundance of more profound features. I should be very glad to feel that we are in agreement over this by no means unimportant matter. The title *Rosenkavalier* seems to strike people as very pretty and attractive, as I hear from all sides. If you agree, I shall call my book edition *Burlesque for Music,* and the definitive title of the whole work is

DER ROSENKAVALIER
Burlesque Opera in 3 Acts
by Hugo von Hofmannsthal
Music by Richard Strauss

Very sincerely yours,

HOFMANNSTHAL

P.S. 'Burlesque Opera' gives us back something of what the title 'Ochs von Lerchenau' was to have conveyed.

Garmisch, 12.(?)9.(1910)

Dear Herr von Hofmannsthal,

Of course I didn't take your letter lightly, but let me reassure you that (1) I have myself made a few cuts towards the end and (2) neither yourself nor Herr Salten can possibly at this stage judge the musical effect which the conclusion, in particular, will have. That it sounds a bit flat in reading is obvious. But it is at the conclusion that a musician, if he has any ideas at all, can achieve his best and supreme effects—so you may safely leave this for me to judge. I am nearly finished and I believe that the last third has come off brilliantly. The weakest spot in the third act is the passage with Annina and later the Police Inspector, which is rather heavy going for a musician. I hope that it'll score its effect through the situation. As for the rest, from the Baron's exit onwards, I'll *guarantee* that, provided you undertake to guarantee the rest of the work. As far as I am concerned, I've sorted things out with the Dresden and Berlin Court Theatre. Perhaps you know that at the last minute Count Seebach did not sign the contract, and now the whole Bühnenverein is up in arms against me because of my unheard-of conditions. I am still fighting, but whether I shall win is, to say the least, questionable at the moment.

With best regards, yours

RICHARD STRAUSS

I shan't win, but the world première is going to be in Dresden all the same.

Subtitle: 'Comedy for Music' is by far the best and freest.

'Burlesque Opera' is impossible: after all, there's nothing burlesque about it. Just think what the public would expect: Offenbach, *Mikado*, etc. 'Opera' by itself would also do.

But let's keep 'Comedy for Music': it's clear and new and free! And to hell with all wisecracks!

Aussee, 17.9.(1910)

My dear Doctor,

Many thanks for your kind letter with its postscript. I hope it is true that Dresden stands; for many factual reasons it would mean much to me.

I felt obliged to put forward my doubts concerning the *longueurs* in the final scene, because I was under the impression you had not yet reached that point in composition. If it is already set to music and if, on top of that, you are so pleased with the result, then all is well. All I remember of the end of Act II I treasure just as much as ever.

For my part I think I can guarantee the success of the earlier scenes, provided the acting is at least adequate. They are invariably effective when read aloud, to *any* group of listeners, and where even three people in a room laugh loud and often, there ought to be roars of laughter in a crowded house—unless something is altogether wrong.

68

If you wish to stick to the sub-title, then this is the only correct form:

DER ROSENKAVALIER
Comedy for Music by H. v. H.
Music by Richard Strauss

but never DER ROSENKAVALIER, Comedy for Music by Richard Strauss—or else it should be: DER ROSENKAVALIER by Richard Strauss.

From the 24th onwards I shall be in Munich, Hotel Marienbad, for eight days. If the weather is good, I should very much like to make an excursion to Garmisch with my wife and my father, staying the night at Partenkirchen, and to hear on that occasion the third act to which I look forward immensely. But will you be in Munich around that time?

Please inform me by postcard.

Sincerely yours,

HOFMANNSTHAL

Berlin, 8th October 1910

Dear Herr von Hofmannsthal,

When your last letter arrived I was already in Berlin, where I shall stay till the end of the month. I much regret not having seen you and send my warmest congratulation on the great success of *Oedipus* in Munich.

All difficulties about *Rosenkavalier* are now straightened out and the bookings are progressing steadily. Now what's the position about your prompt-book, which you wanted to work out with Roller? The matter is very urgent, since the first setting rehearsals in Dresden must start about the middle of November, or certainly not later than December. It's important therefore to have your detailed prompt-book available by then. It is equally important that you should be present in person at the setting rehearsals in Dresden, as the producer there is only an ordinary run-of-the-mill operatic producer and presumably hardly capable of staging a comedy like ours.

With warmest regards, yours sincerely,

RICHARD STRAUSS

The time has now almost come to think of *Semiramis*!

69

Schloss Neubeuern am Inn, 12.10.(1910)

My dear Doctor,

Roller has completed preliminary work on the prompt-book, and within three days I shall be back at Rodaun and ready to tackle this job with him energetically—but it is essential that Fürstner should send him the music for Acts I and II in some form, since the prompt-book is a pointless amateurish affair unless each step and each gesture is in absolute consonance with the music. Roller and I will then hire a pianist and this will give us a prompt-book which will make it virtually impossible even for the most obtuse of provincial opera producers to miss as much as a posture or a small detail. *Therefore please arrange for despatch at once!!*

I realized how absolutely essential it is to settle everything with Roller for this music (and that applies also to anything we may do together in the future) when I saw the other day at the Prinzregententheater the truly appalling décor for *Elektra*, in the taste of a pastrycook.

In haste, yours sincerely,

HOFMANNSTHAL

Schloss Graetz near Troppau, 31.10.(1910)

My dear Doctor,

I return to Rodaun tomorrow and count definitely on seeing you early in November in Vienna, where I would like to submit to you for discussion a few proposals for the casting of *Der Rosenkavalier* which are based on my personal knowledge of the company, especially for the smaller parts like Faninal and Valzacchi where the acting is so important.

Mme Gutheil is canvassing energetically for the leading part (Quinquin), and has already, I hear, tried to get at you through Mahler, Roller, and Walter. I must say myself that, so far as acting goes, she is the *only* person worth considering, and she also looks the part. But we can talk this over. (Mme Kiurina, who is suggested by Weingartner, is a nonentity and plump.)

Semiramis is miles away; no intellectual or material inducements could extract from me a play on this subject, not even a most determined effort of will. Will-power anyway is of no use in such matters. Actually, apart from the scenic prologue which I had quite complete in my mind, it never amounted to a plot, but only to the possibility of one. What is more I would not be quite happy about it, in any case, from the musical point of view, or shall we say the point of view of musical policy and style.

Since last spring, on the other hand, I have been hatching the subject of a fantastic play, a simple action divided into three acts, with strong obvious contrasts and strong, striking curtains to each act; sombre but not monotonous in temper as a whole—a subject which might very well invite music, although at the outset I thought of music as merely accompanying and subordinate.

And so *au revoir*.

Yours,

HOFMANNSTHAL

St. Moritz, 30.12.10

Dear Poet,

Wholeheartedly share your misgivings about Perron and am entirely of your opinion that the opera must not be allowed out with a merely *adequate* Ochs. Whether Mayr will be ready to take it depends largely on Schalk; to snatch him away from Weingartner would be a *cura posterior*. That leaves Bender (Munich), who is available. Couldn't you attend a few Munich rehearsals: then you'll see at once whether Bender is conceivably suitable for Dresden. Please get in touch directly with Hofkapellmeister Cortolezis (Munich), who is producing the opera together with Mottl and who will assist you in every respect. I have now written to Schuch, asking that you, Roller and Reinhardt be invited to the setting rehearsals after 9th January. In case you and Reinhardt do not succeed in grooming Perron for the part, I give you full powers of veto to cancel the première with Perron on the 26th. The latter is such a first-class artist that he will understand and share our misgivings. Do treat him tactfully—he's trying terribly hard—but at the same time be implacable, for the fate of our opera is at stake.

Wire me your impression at once and be strict. Schuch has been informed of our misgivings, but *no one* else in Dresden. Therefore: tact and circumspection!

I may possibly attend a rehearsal in Munich on 16th January, in order to take a look at Bender, and on the morning of the 17th January I shall be in Dresden.

With best regards, yours

RICHARD STRAUSS

1911

My dear Doctor,

I am very glad to know that you feel exactly as I do on these matters (I mean the importance of this role, the danger involved for the whole piece and the paramount significance of just *this* point). You may rest assured that in Munich and later in Dresden I will do exactly as you suggest in your letter. Mayr will not be ready by the 26th; Schalk made it clear to me that there is no prospect of that. But a fortnight later he will be free, and he is not only a good, but almost an ideal *actor* for the part and musically, too, according to Schalk, he will leave *nothing* to be desired. Coming from Schalk, that is a great deal, a very great deal, to say.

The elements most vital to this character, the buffo quality, those Falstaffian, self-satisfied, ludicrous touches, they are exactly the ones which no author and no Reinhardt can possibly instil into Perron. Act III with an Ochs who fails to amuse and who looks almost spectral instead of smug and self-satisfied, that would be the end! Such casting is absolutely incomprehensible to me. If only I had heard of it sooner! For eighteen months I have been preoccupied with nothing but the immense importance of finding the right man for this very part—a buffo, and, for all I care, even a foreigner, an Italian, anything (it was I who suggested Pini-Corsi!!)

Well, I shall wire you my impressions of the situation exactly as I find it.

Au revoir!

Yours,

HOFMANNSTHAL

P.S. On my recent railway journey I hit upon what I believe to be the *decisive ideas* for *Das Steinerne Herz.*

St. Moritz, 5.1.11

Dear Herr von Hofmannsthal,

Letter received with thanks. Are you going to Dresden for the setting rehearsals after 9th January? Reinhardt will be arriving on the 10th. Enclosed I am sending you Mottl's rehearsal schedule. I would urgently ask you (perhaps after Dresden) to attend a few stage rehearsals in Munich. Have already informed Mottl. I shall probably be in Munich on the 16th, and in Dresden from the 17th onwards, so I shan't return to Munich until the dress rehearsal on the 28th.

At all events have a good look at Bender as Ochs (in Munich), because he might possibly take the part over from Perron at short notice.

Cheers for *Das Steinerne Herz*! Plenty of nature atmosphere, please: German forest. Thunderstorm as Holländermichel fells his trees: this is how the thing might start. I am very curious to hear further details from you soon. The love story in Hauff is flat and uninteresting.

With best regards, yours

RICHARD STRAUSS

Before you leave for Munich better confirm again with Mottl. What's this about the Vienna censorship?

Schloss Neubeuern am Inn, 8.1.(1911)

My dear Doctor,

Tomorrow morning, then, I shall be in Munich to watch the rehearsals; I have already informed Cortolezis and Mottl and will do everything in accordance with your wishes. After that I have to go to Berlin for three days and shall be in Dresden on the 16th. This arrangement is just as well, since in any case no major decision can be taken except by us *jointly*.

I have just learnt to my sorrow that Bender is also no Falstaff, is in fact anything but, and therefore no Ochs—at least in no way naturally fitted for the part. Oh well, if all bass buffos are long and lean and only the Quinquins thick and fat I may as well close down!

Although *Das Steinerne Herz* is for the time being purely a *cura posterior*, a passage in your letter has suddenly made it for me a *cura proxima*. What a confounded fool I was to tell you the title and the subject and so direct your imagination to Hauff's fairy tale which, except for the central germ, has nothing in common with what exists in my own imagination. In this way I have raised definite images and desires in your mind which my scenario is bound to disappoint. I am really quite inordinately vexed. What makes it worse is that my scenario is in fact very beautiful, truly the happiest idea, I feel, I could have had for you:

a romantic opera of the old type and yet something that could have been thought of only today, real and symbolical, capable of capturing the most difficult audience and of making an impression on the very simplest; only a few strong leading characters and an action which is beautifully and firmly divided into three acts. Around these characters a whole world of houses and narrow lanes, churches and banquets, a scene of conflagration, a cemetery of the dead, human voices and the voices of spirits, organ and cloister, death and the devil. The end of Act I very much in the manner of the final scene of the first act of *Der Freischütz* (which for good reasons you value so highly) and scarcely anywhere a scene or a situation which does not meet your art half way. But it is decidedly not Hauff's fairy tale; there is no Holländer-michel, no Little Glassman, and none of Hauff's Black Forest peasants of whom I can make nothing. There is, above all, *no forest*; a forest does not fit in with my conception at all, so please do not let your imagination expect a forest when I am on the point of offering you something rich and strong, though not, of all things, that. Although Wagner has practically exhausted the possibilities of scenic nature effects, the heart that beats and the heart that is frozen remain a fundamental, an almost inexhaustible theme. All else by word of mouth.

Very sincerely yours,

HOFMANNSTHAL

Hotel Marienbad, München, 12.1.(1911)

My dear Doctor,

My impression of the rehearsals here is *not* good.

Bender is not an ideal Ochs, but still a very good one, all the same; he does not mind how much one tells him and, as an actor, possesses a rich store of shades of expression. In an emergency, at any rate, his taking over is a way out. (I have made no mention of this plan here.) Fuchs, the chief producer, spares no trouble and does quite a lot that is good. A certain exaggerated subtlety of his I have pared away.

And so until I see you in Dresden on the 16th.

Yours,

HOFMANNSTHAL

Your music gives me immense pleasure. It is like a festoon of many pretty flowers and so marvellously organic in the transitions.

Dear Herr von Hofmannsthal,

I ought to have written to you long ago, and I wanted to write to give you an account of the battle royal in Milan[1]—if only writing weren't such a bore. I'm saving my report for Vienna, where I am arriving on 3rd April. Nevertheless, I must tell you today that, after reference to the Kaiser and after all the stupendous success, special trains to Dresden, etc., Herr von Hülsen has now also accepted *Rosenkavalier* for the beginning of the next season, provided I decide to allow him to wield his 'mitigating' and 'refining' hand over the whole thing.[2] Well, it probably won't be too bad; it's all talk mostly, designed to belittle the achievement of Dresden and to outshine it. Details verbally! You are also in Vienna, I trust, after 3rd April? I hope that you and Roller are taking an active part in the setting rehearsals in Vienna. I am most anxious to hear what you have to tell me about *Steinernes Herz* and the little Molière piece. Don't forget: I've still no work for the summer. Writing symphonies doesn't amuse me at all any longer.

I hope you're well and working vigorously!

Looking forward to seeing you! With best regards from us to you all, yours most sincerely,

RICHARD STRAUSS

Rodaun, 20.3.(1911)

My dear Doctor,

It was very nice of you to write to me; I too have thought several times of writing to you, but had no idea at all where you were. About Milan I had a full report from Placci; besides, I read the *Corriere* and *Secolo*. There is always something to be learnt (at least for me) and I feel that the public is never *altogether* wrong. True, so far as the music is concerned, these are questions of style which are always the most awkward. My libretto certainly has one *grave* defect; so much of what sets it apart and gives it charm *must* fade, or almost disappear, in translation. If we were to work together once more on something (and by this I mean something important, not the thirty minute opera for small chamber

---

[1] For the controversial reception of *Rosenkavalier* at the Scala, Milan, see *Richard Strauss: Betrachtungen und Erinnerungen*, 1949.

[2] Examples of Hülsen's revision of the text were quoted by Julius Kapp in *Richard Strauss und die Berliner Staatsoper*, Berlin 1934.

orchestra which is as good as complete in my head; it is called *Ariadne auf Naxos* and is made up of a combination of heroic mythological figures in 18th-century costume with hooped skirts and ostrich feathers and, interwoven in it, characters from the commedia dell'arte; harlequins and scaramouches representing the buffo element which is throughout interwoven with the heroic); well now, if we were to work together once more on something big, it would have to possess colourful and clear-cut action, and the detail of the libretto would be less important. I have something quite definite in mind which fascinates me very much and which I shall certainly do, either for music or as a spectacle with accompanying music—we shall have to decide about that. It is a magic fairy tale with two men confronting two women, and for one of the women your wife might well, in all discretion, be taken as a model—that of course is wholly *entre nous*, and not of any great importance. Anyway, she is a *bizarre* woman with a very beautiful soul, *au fond*; strange, moody, domineering and yet at the same time likeable; she would in fact be the principal character and the whole thing a many-coloured spectacle with palace and hut, priests, boats, torches, tunnels through the rock, choruses, children. The whole thing assails me with real force and even interferes with my work; it has pushed that other project, *Das Steinerne Herz*, quite into the background because it is so much *brighter* and more *joyous*. The whole idea as I see it suspended before my eyes (though it is still incomplete, with important links missing) would, incidentally, stand in the same relation to *Die Zauberflöte* as *Rosenkavalier* does to *Figaro*—not, in either case, an imitation, but bearing a certain analogy. One cannot, of course, hope to equal the enchanting naïvety of many scenes in *Die Zauberflöte*, but the whole conception is, I think, a very happy and very promising one. When you come here, we must set aside for ourselves, more than once, a couple of quiet hours, so that I can explain this project[1] to you in all detail. (. . .)

About *Ariadne*, too, we must talk; it can, I believe, turn into something most charming, a new genre which to all appearance reaches back to a much earlier one, just as all development goes in cycles.

I am also inclined to think that this interim work is necessary, at least *for me*, to make myself still more familiar with music, especially with your music, and to achieve something which brings us even closer together than in *Rosenkavalier*—which as a fusion of word and music

[1] *Die Frau ohne Schatten.*

satisfies me *greatly*, but not *wholly* (and which, I hope, will keep its place on the stage, at least on the German stage, for several, perhaps for many decades).

This slight interim work will perhaps make it still clearer to me how to construct a dramatic piece as a whole so that the *set numbers* regain more and more their paramount importance, and help me to find the right treatment for that which lies between the numbers, where one cannot fall back upon *secco* recitative and prose. (Or perhaps one can, after all. But how? and how far?) After all, one thing is quite clear: if possibly we are to collaborate further, and again, everything must follow a definite line of development in the matter of style. (Of course I do not mean this as dry theory, but as something one feels, an instinct, an inner compulsion.)

Therefore *au revoir*. Please be sure to come by the 31st, and not as late as the 3rd, for we must work here with both the Marschallin singers. You will be conducting a few times and I need your whole attention for discussions. Later on will be too late! Therefore *please* on the 31st, with Levin.

Yours sincerely,

HOFMANNSTHAL

Garmisch, 15.5.11

Dear Poet,

I want to inquire how *Frau ohne Schatten* is doing: can't I get a finished draft or maybe even a first act to look at some time soon? I'd also be interested to know what's happening about the Molière. At the same time, to make sure you don't suspend your work for me, I want to reassure you that I am not yet setting any d'Annunzio text to music, but am waiting for you as anxiously as ever.

Some time ago d'Annunzio sent word to me through Sonzogno to the effect that he'd like to do some work for me and inquired what kind of subject I should prefer. I had a few ideas passed on to him, in particular my wish for an entirely modern subject, very intimate and psychologically extremely nervous: let's wait and see what he brings off. I've no great hopes of him, but one's got to pull all strings. Levetzow too is going to send me a new drama, possibly—as *he* thinks—suitable for music. The definite arrangements with d'Annunzio reported by the newspapers are therefore pure *canards* for the time being. I am waiting for you and am meanwhile torturing myself with a symphony—a job that, when all's said and done, amuses me even less than chasing may-bugs. With Seebach I am entirely at loggerheads because of the (infamous) Dresden cuts; but in spite of its mutilation *Rosenkavalier* has prospered there and reached its 28th sold-out performance. Have you read Wagner's biography yet[1]? A genuinely stirring book that one can't lay down without tears of emotion. What creative vigour in spite of a truly desolate life: a fate that represents one of the saddest chapters in the history of German culture.

Work away, then; work away, and give some pleasure soon, by delivering something 'positive', to your

RICHARD STRAUSS

Rodaun, 15th May (1911)

My dear Doctor Strauss,

I like you very much indeed, I enjoy working for you, and I owe you much that is beautiful, agreeable and good, and so I was exceedingly sorry when, some time ago, I had to send you away empty-handed for the moment.

The fact is that with so fine a subject as *Die Frau ohne Schatten*, the rich gift of a happy hour, with a subject so fit to become the vehicle of beautiful poetry and beautiful music, with a subject such as this all haste and hurry and forcing of oneself would be a crime. Every detail must be present in the imagination clear-cut and definite, succinct and precise and *true*. Quietly, beyond the threshold of consciousness, the relation of the characters to one another must take on shape and realize itself naturally in colourful action of an effortless symbolism; the profound must be brought to the surface, nothing be left empty, nothing remain in a state of mere unaccomplished purpose and good intention. Once this is achieved, everything will have been made ready for the music, so that it need only pour into the bed prepared for it and reflect in its stream the likeness of heaven and earth. But all this depends on fertility and the concrete intensity of real inspiration, and *le temps ne fait rien à l'affaire*.

Had you made me choose between producing this work on the spot, or doing without your music, I should have chosen the latter.

[1] *Mein Leben*, first published 1911.

78

But now for something different: I *have* the Molière. I had never thought of anything except his less well-known plays, but in Paris suddenly it came to me how splendidly the *Bourgeois Gentilhomme* would lend itself to the insertion of our operatic *divertissement*. There are five acts, which I shall easily concentrate into two. I shall leave out the Turkish ceremony (being in *lingua franca* it is untranslatable and no German audience can enjoy the fun which the French get out of this barbaric pidgin-French), and, together with the Turkish ceremony, there will disappear as a matter of course the whole subsidiary plot and the figures of the daughter, Cleante, Covielle—more than one third of the whole comedy. The *divertissement Ariadne auf Naxos* itself is to be performed after the dinner, in the presence of Jourdain, the Count and the dubious Marquise, and will be punctuated now and then by brief remarks from these spectators. It concludes the whole work. The play-bill looks like this:

DER BÜRGER ALS EDELMANN

A Comedy with Dances by Molière, arranged by Hugo von Hofmannsthal from the old translation of Bierling (1751)

Cast. . . . .

At the end of Act II

Divertissement:

ARIADNE AUF NAXOS

(Music by Richard Strauss)

Ariadne	Harlequin
Bacchus	the first Scaramouche
Echo	the second Scaramouche
first Nymph	Tartaglia
second Nymph	Brighella, and so on.

The short dances in the play will be preserved (not all of them, but certainly the tailors' dance and the brief scene of the musicians). During the dinner I should like instrumental music: no singing, since the opera is just about to begin.

I suggest you get hold of the old Bierling translation at once; you will find it in Cotta's *Bibliothek der Weltliteratur*, Molière, volume 3, *Der adelige Bürger*. Perhaps this will give you some ideas for the dinner music, and for the small ballets which must be very brief. I should like to omit the protracted song scene in Act I, or at least to reduce it to a minimum, since all these scenes will have to be severely pruned. Wassmann will make an excellent Jourdain.

I dislike writing into the blue, so please let me have a line on a post-card as soon as this letter reaches you. I shall then send you the *Ariadne* sketch at once. The full libretto, for which I still need a few more ideas, I can promise you (in so far as one can promise anything at all) for the *beginning* of July, perhaps even the end of June. That will give you work for July/August.

Let me hope then that this news will please you and that I shall hear from you soon.

Very sincerely yours,

HOFMANNSTHAL

Rodaun, 19.5.(1911)

Dear Doctor Strauss,

Please read through the enclosed and tell me how it appeals to you. This is how I imagine it: not as a slavish imitation, but as a spirited paraphrase of the old heroic style, interspersed with buffo ingredients. I imagine the character of Ariadne gently outlined, but altogether *real*, as real as the Marschallin. There is ample opportunity here for set numbers: duets, trios, quintets, sextets. It would be good if you were to indicate to me points where you mean to place definite *numbers*, and where you intend merely to suggest them as you did repeatedly in *Rosenkavalier*. This slight scaffolding for your music will have served its purpose if it gives you an opportunity of expressing yourself on a deliberately reduced scale, half playfully and yet *from the heart*.

Most sincerely yours,

HOFMANNSTHAL

Garmisch, 20.5.11

Dear Poet,

Have read *Gentilhomme*: the first half is very nice, especially the first scene: Composer and Dancing Master—perhaps you will accentuate it a little with topical points. One might cock a pretty snook here at the critics. The second half is thin, and in my opinion you would have to add a good deal here to round off the action more and to point it towards a climax. It seems to me that the piece lacks a proper dénouement.

You're quite right: from Act III, Scene 8 onwards it becomes weak. The last really good bit is the second scene of Act III; the rest would have to be invented anew. The musical conversation—Act I, Scene 2— is also thin; here too you would have to shape something new.

For the dances of the Dancing Master, tailors and scullions one could write some pleasant salon music.

I shall enjoy the thing very much, and I am sure I can bring off something striking. I am impatiently awaiting your consignment.

Mahler's death has been a great shock to me: no doubt he'll now become a great man in Vienna too.

With best regards, yours

RICHARD STRAUSS

Not a word, please, to anybody about the *Gentilhomme* except Reinhardt (to him alone, no producer or director)!

Not to anybody! I'm not breathing a word either!

(after 20.5.1911)

Here, for your information, is the rough sketch of the two-act adaptation, without any cuts as yet. The play, as you quite rightly say, possesses no real point and this is exactly what serves our purpose—the insertion of our *divertissement*—so well. One could hardly tack an opera on to a play which culminates in an effective and pointed curtain. I have already discussed the conclusion with Reinhardt, and the whole thing will be excellently filled out on the stage, with a lot of amusing ceremonial and so on.

(HOFMANNSTHAL)

Garmisch, 22.5.11

Dear Herr von Hofmannsthal,

Ariadne may turn out very pretty. However, as the dramatic framework is rather thin everything will depend on the poetic execution. But with you one doesn't have to worry about flowing verse. So get your Pegasus saddled.

81

Ariadne I imagine as	.	.	contralto
Bacchus	.	.	. lyric tenor
Najade, Dryade	.	.	. ordinary sopranos
Zerbinetta	.	.	. high coloratura soprano
(star role)			(Kurz, Hempel, Tetrazzini)
Harlekin	.	.	. light baritone
the other three	.	.	. buffo tenor and two basses

Set musical numbers, from the beginning:

(a) Recitative and aria of Ariadne,

(b) Harlekin's song

(c) Great coloratura aria and *andante*,

then rondo, theme with variations and all coloratura tricks (if possible with flute *obbligato*) for Zerbinetta, when she speaks of her unfaithful lover (*andante*) and then tries to console Ariadne: rondo with variations (two or three). A *pièce de résistance*.

(d) Male quartet (Harlekin): 'Komm mit mir' going over into quintet with Zerbinetta.

(e) Male trio (buffo), after Harlekin and Zerbinetta have disappeared.

(f) Finale (unbroken and continuous), beginning with the Naiad's warning. (A hymn-like march theme, add the duet of Ariadne and Zerbinetta, rising towards a climax and concluding with Bacchus's entry.)

Love duet.

Final ensemble.

As for the form of well-known coloratura arias, perhaps you could get Kurz to sing you *Sonnambula*, *Lucia*, the aria from Hérold's *Zweikampf*, Gilda, or some Mozart rondos. But if Mme Kurz lets me down again with this thing I shall be forever cross. And remember: utmost discretion all the time: no names, no mention of the subject. Best not say anything at all, just let her sing to you.

Orchestra *on* the stage impossible: for this kind of chamber-music piece I need first-class people (only from the Royal Court Orchestra in Berlin) and they wouldn't play-act.

Reinhardt, on the other hand, must start right away in the summer having the orchestra pit of the Deutsches Theater reconstructed in such a way that we get an open, raised orchestra as in the Munich Residenztheater.

I'm thinking of the following composition of the orchestra: 2 violins, viola, cello, double-bass, 1 flute, oboe, clarinet, bassoon, 1 or 2 horns, harpsichord, harp, celeste, harmonium (perhaps also a trumpet and some percussion instruments; 15 to 20 players).

Well: May Dionysus illumine you! I'm waiting!

Best regards, yours

RICHARD STRAUSS

Rodaun, 25.5.(1911)

My dear Dr. Strauss,

Thank you very much for your two letters. Discussions of this sort, which show how each of us visualizes the joint work, are indispensable and will be necessary again from time to time. Your list of the set numbers you would like is helpful and stimulating, and the same will certainly be true of all other specific musical wishes and intentions you may communicate to me. This is the only way to collaborate. There will be other occasions when I shall ask you to comply with requests of mine: where, in certain episodes, a given text requires a more subordinate attitude from the music, as was the case in the Marschallin's scene. Here, on the contrary, the whole thing is to be simply a frame-work on which to hang the music, well and prettily. We must not merely work together, but actually *into each other's hands*.

That you intend to place Zerbinetta so distinctly in the musical lime-light surprised me at first, but finally quite convinced me. I shall make myself acquainted with the formal requirements of coloratura, though not through Mme Kurz with whom I am not on those kind of terms and whom I would definitely not like to bring into anything. Alto-gether I am somewhat perplexed to find you putting down the names of Kurz, Hempel, Tetrazzini. For even apart from the fact that they are financially out of the question (the fee for *one* such star would swallow up half of Reinhardt's gross takings each night, and how could a budget so over-taxed leave us any chance of a long run of repeat performances?!), but leaving that aside altogether, the prospect of work-ing with women who cut such appalling figures on the stage, with prima donnas devoid of all talent as actresses, would literally paralyse my imagination, especially when it comes to a part like Zerbinetta's. If I am to write this with relish, I must think of it as something most subtly contrived both in style and production (this is surely also your idea), something thoroughly à la Reinhardt, and nothing in the slightest way reminiscent of court opera. Preferably an exotic cast, a charming American girl, a Dane or Italian with an exquisite (not an unduly big) voice, a Farrar, Mary Garden, or a young Bellincioni—this is surely your idea too, is it not? Please let me have a word about this.

You call the scenario a little thin—that is quite true. Perhaps a still better way of putting it would be: a little rectilinear, possibly a little too rectilinear. There is no turning, no proper dramatic twist. When I think of heroic opera, whose spirit we mean to invoke, when I think of Gluck, of *Titus* or *Idomeneo*, this kind of thin, rectilinear quality, does not seem to me a fault. The intermingling with the other, the buffo element, possesses moreover great attractions and disposes of monotony. I am flattered that you should promise yourself so much from my poetic diction, but we must not expect too much from the diction *alone*. 'There is nothing in the skin but what was bred in the bone', Goethe says somewhere. A framework which *failed to satisfy* your imagination, *if* it were to fail in that, could never be made to appeal to you, and to inspire you, by diction only. Let us never forget this. Even in a dramatic trifle like this it is the peculiar poetic quality of the text which must inspire you to composition, its relative emotional wealth, the contrasts, the structure—and not just the diction, which is to be compared to a nice complexion that only becomes pleasing in a woman with a good figure. Besides, my verse is not really rousing or glowing. Its true quality, which can hardly be questioned, is something else: it is meaningful, concise, rhythmically flexible; never flat, sugary or vague—works as diverse as *Elektra* and *Rosenkavalier* have sufficiently proved that to you.

And so please think it over again, weigh it carefully, and be as objective and severe with me as you are with yourself. We do, after all, mean to make something really good of whatever we undertake, don't we, even if it is only an interim work—this duty we owe above all *to ourselves*.

And please have a copy made of my draft and return the original to me (or the copy if it is absolutely correct).

One more thing: we must have a clear division of responsibilities. Everything connected with the stage sets, including style and design, the dances and so on, is my affair. All other requests—like the alterations in the orchestra pit—should be addressed to Reinhardt. Please send them to him direct or through Levin or however you like; in the summer he will in any case be in Munich for a long time, and at your disposal. I have mentioned the matter only to him and not to any producer.

Sincerely yours,

HOFMANNSTHAL

P.S. Many thanks for taking up the cudgels so forcefully on my behalf over this impropriety of a Viennese newspaper—of which, incidentally, I was not aware at all.

Garmisch, 27.5.11

Dear Herr von Hofmannsthal,

Of course a Farrar or young Bellincioni would be best: indeed for Reinhardt's production we shall have to find some such 'budding speciality'. But where? And if, after Reinhardt, the Court Theatres with associated playhouses (such as the Munich Residenztheater) are to take up the piece with any success or profit there must be some star singing parts in it, for the plot as such holds no interest and interesting costumes won't turn the scale either. Personally, I am not particularly interested by the whole thing myself: that was why I asked you to spur your Pegasus a bit, so that the ring of the verses should stimulate me a little. You probably know my predilection for hymns in Schiller's manner and flourishes à la Rückert. Things like that excite me to formal orgies, and these must do the trick where the action itself leaves me cold. Soaring oratory can drug me sufficiently to keep on writing music through a passage of no interest. The interplay of forms: the formal garden must come into its own here. Otherwise we are *d'accord*!

Best regards, yours

RICHARD STRAUSS

I hope to have *Ariadne* all ready by 1st July. Overture and first dances and quite a bit besides already sketched out.

28.5.(1911)

My dear Doctor,

We have always understood each other well, but on this occasion I feel we are in the best way not to understand one another.

85

Since one can give one's whole mind only to one thing at a time, I have in the past few days put aside, for your sake, everything else in order to occupy myself most intensively and exclusively with *Ariadne*. What induces me to undertake this work is chiefly the desire to do you (and in the second place Reinhardt) a favour and a service. I am deliberately putting it in this way which I should never apply to our collaboration on a major work (like *Rosenkavalier* or *Die Frau ohne Schatten*); in the case of *Ariadne* there can be no question of any other inducement. The material gain I myself may derive from it does not stimulate me; for the rest, the better, the more stylish and delicate the whole thing turns out to be, the more vulgar the incomprehension it will earn me.

During the past few days (before your letter arrived, the effect of which would have been to put me off rather than to encourage me) I have got through the hardest and most attractive part of the work; namely, to settle the psychological motives of the action, to establish, in my own mind, the relations between the various characters and between the different parts of the whole thing—in short, to sketch a detailed outline of the underlying motives which the poet must have before him (rather as you must have to picture your symphony) if he is to be attracted, roused and held by the work. The essence lies in this tracery of ideas, and all the rest (what you so strikingly call the formal garden) is mere trimming, just as in *Rosenkavalier* the period flavour, the ceremonial, dialect and so on lie merely at the fringe of the essential meaning. Now, this essence of the relationship between Ariadne and Bacchus stands before my mind's eye so finely graded, so delicately animated, psychologically so convincing and at the same time so lyrical, that my execution would have to be wretched indeed if in the end it failed to arouse your interest as much as the lyrics of your songs, or the scenes between the Marschallin and Octavian. An ordinary composer could not have made anything of these, and yet you created something entirely original and wholly enchanting which does full justice to the words.

That is how I feel about *Ariadne*—and about the trimmings, Zerbinetta, and so forth, we are in any case already entirely *d'accord*. But if my libretto, when you have it, does not attract you in this way, then by all means leave it alone; there will be no hard feelings. What matters is the central idea of the piece and though two men like us who know their job should not despise the flourishes, they can never be a substitute for the main thing. It occurs to me, incidentally, that Hermine Bosetti might, *faute de mieux*, make quite a charming Zerbinetta. Wouldn't she?

And now, if you will please mark in the libretto which I enclose the coloratura aria with rondo, I shall be able to make myself familiar with its scheme. Perhaps you could at the same time get someone to copy for me the text (without the music) of the corresponding aria from Herold's *Zweikampf* (for I cannot get hold of the *Zweikampf* libretto).

It was actually quite wrong of me to expect you to read more into the scenario than there is at present in it—to any except my own eyes.

Most sincerely yours,

HOFMANNSTHAL

P.S. The following is most important so that your imagination should not go astray from the very outset over the character of Bacchus: this lyric tenor will have to be interpreted in the most delicate manner, almost boyish. (But it is quite correct to compose the part for a man, not once again for a soprano.) This Bacchus is but lately fledged, he has only had his one affair with Circe and is shy. I think this could make a charming one-act piece!

Garmisch, 1st June, 1911

Dear Herr von Hofmannsthal,

We don't misunderstand each other at all. It was foolish of me to refer you to those idiotic coloratura arias from whose texts you can't learn a thing. I merely wanted to refer you to the musical scheme as it emerges, for instance, from Donna Anna's letter aria, or in Gilda's aria (*Rigoletto*).

The form of coloratura variations sprang to my mind unwittingly as I read your draft of Zerbinetta's first aria. So please, don't let me confuse you any further. I pictured Zerbinetta's first speech—when she tries to ingratiate herself with Ariadne—as recitative with slow accompaniment, added to it then the speech of the four men, and finally an allegro with variations as she finds something irresistible in each of the four. But so far as you're concerned, it's quite enough if you characterize all this with a few melodious verses (in the manner of Ochs's account of his wenches). The rest will be up to me. The main thing, of course, is Ariadne and Bacchus. I already have a short overture for the play and another for the opera itself, and the dances of the tailors, etc., are sketched out. The whole thing will be ready by the autumn. Bosetti as Zerbinetta most suitable. Just go on working happily and don't worry about me.

With best regards, yours

RICHARD STRAUSS

Please let me have at once anything you finish in detail of the first few scenes.

Rodaun, 5.6.(1911)

My dear Dr. Strauss,

No, we did not misunderstand each other for a second; that was a very unfortunate expression for me to have used.

I am marshalling all my strength for this slight but by no means easy piece of work. I am thinking of nothing else and have abandoned all correspondence even, so rest assured *I am doing what I can*. To hear of your wishes and suggestions for set numbers did not in any way irritate me; on the contrary they can only be useful and stimulating; I beg you once again to send me the exact text of a coloratura aria with rondo and variations, absolutely exact, however silly the words, and to send it at once—it is bound to be useful since it will give me some indication of length, structure and so on.

Best regards,

HOFMANNSTHAL

P.S. Gilda, or whatever aria you like; best of all Mozart or Gluck.

Garmisch, 7.6.11

Dear Herr von Hofmannsthal,

Don't grow any grey hairs over that coloratura aria: I've nothing of the kind to hand. The outline I have given you for Zerbinetta's scene with Ariadne is quite sufficient. I am conducting *Rosenkavalier* in Cologne on 17th and 18th June, and shall be back here and ready for work on the 26th. With best regards, yours

RICHARD STRAUSS

Dear Herr von Hofmannsthal,

How is the transition effected from play to opera: change of scene on the open stage? Or does the curtain fall? Can an overture of some length be played before the opera? Or would it be better to have just a few introductory bars and then start off with: 'Schläft sie'?

To precede the play itself I had a little rustic overture in mind, with transition into the little song which the shepherd is just composing. This is all ready. Maybe in that case a longish piece before the start of the opera would be too much and would result in a dead point with an open stage. Please drop me a brief line about this to Cologne, Neumarkt.

Yours,

RICHARD STRAUSS

Do you know Lorenzo the Magnificent's song from *Bacchus and Ariadne*, whose refrain:

> Quanto è bella giovinezza
> Che si fugge tuttavia!
> Chi vuol esser lieto, sia:
> Di doman non c'è certezza

is mentioned by Burckhardt in Volume II of his *Civilization of the Renaissance in Italy*, page 150?

Altogether the account given there of Italian festivities and processions is most interesting. That would be something for Reinhardt and Roller.

Rodaun, 15.6.(1911)

As agreed: no form of address![1]

Delighted to hear you are pleased with the beginning of *Ariadne*; hope it will get better and better as it goes on. Though unwell, I am working every day; yesterday I wrote Zerbinetta's aria which will give you no cause for disappointment. Altogether, when two men like us set out to produce a 'trifle' like this, it has to become a very serious trifle: we must strive to put our *best* into it; some time, somewhere, somehow we are sure to receive our reward.

The sheet with Harlekin's little song, which fell out, has gone off to Garmisch by express letter.

[1] Strauss had suggested dropping the opening address in the 'workshop correspondence.

The transition to the actual opera takes place on the open stage; I shall lead up to it by a short scene in prose in which Dancing Master and Composer—who are responsible for arranging this opera performance at Jourdain's house—talk about the public, critics, etc. During this conversation the stage is being set for the opera in the big hall; Harlekin and Ariadne are making up, others are bustling to and fro half dressed for the performance. The lights are being lit, the musicians are tuning their instruments, Zerbinetta tries a few roulades, Jourdain and his guests appear and take their seats in the fauteuils—and at this point, I must say, a little overture seems to me stylistically indispensable; a little symphony of the old kind which brings together the main themes from the opera would, I feel, be charming. Perhaps, however, it might be better to leave the writing of this to the very end, for the second part of the text is sure to suggest to you certain themes: the strange aura of the fabulous East which surrounds Bacchus, the vibrating sense of the realm of death and shadow, that delicate, lyrical, unearthly atmosphere to which Ariadne still clings—and all this in most distinct contrast to the melodically pellucid world in which Zerbinetta and Harlekin have their being. My special qualities as librettist are perhaps not so hard to define—I build on contrasts to discover, above these contrasts, the harmony of the whole; that is to say they are perhaps of a general artistic order (and such artistic qualities are rare among Germans). (*Die Frau ohne Schatten* might, I sometimes imagine, become the most beautiful of all existing operas.)

As for the obscure passage in the text: Ariadne endeavours to recall in her bewildered brain the picture of her own innocent self, of the young girl she once was (and who, she fancies, is now living again, here in the cave), but she refuses to employ the actual name of Ariadne in this process of recollection, because that name is for her all too closely bound up, grown together with Theseus; she wants the vision but without the name and therefore, when the three nymphs call her by that name, she fights shy of it: 'Not again!' (Do not let me hear that name again!).

With best wishes, yours,

HOFMANNSTHAL

P.S. Have asked Schalk about Windheuser; voice very good, acting helpless, looks pretty unsuitable. (But possibly both troubles might be remedied.)

My dear Dr. Strauss,

What is the matter with you? I get quite anxious when I do not hear from my alter ego for such a long time. In spite of an abscess in a tooth and workmen laying slates on the roof next door I have been most industrious: Zerbinetta's aria, the big ensemble for the five comic figures, the nymphs' account of Bacchus, his approach and his song are all finished. Tomorrow I shall turn to the Zerbinetta-Ariadne scene (when Ariadne is being dressed) and then comes the big scene for the end. I hope it will all turn out well.

Can you be found in Garmisch or Munich early in August? I should very much like to know.

Sincerely yours,

HOFMANNSTHAL

(*Garmisch, early July, 1911*)

Dear Poet. You are funny. You want to hear something from me! But I want to read something from you, and only then will you be able to 'hear' something from me. Go write your poetry, please, and wait! In any case send me all the poetry you've written without delay! I'm here in Garmisch till 8th August, then part of the time in Munich conducting! Now I want to work hard! So please deliver: then you'll hear! —*Rosenkavalier* in Cologne without any cuts a brilliant success. Berlin première (with very beautiful décor) on 7th November.

Yours,

RICHARD STRAUSS

Rodaun, 5.7.(1911)

My dear Friend,

Was I really so funny? Was it so hard for you to understand that I was waiting for some sign of life, for a simple word that you were back at Garmisch and at leisure? that I did not want to send my manuscript into the void? I had, after all, taken very great pains; I had even kept, to the dot, the date which you yourself wished—with growing pleasure, as the conclusion rose more and more to a higher spiritual plane from something which was merely meant to amuse. The whole thing was after all devised purely for you, purely for your music! Is it then so difficult for you to understand my desire, just at this moment, to feel in contact with you, the desire to know that *you*—not just an empty writing desk—were there, ready and able to welcome what had been produced for you alone!

I am still giving a last polish to the big scene between Ariadne and Bacchus and will send you the rest within a day or two. What you now have is (including today's) about one half, perhaps slightly more.

Sincerely yours,

HOFMANNSTHAL

(Note on the Manuscript of Ariadne auf Naxos):

R(odaun), 12.7.(1911)

Here is the conclusion. I have done it, the whole thing, as well as I was able. I hope that setting it to music will be a joy for you, and that I have not failed.

Am very keen and impatient to have a word from you which will reach me after Thursday at Aussee, Obertressen 14.

Sincerely yours,

HOFMANNSTHAL

Garmisch, 14th July, 1911

Dear Herr von Hofmannsthal,

The whole of *Ariadne* is now safely in my hands and I like it well enough: I think there'll be some good use for everything. Only I should have preferred the dialogue between Ariadne and Bacchus to be rather more significant, with livelier emotional *crescendo*. This bit must soar higher, like the end of *Elektra*, sunnier, more Dionysian: harness your Pegasus for a little longer, I can give you another four weeks at least before I've caught up on you with the music.

I have just finished the entertaining dance scene: 'Die Dame gibt mit trübem Sinn.' Ariadne's expectation of the messenger of death has also come out well.

Zerbinetta's rondo is partly sketched out: you see, I'm not idle; but for the conclusion I need something more soaring: 'Freude schöner Götterfunke.'

Shall I see you in Munich in August? Have a good rest now, stretch out under the beeches and dream a little more about Dionysus and Ariadne!

With best regards, yours

RICHARD STRAUSS

Aussee, Obertressen (mid July 1911)

My dear Doctor Strauss,

I must confess I was somewhat piqued by your scant and cool reception of the finished manuscript of *Ariadne,* compared with the warm welcome you gave to every single act of *Rosenkavalier*—which stands out in my memory as one of the most significant pleasures connected with that work. I believe that in *Ariadne* I have produced something at least equally good, equally original and novel, and although we certainly agree in wishing to shun anything like the false show of mutual adulation in which mediocre artists indulge, I cannot help asking myself whether any praise in all the world could make up to me for the absence of yours.

You may of course have written your letter or read the manuscript when you were somewhat out of sorts, as happens so easily to creative artists; nor do I overlook the fact that a fairly subtle piece of work like this inevitably suffers seriously by being presented in manuscript rather than clear typescript (unfortunately my typist was ill). And so I am not without hope that closer acquaintance with my libretto will bring home to you its positive qualities. Set pieces like, say, the intermezzo, Zerbinetta's aria and the ensemble will not, I venture to say, be surpassed in their own line by anyone writing in Europe today. The way in which this work—though it adheres to the conventional form (which, properly understood, is full of appeal even to the librettist)—indicates and establishes its central idea quite naturally by making Ariadne and Zerbinetta represent diametrical contrasts in female character, or the manner in which I have led up to the arrival of Bacchus, first by the trio of the three women cutting each other short, next by the little Circe song, and finally by Zerbinetta's announcement which, though important in itself, gives the orchestra predominance in that hymn-like march theme—all this, I must say, seemed to me to deserve some expression of appreciation on the part of the one person for whom my work was visualized, conceived and executed. I doubt, moreover, if one could easily find in any other libretto for a one-act opera three songs of comparable delicacy, and at the same time equally characteristic in tone, as Harlekin's song, the rondo for Zerbinetta and the Circe song of Bacchus.

Not unnaturally I would rather have heard all this from you than be obliged to write it myself.

No doubt it will be possible to find a way of heightening the intensity of the end along the lines you indicate, but before we proceed to settle the degree and the manner of any such climax-building, let me try and explain in a few sentences the underlying idea or meaning of this little poetic work. What it is about is one of the straightforward and stupendous problems of life: fidelity; whether to hold fast to that which is lost, to cling to it even unto death—or to live, to live on, to get over it, to transform oneself, to sacrifice the integrity of the soul and yet in this transmutation to preserve one's essence, to remain a human being and not to sink to the level of the beast, which is without recollection. It is the fundamental theme of *Elektra*, the voice of Electra opposed to the voice of Chrysothemis, the heroic voice against the human. In the present case we have the group of heroes, demi-gods, gods—Ariadne, Bacchus, (Theseus)—facing the human, the merely human group consisting of the frivolous Zerbinetta and her companions, all of them base figures in life's masquerade. Zerbinetta is in her element drifting out of the arms of one man into the arms of another; Ariadne could be the wife or mistress of *one* man only, just as she can be only *one* man's widow, can be forsaken only by *one* man. One thing, however, is still left even for her: the miracle, the God. To him she gives herself, for she believes him to be Death: he is both Death and Life at once; he it is who reveals to her the immeasurable depths in her own nature, who makes of her an enchantress, the sorceress who herself transforms the poor little Ariadne; he it is who conjures up for her in this world another world beyond, who preserves her for us and at the same time transforms her.

But what to divine souls is a real miracle, is to the earth-bound nature of Zerbinetta just an everyday love-affair. She sees in Ariadne's experience the only thing she *can* see: the exchange of an old lover for a new one. And so these two spiritual worlds are in the end ironically brought together in the only way in which they can be brought together: in non-comprehension.

94

In this experience of Ariadne's, which is really the monologue of her lonely soul, Bacchus represents no mere *deus ex machina*; for him, too, the experience is vital. Innocent, young and unaware of his own divinity he travels where the wind takes him, from island to island. His first affair was typical, with a woman of easy virtue, you may say or you may call her Circe. To his youth and innocence with its infinite potentialities the shock has been tremendous: were he Harlekin, this would be merely the beginning of one long round of love affairs. But he is Bacchus; confronted with the enormity of erotic experience all is laid bare to him in a flash—the assimilation with the animal, the transformation, his own divinity. So he escapes from Circe's embraces still unchanged, but not without a wound, a longing, not without knowledge. The impact on him now of this meeting with a being whom he can love, who is mistaken about him but is enabled by this very mistake to give herself to him wholly and to reveal herself to him in all her loveliness, who entrusts herself to him completely, exactly as one entrusts oneself to Death, this impact I need not expound further to an artist such as you.

It would be a very great joy to me if, by an early reply to this personal, friendly letter, you were to restore to me that sense of fine and intimate contact between us which I so much enjoyed during our earlier collaboration, and which has by now become indispensable to me.

Very sincerely yours,

HOFMANNSTHAL

Dear Herr von Hofmannsthal,   *Garmisch, 19th July, 1911*

I am sincerely sorry that in my dry way I failed to pay you the tribute you had hoped for and which your work certainly deserves. But I confess frankly that my first impression was one of disappointment. Perhaps because I had expected too much. I have now had your manuscript typed out and, upon a quick perusal today, got indeed a vastly better impression (except for the final conclusion, where I certainly need a bigger *crescendo*); but even so the piece did not fully convince me until after I had read your letter, which is so beautiful and explains the meaning of the action so wonderfully that a superficial musician like myself could not, of course, have tumbled to it. But isn't this a little dangerous? And isn't some of the interpretation still lacking in the action itself? If even I couldn't see it, just think of the audiences and—the critics. The way you describe it it's excellent. But in the piece itself it doesn't emerge quite so clearly and plainly.

I am doubly pleased that I have again been incapable of dissembling and that my coolness has coaxed this marvellous letter out of you. I shall send you the play *and* your letter in typescript in about three days. Will you then, please, compare the letter and the play once more, and see if some of the points in the letter couldn't be put into the play so as to make the symbolism clearer. An author reads into his play things which the sober spectator doesn't see, and the fact that even I, the most willing of readers, have failed to grasp such important points must surely give you pause. Reading your piece now, after your explanation, I do indeed find in it everything, but as for the explicitness needed by any theatrical work—just think of those asses of spectators, the lot of them, starting with the composer!

Zerbinetta's scene is indeed very pretty and the scene before Bacchus's arrival, and also his song, quite excellent—as I have to admit now that you've pushed my face in it. But is this quite right? Surely, the symbolism must leap out alive from the action, instead of being dug out of it by subsequent laborious interpretation. Besides, I'm only human: I may be wrong, and am indeed out of sorts; I've been here alone without another soul for the past four weeks, I haven't touched a cigarette for four weeks—let the devil be cheerful in such circumstances! Be patient therefore: maybe my incomprehension will spur you on after all—and don't take it as anything else. After all, we want to bring out the very best in each other. As for the conclusion, we can have a chat about that in Munich. Enjoy the fine summer to the full and accept the best wishes of yours,

RICHARD STRAUSS

Aussee, 23.7.(1911)

My dear Dr. Strauss,

This frank exchange of views is most welcome to me; I am grateful to you for your letter. Nothing you might have said could have appealed to me more than that we must try to bring out the very best in each other. Therefore send me the copies of the letter and of the libretto as soon as possible; I shall read, examine and compare with the best of good will. Please let me have two copies of the play so that I can return one of them immediately to you, purged of the mistakes which have crept in during copying; in a work in rhyme which has been so carefully polished as this the alteration of any syllable would be painful to me. I was quite vexed enough over *Rosenkavalier* where, owing to the rush, I was unable to arrange with you for the deletion in the score of certain slight changes from my wording; it is a matter of minor contractions, even single syllables which slip by perhaps without your realizing it, yet from my point of view they seriously disrupt the impression of dialect and diction, almost exactly as you might feel if in the course of copying your score individual notes were altered here and there.

To your kind letter, let me first of all reply this: there exists a certain productivity not only of creation, but also of reception. One day I may take up my Goethe or Shakespeare and find that they produce in my imagination a heightened response; another day the essence may be missing, the contact between mind and mind, that luminous, scintillating medium through which alone the image takes full shape in the imagination. Now in so delicate a matter as the production of a poetic text intended for music I must be able to count on this kind of productive receptivity on your part. During the past few weeks you have lacked it. Being alone at home without your wife; a chronic and irritating, though slight, nervous depression which has resulted from your giving up cigarette smoking—each one of these causes would be quite enough by itself to make this negative condition understandable; how much more, then, the two coming together. I knew of it, or felt it, when I sent you the *Ariadne* sheets. I felt we were not in contact when you failed to inform me, of your own accord, that you had returned to your home and were impatient to have the text. Two years ago, when I sent you the first fragments of *Rosenkavalier*, your frame of mind was just the opposite; at that time the welcome you gave to what I had done exceeded my expectation and I was well aware how much of this delight was due to your own receptive productivity. That this time I was obliged to 'rub in' the merits of a really successful achievement is for me a matter of momentary disappointment; but it cannot seriously depress me, just as I did not attach undue and exaggerated importance to your enthusiasm on the former occasion.

I have no doubt that things like the intermezzo and the passage for the three nymphs will be grist to your mill as soon as the main sluice is no longer blocked; I also know that the three little songs, the tender, the frivolous and the dreamy one, will one day be among your most beautiful Lieder.

Let me now say something about the point which agitates you at the moment, about the question of understanding and not-understanding, about your own original non-understanding, about the probable incomprehension of the public, the certain incomprehension of the critics. The pure poetic content of a work of art, the real meaning it contains is never understood at first. What is understood is only that which needs no understanding, the obvious, plain anecdote: *Tosca*, *Madam Butterfly* and such like. Anything more subtle, anything that really matters, remains unrecognized, *invariably*. May I remind you of the book Wagner wrote in 1851[1] where he describes (what is almost inconceivable to us today) how works so simple, and constructed with such unfailing stage sense, as *Lohengrin* and *Tannhäuser* failed to be understood—not the music, but the poetic texts. His audiences lacked the slightest inkling of the broad and simple symbolism, based though it is on popular fairy tales, and they actually asked themselves: 'What is all this about?'; they thought the action of the characters absurd and incomprehensible. And what about my own straightforward libretto for *Rosenkavalier*: is that understood—or rather, is it understood by the critics? Everyone who does understand it has discovered its charm, yet the critics have never seen any charm in it. And is it not true that, bogged down in irrelevancies—the frequent occurrence of the word 'blood' and the violent, vehement diction—less than one tenth of the critics recognize or apprehend even today the true basic theme of the 'famous *Elektra*'? No, my dear friend, the essence of poetic meaning comes to be understood only gradually, very gradually; this understanding emanates from a very few people who are in close touch with the world of poetry, and it takes decades to spread.

But it is equally true that the poet's text must possess yet another attraction, through which it can effectively reach even the non-comprehending majority, and such attraction lies in the fact that it exhibits something which is neither insubstantial nor commonplace. This is what made *Elektra* and *Rosenkavalier* effective. In the case of *Ariadne* the attractive style of this supporting opera, the bizarre mixture of the heroic with buffo elements, the gracefully rhymed verses, the set numbers, the playful, puppet-show look of the whole piece, all this gives the audience for the time being something to grab and suck like a child. I have, what is more, been at pains to treat the main action in such manner that it is something thoroughly familiar to the average spectator:

[1] *Oper und Drama.*

Ariadne, deserted by Theseus, consoled by Bacchus, *Ariadne auf Naxos* is in fact, like *Amor and Psyche*, something everybody can picture to himself, even if it be only as a plaster of Paris ornament on the mantelpiece. As for the symbolic aspect, the juxtaposition of the woman who loves only once and the woman who gives herself to many, this is placed so very much in the centre of the action, and is treated as so simple and so clear-cut an antithesis, which may be heightened still further by an equally clear-cut musical contrast, that we may hope at least to avoid utter incomprehension by the audience (and it is on them, and not on the critics, that our success depends).

I have, furthermore, another vehicle to bring home to people this central idea; I mean the prose scene which is to precede the opera. In this scene the stage is being set, the singers are about to make up, the orchestra tunes its instruments. Composer and Dancing Master are on the stage. The Composer, we are told, is to conduct a short heroic opera: *Ariadne auf Naxos*; Ariadne is to bewail her lot and to long for death until Bacchus appears and carries her off. After the opera, a light-hearted afterpiece is planned for the Italian comedians (Zerbinetta and her companions) who are to dance and sing under the direction of the Dancing Master. That is how the programme reads. And now Jourdain suddenly sends his footman with the message that he wishes the two pieces to be performed *simultaneously*, that he has no desire to see Ariadne on a deserted island; the island is on the contrary to be peopled by the Italian players who are to entertain Ariadne with their capers. In short Jourdain asks them to arrange one show out of the two operas. Consternation. The Composer is furious, the Dancing Master tries to soothe him. Finally they summon the clever soubrette (Zerbinetta); they tell her the plot of the heroic opera, explain to her the character of Ariadne, and set her the task of working herself and her companions as best she may into this opera as an intermezzo, without causing undue disturbance. Zerbinetta at once grasps the salient point: to her way of thinking a character like Ariadne must be either a hypocrite or a fool, and she promises to intervene in the action to the best of her ability, but with discretion. This offers us the opportunity of stating quite plainly, under cover of a joke, the symbolic meaning of the antithesis between the two women. Does this appeal to you?

Sincerely yours,

HOFMANNSTHAL

Dear Herr von Hofmannsthal,

Many thanks for your very interesting letter. Further proof that I was not entirely mistaken, and that it is better to discuss all possibilities of a theatrical flop before a piece is staged rather than afterwards, has been provided by our friend Levin who said to me after reading *Ariadne*: 'I haven't a clue what it all means, or what connection it is supposed to have with Molière.' Ecco! Have you read Bahr's chilly review of *Rosenkavalier*? I was quite taken aback; because as a rule Bahr has a good nose even though he doesn't know anything about music. I think that Bahr too has foundered on the slogan 'comic opera', without reflecting that there is no such thing as a really comic opera. When has music in the theatre ever aroused laughter? At two or three places in the whole of operatic literature; otherwise only at actors' extemporizations or in the spoken dialogue (as in *Wildschütz, Zar und Zimmermann, Fra Diavolo*). I am firmly convinced that if one served them up *The Merry Wives* or *Figaro* as a novelty today, they would all declare there was no humour in them.

In your letter you moot the brilliant idea of preparing the ground for *Ariadne* by a big scene which would explain and motivate the whole action. That's excellent. The best thing would be if your last letter to me could be read out. The Composer and the Dancing Master are anyway two Molière figures which could be enormously expanded. They are well conceived, but only you can make them topical.

Give your sense of humour its head, drop in a few malicious remarks about the 'composer'—that sort of thing always amuses the audience and every piece of self-persiflage takes the wind out of the critics' sails. Molière's piece is a little silly, but it can become a hit provided you develop the two parts of Composer and Dancing Master in such a way that everything is said that can be said today about the relationship of public, critics and artist. It could become a companion piece to *Meistersinger*: fifty years after. Pack into it everything that's on your chest, you'll never get a better opportunity! Is there enough malice in you? If not, take a collaborator; such things are usually best done by two people. I was very unwell for a couple of days; I'd overdone things a bit and shall have to let up in my work a bit now!

The only purpose of this letter is to confirm you definitely in your intention: the scene preceding the opera must become the core of the piece. Zerbinetta might have an affair with the Composer, so long as he is not too close a portrait of me.

Best regards then! See you soon in Munich: I shall be there on 8th, 9th, 10th August; 14th, 15th August; and 29th, 30th August (4 Jahreszeiten).

Yours very sincerely,

RICHARD STRAUSS

Aussee, Obertressen 14, 26.7.(1911)

My dear Dr. Strauss,

Even friend Levin (for whom I have the highest esteem and regard)! Yet it seems to me that his two negative judgements cancel each other out. He does not know what the whole thing is about: that might give one pause. But at the same time he does not understand how this can possibly be joined with a Molière piece. And here he is demonstrably wrong. Here his imagination somewhat fails him. For the whole affair is after all actually distilled from the two theatrical elements of Molière's age: from the mythological opera and from the *maschere*, the dancing and singing comedians. Lully might have set it to music, Callot might have drawn it. At first sight indeed one would hardly be surprised to find this whole *divertissement* printed as part of the text—the original text of our comédie-ballet *Bürger als Edelmann*.

Here then friend Levin is demonstrably wrong. Still I was taken aback, since I felt I might be opinionated or deluded, and so yesterday I invited a small group of pleasant, but by no means unduly erudite people who were not prepared in any way and told them: 'Here is something, an impromptu, or I daresay it is nothing at all; let it produce an impression on you and tell me frankly what you think of it.' I gave them first a brief outline of the introductory scene and then briskly read the whole libretto through—they were, as I said, almost naïve people (my wife who is inclined to be severe and not easy to win over, the dancer Grete Wiesenthal, a young painter, Countess Degenfeld from Neubeuern), and the result was so great a delight, so whole-hearted an absorption (on this point a practised reader can never be deceived) and such astonishing comprehension! I asked them: 'Do you miss something? Is there anything you do not understand? Do you see what the Circe business is about?' and the answers I received were most encouraging. Spontaneously, without any prompting from me, they saw and appreciated the charm of the ending, the humour which lies in Zerbinetta's simply saying to herself: 'Well, what of it? She, too, has changed her lover after all—but what a lot of fuss she made about it!' . . . In short I was highly satisfied. Now I am really not a complete idiot, nor am I by any means deficient in self-criticism; but nothing can shake my belief that, so far as in me lies, I have created something really good and ingenious here which, in the special circumstances, will prove most felicitous on the stage, especially for the combination of your art with Reinhardt's theatre. Of this we shall of course have to talk in greater detail, at first between ourselves in all candour and good temper, and then with Reinhardt whose instinct and vision in matters theatrical are so entirely to be depended on, who like us risks his skin and is not likely to let an altogether unique chance slip through his fingers. But I want to get this settled soon, as soon as possible, and I am sure you will be glad of that too. I should like to have a few pleasant days with you, at our leisure, preferably at Garmisch before you go to Munich. I propose to spend the night of the 5th or 6th in Garmisch or Partenkirchen and shall bring my work and books, looking forward to many hours by myself; but towards the evening, or whenever it suits you, we shall go for walks together and straighten out these things. Once we are agreed between ourselves, we shall discuss what is necessary with Reinhardt. I suggest I arrive in Munich on the evening of the third (Hotel Marienbad); I would be busy there on the 4th and come out to you on the 5th. Please fall in with this, it would be very difficult for me to change plans. Therefore please let me have your consent at once on a brief post-card and give me the name of the best hotel in Garmisch-Partenkirchen (I do not care at all for staying in small, soi-disant *gemütlich* inns). One more request: will you reserve for me two seats for the first Mozart evening which you are going to conduct (on the 8th or 10th?), I am very much looking forward to that. And so *à bientôt*, and for God's sake please work little or not at all while you feel run down. It would be too absurd for me to write something expressly for you, just because you are in the unhappy position of having nothing to do, and you were then to make yourself ill over the work. What does it matter when this thing gets done?

Sincerely yours,

HOFMANNSTHAL

P.S. Please do not ask me to stay at your house, I would like us both to be entirely free. If Levin is about, I would very much like to see him.

With the MS. copy which I now return (it contained many distorting mistakes, so please read it through) I enclose a feuilleton by Bahr on Siegfried Wagner, from which you will gather how the wind blows in this particular case, and why *Rosenkavalier* cannot be a very good nor, above all, a comic opera. The sooner you see through the fickle and insufferable character of a renegade like Bahr, the better I shall be pleased. Moreover, since he has dedicated a book[1] to you, you are predestined to be betrayed by him soon and thoroughly, just as in this glorification of Siegfried Wagner he repudiates Reinhardt without mentioning the name, a man whom he has idolized for five years (just as he did me for fifteen!). Such men do not lack judgement, but are far, far worse and more dangerous than those who do.

(Enclosed: Prose insertions for *Ariadne*.)

Rodaun, 22.10.(1911)

Dear Dr. Strauss,

After all those letters we exchanged in July, we both laid off for a while: what a pleasant surprise it was, therefore, at Neubeuern, suddenly to come across the most unexpected news in the *Münchner Neueste Nachrichten* that you have actually finished! But surely not the scoring yet? This presumably means that I must make haste over the gay short transition scene? If this is the case I have one or two things to say and ask. What is it that the Composer plays for Jourdain in the opening scene of *Le Bourgeois Gentilhomme* (instead of that conversation about music)? I must know this in order to refer to it. In this scene I am leaving out the Composer's pupil, who is not wanted; or perhaps I shall use him as a young musical genius and make him the author of *Ariadne*, because the figure of the Composer himself, smug and bourgeois as Molière has made him, is of little use—the character is so inflexible.

Further: I am leaving out the *entrée de danse* introduced by the Dancing Master. The first *entrée de danse* which will remain is where the journeymen tailors put him into his coat; this one will be funny where the other one would have to be treated seriously, as a pure historical imitation of an old dance, and I would not care for that.

With regard to the financial aspects, I was under the impression last summer that we would both rather like to have this arranged through Levin—but if you prefer to do it direct, we can just as well settle it

[1] The comedy *Das Konzert*.

between ourselves in a quarter of an hour; we have, after all, the *Rosenkavalier* contract which needs only a few minor adjustments.

Only one thing I should like to say from the outset, so that it is said in good time: neither in this nor in any future case will I part with the full right of advance publication. Financially this is of no importance, but it is important to me in other respects, and I have no intention of relinquishing this right ever again purely for reasons of organization. If Fürstner sticks to his somewhat chimerical point, he will have to make arrangements accordingly and print a small edition of the text in France before it is too late; I in any case reserve to myself the right to publish my work in a daily newspaper (Christmas number) or in a periodical some weeks before the première.

I know how very meticulously, in every possible way and on all occasions, you see to it that justice is done to my share in our joint productions, that share which is so hard to define. And I do not fuss and fidget when I find that, in gross disregard of your invariably most correct and careful choice of words, every reference in print, in telegrams and so on is always right from the start and so *ad infinitum* to a new Strauss opera, and not to a work somewhat out of the common run produced by two artists who, with imagination and delicacy, are seeking new ways of expression. But all the more acute is my need to make manifest, at least once before the opening of hostilities, the existence of my own work as such, and my right to bring it before the public.

I am sure you understand what I mean, appreciate the justification of what is implied in my wish, and realize for the rest how great and pure a joy it is to me to work for you, or to make you work for me, which to my mind comes to the same thing. The thought of the beautiful music you are sure to have written makes me look forward to the rehearsals with immense pleasure.

Very sincerely yours,

HOFMANNSTHAL

Berlin (early November 1911)

Dear Herr von Hofmannsthal,

Have unfortunately been suffering for the past eight days from a loathsome intestinal catarrh, moreover daily rehearsals for concerts or *Rosenkavalier*—otherwise I'd have written before and thanked you for your letter. *Rosenkavalier* is coming along here very well, both cast and music; whether scenically as well I can't judge yet, since Hülsen only got down to producing two days ago. We'll see. Première on the 14th, dress rehearsal on the 13th. May I expect you here for the event? If so, it would be best to discuss the whole *Ariadne* affair, including the business side, verbally. Otherwise I would write to you. I'm here till 15th November, then at the Hague till the end of the month.

With best regards, also to your wife, yours

RICHARD STRAUSS

On Friday I'll discuss with Reinhardt whether he is in a position to stage *Ariadne* at all; I still don't see where he's to get his orchestra and singers from. The best hope might be Munich in the summer.

Rodaun, 4.11.(1911)

My dear Doctor Strauss,

Many thanks for your kind letter and for the invitation to the première. But I must not squander quiet periods of concentration like the one I am now having. It is *Die Frau ohne Schatten* that benefits from this one. Occasionally a happy thought drives a tunnel through the dark mountain of the very difficult middle act.

Between you and me I am terrified what may happen to certain parts of *Rosenkavalier* in Berlin. I would ask you to make sure at the stage rehearsals that there will be no arbitrary and violent departure from the *authorized* production, and above all that the ceremonial at entrances, taking of seats and so on is strictly adhered to, for that will hold the whole thing reasonably together.

About the *Ariadne*-Reinhardt question, I would like to say only this today: you know I am not obstreperous, but wild horses will not get me to carry out this adaptation of Molière and the introductory scene, unless Reinhardt is to produce it; I say this not for sentimental reasons, but because the whole bizarre piece of work can only exist in the special atmosphere of Reinhardt's theatre for which it is designed. A world première of this work at some Court theatre or other would mean a complete flop, or a dreary *succès d'estime*; with Reinhardt it can be and will be a brilliant first night. But this year Reinhardt is over-taxed; this thing needs quiet preparation and buoyant spirits, no intestinal catarrh, so let us *for Heavens sake* do it twelve months from now and not before.

If you wish, I'll write you the first act of *Die Frau ohne Schatten* for next summer, and in the autumn we will cheerfully tackle the *Bourgeois Gentilhomme*.

With best wishes, yours,

HOFMANNSTHAL

P.S. The idea of bringing out *Ariadne* in Munich during the summer would have much to commend it, i.e. with Reinhardt at the Residenz-theater, if that could be done. But it would perhaps have to be mentioned to Reinhardt now, so that he does not enter into any agreement with the gang of shady businessmen who hired him last year for their Arts Theatre, which would prevent him from undertaking any other production. Reinhardt's own actors would of course have to take part in the Molière! *En somme* I am much more in favour of a small company assembled by a good energetic Kapellmeister (Fried?) in Reinhardt's own theatre.

Rodaun, 18.12.(*1911*)

My dear Doctor Strauss,

I am writing this letter at leisure, quite alone here, after due deliberation and in high seriousness, and ask you to read it in the same spirit, to re-read it and to remember how much is at stake between the two of us who have been brought together by something higher, perhaps, than mere accident; between the two of us who are meant to derive joy from each other and who must do all in our power not to be deflected from this purpose—a danger which seems to threaten us at this critical juncture. I have received a cable from Max Reinhardt in London which showed me just *how* hard it would hit him if *Ariadne* were to be taken away from him; the Deutsches Theater in Berlin has at the same time sent me the enclosed entirely futile notice which, I am afraid, must be the outcome of some accidental indiscretion on the part of a friend. Meanwhile I have had time to think over my Berlin impressions as well as our conversation and so on, and I must tell you that you would be doing a grave injustice to the work *and to me* if, without absolute and compelling necessity (such as cannot emerge for several months), you were to take away the original première, which is decisive for the impact of this work, from the one theatre for which, and for the special qualities of which, I have devised and executed it in every detail. This 'opera', with its subtle stylistic make-up, with its profound meaning hidden beneath the playful action, framed as it is by the Molière piece, a fact itself symbolic in intention (for Jourdain stands for the public), is a conception of the most fragile, the most uncommensurable kind. It is one of my most personal works and one I cherish most highly. It is conceived as a whole composed of several parts, and can only exist, or come into being, where a theatrical genius of a superior order knows how to weld the parts together; were it to fall into the hands of some colourless routine producer, then even the man in charge of the production himself would not feel, or even suspect, the unity of the piece as a whole—so how could there be the remotest chance of projecting it into the minds of the audience? A performance like the one in Dresden with Perron made nonsense of one individual character of mine, and in that case I was able to show myself tolerant and accommodating; but here my whole conception is jeopardized: instead of a spirited entity I shall get a miserable patchwork. Here I must dig my heels in, or show myself as an amateurish bungler and worse.

Let me speak my mind. I am quite willing to display an amiable disposition, I did not object to sending a telegram at your request to Hülsen, I have spoken kindly to you and to other people about that which is praiseworthy in the *Rosenkavalier* production; but if I stop to think, and tell myself quite soberly how this production is pervaded with the most thick-skulled barrack-room spirit, how drill-sergeant thoroughness and vast expense of money literally trample out all subtle charm, blur all contrasts and flatten all emphasis to drab monotony— if I add to this the insult of the crude blue curtain on to which a painter, practised in lavatory decoration, has daubed figures *from the work itself*— this, translated into your sphere, is like a player-piano strumming the principal passages of your music in the theatre bar or in the cloak-room while people are taking off their coats and hats—if on top of all this I tell myself that, whereas the Berlin Opera at least enjoys an occasional gust of cosmopolitan air, the Schauspielhaus is the embodiment of the dreariest mediocrity and provincialism, then I must inform you that I am incapable of stooping so low as to entrust to such hands a work of extreme delicacy and subtlety like this; that I would therefore *in no circumstances* give my consent to a première with Hülsen. Sooner Dresden or Munich or Vienna, if need be.

On more than one occasion you have been good enough to tell me in your kind and friendly manner how distasteful you find the fatuous and crude attitude of critics and scribblers towards *my* share in the

Rosenkavalier. I do value your kind and well-meant desire to counter this, but to tell the truth the fact itself leaves me cold. I know—and I say this with all humility towards the imperishable masterpieces of our literature—I know the worth of my work; I know that for many generations past no distinguished poet of the rank with which I may credit myself amongst the living, has dedicated himself willingly and devotedly to the task of working for a musician. So long as the value of this collaboration is recognized by almost everyone whose judgement matters to me, and while it is so singularly welcomed by the public at large, I can afford to treat with contempt a few hundred pen-pushers up in arms against me for some reason or other; their shafts cannot touch me, or touch me only where I am proof to them.

But that in this case *you* should find it possible to disregard everything that matters to me, to disregard all that the realization of this work of my imagination means to me, to force me into a theatre where I could not appear without a sense of debasement, this *does* touch me; the mere idea that you on your part should entertain such a possibility does hurt me, and hurts me more than just momentarily. Here I find myself misunderstood and injured by you at the most vulnerable point in our relationship as artists. How, if you have so little regard for the unusual nature of this work beyond your own share in it—I mean for the poetry-cum-music aspect, which you must after all bring to fusion if our collaboration is to produce anything of value—how in such circumstances am I to devote myself with joy to the task of working out another project of a similar kind? How am I to write a single line of *Die Frau ohne Schatten* if, over this affair, you not only upset my own relations with Max Reinhardt—and who, in the feverish world of the theatre, would ever get over a disappointment like that?—but face me with the certain prospect of having to abandon altogether every hope of Reinhardt's assistance in the preparation of this future work, subtle and allergic to all routine as it is bound to be, and so of having to do without the very help I need above all else?

Indeed, why should I continue to write libretti for music, which anyhow antagonizes half the world, including even friends I value? Even if by nature or inclination I could be swayed by such considerations, a change in my private circumstances has placed me above the need to do it for financial gain.

(. . .) What stimulates me, and can stimulate me again and again, is the prospect of the beauty which will be called into being by a union of our two arts, the pleasure I promise myself from a perfect harmony of seeing and hearing. Such anticipated joy inspires me while I am producing these works. But there are also recollections and anticipations which have the opposite effect. The painful memory of the spectacle offered at the Dresden and Berlin productions of *Elektra*, by the acting as well as by the stage décor, is one thing I have repeatedly had to suppress by force, otherwise I might have stopped working in the middle of the second act of *Rosenkavalier*; here is your chance to deprive me for ever of all desire for similar undertakings.

Over *Ariadne* you did not vouchsafe me that purest of pleasures, that most personal pleasure between us which you conferred on me so abundantly over *Rosenkavalier*: I mean the joy of knowing you were pleased with what I had done. You were not in a happy mood when the manuscript reached you, and you gave me some gloomy days as a result. Then, nonetheless, you proceeded to make something of this little work which is beautiful beyond compare and fills everyone who has had the privilege of hearing it with most genuine, most rare delight. Today I may surely remind you that last summer I sacrificed to you my own work, my prose comedy. In May you wrote several letters so sad and disappointed that I put aside my *Jedermann* and wrote *Ariadne* for you. Later I had considerable difficulty in getting over this violent interruption of my work on *Jedermann* and in bringing it to the clear and simple conclusion it now has. Then my strength gave out for the time being and I had to leave the comedy, had to postpone it by another year. I am not saying this as a reproach to you, but I am saying it because it is true. *I beg of you, do not inflict on me this injury*; do not injure us both, do not injure our relationship! If you now estrange me from yourself, you can find in Germany and abroad men of talent and rank who will write opera libretti for you, but it won't be the same. And don't injure our work simply by meaning to benefit one aspect of it. Even if I think only of *Ariadne* and not of the seventy-five minutes which precede it and are inseparable from the whole evening's performance, even if I think only of the opera, only of the two groups: Ariadne-Bacchus, Zerbinetta and the four men—even then I must tell myself that they need a mysterious power higher than music alone in order to reveal their ultimate significance at all. The subtly conceived exiguity of this play, these two groups acting beside each other in the narrowest space, this most careful calculation of each gesture, each step, the whole like a concert and at the same time like a ballet—it will be lost, meaningless, a tattered rag in incompetent hands; only in Reinhardt's, yours and mine, can it grow into a singing flower, the incarnation of dance. *Love* is what it needs, enthusiasm, improvisation; it needs a theatre conscious of its ability to achieve something which is today altogether out of the ordinary; it needs a real man at the conductor's desk whose heart and soul is in it—not that appalling atmosphere of the commonplace, the drab routine, the conductor with the cold heart, the opera singers who get through their music somehow. Everyone concerned must stake his life, the impossible must become possible; Reinhardt must sacrifice the space you need for the orchestra; Fried will get together the thirty-six first-class musicians; an Ariadne you have already found; for the smaller parts we shall engage concert singers who will be transformed in Reinhardt's hands (just think of Margarethe Siems!). One difficulty remains —Zerbinetta. And why should we not still get the one person we must get for the première? (For it is the launching of the whole piece which alone matters to you and to me; about the rest, the exploitation of a success, we need not concern ourselves.) We shall just have to get her, whether she be an Italian or an Englishwoman, or Frieda Hempel from America before the opening of the Scala; this is merely a matter of trying hard enough, of tenacity. I will go with you through anything, my dear Dr. Strauss, but never let me see you, in matters of art, choose the more convenient alternative in preference to the higher, the richer possibilities; it would not be like you. It would be acting against your own anarchic nature as a genuine artist. As soon as this were to happen, you would cut yourself loose from me for ever; for I am meant to associate myself with what is best in your character, and not to do convenient business with you. And now farewell, and remember me kindly; I shall always try to deserve it.

Yours,

HOFMANNSTHAL

P.S. One more thing which aggravates my situation towards Reinhardt most painfully. Before you arrived in Berlin, and before it occurred to me that you might wish to alter the course mapped out in this matter, Reinhardt told me that one of his authors had suggested making a big ballet and spectacle out of Molière's forgotten *Amants Magnifiques* (which would have had very good chances); he asked whether this would strike me as inopportune in view of *Ariadne* with its Molière framework, in which case he would drop the idea at once. My answer was 'yes' and so he wired a refusal to the person concerned the very same day.—One cannot and must not treat a man like Reinhardt in such a way; it is madness for the few of us, of our kind, of our rank, scattered in this desert crowded with mediocrity, to act in such a manner; for then we lose our last hold, and before that is lost I would rather stop writing for the theatre altogether—I tell you this quite calmly.

Garmisch, Villa Richard Strauss (late December 1911)

[1] . . . (Edmund Reinhardt) who is of course furious that *Ariadne* can't be done in the Deutsches Theater; but that must not queer our pitch with his brother who is a real artist and not a theatrical manager. Surely it's not my fault that the theatre in the Schumannstrasse isn't an opera house.

I sent a long letter to Max Reinhardt yesterday: I told him how sorry I was, but I was also quite definite that neither the world première nor any subsequent performance is possible in the Deutsches Theater. This fact is unalterable, and we've *got* to reconcile ourselves to it. From now on we'll discuss what our next step could be and what it ought to be. *Not without Reinhardt!* But where with Reinhardt and an operatic cast with whom I wouldn't risk failure? Because not even Reinhardt can produce without an orchestra and singers.

For the moment the matter must rest until Reinhardt's return from London. I shall be in Berlin about the middle of February and in Vienna about 21st February—so we can finally settle the matter then.

Would you agree to *Dresden incl. Reinhardt* and all the rest of our conditions?

I'm sitting over the score for seven or eight hours every day; it's making vigorous headway.

With best regards, yours

RICHARD STRAUSS

Rodaun, 26.12.(1911) After Friday: Schloss Neubeuern am Inn, until 8.1.
My dear Dr. Strauss,

This is supplementary to today's telegram. I expect you to believe and accept my: 'Impossible without Reinhardt', just as I accept your position. About the rest, with Dresden as the basis, we are agreed. To let

[1] Beginning missing.

Levin and Edmund settle the business side—money and so on—is good; but towards Max Reinhardt, who is extremely sensitive, indeed exceedingly touchy concerning the modus of the negotiations, I would urge you to spare no personal effort, just as you never see me sparing myself in letters and telegrams to you or anyone else over a matter of artistic importance. I wrote to Edmund Reinhardt, and to Max Reinhardt (through Gersdorff) as long as four days ago, to appease them, but turning over all the negotiations to you.

To repeat: Reinhardt is indispensable (a) for *Ariadne* itself (in anyone else's hands the work will burst like a soap-bubble), and (b) for the transition scene which must be gay, brilliant, spirited and elegant; as well as for the Molière. The latter, with all its difficulties, you greatly underrate; this 'little bit of Molière' is just as difficult as Mozart. Hitherto Molière has never really existed on the German stage: he has invariably been flogged to death. This 'little bit of Molière' fills three-fifths of the whole evening, and on it I am risking my skin—since this dovetailing of the two works which I have devised will prove an amusing conceit only if the overall intention comes out; otherwise it is rubbish.

About our meeting, please remember that I shall not be in Vienna around the 21st February, but I shall be at your disposal in Berlin about the 15.2., and would willingly accompany you to Dresden. I reserve to myself, *bien entendu*, the choice of the stage-designer and will gladly take responsibility for it. Please do not leave me long without some sign of life; it makes me uneasy and from time to time I shall have things to communicate to you.

Sincerely yours,

HOFMANNSTHAL

P.S. I should be most grateful if some time you could find the opportunity of dropping a hint to Speidel by letter or by word of mouth concerning *Jedermann* (assuming he has got it already); only a hint that it is a work deserving of every respect, that the Berlin music is useful and that he must find good executants for it, and also a hint about my competence regarding the décor and so on.

1912

Dear Herr von Hofmannsthal,

From the enclosed letter you will see that the proprietor of the Deutsches Theater is even more strongly opposed to it than I am. Nor do I think that *Ariadne* would be possible within the framework of the Deutsches Theater, unless in the meantime it changes into a Royal Court Opera House, but would be quite prepared to let the matter rest till Max Reinhardt's return. Levin, however, is pressing me and sees our salvation in Dresden. Of course Reinhardt must be in it with us: you might do some good by exerting a little calming influence on Edmund Reinhardt, who doesn't seem to believe in my good will. Ten days ago I sent a letter to Max Reinhardt in London, as friendly and respectful as possible, but have had no reply so far. Fried and Edmund still believe in the possibility, but I know that it is impossible. Belief against knowledge! Who's going to be right in the end? I had a word with Speidel about *Jedermann*: he has already sent a producer to Berlin, but naturally he doesn't want to copy but to 'create' for himself. He has great hopes of the piece; you had better come for the rehearsals yourself and make sure the producers there aren't too independently creative.

The full score of *Ariadne* is finished as far as half-way; by 1st April everything will be all right. I shall now soon need the absolutely accurate text of the Molière, because of pre- and inter-ludes, songs, etc. —but believe me, it's the end that will determine its success, i.e. the opera by Hofmannsthal-Strauss and not the Molière-Reinhardt. Please be patient, therefore, but make sure of Reinhardt so he doesn't let us down.

Believe me, it cost me a hard inner struggle before my conscience would let me tear the piece, which after all had been conceived from the start solely for Reinhardt and the Deutsches Theater, away from this destination. But art comes first and all other considerations come afterwards! I wish you a good 1912 in health and happiness and steady progress, and in it a fine *Frau ohne Schatten*.

Sincerely yours,

RICHARD STRAUSS

Best regards from us to you all.

R(odaun), 18.1.(1912)

My dear Dr. Strauss,

Many thanks first of all for the nice things you say in your New Year's letter.

Now about the meeting in Dresden: in accordance with your letter and Levin's corresponding advices I have settled everything for Dresden on the 18th. I might possibly be available there on the 17th, too, and on the 19th or 20th, but *definitely not before* the 17th. Naturally I attach the greatest importance to this discussion, to this joint meeting between us two and Reinhardt (on whom, encouraged by Levin, I count most definitely), for we must at long last settle everything there, including the *mise en scène*, before I (working hand in hand with Reinhardt) can get down to the writing of that 'transition scene'. Please for my sake try and let us stick to the 18th for the Dresden conference—or else let us have it at the very end of February, in which case I must know at once. I should be particularly grateful if it could be left at the 18th. (. . .)

One more request—outside the contract: *for good reasons* (of a purely literary kind, into which financial considerations do not of course enter in the least) I am *most* anxious to be able to arrange for the pre-publication of *Ariadne* (e.g. in *Neue Freie Presse* or *Neue Rundschau*). Believe me, for I do know: such pre-publication will at the same time be of the greatest benefit to the opera itself.

There is nothing to prevent it except those altogether ludicrous formalities concerning copyright in France—God knows how many years after we are both dead! In France, what is more, of all places in the world where, thinking merely of the sacrosanctity of Molière, this particular work has the poorest prospects! So please let me take it for granted that in this special case you will rid me of this unnecessary obstacle (in the case of *Die Frau ohne Schatten* I would find it easier to respect an arrangement of the kind)—it matters very much to me.

Au revoir, then, I hope, in a month's time, and *before then* by letter.

Yours,

HOFMANNSTHAL

P.S. I will shortly write to you concerning the first scene of *Le Bourgeois Gentilhomme*—which music is it to be? I do *not* fancy Harlekin's little song there at all!

Dear Herr von Hofmannsthal,

Levin writes that the little house in Dresden is impossible and that only the big opera house is available for *Ariadne*. This would be suicide, the more so as we should have to expect no end of difficulties from Seebach over a star cast. I have therefore written off to Stuttgart and offered them the world première, provided they agree to the cast chosen by yourself, Reinhardt and me (Hempel as Zerbinetta, Destinn as Ariadne), Reinhardt as the producer, any stage designer of your choice, etc., in fact everything the heart desires and generally full powers. I have today received the enclosed letter, which I am passing on for your information. I believe we couldn't ask for anything better. The only thing now is that Reinhardt's got to come in with us, that Hempel and Destinn must accept, if necessary I'll conduct myself—and then it could be launched with two model performances in Stuttgart about the middle of October. After that we can have Dresden—the big opera house; Munich—the Residenztheater; Berlin—the Schauspielhaus—anything you like. The piece will have been staged twice in an exemplary production and that's the main thing. I am writing at once to Hempel and Destinn; Levin's got to get us Reinhardt; and you let me know your own list of requests.

With best regards, yours

RICHARD STRAUSS

Rodaun, Tuesday, 30.1.(1912)

My dear Dr. Strauss,

Levin wires me the good news that Reinhardt is willing to work with us in Dresden, so I ought to be overjoyed to feel that we are out of the wood at last. You can perhaps hardly imagine how I have set my heart on this little piece and how greatly these difficulties, which have dragged on for five weeks, have preoccupied and hindered me in my work; now at last I could be quite happy and relieved—were it not for this new idea about Stuttgart, for which I can raise no enthusiasm whichever way I look at it. Even assuming Reinhardt were willing to accept yet another change of plan and to follow us to Stuttgart; even assuming we can gain one or other of the two stars for *Ariadne*, i.e. for two performances—I am still left with the thoroughly depressing thought that all our labours, including Reinhardt's and Stern's, will have been undertaken for *no-one* except twice eight hundred people, ninety-nine per cent of them critics, envious colleagues, professionals: for the real public there will be literally no seats. After that *no-one* will see what we have created, indeed it will have ceased to exist as soon as the stars, or the star, have left; and as for what remains, whoever is going to see it in Stuttgart, that most God-forsaken spot on earth? In Dresden, on the other hand, whatever one may think of the place, what we four have built up will exist for at least a season; thousands and thousands of people will see it, and among them the anonymous, truly receptive, distinguished section of the public; you realize, don't you, that I want to feel I have created a thing like this for someone to see— you will grant me this. For you to expect me even for a single moment to agree to a performance without Reinhardt, after he has so generously accepted our suggestion as soon as it was made, that would be flying in the face of your pledge, and of something more delicate and binding still, the reliance on complete respect and consideration for each partner's share in the work, without which a collaboration such as ours would break up at once—would, indeed, be broken off already, by implication.

I would not dream of voicing all this, were it not for one of your letters to friend Levin which mentions, among other unthinkable possibilities, the possibility of an original première under Hülsen—a 'possibility' which is no 'possibility' at all, since it is excluded by the promise you gave me.

Perhaps since you live, move, and have your being more in the musical than the visual side of *Ariadne*, you do not yet quite realize the difficulties and secrets which—not to speak of the evening's entertainment as a whole—are involved *even in 'Ariadne' alone*, points where only a producer of genius can bring to life what we have created. I am thinking above all of the Bacchus scene. Up to that moment the acting, the stage upon the stage, the hooped skirts, the wax candles, the reminiscences of Händel are a chief ingredient. As soon as Bacchus appears on the stage we are at once in the regions of great poetry, of sublime music. Here I know exactly what I have in mind, but only Reinhardt (Reinhardt and Stern) can make it reality. Here we want a miracle of lighting (darkness everywhere, a magic light from above) to transform the miniature stage into a dream-like big stage—perhaps the wings must disappear altogether—once the duet in the cave has died away, the stage contracts again—these sort of things must be done, but

116

they must be done where they can continue to be seen and serve as a model, just as the *Rosenkavalier* production in Dresden did an immense amount of good for the general level of production elsewhere (see Berlin) by creating the desire to surpass what was there accomplished. The production of *Ariadne* will need an infinite amount of working out and directing.

So let me beg of you, since I am, after you, the person most closely concerned, to admit of no other consideration but this one: where, and how, can we realize most perfectly the *whole* (not any single part, any one element) of our work. I hope for early and good—if possible definite—news, and for a harmonious, happy meeting in Dresden.

Sincerely yours,

HOFMANNSTHAL

St. Moritz, 3rd February, 1912

Dear Herr von Hofmannsthal,

Schillings (with full power of attorney from Baron Putlitz) and Levin were here for three days. Your kind letter also to hand. What you say about Dresden and Stuttgart is certainly correct—but more important than anything else is a truly perfect performance which in Dresden, under the prevailing conditions (restriction to the resident opera ensemble), would be impossible. The outcome of our consultation: if Reinhardt agrees and comes in with us—*and this is always a conditio sine qua non*—three gala performances in Stuttgart about the middle of October with the entire personnel of the Deutsches Theater!!!

> With Hempel (Zerbinetta)—has as good as accepted
> Destinn (Ariadne)—no reply yet
> Erb (Stuttgart) Bacchus—eminently suited for the part
> Designer: Stern
> Orchestra reinforced by first-class artists hand-picked by me.
> I'll conduct the première myself.
> Reinhardt and you to have unlimited full powers.

What more do you want?

Dresden can follow at the beginning of November with an ordinary production; then Berlin-Hülsen, six months later, as in the case of *Rosenkavalier*. Levin is now negotiating with Reinhardt: if he is willing I hope you too will agree to Stuttgart. Thanks to Putlitz's understanding and Schillings's helpfulness we shall have an opportunity there for a really model performance such as we shall never find again. Against this all practical considerations must stand aside. I am in Berlin on 11th February.

With best regards, yours

RICHARD STRAUSS

When shall I get the final text of *Bourgeois* with the musical interludes?

In Stuttgart, where I'll have absolutely full powers, everything's going to be tip-top: you may confidently leave that to me!

St. Moritz, 6th February, 1912

Dear Herr von Hofmannsthal,

Reinhardt has accepted for Stuttgart—with his whole ensemble! Putlitz is signing the contract with him in Berlin today. Hempel as good as certain. Destinn wired her acceptance yesterday. This is going to be something that, Bayreuth apart, has never been seen before, and certainly not at a Court theatre. The Stuttgart theatre is new (seating 800), with all modern facilities for décor and lighting. Middle of October. Dresden can then follow suit at the beginning of November with an ordinary performance by its 'own efforts'.

What do you say now? Are you agreed?

Best regards, yours—not such a fool after all—

RICHARD STRAUSS

In the spring the whole Stuttgart crew with Reinhardt, the Deutsches Theater, Hempel, Destinn, to Paris, England, Holland! That would be my plan!

Semmering, 7.2.(1912)

My dear Doctor Strauss,

Thank you for your good letter. Of course under these conditions I agree to Stuttgart without reserve. I am signing the contracts at once and am sending them to Fürstner.

Now the following: an early meeting between us is indispensable. I know that you are in Berlin from the 11th to the 17th, but at that time I cannot get there. I shall be in Berlin from February 21st to the 29th and could stay until March 2nd or 3rd. Will you be in Berlin on any one of these days? or can I meet you in Vienna during the first few days of March? Please reply at once by postcard to this address.

If you see Stern in Berlin, please refer him exclusively to me for instructions (which I shall give him verbally) and on this point rely altogether on me (and Reinhardt).

You write: how about the Molière and the insertions? I do not quite understand this question. You already have the Molière with all the proper cuts. For my part, I shall make no changes whatever in it (except for a few details in the *first* scene of the play). The transition scene between the Molière and *Ariadne* (where the actors make up and the combining of opera seria and opera buffa is explained) I mean to write in March. There is nothing in this scene for music.

The remainder of the musical interludes (the tailors, the cooks) are obvious from the Molière.

For the supper music during the meal I would urge only instrumental music and no singing (since the opera is to follow).

About the first scene, which requires a quotation from *Ariadne* (but please not Harlekin's little song), we shall have to talk; the dancers will be out of this scene since we are not having a ballet, but an opera.

One more thing: the pre-publication in *Neue Freie Presse*.[1] I am very glad, and grateful to you for conceding me the point so far as it depends on you. There are only few occasions (and this is one of them) when you can, by some small gesture (like this concession), lighten my difficult and rather thorny position as poet-librettist (who is being reviewed exclusively by music critics). Such assistance (and also possibly the prompting of an article by Bie) is of tactical value only *in advance*; afterwards, when all the stupidities and irrelevancies of a thousand critics have hardened, it is of no use at all.

(...) Such pre-publication offers me a chance to explain the meaning of *Ariadne* (analogous to my letters last summer) by means of a preface to the transition scene. I *really do need that*; as soon as I say this, I know you will concede it. (...)

Therefore please drop me a line; *I am delighted* that (thanks to Levin) we are all at long last at one.

Sincerely yours,

HOFMANNSTHAL

Last night I had some excellent ideas for *Die Frau ohne Schatten*. This could really become a *very very beautiful* thing. Let us hope!

[1] *Ariadne auf Naxos* appeared in the issue of 26th May 1912.

My dear Dr. Strauss,

Herewith the contracts. My insistence on pre-publication (towards you it is a request) remains as urgent as ever. I need a place where, together with the libretto, I can make known my authentic explanation of the how and the wherefore of this combination with the Molière, before all manner of opinions and errors gain currency. Otherwise I am exposed to quite unnecessary misinterpretations and attacks.

When and how can I see you between 21.2. and 5.3.? Please wire. We must discuss the insertions for Act I, scene 1, and many other things. And I do not think Act I can end without some musical epilogue, however short—a few bars repeated from the overture, or something like that. I believe, furthermore, that in place of the conversation about music on p. 67 I shall have to write something new; something written specially would be better than a scene from *Ariadne*, but I must hear from you what you want, a duet, a quartet or what. I even think it ought to be something specially beautiful and splendid, a sort of concert number.

With best regards from your librettist, who considers you by no means a fool and is very well disposed towards you.

HOFMANNSTHAL

Rodaun, 10.2.(1912)

My dear Dr. Strauss,

I am in despair at the sudden news from Schalk that you are *not* coming to Vienna early in March, as I had mistakenly assumed. Where then can I catch you? I am to give a reading in Prague on the 16th—I could be in Dresden on the 17th and 18th, if you would, for my sake, stop off there and spend a few hours with me incognito! And then, I am told, you will be in Prague on the 19th! Or are you going back from there to Berlin?* Please wire!

Yours,

HOFMANNSTHAL

*Then you would meet me in Berlin.

Dear Dr. Strauss,

Today about something which is not *Ariadne*!

I have often felt that those of our subjects (*Rosenkavalier, Ariadne, Die Frau ohne Schatten*) which treat of purification, of a Goethean atmosphere, and in which your profound understanding has given me infinite satisfaction—that all these subjects arouse aspects of your genius, the spiritual and the lovely, which, though hinted at in *Elektra* and *Salome*, are not seen there as an integral part of your equipment. These same subjects also arouse much that has an affinity with your Lieder, with *Don Quixote*, with *Eulenspiegel*; but at the same time they offer only small scope to other sides of your fecund nature—I mean to those massive, grandiose, wholly compelling qualities which chiefly distinguish you from every other living composer and give you a position without equal anywhere.

It was deliberate intention which made me refrain from continuing in this direction after *Elektra*, just as I put the *Semiramis* plot deliberately aside; for here as always I was obliged to pursue a line which is my own. To be your librettist in a higher sense, I had to begin by not being it in the banal sense.

But for all that, the other element in which you are equally at home, that mastery over the dark, savage side of life—which I deliberately refused to nourish—remains nonetheless one of your most precious gifts; and at times, when discussing a plot with you, I have felt you hankering after nourishment for this element, have felt your desire for an opportunity to work again and anew a mine which yielded so much for *Salome* and *Elektra*, your desire for a counterpart once more in the sombre mood, for a *furioso* perhaps—and *furioso* is derived from furia, furies are stupendous avengers of crime who before now inspired Gluck with overwhelming musical passages . . . will you, my dear Dr. Strauss, allow yourself to be inspired by the vision of this central event in ancient tragedy and write a tragic symphony, a symphony of thirty to thirty-five, at the most forty minutes duration, *Orestes and the Furies*? Please read the enclosed sketch and tell me whether this is not an occasion for wonderful, sombre, grandiose music— a synthesis of your symphonies and your two tragic operas. And now imagine Orestes created by Nijinsky, the greatest miming genius on the modern stage (next to Duse, and as a mimer above Duse)—the whole thing, as a pantomime, as a scene, as a tableau based on your music—just as a symphony of yours would be based on a vision, and growing out of it—think it over and please don't refuse me this.

After the delicacy of *Ariadne*, and before *Die Frau ohne Schatten*, I can think of no finer and more contrasting subject for you than these Furies! Hitherto I have always written my libretti because you wanted them and were waiting for them; this time I come to you with a subject because I want it, because I would like to work with this wonderful picturesque artistic tool, with this incomparable body of artists— so don't say no! If you turn it down, the Russians will do it with some French or Russian musician—but in that case it will no longer be what I dreamt of. Canaries, says Hebbel, should never try to imitate a thunderstorm.

The purely superficial affinity between this plot and *Elektra* must not and will not put you off for a minute. The tragic events of the House of Atreus are, after all, the staple subjects of tragedy. No stress lies in this case on the figure of Electra; she and Chrysothemis may figure as nameless daughters of Clytemnestra. The affinity between the two plots is no closer than that between the *Elektra* of Sophocles or Euripides, and the *Eumenides* of Aeschylus. Into the character of Clytemnestra you might, as Wagner did, work some of the themes you have so wonderfully created for her, or you might not. The main emphasis, in any case, is placed on Orestes, on his terrible deed and his terrible suffering; this—with the Furies which lurk and lie in wait for him, only to burst forth in the end horribly and triumphantly—this I feel is a theme for a tragic symphony no less great than Leonora's deed and suffering was for the Leonora Overture No. 3.

Now please read it, think it over and let me know. A note is enclosed which contains an outline of the terms which Diaghilev, the artistic director of the Russian ballet, takes the liberty of submitting to you for the composition of these Furies.

All further details we could, if you accept, discuss in Vienna.

Yours ever,

(. . .)   HOFMANNSTHAL

Garmisch, (mid-April 1912)

Dear Herr von Hofmannsthal,

You have sent me Sternheim's *Ulrich und Brigitte*: what's the idea? A mistake of the packer, perhaps?

What I really do need in order to finish my score is the last concluding words of Jourdain. I'm asking you urgently to send them! Bahr tells me that you could give me accurate information about the Hotel Excelsior on the Lido. Could you do this, please? We may be going there. When shall I get the definitive version of *Bourgeois Gentilhomme*?

With best regards, yours

RICHARD STRAUSS

Garmisch, 19.4.1912

Dear Herr von Hofmannsthal,

I *must* have Jourdain's final words. Also the exact text of the whole play: otherwise I can't carry on with the work.

I hope the scene before the start of the opera is going to be very humorous: do, please, let off rockets of malice and satire and every kind of self-persiflage.

To have Jourdain make his entrance to music, before the opera, doesn't suit me: I want to let the music be silent for a good while before the beginning of *Ariadne*.

Must there be music for the entrance of Dorante and Dorimène? Is this the start of Act II? If so, we might have some slight entr'acte music and make the two enter as the curtain rises upon the final bars. Also in Act II, music for the cooks and the supper. But that'll be all.

Will it suit you if, as an entr'acte to Act II, I have courtly music accompanying the wine until the rise of the curtain? Then a long pause: Footman: 'Herr, der Herr Graf kommt', etc. Jourdain: 'O mein Gott! Ich hab' noch Verschiedenes anzuordnen. Sag' Ihnen', etc.

Three or four final bars during which Dorimène and Dorante make their entrance. When the music has finished the footman says: 'Mein Herr sagt, er würde den Augenblick bei Ihnen sein.' I'm asking you once more for the exact final words of Jourdain.

When are you going to Italy?

Are you going to be in Stuttgart with Reinhardt and Stern about the middle of May, so that you can discuss the last and most important points on the spot? For God's sake see to it that Stern doesn't produce any trashy effects. The last Reinhardt productions of *Turandot* and *Dandin* are to me inspired trash: inspired, but nevertheless trash. I'm still in favour of Roller who is a much more solid and thorough worker. With Stern everything looks *dashed off quickly for cheapness*. Please keep at him. I'm holding you responsible for seeing that it turns out *very* beautiful. Go on prodding Stern and make sure that everything is ready before July so we don't have the usual Reinhardt rush at the last moment. I absolutely detest this business of putting the final touches on a theatrical production at the dress rehearsal. Costumes and scenery must be all ready in Stuttgart on 1st September. Everything must be worked through slowly and painstakingly, the way I work through my full score. Not à la Nelson.

Best regards,

RICHARD STRAUSS

(Notes by Hofmannsthal on the above letter)

After the words:
　'To have Jourdain make his entrance to music, before the opera' etc.:
　'Quite right.'
After the words:
　'Must there be music for the entrance of Dorante' etc.: 'Very good.'
After the words:
　'Also in Act II, music for the cooks' etc.: 'Details in the libretto. Supper music to end with the scullion's dance (Wiesenthal).'
After the words:
　'Will it suit you if, as an entr'acte' etc.: 'Yes.'

Rodaun, 19.4.(1912)

Dear Dr. Strauss,

Please forgive my apparent slackness; I had not realized that you were in any particular hurry about the insertions and the concluding words. Here they are, I am sending you the manuscript, as having them typed in Vienna would mean a delay of three or four days. Please pass on a copy to Fürstner afterwards and see to it that the passages are correctly inserted into the libretto. I have done them in strict accordance with your very valid suggestions, and have drawn forward everything else that happens between Dorante and Dorimène, so that what we need here is the mere dumb-show of their exit; for perfectly understandable reasons you have left me no further space for insertions.

I have, incidentally, worked like a cart-horse at these various unobtrusive, minute additions and alterations in the Molière—especially over the much-discussed 'transition scene', which ought to be concise and colourful, discreet and at the same time gay, which must not jar with the Molière and must yet contain the whole key to *Ariadne*: a hellish chess-problem. Still, I think it has turned out well. Today I have dictated Act II, now I am going through Act I (where for the most part Molière will be left intact); within eight days at the most the whole play will be in your hands, finished and done with.

About Act I, I would like to say that it seems to me not in keeping for the Prima Donna (the actress of *Ariadne*) to appear in the morning at Jourdain's house with the Music Teacher. I should bring on only the three singers Naiad, Dryad and Echo; two of them sing the duet (*berger* and *bergère*), the third, being a soprano, might sing, in place of the Prima Donna, a short passage from Ariadne's recitative. This seems to me at the same time better theatre than bringing the person who is to sing Ariadne on to the stage at this early point. Try as I may, I cannot find any better or more fitting verses for the *berger-bergère* duet than those in the Molière; there they form a trio; I am adapting them, of course, for a duet.

The Excelsior-Lido is an excellently run, very elegant hotel (with prices on the scale of St. Moritz, and outstanding cooking). The manager (Herr Steinschneider) is most obliging. Take a room on one of the upper floors, much more airy. Essential to book your own *capanna* in advance, in the first row.

Sternheim asked me to send you that particular play as specially suitable for music. He is certainly a very gifted poet, not lacking a touch of that higher quality which falls only just short of the fire of genius, and one of the few people whom I could imagine doing useful work with you. In any case please read the play; it is one that I do not know myself.

With best wishes, yours,

HOFMANNSTHAL

21.4.(1912)

Dear Dr. Strauss,

The day before yesterday I received the enclosed letter from Stern, and just as I was on the point of sending it to you, with an urgent request for intervention, you write today asking me to press Stern still further. This is really throwing out the baby with the bath water! If a highly gifted man is being driven and pressed, day in, day out, to improvise, and to produce cheap work, the result is bound to be trash of a sort. He longs to work for us with care, solidity and splendour. Do send him word again at once, authorizing him to do just that! *Il ne demande pas mieux*. I perfectly understand your dislike of work done, à la Reinhardt, only just in time for the première—but the reverse, not giving people enough time from the outset, is equally mad. Stern is faced here with an infinitely subtle and complicated task. His designs and colours must, in a spirited, half-historical, half-anachronistic manner, balance against each other two different conceptions of the world—a task which is quite beyond the solid, but altogether unimaginative Roller. Apart from Stern, we might have had Bakst or Benois, but I fought shy of adding linguistic and geographical difficulties to a situation already sufficiently complex. On top of that, Russians are not very reliable. Please intervene in such a manner that the thing is done properly, but so that the man has sufficient elbow room to use his imagination and not have to rely on mere routine. Why not give Stern until, say, July 20th?

Yours,

HOFMANNSTHAL

About Act I: Since one of the singers is to sing the little song which the pupil (in my text: a young Composer) has composed to your tune, while the other two (contralto and soprano) have the shepherds' duet, the singing of a passage from *Ariadne* becomes, so far as I can see, unnecessary. It will perhaps be as well if here, in the first act, we get only a mention of *Ariadne* and no singing from the opera.

Dear Dr. Strauss,   *Rodaun, 22.4.(1912)*

Herewith first of all your little song (Act I, scene 1). Groping rather in the dark, I have stuck to your metre scheme and merely added period flavour. I enclose at the same time the big duet for soprano and contralto which has, I think, come off rather nicely, and I hope will suit you. The material necessary for the other numbers in Act I (minuet for the dancing lesson, wild music for the fencing lesson, and the tailors' scene) is in the Molière; there will be no change. Within four or five days you will have the full text of both acts anyway.

As for the tailors' scene, I would like to remind you of what we discussed in Berlin: at first, when the tailors come hopping on (goat motif?), and for the jerky attempts to put on Jourdain's court suit, we need something with very marked rhythm; then follows a pretty, stately minuet-like tune (of one or two minutes) for the first journeyman tailor, who shows him how to wear court dress, and with it some parallel-contrasting orchestral music for Jourdain himself as he clumsily tries to get the idea. Don't begrudge the labour spent on this scene: it will benefit the whole work and is indeed needed to establish it, let us hope for many years to come, as a complete piece of a bizarre kind.

On May 17th I shall be in Siena and cannot therefore possibly be in Stuttgart with Reinhardt and Stern—as I informed you, Reinhardt, Stern and Fürstner many weeks ago. In any case my presence at this technical inspection of the stage will not be in the least required. I have explained my intentions in all possible, precise detail to Reinhardt and Stern, and have moreover given you full liberty to decide, where necessary, between two sets of alternatives, according to the technical resources of the stage. Rest assured that there is no other poet or librettist in the whole of Europe whose stage directions, down to the minutest detail of lighting or the feather on a hat, are as accurate and technically precise as mine. Reinhardt will bear me out; he has often told me that I am the only person he knows whom he believes capable of producing a prompt book as complete as his own (and that is something). I have a gift for it—not unlike your own innate facility in orchestration; what I lack is the ability *to carry it out*, especially to *demonstrate* anything. So let me go off quietly to Italy; I badly need to do so, and nothing short of illness in my family will stop me. My head is in a poor way, I don't sleep well, my imagination is stagnant; what I need is cheering up and freedom, not fifteen business letters on my desk every morning. Since we met in Berlin, that is for the past two months, I haven't had a single idea, neither for *Die Frau ohne Schatten*, nor for any one of my other subjects—not a single, in any real sense, productive minute. A dog's life. On the morning of the 28th I shall get to Munich (Hotel Marienbad) and for anything urgent I am at your disposal on the 29th. On the 30th I shall go South.

Sincerely yours,

HOFMANNSTHAL

Dear Herr von Hofmannsthal,

Have already written to Stern and Fürstner, confirming that Stern is to be allowed all the time he needs for a sound, well-matured job. He himself must guarantee that everything will be ready in time. I hate this completion of productions between dress rehearsal and performance, somewhere about 6.30 p.m., half an hour before the box office opens!

Now the little songs: the first stanzas: The Prima Donna (couldn't you write me a few lines to the enclosed tunes?) can sing Echo. The duet between shepherd and shepherdess could then be Naiad (soprano) and Dryad (contralto).

All I want now is the exact version, please, because in Molière it is a trio.

These two things at once, as I'm working on them.

With best regards yours

RICHARD STRAUSS

At the most I shall be going to Northern Italy (Vicenza, Ravenna) by car for three weeks in May: otherwise I'm always in Garmisch.

Jourdain's final words can all be fitted in; likewise the preceding dialogue.

Dear Dr. Strauss, *24.4.(1912)*

Here is the second act complete.

The opening scenes of Act I (up to the dancing lesson; from there onwards we have Molière without significant alterations) I have today sent to Fürstner in Manuscript and he will let you have a typescript copy by return. For the dance of the scullion in the second act, for which the music might grow out of the supper music (especially out of the bird song during the last course), I shall send you tomorrow further indications. I hope the menu: fish, mutton, song-birds is in accordance with your ideas.

With best regards, yours,

HOFMANNSTHAL

P.S. On reading it through I find the transition scene quite good. If you, Reinhardt or I can think of anything to add, this can easily be done during rehearsal. In Reinhardt's hands too much rather than too little tends to be made of such an outline (and for the other theatres we can lay it down in the prompt book).

26.4.(1912)

Dear Dr. Strauss,

Many thanks for your kind letter, which pleased me greatly by telling me of the pleasure you feel over what I have done. Perhaps we shall meet in Munich on the 29th. Unfortunately I cannot travel via Garmisch but hope for a meeting in Italy. My eventual destination is Umbria and Southern Tuscany, down towards Rome: Viterbo, Terni, Orvieto. From May 5th to 7th I shall be in Florence, Hotel Minerva, and from there will make an excursion to Lucca, Pisa.

Correct is: Pagliazzo   zz

Cavicchio   v

Just another word or two about the scullion's dance in Act II. This, together with the supper music out of which it springs, can certainly develop into quite a fine number; Grete Wiesenthal (and in every other town the most gifted and the prettiest ballerina) must then make something really attractive of it, not least because from now on we get not a breath of music for twelve or fifteen minutes. This dance is therefore the last beautiful foot-hill as the mountain chain of music runs into the plain of prose, or the point which marks its arrival in the plain. On the enclosed slip of paper I have indicated the action of the dance, which is also referred to by Dorante.

With sincere regards, yours,

HOFMANNSTHAL

Dancing scene of the scullion (two or three minutes of music):

At first, having got down from the little cart, he is timid at finding himself in such company. Snatches with furtive avidity a glass of sweet wine and sips it. Now he grows bolder and scrutinizes the noble company. Soon he sees everything through the golden haze of slight drunkenness. He is intoxicated by the beauty of the Marquise: he expresses in his gestures that she is driving him out of his senses, that she makes him fly. Now he takes another bold and lusty drink. He kisses his own hand; the whole situation strikes him as more amusing, Jourdain's presence as increasingly droll; the atmosphere between the two lovers is an element which he seems perfectly capable of understanding, which intoxicates him more than the wine—finally he spins several times round the table like a madman and off.

(Siena), 18.(5.1912), evening

My dear Dr. Strauss,

I could not be more sorry! Arrived here a few hours after your departure. Of course I did not know you were coming so far South—or else I would have tried to get in touch. Tomorrow I am going for a long-arranged and long-promised visit in the Apennines near Lucca; from there (Castelnuovo Garfagnana) I shall drive on Tuesday morning straight across the mountains via Modena to Padua (that night at Stella d'Oro, Padua). In the evening of the 22nd I shall be at Cortina d'Ampezzo, next evening at Hotel Post, Kufstein; by midday on the 24th I shall have to be in Munich (Hotel Marienbad) in order to reach Paris on the 25th for a definite performance by the Russians (staying at Hotel Castiglione until about June 7th). Unfortunately I cannot drive via Zell–Garmisch (since Countess Degenfeld, who is with us, must get back to Neubeuern).

Is this talk about *Ariadne* urgent? I hope nothing unpleasant at the eleventh hour! Could you be in Padua in the evening of the 22nd? Or in Munich in the afternoon of the 24th? (I am not leaving for Paris before the evening). If this should be impossible and the matter urgent, I might get out of the train at Stuttgart on the way back from Paris! Please send word to Padua, Stella d'Oro.

Sincerely yours,

HOFMANNSTHAL

Rodaun, 14.6.1912

My dear Dr. Strauss,

How are you? And what did you think of the Stuttgart rehearsals? I hope you were very pleased with them, and enjoyed hearing your music for the first time. This is one of the purest joys granted to people like us, and I for my part am already looking forward to the delight which the days in Stuttgart will bring me, too.

As you will have seen from the libretto, I have adopted all your additions with the exception of one (the King's remark that all modern operas lack melody), and this for a reason with which I am sure you will agree. In the first place this remark, directed as it is against everything modern (or against all detractors of that which is modern) weakens, it seems to me, instead of reinforcing our point. According to our original idea our target in this humorous pastiche of ourselves ought, to my mind, to be always to make fun of our own work, especially the present one; once we begin to talk 'of all modern operas', the joke evaporates.

What is more, in Molière one associates the word 'King' invariably with Louis XIV, whose attitude was the exact opposite (he patronized only what was modern, what was produced in his own reign). This serious anachronism (all the other intentional anachronisms are mild, and not one as clear-cut) so displeased me that I thought it too high a price to pay for a not very effective insertion.

I would like to say once again how much I regretted the seemingly unfriendly haste of my return from Italy. But I had promised to be in Paris on the morning of the 25th and was fully rewarded there by the almost boundless enchantment of the senses which the performances of the Russian ballet presented to me.

Sincerely yours,

HOFMANNSTHAL

P.S. Please let the dedication of the score to Reinhardt be written in both our names. I shall gladly associate myself with any formula which seems fitting to you as an expression of the delight we take in the existence of such a man, and of that sense of gratitude which creative artists should be the first to voice to their contemporaries. This is no more than is due to an exceptional person whose collaboration in our joint work promises to be of incalculable benefit to us.

Garmisch, 20.6.12

My dear Herr von Hofmannsthal,

I have inscribed the following dedication to Reinhardt in the full score:

Max Reinhardt in deep respect and gratitude

followed by both our names; mine first, in accordance with your wish, though I should have liked it better if the poet's name had stood first.

If you can think of a poetic dedication, please send it straight to Fürstner.

The rehearsals in Stuttgart have given me very much pleasure. I believe the score is going to signpost a new road for comic opera, for those who are capable. For with this chamber music style the white sheep will quite clearly be divided from the black. The whole artistic milieu in Stuttgart is exceedingly pleasant. All of them very earnest artists; the soloists very respectable. An ideal manager; and Gerhäuser and Schillings both artists who, anyway, know what's what. I am quite confident now even if Hempel refuses: because of America she is still uncertain. My score is a real masterpiece of a score: you won't find another one like it in a hurry.

There's only one point I'm still anxious about. Exceedingly pleasant and charming though Littmann's little theatre is—and judging by the first rehearsal from the front of the house the acoustics seem to be very good too—I still fear that, with your arrangement of the *Ariadne* stage, the whole opera (especially with its frequent and highly important songs off-stage: Bacchus's song and the final duet) will be acted much *too far up-stage*.

Wouldn't it be possible to set the new dressing scene in a separate room, and then, prior to the entrance of Jourdain and his guests, to have a change of scene so that the *Ariadne* stage and the theatre stage proper are, as it were, identical; in other words, the *Ariadne* stage would be moved forward as far as possible. Do think it over, please. An opera played right at the back of a theatre is a very unsatisfactory business.

Please see that Grete Wiesenthal's contract is sent to Stuttgart, signed.

Jedermann is having a colossal success in Munich: every performance sold out. How are you otherwise? How is *Frau ohne Schatten* going? With kindest regards and best wishes for a productive summer, yours.

RICHARD STRAUSS

Where are you spending your summer?

Rodaun, 23.6.1912

My dear Dr. Strauss,

Your letter has given me real pleasure. The satisfaction you express with what you have achieved, that calm assurance of the mastery displayed in your work, this has done me good and has, in a sense which you will understand, moved me. It does me good to think that I, who hardly consider myself as standing even at the extreme periphery of your art, should have found—with that instinct which is the common bond between all creative artists, over the heads, so to speak, of the rest of the crowd—the right thing to do in producing this particular work which literally forced upon you a definite style, only to give you back your freedom more fully on a higher plane; and that I should in this way have fulfilled the promise I made to myself in devising this plot, a promise affecting the musician which incidentally I mentioned in the short introduction to the publication in *Neue Freie Presse*, which I assume must be in your hands.

The enclosed cutting sent to me by some diligent agency shall be welcome, with reservations, if I may take it as symptomatic of the attitude of the press towards my work. It shows understanding and a certain amount of good will towards at least one part of my intention— the purely theatrical one. As soon as it comes to the more sublime aspect, to the essence of the contrast between Ariadne and Zerbinetta, comprehension, alas, is wanting. I believe your music will make it absolutely clear that what was intended, as far as the figure of Ariadne is concerned, is nothing baroque, nothing pseudo-pastoral, but something real and true in the realm of mind and emotion.

Please set your mind at rest about the scenic difficulty you mention. *Ariadne* is the *raison d'être* of the whole thing; nothing, therefore, will be allowed to cramp her, either in sound or acting. This must be the paramount consideration, and I do not mind if the dressing scene is assumed to take place behind or beside the stage, and if another scene change becomes necessary. In saying this I only mean to express that my mind is completely open in this respect, not to anticipate or prejudge the solution which Reinhardt is sure to produce. For it is one of his outstanding qualities that he can, in the most brilliant fashion, make a virtue of necessity; that he can solve a purely technical difficulty like this in such a manner as to make it appear an imaginative touch. This is where we should have to call him in, if he were not already with us; and I am really looking forward to what his resourcefulness will do for our enterprise.

At the time of my *Orestes* suggestion, which I sacrificed quickly and readily enough to your objections, I said all that is necessary to broach the ballet question. You were by no means altogether disinclined, and I have an idea that such a symphonic piece, of twenty-five or at the outside thirty minutes duration, might not be wholly unwelcome to you as an interim work. Every development, yours included, proceeds after all by way of a spiral; it leaves nothing altogether behind but with each mounting turn comes back to the same point.

As you advance steadily towards a new style of opera which will be wholly your own and yet wholly operatic, it might not be altogether unattractive to you to take up again, at a higher point in the spiral as it were, and with the freedom it gives you, the type of work where the rich resources of a big orchestra generate in complete self-reliance a whole world of a thousand colours. For *Die Frau ohne Schatten* I have actually in mind a blend of these two processes—but I must stop before I chatter more, and more brashly than is proper, about the secrets of your creative work which are, after all, wholly sealed to me.

Together with Kessler, who possesses a most fertile, and quite specifically a designer's imagination, I have produced a short ballet for the Russians, *Joseph in Egypt*, the episode with Potiphar's wife; the boyish part of Joseph of course for Nijinsky, the most extraordinary personality on the stage today.

Tomorrow or the next day I shall send you the sketch in typescript. Please read it through, without overlooking the visual aspects, the beauty; read it in the same spirit which once moved you to devise a Boucher-Fragonard-Watteau ballet.[1]

The sketch has, if I am not mistaken, two good points: the idea of dressing a biblical subject in the costume of Paolo Veronese and of treating it in his spirit; and, dramatically, the sharp antithesis between the two main characters which in the end leads them to opposite poles: one upwards to a bright heaven, the other to sudden death and damnation. How far this is successfully worked out you will judge for yourself; read it and let me have your opinion in a few days. Even if you are not willing to set it to music, I cannot withdraw yet another piece from the Russians (Diaghilev and Nijinsky know the sketch!). But I would endeavour to modify, as far as possible, my collaboration with the Russian or French musician of Diaghilev's choice, so as to make it quite clear that I was concerned to be of assistance only to the dancer, and not to the musician concerned.

The reply signed by Grete Wiesenthal I sent to Baron Putlitz a week ago, apologizing for the delay.

With best regards, yours,

HOFMANNSTHAL

[1] *Kythere.*

134

Dear Herr von Hofmannsthal,

In your contribution to the *Neue Freie Presse* I very much missed your introduction and detailed explanation of the *Ariadne* problem, which you had supplied so beautifully in the enclosed letter to me.

This is very important if *Ariadne* is to be fully understood—which is by no means easy. Look at the enclosed letter from Leopold Schmidt, in whose Almanach the omission might be rectified. Please, write him a good introduction to the style and subject of our piece, not later than mid-August. It's always better to tell the people in advance what to look out for and what to write.

I have neither the inclination for it, nor, what's more important, the necessary skill.

With kindest regards, yours

RICHARD STRAUSS

Rodaun, 28.6.(1912)

My dear Dr. Strauss,

I talked today on the telephone to Dr. Leopold Schmidt and promised him something of the kind for his Almanach—just as I made a similar promise some months ago to M. Ecorcheville for his *Revue Musicale S.I.M.*[1] to pacify the French musical world. You see I am glad to do what I can. But that introduction in *Neue Freie Presse* was never intended to do more than enable me to speak authentically about the ticklish question of the link with Molière; what could have given you the idea that I ought there to have commented, and given explanations, about *Ariadne*? Everything I was obliged to tell you in that letter of mine is now, in the transition scene, being driven into the heads of the audience with a sledge-hammer, point for point. Nor can anyone fail to understand it except conceivably those who, like the Frenchman whose twaddle you have sent me, distort everything out of obvious malice, and make it appear as if we meant merely to raise a laugh. Anyway, as I have said, I shall comment upon myself once again, as a work of supererogation, in the Almanach; only let us make sure that the daily papers reprint as much of it as possible, so that it gets known.

[1] *Revue Musicale de la Société Internationale de Musique*, Année VIII, Paris, 1912. Reprinted in *Gesammelte Werke* (Prosa III).

I am very glad that you take to the idea of *Joseph* as an interim work; this will greatly please Kessler and the Russians are very keen on it. Diaghilev will come to see you in Garmisch from London to settle the business side, but will inquire beforehand when this discussion would suit you best. He is a Russian of the most attractive kind, much more like a country gentleman than a manager, and yet not a bad man of business, neither vague nor ungenerous; I believe you will get on very well with him and quickly come to fair and proper terms.

The similarity with Salome-Jochanaan is definitely only an apparent similarity. In fact, each figure of this pair differs fundamentally from the other two, and so does their relationship. The similarity between Electra and Hamlet is far greater, for in that case all the underlying motifs are identical—yet who would ever think of *Hamlet* when seeing *Elektra*?

You would have to go to considerable pains before you could make the two subjects really similar in music, and even then you would hardly succeed. Do read in my enclosure what Kessler has to say on this point; it is very sensible, like everything he says.

Sincerely yours,

HOFMANNSTHAL

Garmisch, 2.7.1912

My dear Herr von Hofmannsthal,

Once again, *Joseph* is excellent: I'll bite! Have already started sketching it out. Count Kessler's remarks, I am bound to admit, do not convince me entirely, but never mind, I'll get over the difficulty somehow, especially if the character of Potiphar's wife is accurately outlined in the libretto (possibly in the list of characters). We can't have *Joseph in Ägypten* as a title, because that's the name of Méhul's well-known opera, which is still in the repertoire. It must be *Joseph bei Potiphar*. That you mean to write something for L. Schmidt is splendid. You are mistaken if you believe that everything's already been said adequately in that scene you've added. Only for the very subtle! But as for the general public, and particularly those gentry of the press, you just can't pile it on too thick or stick it too close under their noses. But it must be done in advance; before those first stupid slogans gain ground from which a man might suffer for the next fifty years. Anticipate all criticism and instruct them in detail just what they've got to think and to feel, and how they've got to take the whole thing. I consider this preliminary job every bit as important as the work itself. And you write so splendidly: so please do make the effort and use the letter you wrote me at the time. It was quite excellent.[1]

In Reinhardt's and my opinion the interval must come before the inserted scene with the actors; that's where the act must end at all costs.

I suggest that both Molière acts should be played consecutively, with only a transformation; end of act and interval not till after the supper.

In that case I'll compose a musical introduction to your dressing-room scene, and Molière and Hofmannsthal will thus be also formally separated. Only the end of the act on page 96 is very weak. Try and see if some improvement couldn't be made there. If there is anything I can do musically to help, I'll be glad to.

The first Molière act ends with the audience hearing the orchestra rehearse the *Ariadne* overture off-stage, through the door by which Nicoline, her face slapped, makes her exit. But the second act, before the first long interval, must be more striking, I feel sure you'll think of some vigorous improvement on Molière.

Or could one bring on all the actors already at this point? Not witty enough. What's wanted here is a vigorous joke. Herr von Hülsen wrote to me yesterday that he finds my new piece 'exceedingly delightful'! All of a sudden—after fifty-eight sold-out *Rosenkavaliers*. Marvellous how one rises in their esteem! Before, one was just so much dirt. Where will you be this summer? Can one see you some time?

With best regards (always, of course, to your wife as well), yours

RICHARD STRAUSS

Hinterbruehl, Hauptstrasse 19. After tomorrow: Aussee, Obertressen 14
9.7.(1912)

My dear Dr. Strauss,

I quite agree with you that the whole thing must be served to the critics on a platter; I discussed it all with Leopold Schmidt last week.

As for putting the interval before the transformation in Act II, instead of at the end of Act I, I don't quite see the point. Wherever we

[1] In the *Almanach für die musikalische Welt*, Berlin, 1912, Hofmannsthal's *Ariadne* letter was first published, an edited version of the original letter to Strauss of 28th July 1911. Included in Hofmannsthal's *Gesammelte Werke* (Prosa III).

have the interval, the audience will not yet be relaxed, they will even be impatient, because they have not yet heard one note of the opera for which they have come. This will happen whatever we do. But the later the interval, the more noticeable this impatience and slight disappointment. Still, I don't mean to be difficult if you and Reinhardt should have weighty reasons which may eventually convince me.

To strengthen the curtain on page 96 (if it is to be followed by the interval), either by new dramatic ideas or through music, does not appear to me called for by the situation. Anything that is not organic invariably looks studied and weak. But if one were merely to change round the last sentence a little (see below), an experienced comedian could surely get a laugh out of it, and it is always safe to bring down the curtain on a laugh. But I would anyway think it best to leave the interval at the end of Act I. What harm can it do there? I cannot see any.—Page 96 might end something like this:

Jourdain: 'Komm her, ich brauche Dich! Ruf den andern auch (the footmen take their places one on each side of him). Ich sage Euch, ich will jetzt sogleich noch etwas anordnen, das sehr wichtig und sinnreich ist, aber ich weiss noch nicht, was es sein wird.' If he stops there with his pretty silly, pompous face, that will be enough to make us laugh, and it will at the same time point firmly towards what is to follow, the chief event of the evening.

I have given thought to the alleged similarity between the ballet and *Salome*, but, try as I may not to deceive myself, I can discover no point of resemblance except that in both cases a lady demands of a gentleman what on the stage we usually see demanded by the gentleman and either granted or not granted by the lady. At this point the action converges, but from here onwards it takes to my mind entirely different directions, since the two ladies, and also the two gentlemen, are poles apart; so is the way they put forward their demand; the whole atmosphere, and the peculiar emotional tension this produces, are altogether different—as a non-musician I seem to hear the sound of quite different instruments when I think of the couple in *Salome* and then of the pair in the ballet.

I am most grateful to you for the delicacy with which you have refrained from pressing me over *Die Frau ohne Schatten*, and have indeed only rarely and gently reminded me of it. In return I promise you that, in the course of the harmonious and productive hours which I so much long to find in the next two months, I shall not forget to direct the eye of my imagination towards these characters and to let it rest there as long as this radiation is needed for their subterranean growth. No reminders and no impatience of yours could add anything to the passionate and sanguine affection with which I am tending this happy, profound subject—and I deeply appreciate your restraint. I am, with my compliments to your wife, yours,

HOFMANNSTHAL

P.S. Grete Wiesenthal will be here with us at Aussee (early) in August. I would be immensely grateful if I could have a copy of the dance pieces, especially the scullion's scene, so that she can play them through on the piano and think out her dances. Thus she will come to the Stuttgart rehearsals more or less fully prepared; improvisation is no more compatible with dancing than with any other serious art.

Garmisch, 21.7.1912

Dear Herr von Hofmannsthal,

Many thanks for your kind letters: after careful consideration I am, after all, in complete agreement with your division into acts. You're quite right. It's better as it stands. The first act of the Molière is long enough and the division into Molière and Hofmannsthal, as suggested by Stern, would be too deliberate. At the same time, an accentuation of the end of Act II, or rather transformation, as proposed by you, would not come amiss. The main thing, of course, is to keep this entr'acte down to a minimum as I'm not having any music before the actors' scene now: I want the ear to be fresh again for the opera. I'm still liking the ballet libretto a lot; it's a masterpiece and I'll get down to it as soon as possible.

Count Kessler and the Russian will be here on 3rd August. Surely I need arrange my conditions with the director only?

Ariadne is now finished. Fürstner is getting the last pages of the full score tomorrow, with orders to send you the two little ballet pieces at once, either copied out or printed, so that you can run through them with Mme Wiesenthal.

With best regards,

RICHARD STRAUSS

My dear Dr. Strauss,

Many thanks for your note and for the good things you say about the ballet, which I welcome both on my own and on Kessler's behalf. When he comes to see you with Diaghilev, please treat him as a collaborator in the full sense of the word. Ballet is perhaps the only form of art which permits real, intimate collaboration between two people gifted with visual imagination, and my share in this one has been smaller, Kessler's larger than you may imagine.

Now for your reply to your own question about Vienna and Berlin. In our obvious joint interest I must urge you to think twice before you place undue restrictions on the right of the Russians to avail themselves of this ballet. The Russians are performing with rising prestige in all the capitals of Europe, at enormous prices in very big theatres—naturally, therefore, for not very protracted seasons. A poor number in their repertory goes by the board at once; but on the other hand they are quite unable to exploit fully, either artistically or financially, their *big* successes (like *Scheherazade* or *Le Spectre de la Rose*, a brilliant work of Nijinsky's to music by C. M. Weber) in one Paris and London season. Their enterprise is forging ahead, they have not yet toured North America, South America or Australia despite most promising offers. It is impossible to foretell how often and where they may be able to perform a work of yours with an outstanding part for Nijinsky—but Paris, Berlin, London must be the foundation, throughout two, three, four seasons, of a constantly renewed success. Please make this view your own, accurate as it undoubtedly is. I say it of my own accord, for I have never discussed such matters with Diaghilev; I have in fact not seen him since the scenario was sketched, and we have only exchanged a few brief telegrams.

Another point: how do you, in any case, imagine such performances in Berlin, Vienna, etc.? Executed by whom?—since Joseph and the Woman, at least, require the combination of an actor's and dancer's highest art. I am not going to brandish a fidgety veto, nor would such a thing be in the least called for between the two of us, but I can't assume that you countenance, any more than I do, the idea that this work should ever be mimed by local companies say in Frankfurt, or Dresden, or Hamburg? What you get in return strikes me as not at all bad: Buenos Aires and Madrid, Warsaw, Sydney, Chicago, and so on.

Please set my mind at ease about this, and tell me how you feel about it. It does not after all affect Diaghilev, but it does affect me, supremely. I am entirely in your hands, since I have no wish to upset the apple-cart by making difficulties. But imagine you were similarly in my hands, and I were to allow your music to be massacred by the vilest fairground musicians on the Prater, by circus bands and the like. Please let me have a short note about this, even before Kessler comes to visit you with Diaghilev and Nijinsky.

Sincerely yours,

HOFMANNSTHAL

P.S. I am glad you agree with me about the division of the acts in *Le Bourgeois Gentilhomme*. The transformation to take no time. I assume a modernized theatre has a revolving stage or some such scene-shifting machinery?

Aussee, 8.9.1912

My dear Dr. Strauss,

Because I know it will give you pleasure I am writing to tell you that *Die Frau ohne Schatten* has now taken a powerful hold on my mind. At long last I have fully possessed myself of this subject, step by step, scene by scene, every transition, every climax, the overall shape of the whole work and at the same time the details, so that I can say to myself 'this is safe'. May it be given to us to carry it through as I now see it before me. I am altogether in a productive mood and look forward to a good spell, provided nothing comes from the outside to trouble my autumn. Ever since the age of eighteen I have known that for me the autumn months are the most creative time of year. Stuttgart I shall regard as an enjoyable break. I mean to get a lot on paper and to make sure of the first act at least of *Die Frau ohne Schatten*; for the time being I hunger and thirst for sun; here we have rain, rain for the past seven days, after a ruined August. My wife is not at all well; if she recovers sufficiently to travel I shall settle down somewhere in the South Tyrol or Northern Italy.

One more thing: I shall shortly send Reinhardt's secretary a copy with as many cuts (in the prose of *Le Bourgeois*) as I can make. Would you please let me have by return the amended, more trenchant passage for the end of Act II (before the transformation) which I suggested to you by letter when we discussed the question of the interval.

Sincerely yours,

HOFMANNSTHAL

P.S. A long Italian press interview has found its way here in which you, as usual, and as is only right and proper, take up the cudgels strongly on my behalf; I am very pleased.

Among the candidates for succession to Speidel is Baron Franckenstein, a childhood friend of mine whom you have met. His qualifications (he is a real musician, a man of the theatre, a man of intellect and character) put him far above all the sycophantic courtiers who compete with him; but notwithstanding all these advantages he still has some chance, for he is related to the Schönborns, Oettingens and so on. Please give him your strong support if the occasion arises; I am willing to vouch for this man in every sense, and you know I do not do that lightly.

Garmisch, 11th Sept. 1912

Dear Herr von Hofmannsthal,

Congratulations on *Frau ohne Schatten*: I'm looking forward to it. *Joseph* isn't progressing as quickly as I expected. The chaste Joseph himself isn't at all up my street, and if a thing bores me I find it difficult to set it to music. This God-seeker Joseph—he's going to be a hell of an effort! Well, maybe there's a pious tune for good boy Joseph lying about in some atavistic recess of my appendix.

The passage in your letter of 9th July, concerning the end of Act I of *Bourgeois* reads:

Jourdain: 'Komm her, ich brauche dich! Ruf die andern auch! Ich sage Euch, ich will jetzt sogleich noch etwas anordnen, das sehr wichtig und sinnreich ist—aber ich weiss noch nicht, was es sein wird.'

See you in Stuttgart. I am tremendously curious about *Frau ohne Schatten*. Best of luck for the rest! Sincerely hope your wife will soon be better. And best regards. Yours

RICHARD STRAUSS

Aussee, 13.9.(1912)

My dear Dr. Strauss,

I am amazed to hear you are stuck over the character of Joseph; to me he is the best and most successfully conceived character, the only thing in the whole ballet which is genuinely unusual and engaging. I must say, however, that the way you describe it, as the 'chaste Joseph' for whom a pious tune must be found, this character bores me too and I should be equally unable to find music for it. As I see him, you would have to look for the music not in some atavistic recess of your appendix, but in the purest region of your brain, where the imagination soars to the heights, to the pure, clear air of mountain glaciers, to keen, absolute intellectual freedom—a region to which, I know, you readily and easily soar. This shepherd lad, as I see him, the gifted child of a mountain race who has strayed among people living in affluence by the river delta below, resembles far more some noble, untamed colt than a pious seminarist. His search for God, in wild thrusts upward, is but a wild leaping towards the lofty fruit of inspiration. The clear, glittering solitude of the mountain heights has accustomed him to strain higher, ever higher towards a lone, pure ecstasy, and to tear off from the unattainable brightness above him (which no art, if not music, can possibly express) a little piece of heaven, to tear it to his heart; this fleeting state of exaltation, this trance, he calls God—and it is this God whom he summons to his aid with outstretched arms when the dark, smothering, stifling *alien* world—a world alien to him to the very marrow of his bones—stretches out her tentacles to entangle him. And the angel is nothing but the forefinger of this God, who is light and all that is most high—the highest that is in you, where could you call it forth if not here?

When, to my amazement, I see you stuck at this point, I can only imagine that the *Alpensymphonie* (which I do not know) is in your way, that you wish to avoid the upward surge, the soaring towards?—well, towards 'God'—which you sought and found there; that in this instance you do not wish to let yourself go. But I am not seriously alarmed, for I remember Clytemnestra and tell myself that with you such stoppages produce what is most remarkable of all.

The motif of blank refusal, which is the motif of the 'chaste Joseph'— though by calling him that you open the door to an atmosphere of parody, of caricature, indeed you have already let it in—what is this but the grandiose and awe-inspiring basic motif of the whole of Strindberg's work: the struggle of man's genius, of man's intensified intellectuality against the evil, the silliness of woman, against her urge to drag him down, to sap his strength? A glance at one of Strindberg's books, perhaps at that strange novel *An offener See*, might help to make you more susceptible to the truth, the symbolic significance of this conflict, where a conventional, parodistic interpretation appears to encumber your imagination and so ends by 'boring' you. I cannot believe that you should be incapable of finding some bridge between this boy Joseph and the recollection of your own adolescence; whether there was a Potiphar's wife or not, there must have been something lofty, radiant, hardly attainable above you, waiting to be taken by force—this is the meaning of Joseph's dance.

Sincerely yours,

HOFMANNSTHAL

My dear Dr. Strauss, *Munich, Wednesday (9.10.1912)*

Many thanks for your kind suggestion, but please allow me to spend this time quite alone, without wife or children, without distraction, belonging only to myself and to my work, pacing up and down the small hotel room for many hours, pursuing my thoughts, my dreams and day-dreams—all this is so precious to me, a real regeneration. So please let me stay here as long as possible; it is bound, incidentally, to benefit *Die Frau ohne Schatten* which will, I hope, establish me once and for all as your 'Leib-, Hof- und Haus-Dichter'. Then by November, if you wish, I shall be able to give you a detailed scenario of all the three acts, the eight scenes; in the spring, as soon as you like, you shall have the first Act. So please go to Stuttgart now by yourself, but take good care not to catch a cold; that would ruin the première.

Will you set Schillings's mind at rest about the various curtains; I am told they worry him. I have already thought out an amusing twist for Act I, but cannot settle the actual wording until I get there—because Jourdain's joke must be made to fit your musical ending, where all the instruments chime in together. The end of the half-act in Act II can perhaps also be made more forceful. As for the final ending, that last little speech of Jourdain's (after *Ariadne*) which once more epitomizes this comic character and then is lost in the final chords of the music, that I consider excellent and I have no intention of changing anything there. You have a concert here on the 15th; could I travel with you to Stuttgart on the 16th?

Yours,

HOFMANNSTHAL

144

Rodaun, Wednesday (9.10.1912)

Dear Dr. Strauss,

I wrote to you only three hours ago, but anger obliges me to take up my pen again, anger about a horrid, typically provincial piece of nonsense from Stuttgart: the official announcement which I have just discovered in my newspaper of the plan to hold a *banquet* there on the evening of the 25th, after *Ariadne*, at which anyone (sic!) can participate on payment of 10 marks. This is really beyond any joke! I hope you can dispose of it by an energetic protest in Stuttgart, and would be much obliged. For my part I refuse from the outset to spend an evening, which I hope to hold precious in my memory, rubbing elbows with newspaper-hacks and Stuttgart philistines who will slap you and me on the back over a glass of champagne. The seating order, I shouldn't be surprised, to be drawn up by one of the clerks of the theatre management, and my wife to sit between Mr. D. and a theatre director from Zwickau! No, thank you! I am a very liberal-minded person, but I do draw the line when it comes to social intercourse. So I beg of you to redeem the situation by word of mouth. The only possible way is the one which proved so satisfactory at the time of *Rosenkavalier*; that is small or medium-sized tables—one for you, Putlitz, Schillings, Reinhardt and whomever else you want, one for Fürstner, one for Levin, and one table for me and my close personal friends. If they will not accept this, I should unhappily be obliged to stay away, to my infinite regret. But I am sure you can straighten this out by a few words, if necessary energetic ones.

Sincerely yours,

HOFMANNSTHAL

Frankfurt, 13.10.12

Dear Herr von Hofmannsthal,

I shall be in Munich on Tuesday at 1 o'clock: would you like to have lunch with me at the Jahreszeiten at 1.30? I shall be going on to Berlin on Tuesday night. Yesterday's rehearsal in Stuttgart most gratifying. Excellent casting in opera and play. If Reinhardt, as it seems, arrives here with his second-best team, without Wassmann, he won't have an easy time.

The piece is tremendously effective. Molière is unspeakably funny. The banquet in accordance with your wishes, with separate tables, already arranged by Putlitz.

With kind regards, yours

RICHARD STRAUSS

Munich, Monday 4 o'clock (21.10.1912)

Dear Dr. Strauss,

Very glad to come to lunch with you tomorrow, 1.30 p.m., and shall travel to Stuttgart on Wednesday. I am immensely pleased to hear that the enormously poetical and dramatic qualities of the Molière have now been brought home to you, and with them also the real significance of this combination of a work not mine with my own. I cannot for the moment make any sense of your remark about Reinhardt (second-best team), because I settled every detail of the cast with Reinhardt last March (Arnold and not Wassmann as Jourdain, because Wassmann is a punster who would blur the character and destroy the whole line of the play, while Arnold is a real comedian and actor and so forth). I am sure Reinhardt has made no changes without my consent; indeed at my request he expressly engaged Rosa Bertens for the small but important part of Mme Jourdain; so—everything else when we see each other.

Sincerely yours,

HOFMANNSTHAL

Auerbach, Vogtland, 2.12.(1912)

My dear Dr. Strauss,

I write to you at the express request of Bruno Walter, and break my habitual restraint in these matters to tell you of my violent distaste for any *Ariadne* and *Bourgeois* performances in the big Munich House (instead of the admirably suited Residenztheater), and to remind you of all the many reasons you yourself advanced to me in Stuttgart in favour of small theatres for this work.

After a talk with me, Walter seems to realize that a letter he appears to have written to you is pretty absurd (this strange man seems to be constantly in a fever, pro or contra, and never able to weigh anything calmly). Now he apparently wants me to attenuate the effect his letter may have on you; hence this note.

There is something wrong between the two of us (you and me) which in the end *will have to be* brought out into the open; but to touch on it and discuss it is so extremely distasteful to me that for some three weeks I have put off the decision to mention it to you—and I shall probably put it off for some time still, the more so since the sombre political situation seems to render everything else almost trivial.

With best wishes, yours,

HOFMANNSTHAL

My dear Dr. Strauss,   *Dresden, 5.12.(1912)*

I have now heard *Ariadne* here, and was once again profoundly moved by the delicacy and beauty of this work.

The Molière in the big house strikes me as absurd. The performance was very poorly attended, and there is something saddening in the comedy being acted in a vast half-empty hall; we must do everything to avoid a repetition of this in Munich. Looking at the whole thing— as it is now performed (not without serious loss) in a manner, and in theatres, different from those for which it was intended—I still draw lasting pleasure from the thought that I forced upon you so unusual and important a work. But at the same time I cannot help realizing that the subtlety and refinement of the whole piece, although they are gains to its musical purity, have made it hard for this work to hold its own in the face of a refractory public, which (even in opera) is prejudiced in favour of verism, and a press which, so far from popularizing the ideas behind this work or even entering into their spirit as it ought, invariably pitches into it like an axe into a tree. That Ariadne is a decidedly well-rounded figure, in the music and in the poetry, far better fashioned and rounded than many thousand Miss Müllers or Mrs. Meiers we get on the stage whose addresses and incomes we are told in detail, no less 'round' than Electra or Salome, this is something which these louts cannot comprehend; any more, so it seems, than they can look upon a genius as lucid and radiant as Molière with anything but inveterate, indeed professional, antagonism.

I understand you are going to be here on Saturday. I leave tomorrow for Berlin, Hotel Adlon, and will stay there until the 12th; I would very much like to see you sometime for an hour to talk over various questions. For the time being I should not wish to touch upon the matter referred to in my last letter, for at the moment I can only concentrate on the more positive aspects of our present, and possibly our future, collaboration.

With best regards, yours,

HOFMANNSTHAL

Hotel Adlon, Berlin W. (9.12.1912). Monday, 7 o'clock

My dear Dr. Strauss,

So we shall meet tomorrow night at the Adlon, and since a telegram from Darmstadt (which concerns the *Jedermann* dress rehearsal and luncheon with the Grand Duke) has just informed me that I need not leave here until Thursday evening, we might lunch together or something—perhaps at Levin's on Wednesday or Thursday (but nothing at night!).

I was very glad of our talk the other day, and about your happy idea concerning the *secco* recitatives (in view of this I shall recast that brief scene and cut out all allusions which refer back to the Molière). I am also glad we have settled this money business by word of mouth, since you have seen the injustice of it and will get it rectified.

Fürstner has sent me a draft contract for *Josephslegende* which has the same ambiguous wording and contains clauses concerning a libretto—whereas I, for artistic reasons, absolutely reject the preparation of a book of words for this ballet. There can be no text for a ballet. A ballet which needs a text would be a mistake,[1] and I should *rightly* be blamed for the publication of such a book of words; I can take attacks and disparagement with equanimity only so long as I feel them to be unjustified and can thus deprive them of their sting. All this will have to be talked over; I doubt whether this contract will get signed before February.

Until tomorrow then, sincerely your

LIBRETTIST

Darmstadt, Friday, 13.12.(1912)

My dear Dr. Strauss,

Ever since you played to me yesterday, I have not ceased to be perturbed; I mean about the style of the Joseph themes (more exactly the first and the second Joseph themes you played). You spoke to me

[1] A 'Book of Words' for *Josephslegende* nonetheless appeared.

148

recently in a good and salutary way about confidence. Now it is true that in matters musical I am an illiterate, an idiot, what you like. But I do possess a feeling for style, a sense of what is congruous or incongruous; and so I beg of you, as a true test of friendship, please accept with an open mind what I am now about to say. It is a vital matter, and nothing is lost so far since we are not yet concerned with anything final, only rough sketches and intentions.

What troubles and aggravates my own sense of responsibility is the idea that I might have confused you by the refinements of this unrepeatable experiment which is *Ariadne*; also that I might once again have sown confusion in your mind by an altogether secondary detail, I mean by our plan to perform this biblical subject in the costume of Veronese, or something of the kind. Please dismiss this detail entirely from your imagination, for it is related exclusively to certain visual aims. I have only mentioned it in order to postulate some sort of ornate costume, and to escape at the same time from archaeological accuracy which is invariably dry. But you, the musician, are in no way concerned with the question of costume. The conception of *Ariadne* actually did make it necessary for you to put *some* of your music into period costume, to treat it as a quotation; and you solved that with wonderful tact. But here nothing of the kind is intended. You are faced with the absolute content of the biblical story, which you have to interpret as music in musical language, in the language of Richard Strauss—just as you interpreted the *Salome* and *Elektra* subjects in your own manner. Do we see eye to eye on this point, my dear Dr. Strauss? When I recall the music you played to us, the finished part, I would swear we see eye to eye over this, to a nicety. The opening, the dance of the women, the grave, threatening bars or figures (my terminology for the technicalities of music is altogether erratic and idiotic) which introduce the boxing scene, and above all the wonderful, monumental theme which immediately establishes Potiphar's wife: this is a definite world, a style, your most personal style, the style which—to mention what is perhaps its finest moment—created Clytemnestra. Now we come to the themes for Joseph (not the incomparable third theme, that of union with God, but the first and second)—here, as you now have it, we are in another world; not, as would be quite correct, its opposite, but a different world altogether, an abrupt break in the *style*, a blow, a slap in the face.

Admittedly you carry within your nature, organically, much that recalls the 18th century, and Mozart. But it is a fact that as a rich, a great musician, you carry within you *much* else besides. It all depends on what is brought out and what is best left dormant. In every task before us the final criterion can only be sensitivity in the matter of style, and of this I must consider myself guardian and keeper for the two of us. In *Rosenkavalier* and *Ariadne* it was right and fruitful to bring out the 18th century in you; in the present case it would be entirely wrong, as wrong as it would be in *Salome*. There may be something absolutely right in these themes for Joseph—I am too incompetent to analyse that —but as they stand they are, or strike one as, dressed up, dolled up, pastoral, *impossible* for this atmosphere, and they put one off fatally. I know perfectly well that interwoven and drawn as they are into the texture of the orchestra, your themes never emerge naked, but this is no consolation—the spirit, the essence of these two themes contradicts the character of Joseph and contradicts the style of the whole piece. Something must have confused you here. I fear it was that idea about the costumes, and that is what made you conjure up the wrong spirit. I am so miserably incompetent at expressing myself accurately and precisely in musical terms, that I can only appeal again and again, and on behalf of the three of us—the perturbed Kessler, the perturbed Nijinsky, as well as myself—to your goodwill, to your open mind, to your willingness to understand. You have drawn a sombre, stifling world: into this world steps a young hero, a boy hero, but he is a figure belonging to the same atmosphere which is, all in all, tragic; he must bear no trace of another, dainty world, the world of the menuet, or else this whole work is ruined.

I fear it is the idea of ballet, of the need for accentuated rhythms which has misled and confused you. Therefore I must make myself the spokesman for Nijinsky who implores you to write the most unrestrained, the least dance-like music in the world, to put down pure Strauss for this leaping towards God which is a struggle for God. To be taken by you beyond all bounds of convention is exactly what he longs for; he is, after all, a true genius and just where the track is uncharted, there he desires to show what he can do, in a region like the one you opened up in *Elektra*.

You do understand me, my dear Dr. Strauss, don't you—and you will not assume that I arrogate to myself the right to tie you down to your own two operas, *Elektra* and *Salome*. Everything in you is progress and development. But here it is a question of style, of a conscious choice between alternatives in your mind. So please set my anxieties at rest by not too short a line to Rodaun. When I visualize how *unusual* a work may here come into being, with executants like these Russians, I am anxious as I have rarely been about any source of danger at the very core of the work itself.

Yours ever faithfully,

HOFMANNSTHAL

Rodaun, 22.12.(1912)

My dear Dr. Strauss,

I am very glad you took my letters in such good part (not that I ever expected anything else, for I took up your reply without the slightest misgiving) and that you have already carried your changed purpose into effect, i.e. into music. For us to be rent asunder, or not to come together, that would be a major disaster, a festering wound, or even a permanent crippling of our joint child. If such conflict of purpose were to occur often and without remedy, it would render our collaboration in any higher meaning illusory and therefore reprehensible; it would prove correct all those friends and strangers who incessantly, by letter and by word of mouth, directly and indirectly, tell me or get others to tell me, write to me or get others to write that I ought to abandon this collaboration. I prefer to take my own counsel which assures me that together we may achieve something valuable, at least here and there, perhaps even do something universally significant in the cultural sense by creating for once a work of art flawless and in every sense harmonious—which would indeed be an immense gain.

I hope we are agreed about the stylistic intention of the ballet, which is simply meant to give you once again every conceivable freedom in polyphony as well as modernism: that is, to express your own personality in a manner as bold and as bizarre as you may wish. You are bound by no law other than the preservation of unity in the style and relative proportion between the parts. Against this second law, it is true, you have 'offended' in the scene of the women's dance. Not that it is particularly difficult to find some visual equivalent for this 'too much' of music, and if that were the only trouble, there would be no need to waste one's breath. But specially where the miming aims very high, as here with what a genius like Nijinsky (I mean Nijinsky as producer) is expected and intends to do, it is immensely important that there should

151

be no repetition of such licence, for this must inevitably ruin the structure of the whole work, it shifts the points of emphasis and something goes flat. But what goes flat (or may do, at least) is by no means the unduly dilated episode itself—it is a later, much more important one; some other scene, intended as the cardinal point of the whole piece, will somehow be deprived, in some mysterious, incalculable way, of its full effect, and the whole work will find itself, for no demonstrable reason, one rung lower.

With this somewhat stern warning I do not mean to read you a lesson; for, of the two of us, quite apart from the compass of our respective gifts, you have beyond any doubt the stronger dramatic instinct. But there is something in you, deep down, which on occasion runs counter to this instinct and makes you sometimes unable to see the wood for the trees. There can indeed be no 'too long' or 'too short', no 'weak' and no 'strong' in isolation; creative genius must yield more and more to the magic of the unfolding situation. Nowhere is this felt more marvellously than in the second part of *Faust* and in the late work of Palladio. (. . .)

Between 28.12. and 5.1. I am at Neubeuern am Inn; perhaps a line from you will reach me there which will settle the whole thing. I should be most grateful. At Neubeuern I mean to take up the *Ariadne* Vorspiel and go through it to cut out all allusions which refer back (to *Bourgeois*) so as to make the whole thing as suitable as possible for treatment with *secco* recitatives as an enduring pedestal for *Ariadne*. I hope your wife has recovered long ago, and wish you a happy time over Christmas.

Yours very sincerely,

HOFMANNSTHAL

1913

Rodaun, 9.1.(1913)

Dear Dr. Strauss,

Your idea about *secco* recitatives for the *Ariadne* Vorspiel strikes me as very promising, and on hearing *Figaro* in Munich recently its possibilities began to gain substance in my mind. I am thinking of rewriting this introductory scene; it will give me quite a lot of work (which I shall not mind), but ought to be a very real gain, perhaps even a solid foundation for the whole future of the piece.

This Vorspiel, then, with the established characters (Composer, Dancing master, singer, tenor, Zerbinetta and others) is to take place not *on* the *Ariadne* stage, but behind it, in a hall where the dressing rooms have been improvised. The scene of the action to be described as: the big country-house of a rich gentleman and patron of the arts. The Maecenas (Jourdain) himself remains un-named, allegorical, in the background, represented only by his footmen who transmit his bizarre commands. More strongly even than before the focal point will be the musician's destiny, exemplified by the young Composer. The action will remain by and large as it is, but I shall make it still more lively and more of a comedy (the Composer as a man in love, fooled, as guest, child, victor and vanquished in this world); it ends with the steward giving the sign to begin. This whole Vorspiel, designed for *secco* recitative, will run to twenty-five or thirty minutes; a not too long entr'acte follows, then *Ariadne* without any cuts—the whole thing to fill a normal evening's bill, for performances abroad to start with, but eventually also here. If you like this little scheme, I feel I could carry it out with success. When would you want it? Please let me have a line.

I did not find a letter about the Fürstner affair at Neubeuern, and should be glad to see this straightened out soon. Between us and around us we always ought to have solid, smooth ground.

Sincerely yours,

HOFMANNSTHAL

Rodaun, 20.1.1913

My dear Dr. Strauss,

Thank you very much for your letter. The words 'to keep me happily at work' made me laugh. But as it is I really am happily at work. In the past eight days *Die Frau ohne Schatten* has made decisive progress. The most important scenes are now organized in every detail, including all the twists and turns of the dialogue; the transitions, seven of them, from one sphere to the other, arouse in me a kind of envy for the composer who will have the chance of filling out with music what I must leave blank, where I can enjoy only the abstract idea of the higher and the nether world.

The profound meaning of this plot, the effortless symbolism of all the situations, its immensely rich humanity never fail to fill me with delight and astonishment. It is indeed a stroke of rare good fortune, for you no less than for me, that this subject with its inherent unquenchable urge towards music should have occurred to me in the present phase of my life, now when I am sufficiently mature to grasp, and not to rush it. Chamberlain, in his new book,[1] has brought together all the references to Goethe's never-ceasing attempts to write an opera, attempts which eventually petered out because he was unable to find an adequate composer. The definition of opera which Goethe tries to formulate for himself, by distinguishing it from mere theatre on the one hand and from mere drama on the other, was the result of many years, of decades of intellectual striving towards that form of art which he describes as perhaps the most promising of all dramatic forms. Significant situations in artificially arranged sequence—this is how he epitomizes the ideal in opera, and it is a phrase which has encouraged me immensely over *Die Frau ohne Schatten*.

Indeed, this phrase looks as if it had actually been coined for the subject which I have had the good fortune to find, and for the kind of treatment which experience and instinct have dictated to me. There are eleven significant, almost pantomimically incisive situations, but it is their combination—in which two worlds, two pairs of beings, two interwoven conflicts take their turn, reflect each other, enhance each other and eventually find their equilibrium—which gives unity to the whole work. Even seen merely as a spectacle, it would be most remarkable and attractive; through the music it will receive its final consummation, through the music which will merge both worlds, will reflect the one in the other, will indeed transform one into the other, as an alchemist transmutes the elements.

It is certainly not chance which made two men like us meet at the same period in history. And I would ask you not to ascribe to a mere freak of creative fancy any single step along the road which we have to travel together, nor any one step which I have taken and which you have had to take with me. What, between ourselves, I would wish you to appreciate above all as a high merit of mine, and one earned with loving care, is not my libretti as such, but that which is implied in them. After *Salome* and *Elektra* had made it obvious to me that certain things, once done, were not to be repeated—for in art everything can only be done

[1] *Goethe* by Houston Stewart Chamberlain, published in 1912.

once—I set out in another direction with *Rosenkavalier*, which on the one hand required an unprecedented degree of pithiness and animation in the conversational style, while it re-admitted on the other, through the back door, so to speak, a seemingly remote stylistic method, the method of set numbers. Now I have felt compelled to probe to their very limits these set numbers and the formal and intellectual possibilities which they offer. Hence the choice of a subject of almost contrapuntal severity; hence the stylizing of emotion and—to make this possible, palatable and, in a higher sense, true—the idea of this archaistic setting; all of them rather intricate, by no means obvious propositions. I know where I now am, yet I had rather not demonstrate it in words, but by deeds—that is through a work of art which possesses complete and pure operatic form. I hope this work, when compared with da Ponte's, Goethe's, Wagner's output, will prove itself true and genuine, not excogitated and entirely uncontrived. (. . .)

The *Elektra* production which awaits you at St. Petersburg has, I am told, very beautiful stage sets (by the painter Golovin). This leads me to hope that you derive pleasure now and then from our older and younger children, and makes me wish that you will think of me always as kindly and with the same warm friendship as I think of you.

Very sincerely yours,

HOFMANNSTHAL

Rodaun, 13.2.(*1913*)

My dear Dr. Strauss,

I should have been in Berlin and at the rehearsals with you long ago if I thought my presence might be of the slightest tangible use—but the piece being what it is, there is no improvising one can do apart from the appropriate cuts in the Molière, and the scope of these we have settled. That the success of the Molière depends utterly upon the availability of comic actors, of real actors, this is plain beyond doubt—the mistake, for which I must take the blame, was that I overrated the capacity of German theatres. 'Yawning' is every second word I see whenever I come across the silly twaddle retailed by these miserable journalists; 'yawns' during the Molière, notwithstanding the 'excellent' Herr Wohlmut or whatever his name may be. Who yawned at Stuttgart, I should like to know! It really mortifies and depresses one, for

155

the moment at least, to hear that a great classic has been hissed in Munich; to discover that people consider they are getting *too little* when, in addition to an opera of the dimensions of *Elektra*, they may listen for an hour to a melodrama with enchanting music, and words by Molière; and that, over the opera *Ariadne*, not one man Jack among these pen-pushers gives the writer of the libretto credit for this singular experiment, for the incomparable purity of the music and for making such singular delicacy and grace possible through the deliberate subordination of the words and through the specific construction and purpose of the whole as a work of art—yes, this does mortify, this can depress one, at least for the moment.

But in the end what remains is the knowledge that something so very beautiful has come into being, which moves one even in recollection, that this work of beauty will last, and this at least that nonsense about your 'extrovert' music, about the 'heaping of resources' etc., etc., has now collapsed at one fell swoop. Strange to remember that two years ago, when I wrote *Ariadne*, I would have much preferred to give her a framework of my own devising: a little comedy which takes place at a castle in Bohemia, a young heiress with three suitors, who, to please her, bring an opera company and a troupe of harlequins to the castle. I suppressed this idea deliberately so as not to endanger your work by combining it with the première of a Hofmannsthal comedy. As it happened, our dear German public could not very easily have given me a worse and more sullen reception than they have given to the greatest comic dramatist of modern times—everything, in fact, would presumably have gone better. But then I thought of Reinhardt; with him I was sure the Molière would vanquish and live—and this is what did happen in Stuttgart. The rest, alas, I did not foresee.

Vollmer in Berlin is said to be a real comic actor. Please send me a telegram about how it goes or get Fürstner to telegraph to me—I am already so very much attached to *Ariadne*, I can hardly tell you how much. Strange, most strange that people are not satisfied—I can't stop thinking of it—why, if a one-act opera contains wonderful music, why shouldn't the words be there merely, let us say, to make this music discreetly possible? All this palaver is concerned only with the music, but when you find what it adds up to, you might think they were looking only for the play and regarded the music as a *quantité négligeable*.

Well, of *Die Frau ohne Schatten*, in which all the essentials have fallen into place during the past few weeks, I can tell myself that it has all the qualities needed to pass as a play too, and to make—more even than *Rosenkavalier*—a deep and widespread impression in human as well as in theatrical terms. But this does not make *Ariadne* less dear to me. There must be cherries and apples, all in due season.

We thank you and your wife most cordially for your kind invitation. But for the time being I must sit tight, otherwise I endanger my whole existence. It would please me greatly to see you here in the not too distant future.

Yours,

HOFMANNSTHAL

Berlin W, Kaiserdamm 39 (1.3.1913)

Dear Herr von Hofmannsthal,

Ariadne was staged in a really wonderful production the day before yesterday.[1] The comedy without Reinhardt's genius, but neatly and finely acted. Vollmer as Jourdain still a great comic actor—the rendering of the opera accomplished beyond all words, décor very charming, cast not to be bettered. Press seems very good, haven't seen much yet: the enclosed review by my old enemy Krebs is significant for the reason that at long last he is doing justice to you, and because with his remark about children and their semolina pudding he has, possibly unwittingly, hit upon the salient point of all dramatic technique. Whether the success here will spread to the broad masses remains to be seen. The performance, accomplished as it was (the acoustics in the Schauspielhaus were ideal), was a cultural achievement in itself. And a thing like that always bears fruit.

Meanwhile, in response to regrettable news from Munich, where it seems they are massacring *Ariadne*, I have launched a letter of protest to Walter and demanded that Jourdain be recast—the part to be given to a comic actor and new rehearsals to be held. The performance of the comedy was so terrible that the first act was hissed. Instead of laying the blame on the actors they cut the text murderously.

The last performance was conducted by a repetiteur: I'm told it was ghastly.

Performance in the big house means complete murder. I have therefore formulated precise demands, including the re-transfer to the

[1] The Berlin première of *Ariadne* was on 27th February 1913.

157

Residenztheater (please support me energetically); unless Franckenstein does this (he moved the piece to the big house without getting my consent) I shall withdraw the piece. Aren't Munich and Vienna always sources of joy!

One other thing: I am arriving at Ala on 30th March, at 8.27 in the morning, and from there am driving alone in my car via Verona, Mantua, Bologna, Florence, Arezzo, Orvieto to Rome, where I shall stay till 14th April and then return to Garmisch by some enjoyable round-about route. Would you like to come along? You'll only do the journey itself with me, otherwise you'll have complete freedom: when we feel like it we'll chat—but silence and contemplative enjoyment also very welcome. It would be very nice, and especially at this stage it would be a good thing to be together for a somewhat longer period, undisturbed, and work out *Frau ohne Schatten*. Perhaps you could reach a stage by then with your work where an exchange of ideas would be profitable. Let me know at once, please, whether you'll come. You could join the car at Ala, Verona, or where you will: on 30th March! On 6th and 13th April I'm conducting two concerts in Rome. Each of us to pay for himself, to choose his hotel as he likes—in short, complete independence.

With best regards, yours

RICHARD STRAUSS

Rodaun, 2.3.(1913)

Dear Dr. Strauss,

I am a little sad not to have had a single word from you either by letter or telegram after the Berlin performance. Was it not beautiful, after all? Nor have I heard anything about the St. Petersburg *Elektra*. The success of *Rosenkavalier* in London has given me great pleasure. Arthur Schnitzler wrote to me after hearing *Ariadne* in Munich by chance, and spoke kindly and beautifully of his impressions, as other people from Munich have done—this has encouraged me a lot in view of the almost unbelievable degree of antagonism this light and poetic work of art has aroused among the scribbling race, which really puzzles me. Is it that these people sense in it what they apparently hate more than anything else: this turning away from merely ephemeral effects, from the mere *semblance* of reality, this search for transcendental meaning? Is that what arouses their hatred and antagonism? If so, the future of this kind of work should indeed be pretty safe.

Do write me a few lines some time.

Sincerely yours,

HOFMANNSTHAL

P.S. Fürstner, i.e. Oertel, wrote to me a while ago that the sale of the piano score also falls short of his expectations; this makes it more puzzling than ever, for, after all, it cannot be due to my libretto and to Molière; and all the world is agreed that the music is among the most beautiful you have ever written!

Rodaun, 4.3.(1913)

My dear Dr. Strauss,

Thank you very much for your kind, most encouraging letter about *Ariadne*; I shall reply tomorrow to that, and also to your kind invitation for the journey by motor car with a precise suggestion how far I could and would like to take part.

Today about Munich. Little as I usually bother about things which are given facts, I am sorry, indeed it actually pains me to think that there is to be a sharp clash with Bruno Walter and Franckenstein. You see, my dear Dr. Strauss, I would certainly not wish to prevent you from speaking out sharply and vehemently if I agreed with you at heart, but in this case I cannot think you are right. I believe that everything in the world will eventually be settled according to right and wrong, and thus, in this instance, it is *Ariadne* which would really bear the brunt. Those who hate and object to the singular character of this work and to its unpopular and aristocratic nature (of which I am aware), would make endless capital out of this quarrel as it is dragged through the newspapers, and everything would be so twisted as to make it appear that it is all about money. So please listen to what I am going to say now, and what I am going to say purely out of regard for you and for justice. This, after all, is my work, too; and my affair, and I am certainly not inclined towards giving way beyond reason; as it is I *cannot* strongly take sides.

By coincidence, you see, I have just received from Munich, apart from Schnitzler's kind, appreciative words, *three* other reports from widely different circles, and far from Franckenstein and Walter, all of them *full of praise* and all annoyed about the newspaper (Dillmann), telling me that the public has received the work with real delight.

Now to the points of dispute:

Concerning comedian: They have not, after all, got anyone else! Nor can they get anybody, and I myself have no suggestion to make. Have Dresden, Hamburg, Frankfurt a Jourdain?? When they moved into the big house, the minor part of the Dancing Master was specially given to the popular Gustav Waldau.

Concerning cuts: I asked Schnitzler: do you consider that barbaric cuts have been made? (He knows the full text). His answer was: *by no means*. Dillmann, after the first performance in the big house, complained that the Molière was still intolerably long (too much semolina pudding), he spoke of yawns and so on. One cannot please everybody. (I do not know from whom you had your report, but I fear he was unjust, somehow indisposed, not in the right mood—or perhaps it was just one of those bad nights!)

Concerning small or big house: How could they have proved their goodwill more plainly than by moving, at my request and against their better judgement, into the little house? Then they discovered that it did not work—we must believe them on this point, after all, since they are both young men, not old stick-in-the-muds and routiniers of the stage. You were in St. Petersburg at the time, and I was not asked either, only informed; but I felt all the less justified in raising a violent protest, because a short while before the little house had not appeared *to you*, as far as I could see, such a vital point; and also because I accepted, and do accept, the reasons both of them gave me by letter.

I had a word with Bruno Walter here not long ago. Without any prompting he told me that the four performances for the tourists in the summer would naturally take place in the little house again. So only the period between March and the middle of May is involved. In the circumstances is it not better to keep the work affectionately on the bill —not too often, for it can't stand that, but enough to keep it going— or is it better to have a scandal? Withdraw it? The whole pack of journalists will be off full cry, poor box office returns from here and there will be publicized, and this delicate, beautiful work will be made to suffer all the virulence stored up since the powerful impact of the *Rosenkavalier* success. For my sake, dear Dr. Strauss, be generous and a man of the world over this detail, as you always are to my great comfort over the major problem (I mean in accepting the whole peculiar situation which results from the nature of this work). Yes, for my sake, who would willingly do the same for you.

Very sincerely yours,

HOFMANNSTHAL

Rodaun, 5.3.(1913)

My dear Dr. Strauss,

Your kind, attractive proposal that I might accompany you on a car journey from Ala was altogether unexpected, and not easy to fit in with everything I had planned. But I should very much like to say 'yes' on this occasion, for as a matter of fact the scenario for *Die Frau ohne Schatten* is so well worked out and definite in my mind, that we could certainly talk about it; and this personal contact (which we have never had over anything we have done before) might greatly benefit our chief joint work (for that is how I see it).

Now, I would have to find a compromise between your proposal and my own plans for that very month of April, which also involve my wife. She is most amenable and easy to please, but I should hate her to be disappointed, the more so since this year, without a murmur, she gave up the annual visit to Berlin which she always enjoys very much in order to let me work in peace. What I had planned was a ten-days' stay on the Riviera with her, at Monte Carlo, about April 18th to 30th; there we were to meet the Russians and Grete Wiesenthal (who performs as guest with Diaghilev's company during April).

Before then I had intended to pay a visit of several days to friends at Lucca which for good reasons cannot be put off, and to travel, again with my wife, but by train since we cannot manage a hired car this year, from Vienna–Florence–Lucca–Genova to Monte Carlo between April 10th and 30th. I shall now venture to make a compromise proposal: you pick me up at noon on the 30th March at Verona (which is easier for me to reach than Ala) and we drive quietly down to Central Italy together (whichever road you like, the route: Bologna–Faenza–Rimini–Urbino–Passo Furlo–Gubbio–Arezzo–Florence, in two days, is most beautiful); around the 8th you take me to Lucca, or drop me somewhere near there, and you go on alone to Rome (or take Placci with you from Florence onwards). On the way back you collect me and my wife (who is the quietest, least exacting and most grateful passenger possible) again at Lucca or Pisa and take us along that glorious stretch Spezia–Portofino towards Genova, or even Nice, or else you turn off at La Spezia for Parma or something like that.

Now how would that suit you, roughly??—or could you in any case think of a better travelling companion (one who can play Skat!); if so, I am also quite willing to come to Garmisch early in May for two days instead of being with you in the car. I have proposed what would be possible and pleasant for me. *Please* be frank about the whole thing, *perfectly frank*!! If, for instance, it does not suit you so well to collect me and my wife at Lucca or Pisa again, then please say so frankly; in that case I would work out where else to meet my wife, and not have her come down to Lucca. I should perfectly understand if, in view of my partial acceptance, you were to withdraw the whole invitation. Please reply soon,

Sincerely yours,

HOFMANNSTHAL

P.S. On second, mature, thoughts I consider any violent steps against Munich on the basis of unreliable and perhaps only half-accurate information both unjust and *impolitic*. What I saw at Dresden made me oppose the big house at the time, because I hoped that in the small one the Molière would make an impression and become a positive gain. Now that its wholly negative effect in the small theatre there is a *fait accompli*, I can see no great harm in their taking the whole thing to a theatre where it looks as if at least the opera fares *better*, and where further performances at normal prices are possible. In the little house, on the other hand, special prices would always have been necessary, and I ask myself whether in that case, with the best will in the world, the whole piece could have been kept going at all?! My belief in the future of *Ariadne* is, to tell the truth, greater than in her present fate.

Rodaun, 11.3.1913

Dear Dr. Strauss,

Reliable I am, thoroughly—always excepting sickness in my family. I would arrive in Verona the day before you come through (i.e. the 29th or possibly the 28th) and wait for you (Hotel Londra). If we can get to Bologna by the evening of the 30th and all goes well, we can drive on the 31st Rimini–Pesaro, on the 1st Pesaro–Urbino–San Sepolcro–Arezzo, or even more beautiful Pesaro–Urbino–Passo Furlo–Gubbio–Perugia, on the 2nd Perugia–Orvieto, on the 3rd Orvieto–Viterbo–Rome; then I shall stay two or three days in Rome and go to Lucca on the 6th by train, where you will pick me up (via Pisa, or via Volterra, both of them scenically glorious roads) on the 15th or perhaps on the 16th. If my wife were then to join us (she is most grateful to you), she will bring a minimum of luggage (we are used to managing four of us in a car, with luggage); but if she were not to come and the Monte Carlo excursion were to be abandoned, I would accompany you all the way back to Germany, and perhaps on this return journey we might go through that part of Northern Italy where the churches are decorated with works by Gaudenzio Ferrari and Lanini (Sacro di Varallo).

If you book in Rome in advance (from April 3rd), please book a quiet room for me too at the same hotel for three days, and please tell me on a postcard which hotel it is. Rome will be overcrowded. (Placci is in Rome and will stay there until the middle of April; letters will reach him via Florence, 17 Via Alfecci.)

Best regards,

HOFMANNSTHAL

P.S. Verona–Mantua–Modena–Bologna is an easy day's journey, whereas Ala–Bologna (with customs taking anything between half an hour and an hour and a half) is a *very considerable effort*. Could you not send car and chauffeur to Verona by train and pick them up there? (Only to save your nerves; to me of course it makes no difference whatever. Especially since one has to drive through so many villages and towns.)

Rodaun, 14.3.(1913)

My dear Dr. Strauss,

Our letters have crossed. If you stick to Verona on the morning of the 29th, I shall arrive there as early as the afternoon of the 28th, staying also at the Hotel Cavour, and will wait for your arrival by car.

Concerning Rome you must have overlooked (or I did not make myself quite clear) that I am obliged to spend at least eight or nine days at Lucca, and that it was only the combination with this project which enabled me to accept your kind invitation at all. It strikes me as fortunate that you will be busy for just about that length of time in Rome, and have enough people there—certainly many Germans, as well as Placci who is an excellent cicerone and companion for excursions into the Campagna. For me to stay in Rome with you, however much I should enjoy it, is impossible, otherwise I should have to give up the whole tour. It is, on the other hand, almost certain by now that my wife will not come out to join us, and that I shall not go to the Riviera and shall therefore be at your disposal for the return journey. Please let me know whether you have been so kind as to book a room for me in Rome. Rome will be overcrowded.

Sincerely yours,

HOFMANNSTHAL

P.S. My most respectful regards to your wife. If you should happen to share the doubts Levin expressed to me here concerning Diaghilev's solvency, I am able to reassure you without hesitation after a conversation I had with his Russian backer and after seeing the Argentine contract.

Rodaun, 14.3.(1913)

Dear Dr. Strauss,

Another letter has crossed with mine, so I recapitulate. I shall be in Verona, Hotel Cavour, from the 28th onwards. We shall drive via Bologna–Pesaro–Urbino–Gubbio–Perugia–Orvieto to Rome, where we shall arrive not later than the afternoon of the 3rd. You will kindly book another room at the Hotel de Russie, for me (for three days only). You will drive on the 14th from Rome to Lucca where I shall expect you. On the 15th we will do Lucca–Modena–Verona, on the 16th perhaps Verona–Brixen, on the 17th Brixen–Garmisch (possibly I may get out at Innsbruck). My wife is definitely not coming to Lucca.

All best wishes,

HOFMANNSTHAL

P.S. Please don't forget to book the room in Rome!

Garmisch, 13th May (1913)

Dear Herr von Hofmannsthal,

Since I am not going to Paris I have offered to conduct *Ariadne* in Coburg on the 20th. Have today received the enclosed invitation which I am duly passing on to you. I shall be in Coburg on Sunday, but presume for the moment that you would prefer to stay with your work at Rodaun. Would you please notify Holthoff direct?

With kind regards, yours

RICHARD STRAUSS

Garmisch, 1st June 1913

Dear Herr von Hofmannsthal,

I've various interesting things to tell you. First of all, Coburg was very pleasant. The ducal couple tremendously simple and cordial, and with a very keen and serious interest in artistic matters. A very well managed theatre, a truly splendid performance of your *Jedermann*, superior in ensemble and style to the Munich performances, and a quite excellent performance of *Ariadne*, preceded by a very pretty Molière.

A pity you weren't there: I'm sure you'd have been pleased—also with the manager, Herr von Holthoff, who is very keen and conscientious about the whole thing. Unfortunately I can't report equally pleasant news from Munich, where I heard a performance of *Ariadne* the day before yesterday: the opera performed very well, but the comedy so unspeakably lousy you'd hardly credit it.

Of all the Molière performances which I have so far seen it was by far the most awful. All parts either entirely miscast or badly cast, with crazy cuts in the text, and without a glimmer of humour. The title part taken by a very ancient, droll Franz Moor from the last century—in short, it was simply unbearable.

Yet a full house and a most willing audience: tremendous enthusiasm after the opera.

I have made no secret of the fact, either to Baron Franckenstein or to Bruno Walter, that this Molière performance is utterly impossible. Fuchs, the operatic producer, is just incapable of producing a Molière comedy.

Herr von Franckenstein has now promised me that he will revise the comedy completely, partly recast it, give the lead to Steinrück, etc.

I have marked in the enclosed book of words the passages which, to my mind, ought to be cut in a good performance. Will you please look at it carefully and make the necessary revisions?

From all I have seen I wouldn't try to dress up the Molière curtains any further, but leave them as unassuming as they are. All improvements along those lines have so far been useless, and I think it'll be simplest to keep to the original and ring the curtain down even when there isn't a proper 'curtain'. On the other hand, I think it's tremendously important to retain your whole dressing-room scene. All this is quite feasible since the comedy is going to be rehearsed anew in June, for the Festival.

At the beginning of August I should then be coming to Munich myself, for the final rehearsals for the Festival, but consider it even more important that you should be present at these rehearsals, in order to bring out all the subtleties and finer points which Fuchs is evidently incapable of bringing to life. To switch the comedy to another producer is impossible. So it only leaves intervention by the authors.

When shall I have some good news from you? I am going to Berlin today and shall be back on 10th June.

With best regards, yours very sincerely,

RICHARD STRAUSS

Rodaun, Vienna, 3.6.(1913)

My dear Dr. Strauss,

Don't, I implore you, get impatient for *Die Frau ohne Schatten* at this moment—and don't let your wife do so!—or else you will jeopardize not only my nerves but, above all, the work itself. It is a terribly delicate, immensely difficult task and more than once I have been in profound despair. I have now rewritten the first half of Act I no less than three times, from the first word to the last, and even now I have not got a final version. Scene Ib (Act I, second half) makes good progress and quite a lot of Act II is definitely settled, even finally it would seem. I never cease being delighted with the wealth of each individual scene, with the immense opportunities for the composer which offer themselves of their own accord in the lyrical passages and in transitions which cry out for music. But the difficulties of compression, of finding the right words and the style were enormous during this final, but in one way first truly creative part of my labours (a scenario is, after all, a mere outline, and not yet creative work). Since the end of April I have lived for nothing but this work; I have altogether interrupted all correspondence, I refuse to have visitors, I see almost no one; but still you must have patience! Of course I want you to have the joy of being engaged in creative work—and what a joy that is!—but June and the first half of July at least are sure to be over before I can let the first act go out of my hands; I cannot let it go before certain parts of Act II (especially Scenes IIb and IId, the scenes 'in the upper sphere') are completely settled. Once they are done, cuts may become possible in Act Ia or expansions may be required there, for Act Ia must establish a thoroughly clear exposition of the situation and of the rather complex state of mind of the Emperor and of the Empress, so that Act IIb and IId may contain nothing but lyrical effusions (as points of repose between the steady progress of the action on earth in IIa, IIc, IIe). All this wants not only thinking out, but doing as well.

That was a brilliant idea you had in the moonlight between San Michele and Bozen, of accompanying the upper world with the *Ariadne* orchestra, and the denser, more colourful atmosphere on earth with the full orchestra. This stylistically most valuable idea has now taken firm hold on my imagination, and the poetic diction will be made to correspond to it: in the upper sphere we shall have heroic recitative throughout (though much more rapid and flowing than in Wagner), while below there is real conversation such as only the Master of *Rosenkavalier* can compose. Wonderful transitions from one orchestra to the other will appear unsought, e.g. in Act Ia: as soon as the Empress has decided to descend to the world of the humans, day breaks (the scene takes place very early in the morning on a roof garden, where the bed and canopy of the Empress are set up). The early morning sky is green, then pale violet, till it reaches the most intense fiery red of sunrise.

AMME: Wahnwitziges Kind,
zu herrschen gewohnt!
Ein Tag bricht an,
ein Menschentag!
Witterst Du ihn?
Schaudert's Dich schon?
Das ist ihre Sonne!
Der werfen sie Schatten!
Ein Verräter Wind
schleicht sich heran,
wühlend im Haar von Schläfern,
klirrend und taub,
ein grüner Himmel,
ein wildes Getümmel,

ein ewiges Trachten,
gierig, sinnlos,
ohne Freude!
Ein Menschentag!

and so on.

New instruments flash out in the orchestra, the musical atmosphere thickens ominously, clangorous bells peal into the morning.

The 'big' orchestra continues and provides the transition to Act Ib.

My chief difficulty is this: in aiming at compression I must not go too far, or else I shall impoverish the subject; the characters would lose their charm (which consists in the broken contours of their psychological make-up), they would look stylized and the whole thing would become trivially operatic. So I must all the time strike the exact balance between too much and too little. If I were to allow myself to think of this libretto being set to music in Wagner's ponderous and turgid *andante*, I could not do it at all, for the opera would last seven hours— it is the recollection of *Rosenkavalier* which keeps me going. The libretto will not, I hope, be very much longer, and a little longer— given such abundance of material, so varied an action, colourful in every sense, and profound—a little longer, say by a quarter or by one third, will be all right.

It is terrifying how short the libretto for *Tristan* is, for instance, and how long it takes to perform.

Now for the unfortunate Molière. While you are cursing (I am sure, and with justification) about Munich, your wife writes very mildly about Berlin; yet twenty people have written to me from there thoroughly horrified about the Molière (I mean the performance), begging me never to see it myself, about the vile interpolations, the arid, vulgar tone of the whole thing. In short, my dear Dr. Strauss, although it is not my fault that there are no comic actors in Germany outside Reinhardt's company, and although it is not my fault that a lightly improvised combination of pieces which was intended for Reinhardt has been done everywhere except at Reinhardt's theatre, I am now nauseated by the whole thing—so enchanting in one's imagination and so disgraceful in performance. What is the use of tinkering, of cutting this scene or that, or patching it up; why should I care whether the philosopher's scene is being done by clods or not done at all, whether they rattle off my dressing-room scene or leave it out altogether? I cannot even think of the whole business, wrecked and ruined as it is, without profound despondency, and this might easily upset me now while this happy productive mood is upon me. Nothing on earth will induce me to come to Munich in August; I cannot imagine anything in the world I detest more than wasting my energy on a lost cause.

What is the use of all these lame attempts to patch the thing up? The only real remedy has been on my desk for the past week. I am now copying it out, a few pages each day, and within a week you will have it, all typed. I have rewritten the Vorspiel, the dressing-room scene, with great zest and vigour; the Composer now occupies the very centre of the scene; he is, symbolically, a figure half tragic, half comic; the whole antithesis of the action (Ariadne, Zerbinetta, Harlekin's world) is now firmly focused on him; everything has been extended and enriched; there are slight, witty occasions for arias, so that it need not be all in *secco*; the genesis of the tune ('Du Venussohn') runs through the whole scene; there is even a hint of a little duet (Zerbinetta-Composer).

Get down to it at once, it is all neat and round, gay and serious; set it in *secco* recitative, put in a few highlights and have it performed from the manuscript in Munich in August after three rehearsals—it will be an enchanting surprise for everybody. It will take a real load off my mind, and, believe me, off yours too, once that unnatural connection between the dead and the living has been severed (I thought the stage would enable me to galvanize the defunct, but the instrument failed me!). Please believe what I say! Imagine how crystalline and complete, how harmonious our beautiful *Ariadne* will emerge once she is placed on this pedestal. Believe me, please.

Your friend,

HOFMANNSTHAL

You will have it by express letter within five or six days.

Semmering, 12.6.(1913)

My dear Dr. Strauss,

Herewith a corrected copy of the new definitive Vorspiel for *Ariadne*; it is only since this has come into existence that I consider the whole *Ariadne* completed.

Everything is intended for *secco* recitative, only round the figure of the Composer a glimmer of something more: music. For this I have provided the following *points d'appui*: first the genesis of the tune ('O, Du Venussohn') from the *Bourgeois*—this twice; then at the end the conversation with Zerbinetta, rising emotionally to something more than mere *parlando;* perhaps the thing might lead up to a tiny duet or something of the kind, but not a proper *number*, on the last few sentences of the text which are lyrical in tone. Thirdly and finally: the lyrical climax (for which the above melody is probably too tender and tame); I mean the Composer's outburst: 'Music!'—a kind of little Prize Song (indeed the whole *Ariadne* with the Vorspiel possesses a remote, purely conceptual affinity with *Meistersinger*). Here the words ought to inspire you to find a new, beautiful melody, solemn and ebullient; let's hope they accomplish their object:

(Properly organized in lines)

> Musik ist heilige Kunst
> zu versammeln alle Arten von Mut
> um einen strahlenden Thron!
> Das ist Musik!
> Und darum ist sie die Heilige unter den Künsten!

(This struck me as the kind of text Beethoven might have liked to use.)

I am satisfied with the whole thing as it has now turned out, and especially with the figure of the Composer as it now stands, tragic and comic at the same time, like the musician's lot in the world; the two fundamental *Ariadne* motifs, anchored or rooted as they are in the heart of the musician, all this I believe is poetic, and has substance, it can last— I am satisfied with it; whereas that improvised misalliance with the prose comedy cannot persist in the long run and in a way ought not to, because it is too much like a centaur or the Siamese twins.

Please take to it kindly, and let me have news (to Rodaun) *how* you have taken to it!

I have come here for a few days with my work on *Die Frau ohne Schatten* which I truly love the more hellishly difficult it becomes—as at times it does; it is cool here, entirely empty at the moment and quiet. Kessler's letter, which tells me that you have found a way out for the character of Joseph and are getting down to work at once, has been a real relief to me. As an artist, you are so precious, as a man by now so close to me, that I could never resign myself to the idea of your being kept waiting in impatience. I, on the other hand, cannot and must not in this case let you have the first act alone, even if it were finished—which it is not, by a long chalk. That would be a flagrant crime; it was almost criminal even in the case of *Rosenkavalier*, but that was a half-improvised farce, while here we have a whole world of the most profound inter-relations and the most inexorable unity. Here one rhythm must kindle the next. Perhaps by the time I come to work on the third act, I may have acquired so precise a sense of the relative proportions, and so much bolder and more concise a style, that I shall recast Act I once again—in short: a bell cannot be cast piecemeal. *Joseph* was thought of expressly to spare us both such a situation. In this case, moreover, it is of paramount importance to me that you should have the whole work before you when you start setting it to music. Its abundance must make you economical in detail.

So please send me good news, and take satisfaction from the knowledge that my best abilities—which are after all among the best our epoch has produced—are in this way, by fate, bound to your work with diamond chains. For so it is.

Sincerely yours,

HOFMANNSTHAL

Garmisch, 15th June, 1913

Dear Herr von Hofmannsthal,

Many thanks for your two most valuable letters. Of course, you are not to feel hurried over the new piece, but to work entirely at your pleasure. Besides, there's no justification really for my impatience: I've got quite enough work that I could do.

It is merely the urge to exchange uninteresting work for the most enjoyable work; but until this arrives I shall content myself with the more dreary. Among the latter I particularly include the scene just received from you:[1] to be quite frank, I have so far not found it to my liking at all. Indeed, it contains certain things that are downright distasteful to me—the Composer, for instance: to set him actually to music will be rather tedious. I ought to tell you that I have an innate antipathy to all artists treated in plays and novels, and especially composers, poets and painters. Besides, I now cling so obstinately to our original work, and still regard it as so successful in structure and conception, that this new version will always look to me like a torso. And to produce such

---

[1] The scenic Prologue (Vorspiel) to the new version of *Ariadne*.

a thing, for which I have no inner urge, I would have to be driven by pressure of circumstances—which, at the moment, is not the case since the *Rosenkavalier* contracts for America have just been signed.

You are angry at present because the critics and the actors have so disfigured the Molière. The misfortune was, of course, that the piece did not go where it was intended, to wit to Reinhardt; but this doesn't alter the fact that, to my judgement, the idea of the whole piece was excellent and will undoubtedly be resurrected with success in this form. I will try, in the meantime, to get down to *Joseph*, which our dear old Count Kessler is doing his best to make palatable to me. It's not because of any lack of goodwill that I haven't got any further, but simply that artistic creation, as of course you know better than anybody, can't be commanded.

At any rate, I am happy and delighted to know you engaged on our piece with such zeal and tenacity: your mild explosions of wrath, your moans over the difficulties of giving shape to the subject, lead me to expect the very best.

When are you going to Aussee? Maybe I'll come over by car one day to visit you.

Perhaps you'll decide after all to come to Munich for a few days and to revise the Molière a little, especially as it would be quite impossible to rehearse the new version by the beginning of August. I, for one, couldn't do the job so quickly, nor would the singers be able to learn and rehearse it during the vacation period.

Moreover, I am so oversated with *Ariadne* after the many performances last winter that I must first regain some more distance from the piece before I can feel any inclination again to work on it.

In any case I can't accept as justified your wish to have this second version regarded as the only valid and definitive one. To me, its first version is still the right one and the second no more than a makeshift.

I should therefore be grateful if you wouldn't mention this second version in public yet, and if you would continue to insist that the first version is the right one and that all it urgently needs is a better rendering of the Molière. Leave yourself time, therefore: I will wait and hope, and meanwhile remain, with kind regards, yours always most sincerely,

RICHARD STRAUSS

The little hors-d'œuvre of verses from *Frau ohne Schatten* is most promising.

Dear Herr von Hofmannsthal,

From my Wagnerian alpine solitude I merely want to inform you that, amidst all this boredom, I have now at last finished the sketch of Joseph's dance. I hope the thing is now going to make vigorous headway and that the piano score will be ready by autumn and the full score by the spring of 1914. Would you be good enough to inform Count Kessler briefly to this effect, as I haven't got his address to hand here. We are staying in the Dolomites till about 25th July and shall be back in Garmisch after then. How long are you staying at Aussee? Perhaps I can visit you there by car one day towards the end of August. Are you working hard? Is the work progressing to your satisfaction?

   With best regards from us to you all, yours

RICHARD STRAUSS

Grand Hotel Britannia, Venice, 24.9.(1913)

My dear Dr. Strauss,

This abortive visit to Aussee distressed me terribly and upset me for days—let me hope you did not feel the same way about it. For the future, if ever such an occasion were to arise again, I beg you to inform me at least four or five days in advance of your kind intention to pay me a visit, even at Rodaun. This time, it is true, you had spoken of it many weeks before and down to the last days of August I expected to hear from you announcing your visit; but August went by without word from you—indeed I heard you had abandoned your idea of a tour into the Salzkammergut and had gone to the South Tyrol. I was planning two visits in the Enns Valley and another to Roller, with whom I had important things to talk over, and both visits had been put off several times on account of the bad weather (promised by me one day and cancelled the next). And then, within half an hour of sending off the last, definite telegram I received your message—so worded that it never even occurred to me to suggest your coming a day later, for I assumed you were travelling south, according to a fixed schedule. Besides, the hotel question thoroughly perplexed me, for I stand in mortal awe of your wife's fastidiousness in this respect: the hotels in the Salzkammergut are, even by our standards, not fit for a dog. In our little tourist inn there was only one room free, quite unworthy of you and your wife; in short it was most distressing for me to have to send that telegram saying no. Later I sent you several more telegrams, to Gmunden and a third to the Hotel Elisabeth, Ischl, and I hope you received these. And my wife, too, has written to yours.

The serious hold-ups I have suffered in writing *Die Frau ohne Schatten* must have astonished you, for when we were in Rome I seemed to see it all so clearly before me. Yes, but only the '*what*', and for the '*how*' there are a thousand different ways. The passages concerned will have benefited from the fact that I have left them for two and a half months; I am sure they will have become simpler. The sections which take place in the realm of the fairies must be very simple, transparent, like a fairy tale; as I had them (for everything has already been written more than once) they were too heavy in tone, too dark, too symbolic; there was not enough contrast between framework and picture, between the lighter world above and the sombre world of the humans. But now I think I have got it right.

Perhaps the careful study of Wagner libretti which I made in May did me more harm than good. What depressed me at the time was not their dramatic structure—in this respect *Die Frau ohne Schatten* can vie with any existing libretto—but the inimitable excellence with which the way is prepared for the music, that consummate quality through which, as the course of a river determines its landscape, so here the poetical landscape is already figured with streams and brooklets of melodies foreseen by the poet. I have now got over this; it was a kind of depression of the spirit, which may show you how deadly in earnest I am over this work. Now I shall tackle Act Ia with renewed vigour and with the determination to give it that lightness of touch suitable to opera. Act Ia must correspond in tone, in the fairy-opera style, to Act III. Acts Ic, IIa, IIc, IIe may be regarded as successfully completed apart from needing greater compression. Send me a few encouraging words to Munich, Hotel Marienbad, for I should like to feel in touch with you when I return to this work.

Sincerely yours,

HOFMANNSTHAL

P.S. I met Bakst here and we talked a lot about *Joseph* which might really become something quite outstanding with its décor inspired by Tintoretto, Veronese and Tiepolo. I hope you have not in the meantime abandoned the work. I do not know anything apart from an enthusiastic telegram I received from Kessler in August about something you had played to him.

Don't leave me without a line.

Garmisch, 26.9.13

Dear Herr von Hofmannsthal,

Many thanks for your kind letter. We were very sorry not to have met you at Aussee. At first I was a little surprised to find you running away from us, but your wife's charming letter—for which my wife asks me to express her particular thanks—naturally forestalled all irritation. We are always rather given to impromptu decisions, besides with a car one always depends on the weather—so it is sometimes difficult to make definite plans four days ahead. I am now looking forward to seeing you in Munich: on 4th or 6th October they are doing a new production of *Salome*, and I shall be there with my wife (Hotel Vier Jahreszeiten) for the rehearsals three days beforehand.

I am exceedingly happy at the good news concerning our future work and ask you urgently not to feel pushed by me. The more frequently such an operatic subject is sieved, the more often it is worked through and over like a vineyard, the more pregnant and concise it becomes. I shall have plenty to do with *Joseph* until the spring of 1914: I'm now at this job without interruption and shall do my best to get it ready for Paris in June: 100 pages are already scored, but it's a big and laborious job.

If I have the first act of *Frau ohne Schatten* by Easter that will be time enough. But work away at it zealously and don't begrudge the effort of going over it again and again—it'll be more than worth while.

See you soon in Munich. With best regards, yours

RICHARD STRAUSS

Can't you get Franckenstein to put on *Ariadne* at the Residenztheater during your stay in Munich? The comedy is now very nicely played there.

Hotel Marienbad, Munich, 30.9.(1913)

My dear Dr. Strauss,

I cannot think of anything more pleasant than being welcomed here by your warm and friendly letter which I found on my desk. It means a great deal to me that you understand so well the cause of my stoppages and realize so clearly the potential and prospective advantages of such a slow method of working, which discards again and again what has already been done. It is a question of finding the right proportions; but then, next to getting hold of a rich, intelligible plot full of human feeling, these proportions are the most important thing of all. The composer cannot change them afterwards—or rather he can only change them for the worse, not for the better; whereas it is in his power to make good nearly all other defects and even to make up, by means of the music, for any weakness in characterization.

You are giving me plenty of time; nevertheless I mean to get down to work today and tomorrow. It would be an immense gain if I could finish the first act and possibly even the second, and then, after leaving them alone for a few months, go through the manuscript for a last time before sending it to you.

I welcome the news that you are hard at work on *Joseph* for several reasons; I cannot imagine you engaged in such vigorous and unremitting creative labour without some pleasure, and early in the summer I was somewhat grieved and vexed when you spoke of this work as 'boring', so that I could not help asking myself why, in that case, you had taken it on at all.

In Venice I saw a lot of Diaghilev, Bakst and the very charming Lady Ripon and the conversation came round to *Joseph*, over and over again. I really do believe that whatever the stage can give by way of visual contrivance to a musical work will here be of the most lavish and beautiful imaginable, and I, for my part, am delighted to have contributed to the creation of something so festive and splendid. It will, I am sure, endure with the Russians in all its homogeneity and precision for many years and lead a roving and triumphant life on the European and American stage by the side of our present and future operas, yet without jostling them.

I entirely approve of Diaghilev's intention to employ Fokine and not Nijinsky as metteur-en-scène of this ballet. As a matter of fact I consider Diaghilev, next to Reinhardt, the only really outstanding personality in the whole European theatre (excepting only Stanislavsky who is restricted to Russia) and I am pleased to see you connected with him through this work.

Incidentally I was most interested to hear Diaghilev say that, in spite of the prejudice shown by French critics, the combination of the opera

Ariadne with the Molière and your incidental music for it had struck him as particularly attractive. I am very much looking forward to *Salome*.

Sincerely yours,

HOFMANNSTHAL

P.S. I am working mainly in the morning between 9 and 1 o'clock.

Rodaun, 25.10.(1913)

My dear Dr. Strauss,

Many thanks for your kind letter and the good news. (Not least for the sake of *Die Frau ohne Schatten* I am glad that your mind will be free next summer.) I, too, have worked well in Munich; the first act is now, I believe, definitely finished and is good. It is not unduly long, in all (balancing long lines against short) perhaps some 100 lines shorter than *Rosenkavalier* Act I. The second act with its five scenes will probably be a little longer, that means longer also than the second act of *Rosenkavalier*, but the third will be considerably shorter than these. That makes us all square, but considering how much there is in it both poetically and ethically, as well as its unlimited musical possibilities, we are vastly ahead. Even I with my wholly inadequate musical imagination can hardly think of the finale of the second act without horror, and out of this horror the third act will rise by degrees to the heaven of music.

Now one word about *Josephslegende*. Judging by Kessler's letters I am not altogether happy about the situation, and this although I have complete confidence in Diaghilev and know that he is obviously bound to do his very best. Kessler now suddenly describes it as doubtful whether Fokine can be engaged as metteur-en-scène. This 'doubtful' cannot be allowed to exist. He must get us Fokine. Nor do I understand, or accept, the suggestion in Kessler's letter of an alternative for the female part: Mme Rubinstein or Frau Vollmöller. Frau Vollmöller is out of the question for L(ondon). She has always failed, except in a walking-on part in *Mirakel* which required no acting whatever. I have my eye *primo* and (almost) *unico loco* on Pavlova; after her, Mme Rubinstein for Paris and London, but hardly for Germany where Pavlova is practically indispensable to give our piece prestige. Please get this accepted straightaway during Diaghilev's forthcoming visit to you.

Sincerely yours,

HOFMANNSTHAL

So I count on seeing you on November 12th.

Rodaun, 8.12.[1](1913)

Dear Dr. Strauss,

The best thing is to take no notice of newspaper reports. Franckenstein, in a long and exhaustive conversation, expressly mentioned that he plans the resumption of *Ariadne* during the summer, and views it hopefully. He is putting *Ariadne* on for me in January, and thereafter at intervals of about six weeks. As far as the *Salome*-Petzel episode is concerned, he maintained that he himself regretted very much Petzel's unavailability on two occasions (once sickness and then leave of absence on urgent family business) which interfered with *Salome*.

Rosenkavalier, so he said, was to have been put on twice (in November), but on the first occasion the Innkeeper, on the second the Singer were unavailable; in view of the volume of work being done, as evidenced by the rehearsal list which you could see in Berlin, it had been impossible to make a change in the cast because of the consequent need for orchestra rehearsal.

About *Elektra* he was evasive, so long as the company was without a performer for Clyt(emnestra).

Altogether he protested against the suggestion that his attitude towards your works was anything other than *warm*. And F. is a thoroughly sincere person; I have known him well for nineteen years. Concerning W(alter), on the other hand, you may well be more or less right in what you hint at in your letter. All in all I consider it more *politic* to take a tolerant view of the situation, but I would not like to be understood as offering you any advice.

Thanks for inquiring about my health. I have been a little better these last few days, but had to interrupt the work on the big prose story[2] which I enjoyed so much, and am at present busy with the Burgtheater rehearsals for *Jedermann*. One of my prose projects, which I have

---

[1] This date is uncertain; in the original it looks more like 8th July.
[2] *Andreas oder Die Vereinigten.*

already begun, is *Die Frau ohne Schatten* as a fairy tale. Would you prefer me to give this story a *different* title? I feel the title should be the same.

I cannot possibly let you have the full first act before February, without endangering the whole thing; dictating presupposes the final revision done; but I shall send you shortly the (shorter) *first half*. As a result of Fürstner's letter, I have disposed of the financial difficulty by yielding unconditionally, although I still consider there is a grain of injustice in the arrangement; I was almost a little surprised that you did not mention the matter, nor my compliance, at all—or am I to assume that Fürstner failed to inform you of it?

Good-bye, and don't ask for an uninterrupted productive mood, that would be asking too much!

Sincerely yours,

HOFMANNSTHAL

15th December, 1913

Dear Herr von Hofmannsthal,

That highly gifted musician Wolf-Ferrari, in conjunction with Herr Batka who is likewise highly skilled in turning out operatic libretti, has written an opera: *Der Liebhaber als Arzt*, after Molière's *Le médecin malgré lui*. This opera was produced in Dresden a few days ago in the costumes of our *Ariadne*, with overwhelming success, and hailed by the press as the finally-arrived, long-awaited musical comedy of our day. To think how many comic operas have been hailed as the musical comedy of our day in the past five years—all except *Rosenkavalier* which had its eighty-ninth performance here three days ago, before an entirely full house. In a press notice from Dresden I read that the piece by Wolf-Ferrari and Batka represents the correct 'rebirth of Molière' from the spirit of the music. In fact the very thing that I have failed to achieve with *Ariadne* because of your 'clumsiness'. The man has evidently heard some vague reference to Nietzsche's 'birth of tragedy from the spirit of music' and has now arranged for Molière to be reborn by Wolf-Ferrari.

My dear friend, must one really take all this nonsense lying down? Oughtn't one at last to raise one's voice against it all, in some form or another—or must I go on waiting patiently until people realize for themselves how stylistically delicate your own work has been in

Ariadne and how of the Molière only those elements have been preserved which, in this as in all his other plays, are immortal—such as the type of Jourdain? How subtly your comedy has distilled from Molière all that which is musical, and how it all leads gradually to the very spirit of music and finally scales heights of which even the reborn Molière could have had no inkling? Doesn't it make you sick to read how the audience of the charming Wolf-Ferrari-Batka musical comedy was kept deliciously amused throughout the whole evening, whereas during our short Molière, in which you have really retained only what is amusing and typical, they were bored to tears and could scarcely wait for the opera to begin? Must one really take all this lying down? Have you no one among your friends—Schnitzler or Bahr or whoever it is— who could at long last utter a little word, forthright and clearly audible, that would explode the myth of the boring *Bourgeois*? A myth which has persuasively spread throughout the world and which was born of the trivial circumstance that, at the world première in Stuttgart with its two entr'actes of fifty minutes each, for which the Royal party was to blame, the audience was kept waiting three hours for the eagerly expected opera by the operatic composer Strauss and interpreted this impatience as boredom with the Molière-Hofmannsthal comedy.

That by way of a little example! Yet none of these louts has had the guts to correct this Stuttgart-born tag of the unending, boring Molière, which in Stuttgart, including the entr'actes, ran for three hours but which now runs for just one hour at all performances. Among the visitors to the Strauss Week here is the good Princess Marie von Meiningen, who is now hearing all my operas for the first time, with the exception of *Salome*. After reading the libretto of *Rosenkavalier* she writes to me that the text is very boring. After the performance on Friday she confesses to me, all astonished, that the text is delightful. This woman has the courage and the decency to revise her earlier judgement after hearing a performance. No critic would ever do such a thing. I'd like to know what people would say if they were asked today to judge the words of, say, *Meistersinger* or *Parsifal*, without Richard Wagner's name. I wager 90 per cent of them would declare the libretti to be unspeakably boring and certainly incapable of being set to music. In short, full justice should be done one of these days to the grand job that we have jointly made of *Ariadne*, a valuable job which I won't have anybody belittle. For this reason also I am against any re-arrangement or separation of the opera from the comedy, and negotiations are now taking place with America to have the piece performed there next winter, in English, in a small theatre, in the way we've written it.

To sum up once more: haven't you anybody who could speak an authoritative and clearly audible word to the general public about *Ariadne*, about the style of the whole work, and about the value of the Molière part in it? The continuous nonsense that one gets to hear about it is beginning to get on my nerves. This afternoon, before the performance, I have summoned Dr. Bie to see me and I shall discuss this same matter with him too. For errors, left uncorrected for too long, establish themselves as truths.

With kindest regards, yours sincerely,

RICHARD STRAUSS

Rodaun, 19.12.(1913)

Dear Dr. Strauss,

Many thanks for both your letters; the second, especially, the typed one, interested and pleased me very much. Concerning *Ariadne* I am particularly delighted to find so much understanding and such warm appreciation on your part for what I have accomplished (including even the Molière); any other reaction would have been most painful and distressing to me. For the rest I am able to view the truly fantastic ill-will and lack of understanding with some equanimity. I feel all one can do is to trust one's ability and one's achievement alone; to try and influence anything else, powerfully and with skill, is not, at any rate, *my* line at all.

Schnitzler has never in his life written an essay, nor a line of journalism, not even *pro domo*, not even an open letter; he has not, as he told me himself, the slightest flair for it.

Bahr wrote about me at least twenty times in the old days, always as a partisan, but it never gave me any pleasure; it was always shallow, biased and fundamentally without impact, without consistency, without the truth of conviction. Nothing more unpleasant could happen to me than for someone to try and induce him now to devote his prattle to anything that involves me.

Wassermann, who is a serious artist and does not often come out of his reserve, wrote a very fine essay about my libretti last year in *Die Neue Rundschau*.[1] It earned him all sorts of attacks—including one from

[1] *Die Neue Rundschau*, XXIV (February 1913). 'Last year' is therefore an error.

(Alfred) Kerr—but has not led to any improvement in the tone or the understanding of the press. Bie certainly would be quite a useful ally in the press. The sections of his book[1] devoted to us are really attractive. He has an eye for quality, but it is a fact that he also sees it where it does not exist at all, and tends, with all his refinement and impartiality, to water everything down.

Only a well-led group of two or three journalists, or even more, active and consistent in one or several papers, could wield real influence in such matters; we did discuss all this one fine evening at Orvieto. Consistency is the whole secret. A view consistently put forward, the consistent exposition of a work, is bound to conquer public opinion, slowly but surely.

To bring this about is in your power far more than mine, for it suits your temperament and your wishes. What is more you, whose work is far less misunderstood than my share in it, are in the vastly more favourable position. Anything that can ever be achieved in this matter (and I do not fail to recognize its importance for the future of our joint works) will depend entirely on the degree of consistency with which you handle it. For you to tackle it *occasionally*, as mood and chance take you, is a waste of energy. Wagner always treated matters of this kind with iron consistency, with passion sometimes and sometimes with frigid calm, according to circumstance, but above all he never let go. It all depends on that.

I am consoled more than anything else by the pleasure which I myself get out of working; next to this by the impression which almost all my works have hitherto succeeded in making, and finally by the appreciation of some twenty or thirty people who really matter. Tonight we are having *Jedermann* at the Burgtheater. At the dress rehearsal yesterday most of the audience had tears in their eyes. Now it will go to ninety German theatres. And yet not a single one of these newspaper louts has dreamt of taking the trouble to compare the original old English piece with my poem. It would have shown them that I have not simply added a few fingers to an old wooden sculpture, but that I have added— not without poetic vocation, I think—a whole body to its one hand and what was at best half a mutilated head. But they just take it as they find it, like cows feeding on grass, and in their ignorance or malice pretend that what I have done to the old Englishman is roughly the same kind of operation as Mr. Batka's when he botches up Molière. That's how it

[1] Oscar Bie: *Die moderne Musik und Richard Strauss*, Berlin, 1907.

always was and always will be. I take this kind of treatment as proof that one is not of the *canaille*.

The prose version of our fairy-tale is most satisfying to do and gives me great pleasure. Once these two works exist side by side, many instructive comparisons might be made (with goodwill, of course) concerning the relation between subject and execution, about narrative and drama. I hope this material in its earlier form (although written later in point of time) will help the subject and the characters, and their interconnection, to gain a real hold on the minds of a receptive public (for it is the public that matters, isn't it, and not the pen-pushers!). In this respect, reasonably well organized Strauss publicity (if you had the energy to organize it) could give me valuable support. Once the fairy-tale is done, we shall discuss again whether it would not, after all, be the only sensible thing to give the prose story the proper name from the start.

The money matter I obviously did handle wrongly. I identified you with Fürstner, and thought I was doing you a favour by giving in. The way you have settled it now is pretty well fair.

Sincerely yours,

HOFMANNSTHAL

Rodaun, 26.12.1913

Dear Dr. Strauss,

I had intended sending you a Christmas present, but now you will not get it until New Year's Eve. It is the first, shorter half of the first act of *Die Frau ohne Schatten*, a section which I feel entitled to consider final and which, I believe, lends itself even more readily to music than anything I have previously done for you. I shall send it to you from Neubeuern in typescript and will add a page of notes on the characters and the poetical motifs which are after all the musical ones as well.

Franckenstein is putting on *Ariadne* for me on the 4th and I am looking forward to it, for I have not seen this dear child properly since the première; a wholly wrecked night at Dresden, which lacked all atmosphere in that vast and empty theatre, does not count. Franckenstein adds in his letter of his own accord that *Salome* and *Rosenkavalier* will *speedily* follow upon this performance.

I know that Diaghilev is coming to Berlin on the 4th and I have high hopes of this conversation, for to my mind—and I do not change once

I have made up my mind about someone—he is a great *valeur*, a Number 1 man of the theatre. What he aims at is, after all, very much what we want, too; therefore I am in good heart despite the inevitable collisions and vexations.

Most sincerely yours,

HOFMANNSTHAL

28.12.(1913)

My dear Dr. Strauss,

Here is my little New Year's gift. I want you to have it by you, and to give your imagination now and then something to play with.

For this introductory scene (Ia) everything depends on the right timing. Since the complete first act must not last longer than sixty to seventy minutes (for the second act with its five scenes is bound to take between seventy and eighty), and since the second part of Act I is far weightier than the first part and half as long again, this first half act ought not to run to more than twenty or twenty-five minutes. You will catch the feeling of the poetry perfectly if you give the music here something light, flowing and ethereal throughout, and this in spite of all inherent contrasts, for their common ground is that the whole scene belongs to the sphere of the spirits.

Of the five main characters in the piece, the Emperor is the least conspicuous; his fairy-tale fate of being turned to stone and redeemed again is his most striking feature. His traits are typical rather than individual; he is the hunter and lover. What the music will have to give him is not so much pronounced characterization as a more truly musical element; his is to be the sweet and well-tempered voice throughout.

Of the threefold nature of the Empress, part animal, part human and part spirit, only the animal and spirit aspects are apparent in this scene; these two together make her the strange being she is. In between there is a vacuum: the humanity is missing; to acquire this humanity—that is the meaning of the whole work, even in the music. Not until the third act will the voice of the Empress gain its full human ring; then the animal and spirit aspects will appear fused in a new being on a higher plane. I have written in the margin of the text occasional notes about the dual facets of the Nurse, who vacillates between the demoniac and the grotesque. From the 2nd to the 5th I shall be in Munich, and look forward to hearing *Ariadne*.

Yours,

HOFMANNSTHAL

31.12.(1913)

Dear Dr. Strauss,

I am really not particularly impressed by the whole business. The only thing that strikes me as odd is that stuff produced by abysmally wretched hacks like Monsieur and Madame Freska should be taken so seriously by the lady writing this letter. For the work is, as you have overlooked, Madame's. To me the whole affair is as queer as if you were to show me a letter which treats symphonic sketches by, say, D'Albert as if they were from the pen of Beethoven. Fairy-tale subjects, poetic fancies like this one of the *Urfelsmühle* are to be picked up anywhere—what matters is the hand which lifts them out of the mire. In my work this subject gains significance only through connection with the shadow-motif, for the secret lies not least in the power to chain various themes together and so to create unity. Such unity reaches transcendental regions, both human and moral, where Monsieur and Madame Freska cannot follow us; they have stumbled on this subject by a fluke, but, wretched creatures that they are, they haven't got beyond making a paltry, trivial anecdote of it. What is more, before Madame Freska has completed her opus, the prose version of my fairy tale, which I have very auspiciously begun, will long be published and in circulation, thus vindicating my priority (by which I set no great store).

If only you could find a small but permanent platform in some periodical which would support our aims and so give them authentic interpretation! Did the talk you had on this subject with Bie come to nothing? I should very much like to know! I look forward to hearing *Ariadne* in Munich the day after tomorrow, and, on the following day, part at least of *Rosenkavalier*. Towards the 10th I shall come to Berlin. Very anxious to hear the result of your conversation with Diaghilev. Many thanks for kindly giving me news of the continued success of the two works in Berlin.

Most sincerely yours,

HOFMANNSTHAL

1914

Dear Dr. Strauss,

Many thanks for your letter. The more you can cut in this scene, and in every other, without making the characters incomprehensible or damaging them in essentials, the better. I think I shall accept every cut you may find possible. Exposition remains exposition, and as such is not the most exciting part; I believe none the less that this exposition is quite successful and that the transition to the second half of the act is not merely very happy and organic, but in the highest degree suitable for music. I further believe that during the composition of these three acts your road will be exactly like Dante's: from hell, through purgatory, into the heaven of the third act. But so as to give you a more balanced impression, I shall most decidedly have to read you the two halves of the act consecutively in Berlin—the second half from the manuscript.

Yesterday I heard *Ariadne* here. It was an enchanting evening for me, even the Molière. How much beautiful and nimble-witted music there is in it! How charming the supper scene, how elegant and pretty and in the most attractive sense entertaining the whole work is!—what morons these newspaper scribblers who have no eyes whatever for something so pretty and so well done! You are quite right: we shall change nothing, not one thing. And you are right too that it must remain in small theatres. The house looked good, all my Neubeuern friends were there, Franckenstein had invited the Kaulbachs and other people; Steinrück was very acceptable, Mme Bosetti brilliant, Mme Fay and Erb very fine. But the box office takings very modest (when I asked, Franckenstein showed me the slip under the edge of the box)—2300 marks.

We are likely to arrive in Berlin within the next three to five days and will invite ourselves to a meal at the earliest occasion; perhaps you could send the car to fetch us? A telegram just received from Diaghilev reports that agreement has been reached on the main points. I am very pleased. And so *à bientôt*!

Yours,

HOFMANNSTHAL

Dear Dr. Strauss, *Hotel Marienbad, Munich. Tuesday (January 6th, 1914)*

Everything is well, we are arriving on Thursday; please let us have a line at the Adlon whether your wife can have us for lunch *Friday* or

Saturday. The car is of course quite unnecessary, there are plenty of cabs.

I have muddled another thing, too: Franckenstein considers the figure of 2300 *very good*, it amounts to four-fifths of a full house; I did not know that, did not know that the maximum at these prices does not exceed 3000; when he showed me the box office account the other day without comment I assumed it to be a poor figure. It was not his fault.

I look forward to seeing you. Make whatever cuts you wish in Act I right away, if you can; I should like *to read to you* the whole of the first act, the first half with the cuts you have already made.

Sincerely yours,

HOFMANNSTHAL

My dear Dr. Strauss,   *Hotel Adlon, Berlin, (January 1914)*

I am really exceedingly sorry to have offended you in so delicate a matter as this joint work of ours—but *please* keep these two things which I have 'committed' apart, for that will make it easier for you to understand.

Bodenhausen is my most intimate friend and adviser, the administrator of my small fortune and so on; his relation to me is rather similar to Levin's *vis-à-vis* you, and it is true, is it not, that you brought the latter into the first discussion about this plot. Bodenhausen knows the subject from a walk we took at Gastein in the summer of 1912, and it was in fact his request that I should tell him what was then but the vaguest outline of this fairy story which helped to crystallize the material in my mind, so that it is to this walk that I owe the decisive and finest ideas. Besides, B. is of granite discretion.

As for Reinhardt, I did read him the short fairy story fragment, not for the sake of the plot but to lead him into a definite poetic atmosphere which might one day yield a fantastic spectacle (with or without music) treating of quite a different subject. Still, it is true that he did at that time get to know the substance of our subject, even if only in exposition, and it was absent-mindedness on my part, for which I find it difficult to forgive myself, that I failed to make a point of asking him not to speak of it. He is absolutely discreet, but incredible as it may seem I forgot to impress on him the need for discretion; on this pleasant social occasion my mind was unfortunately miles away from the stupid, indiscreet newspaper world and all that sort of thing. Of course you are absolutely right, and all I can say is that I will not do it again, especially not if you mind as much as this! We will talk about it again tomorrow at length; I am expecting you any time after ten, but please let me ask you to forgo your anger now. B. as a confidant in the secret counts for as little as my own shadow, and Reinhardt can be relied on not to mention it again to anyone; he suffers too much himself from loose talk.

Very sincerely yours,

HOFMANNSTHAL

Rodaun, 24.1.(1914)

Dear Dr. Strauss,

I forgot to speak to you, when we met, about a new Vienna production of *Elektra* and must now make up for it by letter. Here, under the (...) aegis of (Hans) G(regor), Schalk is now the only person who does anything for us—forgive me for saying 'us', I mean for your works. Already last year, G.'s maxim was: *Rosenkavalier* has had its day—why bother with it? It is Schalk who sees to it, from one performance to the next, that this opera is kept intact (it is on the bill again next Thursday); it is he who fights against the famous 'difficulties', such as Mayr's laziness and his dislike of the strenuous part and so on. I don't have this information from him, but have also heard it repeatedly from other sources. Personal considerations, ambition and so on may have quite a lot to do with this, but undoubtedly well-founded appreciation of the value and importance of your work enters very largely into it.

Now it is his wish to produce in 1916, as a cycle, at least the three works *Feuersnot*, *Elektra* and *Rosenkavalier* which are available at the Hofoper, and to *keep them there*; and he undertakes (*il se fait fort*, as the French say so well) to get this through, on the sole condition (*sine qua non*) that you write a letter to the management or to him, demanding a new production of *Elektra* (with Mme Schoder)—a new production by Schalk. I do not overlook the fact that this implies a reflection on Reichenberger, but Reichenberger is a very weak gentleman in every way, while Schalk is a man of burning ambition and great will power. What matters with operas is that they must be performed in the theatre in order to keep alive; everything else is personalia and, worse still, personalia theatralia—please let me know in any case what you think of the scheme.

When I came to Berlin, I looked forward to hearing something of the music for *Joseph*, and in the course of conversation I was always on the look-out for a turn of phrase which would indicate your willingness to let me enjoy some part of its still hidden beauty. But nothing happened; and I am always too diffident to ask outright. The fact that I am 'unmusical' gets in my way; the idea that it might be not worth your while to play something for my inadequate comprehension. That is why I am always delighted when it so happens that you play to someone else who does 'understand something about it', and I can listen. This time, unfortunately it did not work out that way, and on the last day but one (my very last day in Berlin I spent in bed with a slight temperature) I heard from Bie that you had played some passages to him; he told me that what had struck him as particularly beautiful and happy was the unusual fact of its giving you for once occasion to write dramatic music without voices. I am pleased to think that such an opportunity will recur in *Die Frau ohne Schatten* (during the many transformations, especially in Act III).

Your cuts and rearrangements in Ia are quite excellent, and I shall simply carry them over into my copy.

Yours,

HOFMANNSTHAL

Rodaun, 31.1.(1914)

Dear Dr. Strauss,

Many thanks for your letter and for the good news that the *Joseph* contract has been signed. A telegram from Diaghilev in Paris expresses his delight over the same news and informs me that Mme Rubinstein is now apparently certain for the female part. *Tant mieux!*

Schalk thanks you very much for your letter, the contents of which I communicated to him, but after careful consideration he prefers to save you the trouble of writing that 'letter' altogether and will first try to settle the matter personally with Reichenberger (by offering an exchange); after that the main point through the intervention of Montenuovo. Schoder-Jeritza are now settled for the two sisters.[1]

I feel neither the slightest cause, nor any temptation to read the fairy-tale to anyone else. You scold me for being a Viennese, and that is pretty bad. But I cannot be too much of one, or else I would not find

[1] In *Elektra*.

the atmosphere here so uncongenial. My big narrative story[1] concerns incidentally exactly the development of a young *Viennese* to manhood (or towards becoming a German).

Best wishes,

HOFMANNSTHAL

Dear Herr von Hofmannsthal,   *Brussels, 17.2.14*

Many thanks for the cantata:[2] the insertion at the end is excellent and already set to music. Just to be on the safe side, is it:

> Er aber droben
> sucht sich selber, welchem er diene
> von den Geistern, welchem strengen . . .

Is 'welchem strengen' correct? Please reply to Berlin. When shall I get the first act of *Frau ohne Schatten*?

I am conducting *Elektra* tomorrow with Fassbender and Mildenburg.

On Sunday I played *Ariadne* to the directors of the Théâtre de la Monnaie: they are charmed with your work and regard the excuse that such an adapted Molière would be impossible in France as a piece of nonsense easily overcome given appropriate instruction of the public. *Ariadne* is being done here next winter, in a French translation by Kufferath. *Elektra*, likewise in French, at the Grand Opéra in Paris in the spring of 1915.

With best regards, yours

RICHARD STRAUSS

Dear Dr. Strauss,   *Rodaun, 18.2.(1914)*

Many thanks for your Brussels letter with the kind good news. The verdict of the Brussels friends concerning *Ariadne* cum *Boùrgeois* is really encouraging and gratifying. Very glad if that improvised cantata, which I wrote down like a telegram without much deliberation, was useful to you as the basis for a composition. The line runs, as you rightly assume

> welchem er diene von den Geistern, welchem strengen . . .

---

[1] *Andreas oder Die Vereinigten.*

[2] 'Kantate' ('Tüchtigen stellt das schnelle Glück'). Poem by H. v. Hofmannsthal on Count Seebach's twentieth anniversary as Theatre Administrator of the Dresden Opera, composed for male choir by Richard Strauss on 22nd February 1914.

That *Elektra* is accepted in Paris also gives me great pleasure. *Die Frau ohne Schatten* Act Ia will be returned to you tomorrow; next week I shall have a typist out here and will produce the definitive text of Act Ib.

                    With best regards, yours,

                                        HOFMANNSTHAL

                                        Munich, 4th April, 1914

My dear Herr von Hofmannsthal,

The first act[1] is simply wonderful: so compact and homogenous that I cannot yet think of even a comma being deleted or altered. My problem now will be to find a new simple style which will make it possible to present your beautiful poetry to the listeners in its full purity and clarity. Perhaps I'll make a few cuts in the first part, so that the second part of Act I, and all that follows, should find a fresh and receptive audience. At any rate, I now have a better perspective of the whole thing, and shall start preparing myself to find the right form of expression for everything. Let me congratulate you therefore on your beautiful and perfect achievement: I only hope the subsequent acts will be on a par with the second half of Act I. I shall be in Garmisch from Monday, and in Paris from the beginning of May.

  With many thanks and kindest regards, yours

                                        RICHARD STRAUSS

                                        Garmisch, 20.4.14

Dear Herr von Hofmannsthal,

The beginning is now dead right, and the aria of the Emperor is very spirited and well-contrived. But I should like the Emperor to make his exit immediately after:

                    ist sie die Beute aller
                    Beuten ohne Ende   (Exit)

I've got a very brilliant ending there, and the falconer's lodge and the whole of page 12 had better also be left out. The Nurse merely says (to the servants):

                    Fort und von hinnen!
                    Ich höre die Herrin!
                    Euch darf sie nicht sehn!

[1] Of *Die Frau ohne Schatten*.

Brief (musical only) transition and at once the Empress:

> Ist mein Liebster dahin,
> ?   was weckt mich so früh!   ?Wie?
> ?   O lasst mich noch liegen.   ?
> Vielleicht träume ich   etc.

But as the whole (rather unimportant) secondary theme of banishment to the falconer's lodge is dropped in this way—and I do want to confine myself to the most essential points, especially in these opening scenes (it's unbelievable, a great pity but true, how little of the text can be caught by opera-goers no matter what pains the composer takes)—the opening words of the Empress would therefore have to be changed a little. Request suggestion from you.

On the whole, I am now gradually getting into the style and melodic character, and shall easily finish the first act during the early summer. So you can already budget for sending me Act II by August, since after a fine summer the autumn is my most productive working season.

How are you yourself—in health and spirit?

Hope to see you in Paris, where I am arriving on 6th May.

With best regards, yours

RICHARD STRAUSS

Rodaun, 22.4.(1914)

Dear Dr. Strauss,

I was just going to write to you tonight to thank you for your earlier letter which gave me great pleasure (for in a collaboration like this I look upon you at the same time as my critic and my public)—when there was your new letter.

I have no objection whatever to your firmly compressing the first half. Only one thing you must not, must never forget: the Empress is, for the spiritual meaning of the opera, the central figure and her destiny the pivot of the whole action. The Dyer's Wife, the Dyer are, admittedly, the strongest figures, but it is not on them that the plot is focused: their fate is subordinate to the destiny of the Empress. I must tell you this, and you should never for a moment lose sight of it, for otherwise the third act will become impossible, where it can and ought to be the crowning glory of the whole work, far surpassing Acts I and II; it is to lead us where music and poetry, without clipping each other's wings, and truly hand in hand for once, shall float lightly over the gardens of paradise, as this singularly happy subject enables them to do.

I am glad you got into your work so well and I will see to it that you get Acts II and III by the summer, because in this case, more than ever before, it is essential that you should bear all the parts of so complex a whole constantly in mind; thus you can master the difficult art of economizing, of giving little at times, because the opportunities are so abundant for giving much.

Not long ago I heard here an opera[1] by someone hitherto unknown, one Franz Schmidt. The remarkable thing about Schmidt's opera, and that is why I mention it here, was that on first hearing I was able to understand almost the whole of the (incidentally absurd) text, and yet the music was by no means thin melodramatic stuff, only whenever the voice was to preponderate, everything else was kept in the background. I must confess it struck me as *very* beautiful, although the libretto was, as I said, silly. I am not telling you this for the sake of my own libretto— you know me well enough by now not to think that—but I want to suggest, wholly unqualified though I am, that there must be ways and means to let the word take command on occasion, and that, to my mind, it would be a *great gain* if you could accomplish this in our present work. (I say this because you yourself complain how little of the text, given the best will in the world on the part of the composer, one can understand. And yet in this opera I caught at least half the lines that were being sung—without any libretto, at the first hearing; how do you account for this? It was, after all, an opera in the modern style, even reminiscent, at times, of your music.)

I am *au courant* with the preparations for *Joseph* and remain very confident (which is exactly what I was *not* over *Ariadne*). The photographs of Miassin as Joseph which have been sent to me I take almost for a guarantee that he will present the essence of this character, that quality of purity which makes up the telling antithesis to the female figure, an antithesis which must be plain to all.

One important request: since your name is bound to impress the manager of a Paris hotel, but mine not at all, and since Diaghilev is not very reliable and Kessler too nervous, would you kindly book for me *a not too expensive room*, on one of the upper floors, not a servant's room,

[1] *Notre Dame.*

but rather a secretary's or librettist's room in the Crillon, from the morning of the 9th. Please do not forget! With many thanks in advance,

Yours,

HOFMANNSTHAL

Garmisch, 25.4.14

Dear Friend,

We shall be staying in Paris at the Hotel Majestic by the Arc de Triomphe—quieter and the air better than in the hotels nearer the centre. My friend Hermann has booked good and reasonably-priced accommodation for me there. If you want to put up there too, please write direct to Edouard Hermann,[1] 2 rue Rembrandt, Paris, and ask him to book accommodation for you either there or wherever you like. I have already advised Hermann that you might do so. Many thanks for yesterday's letter: entirely share your opinion and will do my best to make the poetry audible. I promise I shan't delete anything essential.

Looking forward to seeing you! I'm already past the falcon's prophecy and am coming down to earth to the humans.

Very sincerely yours,

RICHARD STRAUSS

Hotel de Crillon, Paris, 11 o'clock. (20.5.1914)

Dear Dr. Strauss,

Kessler said you would come to see me once more—but unfortunately you have not come; I should have liked to see you before I leave, and would have preferred to say rather than write what follows. Kessler handed me, as from you, a letter from G. Brecher which has somewhat annoyed me, and it did so because Brecher is a member, even if a subordinate one, of your circle. Coming from a writer who is fairly close to you, I consider this letter lacking in respect towards me and therefore objectionable. I can easily overlook the fact that malicious journalists make my share in our work from time to time (as happens again and again) the butt of some of the resentment which is really meant for you (it was you yourself, I think, who used the very telling expression 'lightning conductor'). I should, on the other hand, take a very poor view if, among the circle of your *protegés*, there were to be

---

[1] The score of *Josephslegende* is dedicated to Edouard Hermann.

any lack of understanding, or lack of appreciation of the significance, to you, of my collaboration in these three stylistically so very different works, significant as they are from your point of view just because of these differences in style (*Rosenkavalier*, *Ariadne* and now, this time, the foundations for this symphonic fresco).

Opinions may differ about the preface to the book of words (why ever does Herr Brecher describe this perfectly ordinary libretto so consistently as 'the pamphlet written by H. and K.'?); it has certainly served a number of critics as a peg for their malice, but on the other hand it provided a most useful signpost for the notices by Schmidt (in advance of performance) by Kalisch, Karpath, Frischauer and others. Your description of it as 'Notes which served the composer as substratum' is absolutely correct, otherwise I would not have left it standing in the book of words to which I have put my name. It might *perhaps* have been just as well to publish the text without comment, that is a question of opinion, but it offers no excuse for such effrontery from subordinate creatures who have never produced anything creative in their lives. This sort of thing is very 'German' in the not so pleasant sense of the term.

Regarding the ballet and the action itself, I should very much like to know what objections can be raised against them as the foundation for music by a real musician? Quite seriously, if you have heard, in discussion or from the press, any objective and reasonably relevant adverse comment on the whole work or on some detail (in conception, not performance), *please* let me know.

Until Saturday my address will be Frankfurter Hof, Frankfurt; after that Parkhotel, Nauheim.

Before you leave, please settle about Mildenburg for Berlin; Mme Kussnetzoff was a flop, and I have only very little confidence in Mme Carmi.

I have the happiest recollection of the hours we spent together at the Trianon and so I am very sorry that the stay in Paris ends on this unhappy note, which annoys me (only in so far as you are involved in it) and which seems to me particularly out of place at this moment, when my initiative has helped to bring about a great artistic and financial success for a beautiful symphonic work of yours.

Sincerely yours,

HOFMANNSTHAL

Dear Herr von Hofmannsthal,

I was at your hotel last Wednesday at 11.30 exactly, but to my regret was informed by the porter that you had left for the station five minutes earlier.

I was sorry to see from your letter that Herr Brecher's letter has rather annoyed you. But since I supposed you knew Brecher always to have been an enthusiastic admirer of your work—and to have publicly expressed this admiration in connection with the London text—I thought you would not take his last letter (which I didn't think I ought to keep from you) too personally.

On the whole I can't blame Brecher too much: because there was indeed a palpable disproportion between Kessler's intentions, as expressed in the synopsis,[1] and what was in fact shown of them on the stage in Paris. Kessler takes the view that, since his intentions were not realized on the stage, the audience must at least be told what he had intended. That is true enough from a literary point of view, but to my mind wrong from a theatrical one. As matters now stand, the spectators are led, by Kessler's introduction, to expect all sorts of things which subsequently they aren't shown on the stage. The resulting disappointment is more detrimental to the effect than if the audience, unprepared by any introduction, were to enjoy and relish naïvely the accepted plot as it is now presented—as in fact they did in Paris.

I believe that much adverse criticism goes back to just that. Kessler's amiable suggestion that I ought to be glad to have him and you as my habitual lightning conductor is not at all to my liking. I am more anxious than you think to see your valuable collaboration in my work appreciated more correctly and more highly, not least by the public and the critics, than has been the case hitherto.

Won't you think the matter over again? Wouldn't it be better after all to leave out Kessler's introduction, or at least to cut it extensively so that the audience's expectations are not raised too high? Besides, much of Kessler's introduction is a personal exchange of views between poet and composer, and really no business of the audience.

Since even in such an accomplished performance (in the opinion of the audience) as the Paris one Kessler's ideas have emerged so faintly, the public is bound to assume that the poet has demanded something which the stage cannot achieve; and Kessler's belief that the audience

[1] Published in the libretto of *Josephslegende*.

will attribute the blame to an imperfect production is therefore mistaken, as evidenced also by Brecher's letter and the review in the *Frankfurter Zeitung*.

I should be in favour of holding Kessler's introduction back until we have achieved a more perfect stage performance.

If in such a performance we find our intentions realized to a greater degree, there would still be time to publish the commentary later.

Anyway, I am extremely sorry you left Paris so suddenly. My intentions were good, in the interests of our cause, and I thought that you would attach more importance to the voices from the public.

If I had foreseen your reaction I should have spared you the contents of Brecher's letter. Please forgive me and accept my best regards. Yours,

RICHARD STRAUSS

After an enjoyable journey returned here last night to enjoyable work on *Frau ohne Schatten*.

Yours very sincerely,

RICHARD STRAUSS

Tuesday, 2.6.(1914)

Dear Dr. Strauss,

On my arrival here on Saturday I found your letter of the 25th and asked Roller to come and see me yesterday for a thorough discussion of the décor and scene-changing question. Musical interludes of three minutes strike me as an appalling idea! And that six times the same night! It would amount to half a symphony! Even two minutes are too much! (Roller, who produced *Parsifal* here, told me that the big transformation music, which seems to take a quarter of an hour, lasts in fact exactly $4\frac{3}{4}$ minutes). He will therefore so arrange things that each one of the scene changes is accomplished within $1\frac{1}{4}$ minutes (75 seconds) and even if for one or two you should leave him with one minute only, he will still manage somehow.

I am very glad this is fixed, for since that excess of music in the boxing-scene and in Joseph's dance, which struck us (and many others) as so unfortunate, I am even more apprehensive of *longueurs* than before.

By chance I came across that letter of Brecher's while I was unpacking, and read it through again. My anger has of course cooled by now, but today I can quite calmly put my finger on the actual point which annoyed me: it is where, not content with fabricating a futile opposition between the two of us (for the fact itself that the musician writes music mutely, while the librettist produces a text consisting of words, is the most natural thing in the world), he attacks the 'high-faluting exegesis which the two gentlemen were pleased to add', and this despite the fact that in my short preface I expressly (though of course quite urbanely) refused to associate myself with that whole document[1] and kept aloof. This promiscuity, this lack of discrimination, this charging one person with what should be imputed to others—these are the kind of liberties, part slovenliness, part ill-will, which one has to put up with from journalists; but it is twice unmannerly for a fairly close acquaintance, an 'admirer of my art', to saddle me in such slovenly fashion with what I have quite unmistakably disclaimed.

What makes me more touchy than usual in this matter is that I consider my part in this book of words not as a 'work' of mine, but as an act of courtesy towards you, a social gesture rather than a matter of art, and it disconcerts me to find it used as a stick to beat me with (the kind of thing to which I am able to submit with much better grace over *Die Frau ohne Schatten*, for there I can always tell myself: I know what I have done.

I realized in 1912 that it would take me another year or two to master the subject of *Die Frau ohne Schatten* fully. You were stranded with nothing to do, the prospect of Levetzow as an alternative, which now greatly relieves me, did not then exist; I was distressed to think of you without any acceptable work; the Russians wanted a ballet from you, and so I drafted this one and brought in Kessler since he had been present at these discussions anyway (and because he had assisted me over sketching out the *Rosenkavalier* scenario, pleasantly and skilfully, though perhaps he tends rather to over-estimate the importance of his help). After that I sent you the scenario and you telegraphed that you would like to do it. I neither asked you to set it to music, nor would it have grieved me if you had not done so—the whole thing pleased me in so far as it would give you pleasure and might lead to something beautiful for the stage and musically valuable. But it really nauseates me to be taken to task over so silly a matter, as if you were a small child that does not know what it is doing, and I a demon or an *entrepreneur* intent on conquering the world stage *à tout prix*, as if, in short, I were Vollmoeller,

---

[1] 'The Development of the Poetic and Dramatic Themes' which precedes the printed 'Book of Words' for *Josephslegende* was written by Count Kessler.

d'Annunzio and Astruc rolled into one. My mind is sufficiently full of ideas and of theatre to produce from time to time something like this with decorum, and stylish and becoming it is, despite inadequate finish. It was an opportunity for you to do a work in a style which interested you, and so amen. Artistically as well as financially, as you well know from the terms of the contracts, it is a very modest affair from my point of view; I have sought advantage neither the one way nor the other, but have rendered a courtesy in the sphere of art. This is the position and for this reason I ask you and, since we are linked in this and in more important matters, expect of you, if it should prove necessary, to stand by me energetically in this affair, as far as lies within your by no means inconsiderable power; I ask and expect you to cover me personally in Germany as well as abroad (the kind of thing I should not dream of demanding where I stand side by side with you as a creative artist like in *Rosenkavalier* or *Ariadne*, and bear the full responsibility for my share) and, if need be, to relieve me plainly of responsibilities which are not mine. About the book of words, a question on which I am strongly inclined to agree with you and, for once, with Brecher, I shall write to you shortly.

Sincerely yours,

HOFMANNSTHAL

Garmisch (mid-June 1914)

My dear Poet,

Many thanks for your kind congratulations![1] I've been very busy. Act I will very soon be finished. Unfortunately I must go to London the day after tomorrow, but maybe the interruption will be a good thing just before I tackle the end of the act.

When shall I get Act II?

With best regards, yours as ever,

RICHARD STRAUSS

Aussee, Obertressen, 4.7.(1914)

Dear Dr. Strauss,

Are you back? And settled again? Have you already resumed work? Are you on the end of Act I? If so, I must hold my thumbs for you, if

[1] On his fiftieth birthday on 11th June 1914.

you are familiar with that Austrian expression. And how was London? good, on the whole, I believe, but I should like to hear the details. What was Mme Karsavina[1] like and what about the mise en scène? The banquet, above all, and so on? And the lighting which so upset me in Paris? Please let me have a few candid lines. And have you by any chance talked to Kessler about the book of words? I do not, *entre nous*, much care for the thing myself. (And made it pretty plain in my preface that I did not wish to identify myself with this book of words.) Kessler is rather obstinate, very touchy and excitable, so I preferred to leave the thing alone.

I am rather proud of the second act (it is now being typed), proud of having succeeded in getting the abundance of material which belongs there into thirty pages. One does, after all, always learn something new in this *métier*, if only one is willing to learn. Do enjoy the work—you will never get a finer libretto, neither from me nor from anyone else, it was a unique favour of destiny—and let this joy benefit your work.

I am counting on a few lines; my wife was very pleased about the kind letter from your wife whose approval, coming from someone so unsophisticated and genuine, I value highly. Please convey my respects to her.

Sincerely yours,

HOFMANNSTHAL

Dear Friend,   *Garmisch, 5th July, 1914*

I am back from London where *Joseph* was a great success, in spite of the fact that most of the press was angry and even the most sophisticated Englishwomen found the piece indecent. The production had been improved in many respects, but the main thing, Joseph's dance, still inadequate and hence boring. Orchestra magnificent, all performances sold out, and advance bookings for the next lot—as Kessler informs me—excellent.

How are you keeping? Kessler was worried about your long silence to him. Perhaps you could drop him a few short lines, just to tell him how you are.

Today I merely want to settle a few minor doubts concerning the text of my first act:

[1] Potiphar's wife was danced at the London performances by Tamara Karsavina and Maria Carmi in turn.

200

On page 16 the Wife says:

> Nun wird er verlangen nach seinem Nachtmahl,
> Das nicht bereit ist.

Nevertheless, the Wife says on page 18:

> Dort ist zu essen

and Barak does in fact sit down on the ground to eat; a moment earlier, however, he says:

> Ein gepriesener Duft von Fischen und Öl.

Won't this suggest that he is about to eat the freshly fried little fishes—which would be rather distasteful and revolting?

Do please consider this food problem—whether one ought not to delete the passage: 'Ein gepriesener Duft von Fischen und Öl' to avoid all misunderstanding.

My second question is: will you permit me to cut out the first six lines of the Nurse on page 15, so that after the passage of the Wife:

> So ist es gesprochen und geschworen
> in meinem Innern

the Nurse would start straight off with:

> Abzutun Mutterschaft auf ewige Zeiten.

This conclusion would suit me better, and the passage:

> Denn sie hat ins Schwarze getroffen, etc.

seems to me dispensable.

Now a third question: page 16, the passage of the Nurse:

> Du bist nicht allein, Dienerinnen hast du, etc.

You say this passage is indispensable to the understanding. I don't quite see why. Why must the Nurse and the Empress be in the house at all costs, seeing that the Emperor has gone away for three days, and why is the passage indispensable? On the strength of the action so far I don't see it.

If this passage could be incorporated in the earlier passage of the Nurse, page 15:

> Tage drei dienen wir hier im Haus

that would suit me very well indeed.

Perhaps you'll think it over.

With best regards, and hoping you are in good health and with good news of your father.

Yours very sincerely,

RICHARD STRAUSS

Dear Dr. Strauss,

Your letter of July 7th which has just reached me via Rodaun must have crossed with mine; I am answering it at once.

The objection to the eating of the fishes strikes me, frankly, as over-subtle. The little fishes are not, after all, the children: they are merely the vehicles of magic. I cannot imagine anyone objecting to this passage; it is invariably like that in fairy-tales, and always has been. I really cannot see any good reason for change here and would hate to lose the juxtaposition

> Nun wird er verlangen nach seinem Nachtmahl,
> das nicht bereit ist
> und nach seinem Lager,
> das ich ihm nicht gewähren will.

The passage which says that the female servants are sleeping some-where else (i.e. in the palace and not in the Dyer's hut) seems to me indispensable, because in both the two other scenes interposed in the second act (outside and inside the Falconer's house, and in the Empress's bedroom) this fact of their sleeping elsewhere enters into the action, and I feel this must be explained to the audience to prevent them from asking themselves: what is all this about?

The objection to moving the passage:

> Als arme Muhmen, etc.
> um Mitternacht nur,
> indessen du ruhest . . .

from page 16 to page 15 is this: the whole big speech of the Nurse is solemn in diction; it contains the covenants. To rearrange a detail like this appears to me rather unsatisfactory. Where it now stands it is not, on the other hand, either poetically or musically, a very important point, that is just why I have placed it there. I beg you to think this over again; I should not at all like to see this passage inserted into the big tirade on page 15.

Please write to me again to tell me the result of objective recon-sideration: these are matters of great importance.

With your suggestion to leave out the first six lines of this same big tirade (page 15) and to begin with: 'Abzutun Mutterschaft', you over-look in the first place that this leaves the sentence incomplete. 'Abzutun

Mutterschaft' finishes the earlier sentence: on the condition that, etc. . . . she has undertaken . . . But perhaps the whole passage could be recast as follows:

Wife (less loud):
> Meine Seele ist sattgeworden der Mutterschaft,
> eh sie davon verkostet hat.

Nurse:
> Heran, meine Tochter, und küss ihr die Füsse in
> Ehrfurcht
> (interposing joyfully, quite softly).

Wife (without looking at her, to herself):
> Ich lebe hier im Hause
> und der Mann kommt mir nicht nah!

Nurse (breathlessly awaiting her words):
> Getroffen ins Schwarze,
> bevor zur Bedingung
> mein Mund sich auftat!

Wife (sombrely):
> So ist es gesprochen
> und geschworen
> in meinem Innern!

Nurse:

A.   In diesem Innern,
     o du Herrscherin,
     dies gesprochen,
     o du Seltene,
     und beschworen.

Here the nurse performs a veritable witch's dance until she proclaims her triumph A, B, C, D, to all the four points of the compass.

B.   (very solemn)
     abzutun
     von deinem Leibe
     Mutterschaft
     auf ewige Zeiten,

C.   dahinzugeben
     mit der Gebärde
     der Verachtung
     die Lästigen,

(or only: mit Verachtung)

D.   die da nicht geboren sind! (End of the witch's dance).
        O du Gepriesene
        unter den Frauen,
        nun sollst du es sehen
        und es erleben . . .

Does this suit you? I am most anxious to hear.

Kindest regards, yours,

HOFMANNSTHAL

P.S. You must make sure that this version does not weaken the whole passage; if it does, I should have to think of something else.

Garmisch, 10.7.14

Dear Herr von Hofmannsthal,

The passage:
        Du bist nicht allein,
        Dienerinnen hast du, etc.

can remain as it is.

   On the other hand, I definitely want a direct transition from:
        So ist es gesprochen und geschworen
        in meinem Innern!

so that the Nurse can go straight into her prophecy:
        Abzutun Mutterschaft

        . . .

        Die Lästigen, die da nicht geboren sind!
        du Seltene, du! du Erhobene!
        o du Herrscherin, o du Gepriesene unter den Frauen:
        nun sollst du es sehen und es erleben:

Is this really impossible?

   You have not dispelled my misgivings about Barak eating his own children. If one didn't hear the children singing you'd be right! But as it is, one is bound to identify the unborn children with the little fishes in the frying pan! Why must Barak eat supper when the Dyer's Wife has clearly stated that she has not got his supper? How would the following version of the scene do, after Barak's entrance?

Wife: Ich geh zur Ruh. Dort ist jetzt dein Lager.

Barak: Mein Bette hier? Wer hat das getan!

Wife: Von morgen ab schlafen zwei hier,
       denen will ich das Lager bereiten zu meinen Füssen
       als meinen Mägden. So ist es gesprochen, und so
       geschieht es.
Barak (putting down his basket and beginning to unpack):
       Sie haben es mir gesagt,
       dass ihre Rede seltsam sein wird
       und ihr Tun befremdlich
       die erste Zeit.
       Aber ich trage es hart,
       und die Arbeit will mir nicht schmecken.

(He drops his hands and sits down on a bale on the floor.) The voices of the watchmen, etc., remain to the end. Thus all ambiguities would be eliminated and the meal is really not necessary. He simply goes to bed without his supper.

Our letters have crossed: I am impatiently awaiting Act II. Karsavina was excellent, much better than Kussnetzoff! You probably know that *Rosenkavalier* will be done at the Opéra Comique on 25th January with a splendid cast, and *Elektra* at the Grand Opéra towards the end of April.

How is your father?

We're off to the Dolomites next week for eight days and shall probably spend a few days at S. Martino.

From about 25th July I shall be back here!

I should like to play my second act to you! Only the end isn't quite right yet, but it'll come!

With best wishes for your health and kind regards from us to you all (my wife was very pleased with your kind remarks), yours as ever.

RICHARD STRAUSS

Dear Dr. Strauss,   *By return of post, Sunday morning (12th July, 1914)*

To open the tirade with an infinitive like this ('abzutun Mutterschaft') is *possible* from the strictly grammatical point of view (it would then depend on 'so ist es beschworen'...), but quite impossible, to my ear, in elevated language; what is more it would be fatal to the understanding of this highly important passage. We must not in any circumstances obscure it by such laboured diction! The Woman has her say, then there must be a distinct break for the Nurse to grasp the good news; then she herself speaks out, decisively and powerfully, but not at once in the tone of 'prophecy' ('asseveration' would be the better word, but I know what you mean), for this comes only at line six of the tirade. First come the words essential for the listeners' understanding. She must begin in a tone of joyful surprise and assent (something like the following trivial phrases: 'Bravo! You've got it! Hurrah . . . Got it! That's it!'); the infinitive (without the lines in between) would literally make nonsense of the whole thing. But perhaps *this* might do (I am recasting the words slightly, but making them stronger):

Nurse (after a significant orchestral passage, prancing about in a frenzy of delight):

> Abgetan in deiner Seele (better: in ihrer Seele)
> Mutterschaft auf ewige Zeiten!
> Dahingegeben den vier Winden
> die Lästigen, die da nicht geboren sind! etc.

Would this suggestion of witch-like dancing around provide a rhythm which you can use at this point? I wish it would, for this is how the passage was seen in my mind, this is the mimic equivalent of what I meant. Please let me have a word on a postcard; this is poetically, dramatically and in the acting one of the outstanding points of the whole piece and I should like to feel altogether reassured about it.

Now for the supper scene. Here, too, small points are of great significance to me; a tiny untimely stroke of the brush can do a great deal of damage where everything has been so very carefully weighed. Very well, let him not touch the fishes, but I need the point of repose where he sits on the floor and eats, instead of always working! Let him then be resigned to what she says and (sure from the outset that there will be no supper) take a piece of bread out of his pocket, and eat it. To make him say: 'die Arbeit schmeckt mir nicht mehr' sounds sentimental and would anticipate a very significant idea from Act II, scene 3.

Therefore on page 18 at the bottom: the woman rises wearily, goes to her bed and says *nothing*. Now he:

> Ein gepriesener Duft
> von Fischen und Öl, etc.

(this passage expressing naïve pleasure I would hate to take away from him), and then *she*, with sharp anger:

> *Hier ist kein Essen.*
> Ich geh zur Ruh . . .
> Dort ist jetzt dein Lager

and so on as it stands, only with this stage direction: '(Barak, resigned, takes a piece of bread out of his coat and sits down, this time on the ground)'. In this way the passage gains both from your point of view and mine.

Many thanks for the rest of what you say. I am glad to report my father came back from Nauheim feeling really better and looking well. His breathing is still not what it should be, but I hope, from what I have been told so often, that this will improve only some six or eight weeks after the cure. You said something of that kind too, didn't you? He is now at Ischl and will come to us next week.

I am, as always, very content here and entirely absorbed in work and productive thinking. The fairy-tale (*Die Frau ohne Schatten*[1]) is making good progress and will, I hope, help to secure understanding for our work not only among the present generation, but also in the next.

Have a good time in the Tyrol with your wife. I shall send off the second act tomorrow, or the next day at the latest, so that you can take it with you and get to know it. Tomorrow I shall also write you a note expressing my, as I think, not very excessive wishes concerning the financial arrangements, generally on the basis of the *Rosenkavalier* terms.

Sincerely yours,

HOFMANNSTHAL

Garmisch, 16th July (1914)

Dear Herr von Hofmannsthal,

Thank you for your kind letters. I would ask you to postpone settling the passage of the Nurse's prophecy until we've talked to each other. The direct link-up of the words 'Abzutun Mutterschaft' with the words of the Dyer's Wife suits me so well that I am convinced you'll agree to it once I've played it to you.

I've adopted your idea of a kind of witch's dance, but it suits me only in the passage after the prophecy, to contribute to the climax. The second act is wonderful: the difficult problem of the Apparition of the Youth is solved with colossal tact and delicacy, the two scenes between Emperor and Empress are quite splendid, and the end of the act is superbly magnificent. Admittedly, it sets me a very difficult task; in

---

[1] The prose version.

particular, I don't know yet how I shall be able to manage the two septets; also, strangely enough, the character of the Dyer's Wife has not yet quite translated itself into music, whereas Barak is right up my street.

However, I shall work hard on it, and I hope I'll manage.

In any case, you've never written anything more beautiful and compact in your life, and it is my merit, I flatter myself, that by our joint work I have made you do it. I only hope my music will be worthy of your fine poetry. At present I am still far from satisfied with myself: true, I am making very high demands on myself, but what I have done so far only partly measures up to my expectations.

I am glad to hear Nauheim has done your father good. Of course, the after-effects of the treatment are felt for a long time, and I don't think your father will have got over them even in six or eight weeks—at least not in my experience. Once more a thousand thanks for everything; I hope after this highly dramatic second act with its foreboding of disaster, I shall now get a beautiful, lyrical, animated third as a final rounding-off.

With best regards, yours as ever,

RICHARD STRAUSS

Aussee, July 25th, 1914

My dear Dr. Strauss,

Your telegram and letter gave me very great pleasure. This spontaneous expression of your approval, just where yours means so much to me and where I believe I have really deserved it, was most welcome. I think myself that I have never produced, for the stage, anything as successful as this work; each act, the first as exposition, the middle one to tie the knot, and now the third act as finale, steadily soaring from darkness into light and, in the highest sense, made for music, must become a model of its kind. While I was at work on Act II, I foresaw to some extent the difficulties with which this act will confront you. But I do take some credit for the fact that the ensembles emerge out of the whole situation in a genuinely organic manner such as you will hardly ever find in a libretto, and that there are proper transitions from scene to scene which will facilitate your difficult task of turning five parts into one whole.

I would like to draw all your attention to the character of the Empress. She has not a great deal to say and yet is the most important figure in the opera. Never forget that. How she becomes a human being, that is the point of the action; she—not the other one—is the real woman without a shadow. The whole of the third act, in which she is the central figure, will hang in the air unless the composer does for her in the second act everything that can be done through the power of his wonderful, sensuous and at the same time spiritual art. She has not a great deal to say, but what she does say is always extremely significant. Throughout a light of spirituality radiates from her, and each stage on her road to humanity is marked, as it were, by flaming beacons. In the first scene it is the cry: 'Ach weh, dass sie sich treffen müssen' etc. (p. 6), in the second scene she does not speak at all, and yet everything turns exclusively on her (she is, indeed, the only character not left out of a single scene in the entire opera). The finale of the third scene is altogether focused on her, in the most delicate but most definite way. This scene merges directly into the fourth which is nothing but a monologue of the Empress interrupted and sustained by a vision. The final words of this monologue set the mood which is maintained throughout the fifth scene, and it might indeed be said that the whole action of this scene is but a projection of what goes on in her mind. For after all the poetic intention is only fully realized if all outward events are given spiritual meaning and all the spiritual meaning is translated into action. In the big septet your mastery must find the way to give her voice that splendour which soars dominant over all the rest, sums up all that has gone before and foreshadows the high significance which this character is to gain in the third act.

That you wince at the prospect of two septets in the fifth scene I can very well understand; perhaps the earlier one may have to be sacrificed to the impressive second septet; indeed there is no reason why the passage which begins on page 24 down to the bottom of page 25 should necessarily be treated as a septet at all. The Nurse might very well sing her passage ('Es sind Übermächte im Spiel') together with the Empress ('Wehe womit ist die Welt der Söhne Adams erfüllt') and this might be followed by a weird, gloomily tempestuous quintet of Barak, his Wife and the three brothers to words which express nothing but brutish anxiety ('Es ist etwas, und wir wissen nicht, was es ist') and might be repeated ad lib. In saying this I do not presume to advise you on the treatment of so important a passage; I only want to point out that so far as the text is concerned there is no necessity here to have all the seven characters singing simultaneously, such as exists for the other passage (the 'big septet') where the words are designed for this and no other purpose.

I only answered your letter and telegram so quickly because you had written you were on the point of leaving on a motor car tour. Have you postponed that, or what is the position? Have you already finished the first act? Is the passage of the watchmen a success? Naturally any information about your progress on a work which means so much to me is most welcome. It is only right and proper that you should set yourself such exacting standards. Who can be expected to make high demands on himself if not a man whom the world calls a 'master'? And where could he do so if not in a case like this which enables him for once in his life to give everything he has and to display, by fusing these many elements, that high order of creative genius with which a kind fate has singled you out among Germans?

I am surprised that, of all the characters, it is the figure of the Dyer's Wife that gives you trouble and I must say it would go somewhat against the grain if I had to comment on a character whose sharp and definite contours speak for themselves. You yourself have repeatedly expressed the desire to depict in music the capricious, flighty aspects of such a basically good woman. I would prefer not to say more than this and have no doubt that it will work out.

Please accept my best wishes and let me have news soon, either of the progress of your work or of the course of your journey which will, I hope, refresh you after so very considerable an effort.

Very sincerely yours,

HOFMANNSTHAL

P.S. I called on Franckenstein and talked to him as requested. He does not deny that the idea would be valuable from his point of view, too, but remarked that it presented certain difficulties so far as the programme for the Festival is concerned; last year *Così Fan Tutte* had to be left out on account of *Ariadne* and this led to a great deal of adverse comment and so on. He definitely intends to give at least one performance in August and one in September.

I shall myself write to Walter about it again some time.

Yours,

HOFMANNSTHAL

Dear Herr von Hofmannsthal,

In bed with a slight feverish catarrh, I received your wife's kind lines this morning. Baron Franckenstein had already reassured me in Munich, ten days ago, that you were no longer at the front but in safety at a quiet post. This was a great comfort to me. And now I think it may give you a little pleasure to know that the first four changes of scene of Act II are finished in the draft. The solo scene of the Empress has just been completed and furnished with a great deal of immanent music. The Emperor's scene, too, has come out very well, and Barak's banquet is merry and lively. Everything very full of variety—but then the text is really brilliant, goes into music with marvellous ease, stimulates me all the time, and is so short and concise: my dear Scribe, you've really pulled off your masterpiece here.

Amidst all the unpleasant things which this war brings with it—except the brilliant feats of our army—hard work is the only salvation. Otherwise the incompetence of our diplomacy, our press, the Kaiser's apologetic telegram to Wilson and all the other undignified acts that are being committed would be enough to drive a man to distraction. And how are the artists treated? The Kaiser reduces the salaries at the Court Theatre, the Duchess of Meiningen turfs her orchestra out into the street, Reinhardt stages Shakespeare, the Frankfurt theatre performs *Carmen, Mignon, The Tales of Hoffmann*—who will ever understand this German nation, this mixture of mediocrity and genius, of heroism and obsequiousness? What's the atmosphere like in Vienna, by the way? One hears so much of downheartedness and treason there that one doesn't really know what to think! We're bound to win, of course—but afterwards, Heaven knows, everything will be bungled again! You needn't hurry about the third act: now that I know you safe I know at least that I shall get it some time. I shan't need it before 15th March.

If I succeed in getting Act II ready this October I shall leave the whole thing till next Easter and then tackle the end with fresh vigour. During the winter I'll score my Alpine Symphony! That's all for today. Kindest regards to you and your family from my wife and your devoted

RICHARD STRAUSS

My dear Friend,

The second act is nearly ready: it's going to be really splendid; almost composes itself, so good and suited to the music is the poetry. I should like to dedicate the work to Count Hülsen:[1] he has done a lot for my works and will, I hope, continue to do so. That is why I should like to be able to inform him of my (or our?) dedication straight away. If you are agreed please send me a brief telegram to Berlin (Hotel Adlon) by 18th October.

How are you keeping? The Alpine Symphony, due to be ready in spring, I shall then dedicate to Count Seebach.

With best regards, yours

RICHARD STRAUSS

Rodaun, 19.10.(1914) at night

In great haste only this to thank you for the kind, good and cheerful news in your letters and postcards. Of Act III there exists a very full sketch with a great deal of text. The act will be very beautiful and short. It ends with an immense upsurge in which my mind has mysteriously anticipated a great many of the stupendous events of this year. Am in entire agreement with dedication to Count Hülsen.

Very sincerely yours,

HOFMANNSTHAL

Garmisch, 27.10.14

Dear Herr von Hofmannsthal,

Second act finished to schedule and, I hope, turned out not too badly. According to my calculation it will play for 65 minutes, i.e. an hour and 10 minutes at the most. First act: 54 minutes—these are good dimensions. When do I see you again? Couldn't you visit us here some time for a few days? We shall stay in Garmisch till Christmas. I very much want to play the two acts to you and discuss the third one together.

Best regards from us to you all!

RICHARD STRAUSS

[1] *Die Frau ohne Schatten* was published without dedication.

1915

Dear Dr. Strauss,

You have not had a sign of life from me for a long time—I simply was not able to write, and even today I could not explain why it was impossible—very general, non-personal reasons.

A few months ago you invited me to come and hear Acts I and II. How much I would enjoy that, but you forget that I am on active service and that there is no chance of getting the leave necessary for such a journey, however short the distance, before the end of the war, or at least within the foreseeable future. And yet it would be so important for me to hear the two acts and also to talk to you about certain points in the third act and not just to give it to you without a word.

I did the sketch for the third act in July. A fortnight before the Serbian ultimatum it was finished. Now, six months later, I have at long last got myself to take it up again and I am working on it: everything essential was already there. This third act is by far the most beautiful and must become in the music, just as it is in the poetry, the crowning piece of the whole work. How lucky I was able to get it that far at the time; today I could scarcely find within myself what was needed to write it. And yet it is quite short, hardly half the length of either of the other two. Do you remember when we discussed it on our Italian journey? You will recognize all the things we talked about then, even the surprising and significant use of the chorus.

Now do please come to Vienna in February for two days and let us exchange our treasures. I count on it.

Sincerely yours,

HOFMANNSTHAL

Rodaun, 6.2.1915

Dear Dr. Strauss,

Our letters (about a fortnight ago) have crossed. You can see from mine that I would not dream of leaving you in the lurch. You will have gathered from my letter, on the other hand, that I for my part cannot possibly travel to Germany, because I am on active service and nothing but sickness could support an application for leave.

213

Now before the completion of the third act, it is a serious disappointment and hardship that I cannot hear Acts I and II, and in saying this I am thinking not of my private curiosity and pleasure but of the need for closest possible collaboration over this, the most important and promising work we have ever undertaken together. That is why I ask once more: won't you have something to do either in Munich or Dresden in the near future; from either of these places a two-day excursion to Vienna for the sake of this matter would surely be well worth while. If no such possibility exists, I shall add to the very concise third act an extensive commentary which will indicate to you the internal organization of the act, the points where the chief, and the lesser, accents lie, the reasons for what I have done, and the thematic structure (in the poetry) of the whole work. For we would run grave risks if we were to be at cross purposes anywhere in this work, as happened for instance, as you know, more than once over *Ariadne*, where what I had meant to be subordinate and even unimportant was often emphasized and drawn out by the music, so that the final product as a whole has about it something of a convex mirror.

In one respect I have been full of confidence for our new work throughout: the way the seriousness and power of this opera befits the right and significant moment in time when we shall bring it before the public. After this war, a very distinct atmosphere is sure to prevail in Germany, with very definite demands (and prejudices) towards everything, not least towards the arts. Leaving aside certain so-to-speak inevitable manifestations of ill-will, it is just *Die Frau ohne Schatten* which, on the strength of both subject and execution, will show up exceedingly well and with great honour in this atmosphere, whereas a more artificial and playful piece like *Ariadne* with its Molière would have met with redoubled hostility just at such a moment. I have always considered this providential, but my sense of satisfaction with this favourable state of affairs has been rudely shaken by a few words of yours which Mme Wiesenthal has repeated to me from a conversation with you. These, though not very precise words, seemed to indicate that you intend to get *Joseph* performed in Germany somehow and with some sort of cast *before* the première of the new opera. I must confess this idea really startles me. That I consider *Joseph* not a very successful, or shall we say not a very happy, work is neither here nor there, and the announcement that it is to be performed shortly, or let us say in the autumn of 1915, at the Scala, or in New York, or anywhere else, does not concern me. But a performance in Germany, the performance of this one-act ballet in *Germany* as the first event after the war, would seem to me impolitic in the highest degree: (1) all ballet as such is alien to the German taste in art and not well received, (2) a distinct prejudice against this ballet has existed ever since Paris, (3) the imponderabilia of internationalism which are implied in it, in this 'commissioned' work (*commissioned* by Russians for Paris).

Please think over this point which weighs heavily on my mind, and discuss it also with your wife whose feeling is so often right; but towards Fürstner, etc., I would ask you to treat this my opinion as confidential. Once you have come, as I hope, to a firm resolve, no conceivable business opportunism of the Fürstner firm will any longer be able to turn you aside from what you have come to consider right.

I repeat: my fears, my distaste of seeing *Joseph* performed in the very special circumstances of the present moment, of the immediate future, before *Die Frau ohne Schatten*, refer exclusively to Germany, and not at all to foreign countries. Once the big work has taken root, I do not care if either a foreign company on tour, or Reinhardt or Hülsen or anybody, picks some unobtrusive, inconspicuous occasion to bring the ballet to the German stage where its general character, being more decorative than profound, leads me in any case to predict for it no happy fate. It is of course quite possible that Mme W. did not understand you right and that I am fidgeting over a mere nothing. So much the better, but I would ask you to set my mind at ease once you have thought over what I have had to say. I must shortly write to you about several other points. I do not think anybody could have foreseen that during our most important joint work we would be cut off from each other for an indefinite period. Please God this stupendous affair, which possibly causes me more violent pain than most people, may soon come to a decisive issue.

Sincerely, and with my best regards to your wife, yours ever,

HOFMANNSTHAL

Berlin (*February 1915*)

Dear Herr von Hofmannsthal,

Many thanks for your kind letter. Let me reassure you at once about *Joseph*: Mme W. has really misunderstood me. Mme Vollmoeller once expressed the wish to dance the piece now (i.e. in New York); but this was impossible, if only because we are contractually bound to the Russians until July. Your warning at any rate did some good in that I definitely and firmly endorse your argument and entirely share your opinion that *Joseph* must not come out in Germany before the opera. It is sad enough that mature and serious artists like ourselves, whose work remains true to artistic ideals, must pay so much heed to people for whom this great epoch serves merely as a pretext for bringing their mediocre products into the open, who seize the opportunity to decry real artists as hollow aesthetes and bad patriots, who forget that I wrote my 'Heldenleben', the 'Bardengesang', battle-songs and military marches in peacetime but am now, face to face with the present great events, keeping a respectful silence, whereas they, exploiting the present 'boom' and under the cloak of patriotism, are launching forth the most dilettantish stuff! It is sickening to read in the papers about the regeneration of German art, considering that only twenty years ago the most German of all artists, Richard Wagner, was accused of 'Latin rut'; or to read how Young Germany is to emerge cleansed and purified from this 'glorious' war, when in fact one must be thankful if the poor blighters are at least cleansed of their lice and bed-bugs and cured of their infections and once more weaned from murder! If one is conscious of always having taken one's art most seriously (even if, just for once, one did allow a ballet to have its first performance in Paris), then one feels a veritable revulsion against all this hypocrisy and ignorance. Enough of this! As far as the war itself is concerned we have, I think, every reason to view the future serenely. In our Navy there is an unbelievable confidence; the Russians will soon cave in; and in England itself the popular mood is said to be very flat already. What is the 18th February going to bring?

I can't possibly get to Vienna before the end of April or the beginning of May. With all incidental emoluments gone I shall have to toil hard for my daily bread. I think the best thing would be if you sent me Act III here as soon as possible: I shall study it carefully, and anything that needs discussing we'll deal with verbally in the spring. I don't want to start composing it before April. It's a pity though I can't play you the two acts. But I think you'll be satisfied, and I can already with a good conscience refute the misgivings you have expressed. I know exactly the shortcomings of my earlier works, and I know your wishes which are also my own—so you can calmly send me your third act even without commentary. I shan't muff anything.

All the best, and let me hear some good news from you soon! Best regards from my wife. Yours as ever,

RICHARD STRAUSS

Some friends, to whom I first read your first act and then played it, were equally delighted with the poetry and the music.

It's a pity though I can't play the two acts to you.

Berlin, 12.3.15

Dear Friend,

When shall I get Act III? I am arriving in Garmisch on 24th March and should be delighted to find it there! We had *Ariadne* yesterday, *Rosenkavalier* next Tuesday, *Elektra* on 23rd March with Gutheil! Kessler was here; called on us. Fürstner shares your and my opinion about *Joseph*.

How are you keeping? I have worked a lot and am looking forward to Garmisch to continue working there!

Perhaps I'll come to Vienna at the end of April.

With best regards, yours

RICHARD STRAUSS

Rodaun, 26.3.(1915)

Dear Dr. Strauss,

I had hoped to send you the finished third act before Easter, yet despite every effort of my depressed spirits a single but important scene which must be concise and at the same time beautiful now refuses to take on final shape. Still, if nothing wholly unforeseen casts me down once more (my father, too, was gravely ill again), I shall hatch out these few stanzas as they ought to be during Easter week. The act will delight you; it is wholly music, meets the music all the way, and at the same time is rich and varied and brief (only eighteen pages). You will and must summon your best strength to make this act hold all that is most rich and most sublime in what we two together have to give.

(. . .)

Sincerely yours,

HOFMANNSTHAL

217

Dear Herr von Hofmannsthal,

Many thanks for your letter. In full agreement with your wishes (. . .). We can discuss the details in Vienna at the end of April.

I shall probably conduct in Budapest on 24th April, in Vienna on 27th April, and in Prague on 29th April. Please send me at once anything that is finished of Act III, so that I have time to get into the spirit—at least the beginning and the first half. I am definitely thinking of starting to compose Act III at the beginning of May.

I am now making a fair copy of Act II and shall play you everything at the end of April. I think you'll be satisfied. I hope the third act will give me plenty of opportunity for lyrical discharges in the manner of the *Rosenkavalier* trio. I shall make an all-out effort to prove worthy of the poet.

Am fresh and rested and full of energy. Why are you letting your spirits droop like this? You may rely on Germany. Of course, I understand that your father's illness has got you down; please convey to him my kindest regards and best wishes for a complete recovery.

But as for politics: I think we'll view them from a little way off and leave them to the care of those concerned with them. Only hard work can console us; only hard work can bring us victory.

Please let me soon have anything that's ready—if possible the first half. I always take rather a long time to get into a thing. Once I've got the beginning things usually move fast with me!

Looking forward to seeing you, I hope, at the end of April!

With best regards, yours as ever,

RICHARD STRAUSS

Dear Herr von Hofmannsthal,

Telegram received. Before you send me Act III I must convey to you a few misgivings which may perhaps still give you some important ideas for the third act.

What happens to the shadow which the Dyer's Wife has lost in Act II and which the Empress does not want to accept? Surely, the Empress sings: 'Ich will nicht den Schatten', etc.

The shadow therefore hangs in the air. Moreover, the Empress's words:

> Ich will nicht den Schatten,
> auf ihm ist Blut, etc.

are lost to the audience since they are sung in an ensemble. It would thus be most important to have the Empress once more, in Act III expressly announce her decision of renouncing the bloodstained shadow.

I have let Hülsen and Seebach read the first two acts of the text. Both displayed total incomprehension of the thing, and Seebach understood it only after I had once more orally explained the subject to him and played the first act to him on the piano. Everything tells me that the subject and its theme are difficult to understand and that everything must be done to make it as clear as possible. I ask you urgently therefore to recapitulate emphatically in Act III (as Wagner often does) the decisive psychological processes so that nothing remains obscure, and in particular the idea that the Empress, because she has learned to feel pity, has earned the shadow, i.e. become a human being. Perhaps you have done all this already; but I thought there would be no harm in drawing your attention to it again. It is so easy, while working on a subject, to identify oneself with it to the point where one believes that everything that's clear to oneself must also be comprehensible to the reader or spectator.

I shall now definitely be in Vienna at the end of April and am looking forward a lot to seeing you again!

Mme Schoder acted and sang an unbelievably magnificent Electra in Berlin and scored a tremendous success.

For me her performance was an experience! Further details when we meet.

With best regards, yours as ever.

RICHARD STRAUSS

Rodaun (early April, 1915)

Dear Dr. Strauss,

You are quite right: at the end of Act II the shadow hangs in the air: the one woman has lost it, the other has not validly acquired it—this pending transaction and its final settlement by a Solomonic judgement of higher forces, whose spokesmen are 'the Unborn Children', this is indeed the focal point of the third act, the big scene of the Empress in the Temple, this is the essential core and meaning of the whole opera which helps us to see Acts I and II in their true light. It was, if you will forgive my saying so, not a practical proposition to give Hülsen and Seebach parts only of so interdependent and admittedly complicated a work. Nor must the public—as we agreed in Italy—come to be faced with this work unprepared. We absolutely must have an introduction— which I will entrust to Max Mell, a young Austrian poet who is very close to me, and which will find its place, brief as it is to be, in the guide to the music—in order to clear the way for proper understanding of the interplay of motives and symbols; I always had this quite definitely in mind.[1] A whole world is implied here, yet a couple of lines from Goethe[2] describes the gist:

> Von dem Gesetz, das alle Wesen bindet,
> befreit der Mensch sich, der sich überwindet.

Of other things soon by word of mouth. I shall probably be sent on active service to the occupied parts of the Russian half of Poland, but hope I can so arrange it that I shall not leave until you have been here.

Sincerely yours,

HOFMANNSTHAL

P.S. If on that legal question (the bargain over the shadow) you would like to dot the 'i's, the Nurse's passage on page 5 might be expanded as follows:

> Und was zu verschweigen,
> das hab' ich heraus!
> Dein wird der Schatten!
> Sie hat ihn verwirkt
> mit wissendem Mund.
> Du greifest ihn nicht,
> so schwebt er in Lüften.
> Herrenlos!
> Doch bindet auch ihn,
> was alle bindet:
> Wo du ihn forderst
> vor Sternengericht,
> wird er dein![3]

[1] Never written. [2] From *Die Geheimnisse*. [3] These lines were not set to music.

Dear Herr von Hofmannsthal,

Your third act is magnificent: words, structure and contents equally wonderful. Only in its quest for brevity it has become too sketchy: for all the lyrical moments:

> Duet between Barak and Wife,
> the Nurse's exit aria,
> duet between Emperor and Empress,
> final quartet,

I definitely need more text. No new ideas, just repetitions of the same ideas in different words and at a higher pitch.

I have put down my doubts, requests and suggestions on the enclosed sheets, which I would ask you to consider by the time I come to Vienna. My greatest misgivings are about the character of the Empress who doesn't touch us closely enough on the human plane:

> her remorse

> her renunciation of her own happiness at the side of the Emperor, confessions of her frivolousness, her guilt, and in particular her vacillation between pity for the Dyer and his Wife and her love of the Emperor—all these ought to emerge much more impressively in a monologue of some length, in the Temple scene.

Keikobad's intervention, too, ought to be much more clearly visible.

Do please think these points over, so that we can discuss them when we meet.

I am arriving in Vienna (Hotel Imperial) in the morning of the 21st. Could we have lunch together? On the 22nd I am conducting in Budapest, and from the 23rd until the 30th I shall be back in Vienna. Probably conducting *Elektra* at the Hofoper. Should also like to confer with you and Roller together.

Looking forward to seeing you! With many thanks and regards, yours

RICHARD STRAUSS

(*Enclosure*)

Criticisms and suggestions

Page 1: The voices of the Unborn Children should be heard, I think, only in the orchestra and not, as is the case later, in actual song; that would cause confusion among the audience.

Page 2: After Barak's 'Weh mir!' insert eight lines of repetitions, sung simultaneously by Barak and his Wife as a duet, the conclusion 'dass ich sie noch einmal sähe' etc. being sung by Barak alone.

By repetition, once and for all, I mean a text elucidating, amplifying and restating more clearly in different words that which preceded it.

Scene 2: As all unseen voices from above are absolutely fatal in opera, because invariably incomprehensible, I would recommend introducing the Spirit Messenger from Act I, possibly with some female colleagues; these could later, on page 3, escort the Empress, utter the warnings on page 13, and generally symbolize active intervention of Keikobad of whom, incidentally, there is far too little mention in Act III.

Page 6: Lead up to

(1) Was Menschen bedürfen,
    weisst du zu wenig,

(2) Was Menschen fühlen,
    fühlst du nicht,

(3) was Menschen leiden,
    fassest du nicht, etc.

(a) Ich habe es gefühlt,
    als ich in Baraks Augen blickte,

(b) ich habe geschaudert,
    als die Frau ihn so tödlich verwundete,

(c) ich habe zu den Sternen gefleht,
    das Grässliche nicht geschehen zu lassen, etc.
    Ich gehöre zu ihnen,
    du taugst nicht zu mir.

Page 9: The Nurse's farewell aria must be much longer; this must become a proper big scene for the Nurse, a companion piece to the scenes of the Emperor and the Empress in Act II. Invocation of Keikobad, return to the pure spirits (?), her love for the Empress whom she has now lost for ever, and a hideous lengthy curse on mankind (similar to Ortrud in Act II); in short, a colourful exit—at least twenty-five lines, with the voices of Barak and the Wife as interjections —at any rate the scene must end with a colourful conclusion of the Nurse's aria.

222

Pages 9, 10: What worries me here is the total failure of the Empress to say more about her relationship to the Emperor: here the entire psychological development of the Empress ought to be outlined in a monologue and all the salient points recapitulated—how she had inherited from her mother her yearning for humans, how she had thrown herself at the Emperor. How she had loved him beyond reason, unthinkingly, idolatrously; that she had lost the talisman, forgotten the frightful curse; how she had tried to acquire the shadow by fraud; and how, at the decisive moment, she had come to know and feel the real love, pity. Repetition of the key words of Act II.

> Da wollte ich nicht den Schatten,
> auf ihm war Blut.
> Meine Hände reckt ich in die Luft,
> rein zu bleiben von Menschenblut.
> Sternennamen rief ich an gegen mich.
> Diese zu retten, geschehe was wolle.

'Da hörtest du mich, Keikobad, Vater, du entrissest ihm das Schwert, sie zu töten, doch die Wunde, die sie ihm geschlagen, trägt er im Herzen. Du führtest mich hierher, werde ich dein Auge schauen, wirst du uns helfen?'

To page 11: What I have just written leads the Empress on to different ground—but I can't help it, I find it very unattractive that the Empress is so full of the idea of her own humanity that her thoughts are only for the sufferings of the Dyer and his Wife and that she has entirely forgotten the Emperor. Wouldn't some compromise be possible here?

Pages 13 and 14: How do the audience know that it is the Unborn Children who are singing? The audience hear children's voices, don't catch the words—all this must be explained and recapitulated by way of repetitions and references on the part of the characters standing on the stage!

Pages 14 and 15: Much more text for the duet between Emperor and Empress: perhaps something might be worked in here about a higher relationship and their former love and the curse—at any rate much more text, identical repetitions. Final quartet: at least twice as much text for all four; repetitions will do.

It seems to me: the insoluble conflict into which the Empress has got and which can be solved only by a superior spirit power, ought to emerge much more clearly and tangibly. After all, the Empress, by declining to acquire the shadow through fraud or through wrecking the happiness of the Barak couple, sacrifices her own husband. This in itself is somewhat unnatural and distasteful. That is why the Empress's renunciation of her love, of the Emperor's salvation, her decision to do penance ought to be motivated much more extensively. Otherwise nobody will understand why Barak's happiness should mean more to the Empress than her own life and that of the Emperor.

Friday (23rd April, 1915)

Dear Dr. Strauss,

I have arranged everything for Sunday, at Schalk's for the sake of the best piano; Roller is informed, but since I have an official appointment with Major Morath at 11 o'clock which cannot be postponed, we must put off our meeting until 12.30 precisely, then lunch, then a rest, and afterwards Act II.

Perhaps you could get your constitutional in Schönbrunn Park beforehand. Our conversation the other day was most fruitful; Act III will develop into something very beautiful.

Other fine pictures are in the too-little-known gallery of the Academy, Schillerplatz. Admission at any time by card through the custodian. I am looking forward to Sunday.

Sincerely yours,

HOFMANNSTHAL

Rodaun, 14.5.(1915)

Dear Dr. Strauss,

My departure for Poland is somewhat delayed on account of the recent big events, so I am able to send you the new version of the beginning of Act III—I hope it is what you want. I should be grateful if you will give me time for the rest of the act in which case it will all turn out far better and still more beautiful than you can imagine. All your suggestions have sunk in, but even more lasting and powerful is the impression made by your glorious music. Your musical treatment of the Emperor is for me the clearest possible pointer how I am to deal with this character in

Act III; after he is woken from his petrification, he must have his aria, his (totally different) 'Gralserzählung'. Far more light must be thrown on Keikobad's significance to the whole opera and on his relation to the Unborn Children; I know already exactly how and where to introduce this. All these changes will benefit greatly the Nurse's impassioned scene. Far more passionate action on the part of the Nurse herself; a violent dispute with Keikobad's Messenger as he sternly turns her back; lightning and tempest and in the midst of this the frightened voices of the Dyer and his Wife will give the Nurse's exit all the massive intensity you can want for it. But so as to prevent your imagination from fastening upon the wrong ideas, let me say at once what I do not intend to aim for: I entreat you not to waste the chorus of the spirits on this scene, for I should like to reserve this crowning effect for that one unforgettable and unique moment in the chief scene, when they sing: 'The woman casts no shadow!' The two Tempters whose voices are heard in this scene will be sorcerers, two mysterious shapes emerging on either side of the petrified figure of the Emperor: they are the guardians of the threshold. For the three calls: 'Hab Ehrfurcht!' 'Mut!' 'Erfülle Dein Geschick!', on the other hand, I should be loth to concede any figures visible on the stage; these exclamations ought, in my opinion, to come from among the orchestra.

One more thing which has given me much concern since your good and enjoyable visit in the spring: it was a grave mistake of mine (which I can only ascribe to the preoccupations of war-time) not to have impressed upon you adequately the fact that the 'strange Youth' is an apparition to be mimed with the greatest delicacy on the stage and to be sung from somewhere else (from the orchestra pit) in an unearthly voice. As it now is you have, alas, taken quite a different view of it which distresses me greatly; I beg of you not to dismiss this point lightly, for this 'strange Youth' emphatically does not belong to the world of the mortals. His world is the same as that of the falcon, and of the Unborn Children who sing with the voice of the little fishes; there you have found the contrast so marvellously that it now makes me quite unhappy it should have gone wrong. Of course I am well aware that you cannot change the theme of the 'strange Youth' since it is woven through everything; but despite my layman's floundering in matters of your art I venture to warn you that instrumentation alone cannot do the trick, for that provides only the turn-out of a character, the atmo-sphere, and cannot change the substance. Therefore I would implore you to try, in this one scene where the apparition opens its mouth, so to recast the modulation of the voice, while preserving the theme, that it becomes singular, non-human, unearthly. Forgive my pestering you with this, but if you can achieve it much will be gained.

Mme Wiesenthal has not heard from Korngold concerning the ballet and is very anxious because Nedbal (since he wants to do a ballet with her himself) cannot be a suitable intermediary and the whole business of negotiation may therefore be in the wrong hands. Would it be too much to ask you to write a letter tipping the wink say to Karpath who likes acting as go-between and has his finger in every pie. Getting good music for this beautiful and well-conceived ballet is such a vital question for her.

Most sincerely yours,

HOFMANNSTHAL

Garmisch, 27.5.15

My dear Herr von Hofmannsthal,

Many thanks for letter and opening page of Act III: there's still not quite enough lyrical stuff for a real duet of lament and remorse. Very fine indeed is Barak's:

> Mir anvertraut,
> dass ich sie hege
> und sie trage
> auf diesen Händen
> und ihrer achte
> und ihrer schone,
> um ihres jungen Herzens willen!

But now I would need at least one more seven-line stanza in exactly the same manner—just different words but the same sentiments for the Wife. Couldn't you let me have this too? When are you going to send me the next batch?

I have in the meantime sketched out a pretty good prelude to Act III and am now starting on the act proper. I am not quite clear what fault you have found with the scene of the Youth. If he sings his few words in the orchestra pit, unseen, the ghostly effect will, I believe, be fully achieved; also, while singing, he can stand with his back to the audience.—Are you going to Poland? Will you come to Garmisch some time?

With best regards, yours very sincerely,

RICHARD STRAUSS

I am quite in agreement about the sorcerers, the way the Nurse's scene is handled, her exit without a soliloquy, and the outlined account of the Emperor, and also about the unseen spirit voices.

I've already written to Karpath about Korngold.

Garmisch 28.5.15

Dear Herr von Hofmannsthal,

I now have the beginning of Act III up to and including:

> Schweiget doch, ihr Stimmen,
> ich hab' es nicht getan!

But before I continue with:

> Barak, mein Mann,
> o dass du mich hörtest!

and the subsequent reminiscences I need about eight lines in which the Dyer's Wife describes her present condition, sadly and haltingly (in F minor); roughly like this:

> Verstossen von ihm
> in Nacht und Grauen,
> allein in Verzweiflung,
> allein in Reue,
> kein Licht vor mir,
> keinen Ausweg,
> o bitterste Not,
> o schrecklichste Trauer!

Could you fit in for me such a sombre moment of repose from which I can then climb upward again?

As for the rest, I'll manage that all right.

Would you mind if in the duet I also let Barak's Wife sing Barak's words:

> Mir anvertraut,
> dass ich ihn hege,
> dass ich ihn trage

auf meinen Händen
und seiner achte
und ihn liebe
um seines treuen Herzens willen!

This kind of thing is always best and more rewarding in a musical duet. But if it doesn't appeal to you perhaps you'll write me some synonymous lines which I could put into the Wife's mouth.

Did you get my letter of yesterday?

With best regards, yours

RICHARD STRAUSS

At this lyrical moment of repose in F minor I would like to have underlying, symphonically, the motives

(1) of 'Abzutun Mutterschaft
für ewige Zeiten',

(2) of all human misery and human impotence.

A few lines might therefore allude to this. Something like:

Geopfert hab'
was all seine Hoffnung war,
aller Menschenpflicht
hab' ich mich entäussert,
nun bin ich ausgestossen
aus menschlicher Gemeinschaft,
verlassen von ihm,
allein in Nacht und Grauen!

Please do not take these hints as instructions, but merely as suggestions and clues to the direction of my musical requirements! After that we continue with:

Barak, mein Mann
o dass du mich hörtest! etc. etc.

Garmisch, 8.6.15

Dear Herr von Hofmannsthal,

I have now finished the music for the first scene of Act III. It's turned out a very well-constructed and beautifully climaxing scene, for which —as you will see from the enclosure—I have laboriously rearranged the text!

I would ask you to decide whether you approve all the dovetailing, transposition and repetitions, or whether you would rather let me have the necessary additional lines for the three passages marked with *. Also, whether you agree with simple text repetitions for the passages marked 'duet': if not, would you please let me have some other words, but with the same content and in the same mood since the piece is already composed. In a story by A. Bernstein, *Mendel Gibbor*, I read on page 81 about the custom of Jewish coroners to ask the dead man's forgiveness for all misfortunes inflicted on him during his lifetime and to sever all past relations with him. This theme might possibly be used in the first passage, or in the third. Except that there must be an element of ecstatic fanaticism in the third passage; something like:

> Komm zu mir, Barak, mein Mann!
> Verzeih mir, bevor ich dich auf ewig verliere,
> sag' mir noch einmal, dass du mich geliebt hast,
> was du auch über mich verhängst,
> ich will dich preisen und segnen—
> schwängst du auch dein Schwert über mir,
> in seinem Blitzen sterbend noch säh' ich dich!

Can you let me have all this soon?

Also the key scene between Empress and Nurse?

Since I'm now stuck in my composing, while you, most unnecessarily, are consorting with lice and bed-bugs instead of writing poetry, I have now started on orchestrating the score of Act I. But I'd much prefer, while the sun shines, to finish composing Act III in one go—so think of me, please! With best regards, yours

RICHARD STRAUSS

Garmisch, 17.6.15

Dear Herr von Hofmannsthal,

I can't get the Judgement of Solomon out of my head. Wouldn't its dramatic climax—i.e. the outburst of the real mother and her renunciation at the moment when the child is to be killed and halved—be applicable also to our piece and its climax in the scene of the Empress before the statue of the Emperor? All the Empress's remarks in it:

> Helft! dieser Blick!
> Ich kann nicht helfen,

Ich kann nicht.
(the Empress is torn by a terrible struggle)
Ich will nicht!

strike me as rather empty and cold.

Surely, there ought to be a big explosion here—such as the first frightful human cry bursting from the Empress's breast at the end of the scene, something like the scream of a woman in childbirth. In short, it ought to be a moment of the kind that has come off so well in *Elektra*, with Electra's cry of 'Orest!'

Different, of course: but still the climax of the piece, after which everything relapses into pure lyricism and fades out on a beautiful *decrescendo*. Do please get that old head of yours working hard: maybe you'll still hit on something specially fine and powerful—the success of the whole thing depends on this moment and on this entire scene. Please get busy on meeting my requests as soon as you're back from Poland, so that I can soon get on with my work. What doesn't come with the summer it's no good trying in the winter.

Can't you come here yourself for a few days? It's most important!

With best regards, yours

RICHARD STRAUSS

Has Duino, the castle of the Princess Taxis, really been destroyed by gunfire?

Garmisch, 19.6.15

Dear Herr von Hofmannsthal,

Since I am allowed to tell you anything that passes through my head: the scene of the inner struggle of the Empress before the petrified Emperor ought to have a more perceptible dramatic climax. Would it be possible for the Empress, after a severe inner struggle—she feels her death to be near—to utter a terrible cry, *the first human cry, rather like that of a mother in childbirth*? This cry, after which she falls to the ground as if dead, redeems the Emperor who then, for his part, awakens the Empress and with her all the Unborn Children to life.

Perhaps you'll hit on something better still, something more poetic: but maybe this 'idea' gives you a useful suggestion.

I hope to have good news from you soon!

With best regards, yours

RICHARD STRAUSS

The Emperor's first words are: 'Ein Menschenschrei'.

The invisible voices answer, aghast, lamenting:

'Ein Menschenschrei', like an echo from all sides.

Rodaun, 22.6.(1915)

Dear Dr. Strauss,

On my return from Poland yesterday, I found here your letters of May 26, May 27, June 8, and June 17. I am exceedingly sorry you should have got into a tight spot now, after all. You had told me you would not need the new material before the *end of June*.

To shorten as much as possible your unfortunate predicament, I mean to put aside all political preoccupations and all other anxieties (my father has once again not been at all well after a few better months) and to concentrate on the scene between the Nurse and the Empress. This I shall send you at the very earliest; everything else, especially the chief scene in the Temple, will have to mature in my mind and come to perfection after I have thought over your ideas and my own.

You have by now finished the first scene, so I shall leave that alone for the time being; if I find that I need to paint over some parts of the text as you have put it together, this can be done later; probably I shall not be able to give my blessing to very much of it.

The present unreliable mails are, alas, certain to delay still further the manuscript of the second scene which I mean to send off as soon as possible.

I do not believe it is true that the beautiful castle of Duino has been destroyed by gunfire, but it is gravely threatened because, so far as I know, it forms part of the Austrian defence line.

Sincerely yours,

HOFMANNSTHAL

Rodaun, 7.7.(1915)

(Postcard)

Finished yesterday the whole big scene of the Nurse up to her grand theatrical exit. Have written it out myself today to save time and will despatch tomorrow by express letter. Hope I have done it to your satisfaction; all your wishes and suggestions (which are always of value to

231

me) are fulfilled, all the motifs are more strongly brought out, in contrast to the earlier tranquil and laconic treatment. The whole scene now full of unrest, surging towards the catastrophe. In a fortnight's time, after finishing some other business, I hope to apply myself with all my energy to the chief scene in the Temple for which the ground is far better prepared by the scene as it now is. The needs of the music had to assert themselves decisively in this act, that's the only way to make a success of the whole work.

Sincerely yours,

HOFMANNSTHAL

Am on temporary leave, hope to take my father to Ischl and to go to Aussee myself with family.

Dear Herr von Hofmannsthal, *Garmisch, 17.8.15*

How is the stage direction to run about the visible appearance of the three Watchmen on the city wall at the end of the first act? My idea is to have the first verse sung unseen, then the Watchmen appear on the wall and sing the second verse. Would you please let me know your wishes as soon as possible since I've got to the end of Act I with the full score!

When shall I get the rest of Act III? As soon as you can, please! Wouldn't you like to bring it here in person—so that we can settle any possible differences? That would be very nice!

Did you get my last two letters? I should very much like to have your opinion on Munich; also whether you have perhaps discussed the matter with Baron Franckenstein! Having allowed myself to be pacified with excuses and tricked with empty promises by him and Bruno Walter for the past three years, I would now require, for the balance to be restored, some definite written guarantees about the upkeep of my works in my native city—or else I shall not enter the Munich Hoftheater so long as its present directors are in office.

With best regards, yours very sincerely,

RICHARD STRAUSS

Dear Dr. Strauss, *Aussee, 21.8.(1915)*

I usually like writing to you (and for you), but the loss of this ill-starred letter about that tiresome theatre business with Munich and the need to write it again at the moment when I long to be done with this constant plethora of letters (fifteen to twenty a day) has upset me for the past few days. Well then, I talked to F(ranckenstein) at the end of July. He assured me he holds every single one of your works in the highest respect and treats them as he considers right and possible in the circumstances and conditions prevailing, including even the works (*Ariadne*, *Elektra*) which are more difficult to keep on the stage and less popular. He asks whether you do not recognize this at all?

He also wanted to know whether in this abnormal year your works have had substantially more than six or eight performances anywhere except in Berlin? I told him I was unable to answer this question. Finally he said he could not imagine anything he would dislike more and find more painful than to get into conflict with you—but if necessary and if he were to be publicly attacked, he would defend himself on his own behalf and on (Bruno) Walter's whom he has to cover.

My dear Dr. Strauss, it is not for me to interfere in any way with your attitude in this affair or with your approach. If you consider it right and justified to instruct your publisher to refuse the next work to the Munich Hoftheater and not to set foot in the place again, you will never have me remonstrating with you. A measure of this kind, taken without wasting as much as a word, presents itself even to my eyes as something in a way dignified and possible. But if you can reconcile it with your dignity to embark, either yourself or through some organization, upon an altogether loathsome theatre quarrel—where regrettably the artist has always, always the worst of it against officials, public authorities or business men (if only because at bottom all the world looks askance at the artist and is delighted to credit him with the kind of ignoble motives which it can understand and so to drag him down, ostensibly, to its own level)—if you intend to enter upon all that and at such a moment (the end of the war), and if you were to pick on this, just on this work as the occasion and bone of contention, and mean to let yourself in for one of these beastly newspaper squabbles in which by virtue merely of their office the officials must inevitably prevail, a squabble which will give the whole pack of journalists the heaven-sent opportunity for publishing figures, for digging up again your earlier, unsuccessful 'attempts at blackmail' and so on, and so on; if you were to launch out on a veritable campaign which can lead to nothing except that you will lose for this work over a period (at least for the first few years) one of the few first-class theatres in Germany and will eventually, after an ignominious to and fro, come to terms again with

233

the *beati possidentes*, so that after all that mud-slinging everything in the garden will be lovely; if you intend to launch out on all that, and over this particular opera, I of course shall not say anything publicly, but I shall be as bitterly hurt and ashamed as I was over certain disgraceful and entirely unnecessary occurrences in Stuttgart—I shall be ashamed to be in any way connected with such goings on and to have anything to do with them. I am writing this so sharply because I am forced, by the tone of your letters (regarding Munich) to do so. You must obey the laws of your character in such matters, and I mine. The only thing I would ask you before you undertake any irreparable step is to think out, and to write out for me on a slip of paper, the advantages (moral or material) which you expect for yourself and for your works from such tactics, while I would be quite ready to write down the fifteen or twenty tangible disadvantages which I can see.

Yours,

HOFMANNSTHAL

P.S. The conversation with F. was of course much longer than my report, but after all nothing ever comes of such conversations because he believes he is in the right, accounts for certain incidents in detail, explains others as accidental, and so on.

Garmisch 11.9.15

Dear Herr von Hofmannsthal,

Please send me a brief note when, approximately, I can expect to have the Temple scene, so that I can arrange my work accordingly, and also how long you're staying at Aussee! I'll be in Garmisch till 9th October, with the exception of 25th to 27th September when I shall be in Stuttgart for the première of Schillings's *Mona Lisa*.

What I have so far of Act III is finished in the draft, in fair copy, and takes about thirty-five minutes; so the rest must not be too long now. When we meet (in Salzburg or in Munich) I can play it to you.

With best regards, yours

RICHARD STRAUSS

Salzburg, Saturday evening (10th September, 1915)

Dear Dr. Strauss,

You do not come, you do not telegraph, I cannot understand at all what is happening.

234

Last Wednesday I wired you, as well as Bahr and other people, that I shall be here at your disposal from Friday morning until Saturday night. From hour to hour I have waited in vain for news from you. Tomorrow morning I shall have to leave, shall have to be in Vienna for the next few days (on official business), then for an undefined short period at Aussee before taking my father, who is not at all well and very weak, back to Vienna. Early in October I shall travel to Belgium officially and on the way there intend to stop in Berlin for two days (between October 2 and 6) mainly for your sake, so that we can talk everything over.

The Temple scene is finished, only a small passage of the Empress is missing which my weary head just would not produce. I shall in any case make you a fair copy tomorrow (leaving out, if need be, that short passage) and will send it to you by express.

Your non-arrival is inexplicable to me: I only hope nothing has happened to you or your family.

Sincerely yours,

HOFMANNSTHAL

Aussee, 17.9.(1915)

Dear Dr. Strauss,

If you will acknowledge receipt of this postcard by telegram, I shall assume that the mails are functioning normally again and will entrust the only copy of the final scene (I no longer have a typist) to the post. I hope that, taking great pains, I have got it as it ought to be and that I have carried out all your wishes. The dimensions are such that it is of paramount importance to preserve the right balance. The Temple scene and the final scene I am sending you are, at any rate, substantially shorter than the rest of Act III which you already have (the proportion is roughly 2:3). I shall try to postpone my journey to Belgium until 9th Oct. so that on my way there we can meet at last.

Sincerely yours,

HOFMANNSTHAL

I have been told of a very beautiful and careful *Rosenkavalier* performance in Munich, by someone who happened to be passing through.

Dear Dr. Strauss,

Since it appears you are receiving neither my letters nor my telegrams, neither those sent from here nor those from Salzburg where I waited for you in vain for three days (from the 8th to the 11th), I am making use of the good offices of the Bavarian Legation in Vienna to transmit to you safely and at long last the final scenes. From Sept. 26th to Oct. 7th I shall be in Vienna, from the 8th to the 10th (absolutely impossible to make it longer) at the Hotel Adlon in Berlin where I count on seeing you; from there I shall go to the Austro-Hungarian Commissariat in Brussels.

I hope you will be satisfied with the Temple scene and that everything is done as you wanted it. For the three guardians of the threshold, who are deceitful sorcerers or demons, tempters, I imagine highly peculiar voices, male/female, alluring and at the same time repellent, as if a serpent were to sing. Perhaps it is possible to use a very high-pitched male voice (falsetto) or a female one of exceptional depth, or something far more beautiful than I can think of. The passage of the Emperor, where he repeats the prophecy which the spirits 'sang to him' at the moment of petrifaction, must sound most unearthly, a wondrous message of one only just returned to life.

The early passages of the Unborn Children 'Hört, wir wollen sagen Vater' will sound so marvellous, I imagine, that it does not matter whether one understands the words or not, like birds bursting into speech from the skies; but the sound is more important than the sense. These passages have the effect of coming swiftly from afar, as on wings of air; then rejoicing as light as silver.

The principal passage later: 'Hört, wir gebieten Euch', this is real singing, and might be repeated by the Emperor and the Empress to make it understood, but in the earlier passage the wondrous, strangely disturbing and seductive sound must predominate.

Please send me a few lines to Rodaun soon.

Sincerely yours,

HOFMANNSTHAL

Dear Herr von Hofmannsthal,

My wife and I shall be in Vienna from the evening of 1st December till 7th December. Karpath is arranging accommodation for us.

I hope we shall see you then. You must hear my Alpine Symphony on 5th December: it really is good! How are you? Don't forget the fairy-tale. What was Flanders like?

With best regards from us to you all, yours

RICHARD STRAUSS

We want to stop in Salzburg on 29th November. Is the Österr. Hof to be recommended?

1916

Dear Dr. Strauss,

(Berlin), 5.1.(1916)

You are quite right when you connect, in your kind and comforting letter, the memory of my dear father[1] with our joint work. For, if people who are my friends and wish me well tend sometimes to stress unduly the more dubious aspects of my working for music or for a musician, and reproach me with it, if they feel even more acutely than I do myself the resulting misrepresentations and disparagement and thus aggravate still further certain already awkward situations, it was my father who invariably saw only the beauty of it and that which seemed to me the essence of this collaboration, and so, by sharing my pleasure in it, increased it. That is now past and can live only in my recollection.

I see in the papers, my dear Dr. Strauss, that you are to conduct Beethoven tomorrow night[2] and beg you to let me be present somehow without fail in whatever form and wherever a seat can be got. One such evening three years ago belongs to my most cherished memories. Therefore please do not forget me.

Yours as always,

HOFMANNSTHAL

Dear Dr. Strauss,

Berlin, 18.1.(1916)

Here is the newspaper! Is it not truly distressing to light upon something like this, *distressing beyond the common run*? Yet it looks to me as if

[1] Hofmannsthal's father had died on 11th December 1915.

[2] On 7th January 1916, Strauss conducted the State Opera Orchestra in performances of the 1st and 3rd symphonies and of the Leonora Overture No. 1.

even Dillmann had *not* mentioned my name. This would have to be established.

I am very glad we had an opportunity yesterday of talking everything over so frankly; the Club is a nice institution, isn't it. Now please send

(1) your telephone number on a postcard

(2) two seats, dress circle, for *Ariadne*

(3) one seat for the concert.

I hope I am right in assuming that after *Ariadne* we shall go to the Club with R. to talk over our impressions. I am now full of hope that this hapless child will be rehabilitated. The incomprehension of the public for anything with a deeper meaning is another matter. But here, after all, quite a lot was wrong with the work itself: between vision and realization, between the libretto, the music, and the possibilities of the theatre there was a hiatus.

Please give my most respectful regards to your wife: I am your sometimes irate but always well-intentioned librettist.

HOFMANNSTHAL

Berlin, 7.2.(1916)

Dear Dr. Strauss,

Yesterday I spoke at length to my publisher, Fischer, about this outstanding business matter. He rejects, on perfectly reasonable grounds, the idea of a subscribers' or bibliophile edition. He still adheres to an exact repetition of what was done in the case of *Rosenkavalier* and supports his attitude by putting forward the almost irrefutable argument that this arrangement has never involved, and could not conceivably involve any loss, however microscopic, either in prestige or financial returns, to the firm of Fürstner (for whom, and for whose senior partner, he feels the highest esteem).

As for the fairy-tale which I may, perhaps!, be able to create out of the same characters, I refuse, as you know, to allow it to be drawn into any legal or business arrangements, for the simple reason that 'subject', 'themes' and suchlike describe altogether *intangible* things, and because only tangible things (a given play, a given plot, a given text) can be dealt with in such agreements. The plot out of which, hypothetically speaking, a 'film' could be made, might be *easier* to find in Dillmann's account of it (which, legally, is altogether indistinguishable from any

238

future versions of the same subject I might produce) than in the forth-coming fairy-tale which develops the action out of the characters them-selves and which is by no means a mere reflected image of the play. Enough, therefore, or already too much of this point which has nothing to do with the present negotiations. Fischer is not only quite ready, but anxious to meet and discuss with Fürstner this whole business and any-thing he can do to safeguard the rights of the Fürstner firm (relating to America etc.). I would ask you, my dear Dr. Strauss, to give Fürstner my best compliments and to induce him to see to it that this conversa-tion between the two gentlemen takes place if possible before the 15th, so that we get it settled at last. I look forward to speaking to you tomorrow of the matter I mentioned the other day.

Sincerely yours,

HOFMANNSTHAL

Rodaun, 18.2.(1916)

(To Frau Pauline Strauss-de Ahna).
Verehrteste gnädige Frau!

Your kind good letter has given me particular pleasure and I hasten to thank you for it most sincerely. It always makes me very glad to hear that my collaboration with Dr. Strauss, such as fate has brought it about, arouses your interest and is, occasionally, a source of pleasure to you.

In the joint work we have done in the past or may do in the future, I consider Dr. Strauss entirely as the principal partner and the music as the dominant one among the elements joined together. But this does not prevent me from pursuing in this whole collaboration quite per-sonal and quite definite intentions of my own whose greater or lesser realization in the performance of each individual work on the actual stage determines my satisfaction or disappointment. For these joint works I have one very distinct ambition which is that they should earn lasting success, the only sure sign that a work of art has something to say. That real meaning needs time to make itself felt and understood, while ephemeral success is determined by all sorts of extraneous and fortuitous circumstances. Just because I do not consider rapid and immediate success any guarantee of a lasting future, or indeed do not look upon it as anything very significant at all, I may perhaps appear to your husband occasionally indifferent to the fate of these works. Nothing, however, could be further from the truth, for I daresay I am as jealous and as eager for their success as Dr. Strauss himself, only in a different way and from a slightly different point of view (which perhaps makes us complement each other rather happily). I am fastidious and intolerant with regard to the quality and style of execution, because I believe that only a work which is unique, a work which possesses a special style of its own can be expected to live and to endure, and that any success achieved by compromise or by blurring its special characteristics must in the end be paid for by postponement or diminution of the *real* success which is its due. Thus I feel that, had I been left to decide, the fate of *Ariadne* would have been *to all appearance* less favourable, but could in truth have been far happier: I should certainly have withdrawn the work from the stage after the unsuccessful performance in Stuttgart, to bring it out again, perhaps years later, as something untarnished and fresh. In only one single city, in Vienna, my intentions were carried out, and the result has been to me a very great delight: I have heard this beautiful production now five or six times and each time it is something festive and truly solemn.

Once more I must say that I am not at all sure it would not have been far better policy last autumn, when we failed once again to score a success in Berlin, to take *Ariadne* resolutely clean out of the repertoire for a year or two and quietly to bide our time until we can get together a cast which will enable us to present the work to the Berliners in all its delicacy and, as it were, new-born. I am only writing all this down as it comes into my head, because your kind letter prompts me to chat about these things at random.

Concerning the new opera I endorse what you say: the pros and cons will have to be carefully and deliberately weighed—if only I had not learnt to be a little nervous of Dr. Strauss's abrupt and sudden decisions. At first sight there is quite a lot to be said for Vienna, but also much, and weighty considerations, against it. This, above all, that Vienna cannot produce a verdict which will be accepted all over Germany; failure would be taken in Germany as settling the matter, but success not. Moreover: nowhere will Roller find worse soil, nowhere will the libretto meet with so little good will, with so much preconceived incomprehension as in Vienna. By now I have perhaps written more than the censor will pass, and I shall add only my and Gerty's best wishes and warmest regards.

All good wishes to Bubi of whom the children also often speak.

Your devoted and sincere

HOFMANNSTHAL

Dear Herr von Hofmannsthal,

Manuscript to hand: everything to be done according to your wish as soon as I get to Garmisch on 23rd April. I am here till Easter (apart from 17th April) and shall be very pleased to discuss with Direktor Gregor anything he wishes. Everything will be ready for the 4th October in Vienna: here, *Ariadne* is to follow at the end of October. That means that Vienna might have the first performance: in which case I must merely get Count Hülsen's official consent.

The part of the Composer (since the tenors are so terrible) I shall give to Mlle Artôt. Only you'll have to consider now how we might further furnish the part for her with, say, a little vocal number; or perhaps you could write an additional pretty little solo scene for the Composer at the end (after *Ariadne*!): wistfully poetical—possibly by making him burst out in despair after *Ariadne*: 'What have you done to my work', and then the Major-domo could appear and pay the poor devil his salary, or the Count might appear and pay him some compliments, announce the acceptance of the opera by the Imperial Opera House in its present form (with the Zerbinetta scenes), or any other amusing idea that comes to your mind—and then a wistfully-poetical final contemplation.

Please let me have this soon: because I can only win Mlle Artôt for our piece if I can offer her a kind of small star part.

As for the song 'Du, Venus Sohn, gibst süssen Lohn', she can sing that earlier. On Wednesday I am playing the second act of *Frau ohne Schatten* to Hülsen, since perusal of the 'longwinded text' hasn't given him much of a clue.

With best regards, yours

RICHARD STRAUSS

My dear Dr. Strauss,

For the past two days I have been thinking over, backwards and forwards, your letter with its astonishing proposal for the end, but I have failed to come round to it; on the contrary. I fear your opportunism in theatrical matters has in this case thoroughly led you up the garden path. In the first place the idea of giving the part of the young Composer to a female performer goes altogether against the grain. To prettify this particular character, which is to have an aura of 'spirituality' and

241

'greatness' about it, and so to turn him into a travesty of himself which inevitably smacks a little of operetta, this strikes me as, forgive my plain speaking, odious. I can unfortunately only imagine that our conception of this character differs once again profoundly, as it did over Zerbinetta! Oh Lord, if only I were able to bring home to you completely the essence, the spiritual meaning of these characters. I am not, on the other hand, quite so opinionated as not to understand what you want to avoid: the frightful tenor! Yes, I can understand that. None the less; in Berlin they happen to have Mlle Artôt, but who is to sing the part elsewhere? in Vienna, for instance? And what is more: if you do adopt this irrational idea of giving the part to a woman, you must not, for heaven's sake cut the part *to fit the performer*. An outstanding woman like Artôt will have to get right into the character of this earnest young man, otherwise you'll have let go of the bird in hand for the sake of the ten in the bush.

And finally, whether man or woman—this idea for the end is truly appalling; if you will forgive me, my dear Dr. Strauss, this letter was not written in one of your happiest moments. Consider the lofty atmosphere which we have striven so hard to reach, rising ever higher from the beginning of the Vorspiel to the glorious opera, then the entrance of Bacchus, reaching in the duet almost mystical heights. And now, where the essential coda ought to be over in a trice (as with Jourdain's famous last words), now some rubbish of this kind is to spread itself once more (the emphasis is on *spread*): the major-domo, the fee, the Count and God knows what else! And all this merely to make the part an inch longer! To say nothing of the stylistic absurdity of this demand for something 'lyrical' in the framework, which, after the opera has just reached its greatest lyrical climax, would destroy the distinctive nature of this framework. In fact, of course, the only thing to do is to return from this lyrical climax to characterization, first the comedians, and then a characteristic brief speech, given now, if you insist, to the Composer, though 'twas better coming from Jourdain. Please send me a few words by express, telling me that you understand me; I feel quite faint in mind and body to see us quite so far apart for once!

Yours,

HOFMANNSTHAL

P.S. I believe if you go carefully through the part of the Composer, with all the high spots, moods and shades: well it *is* a star part!

Dear Herr von Hofmannsthal,

Why do you always get so bitterly angry if for once we don't understand each other straight away? You almost act as if I had never understood you! After all, two opinions are possible about the character of Zerbinetta: my suggestions concerning the end of *Ariadne* were, as you know, only quite unconsidered suggestions which you could have thrown into your wastepaper basket without another thought: their only purpose was to induce you to reconsider seriously the closing words of the Composer—and how was I to know that you might not think of something particularly brilliant for the ending if I told you that Artôt was to do it? Well then, you do whatever you like about the ending, only do it soon, please! But as for Artôt—as a young Mozart, say, at the Court of Versailles or among the philistines of the Munich Court, for whom, at the age of sixteen,[1] he composed *Idomeneo*—I am not going to budge on this point, for artistic as well as for practical reasons.

A tenor is impossible, if only because I can't get the primo tenore even for Bacchus because he would cost the management too much, and the part would be too small for him, and the two buffos are already booked for Brighella and Truffaldin.

A leading baritone won't sing the Composer: so what is left to me except the only genre of singer not yet represented in *Ariadne*, my Rofrano, for whom an intelligent female singer is available anywhere: Artôt in Berlin, Sanden in Leipzig, Schoder in Vienna, Krüger in Munich, and a score of others. As a rule she is the most talented woman singer in the theatre, who will look forward to the little cabinet part and will make something of it—so what does it matter if, in the end, the effect is a little more masculine or a little more delicate? Believe me, the *Rosenkavalier* is the only possible casting for the young Composer; just think of all the singers I require for the Vorspiel: the Music Master (bass), the Dancing Master (tenor), an Officer, etc. Surely, we don't want to do something again that'll be wrecked by casting difficulties or bungled by second-rate and third-rate singers. Don't forget that the best singers aren't available for the operas of living German composers, or only in exceptional cases, but are kept for Verdi, Meyerbeer and Flotow! So we stick to Artôt, and it's got to be a delightful part! That's final!

With best regards, yours,

RICHARD STRAUSS

[1] An error: Mozart was twenty-four when he wrote *Idomeneo*.

Dear Herr von Hofmannsthal,

I had two copies of the Vorspiel, which I have now arranged identically in accordance with your notes: one of these I enclose for you herewith. I've been here for the past eight days, quite well again—shall finish the full score of Act II of *Frau ohne Schatten* tomorrow and then I'll get down at once to the Vorspiel. Naturally, I shall have to wait for a good idea, but I hope to manage to complete the whole thing by the end of June so that Direktor Gregor gets the material no later than the beginning of September, and earlier if possible. The Vorspiel can easily be memorized by the singers in a fortnight. The main thing is: rehearsals for the *Ariadne* opera proper must be energetically taken in hand before the vacations. That is why I am asking you urgently to let me have, as soon as possible, the following cuts in the opera:

(a) 2nd dance ensemble after Zerbinetta's aria,

(b) the scene after the first Bacchus song, before his entrance proper (how, by the way, is this now to be effected?), in whichever way you consider it possible.

The other day I let Bacchus sing his Circe song on the stage, visible, and it was most effective: I would only ask you for detailed stage directions on what the three Nymphs and Ariadne are to do.

And then the final conclusion: exit of the comedians and closing words of the Composer!

I am very glad that the piece is at last being done in Vienna on 4th October and I shall do everything in my power to see all goes well.

With best regards, yours

RICHARD STRAUSS

Dear Dr. Strauss,

I can well understand that you can't do anything now until you light upon the right idea for the style of the Vorspiel; still, something admirable and original is sure to come out of this tentative toying with ideas and without exerting oneself one never gets anything worthwhile, nothing that endures beyond the moment. Recently I heard the new opera by K(renek). Horrible stuff, *au fond*, like some witchery which reflects only the repulsive realities of the present, and nothing else. And how uninspired, for lack of real impulse, the whole thing is.

Now for *Ariadne*:

About making an early start with the study of the parts please write to Schalk direct (. . .); he is full of goodwill.

Re cuts: in the quintet which follows Zerbinetta's aria I entered, in Berlin, the following cut from Hülsen's score: from page 136 of the libretto:

> Mir der Schuh,
> Mir der Blick!

down to page 137 including 'Verdammter Zufall, aber man erkennt mich nicht!' I would ask you definitely to retain this cut; then after Bacchus's last stanza (he sings his song in front, right, visible to the audience but hidden from Ariadne by the rushes) cut from: Ariadne: 'Belade nicht zu üppig' (p. 147) to Ariadne: 'Theseus!' (p. 151); then, as Bacchus steps forward out of the rushes, the Nymphs retire, otherwise there is no change. (This excellent cut was suggested by you in Berlin, in conversation.)

It is quite extraordinarily difficult for me to put into the mouth of the Composer the final words which belong to the very fringe of the framework. Coming from Jourdain, the man of prose, that *Monsieur tout-le-monde* who hasn't an idea of what he has been up to and what he has set afoot, the words were organic. But coming from the Composer! For him to complain where the opera has after all succeeded in forging harmony out of the two components, that would be absurd; for him to rejoice would be more absurd still. There is a risk that this will make nonsense of the whole thing. A curse on all revision! I shall try my best to find a possible solution. What if the Major-domo were to speak these final words with an air of smug satisfaction, to the Composer? In prose, like Jourdain?

Yours,

HOFMANNSTHAL

P.S. The part intended for Mlle Artôt is a good round complete character; I am altogether averse to padding it out, as if one could add another muscle to a properly drawn nude. But the following two passages are suitable for lyrical, i.e. musical expansion:

(1) 'Vergisst sich in Äonen ein einziger Augenblick!'
    Duet on this line, capable of endless repetition in various moods.

(2) 'Lass mich verhungern, versteinern, erfrieren in der meinigen!'
could be expanded into a touching, plaintive little aria.

Dear Dr. Strauss,   *Rodaun, 15.5.(1916)*

As I said in my telegram, I am in complete agreement about the end
and with your suggestions on the main point; the cave disappears, both
remain visible as they step down towards the sea and so on.

All well and good, and even does away with an almost insuperable
difficulty (I mean over the Composer's final words). But—it would be
a shameless betrayal of the work and its future for me to concede—out
of pusillanimity—that the human counterpart (Zerbinetta) should be
deprived of some last word!

That would be, allow me to say so, deliberately and openly sacrificing the fundamental idea, the spiritual meaning of the whole work
for the sake of an effective curtain; we might possibly get away with it
on this occasion, but I doubt it, for the critics have the first version of
the libretto at hand. They have had the symbolic meaning of the whole
work dinned into them so often in the past that they will not be such
fools as to miss the opportunity of attacking us with glee for sacrificing
so capriciously the point of the whole piece on which the spectacle was
avowedly based from the outset (that contrast between the heroic ideal
and its denial, or whatever you may wish to call it), for sacrificing it just
for the sake of the 'curtain'.

Even if we now succeed in getting it past with tolerable success, the
time will come when an aging work of art, like an aging face, is left
only with its spirit—and then the fact that for a moment we were
pusillanimous and irresponsible will be taken out on our *Ariadne*.

Where then is the compromise between your legitimate proposal
and my: 'Thus far and no further!' I believe it is here: I will only insist
that the counter-voice, represented by the sole figure of Zerbinetta,
should be heard at the end for a second. Something like this: while
to the rear of the stage the couple step down towards the sea, and
before the orchestra opens the epilogue, Zerbinetta appears in front,
right, in the wings, but visible, waves her fan mockingly over her
shoulder towards the back and proceeds to sing her couplet:

Kommt der neue Gott gegangen, hingegeben sind wir stumm,
Und er küsst uns Stirn und Wangen, etc. . . . . gefangen . . .
Hingegeben sind wir stumm!

If need be let her only begin to sing, sing the first line—then let the
orchestra drown her, so that the rest is to be found only in the libretto;
I am satisfied with her symbolic, mocking presence and exit. I am even
inclined to believe that such spicing of the sentimental with its opposite
is quite in your spirit, like that charming touch of irony in the sentimental little duet at the end of *Rosenkavalier*; in short I can only hint at
a solution, but something of this kind is indispensable. I am sure you
will admit I am right once you have thought the whole thing over, as
you would have to do if you wished to tell the whole story to somebody and wanted to make it plausible to him. Please let me have just
two lines on this point, as soon as possible.

Yours,

HOFMANNSTHAL

Dear Herr von Hofmannsthal,   *Garmisch, 18.5.1916*

Your wish is my command: at Number 326 Zerbinetta shall softly step
from the wings and sing mockingly: 'Kommt der neue Gott gegangen,
hingegeben sind wir stumm—stumm—'; the bassoon hints at the rondo
theme from her aria, and at Number 327 she vanishes, whereupon
Bacchus's 'flower-decorated' (correct?) ship appears on the sea. Does
that suit you?

And do you agree that the three Nymphs should at Number 326
take their leave of Ariadne with a deep bow (from a distance, of course)?
Further, Number 215: 'Bacchus appears on a rock by the sea, invisible
to Ariadne and the three Nymphs': have I your permission to put these
stage directions into the full score?

The draft of the Vorspiel will be ready in three days. The little love
scene between Zerbinetta and the Composer has turned out particularly pretty!

Do write me a libretto again some time with 'a lot of love'! That
always gives me the best ideas: Act I and end of Act III *Rosenkavalier*;
Salome—here's a case in point! By the way: have a look at the enclosed
reviews and wave them under Franckenstein's nose when the opportunity arises. They were in no way influenced by me. They'll show you
better than anything what the general atmosphere in Munich is like.

With best regards, yours

RICHARD STRAUSS

Dear Dr. Strauss,

I am delighted with your letter. When you say that a scene has turned out 'quite pretty', I know it is very beautiful. From the style in which you have written this little love scene I anticipate a special gain for myself (as indeed from the whole Vorspiel); I could imagine that I might draw from it the inspiration for a future libretto, a delicate comedy with a great deal of love; I am glad you are mentioning this just now.

Please enter all you suggest into the score, with my consent. Only one question: must the ship really be seen? Ships on the stage are pretty awful, even the fearless Reinhardt fights shy of them; the dimensions are never right, any going-aboard presumably quite impracticable— in short I would urge you not to postulate the ship as *indispensable*; in Vienna we can then try and see how it might be done!

Sincerely yours,

HOFMANNSTHAL

Dear Herr von Hofmannsthal,

Many thanks for your card: but you've still not sent me the alterations to Ariadne's cave: Numbers 315, 320, 321. Or is the cave to stand as it is? How is the final direction to run if the ship is to be left out? 'As Ariadne and Bacchus, in close embrace, walk towards the sea the Curtain falls!' Or how else?

The scene between Zerbinetta and the Composer has really come out very delightful: it is one of my very best ideas. The whole thing is, in my opinion, rather well organized and climaxed, and should be successful in its own right, without oppressing the opera proper.

As for a new opera, I have the following two things in mind: either an entirely modern, absolutely realistic domestic and character comedy of the kind I have outlined to you before, when you referred me to Bahr—or some amusing piece of love and intrigue, somewhere halfway between Schnitzler's *Liebelei* which, of course, is too sickly and boring, and Hackländer's *Geheimer Agent* or Scribe's *Le Verre d'Eau*— a type of play of intrigue for which I've always had a special predilection.

Say a diplomatic love intrigue in the setting of the Vienna Congress with a genuine highly aristocratic woman spy as the principal character

—the beautiful wife of an ambassador as a traitor for the sake of love, exploited by a secret agent or some such rather amusing subject, and then add to it the famous session of the Congress when Napoleon's return is announced.—You'll probably say: Trash!

But then we musicians are known for our poor taste in aesthetic matters, and besides, if you were to do a thing like that it wouldn't be trash.

Hearty congratulations on Austria's fine success in the South Tyrol: we are delighted!

Kindest regards, yours

RICHARD STRAUSS

30.5.(1916)

My dear Dr. Strauss,

I could not help having a good laugh over your letter. The things you propose to me are to my taste truly horrid and might put one off becoming a librettist for the rest of one's life—I mean put off not just anyone, but me personally. But, you know, it's best not to trouble our heads about it, for the kind of thing you have in mind I could never produce with the best will in the world; even if I did want to do it, I could not bring it off. But—*if it is to be*—I shall hit on something that does appeal to my imagination and holds out the prospect of giving me a certain amount of pleasure in the actual execution (possibly along the lines you have now adopted for the Vorspiel); anything conceived in this way is sure to have inherent qualities which will engage your powers in a fresh and unusual manner—that is how it has been every time hitherto, has it not?—and that, after all, is the best we can expect of each other.

When you write to me about a given scene, like now about the one between Zerbinetta and the Composer, that is worth more to me than any actual words of praise from you (however delighted I often am with these). You must guide me, I must guide you: perhaps in this way we shall one day reach wholly new and unexplored regions. You have every reason to be grateful to me for bringing you (as now once again with *Die Frau ohne Schatten*) that element which is sure to bewilder people and to provoke a certain amount of antagonism, for you have already too many followers, you are already all too obviously the hero of the day, all too universally accepted. By all means get angry with me and keep harping for a while on this 'incomprehensibility', it is a mortgage to be redeemed by the next generation, just like that which appears problematical in *Ariadne*, that which today still provokes people to snort their sullen What then? and What for?

The final direction: A(riadne) and B(acchus) in close embrace etc. is quite correct.

I would leave the references to the cave as they are; better a slight incongruity like this than verses tacked on as an after-thought. You must mark the exact moment for the change of scene, for the chandeliers to disappear, for the cave to vanish, and so on.

I shall shortly go to Warsaw and may *possibly* be able to come back via Berlin and Munich. There about July 10th. If this materializes, could you perhaps play the new things to me then? This might kindle my imagination. Please reply to this last question at once on a postcard.

Yours,

HOFMANNSTHAL

Garmisch, 5.6.16

My dear Herr von Hofmannsthal,

You may laugh: but I know only too well what I want. When you've heard the new Vorspiel, which will be ready in the full score by about the 20th June (I'm therefore expecting you definitely some time before 10th July, here in Garmisch: a guest room's all ready and we hope you'll stop with us for a few days at least) you'll understand what I mean and will realize that I have a definite talent for operetta. And since my tragic vein is more or less exhausted, and since tragedy in the theatre, after this war, strikes me at present as something rather idiotic and childish, I should like to apply this irrepressible talent of mine— after all, I'm the only composer nowadays with some real humour and a sense of fun and a marked gift for parody. Indeed, I feel downright called upon to become the Offenbach of the 20th century, and you will and must be my poet. Offenbach's *Helena* and *Orpheus* have reduced the ridiculousness of 'grand opéra' *ad absurdum*. What I have in mind with my impromptu suggestions, which you resent so much, is a political-satirical parody of the most trenchant kind. Why shouldn't you be able to write that? Altogether you write far too little: put your Pegasus in tight harness for once. You'll see how the beast can run. Our road starts from *Rosenkavalier*: its success is evidence enough, and it is also this genre (sentimentality and parody are the sensations to which my talent responds most forcefully and productively) that I happen to be keenest on.

What about the magnificent types that have emerged from this war: the profiteer as a Maecenas, the spy, the diplomat, Prussian and Austrian each against the other and yet each with the other—surely they'd make a splendid comedy and you've got the talent for it: this is proved by your *Rosenkavalier* and your *Cristina*. We'll talk about this at length in July: maybe you'll bring some subject with you from your Warsaw trip. Why don't you study the Jewish-Galician interpreter and middleman on the spot: he, too, is a magnificent figure. Looking forward to seeing you! *Bon voyage*, and take care of your health. Best regards, yours,

RICHARD STRAUSS

What *Rosenkavalier* lacks in compactness you have learned in the meantime (as shown by the superb brevity and balanced structure of *Fr.o.Sch.*) and what it lacks in lightness I have learned in *Ariadne*.

Long live the political-satirical-parodistic operetta!

Rodaun, 11.6.(1916). Whit Sunday

(Not sent)

Dear Dr. Strauss,

All you tell me interests me greatly. We shall see whether anything can be done along this line. In any case I am pleased, for it is along the road (only further along) which I intended to take at an earlier stage, in *Rosenkavalier*. At that time you wholly failed at certain points to enter into my ideas and treated quite a few things in the wrong style altogether—a fact that grieved me much at the time but which I always kept to myself. (For it is not only over Zerbinetta that we have been at cross purposes, but on many other occasions, and I am afraid there are some again even in the new opera; I am referring to the figure of the Nurse, but don't let it worry you, it will not affect the overall impression.) Take for instance *Rosenkavalier*, Act II, the burlesque chorus of the Faninal servants

> G'stochen ist einer? Wer?
> Der dort? Der fremde Herr?
> Welcher? Der Bräutigam?

was written only to be rattled off in burlesque fashion, i.e. in the transparent Offenbach style; what you did was to smother it with *heavy*

251

music and so to destroy utterly the purpose of the words, the deliberate pastiche of an operetta. The fun of this passage has simply ceased to exist, the very thing a man like Offenbach would have brought out as a point charged with humour as a joke.

And similarly at the end of Act I. Out of the footmen who turn up one after the other, uttering their brief messages with a pronounced Bohemian accent, you have made a sort of brief chorus of huntsmen, which always strikes one as quite terrible at this juncture.

The exit of the Baron in Act III offends, I feel, no less gravely against the style of the whole work. Forgive me for speaking out like this; it is your letter which drives me to it with its desire to rush into something novel, something which most probably I may not have the talent to solve *properly* (so that the solution can last and is not dross momentarily mistaken for gold), but which, quite likely, you for your part would lack the determination to carry through in a consistent and clear-cut style.

In one work you did manifest the determination to achieve this distinct style with complete consistency: it was the incidental music for *Le Bourgeois* and that is why I am so fond of this work of yours.

Once again please forgive me: I am somewhat under the shadow of events on the Eastern front and am writing for this reason perhaps more severely and coolly than one would normally write to an artist with whom one is on friendly terms.

I should prefer not to enlarge upon your remark that I am working too little (if only because the upshot would be that at any rate I ought to work more for myself and ought to stop writing for music). Nor can you know what I am working on, how far I have got with my big novel and so on. Even Reinhardt, if he were free to speak of it, could astonish you by an enumeration of plans, finished acts, etc., which he knows. It is only 'publishing' that interests me less and less.

Incidentally, in strict confidence: for the past six weeks Reinhardt has been performing every night a Molière piece, *Die Lästigen*, which contained, apart from the title, not a line of Molière, but every word from first to last was by your devoted librettist, without one peep from the critics. But please keep this to yourself, like a good friend, and do not spoil my joke which I may perhaps repeat again.

Now something very unpleasant, especially to me, for I had looked forward to hearing the Vorspiel and promise myself a lot from it, perhaps even a hint for another joint work; but I have just been informed that I shall have to return from Warsaw (via Berlin) to Austria. I may be able, I hope, to go to Aussee afterwards, but I absolutely cannot make myself apply at this point again to *three* different authorities for permission to cross the frontier for private reasons; so please see to it that you can get to Salzburg. I can't help it, it is terribly disappointing to me too; if there were to be a chance, I would still come to Garmisch, but I am not hopeful.

Yours,

HOFMANNSTHAL

Warsaw, Jerzolymska U 70. Friday, 7th July (1916)

Dear Dr. Strauss,

What you wrote to me about the Vorspiel and your ideas and hopes arising out of it was very good and kind. But I was too much under the cloud of events to be able to reply. I wrote to you once, early in June,[1] but the letter was sullen and ill-inspired (not least as regards the two of us), so that in the end I threw it away. The position now is that I shall probably be in Berlin on Tuesday or, at the latest, on Wednesday of next week (July 11th, 12th) and hope to obtain an official permit which enables me to travel home via Munich. In that case it would give me great pleasure to come to Garmisch for twenty-four hours (around the 15th).

Please wire me to the Adlon whether this suits you, and word your telegram in such a manner that I can use it as evidence ('purpose of journey'), something like this: 'Your presence urgently required for final conference . . . or so . . . R. Strauss.'

With best wishes, yours,

HOFMANNSTHAL

P.S. Fixed all the décor in Vienna with Gregor-Wymetal before I left and will try to see Kaufmann in Berlin. Discussed various things concerning *Ariadne* and *Rosenkavalier* with the rising new Teatr polski (Kapellmeister Birnbaum), of which more when we meet.

Hotel Adlon, Berlin W. Wednesday (12th July, 1916)

My dear Dr. Strauss,

Many thanks for your telegram. I hope to receive tomorrow the official telegraphic permission to make my return journey via Munich

[1] The letter referred to is that dated 11.6.(1916) which was not posted.

and have booked a sleeper for Friday night. That means I shall be in Munich on Saturday morning and shall come to you (depending on certain circumstances) either on Saturday afternoon, in which case I could stay until Sunday towards the evening, or on Sunday morning until Sunday afternoon. (The former is more likely.) I have been to see Oertel and have discussed with him what was necessary, but we two will still have to settle a number of points concerning the definitive text of *Ariadne*. I shall see Kaufmann tomorrow.

I am looking forward to a few hours far from the war in your good company, and especially to the Vorspiel.

Very sincerely yours,

HOFMANNSTHAL

Garmisch, 18.7.(1916)

My dear Friend and Poet,

Thank you again for your pleasant visit: it was most refreshing and enjoyable for me. I hope we shall meet again soon—you with the new Singspiel in your case. Today I have a request again: I am as determined as ever to treat the whole passage of the Empress, after she has caught sight of her petrified husband until her outcry 'Ich kann nicht', as a spoken passage.

Only I don't want to lose, as a tune, that beautiful passage you wrote for me additionally—and I have now found a very good place where I can fit it in earlier. The point is that I have composed the earlier words of the Empress (in her scene with the Nurse):

Was er leidet,
will ich leiden,
ich bin in ihm,
er ist in mir!
Wir sind eins!
Ich will zu ihm!

in an entirely similar manner of heroic, ecstatic resolution (E flat major) to the later passage for which you supplied the words additionally. Now the former passage, unfortunately, is very short and is over so quickly that it could do with considerable expansion: just before there is therefore a wonderful opportunity for inserting the great, beautiful melody of 'mit dir sterben, auf, wach auf'. You would merely have to be good enough to adjust it to the slightly altered situation by re-fashioning it again.

The pattern is as follows:

> Hör mich rufen,
> auf, wach auf,   (other words!)
> an den Stufen,   (vor den Toren)
> auf, wach auf.
> Vor dem Grabe,
> vor dem Throne,
> auf, wach auf,
> dass mein Sterben,
> auf, wach auf,
> mich belohne,
> zu dir dringe,   (strömend Leben)
> Tod bezwinge—   (ganz gegeben)

Now follows:

> Was er leidet,
> will ich leiden,
> ich bin in ihm,
> er ist in mir!
> Wir sind eins!
> Ich will zu ihm!

Earlier the Empress sings: 'Mein Herr und Gebieter! Sie halten Gericht über ihn um meinetwillen, was ihn bindet, bindet mich!'

Here is where the interpolation would come. Would you be good enough to reshape the bits in brackets above so they go with the conclusion? Many thanks in advance and the best of luck for the 'operetta'!

With best regards, likewise from my wife who was also delighted to have you visit us, to yourself and your wife (regards also from Bubi), yours ever sincerely and gratefully,

RICHARD STRAUSS

I have today written to Direktor Gregor along the lines agreed between us. How is the later passage, the one that's now only to be spoken, to run in the new version? Is:

> Mit dir sterben,
> auf, wach auf!
> Aug' in Aug',

Mund an Mund
mit dir vereint
lass mich sterben!

to stand, or do you want to alter this too?

My dear Dr. Strauss,

Thank you most cordially for your kind good letter which harmoniously rounds off my days in Munich and Garmisch. Tell your wife
how grateful I am for her hospitality and for her constant kindness
towards me. Warmest greetings to Bubi.

I found Bahr in an unbuttoned and pleasant mood, full of ideas, and
since it entered his head to tell me the scenario of a very pretty comedy
(after the charming *Novelle* by Goethe *Der ehrliche Prokurator*), it was
easy to bring the conversation round to your wishes and intentions in
the field of the Singspiel. The result is that, if he can think of anything
he will, on the spur of the moment and without any obligation, submit
to you a scenario or a plot. He spoke very intelligently of you, of that
mixture of the hearty, Bavarian aspect of your nature with a subtle,
witty mind and in this connection described your music for the *Bourgeois*
as the finest thing you had done; a commendation with which, less
exclusively formulated, I would agree. Please, dear Dr. Strauss, do not
rashly waste these pieces of music; I am sure I shall succeed in inventing
a second delicate action for this comedy (centred on the daughter)
which lends itself to music, to replace that conventional subsidiary plot.
I will make the whole thing into a genuine, half fantastic, half realistic
Singspiel, with a burlesque ceremony at the end where Jourdain as
Pasha finally launches out on the pond in a Turkish carnival bark while
the lovers remain behind in the moonlight—just the thing for Reinhardt.

The music for the Vorspiel is as enchanting in recollection as anything could be; like fireworks in a beautiful park, one enchanted, all too
fleeting summer night. What remains in my ear of the scenes from the
third act (of *Die Frau ohne Schatten*)·(with the exception of the first
scene), leaves me, I cannot help it, somewhat oppressed and gloomy,
my dear Dr. Strauss. Such an unexpected reaction on my part, such
a feeling of depression, exactly what one experiences oneself when
a piece of work has not quite come off, such a feeling cannot, I am sure,

be mistaken. It is a great relief to me to know that you intend to reduce the last part of this grave, sombre work to *secco* recitative! Even so: are we really to have yet another spinning out of the original passage? More and more! Must that be? My dear Dr. Strauss! However grand and beautiful this melody in E flat major is sure to be, do think about it twice! Remember our talks; remember the conversation we had in the Park at Versailles, when you coined that striking simile of the magnifying cow's eye!

I enclose the new text. But do remember: once a melody seeks to dominate the scene, and the scene dominates the act, instead of the other way about, that is invariably the beginning of the end. Forgive me, for I do not believe there is anyone—perhaps not even yourself— who means so well as I do by you, by your work and by its eventual fate.

Yours,

HOFMANNSTHAL

Blindly to tear apart, as you suggest, a perfectly homogeneous verse sequence:

> Was ihn bindet,
> bindet mich.
> Was er leidet,
> will ich leiden.

and to cram into it fourteen lines is out of the question. So I suggest something like the following:

(passionately turning to her invisible husband:)

> Mein Herr und Gebieter!
> Sie halten Gericht
> über ihn
> um meinetwillen!
> Was Dich bindet,
> binde mich,
> was Du leidest,   } Both or none!
> will ich leiden!
> Hör mich weinen
> Du, o Du!
> Auf den Steinen
> Du, o Du!

Die Verstockte,
die Erstarrte
Du, o Du!
Fühl mich leben,
Dir mich geben,
Du, o Du!
Zu Dir dringen,
Tod bezwingen.
Du, o Du!

        Follows transition to highest pitch!
Or again: Was Dich bindet, binde mich, was Du leidest, will ich leiden!

Ich bin in Dir,
Du bist in mir,
Wir sind eins,
Ich will zu Dir!

Garmisch, 28.7.16

Dear Herr von Hofmannsthal,

Many thanks for your kind letter and your admonitions which shall fall on fertile soil. I entirely share your opinion that the Vorspiel to *Ariadne* marks the peculiar new road which we must follow, and my own inclination is for realistic comedy with really interesting people—either like *Rosenkavalier* with its splendid Marschallin, or with a burlesque, satirical content, something in the manner of Offenbach's parodies. But to change the style in *Frau ohne Schatten*, a style that pleases you and at which we must both aim—that's quite impossible. This isn't a case of a little more or less music or text; the trouble is the subject itself with its romanticism and its symbols. Characters like the Emperor and Empress, and also the Nurse, can't be filled with red corpuscles in the same way as a Marschallin, an Octavian, or an Ochs. No matter how I rack my brain—and I'm toiling really hard, sifting and sifting—my heart's only half in it, and once the head has to do the major part of the work you get a breath of academic chill (what my wife very rightly calls 'note-spinning') which no bellows can ever kindle into a real fire. Well, I have now sketched out the whole end of the opera (the quartet and the choruses) and it's got verve and a great upward sweep—but my wife finds it cold and misses the heart-touching flame-kindling melodic texture of the *Rosenkavalier* trio. I'm willing to believe her, and I keep probing and searching—but believe me:

> Schatten zu werfen
> beide erwählt etc.

does not go to music like:

> Hab mir's gelobt
> ihn lieb zu haben.

I shall make every effort to shape Act III in line with your intentions, but let's make up our minds that *Frau ohne Schatten* shall be the last romantic opera. I hope you'll very soon have a fine, happy idea that'll help me definitely to set out on the new road.

Of course I'll keep the music to the *Bourgeois G.* for Reinhardt! Here's to new deeds! Have a good holiday!

Best regards, also from my wife and Bubi to you and your wife, yours very sincerely,

RICHARD STRAUSS

I've bought the 'Salome' at Böhler's![1] In Munich they are doing *Salome* and *Rosenkavalier* on 10th and 12th August in honour of Mme Schoder. So I shall owe it to this Viennese singer alone if now and again a work of mine is allowed to be performed in my native city. It's a bit thick.

Any present from H. Bahr I shall, needless to say, accept with due gratitude and examine sympathetically. But a new genuine Hofmannsthal would be even more welcome!

1.8.(1916)

Dear Dr. Strauss,

Were I not acquainted with your music for the first two acts, your letter would be bound to cause me anxiety. As it is, I remember them most clearly as a highly successful piece of work, beautiful beyond all expectation, a real solution of the problem of style which brings all the different elements into synthesis. You blend there so happily the need for melody with characterization and carry the style you originated in *Rosenkavalier* still further with such assurance that I cannot be anxious, only astonished when I discover from your good and frank letter that

[1] The large painting of Salome (Catalan school, fifteenth century) which later hung in Strauss's study at his home in Vienna (Jacquingasse 10).

it is just while working on the third act (which to my mind meets the demands of music best) that this slight depression, which even the mature artist does not escape, has come over you—this touch of discouragement and despondency—grieves me though it is not in my power to supply a remedy. Let me say just one thing, my dear Dr. Strauss: the first two acts have already done the vital part of the job. The wealth of content in these two acts, their compelling human appeal, the tension steadily rising to the sombre quartet or septet at the end, the wonderful music you have given even to a figure which, as you say, makes no great appeal to you (I mean the Emperor)—all this creates, in its impact on the audience, quite a definite situation at the end of the second act. In the third act it is the spiritual element which offers the solution, that soaring into the regions of light and harmony, the succession of fairy-tale pictures, the intervention of the Children's voices, all these varied elements combined will not fail to engage the public, even supposing the music were to fall off (and I am sure it will not). Do not on any account let yourself be daunted, either by your own doubts (how often have I known it to happen that your own, your most delicate and beautiful inspirations have appeared to you 'not good enough'), or even by the possibly rash, all-too-spontaneous verdict of your wife (important though that always is to me, too).

A direct comparison between what still remains to be done and what has already been successfully accomplished, in this case with the trio in *Rosenkavalier*, is invariably dangerous. There the situation is a sentimental one, here it is heroic and spiritual, akin to the atmosphere of *Fidelio* or *The Magic Flute*. One lesson, it would seem, I shall have to draw from what you say, namely that it is not the situation itself so much which compellingly operates upon the composer's imagination, but the actual wording of the libretto. (For the future it is quite easy to act on this, but for the moment nothing can be done.) A passage like:

Schatten zu werfen ‖ beide erwählt

you could mentally formulate more tritely, but closer to the heart, like this:

Selig zu werden ‖ beide vermählt

Perhaps you respond to this better. What you say is very severe: in the first act not a single passage was 'chilly'; but 'chilly' I did consider *Joseph* and equally the Hymns which you played to me once in Berlin; neither verve nor upward sweep can get me over that. How you did find, and do find, your melodies (like that trio in *Rosenkavalier*) I have no idea . . ., but do please write to me again soon, perhaps I can help after all. If the situation in itself were to throw up a happy tune, well then I shall have to alter a passage in the text, even if it is difficult.

Very sincerely yours,

HOFMANNSTHAL

(*early August 1916*)[1]

Dear Dr. Strauss,

Should like to know what grounds there could be for 'consternation'! W(ymetal)[2] is the type who perpetually raises futile objections, (. . .); they are all out to make trouble for others, to push themselves forward and so on. Please stick to it firmly that some stage device which envelops (isolates) the two main characters at the end of the trio is indispensable, and that is that!

Sincerely yours,

HOFMANNSTHAL

Bad Aussee, 13.8.(*1916*)

Dear Dr. Strauss,

How are you and your work? Recently I read through the whole of Act III and it left me with quite a satisfactory impression; I hope all will be well. From time to time I look through the libretti of *Figaro, Così Fan Tutte* etc., I hope with real profit. I quite understand why the latter never had any success: there is hardly a single sentence in the whole piece that can be taken seriously; all is irony, deception, lies, the kind of thing the music cannot (except rarely) express and the public cannot stand.

If Wymetal were to write to me about the final scene in *Ariadne* I shall refer him to you, or else we might get *ordre-contreordre-désordre*. It is after all merely a question of arranging some stage effect in the duet

[1] The following lines were written in the margin of a letter from Direktor Hans Gregor to R. Strauss which Strauss sent to H. for information and which H. now returned to Strauss.

[2] Erich von Wymetal, the producer of *Ariadne*, had written to Gregor that he felt consternation after a conversation with Hofmannsthal.

which emphasizes that particular moment and at the same time isolates B(acchus) and A(riadne).

Please insist on this.

Yours,

HOFMANNSTHAL

Garmisch (early September 1916)

Dear Herr von Hofmannsthal,

The enclosed letter will interest you. Your kind card and letter received with thanks. Act III is now finished: but, thanks to our highly beneficial conversation, I have become so uncertain that I no longer know what's successful and what's bad. And that's a good thing, for at my age one gets all too easily into the rut of mere routine and that is the death of true art. Your *cri-de-cœur* against Wagnerian 'note-spinning' has deeply touched my heart and has thrust open a door to an entirely new landscape where, guided by *Ariadne* and in particular the new Vorspiel, I hope to move forward wholly into the realm of un-Wagnerian emotional and human comic opera. I now see my way clearly before me and am grateful to you for opening my eyes—but now you go ahead and make me the necessary libretti à la *Domino Noir*, *Maurer und Schlosser*, *Wildschütz*, *Zar und Zimmermann*, *La Part du Diable* à la Offenbach—but peopled by human beings à la Hofmannsthal instead of puppets. An amusing, interesting plot, with dialogue, arias, duets, ensembles, or what you will, woven by real composable human beings à la Marschallin, Ochs, Barak. In any form you like! I promise you that I have now definitely stripped off the Wagnerian musical armour.

See you in Vienna on 26th September!

Best regards, yours,

RICHARD STRAUSS

Aussee, 16.9.(1916)

My dear Dr. Strauss,

Yes, that was a very good letter of yours—I have just re-read it once again with great pleasure. It is good to find a man like you determined not to stand still and get stuck in a rut, but to change and forge ahead, and it is good to know that you and I can occasionally instruct one another in a world where everyone rushes madly on, stupid, stubborn and opinionated, uninstructed and without discipline.

Your letter offers much food for reflection, and I have reflected, but the censorship does not care for long letters and anyway we shall see each other reasonably soon. When we do meet let us see to it that we can make it a calm, dispassionate conversation and help each other on. A true collaboration between two mature men would be something most rare, ours is as yet only a shadow of what it might be, but we both have good will, seriousness and consistency, and that is more than the God-forsaken 'talent' with which every lout is nowadays equipped. And I am of course delighted that you are holding on to me so faithfully, it warms my heart and ties me in turn to you; so does every revelation of a new aspect of your talent like this light and spirited vein which may develop into a 'third manner' and perhaps produce works of lasting value in a yet almost unknown genre.

Enough; I shall do what I can to fulfil your wishes. You will be amused to learn that I have the libretti of *Le Domino Noir, Der Wild-schütz, La Part du Diable* and others by me here and study them occasionally in bed at night. I am beginning to discover a lot, but also many new difficulties, some of which you will be able to dispose of by a good talk and by examples on the piano.

But there is one thing I am sure you will understand: I cannot tackle a new work for you until one of my own comedies, which has not ceased to occupy me since *Cristina* and *Rosenkavalier*, is out and on the stage. This summer my hopes were not fulfilled, but you do not know and cannot judge how much I expect of myself and how hard I work and will work when I am sure of my goal.

In the past two weeks I was fortunate in being able to resume work on the fairy-tale *Die Frau ohne Schatten* successfully after an interval of two years. Every day is precious, it will be painful to break off on the 29th to go to Vienna, but I look forward to seeing you and *Ariadne* of whom I am very fond.

Sincerely yours,

HOFMANNSTHAL

(*October 1916*)

My dear Dr. Strauss,

I know you willingly trust me in matters of art, so please do in the present instance: my own feeling grows from rehearsal to rehearsal, and is wholly confirmed by the judgement of people of taste, that scant justice is being done, either by the music or on the stage, to the gay figures at the end—they are being dropped—so that one has, unfortunately, a sense of being left in mid-air. The music cannot be changed, but the production on the stage can, and you must settle it by a word with W(ymetal), as your (and my) express wish, that *Zerbinetta* (coming up the staircase) *must be accompanied by her companions* and they must all stand there for a moment, receiving the spot light. Please oblige me over this; it looks unimportant, but is not.

Are we not to see each other again? Please telephone! It is a pity you have booked yourself for every luncheon. Why don't you come tomorrow morning in Hellmann's car?

Yours,

HOFMANNSTHAL

Garmisch, 9th Nov. 1916

Dear Herr von Hofmannsthal,

Have a look please at the essay '*Ein antiker Schwindler*' in the enclosed *Scherz*. Perhaps you could use the man who sets fire to himself for our comedy. What's happening about it? Is it already being born? I'm looking forward to it immensely. *Ariadne* in Berlin was quite a fine performance,[1] but not a real success. The Vorspiel wasn't properly understood at all. Maybe the trouble was that they didn't have two such brilliant voices for the little love duet as Kurz and Lehmann. Count Hülsen, however, had made every effort and given much loving care to both acting and décor. Perhaps you could write him a few pleasant lines to thank him on your part. It'll encourage him to keep the delicate piece above water, as far as is in his power, and to make amends on his part for the grave wrong done to it by the stupid, uncomprehending Berlin press—with the exception of good old Bie and Wilhelm Klatte. *Ariadne* comes to Dresden at the beginning of December—couldn't you come over for the occasion? Then follows Breslau, Leipzig, Düsseldorf.

Bruno Walter, whom I happened to meet on the train the other day and with whom I had a long talk and a conditional reconciliation (i.e. to be revoked if conditions in Munich still do not improve), wants to stage *Ariadne* in the autumn of 1917.

[1] The Berlin première of the new version took place on 1st November 1916.

264

I am now getting down to scoring Act III of *Frau o. Sch.* From 26th Nov. till about 9th December I shall be back in Berlin. When are you coming there? I should like to see you again soon!

Best regards, yours

RICHARD STRAUSS

Kind regards also to your wife and children, also from my wife.

1917

Garmisch, 7.2.17

My dear Friend,

I have just concluded a magnificent triumphal progress with your works: first *Rosenkavalier* at the Hague and in Amsterdam with the Dresden crowd and Knüpfer; full houses at unheard-of prices; a Strauss Week in Mannheim with *Salome*, *Rosenkavalier* and *Ariadne*, staged very prettily and wittily by Dr. Hagemann, the Vorspiel botched completely at the most heavy-footed pace by F., otherwise a very gifted conductor, and eventually put right by me for Switzerland in three rehearsals: it's odd how difficult it is even for the most gifted people to get into a new style.—Finally *Ariadne* and *Elektra* in Switzerland, with a downright triumphal success. *Elektra* in particular has knocked the honest Swiss all of a heap. In spite of an orchestra of only sixty men (or maybe the drama achieved its profoundly shattering effect just because of it) Kessler declared it to have been the finest performance he had ever heard. You would have enjoyed it too! Schoder was particularly outstanding, cutting a splendid figure also as the Composer; Mildenburg moving as always: Jeritza and Oestvig as Ariadne and Bacchus positively ideal. Very charming and piquant the Mannheim Zerbinetta Mlle Eden. A pity one can't tour the whole of Germany with such performances, or at least all the smaller towns. How much misunderstanding could be cleared up!

I am here for ten days; on 19th February I am leaving for Scandinavia and shall try there, and also discuss with Kessler, if one couldn't make a similar Thespian journey there in May as in Switzerland. In Switzerland I received the most pleasing greetings from abroad: for instance from Romain Rolland who was prevented only by an indisposition from coming to Berne, from the beautiful Princess Piccolomini at St. Moritz, from Ottone Schanzer in Rome—it's refreshing to know that there are a few human beings also beyond the frontier. At the Swiss performances there were plenty of Frenchmen and Russians! Pray God the world will come to its senses again. I shall be in Berlin (Adlon) from 5th March to 7th April. Shall we meet there?

How is the new Jourdain doing? I'd like to have him for the summer (from June onwards).

And the new Lukian? Are you well and working hard?

I wish I were sitting again over the full score of our Act III!

Goodbye for now and best regards to yourself and your family from my wife and me. Always very sincerely yours,

RICHARD STRAUSS

Garmisch, 10.4.17

My dear Friend,

Delighted to hear you are quite well again and, I hope, full of creative energy and vigour. With Edm(und) R(einhardt) everything's settled: the première is on 1st April 1918.[1] The piece is then to run for two months. The conductor of the Deutsches Theater was present at the conversation and is fully informed. Edm. R. extremely generous, so I think you can get down to your work without any worries. I am meanwhile gradually re-training my charger to a Turkish trot; I've also got old Lully handy, but there's hardly anything in him that's any use, except a little distilled mustiness as a stimulant, like Schiller's apples! I'm awaiting some good things from you soon and remain, with best regards to yourself and your family, sincerely yours

RICHARD STRAUSS

Garmisch, 11th May 1917

My dear Friend,

Beg to report that the full score of Act III is approaching completion. I am now leaving for Switzerland, but I shall be back again at the beginning of June when I should very much like to work on *Bürger als Edelmann*. I'm tackling the Turkish comedy straight away, but should be glad if I could get your further manuscripts fairly soon.

[1] The first performance of *Der Bürger als Edelmann* at the Deutsches Theater in Berlin was on 9 April 1918.

How are you otherwise? Did you get the etching by Orlik which I had Fürstner send to you in April? We are quite well, except that my Bubi will probably have to join the army soon.

With kind regards from us to you all, yours very sincerely,

RICHARD STRAUSS

Address: till 29th May, Zürich, Mythenstr. 24.
30th May to 4th June, Darmstadt (*Rosenkavalier*), Hotel Traube.
From 5th June back in Garmisch.
Try and read Plautus's comedies in Reinhold Lenz's adaptation. They contain some good types.

Rodaun, 19.5.(1917)

(Postcard)

Received yesterday your kind note from Garmisch of the 11th. Realize with horror that I have not thanked you for the etching. I think it is excellent on the whole, especially the part round the eyes; only I do miss the massive element (as already in the oil painting).

Since April 20 I have been engaged on the adaptation of the *Bourgeois*. It makes a great deal of laborious and minute work and, despite anonymity, will earn *me* nothing but unpleasantness and insinuations, but it will be a remarkable, well constructed burlesque comedy. In Act II there will be a certain amount, in Act III quite a lot to do, especially the *Cérémonie turque*. I hope to send you all three acts by June 10th or 15th. Please let me have your suggestions for the financial arrangements which we have failed to discuss so far.

Best wishes,

HOFMANNSTHAL

Rodaun, 15.6.(1917)

Dear Dr. Strauss,

I wrote you a postcard some while ago to the Zürich address you gave me, but perhaps it did not reach you. By now I assume you are back in Garmisch.

Since the end of April I have been at work on the adaptation of the *Bourgeois*, and now I am pretty well done with it. It was quite a lot of work and gave me some trouble, but I enjoyed it. I believe that, without

267

any harm being done to the basic structure, it has become enchanting, richer, more glowing than the original play where the author's genius comes out chiefly in the central character, while a lot of the rest gives the impression of having been knocked together in a hurry and so to speak with the left hand. The new version will, I hope, come across the footlights as something full of life and captivating. To know this is, however, the only reward I shall have; given the gross want of perception among critics, there is nothing more to be expected and a decent anonymity is all that is left to me.

But now I shall have to set out immediately, and for an indefinite period, for Prague where I have—business of another kind, and I find it impossible to dictate the whole three acts of the comedy onto the typewriter before I leave. The first act, moreover, is so arranged that all the music you have written for it is preserved and you have nothing more to do; in the second act there will be a certain amount, in the third quite a lot for you to do. In addition to the burlesque 'Ceremony' we shall want a delicate melodrama for Jourdain and some sylphs or spirits, and at the end the other melodrama in which seriousness and jest, sentiment and caricature are mingled. I have made a fair copy of the second half of Act II which includes the dinner music (unaltered) followed by a lively informal dance (I have here put down 'Courante' which you will have to compose). (. . .) If you telegraph to my wife, she will send you the typed MS. of Act II, second part.

Best wishes to you and your family,

HOFMANNSTHAL

Garmisch, 28.6.17

Dear Herr von Hofmannsthal,

Many thanks for your letter of the 15th. I've received the manuscript of Act II and read it with much pleasure. What does Act III bring? This ought to be very vigorous since I don't expect Act II, pretty though it is, to have an over-great success with the audience.

As far as our contract is concerned I should much prefer to discuss the matter with you in person: writing about these things is always rather troublesome and invidious. Are you in such a hurry? After all, we've always reached the most amicable agreement orally. (. . .)

Will you be at Aussee in the summer?

I may come to Salzburg at the beginning of August, for the Mozart Festival—in that case could we meet either there or at Ischl?

Have you read Goethe's draft of *Iphigenie in Delphi*? Wouldn't that attract you?

Do read Reinhold Lenz's adaptations of Plautus's comedies in the second volume of his Works. They contain some splendid characters: the wenchers! the 'little father' who idolizes his son to the point of idiocy—very amusing situations which might perhaps suggest to you an idea or two for our 'Roman comedy'.

The full score of *Frau ohne Schatten* is finished.

With kind regards and best wishes for a productive and rich summer, yours very sincerely,

RICHARD STRAUSS

What about the fairy-tale of *Frau ohne Schatten*?

My dear Dr. Strauss,

Rodaun, 30.6.(1917)

In spite of your nice letter—this is not the way to set about it, and even the conversation during the summer is not by any means to be counted on, since the little time I am left with must absolutely belong to me and to my work, including the fairy-tale. As for your doubts concerning the effect on the public, you cannot form any sort of judgement until you have the full sequence of scenes for both acts. The play possesses no more and no less than a Molière comedy can possess, that is the chance of making a fine and powerful impression given a very able comic actor (that means on Reinhardt's stage). I will not assume for a minute you would ever dream of having this play ham-acted in other German theatres, of course not. There it would obviously be a complete flop; that is an experiment we have already made, after all.

Please reply by return; I should very much like to have this straight.

Sincerely yours,

(. . .)

HOFMANNSTHAL

Dear Herr von Hofmannsthal,

Garmisch, 1st July 1917

May I send you a few observations on Jourdain, concerning the musical exploitation?

Jourdain's little melodrama, now at the end of Act II, is very well placed. However, each act ought to be introduced by music and effectively concluded with music. Wouldn't it be possible to alter Molière's rather weak ending of Act I in such a way that Nicoline, before being chased out, hears only part of the arrangements between Dorante and Jourdain, and to leave the rest, relating to the delights of the imminent dinner and Dorimène's company, to be fitted into a little melodrama while the two men are bowing each other out of the door? I would remind you of the charming scene between Falstaff and Ford in Verdi's opera. I am enclosing a little draft.[1]

Surely the young lovers, Cleonte and Lucile, appear in Act III? A little prelude to Act III might be devoted to them.

Does your conclusion of Act III remain similar to Molière's? I find Molière's original very amusing, especially Jourdain's remark: 'Is it to hoodwink her?' Does the little dance remain at the end, while the notary is being sent for? For this I would make the following recommendation: From Act I we have two female voices (soprano and contralto), the Mufti is a baritone, so we only need a small tenor part to make a quartet which at the end would sing a pretty wedding madrigal (in the manner of the earlier Italians) while the ballet people—available from the dance of the tailors and the scullions—could perform an entertaining *Pas de deux* as a *Pas à trois*, paying homage to the bridal couple. Such a ballet, with singing, would make a delightful conclusion and I feel sure that you'll hit on something pretty for it. Since we've already got the singers and the ballet we must not, in my opinion, omit to use them for a favourable final effect—the more so as the Turkish comedy, being pure burlesque, is not very profitable for the musician nor very endearing to the ear of the listener. Do please think over my humble suggestions! With kindest regards, yours

RICHARD STRAUSS

Rodaun, 5th July, 1917

Dear Dr. Strauss,

Suggestions of yours, like those contained in your letter of July 1st, which reached me today, on the 5th, are always interesting and stimulating, but this time they have come too late since, with a great deal of trouble and thought, I have happily, as I believe, and attractively rounded off the whole thing and brought it to an end. There is no point in your reading up your Molière since as a result of recasting or at

[1] Not extant.

270

least rearrangement almost everything is changed and you can have no idea whatever what the whole thing looks like until, I hope within a fortnight, you have it in your hands.

To your letter only this: the suggestions for the end of Act I are not relevant, since the act does not end with Nicoline at all, but with quite a different scene, and that without music. More of this later. Your suggestions for the end of Act III are due to a lapse of memory on your part; we had already settled between us, and quite rightly, that this act was to end on a mixture of burlesque and sentiment; a ballet would be out of place there. The whole point of the way I have done Act III is that it provides, most successfully, three quite distinct openings for music: first melodrama, lyrical-fantastic, for Jourdain and the spirits; then the middle part, the Turkish ceremony, operetta-like; then melodrama for the last part, burlesque-sentimental.

Generally to be borne in mind:

The structure of the whole play (and there are, in fact, three well-constructed acts) rests on an interweaving of the comic character study of Jourdain with the affairs of the couple of lovers (Lucile and Cleonte). I assume the (musical) prelude for Act III, as well as that for Act II, will be concerned with the lovers.

Your librettist's basic idea for what you call the 'musical exploitation' was this: into Act I the music enters often, but episodically. (This act corresponds largely to the Stuttgart version, but at the end of the new arrangement the daughter Lucile confronts her father.) This act ought in my view to end without music, but I have of course no objection if, after seeing the text, you wish to add some musical flourish for the moment the curtain falls. Into Act II the music enters more strongly, especially into the second half which you have. It contains the fine, already famous dinner scene, the dancing scene with its music and at the end the short monologue, the preservation of which I consider rather a feather in my cap. In the first half of this act the composer's chief task, apart from the prelude, will be to provide some Turkish music for the entrance of Cleonte in disguise. (Similar in style to the Turkish ceremony.) Act III is then, as I mentioned above, wholly given over to the music; it must be fairly steeped in 'it. Altogether, you have nothing to worry about, just as I cease to worry when you say that something is good.

I hope to have a reply from you soon to my other letter. My bookseller is unable to get hold of the Plautus adaptation by Lenz; would you send me the volumes to Bad Aussee, Obertressen 14, in August? With kindest regards (all good wishes also to Bubi),

Yours,

HOFMANNSTHAL

P.S. Since you mention ballet, I would like to draw attention to the fact that there is a mixture of operetta and ballet in the Turkish ceremony, and that a ballerina can again find something to do in the small melodrama of the sylph (at the beginning of Act III). Another ballet at the end of Act III would be too much. As one grows more mature, everything depends on balancing the different parts and finding the right mean and equilibrium between the various elements. This is what the French invariably do to such perfection; we must strive to learn it from them.

Munich, 10.7.17

Dear Herr von Hofmannsthal,

Our letters are crossing all the time this summer: yesterday I received your interesting letter of the 5th. I've been having medical treatment for eight days and am going back home to Garmisch tomorrow.

Your observations about the new arrangement naturally interest me tremendously. But even without knowing it in detail I should like to voice my strongest doubts about all melodrama right away: it is the clumsiest and most idiotic art form that I know. Since all music in melodrama must be limited to a minimum, as otherwise one would catch even less of the words than in an opera, it offers the least rewarding task of all to the musician and, as an invariable consequence, not much of a treat for the audience's ears. A little bit of it at the end of Act II is excellent. But for nearly the whole of Act III extremely risky!!! I can tell you that right now, unseen! Especially as the Turkish comedy is very unrewarding for the musician. Besides, I ask you, a first curtain (Lucile) without music—with, at the most, 'a flourish'! I still remember with horror all the various 'attempted flourishes' in Stuttgart and Berlin, when the 'humour' was enough to make you cry and I felt so embarrassed at each performance by the few pitying handclaps after the fall of the curtain that I could have crawled under my music desk.

I implore you: curtains definitely based on music from the outset, and at the end of the piece some enjoyable vocal conclusion, a solo quartet—a dash of really pleasant music, not just a few stop-gap squeaks. I've had enough of these with the present endings of Acts I and II.

I'm writing this in greatest haste, before I've even seen your work, because I know exactly what, if I'm to have a share in this business, the public expects of me. In fact, everybody is saying to me about the two acts of Molière we've got now: Why so little music?

Without having seen your work I believe I can already say that the tasks you seem to have mapped out for me in the third act are not the kind of thing that ought to come as a climax after the brilliant pieces of the first two acts (tailors' dance, minuet, dinner). Melodrama at the curtains of Acts I and II: yes! But at the end of Act III a vocal ensemble with ballet, and if you insist melodrama as well—in short, a finale, i.e. a hit, an effective piece of music in which all participants are engaged simultaneously. But for the love of God: not a succession of three curtains after which not a hand will stir. And believe me: the moment the bill says 'with music' the audience goes all wanton, especially for vocal music. No Reinhardt can help you then, and no Pallenberg: this is where the troubadour conquers! No ill feelings, I hope. I am sure you'll hit on something if you don't dig your heels in stubbornly! In Act III of *Frau ohne Schatten*, didn't I, at the mere bat of your eyelid, tear out the largest chunks of meat and turn the Empress's main scene into—melodrama?

That time there was too much music!

Here there seems to me too little. Unseen!

With best regards, yours,

RICHARD STRAUSS

Aussee, Obertressen 14, 16.7.1917.

Dear Dr. Strauss,

A dry statement of facts like that contained in your first and longer letter is quite a good thing from time to time, and enables the recipient to put forward his views in the same manner. The important part which Fürstner has played in obtaining higher royalties for you becomes clear to me now for the first time and so I understand the justification for his big share in the profits. This consideration does not in any way apply to the matter in hand and it is only your letter which tells me that, as regards printing of the score of the stage work (which I regard as a completely new one) and other things, you have from the outset been bound to him by agreement identical with that for *Ariadne*. I regret this but will make the best of it and am prepared to accommodate myself over this latest work altogether to your views about the division of profits. I advise most strenuously against asking more from Reinhardt. Max Reinhardt's predisposition to the thing, due either to pure idealism or to the fact that it stimulates his imagination (for as you yourself quite rightly point out, financially he has little to gain from it and would achieve the same result with my adaptation and an arrangement of the Lully music) might conceivably enable us to get the extra two per cent, but this additional burden would automatically reduce Edmund R(einhardt)'s incentive for arranging tours here and abroad. In short we should decidedly get the worst of our apparently clever business manœuvre.

I do not mean to oppose altogether the possibility of producing this comedy with music at other theatres later. But it must be so handled in practice that it cannot possibly spoil the chance of Reinhardt or possibly even Pallenberg going on tour with it (that is in our own interest, artistically as well as financially). At least for the time being, Fürstner will have to subordinate his own interest, which is to dispose of the material to other theatres, to the common good. In a matter of this kind one cannot put forward financial considerations as distinct from the artistic ones. Only by intransigently upholding the highest interests of art can lasting success be achieved, even if it has to be done in novel ways which might never seem feasible to the business man. It is to this principle that Reinhardt owes his intellectual and material success which has now been continuous over sixteen years.

You are perfectly right in pointing out so fairly that from the purely practical point of view, to use once again this overworked word which I dislike, Reinhardt and I would be, or would have been, far better off—incomparably better—if we had brought out the adaptation of this comedy with a mere thin varnish of rearranged Lully music. But you distort the whole position by quasi offering us this alternative now, for from the outset I undertook this whole thing solely and exclusively to create for your already existing music, which I value exceedingly, a proper and worthy outlet (on the stage and not in the concert hall). I have therefore done this for your sake and for the sake of your music, that was the primary purpose. If my first purpose had been to adapt this play for the stage, I might have constructed the action quite differently. As it now stands it is written in such a way as to give due justification and emphasis to the show pieces of your already existing music (e.g. the supper scene). It is therefore wholly unfitting for you to say: *If* Reinhardt and you want me as collaborator, then . . . That is not the true situation. I have adapted the play in this form only to create, according to your wish and for your already existing music, the following opening: a stage comedy by Molière into which musical pieces are inserted, musical pieces of which some six or eight extremely valuable ones are already available, while some five or six more are to be added by you in the same style, a style which you have created and which is by now already settled. It is a work of a unique kind, neither Singspiel nor operetta, but in a genre of its own, though one which is already clearly and plainly mapped out in the existing act and a half.

This genre I shall not allow to be adulterated or bent towards operetta, and all your suggestions tend towards such adulteration and confusion of the different genres. And on this point I shall stand firm, for although you are my superior in many artistic gifts and abilities, I have the greater sense of style and more reliable taste with which to create what is sure of enduring for some time though it is not for the time being wholly in line with the taste of the crowd. I must warn you against an aspect of your personality which you yourself tried to exemplify to me by that simile of the cow's eye, and which produces in you the desire to overload this comedy with music instead of giving it music as an ornament. If what you remember is that people found too little music in it, the reason is that they came to it expecting from the first bar an opera. Now that the two components are separated, this part presents a play which the actors alone, headed by a first-class comedian, must be able to carry and which depends for its effect, not least the curtains, on this comedian. To introduce operetta ensembles for the curtains, to make all the ordinary dramatic actors suddenly burst into song, would only produce a repulsive mongrel, a proper moon calf.

Two of my expressions have obviously misled you: flourish and melodrama. One of the flourishes, that musical backcloth painting for Jourdain's monologue, I have retained, because it had proved itself successful and since it was, after all, my purpose to save what had proved successful. Act I ends with a proper comedy curtain entrusted to the comedian, who also has the curtain of Act III. I must ask you to leave to Reinhardt and me for once the responsibility for curtains, for the effectiveness of the work on the stage and so on; I have, after all, some notion of theatrical style and Reinhardt of practical stage craft. Since this is a play, and not an opera or operetta, and since you do not have to figure as the author of the substance, but only of trimmings, why shouldn't you let other people take care of these things?

I have caused another confusion by using the word melodrama in a loose way. As far as I am aware there are only three or four lines of melodrama in the sense which you fear and detest. I used the word to describe a manner of which the supper scene and the scene of the Fencing Master are examples. For the rest I would ask you now, as soon as the manuscript reaches you, to devote yourself a while to a study of the overall poetic intention of my adaptation as a whole, as you have always done in the case of our earlier, much more significant joint productions. First, knowing that I can be relied on, you urge me to get the work done by the end of June, and then, when it is finished, you send me a number of suggestions which naturally do not in any way square with the intentions of what I have already done! That makes no sense, does it?

I should never have expected that the Turkish comedy would cause you so much trouble and vexation, and I am very sorry to hear it. But mortifications of this kind happen to every creative artist; I myself was unable for eight years to complete the third volume of my prose writings simply because I found it so hard to get two prose essays done which seemed to exist quite distinctly in my mind. And so you, too, will get over the difficulties of the past two months for which your health, your unsettled life and Bubi's call-up are no doubt in part responsible. That Turkish comedy is part of the play; there it is, we cannot get away from it. Somehow it must be possible to get it done in a style which matches the other pieces. The style which you give to your music for just that Turkish comedy might conceivably provide you in turn with an opportunity of bringing the chorus on the stage once again for the end of Act III, and so to achieve a kind of finale; although a proper finale where all the chief actors join in the singing strikes me, as I have said, as utterly out of the question. I have a great deal to do and would rather have devoted this morning to dictating the first, still untyped act than to this letter, for I would like you to have the whole piece as soon as possible. Please let me know at once on a card whether you are going to remain in Garmisch; you once mentioned something about a summer holiday at Mainz.

And so for my part too: 'no hard feelings', please, and with best wishes, yours,

Garmisch, 17.7.(1917)

My dear Friend,

I am arriving in Salzburg on 6th August, to perform there on the 7th. From the 8th onward at your disposal, could come to Ischl or wherever you think we might arrange a meeting. When, at long last, shall I get the whole manuscript of *Bürger als Edelmann*?

The Turkish comedy is now slowly beginning to move: but I should very much like—for inspiration—some more of the remaining material.

See you soon! Best regards, yours,

RICHARD STRAUSS

Aussee, 17.7.(1917)

Dear Dr. Strauss,

I am waiting for a line to tell me whether I am to send the manuscript to Garmisch or elsewhere.

On thinking it over, meanwhile, it occurs to me that as musical finale in the last act an ensemble in vaudeville form, with most of the characters on the stage joining in, might very well be developed out of the existing figures. What I have in mind is a soprano solo (by one of the sylphs, while the other sylphs are dancers), then the chorus of the Turks, Jourdain himself, and so on. Please wait until you have my manuscript, then you will see what I mean. I mean actually a *Vaudeville* of one or two stanzas; how does that fit in with your ideas?

Greetings,

HOFMANNSTHAL

Aussee, 21.7.1917

Dear Dr. Strauss,

Enclosed Act I. In the second envelope by the same post you will find the part of the second act which you have not yet had. Please read the whole thing at leisure and let it sink in merely as a comedy without any thought of the music. Try to make clear to yourself, perhaps by comparison with the Molière, how far I have succeeded, by the introduction of new scenes as cognate as possible to the original, by subtle transposition and so on, in surpassing the original work rapidly thrown off as it was, and obviously improvised in construction. The two parts of the action, the comedy of manners and the love intrigue, which are quite unconnected in Molière and run side by side without any inherent suspense, are here linked together into one fairly exciting whole. The third act will strike you as short only at first sight, for in fact, including the Turkish ceremony, it will run for at least twenty-five to thirty minutes which is ample since the first two acts are long, each at least fifty minutes, and two hours in all would be the ideal length for a comedy of this kind. Two and a quarter hours or even two and a half, which it might run to, are already too much. Please give a little thought to the kind of thing you imagine for a musical finale in the last act, so that you can explain it to me on August 9 at Ischl, and in talking it over we can settle this slight difficulty by a short conversation. But do leave it over until we can discuss it by word of mouth, for however glad I usually am to get letters from you, this summer I must concentrate all my imagination on my own various and by no means easy works, and since everything which comes from the outside confuses and disturbs me for hours, or even days, I leave incoming letters unopened for weeks, sometimes for months.

Many thanks for your telegram received today. I have considered the business arrangements and perhaps I shall write to you again, before we meet, to make a compromise proposal which I am sure will be acceptable to you.

With best wishes, yours,

HOFMANNSTHAL

Garmisch, 25.7.17

Dear Herr von Hofmannsthal,

The whole manuscript (except for Cleonte's entrance scene) received with many thanks: read the whole thing zealously and with interest (three times) and find it very nice and fine. There's no doubt much of it has gained a great deal. May I criticize briefly? Only as a suggestion! Perhaps you'll reflect on my critical observations and we may still arrive at some mutually satisfactory result when we meet.

1. The end of the first act is as flat as ever, and I keep returning to my wish, which I've uttered repeatedly, that it should end with music at all costs. The most amusing solution would be to shift the tailors' scene to this act-ending and to have Jourdain strutting out into the street in his new suit, accompanied by the footmen.

If this cannot be achieved by suitable transpositions you'll have to find some other way of making the business end with plenty of music— possibly with the dumb-show of the opening of the carriage door, which could very well be accompanied by music, letting the act end on this note. I am rather sorry to see that many highly comical passages, such as the spelling lesson with the philosopher, have been left out. On the other hand, some of the scenes, especially the first one between Dorante and Jourdain, are rather long.

Now the main point: but please don't kill me. It seems to me that the piece ought to have a fourth act. The third act with the simple wedding of Lucile and Cleonte is absolutely no ending for a play that is entitled *Der Bürger als Edelmann* and represents a comedy of manners, fitted almost exclusively around that one figure. Besides, Dorante and Dorimène now just fade out and all connection with the other comedy, which is hinted at very prettily in Molière, at least towards the end, is lacking in your version.

To my mind the piece ought to end quite grotesquely, either with a merry eye-opener and cure for Jourdain, like Don Quixote, or as a tragi-comedy with the eye-opening being followed by Jourdain's complete collapse and possibly madness. Do think it over, please! Don't be angry with me!

I'm arriving at Aschau near Ischl on 9th August and will either come to see you at Aussee or else we'll meet in Ischl to discuss everything in person like old friends. From 6th August onward in Salzburg, Österreichischer Hof.
                    With best regards, yours sincerely,

                                        RICHARD STRAUSS

Dear Dr. Strauss,   *Aussee, 28.7.(1917)*

For the meeting on August 9 I would propose Ischl. Hospitality, alas, I can no longer offer you here; we have neither the room nor even a piece of bread beyond the mouths we have to feed. Salzburg would cost me two days and more, since any change affects me for days (in this I am quite different from you and consider you a better organized person). I have a train for Ischl which gets me in at half past one; I shall have to make a few other calls there (an aunt) while you are presumably busy with the Steiners; so I shall reserve for you an hour and a half or two hours in the late afternoon and take a train back at 9 o'clock. Does that suit you?

The reasons which make it not quite easy for me to write the finale with vaudeville and so on, are inherent in the matter itself. Perhaps on first reading of the text you have not realized fully quite how much the *whole* play as I have done it aims at this half burlesque, half sentimental finale. The whole drift and purport of the piece (in the new version) is to make the culmination of the love intrigue coincide with the climax of Jourdain's foolish experience so as to pull the play together, whereas Molière lets the two plots amble along stolidly side by side without attempting any synthesis. Such an end is impossible by our present-day notions; it is bound either to upset people or to be accepted as 'historically interesting' and so to leave them quite cold. My finale, that blending of the two themes in bitter-sweet harmony, is what I have aimed at throughout the three acts, especially by my treatment of Lucile, by that touch of wordly jesuitry which I have given to Cleonte, and so on.

What matters is to wed organically the musical finale with this ending, into the spirit of which I beg you to enter. With all the vaudeville and so on, it must not in any circumstances become too long, or else it will look like a paper-tail tacked on. Could you not perhaps begin your whole musical finale *earlier*, at the point *where the lovers re-enter*, then continue it with the melodrama passages which now form the end and finish up with the vaudeville, a few lines sung by the nymph (who would come on the stage once again with a mirror), a few lines by Jourdain and ensemble? Perhaps you already have a melody in mind and with it a metre scheme on which I am to base my vaudeville! I await your news.

Sincerely yours,

HOFMANNSTHAL

Garmisch, 30.7.17

Dear Herr von Hofmannsthal,

Letter of 28th received with thanks. I've got ready: the Turkish comedy with an effective, operatic ending, the courante, Cleonte's entrance, as a prelude to Act II the charming well-known minuet by Lully, which could also be used successfully for the melodramatic ending of Act III, and a fast *alla-breve* madrigal which could be fitted very nicely as a sing-song into the little wedding scene at the end.

I'll bring everything with me: you only make sure we have a piano in Ischl.

Otherwise I could come to Aussee, and you needn't be afraid that we would be a burden on you. Surely there is some hotel or inn at Aussee. We—i.e. with my wife and Bubi—want to spend six or eight days either at Strobl, Aschau or Ischl, starting about the 9th or 10th. As soon as I've had details from Steiner about some decent accommodation there I shall let you know. You can then choose whatever day is most convenient to you. From the 6th in Salzburg, Österreichischer Hof.

With kindest regards, yours,

RICHARD STRAUSS

Aussee, 2.8.(1917)

Dear Dr. Strauss,

I entreat you to let me know at least forty-eight hours in advance by telegram which day you have chosen for our meeting at Ischl and to which hotel and at what hour I am to come. I suggest after your afternoon rest, towards 5 o'clock.

(. . .)

The fact that I do not intend to put my name to the book of words has of course nothing to do with the question of collaboration. Even if I had undertaken the adaptation for Reinhardt alone, I should still have preserved my anonymity, just as I did in the case of *Die Lästigen*.[1] It is a question of tact on which I must be guided by my feelings alone. For a living poet to see fit to make a free adaptation of a classic dramatist is an altogether singular event; in this I am responsible to myself alone and my anonymity is dictated both by respect for the author and by tact.

Must I really give it to you in writing once again that I am not ashamed of our joint works but rejoice in their existence? Do you

---

[1] *Die Lästigen*, freely adapted after Molière, performed at the Deutsches Theater, Berlin, on 26th April 1916 (cf. p. 252), together with *Die Grüne Flöte*, anonymous scenario also by Hofmannsthal.

really know me so little as a man after all these years of friendly intercourse that you could suppose I would not abandon anything of which I am ashamed? Nobody but I myself can know what I have in the meantime produced on my own (fairy story, comedy, prose) and what I have not produced, what I have finished and what I have not finished, what I have published and what I have not. By reason of my character (and by dint of conditions peculiar to my art) my attitude to these things is quite different, indeed diametrically opposed to yours. Publication interests me only in the second place, stage production in the third; all this is wholly irrelevant to the value of my works and their survival. My *œuvre* will either exist and justify my very distinct pretensions, or it will not exist; the stage, even the printed book, the thing one calls 'success' and so on, none of these have anything whatever to do with it. But I know my course and I shall follow it.

And so *au revoir*.

Sincerely yours,

HOFMANNSTHAL

P.S. My wife now hands me your letter.[1] Your proposals I consider, if you will forgive me, beneath discussion. They demonstrate to me that your taste and mine are miles apart, at least as concerns possibilities of this kind. Pray let me have in due course your decision whether I am free to dispose otherwise of this Molière adaptation, of which I do not intend to alter one iota.

Aussee, 3.8.(1917)

Dear Dr. Strauss,

Your critical remarks and 'proposals' reveal such absolute incomprehension, indeed such diametrical anti-comprehension of what I have tried to do, and have accomplished with this Molière adaptation by devoting to it for two months every effort of my imagination, my artistic sensitivity, my tact and self-effacement; there was something so devastating in the vista opened up by your finding it possible, after reading this play three times, to put forward proposals of this kind which make nonsense of the whole thing, that it was my first impulse to wire and ask you to leave the whole thing alone and never to speak to me, or write of it again. But that would have been a sad discord after so many years of amicable and often beautiful joint efforts. A few hours

---

[1] 25th July 1917.

later, moreover, there arrived your letter of July 30, which, quite guilelessly, and without even as much as mentioning these 'proposals' again, reports good progress—and so I would not like to make our meeting and discussion of this work impossible, but will endeavour to take the offensive sting out of my absolute and harsh rejection of your ideas and proposals by a calm explanation (not an exhaustive one of course, but the chief points) and so lead you, by the roundabout way of theory, a little closer to the poet's point of view.

(1) The end of the whole piece. The great critics of the seventeenth and eighteenth century (Boileau, Fénelon, Vauvenargues) already stressed Molière's wisdom in portraying this most highly charged of his dramatic characters successfully as a real fool without ever evoking any association with the *petites-maisons* (the madhouse)—in other words in separating, by a hair's breadth, foolishness as an extreme subject of the comedy of manners from the pathological, from madness. (The kind of thing Regnard, for instance, in his *Le Distrait*, could not do.) This is achieved by a hundred little devices, by a hundred small incidents most tactfully calculated, one of the most important of these the unemphatic, imponderable treatment of the ending; the pretty ambiguous behaviour of Lucile and Cleonte, Jourdain's foolishness, the Turkish comedy and the feast (with the prospect of a ballet), all these are, with a light hand, brought together into a loose garland of motives and wisely none of them is forced, none of them over-worked. The adaptor had to be guided by this.

I have endeavoured to preserve that imponderable, variegated, so to speak iridescent aspect of the final situation (without which it degenerates at once into mere intrigue, into bourgeois ponderosity and so becomes offensive). I have succeeded in this by calculating every shade of the characters of Lucile and Cleonte (who is not as blameless as she is, but has something of the practising Jesuit about him); by telescoping two festive occasions, the ceremony and the signing of the contract; by Lucile's serious qualms of conscience which anticipate her confession and the pardon from her father whom, despite everything, she has always loved. In introducing the sylphs with their looking glass I have raised the festive element by an admixture of the fantastic and have lifted what was light-hearted to the ethereal plane; but so as not to fall out of Molière's style into Shakespearizing romanticism, they could not be real fairies or elves but, to remain within the Latin convention which derives from the classical stage, a machination of the servant who manages the whole intrigue (in this case Covielle). Folly and destiny, the duplicity of the world and the fulfillment of love, successful intrigue and bitter philosophy all come together here as it were on a needle's point, and this, only this is why it is so difficult to find the right style, the right shade for the final vaudeville, for a finale such as you want it.

(2) What had to be excluded from the ending, so that the dubious and undesirable elements should not dominate the atmosphere and contaminate the mixture, was the presence on the stage of Dorante and Dorimène. (Here again your proposal flies slap in the face of what I have aimed at.) The position of these dubious characters is this: similar groups (derived from the parasites and hetaerae of classical comedy) which vacillate between people of quality on the one hand, and confidence tricksters and swindlers on the other, are to be found also in Regnard (in *Le Joueur*) and in Le Sage (in *Turcaret*) and there their outlines are not very clearly drawn either; obviously contemporary audiences knew exactly what to make of such figures. But we do not know it and so we are painfully bewildered when confronted with such thoroughly *demi-monde* characters like Dorimène and Dorante. It was the adaptor's task to make these figures more specific and definite, and to concentrate them into one distinct episode. I have made them definite (morally and socially), have placed Dorimène the highest (she is far more dupe than accomplice), Dorante in the middle as a confidence man, but a dashing and not altogether repellent figure and, to throw him into stronger relief, have surrounded him by worse sharpers still; yet I have packed the whole thing, and finished it, in one clear-cut episode (Act II, second half). This episode is finished and done with and that alone is reason enough to keep these two characters out of the ending. But their exclusion is vital for two reasons above all: first so as not to complicate the various strands of the ending to an intolerable degree, and secondly for a moral reason far more significant still, because any connection (even if established only through Covielle) between this group of base scoundrels, and the story of the lovers would inevitably debase the young couple, and Cleonte especially would become odious as soon as the slightest trace of suspected complicity with such shady characters falls on him.

Folly surrounded and beset by deceit and greed of every kind, that is the theme, or one of the themes of the play, and so we get the Fencing Master's and the Tailor's artful tricks and those of the Philosopher, the rather different tricks of the confidence man and finally the daring intrigue of the lovers. Blend all this with a heavy hand and everything immediately becomes detestable, and any possible effect of the play on the stage is poisoned *for inherent reasons*.

(3) The philosopher. Opinions may well differ on the absence of the spelling lesson. Reinhardt and I find it clumsy and tedious (although it does raise a laugh or two; this is quite irrelevant, since the secret of comedy is in the rhythm and not in occasionally titillating the sense of the ridiculous) and so, without discussion, we agreed that it had to go. The essential gain of my treatment of the philosopher has unfortunately escaped you like *everything*, *everything* else in my work (for since you are invariably kind and courteous, you would certainly have mentioned one of the gains of my adaptation, if any single one had convinced you). The point is that over this 'logic and rhetoric' business I found a transition to the subsidiary plot (Lucile) and this enabled me to allow the philosopher to play some further part in this action (Act II, first half). This is another essential gain, since it helps to remedy and entirely to rectify the lamentable lack of all connection between the characters in the various episodes from Acts I and II (of the Molière original) and the characters in the love story (which only begins at the end of Act III).

Well, I cannot go on filling sheet after sheet with interpretations of my dramatic intentions. All in all I am profoundly saddened by this affair. Taking a lot of trouble I have altered for you, and improved, the structure of an old, somewhat ill-constructed summer house; out of a couple of windows which were awry I have made a balcony; I have taken out the ugly back-stairs, have given decent proportions to the whole building and have made all the rooms and the main staircase open into a large winter garden which has always been the chief attraction of the whole place. You go over the entire building with me and you don't find one word of approval, you don't even notice any of the improvements I have made in this old refractory structure: the lofty chambers, the fine perspectives, the comfortable rooms. We enter the state room with its fine view out on to the garden (and you throw a brick at the big mirror in passing), and then you, without more ado, you request me to put up a party wall and so shut out the view over garden and landscape, or at least put a big dung-heap where the fountain now is. My comparison is bitter, but it is in no way exaggerated. The wall is your appalling idea of introducing real madness, the most horrible thing there is in the whole world, as the crowning point of a light and elegant comedy of manners; the dung-heap is the 'eye-opening' and 'reconciliation' where in fact the various elements face each other as incommensurables and can be reconciled only in the rhythm of the comedy.

I feel as your architect would, exactly. In conclusion I can only ask you—and not for the first time—to make up your mind now, before we meet, whether or not you are willing to decorate with your music *this* my adaptation of the Molière comedy as you now have it, well-rounded, well considered work as it is. These are the only alternatives. Should Reinhardt, who knows his *métier* and shares with me the responsibility for the *play* (from which, in this case, you are free), desire any alterations which strike me as justified, we still have six months, from October to April, to deal with them! Your remark about the length of a certain scene is irrelevant; when it comes to the point, Reinhardt will leave out what he does not want. To transpose the tailor's scene to the end of Act I is of course, where the whole thing has been so carefully balanced, just as impossible as all the other proposals.

Since I have now been able to unburden myself in this letter, we can meet and I shall be capable of enjoying the various pieces of music, highly successful as they are sure to be. I doubt whether there is a reasonable piano in any hotel at Ischl. I therefore suggest coming to Aschau in the afternoon of the 9th, or of the 10th (leaving Ischl about 3 o'clock or 3.30) and after I have been with you for a few hours, returning to Ischl for the night. This proposal is made regardless of the weather; please let me know.

All good wishes for your family; I am delighted that your son is still free to move about, and may God keep him thus as long as possible.

Yours,

HOFMANNSTHAL

Dear Dr. Strauss,   (*Aussee, 10.8.1917*)

I hope you found at Salzburg the very long letter of mine by which I attempted, as best I could, to make up for the asperity of my earlier letter (which I regret) by entering into a detailed explanation of the aims of this my adaptation.

I shall willingly come over for a day; it will be no trouble and I shall look upon it as a country outing. I would suggest that instead of spending an afternoon with you, I might come over for the morning, including lunch if this suits you. I would take the train to Ischl in the evening, spend the night there and come to Aschau next morning between 9 and 10, returning to Ischl in the afternoon. There I can see to my aunt and other engagements. So please tell me by telegram when it is most convenient for you.

Yours,

HOFMANNSTHAL

Dear Dr. Strauss, *Aussee, Saturday, 11.8.(1917)*

Have received you know what I mean[1] and shall do my best to read it through, but I must say right away that I am not the public nor, since I lack all sympathy for the genre of realism, a competent judge of the whole thing.

If it suits you, I should like to arrive on Wednesday early in the forenoon, so that we can discuss, either in the woods or indoors, all that is necessary, especially the end of Act III which must definitely be an unemphatic finale and not a massive one.

As regards the end of Act I, I am against giving the dumb-show a background of music, because a dumb-show of absent-mindedness of this kind is one of the most promising opportunities for P(allenberg) and because the broad comedy of the action, and the laughs, would be foiled by music and by any linking of the dumb-show with music. But perhaps Act I might be *concluded* with this dumb-show; this kind of decision I shall leave to Reinhardt, for each one of us must deal with what he knows best.

Yours,

HOFMANNSTHAL

My dear Dr. Strauss, *Aussee, 4.9.(1917)*

Now you may laugh at me if you like, but don't get angry if I venture to come forward as a critic of your music! But I simply must ask: Isn't there something wrong with that madrigal? Is it really in the right order the way you have sent it to me?? The words you have put to it are rhythmically so utterly unconvincing, especially where I have put

[1] The draft libretto for *Intermezzo*.

287

the little crosses! I have had it played over to me again and again, last of all by Schalk, and even in listening it fails utterly to convince me; at these points I feel as if something must have gone wrong. So once more forgive my criticism, but when it comes to the few little verses which have to be written for this passage the truth is that they would be much easier to find if they could be a little more clip-clop, clip-clop, especially when one considers the old-fashioned style of the whole work. Perhaps you could go a little way to meet me over this!

One more request to trouble you with: I have irretrievably lost my Manuscript of Act I of the *Bourgeois*; please have the act copied by a typist in Garmisch or Munich and send me one (or preferably two) copies. I beg you not to forget this!

Yours,

HOFMANNSTHAL

P.S. I am more and more convinced that Munich might be the one place which offers us at least a hope of finding an audience so composed as to appreciate a work like *Die Frau ohne Schatten*, concerned as it is with spiritual values far beyond the horizon of the average Viennese-Jewish crowd; I mean a chance of finding not that detestable 'wanting to have it made plain', like twice two is four in the multiplication tables, but a receptiveness for a higher meaning where the secret lies in the 'fractions'. (. . .)

Garmisch, 7.9.17

Dear Herr von Hofmannsthal,

Don't be angry with me if I trouble you once more about the end of Act I which, after careful examination (and in spite of Reinhardt), still seems to me ineffective! I am therefore reverting to it with the following proposal:

Either we cut a little off the end of the scene between Dorante and Jourdain and fit it to the conclusion; let Dorante depart, then—following the scene between Lucile and Jourdain, instead of the servant who says: 'Der Herr Graf fragen, wo der Jourdain so lange bleiben'—bring back Dorante himself and let him watch Jourdain still practising the opening of the carriage door; then, after a few words, the brief bowing and scraping scene, which I've already sketched for you—with music!

Or possibly Dorante's scene might even remain unabridged in case you still have some amusing idea for the end.

But I'm sure of one thing: my closing scene with music is more effective and would, moreover, provide a better structural framework than if the first act alone were to end without music.

Do please think it over and don't be angry with me.

Best regards, yours

RICHARD STRAUSS

Garmisch, 11.9.17

Dear Herr von Hofmannsthal,

From the enclosed original by Lully you'll see that the rhythmical irregularity which you've found fault with is in fact the main charm of this madrigal-like form. It is just the same in Lully as in my imitation, which does of course make great demands on the poet whereas Lully simply resorted to such meaningless padding as 'sus, sus, du vin, du vin, versez, versez, partout' whenever things didn't work out smoothly. So that great master of words and verse Hugo will have a bit of a struggle here to squeeze himself into the Spanish boot—which he must now take as it is. Besides, when I've played it to you you won't ask for it to be changed. Maybe even Schalk wouldn't know what to do with the melodic line alone, without accompanying and contrasting voices. But my verse pattern gives an accurate picture of what it ought to be like, provided Herr von Hofmannsthal hits on some fine lines for it.

(a) goes clip-clop;

(b) and (c) are irregular interpolations, possibly in question form!

(d) resumé, coda, amplification, ornamentation and conclusion, the same as the beginning.

With the exception of the three act-endings I have today sent off the completed full score to Fürstner.

One other question: Couldn't the song of the kitten remain? It's always thawed the atmosphere at the very start.

The end of Act I must be like all the others and must end melodramatically. Please don't be obstinate on this point. You're usually so touchy on proportions and good equilibrium. It would be a downright stylistic fault if Act I alone were to end without music! Seeing that every other act has a prelude and ends with melodrama and music.

Enclosed I am sending you Act I which I no longer need: I haven't got a good typist here at the moment.

With best regards, yours,

RICHARD STRAUSS

20.9.(1917)

Dear Dr. Strauss,

My wife is upset about a wholly needless misunderstanding which has arisen between us, needless because there are no points of real disagreement.

Now with regard to Act I, I asked you to consider the work as terminated for the time being, until we meet in November. I did so not out of obstinacy, but because I am certain that in collaboration with Reinhardt I shall be able to think of a better ending for the act, possibly even a musical one, whereas your proposals are nothing better than makeshift solutions. Surely you will be able to get this *one* trifle done between November and March! Over Act II—no disagreement! Over Act III there is also *no* disagreement, since we were perfectly agreed at Aschau that it must end with music, dance and song. You even enumerated to me the individual pieces of music out of which you mean to build up the finale: the madrigal, parts of the minuet, and so on. So now I shall get you the words for the madrigal, difficult though that may be (when must you have them?) and you can get the whole thing on paper in its final form. Once the music is settled in this way, Reinhardt and I will find the appropriate dumb-show and setting for it without any need for you to alter a single bar, and if Jourdain were to be given some more words to fit the existing music, Fürstner would have to print an addition (assuming this finale really must go to press as early as November).

The song of the kitten I urge you to omit. Have carefully thought it over: the German words are flat and clumsy, tending towards low comedy, towards the trivial; that is not what we want, nor does it serve any useful purpose, for we have plenty of gay and truly funny moments in the first act, and broadly comic action too.

I am still pondering your proposal for Act I (for I am, after all, no stubborn mule, as you must have discovered during the past six years!) But what exactly do you mean when you speak of the 'bowing and scraping scene'? I know you sent me something of the kind a while ago (and I could no doubt find your letter again), but then you made them both suddenly burst into song as if this were operetta, and that · of course is entirely out of keeping with the style of the work and therefore impossible (whereas in the finale of Act III it will do well enough, because gradually a fantastic-burlesque atmosphere has been reached). It would be better to try and find something *good* in co-operation with Reinhardt, and surely a master like you can produce such *a tiny bit of music* even at a time when he is otherwise occupied. I cannot get to Berlin before November 15; not out of cussedness, but because I have so far done nothing except a detailed *sketch* of Acts I and II of my comedy,[1] and have not yet written a single line of it.

Best wishes, yours,

HOFMANNSTHAL

Aussee, 21.9.(1917)

Dear Dr. Strauss,

Have gone through the Jourdain-Dorante scene once again. I really cannot see that it is too long, since it is all action and nowhere mere dialogue. Besides, mere episodic characters like Dorante and the philosopher must be made into real parts, or else nobody will care to act them and nobody will be able to make anything of them. Now, of course, Dorante could appear again at the end, but what do we gain by that? Surely it is unthinkable for these two characters suddenly to break into singing a vaudeville in the middle of a sedate prose comedy; people would think they had gone mad! That would be pure operetta, and to this style we would have to stick right through—which is not what we are doing here. Could we not solve it like this: Exit Jourdain with the words: 'Coming, coming', quite in a trance, immersed in his dream of the approaching carriage; then follows a brief, brilliant orchestral epilogue *with the curtain still up*, describing the arrival of the carriage and the welcome? The fragrance of his dream, his vision turned, so to speak, into music!!

Yours,

HOFMANNSTHAL

[1] *Der Schwierige.*

Dear Herr von Hofmannsthal,

You may rest assured that there's nothing I'd dislike more than to cause you unnecessary correspondence or distraction during a fine working spell. I'm too anxious myself to see a new original Hofmannsthal comedy to worry the good author at the time of its birth. I am therefore asking only for what is most indispensable—i.e. the end of Act III, how the music is to link up with the present melodramatic ending, and an approximate outline of what action and what dances are intended, as well as the words for the madrigal and those to be spoken melodramatically by Jourdain during a *pianissimo* repetition of the madrigal.

I shall be in Berlin from 14th to 19th October: am I to talk to Reinhardt about the curtains of Acts I and III and report to you about the outcome of this conversation?

From 23rd October till 5th November I shall be in Garmisch again and might then complete at least the end of Act III, provided I can now sketch it out on the basis of the outline I am asking you for. As for the end of Act I, we can leave that for our meeting in Berlin: to think that I wanted it sung is a mistake; it was also to end melodramatically, like the 2nd and 3rd acts.

Enclosed I am sending you my draft once more, to save you the search. With kindest regards and best wishes for satisfying work, yours

RICHARD STRAUSS

30.9.(1917)

Dear Dr. Strauss,

Herewith the sketch for a melodramatic ending to Act I. There is absolutely nothing to be said for bringing in Dorante at the end: (1) all his motifs are exhausted, he has nothing new to say or to contribute—this sort of thing is always unsatisfactory since it looks tacked on and puts people off; (2) he is a wholly realistic figure and as such hardly to be combined with music; (3) musical melodrama can be introduced only in connection with burlesque episodes or with fantastic or sentimental elements; the Fencing Master for instance (who is a burlesque figure), the spirits or Jourdain's other visions or fantasies. I have taken in this case the tailor's scene, because it has music anyway; to shift this scene altogether would be impossible without damaging the middle of the act and unhinging the whole thing; but I have detached from it the tipping incident. The tailor's scene itself remains as it is, only as soon as the dance of the journeymen is over, Dorante is announced so that the journeymen tailors are disappointed in their hope of a tip (disappointment which they express in dumb-show). They have waited outside and now, at the end of the act, they rush in and make for Jourdain. If this were to suit you, as I hope it will, we could finally complete the act.

Tomorrow I shall think over Act III. My comedy is progressing. It took me all the time from the middle of July to the end of September to produce merely a detailed sketch of the three acts.

Yours,

HOFMANNSTHAL

P.S. Please send the wire telling me whether you approve of my suggestion to Bad Aussee, Ramgut.

N.B. The mirror from the end of Act III I have intentionally introduced at this early stage, since the mirror is, in the fairy-tale tradition, the chief attribute of the fop.

(*Postscript, 1.10.*)

Your postcard of Sept. 25th just received (1.10); the mails are terrible. My new ending is, I feel, still happier than the former idea. It is for you to choose upon careful consideration.

Everything necessary for Act III will follow tomorrow.

Yours,

HOFMANNSTHAL

P.S. Overleaf the text which follows upon the former ending of Act I after the dumb-show.

'. . . Es fällt ihm der Hut aus der Hand' (here the first illustrative music breaks off)

Lucile (flabbergasted): 'Was tun Sie, Vater?'

Jourdain (waking from his dream): 'Ich öffne einen Wagenschlag, was weiter?'

Lucile: '. . . und in der Hoffnung zu verharren, dass die ungnädigen Worte, die ich habe hören müssen, nicht unwiderruflich die letzten sind' (runs off the stage).

Jourdain: 'Wie? Was? Unwiderruflich, das sind sie! und unumstösslich'. (Rings the bell) . . . 'Man soll meine Tochter hereinholen und man soll mir den Lehrer herbeirufen.'

Footman: 'Welchen . . . etc.' down to the entry of the small Footman: 'Der Graf wartet.'

Jourdain: 'Sogleich, sogleich—ich will sogleich bei ihm sein und alles mitbringen.'

Exit. Musical epilogue.

But I consider my new sketch better still. Perhaps even in that you might be able to use the musical epilogue (if already written) as *the very end*.

Garmisch, 4.10.17

Dear Herr von Hofmannsthal,

Both act-endings received with thanks today: the third seems to me very good, but I don't quite understand from the manuscript whether there can be dancing while the madrigal is being sung, or only afterwards, or during as well as after the madrigal—because you say: elegiac, whereas the character of the madrigal is lively. We have three female Sylphs from the beginning of Act III, of whom one can now act as a dancer and the other two as singers (soprano and contralto, as in the duet in Act I). For a third singing sylph I shall then take the earlier Mufti. At any rate the whole thing can be concluded very nicely with the melodrama ending and the Lully minuet.

I am less keen on the newest ending of Act I with the tailors. This somewhat foolish and old-fashioned scene with its ceaseless stepping up of titles struck me as fatal even in the original Molière and I don't know whether it'll be effective enough, especially as an ending.

Your second ending, which you suggested in a letter recently—with the repetition of the dumb-show of the carriage-door being opened by Jourdain, who is left alone on the stage and who is carried away by his day-dreams into ever greater ecstasy, opens the carriage-door, bows, assists the arrival out of the carriage, and finally rushes off in delight— was much more to my liking and also certainly offers a Pallenberg a much more grateful opportunity. Besides, I've already sketched some rather pretty music for it. As we evidently can't agree on Act I at this distance I suggest that we leave the final version till November, when we've spoken to Reinhardt in Berlin.[1] Whatever decision we then take, it'll be no trouble to me to implement.

I am now getting down to the ending of Act III which requires rather more work.

[1] In the final version the dumb-show of the opening of the carriage-door was used.

294

I am glad for your sake that you're now staying at the delightful Ramgut: I'm sure it'll do you good and inspire you to fine work.

I hope I'll have the new comedy read to me in November!

With best regards and with respectful compliments to the amiable proprietress of the Ramgut, also from my wife, yours

RICHARD STRAUSS

Garmisch, 6.10.17

Dear Herr von Hofmannsthal,

I have already composed your very pretty third act-ending and would make only these suggestions: let the sylphs (of whom one carries the looking glass) enter dancing, I have a charming round-dance for this entrance; let the sylphs and the Turks perform a joint dance of homage during the madrigal, and let them make their exit not as you've laid down, but in the following order: first the Turks and only then the Sylphs and the young couple.

This would give me a much better transition to the wistful conclusion which, I believe, has come out very well and will have a great effect. If you agree no reply is needed.

As for Act I, we'll discuss that in Berlin!

Best regards, yours,

RICHARD STRAUSS

Berlin, 19.12.17

Dear Herr von Hofmannsthal,

Dr. Bruck thinks the one-act play[1] charming, full of sensitive atmosphere, and is going to recommend it to Hülsen most warmly and believes that Hülsen will like the piece too. The only difficulty he sees is in what ought to go with it. Perhaps you could make me a few suggestions on those lines. Direktor Leopold Sachse (Halle an der Saale) is also interested in the piece. Could you send it to him to look at some time?

On Monday the one hundredth *Rosenkavalier* came off gloriously in Dresden, with a full house and an impeccable performance. Afterwards,

[1] By Robert von Ehrhart.

in cheerful company, we thought of you gratefully with much admiration.

With best regards, yours,

RICHARD STRAUSS

I have begun, slowly and carefully, to sound about in Dresden concerning *Frau o. Sch.*! If one could only transplant the Dresden orchestra to Munich. They've still got that splendid old man Schuch! Siems and Osten were magnificent, as on the first day!

All good wishes for a merry Christmas and fruitful work!

25.12.1917

Very many thanks, *my dear Dr. Strauss*, for the kind and gratifying words of your letter. First of all for remembering me so amiably in Dresden, and then for the outcome of your good offices on behalf of my friend's play, which is really a great kindness to me and for which I am much obliged. Please give the string just one more slight pull, perhaps by sending a line to Hülsen himself; I am sure that will make all the difference. On searching my mind for a second play to fill the evening's bill, the following suggestions occur to me on the spur of the moment: Goethe's *Die Mitschuldigen* (three acts) had a great success last year at the Burgtheater and was very often repeated. Büchner's *Leonce und Lena* would be a fine experiment. Perhaps *Clavigo* if they have a Clavigo? Something by Benedix or Bauernfeld (*Bürgerlich und Romantisch, Die Bekenntnisse*) in period dress? (Ehrhart and Bauernfeld together would make a *Viennese Night.*)

And now for the *Bourgeois* production in Vienna. Reinhardt made it quite clear to me that he could and would undertake this only if he gets one of the few real comic actors for the title part, and one whom the Viennese really like. Since the death of Maran and because Girardi is entirely out of the question (G. is in fact no comic actor anyway, but a man for character parts), there is *nobody* but Thimig. I went to see him and found him hardly out of bed after pneumonia; he was half anxious to do it and half afraid of it. He did not dare say yes or no. I believe he will end up by saying yes. That gives us our sheet-anchor. In the meantime I have taken up with Karpath again; he is 'of course' willing to do 'anything'. I shall initiate the whole business as adroitly as I can, bearing in mind all the various interests and susceptibilities.

One more thing: would you drop a line to that accursed man Gregor about *Ariadne*; some dreadful person is nowadays singing all the time in place of Mme Kurz. Everybody complains to me about it—and how tiresome that is. All best wishes to you and your wife from us both.

Yours,

HOFMANNSTHAL

Munich, 25.12.17

Dear Herr von Hofmannsthal,

I am now scoring the end of Act I of *Bourgeois*. Will you please send me the exact text of this and the version of Pallenberg's exit so that your exact words can go into the full score.

On 3rd January they're doing *Ariadne* here, which promises to be very nice. This is followed by a Strauss week with *Feuersnot* on 6th January, *Salome* on 9th, *Elektra* on 11th, and *Rosenkavalier* on 13th. Wouldn't you like to come over for it?

I wish you, together with my family, a good, peaceful New Year, blessed with work, and send my best regards to you and your family. Always sincerely yours,

RICHARD STRAUSS

The name of the Brentano novel is *Godwi*, isn't it? Very fine and exceedingly modern in content.

31st December, 1917

Dear Dr. Strauss,

Many thanks for your kind letter and wishes which we reciprocate to you, your wife and Bubi.

I am delighted to hear that the situation is so favourable in Munich (which, for personal and geographical reasons, I consider the most promising of the Court Theatres). Alas I cannot come, on account of considerable creative activity; I must try to make hay while the sun shines.

This is how I saw the end of Act I: all as before up to the last line. Then: he bows ceremoniously to the little footman and is about to go off left. Once again he imagines he sees the carriage driving up, he

297

steps forward with alacrity, meaning to lend his hand to the beautiful Marquise as she descends—and the curtain falls.

Sincerely yours,

HOFMANNSTHAL

P.S. The Manuscript, with all the proper cuts, will go off tomorrow to Oertel. *Godwi* is a strange book; but what I recommended to you was Arnim's *Gräfin Dolores*, on account of the poems which are interspersed. There is a good abridged text in the Insel Verlag edition of Arnim.

1918

Dear Dr. Strauss, *Saturday evening, (late April/early May 1918)*

Do let us think twice, the mischief is soon done! Schnitzler, who is sincerely devoted to your and my works, warned me today during the *Ariadne* interval to be most careful not to give the difficult critical title part of *Bourgeois* to a comedian who has not got the power to *carry* the play (and especially the critical curtains). He said we ought not to think of Forest (it is of him I had thought), because Forest was an actor only for an episode, no pivot for a whole play; Thaller, he said, was impossible; a vulgar comedian from the suburbs like Strassmayer, unthinkable. So I come back to the proposal I made in my letter the day before yesterday, namely to negotiate with Bernau only on the basis that he engages Pallenberg for two or three or four weeks and puts the play on, say, four or five times a week. He can quite easily do this and Pallenberg will be glad not to have to act every day. This strikes me as the only possible basis of negotiation, all the rest— ballerina, ballet master, Godlewski, Stern's décor—is of secondary importance. Without a really strong actor for the title-part this play is in dire danger of proving a flop by way of a *succès d'estime*. I feel it in my bones. It is not safe by any means; on the contrary.

Ariadne was wonderful. You have done nothing finer, and it is worth while making every effort to search for something new in style along the lines of the Vorspiel—and find it I shall.

Adieu, all best regards to your wife,

Yours,

HOFMANNSTHAL

Dear Dr. Strauss,

I have your letter of May 6; in the meantime my days have been profoundly sad. The death of the best, most faithful and most noble of friends[1] has brought me bitter sorrow and utterly irreparable loss. You too count among my friends, and not only as an artist; I know your feelings towards me are kind and warm-hearted and I become more certain of this every time we meet. This is why I am telling you of my loss and am sure you will think of me with sympathy.

I am still without a single word from Bernau. Weeks ago Schnitzler asked me on his behalf what I thought of Thimig for the part of Jourdain. I replied that I could not possibly be against him, since I had thought of him for the part right at the beginning. But I have seen in Berlin what unusual demands this part makes, on physical agility in the dancing and fencing scenes, and then again, at each curtain, on the ability to establish this character so that it borders on the touching. Altogether, now that I have seen how problematical the whole work is even on the Reinhardt stage, since it presents such an exceptional mixture, I am—*entre nous*—once again nervous and sceptical of any performer who is not Pallenberg.

If Eger were to approach me, which so far he has not done, I shall reply to him in strict accordance with your wishes.

I am glad you look back on your stay in Vienna as a happy one. From my point of view, too, these days meant a great deal and the *Ariadne* performance, which rounded them off, gave rise to important ideas which I shall try and elucidate to myself and to you at an early occasion. Of all our joint works this is the one I never cease to love best, every time I hear it. Here alone you have gone wholly with me and—what is more mysterious—wholly even with yourself. Here for once you freed yourself entirely from all thought of effect; even what is most tender and most personal did not appear too simple, too humble for you here. You have lent your ear to the most intimate inspiration and have given great beauty; of all these works, this is the one which, believe me, *possesses the strongest guarantee that it will endure.* From this point the road leads on, even for me, when I think of you; not one road but several.

Sincerely yours,

HOFMANNSTHAL

[1] Eberhard Freiherr von Bodenhausen-Degener who died on 6th May 1918 on his estate Meineweh. Cf. Hugo von Hofmannsthal—Eberhard von Bodenhausen: *Briefe der Freundschaft*, 1953.

My dear Friend Hofmannsthal,

It was by mere chance that, a few days before receiving your letter, I heard of the death of the excellent Bodenhausen, and I thought of you with most sincere sympathy. I knew very well how much he meant to you and how deeply you must feel the loss.

How many of the best and most valuable people have to depart this life thus prematurely, before they have accomplished their task!

I too have pursued in my mind many recollections of my pleasant stay in Vienna, and in particular have discussed with my wife (who agreed sympathetically) the possibility that, in the event of Gregor's departure, I might share in a possible Schalk directorship, perhaps as co-director, in such a way that I would spend two or three winter months in Vienna over a number of years.

Exactly how this would have to be arranged I am at the moment unable to judge: perhaps you could discuss the matter quietly with Schalk some time. I should gladly make a personal sacrifice to prevent some Weingartner from trying his destructive hand again on that fine artistic institution. I have no news whatever from Bernau, but shall write to him today along the lines you suggest—especially concerning Pallenberg.

Heller, too, keeps interfering in the business, although he's got no mandate from me to assemble the orchestra for Bernau.

Eger can't even consider a performance because of inadequate orchestra space. I am still in favour of leaving the piece to Reinhardt alone (with the one exception of Bernau) and waiting to see how far he'll be willing or able to exploit it, either in Berlin or on tour (possibly in the neutral countries).

I am very pleased to hear that you believe in *Ariadne* and love it: unfortunately this love and faith are shared so little by the public and the managers of German theatres that this delightful piece has vanished from the repertoire almost everywhere, with the exception of Vienna and Munich. We'll just have to put our hopes in good old posterity!

May the summer grant you at any rate fresh creative energy; after the turmoil of the winter I too am happy to be landed again amidst the tranquillity and beauty of my beloved mountains and in the bosom of my family.

My son was declared 'fit only for limited service at home stations' at his last medical and is therefore as good as exempt from military service—which is a great load off my mind. He can now calmly continue his studies at the university, and his frail health can be taken care of until he's got over his years of development. All good wishes and best regards to yourself and your family, also from my wife—always yours sincerely,

RICHARD STRAUSS

Garmisch, 31.5.18

My dear Friend,

This letter from R. may interest you as being symptomatic. I have answered all that could be answered factually. Denied, to start with, that the terms demanded from Bernau had been stiffer—apart from Pallenberg—than those from Reinhardt, argued that poor attendance of a play proved nothing against its worth, that *Ariadne* was sold out in Berlin as well as in Vienna, that 'cultured Vienna' would therefore have a particularly good opportunity of proving its superiority over 'boorish Berlin', that Reinhardt's second cast was as a rule a good deal better than first casts elsewhere, and that if Herr Bernau didn't like it he could, as far as we're concerned, follow Götz von Berlichingen's injunction.

There is of course just a chance that Reinhardt has allowed a performance to fall off, which would be a great pity indeed: perhaps you could ask for a complete set of playbills to be sent to you as a check. It would be a pity if our fine work were once more to be dead as a doornail, after such a brief life. The age, you know, doesn't favour us. Lothar and d'Albert are now holding sway. Yet things don't ever seem to have been any different. Goethe's diaries, which I've just been re-reading, offer no comforting indication that things were any better in the old days.

Kind regards! Yours,

RICHARD STRAUSS

Garmisch, 6.6.18

Dear Herr von Hofmannsthal,

Frau von Mendelssohn, who was ill here for a long time, has just left me. I have played her a large part of *Frau ohne Schatten*, and she was

301

highly enthusiastic about the poetry and the music. I had not taken the piece up for some time, and I too like the whole thing very much indeed. It is good—even though it is probably above the head of today's cultured society, or at least of those who ought to fill the theatres. But no matter: for the moment it is the turn of Lothar and d'Albert.

What do you think about Fürstner's suggestion? I don't think that Reinhardt could, or will, tour Germany with *Bürger als Edelmann*, if only because of the difficult apparatus. Except perhaps Holland, Switzerland, Scandinavia. Shouldn't we now after all release the piece for those German theatres which are interested in it? To begin with, I think, Halle, Altenburg, Cologne. But eventually, surely, it could be done by Munich, Dresden, Karlsruhe, Hamburg, Frankfurt, etc. Let me know about this, please. Best regards, always yours very sincerely

RICHARD STRAUSS

The composition of my little domestic opera[1] is making excellent progress. The whole thing is very well planned, and its structure and music will no doubt make up for what the piece lacks in poetic power. I'm getting on with it for the time being, until—I hope very soon—I get a new Hofmannsthal. I wish you a good productive summer and hope to see you at Aussee in August.

Garmisch, 12.6.18

Dear Herr von Hofmannsthal,

Do please read Plautus's *Miles gloriosus* (in Lenz, Volume II) and also the chapter on Sparta in the first volume of J. Burckhardt's *History of Greek Civilization*. I hardly think there could be a better setting for an operetta than this late down-at-heel Sparta.

With best regards (telegram received with thanks yesterday),

Yours,

RICHARD STRAUSS

Rodaun, 8.7.(1918)

Dear Dr. Strauss,

I am delighted to hear that, in playing *Die Frau ohne Schatten* to a receptive friend, you have drawn pleasure and encouragement from

[1] *Intermezzo.*

302

your own impression and from the effect on the hearer. This is undoubtedly one of the purest joys we can experience. A few days ago I discovered in one of Goethe's letters to W. von Humboldt the following sentence: 'To keep on working with any satisfaction, one must pay no heed to the reactions of the German public.' That's how it was and always will be.

About *Ariadne*, on the other hand, I don't feel as resigned as you do. I know, and I know for sure: this opera may not have the public of today, but it has the public of tomorrow. This assurance I have gained not only from the way the work came to life here; it was precisely in Berlin, too, that I felt how the people who really matter in our audiences are coming round to it. What prevents them for the time being from making themselves more distinctly felt is this: the Berlin Opera, under its present Philistine management, addresses its appeal exclusively to the obvious, ephemeral predilections of public taste and is contemptuous of the element of novelty which looks to the future. Besides, an all-too-plainly uninspired production actually prevents the whole piece from making a real impact. Yet none of this can deter me from taking an optimistic view. If I may offer my advice, I would for the time being let things go on in Berlin as they are, with a very few performances each year, and without any tinkering about with it by changes in the cast or that sort of thing; but in a few years' time, at the very first opportunity, I should insist on a careful new production with a first-class cast and with an entirely different set-up for the whole thing.

Another suggestion has occurred to me so often that I should like to mention it just once, though humbly: would it by any chance be possible for you, whose steady development also extends to matters of taste and sensitivity, to compose entirely new music for one number in *Ariadne*, a single one: I mean Zerbinetta's big aria? Here, it seems to me, is a concrete obstacle in the way of the opera's future prospects: the enormous difficulty of doing justice to the coloratura which actually, half ironical as it is meant to be, fails to make any vital contribution to the over-all effect. The immense demands made by these coloratura decorations lead to peculiar difficulties in casting the part: almost every one of the younger and more attractive singers of the soubrette type, whose appearance would naturally fit them for the feminine frailty of Ariadne's unheroic counterpart, are debarred from this role because they cannot manage this elaborate aria. If, on the other hand, you were to take the words of this aria which builds up a whole feminine type, perhaps the archetype of the feminine, and were to write new music of the smooth melodiousness of *Le Bourgeois* for its various phases with their distinct variation in rhythm, the whole aria would, I imagine, all at once gain a firmer hold on people's understanding and make this understanding a delight. At the same time a perpetual obstacle to the performance of the opera, especially in smaller theatres, would be removed. I do realize how annoying suggestions of this kind always are at first sight, so I ask you in any case, to forgive me for making this one!

Der Bürger als Edelmann I consider a failure—I must use this blunt word, for it is no use deceiving oneself—and the fault is, if anyone's, mine. I ought to have realized that the public, especially in Northern Germany, will take to anything elaborate and complicated, because it impresses them, as well as to the vile and the commonplace, but will not put up with old-fashioned works like this one which are meagre and, for all their delicacy, naïve and puppet-like. And so I went wrong when, instead of inventing my own framework at the time (for which I had already completed a scenario *Die artige Gräfin*), I fell back upon Molière out of sheer modesty and a desire not to encumber the work with an undue number of precarious Hofmannsthal ingredients. I repeated my mistake when, acting once more from wholly unexceptionable and selfless motives, I brought up the Molière play once again in order to rescue those enchanting fragments of incidental music— though in this case I must say I was encouraged and confirmed in my mistake by the great and lasting success scored at the same theatre, with the same comedian, by an equally naïve prose comedy of Molière's, *Le Malade Imaginaire*. It was only this success which, in the spring of 1916, decided me to arrange *Le Bourgeois Gentilhomme* for you. And so we arrive at the paradoxical result that the interposition of your music, music which receives the highest possible praise, has turned a Molière play, with Pallenberg in the title part, into a definite failure. A failure I call it because, given the enormous theatrical boom of 1918, it is difficult to avoid the word when one learns that Reinhardt was unable, with the best will in the world, to keep this piece going for more than thirty-five or forty performances (I don't know exactly how many),[1] and even that with very poor houses towards the end.

This result is certainly something to ponder over, for thinking makes one wiser. In a specific 'cabal' I do not believe; this sort of thing may serve as consolation to Pfitzner and his like, to people unwilling to

[1] Only thirty-one performances took place.

304

acknowledge that their work is essentially unsuited to the stage, but it will not do for us. It is hard to imagine more decided antagonism than that which at the time faced *Rosenkavalier*, I mean the libretto or in other words that part which corresponds to the Molière in our present case: it was reviled as 'crude' and as 'precious', as 'indecent' and as 'dull' all at once, and yet the effect, the success, made a clean sweep of all these objections. When all is said and done, effect and success on the stage are the outcome of a bargain struck directly between the public and the work itself. And the opposition to *Le Bourgeois* emanated from the public, of this I am absolutely convinced. It was the audiences we failed to win over; they were somehow chilled, their fun was marred, they were almost put off—quite spontaneously too, and without reflecting, and so it went on from act to act and from performance to performance. People never really enjoyed it and I believe, on thinking it over and re-examining my own feelings, I have discovered the true reason. The proper foundation of all drama is action, action which may be thrilling, or like a gentle puppet-show, or may turn upon psychology. In opera it is the music which becomes the vehicle of the action; dramatic action and music are so to speak two streams which mingle and flow on together. In this particular case, however, in the kind of thing we have for once done here, the music actually fails to contribute anything or to play any part in the progress towards the dramatic aim; it is on the contrary a retarding element (not everywhere, but at most points by far). The meagre and rickety action is constantly interrupted by passages of descriptive music and the audience, whose unsophisticated impulse is to get on with the plot, becomes restive and chafes at these retarding moments. It is, indeed, the constant interruption of the action which brings home to the public what otherwise it might not notice at all, I mean how meagre the plot is; they feel there is no need here for any relaxation of tension, for any retarding passages. This is my own explanation, and it would take pretty solid factual arguments to convince me that there could be any other reasons why a Molière comedy with Pallenberg, produced at the most popular theatre in the Metropolis, with music by the foremost and at the highest level even the most popular composer—why a comedy charmingly staged and brilliantly cast should turn out an unequivocal failure.

What conclusions ought to be drawn from these facts is not quite easy to say. I am afraid we stand to gain very very little, either financially or morally, from repeating this barely concealed failure at a number of smaller theatres. I wonder whether it would not be better, however painful, to hold this work back for special occasions? Or would it not be possible (you know you can count completely on my indefatigable goodwill, especially in cases like this), to take up this work again at a later stage with a fresh mind (which I, for one, lack at the moment) and make an opera of it? with *secco* recitatives? Or to find some other way of rescuing this enchanting music to which I am whole-heartedly attached? In any case I only wanted to speak my mind frankly; I do not venture to give advice.

Rest assured of my lasting goodwill in all our future joint concerns. Your personality, such as you are with all your energy—and still more your ideal personality as I distil it for myself from your music—has won my genuine friendship, that is all I can say to you, for that is the best I have to give. I am a much more bizarre kind of person than you can suspect; what you know is only a small part of me, the surface; the factors which govern me you cannot see. And so I am grateful to you for not prodding me, I am very grateful to you for that. Please do not do it, even indirectly, and do not remind me of things, for then I shall remind myself and as a result admonish myself. So bizarre is my constitution in such matters that, having once spoken to you of a certain possibility (a subject taken from late classical antiquity), your repeated allusions to this idea, your taking it up, your acquaintance with it, made the whole period distasteful to me and have driven it out of my thoughts and dreams, perhaps for good. So please take me as I am, and take me kindly.

Yours,

HOFMANNSTHAL

Garmisch, 12.7.18

My dear Herr von Hofmannsthal,

Thank you very much for your beautiful, extremely valuable, letter over which I am meditating seriously. I suppose I must endorse your judgment on *Bourgeois*, without at the same time entirely sharing its damning harshness. The whole thing, after all, is so attractive in form and content that I cannot believe that a more cultured public than exists today will not some time appreciate its value more fully—in spite of the fundamental shortcomings which you criticize and which are probably difficult to remedy at this stage. That is why I would suggest that we stop doctoring it and why I should find difficulty in applying the surgeon's knife to Zerbinetta again. Shall we write something new in the same manner and form? If ever you have an idea that needs accompanying and—as you very rightly discern—'retarding' music, like for instance *A Midsummer Night's Dream* or *Manfred*, to name only the most outstanding examples of this type among the older pieces—then you may count on me for a genuine new Hofmannsthal, but not some arrangement whose value no one will appreciate simply because it is an 'arrangement'. Reviewers' rot!

Don't be angry that I have 'prodded' you. It was not meant as a reminder—but you cannot blame me for dying to get something from you again soon. I am fifty-four years of age—how long my productive vigour will continue to yield something good, who can tell? And we could both give the world a good many fine things yet. What was it you said at the time? Every few years a delightful little Singspiel, in between a comedy with music (similar to *Bourgeois*), then a satirical operetta, and then—as it goes in the *Magic Flute*—another little Papageno, then another Papagena, until the spring runs dry.

We are going to Aschau on the 19th. Will you be at Aussee then? Can we see each other? If a meeting doesn't suit you or would disturb you in your work, please don't be afraid to say so. With best wishes for a good rest and kindest regards, in sincere gratitude for your valuable friendship, yours very sincerely,

RICHARD STRAUSS

1.8.1918[1]

Dear Dr. Strauss,

Your letter did me good and I am very grateful to you. In our relationship there is no need for many words and arguments. The passing reference to your fifty-four years does more to prompt me than any amount of persuasion. Rest assured that, whenever I feel in a productive mood, I shall always turn my imagination in the desired direction, in so far as this can be done by an effort of the will. At present I am not at

[1] When the two authors looked through their letters prior to the original publication of this correspondence (in 1925), Hofmannsthal wrote in the margin of this letter: 'I should very much like to include this letter if Dr. Strauss agrees, since it expresses what is best in our relation, I mean our mutual sincerity.' Strauss countered this with the following marginal note: 'Please omit this letter since its trend of thought is based on false assumptions. Strauss at Berlin, and Strauss at Vienna were two wholly different people.' The letter was eventually excluded from the first edition.

all well. Such depressions arise in my case either out of my work itself, or spring from some deep source in my physical constitution. All contact with the outside world, all social activity, business, sympathy, the newspapers, things in the gross aggravate this state; only rest, solitude and the right books can restore me.

Circumstances oblige me to speak of something else. I hear you are not unfavourably disposed towards accepting a possible invitation to Vienna. Indeed the plan to call you to Vienna may quite conceivably have cropped up there. I cannot help saying that this plan has an opponent who, though no musician and lacking other relevant qualifications, would still be listened to in this matter, would be listened to especially if he were to speak against your appointment, though less if he were to speak in its favour: I am that opponent.

Forgive me if I use very harsh and unduly strong language in order to explain to you my attitude. What I am concerned with are the merits of the case, and it is on the merits of the case, in this case, that I have no confidence in you.

I believe that about fifteen years ago you would have been the ideal person to bring about the urgently needed renaissance of the Vienna Opera, but I cannot think that you still are today. I believe—and what has given me this impression is the manner in which you yourself, with hundreds of little brush strokes, have painted the picture of your activity in Berlin—that today you would put your own personal convenience, and above all the egoism of the creative musician, before the uphill struggle for the ultimate higher welfare of that institution. I believe that, though you are still eminently *capable* of throwing yourself whole-heartedly into the task of building up the repertoire, into a Mozart or Wagner cycle, into protracted serious rehearsals (the ever-renewed youthfulness of your mind is the finest aspect of your personality and the most obvious assurance that you are a man of superior qualities), you would no longer be willing to do so. I believe, when it came to engaging artists, making enemies, friends, etc., etc., in short in handling the whole policy of the theatre, the advantage to your own works would be uppermost in your mind and not the advantage to the institution. All in all I feel that your appointment would add outward lustre to the Opera by giving it an important and famous conductor, but would not offer it any true, decisive, intrinsic benefit and must therefore, in the last resort, on careful and conscientious consideration be *rejected*, for the sake of the institution itself.

I do not find it easy to argue in this fashion. But I can't help it. I abominate all these personal things; it is the idea embodied in this institution, woefully debased and prostituted though it almost constantly is, which means everything to me. Only thus can I live at all, and the more I see through the wretchedness of human actions and relations, the more uncompromising my attitude.

I am very fond of the good and fine aspects of your personality where I meet them in the artist or, by sudden flashes, in the man as well. Without goodwill towards you I could not possibly speak so frankly, and you will be able to accept what I am saying in this manner only because you feel my goodwill underlying it all. The great danger of your life, to which you surrender and from which you try to escape in almost periodic cycles, is a neglect of all the higher standards of intellectual existence. Any attempt to place oneself above ideas and institutions is an utter negation of what matters to civilized human beings and, in so far as your works themselves form part of what matters in intellectual life, it is they, however much you mean to foster them, which will have to pay the eventual penalty. But I do not think that you have yet reached the point at which you can understand the connection.

I wish you well, better than most people have done in your life. You have not looked for many friends, and have not had many.

I wish you could convince me that I am wrong in what I have written above, and that your presence in Vienna would be beneficial. Nobody could be better pleased and more delighted than I.

I should very much like to go for an afternoon's walk with you tomorrow or the next day. I am at your disposal any time after four o'clock.

Yours,

HOFMANNSTHAL

Aschau, 5th August 1918

My dear Herr von Hofmannsthal,

Many thanks for your kind letter. Though it rather anticipates matters which have not yet in any way taken concrete shape and have scarcely more than flitted through my head from time to time—I am quite prepared to accept the news here and now, and without any offence, that you are an opponent of my accepting the post of Director of the Vienna Court Opera. You are entirely correct in saying that I neither could, nor would want to, accept this post today in the way Mahler filled it. That would have been possible fifteen or twenty years ago.

The few years that are left to me I must devote principally to my productive work. Nevertheless, since I compose only in the summer, I have resolved to devote five winter months for the next ten years or so to my work as a conductor—and since Berlin claims a little more than two months, I could well imagine myself spending the other, longer, half—and if necessary even part of the spring—in Vienna in a kind of advisory capacity (*along with* a full-time Director) in the building up of a truly artistic repertoire, with a say as to the manner of its execution, possibly the necessary new engagements of singers and young conductors (in lieu of Messrs. Reichwein and Tittel), the reorganization and rejuvenation of the magnificent orchestra, and so forth; moreover making myself useful to the institution as a practising artist, by the direction of some twenty to thirty operatic evenings each year, by undertaking each month a completely new production of an outstanding masterpiece and by conducting, upon my own choice and in a fully authoritative manner, either such operas of the current repertoire as appear to me valuable or first performances of domestic and foreign works that are deserving of support. Since I am generally regarded as a very good Mozartian and Wagnerian conductor, the works of these masters (in addition to Gluck and Weber) would be the first to be chosen for revival.

I think you will see even from these remarks that the premises of your letter were largely not correct. This is due to a faulty assessment of my past work at the Berlin Opera House, which, *if it were really in accord with my innermost inclinations*, must indeed throw a false light on my character as an artist.

Let me tell you therefore that it has been my devoutest wish for the past thirty years to assume the *de facto* supreme direction of a big Court Opera House on the artistic side. It was denied me: either because I was always regarded as the opposite of the so popular routine official, or because as too independent an artistic personality, as a composer of some reputation, I was not credited with sufficient interest in the routine running of a theatre and its everyday requirement, such as a purely reproductive artist would have. During twenty years' work in Berlin, under the utterly autocratic Count Hülsen, a man inaccessible to all influence, I finally gave up any attempt to have a say in the management of that institution and have thus become the kind of person that you are now judging so severely. What still keeps me in Berlin is my duty not to withdraw the father's loving hand from my own works at Germany's premier artistic institution, and a delight in a magnificently disciplined orchestra that is wholly attuned to me and from which, by working with it in continuous contact as a composer, like Antaeus with his instrument, I derive new inspiration. *Voilà tout*.—

If therefore a modus were to be found for such an 'Indian summer' enabling me to pursue in Vienna the kind of directing activity adumbrated above, say from about 15th December till the beginning of March, and again from Easter till the middle of May each year, a modus that would meet equally the requirements of the institution which is so much in need of reform, and the wishes of the public and the press, then I would cheerfully undertake to prove to you even today that my idealism, my energy and my objectivity are still the same as thirty years ago, or at most have been suitably mellowed to their advantage and restrained from over-extreme application by more mature experience.—I would ask you to content yourself for today with this rough outline of my justification which I shall be very glad to develop and prove to you in greater detail verbally at any time you like.

With best regards, yours very sincerely,

RICHARD STRAUSS

Alt Aussee, Friday 2 o'clock (first half of September 1918)

Dear Dr. Strauss,

I am very sad to hear you are ill. It is also a little unfortunate for the matter in hand, but we shall manage somehow.

It is just during the next three days that certain circumstances, which I know and understand, make it impossible for Andrian to be absent from here. For me alone to come over is pointless and would lose me another working day; where would this get me in the end?

This then is the position: Andrian was at first very sceptical of our schemes; advice he had received in Vienna from all sorts of quarters was very much against Schalk. Gradually I explained our ideas to him. He was cheered by the thought of your coming (to start with for those three and a half months, and later perhaps a little longer). The financial terms will *not*, I feel, present an insurmountable obstacle. But he must have reason to feel and believe that you have every wish and intention to give new impetus to the institution and that you will put all your energy into this without consulting your own interest. He considers it an obvious duty of his to promote your works, but says you must reassure him that, even when, let us say, *Die Frau ohne Schatten* is on the repertoire, you will refrain from conducting predominantly your own works only, and not the classics. All this needs talking over; we must get there gradually. I am most anxious for it to come off, but I am not glossing over the difficulties and differences; I mean to remove them. To both of you I say: don't be narrow-minded, but do strive, both of you, for what is best and most beautiful. Andrian considers October 14 too late for the suggested discussion. He would very much like your advice how to deal with Gregor for the rest of the time, since he is supposed to restrict that gentleman's pernicious activities as much as possible!

I have only one idea to get us out of this impasse (for I am nervous of all the intermediaries, projects, and subsequent schemes): how about coming to Vienna from Salzburg for twenty-four hours? Andrian will be in Vienna at your disposal from the 18th onward. As soon as you are well enough, please let me have a reply by express. I feel this might be the best way out—and how often you have travelled a very long way for one silly concert!

I believe I have paved the way for this matter as well as one could. (. . .)

(The end of this letter is missing.)

Rodaun, 5.12.1918

Dear Dr. Strauss,

Schalk has shown me with great delight the admirable letter you have written to him, and I was delighted with it myself. For I am convinced that, whatever regime we may get here, the idea of inviting you will not be abandoned. I firmly believe, on the strength of many years' acquaintance with both of you, that you and Schalk will be able to work along with each other perfectly and so to usher in a promising new era for this most valuable institution which to me personally is so exceedingly precious. You, of course, tower above him not only in creative capacity (and by how much!), but also in strength of will-power and flexibility of mind. Still, what he has to contribute is by no means inconsiderable: he is a mature artist, and in his case respect for a high and great tradition is not window-dressing, but scrupulous conviction. His feeling for quality may in the last resort fall short of yours, but his judgement might conceivably be more stable, since he is perhaps capable of forming more vivid first impressions than you are. (. . .)

If I understand aright your present situation in your life and as an artist (and your letter is to me confirmation that this is precisely the view you yourself hold), you mean to devote your best efforts to the Vienna Opera, without however putting the whole of your time and energy into this activity as a director. Schalk's case is just the opposite; he cannot expect to round off his life's work anywhere except here. It is from your share in the job, nonetheless, that the decisive impulse will have to come, not only during the years you are here, but for the future, too: the approach, and the type of your and Schalk's successors will have to bear your impress (and his, but yours much more). Today you are ripe for this, yet not over-ripe: to be ripe means to seek what is highest not in the bizarre, but in what may seem obvious, and to set out to achieve it fully.

You draw my attention to Fritzi Massary[1] and your letter shows that you have been deeply impressed. She is indeed beyond doubt a person who has genius. My own thoughts, which often, and with pleasure, turn upon our joint enterprises, are nonetheless running in a rather different direction, towards the development of new forms in the sphere of lyrical comedy, the Singspiel, the comic opera, yet of a kind that can be performed within the given set-up of our opera houses. I would rather do that than follow you into alien territory, but let us not exclude any possibilities, since all these fields are after all close to each other.

As always, yours sincerely,

HOFMANNSTHAL

(Telegram from Hofmannsthal to Strauss)　(*Rodaun, 7.12.1918*)

ABSOLUTELY REJECT KARPATH'S MUDDLES. FOR OWN AND OPERA HOUSE SAKE WISH AND HOPE FOR YOUR COMING WITHOUT WHICH COMPLETE COLLAPSE HERE. HAVE CONSTANTLY

[1] Fritzi Massary's immense success at the time was chiefly in musical comedy. (Translator)

My dear Friend,   *7.12.(1918)*

I am re-opening my envelope. Am utterly shattered by your hasty letter dated November 30,[1] but bearing postmark Berlin December which has just reached me. Have sent you an urgent telegram along these lines: Reject absolutely Karpath's muddles, have constantly desired your coming here for own as well as Vienna Opera's sake and have constantly worked for this!

Muddle-makers in such troubled times are real hell. Karpath is not an evil person, but a *stupid* one and therefore useless. Why for goodness sake didn't you send me a telegram all that week?

Karpath came to see me one day in great excitement, saying it looked as if you did not wish to come, that you preferred Berlin and so on. Quite possibly my answer may have been: If Strauss does not want to come, then one would have to think, etc. He must have totally misunderstood this, like every other shade of meaning. Have I not worked all these weeks like a cart-horse for one thing: to save the Strauss-Roller-Schalk combination? I am, in fact, full of hope for this regime, I *want* you here—so what is all this nonsense about? I am entirely in agreement with a Vienna première, have never received a letter inquiring about it and wonder why, since I invariably reply to everything, you did not repeat your inquiry by telegram?

Let us hope that we are now done with these muddles!

Very sincerely yours,

HOFMANNSTHAL

Dear Dr. Strauss,   *Rodaun, 25.12.1918*

We send you and your family our affectionate good wishes of the season. May the coming year treat us kindly as it progresses and offer us the bare bones of a new, if modest existence, the chance to do our work and to influence others. For the time being at least you and your wife are freed of the constant, nagging anxiety about Bubi's immediate future.

[1] Not extant.

314

With regard to Vienna, I hope you have received my express letter of Dec. 7, as well as the telegram I sent you immediately on receipt of your letter, in my boundless astonishment over this misunderstanding. What touched me profoundly on this occasion was the infinite kindness and forbearance with which you reacted to my (supposed) opposition against your coming to Vienna. My pleasure over your amiable reaction was all the purer, since in fact my attitude throughout had been the very reverse, as you will have seen from my letter of Dec. 5th which was ready for posting before I heard from you and which I enclosed at the time, a letter full of the prospect of your coming here and your collaboration with Schalk and Roller.

Korngold misses no opportunity of kotowing to Strauss the composer, while at the same time he burrows and agitates against Strauss the Opera Director (who 'from starry heights' intends to direct both theatres). When one comes to consider the incompetence of all concerned and the fickleness of public opinion which by inveterate instinct inclines towards the baser of two alternatives, when one takes into account that in the immediate future the Schalk regime is bound to be, through no fault of his, rather lack-lustre, I must say it would be a relief to me to know this whole thing finally settled. At the same time it would seem to me a good idea if, perhaps by a letter to the editor of *Neue Freie Presse*, you were to make it plain once and for all, as plain as you made it in your letter to me, that strictly speaking you do not intend to *continue your activities* at the Berlin Opera, but mean only to conduct concert cycles in Berlin, and that you will devote all your energy—apart from your work as a composer—to the Vienna institution and its regeneration, and not least to the conductors of the rising generation.

Some of your telegrams were really misleading, even to me, until your letter made everything plain by the straightforward, wholly convincing sentence that obviously you did not in any circumstances whatever intend to carry on under Droescher in a conductor's position which had already proved pretty well impossible under Hülsen. I should be inclined to represent your half-stunted activities in Berlin (problematical as they must be in any case, given the present unstable political conditions) as *even less* than they are, rather than as so promising and extensive as certain telegrams seem to suggest. This would at last deprive those who oppose you of the argument that you mean to do a balancing act between the one place and the other.

As a matter of fact there is an immense amount that can be done here, any number of friends and supporters to be won over. From here, much more than from Berlin, the whole theatrical outlook might be revolutionized for a generation to come by just such a combination as Strauss-Schalk-Roller, which has something symbolical in its fusion of tradition with progress, of Viennese elements with modern German ones, on the common basis of the sensuousness and rhythmical sense which are the special gifts of the South Germans. Your presence here will at the same time provide the *point d'appui* for Salzburg, for Reinhardt's drawing closer; it will greatly strengthen my hand in questions affecting cultural affairs. In short, to sum up once again the strange truth behind Karpath's muddle: I could think of no greater disappointment than the failure of this scheme.

Please read these lines to your wife with whom I should always wish to be *d'accord*, especially in the practical matters of life.

One thing I should like to say *en passant*, since it is often on my mind: if only, yes if only it could be managed that Anna Mildenburg sings the Nurse—but probably this is quite out of the question! What a gain this would be to me so far as Bahr is concerned, whose relations with Andrian were poisoned like a plague spot purely for the sake of this woman. Let me have a word about this and forgive me for referring to it again.

Another telegram of mine contained my consent to the Vienna world première. An earlier inquiry directed to Aussee never reached me. I am never discourteous, least of all towards you; such silence therefore is a sure sign that a letter has failed to arrive.

Roller reports to me your letters and wishes. His sense of duty and his devotion in questions of art is matchless. And so he will do everything that can be done and with the least possible delay, taking into account at the same time the reduced resources and all the rest, and doing the designs accordingly. This is exactly what makes him so unique that, with utter disregard of the artist's egoism, he invariably and with a real sense of responsibility aims at the final result, at that which is really feasible. Let me hear from you again soon. In friendship yours,

HOFMANNSTHAL

1919

Dear Dr. Strauss,

Received your letter today and, being in bed (with a slight cold), I read it through with great care. I understand now what you want. Certain contradictions remain irreconcilable. In your letter of November 30, 1918, you say (I quote) ' . . . Berlin, where a subordinate position as conductor under or with Dr(oescher) is even more impossible now than it was under Hülsen when, as you know, I held on only for the sake of my works.' In today's letter you develop the plan of very intensive activity in Berlin under or with Dr(oescher). Either the facts, or your opinion of the facts must therefore have undergone a decisive change. This and other things you must explain to me by word of mouth at the end of January.

You remind me of our talks at Aussee which envisaged a divided sphere of activity. True, but at that time everything depended on a single person—on Andrian; provided one could make this plausible to him, and get him to accept it, all would have been well. By now the whole thing hangs much more in the air; all sorts of people (Sylvester etc.) have a say in the decision and yet can decide nothing, while at the same time that elusive thing the *vox populi*, carries more weight. Even so I believe in the feasibility of what you have in mind. I believe in it because, apart from everything else, I wish to think it feasible—but nobody except you yourself can put this plan to Sylvester or to anyone else; you alone have the right manner, and the authority necessary to advocate successfully this sort of rather uncommon set-up, which involves special demands of a financial order as well as others. The financial aspects alone, which loom so large in this, render me altogether unfit as a go-between.

Quite apart from this, however, I agree with Schalk that it would be best to do nothing for the time being, not even a note in the newspapers. I believe you will have gone a long way if towards the end of January you ask young Korngold, who is after all a young artist and not a petty haggler, to come and see you for an hour and do him the honour of explaining what you have in mind. Moreover, I have every reason to expect that a new, very serious newspaper is to be founded, which will presumably reduce the preponderant influence of the *Neue Freie Presse*.

But now between ourselves, strictly between you and me, I come back to the doubts I expressed candidly during our first talk at Aussee: will you really be able to raise the energy to permeate with your spirit that fine Viennese institution—of which you speak in your letter in somewhat harsh a tone? Have you not taken on rather too much? Never forget one thing: for you, as a composer whose works are intended to last (whether for thirty years or for more than thirty years), there can be only one *sound* policy: to do everything possible for the advancement of these institutions, putting aside all momentary egoism; to maintain and to raise their standard; to think and plan not in terms of a season but of decades. We must talk about this when we meet.

I don't think much of participation in the management by letter. That remains invariably a sort of monologue into the void, and leads to errors and misunderstandings *en masse*. To mention one right away: Schalk tells me that you are resolutely in favour of disbanding the Ballet, and asks me to discuss this carefully with Roller. After a very thorough conversation with Roller we—starting from the opposite opinion—eventually arrive at the conclusion that we would also advocate the dissolution. Now I discover in your letter a line concerning Fokine which shows me that you mean to preserve the Ballet after all. I only mention this to tell you how much I hope that you will come here, first of all, on a visit soon; and later on in the way you have in mind. If so, I shall willingly take part in everything and hope that this new era will prove a good productive era for us, too.

Now for something personal, entirely between ourselves, relating to *Die Frau ohne Schatten*. You, my dear Dr. Strauss, never mean to vex me, your collaborator, I am sure of that—on the contrary you wish to keep me close to you and to strengthen our ties. In my case, however, everything hinges upon the imagination; little turns on persuasion and goodwill, and least of all on pecuniary considerations. But when I am faced with ugliness, as in the case of the décor of all our productions in Berlin, and when these disagreeable sensations impress themselves on the eye, my most sensitive spot, when they recur again and again and become to me a sort of symbol for the prostitution of the child of my imagination in sordid, vulgar 'business', then this exasperates me, and this exasperation might for a long period or even permanently incapacitate me for this kind of work.

Under the Hülsen regime the situation was such that, very much against my better feelings, I acquiesced in the way you conducted our relations with the theatre, and thus I did not, for instance, even hear *Ariadne* there. But if the same thing is now to happen all over again, if these (. . .) Droeschers and Kautskys are to botch Roller's designs in the same old way, if one's eyes are once again to be outraged by these disgusting colours, as happens always and invariably at this Berlin Opera which I loathe (*Salome* not to be forgotten, a sight to make anyone retch who has eyes to see)—I must enter the most vehement protest, and must address it to the only authority whom I consider competent, namely you. No, here I must draw the line! This is flying in the face of our whole relationship, whose best terms are the unwritten ones. There are two acceptable alternatives: either Roller's designs are scrupulously followed in Berlin, especially in every minute detail of colour and lighting, so that we get something of which neither he nor I need be ashamed; or, if local pride insists on changing them—all right, but only with the concurrence of a Berlin painter who accepts the responsibility. Walser is available there, and he would be ideal for *this* opera, especially for the costumes—better than Roller. Therefore either the one or the other. This is my unalterable point of view. And I do not wish you to give in to me merely as an act of friendship, or out of fairness, or respect; sound common sense must make you support me.

As a matter of theatre policy in the case of a work of yours and mine, a work which is exacting, which must first be understood by a minority and gradually make its way to success, nothing could be more foolish than to alienate from the outset all the vital groups which are generally considered sophisticated, well educated and authoritative; in Berlin—in complete contrast to Vienna—these are the circles, groups, salons, cafés, and so on, dominated by painters. The Liebermann circle, the Slevogt circle, the circle round the Cassirers, the Gurlitt and Corinth circles, the circle of Reinhardt and the studios of the younger men—these are the receptive and truly leading groups; they will determine the 'tomorrow' and the 'day after tomorrow'. How could we—Strauss/Hofmannsthal—we of all people!—contemplate rebuffing them and exposing ourselves from the outset to the ill-will and indifference of those who should be our natural allies; how could we possibly, by the whole visual make-up of the work, and in Berlin of all places, throw in our lot outright with the Philistines! No, such a policy is too foolish. If you but realized the impact of visual impressions on people of sensitive sight (musicians do not generally know this, but you for one might suspect it), you would rather let that voiceless

Mildenburg sing the Nurse—which would presumably be a cardinal mistake—than allow yet one more work to be at the mercy of this gross barbarism. I beg of you to let me know your resolve on this point soon, so as to set my mind at rest. For years I have restrained myself in this respect, knowing that you were unable to contend with the existing situation; but now you *must* contend with it: there is a limit to everything, and surely the whole regime cannot have collapsed just to leave us with this mess.

I have written the synopsis[1] in the last few days and will shortly send you and Fürstner a copy each. The fairy-tale,[2] the most difficult piece of work I have ever undertaken, and the one which makes the highest demands on my character, I hope to complete by the spring. It is of course to be published, if at all, a few months before the opera. To work in present conditions here, in almost unheated rooms, with no gas and practically no electricity, is virtually impossible. Gradually we have reached a point where one must assume that things can only get better, not worse than they are.

Au revoir, then. Ever yours sincerely,

HOFMANNSTHAL

P.S. If the Vienna première[3] is to take place on October 1st, I cannot, with the best will in the world, return from the country except for the last three rehearsals. The reason is of course that September/October is my chief productive period, almost the only time which makes my life worth living. This will not cause any practical problems; together with Roller I shall produce, with the assistance of a repetiteur, a detailed prompt-book. Roller who, after Reinhardt, is one of the most competent of producers and quite capable of demonstrating each gesture, will then produce it together with one of the producers from the Opera to be nominated—but not with Wymetal, with whom he has always refused to work. I guarantee that this will work out perfectly.

Have you ever given any thought to a second cast for Vienna? It is, after all, quite on the cards that Jeritza, unpredictable as she is, may leave us in the lurch four weeks after the première.

P.S. Very glad about your wife's recovery. Did not know anything was wrong.

---

[1] Of the libretto for the opera *Die Frau ohne Schatten.*
[2] The prose tale *Die Frau ohne Schatten.*
[3] The première of *Die Frau ohne Schatten* took place on 10th October 1919.

My dear Friend,

Many thanks for your splendid letter of the 4th.

I hasten to clear up the most important misunderstandings, once and for all, I hope.

1. I don't understand how Schalk could believe that I was in favour of disbanding the Ballet. I consider the Vienna Ballet highly necessary—if only to relieve the rather scanty operatic personnel. The only question is whether it wouldn't be permissible to reduce the staff by eliminating unusable and superfluous elements.

I continue to share *your* point of view: reform and modernization of the Ballet, possibly Fokine, Bolm, or whomever else you recommend for it.

(. . .)

2. I refused to continue my conducting activities in Berlin *under* Droescher. In the meantime it has emerged that, while Droescher is sole Director, I have a special position *directly under the Ministry*, can conduct and produce whatever I want and whenever I want to, and have a decisive say in all matters of importance—such as new works, engagements, the trend of the repertoire, and *productions*. I have already spent the whole of November wielding a reforming hand in the Berlin 'mess', as you rightly call Hülsen's 'art of production', and have moreover met with much helpfulness on the part of Droescher and Kautsky who were also largely victims of Hülsen's 'know-all attitude'. I have already had the *Ring* simplified; I have totally eliminated Hülsen's *Magic Flute* and am having the Schinkel scenery repainted; Hülsen's already completed *Don Giovanni* I have revised from scratch; etc. etc. The only reason why I can't proceed too radically is that, to begin with, Kautsky is the brother of the Minister and has political influence on the whole future character of the Opera House. For the moment, therefore, I must manœuvre carefully and try to achieve by means of amicable persuasion whatever lies within the bounds of present possibilities. *In principle I am entirely on your side!* As a first step towards getting Roller's designs[1] accepted in Berlin I have asked Droescher and Kautsky to have a look at Roller's sketches.

My conditions are these: if the sketches meet with their approval they must be *put into effect unchanged*. It was invariably only Hülsen who messed about with everything. If they are not approved, then new

[1] For *Die Frau ohne Schatten*.

designs must be submitted to me which I, in turn, can reject. In which case I would put forward Walser!

But I am firmly convinced that Roller will be accepted without difficulty. For that is what I am out to achieve, and I only chose this diplomatic approach in order to establish Roller the more surely. We'll talk all this over more fully in Vienna. If it is possible by train, I should like to come to Vienna for the meeting of the Salzburger Festspielgemeinde on 21st January. In any case I believe I can assure you that I have the energy and the goodwill to achieve in Vienna all that you expect of me; neither do I intend to practise my directorship by correspondence or to pursue a one-season policy—indeed I am a little surprised that I have to make a point of giving you these assurances. But evidently misunderstandings do arise in letters, which will no doubt be cleared up by personal contact.

As I've said, it is for the sake of the reforms which your eye so much desired that I should like to keep a finger in the Berlin pie for a little. But if this cannot be reconciled with Vienna, and when once I see that my activity in Vienna promises to be congenial and of some duration, then my choice is made already. I shall not be guided by any personal selfishness in this matter, and material interests too must take second place. You may rely on me absolutely in this matter.

An alternative cast for *Frau ohne Schatten* in Vienna is difficult. Would you consider Kiurina capable of the second Empress and Schoder of the Dyer's Wife? Or the other way round? The Empress needs a lot of dramatic force in Act III and the Dyer's Wife much vocal brilliance in the top range. 'Accursed dilemma!'

Let me finish by wishing you a speedy recovery and the best possible mood for the completion of the fairy-tale, to which I am looking forward with tremendous curiosity. With best regards from us to you all (my wife is quite well again), yours very sincerely,

RICHARD STRAUSS

(P.S. to a letter by Professor Kautsky) Garmisch, 5.2.1919

My dear Friend,

This letter from Kautsky is so true to type that I must send it to you. I hinted to him once about Chinese fairy-tale motives: now this disciple of Hülsen wants to haul me off to the Ethnographic Museum. Always, at all costs, historical and never artistic! Naturally I shall now insist that Roller's designs are executed unchanged also for Berlin; to this end I would ask you for a few factual points with which I could face Kautsky tactfully but crushingly, since, as you know, I'm not too ·well up on pictorial art and history myself. I managed to get as far as Innsbruck in a heated special coach, reached my Garmisch idyll yesterday afternoon and am thinking with much satisfaction of the good work done in Vienna together with you, Schalk and Roller.

The enclosed article might give you pleasure.

With best regards, always yours very sincerely,

RICHARD STRAUSS

Rodaun, *12.2.*(*1919*)

Dear Dr. Strauss,

The confusion in the minds of these North Germans is vast and pretty hopeless. The reason is that these people have no immediate relation to art whatever, but perpetually confuse art with education, i.e. with learnedness, two things which have nothing whatever in common.

I would ask you to reply roughly in the following sense: the lack of consistent style in the décor (i.e. this suggestion of various styles drawn from the ancient Orient) is by well-considered intention. Since the libretto presents not a historical anecdote, but an eternal or timeless, symbolic subject, it requires idealized costume and an idealized setting. Almost until the close of the 18th century our civilization possessed an accepted convention with regard to idealized costume—it was that of antiquity, its dress and architecture modified according to the taste of the time, a kind of purely conventional 'Orient'. Goethe, for instance, employed elements of this style right down to the time of the Empire for works of an *idealized* character. In the course of the 19th century, that century of historiography *par excellence*, the spirit of the time undermined this unsophisticated approach to 'idealized' décor and its place was taken by every conceivable variant of 'historical' stage sets. Yet, the more exacting the sense of historical and ethnographic accuracy, the more inexorable the consequent impossibility of building up, out of these elements, the idealized or universal setting. This very over-stressing of historical accuracy in theatre décor brought about a crisis. To achieve today what, prior to 1800 could have been expressed in a conventional, only seemingly historical idiom, we have no alternative but to avoid everything that is historically and ethnographically precise and—so

323

as not to drift into vague shapelessness—to gather together hetero-
genuous elements and by their combination to suggest remoteness,
mystery, grandeur and religious feeling. As in all matters of art, the
vital thing here is tact, that universal quality which is poles apart from
Berlin intellectual life.

Ceterum et iterum censeo, if you intend to conduct in Berlin opera
policy on the grand scale, and if you wish to prevent the significant
circles of the public from deserting opera wholly for the concert hall
and to prevent the Opera in the very heart of the Capital from degenerating into a provincial enterprise, you will have to endeavour to take
all matters of décor systematically out of the hands of people whose
impotence is almost beyond your comprehension, and to put them into
the hands of artists. Opera is after all a Gesamtkunstwerk, not just since
Wagner, who merely, most boldly and audaciously, gave shape and
substance to old universal trends, but ever since its glorious beginning,
since the 17th century and by the terms of its fundamental purpose: the
rebirth of the Gesamtkunstwerk of antiquity. How simple all this is,
how easy to understand except by ponderous North-German brains.

North-German and ponderous also is this most long-winded treatise
on *Ariadne*[1] which you have sent me. My God, how dull of perception,
how clumsy and heavy-handed! What can be the point of tracing the
derivation of my libretto from (North-German) romanticism, when
both my art and yours derive so effortlessly, so naturally from the
Bavarian-Austrian baroque with its mixture of different elements and
their fusion in music. And on the heart of the matter—the relation
between Ariadne and Bacchus—not the slightest light is thrown
throughout the whole twenty pages of these ponderous and yet complacent cogitations. What pathetic and dull-witted human beings! A
man like Roller stands out as a phoenix, simply because he is not an
enemy of the imagination but means to serve it.

Sincerely yours,

HOFMANNSTHAL

Dear Dr. Strauss, *Wednesday (towards the end of March)*

I hope you are well again. From Friday afternoon onwards I am once
more available. Best through a line to the porter, Stallburggasse 2.

[1] *The Ironic Ariadne and the Bürger als Edelmann* by Bernhard Diebold.

324

My dear friend, I do not mean to weary you with matters that bore you and personally I myself do not care a straw about that sort of thing. But for the sake of all these intricacies of policy in matters of art it would be most opportune if, given Bahr's peculiar and dangerous character, you were one of these days to devote twenty minutes to visiting Mme Mildenburg. Her position, not *vis-à-vis* the management, but towards those who do the individual dramatic coaching is such that even a crumb like that (the prospect of her being wanted in next year's repertoire) would do a lot of good. In this instance I do not altogether agree with your wife's judgement, except in so far as *a certain degree* of insincerity usually belongs to the make-up of gifted theatrical people.

Yours,

HOFMANNSTHAL

(*P.S. to a letter from Kautsky*) *Garmisch, 8.6.1919*

My dear Friend,

I should like to try Kokoschka in Berlin after all: there's no doubt he'd bring fresh life into that bogged-down Berlin scene. I hope you've got my letter about Fried. I am hoping Schalk and his wife will come and see us next week.

Best regards, yours

RICHARD STRAUSS

Garmisch, 17.6.1919

My dear Friend,

As you see, Direktor Droescher has already been active: would you please let me know how you stand in regard to this idea?

The fact is that Kautsky is reluctantly executing Roller's designs: the great question is whether the producer Holy, together with a rather mediocre chief machinist, will be able to bring them properly to life in the theatre. To what extent the absolute freedom that he demands is *in line with your intentions* I would ask you to decide and, perhaps, confer with Kokoschka in person. At present he is at the Weisser Hirsch near Dresden: I am going to write to him and refer him to you. Everything, in fact, will depend on how far K. can come to terms with Roller's decorations on which work is already progressing.

325

As for the invitation from Salzburg, that I should go there at the beginning of July, I can't accept it in view of present travelling conditions and my urgent need for rest. Surely it'll be enough if Roller and Reinhardt consult with you there on the spot. And surely there's no sense in the proposal of the Gemeinde to co-opt Professor M. to the Artistic Council! What do we want a Mozart pundit for? What's your opinion?

With best regards, yours very sincerely,

RICHARD STRAUSS

Dear Dr. Strauss, *Rodaun, the 21.6.1919*

The Kokoschka experiment meets with no artistic objections on my part whatsoever. For years I have hoped in vain for something like this in Berlin. He will introduce the fantastic, baroque, timeless elements and, since he is a really gifted artist, there is no reason why he should not reign supreme over the whole décor and alter Roller's designs; I shan't mind in the least, nor will Roller; he begrudges nothing to Kokoschka who was once his pupil anyway. For the *artistic* aspect I therefore willingly accept responsibility. But I can certainly not do so for the practical aspects of the staging. K. is an absolute amateur in matters of the theatre, and, as I am learning to realize just now during the preparation of the prompt-book, the opera involves most complicated stage machinery and requires for this reason an absolutely reliable expert, who can expertly and with unquestioned authority give instructions to the chief machinist, the chief electrician and all the rest, otherwise nothing will go right.

Kokoschka is, as I am told on all sides, a man of genius but by no means reliable; he takes no notice of contracts, stays away from his job for days, treats everything as an improvisation and so forth. It is essential therefore that you should get one of the local experts, either Kautsky or the chief machinist, to vouch unreservedly for the practical side of the production. In this respect I, as an outsider, must decline all responsibility. The discussions with Breuer, who has given a great deal of most penetrating thought particularly to the acting in this production, reveal that the performers of two of the leading parts will leave much to be desired. (. . .)

Since the opera has unfortunately been billed for the beginning of the season, so that during the preceding months the cast will be God knows where, I would ask you most earnestly to keep young Breisach with you as long as possible, and then, quite in the Bayreuth manner, to ask especially Weidt (whose part depends entirely on good enunciation) and if possible Lehmann as well to come and study their parts under your supervision, so that these two, who are the least gifted as actors, will be almost perfect by the time they come to rehearsal. Otherwise I foresee trouble. Jeritza, Mayr and Aagard should not present any problem.

I agree with you that the Artistic Council[1] has its full complement and that taking on this man M. or anyone else would only increase the difficulties. Perhaps you and Schalk together can contrive to find some felicitous and inoffensive formula to reject M. I also agree with you that your complete recovery is important and that your presence at Salzburg can be dispensed with; if Reinhardt, Roller and I do discuss certain questions, nothing will be settled which you could conceivably disapprove of. With my respects to your dear wife, I am in friendship yours,

HOFMANNSTHAL

Rodaun, 23.6.(1919)

Dear Dr. Strauss,

I am flabbergasted by Sch(illings's) appointment to Berlin. It looks like a repetition of the Vienna coup à la W(eingartner)? (. . .) Please tell me frankly what repercussions you expect so far as your works on the repertoire are concerned.

Are we decided on Kokoschka? My express letter of yesterday which contains my consent has, I hope, reached you.

Sincerely yours,

HOFMANNSTHAL

Garmisch, 27.6.1919

Dear Friend,

Many thanks for your letter. I've no reply yet from Kokoschka, but fear that nothing much will come from personal negotiations, especially as Reinhardt is also negotiating with K. and Max Schillings will probably become Droescher's successor. (. . .)

[1] Of the Salzburg Festival.

327

Concerning *Frau ohne Schatten*, I am hoping to get Mlle Lehmann to come here for private study at the beginning of August and Mme Weidt at the end of August. Schalk is with me and we have had extensive talks about all the important questions. I intend to be in Vienna on 28th August for the first setting rehearsal. But before then I must have your and Roller's prompt-book and study it thoroughly: I'm asking you therefore to send me a copy here for my private use as soon as you've got it ready, possibly even before you send it off to Fürstner.

Best wishes for a good summer (may it bring you some good operatic subjects for me: I should so much love to have a political satire in late-Grecian garb, with Jeritza as a hetaera from Lucian—today's musical-comedy governments are downright asking to be set to music and ridiculed).

With kindest regards from us to you all, yours very sincerely,

RICHARD STRAUSS

Garmisch, 30.6.1919

My dear Friend,

Six months ago the staff of the Berlin Opernhaus unanimously elected Dr. Droescher; today, on the motion of Mme Kemp, its leading singer, (. . .) it elects Max Schillings. This, one would think, has now definitely reduced the Artists' Self-Government *ad absurdum*. (. . .)

I suppose my closer connections with the Berlin Opera will now have come to an end.

Schalk was very helpful and charming, and we worked hard together and made progress in several directions. We too may come to the Ötztal about the middle of July and hope to see you there.

With best regards, ever yours sincerely,

RICHARD STRAUSS

Rodaun, 1.7.19

Dear Dr. Strauss,

Thank you for your kind letter of June 27. The mails are at last beginning to get better. Regarding Berlin, which is after all the key point for the fate of the new opera, it seems to me essential that you should keep matters of art in your own hands—not the detail, but simply the choice of executants. Kokoschka was acceptable to me, and

328

so would be any other reputable painter, or as an alternative the *scrupulous* reproduction of the Roller designs, but not their half-hearted reproduction, ugly colours—another Hülsen affair. I must insist again and again how much is at stake there, not least because the attitude of the painters (Slevogt circle, Liebermann's salon, the Cassirer circle) to the opera will be determined to a considerable extent by visual impressions (even if this is quite an irrelevant approach to a work of music) and it is these people who determine one way or the other the climate of the reception by the intellectual half of Berlin.

With regard to the prompt-book, Roller and I have come to the definite conclusion that, in contrast to *Rosenkavalier*, no such thing can be produced except as part of the piano score. The reason is that in *Rosenkavalier* there was quite a lot of play-acting independent of the music: ceremonies like the levée and the solemn entry, burlesques like the duel, the *quodlibet* at the inn, the whole by-play of the two sets of footmen, the pantomime in the third act and so on.

In *Die Frau ohne Schatten* little more than the gestures of a few leading performers need settling throughout and these will have to be exactly fitted to the music; the outcome of Roller's and my joint labours with Breuer, who is mimically very gifted, consists therefore of a close network of notes and entries in Breuer's piano score. Will you please get Fürstner to send another piano score for your personal use immediately to Kammersänger Breuer, Rodaun bei Wien, Elisenstrasse; I shall then ask Breuer to prepare for you an exact copy of the numerous production notes and to send it to Garmisch by registered post.

In July, when he is in the country, Roller will draw up precise instructions for all stage producers concerning the transformations, the magic contrivances and so on. But this big, strong man is at present so over-worked and under-nourished that he looks pitiable and is constantly, so I am told, on the point of hysterics. He vitally needs five or six weeks of real rest, otherwise he will collapse in the winter, and that would be a bad beginning!

I am myself pretty run down, but if I get a chance to spend a few weeks in high altitudes—and luckily I have found room at the Tauernhaus at Ferleiten, 1150 m. high and good food—I shall pick up again and pursue vigorously the scent of the three or four subjects (opera, singspiel or operetta) which I have in mind, and I hope to track down *more than one of them*.

Since Ferleiten is only three hours rail journey from Salzburg, I can easily get there if Reinhardt should need me, and can keep an eye on the Salzburg project which is so very important even for our own future (yours and mine). I shall let you know before I leave this address.

All the best,

HOFMANNSTHAL

Bad Aussee, 18.9.19

Dear Dr. Strauss,

The decision to settle on a date in autumn for the première of *Die Frau ohne Schatten* always appeared to me a mixed blessing, for ever since the age of twenty I have known that these months, August and September, are my truly productive ones each year; they determine the harvest of the whole year, often of several years even. What I could not foresee in the least, however, is that this year would prove so fortunate a one for me, that slow recovery from lingering and fairly deep-seated physical disorders would coincide with recuperation from manifold despondencies of mind, and that I would regain that natural affluence of my resources which I have missed year after year.

This is what has actually happened. I find myself in the midst of a phase from which I would not wrench myself away for anything, literally not for anything in the world, for every day presents me with invaluable treasure—you will not consider the expression presumptuous, since it is after all the fitting word for the best that is granted to each of us. Therefore you will not fail to understand perfectly why I deprive myself of the joy of listening to the rehearsals, except the last three or four. What I am giving up is pure joy, the magic of seeing my words and characters blossoming out in your music, and the incomparable enrichment which I gain each time in the purest intellectual sphere from this collaboration by drinking, as early as possible and as near as possible, from the still undesecrated source. Yet a life of vibrating work and inspiration, such as I am leading here among my five trees or in an attic of the Ramgut farm, half enraptured and half almost disturbed by these heavenly autumn days—for perhaps if it were wet and rainy I might still more intensively commune with myself and create out of myself—such a life cannot be combined with the world, it does not go with Rodaun, Vienna, rehearsals, people, reality; it would be a veritable fall from paradise into hell. Since you, discerning and generous as you are, have always and in every way taken me as I am, please take me so once again, to welcome me, afterwards, however belated, as very possibly the best friend you yourself and your work have in the whole world, apart from your wife.

In return I promise you, with the fairy-tale finished and due to be published within the next few weeks, with the comedy[1] under final revision, the novel[2] a mighty step forward, a new comedy[3] auspiciously begun, and a new work of a very special kind[4] advanced far beyond the scenario in close collaboration with Reinhardt, that now I shall tend and foster most warmly the germs for the three wholly different works for music which I have engendered, so as to submit to you one of the scenarios in the winter, and a major part of the full text by the spring when you begin your work.

One thing is clear in my mind: that all three, however diverse, are to be works in a light genre, not gigantic burdens on your shoulders, such as *Die Frau ohne Schatten* must have been—although it is true that you carried it up the very steep mountain as if it were child's play. Everything I may still do for you must be a thing of its own kind: each one of the earlier pieces constituted a genre of its own, only *Elektra* perhaps is rather too close to *Salome*, a mere variation. I am pleased by the idea that the little opera which you wrote for yourself in between[5] fits very beautifully into this series of ever-new diversity. That is how it is with Mozart and Wagner: each work is unique, in contrast to a series of generically identical works like Meyerbeer's or Puccini's.

One word only about the rehearsals: as every single individual gesture springs inevitably from the libretto, everything is settled there and laid down in the prompt-book. The final details will depend throughout on the music and on the physical equipment of the performers. In this respect I will accept everything you and the highly conscientious Roller see fit to direct or leave out.

Only one thing: I am told you wanted to make the Nurse and the Empress *vanish through the trap door* at the end of the first scene instead of running off into the bed-chamber. This really will not do, for five reasons:

1. It expressly says there: the orchestra takes up their 'flight to the earth', i.e. a flight through the air, gradually approaching the sphere of the humans—no plunging through the dark centre of the earth.

---

[1] *Der Schwierige.* [2] *Andreas.* [3] *Der Unbestechliche.*
[4] *Das Salzburger grosse Welttheater.* [5] *Intermezzo.*

2. In the second scene the two alight somehow as if through the chimney and certainly not out of the trap-door!

3. Even in the second scene they are not present at once, but after a quarter of an hour—the time necessary to change quickly and to fly down to earth.

4. In the fourth scene (Falconer's Lodge) they again come floating in through the air: how can one possibly chop and change their manner of approach!

5. Anyway who could conceivably sink down from a roof-garden, from the top story of a house! That means falling through the whole house first!

I hope the pleasure you get out of this opera will be greater than the annoyance which notoriously arises out of the inevitable frictions. I look forward to hearing it immensely. I am quite prepared for the certain incomprehension of the subject, for the stupid and aggravating interpretations and the guess-work where everything is simply picture and fairy-tale. All this will pass, and what really counts will remain. Publication of the fairy-tale will excite further speculations, but within the year this will have run its course.

With very best regards to your wife and every good and affectionate wish to yourself,

HOFMANNSTHAL

P.S. Without meaning to interfere in Fürstner's excellent handling of our foreign relations, I should very much like the opera to be given to the *Czech* National Theatre at Prague, which has exactly twenty times as large an audience as the other. As a matter of general policy, too, this strikes me as the right course.

Bad Aussee, 30.9.1919

My dear Frau Strauss or dear Dr. Strauss,

My old friend Franckenstein intends to embark on the fifteen hours' journey to Vienna especially for the première. He has taken the liberty of writing to you, Frau Strauss, with the request to procure for him two seats (for himself and his wife) through your kind good offices. Having received no reply he is afraid that the letter might not have reached you. May I in the circumstances be permitted to repeat the request so as to make sure, and to ask either you or Dr. Strauss to keep the tickets for him? He asked of course to buy the tickets, but courtesy, it would seem to me, demands that the Vienna Opera should treat as a guest its

332

former Director General, who is sure to become the head of a big theatre again.

With all my respects,

HOFMANNSTHAL

P.S. Sunday morning I shall be in Vienna, Stallburggasse 2.

1920

Vienna, Stallburggasse 2, (2.2.20)

Re *Divertissement*!
Not Urgent! To be read at leisure!

Dear Dr. Strauss,

Enclosed the sketch for a *Divertissement* of thirty to forty minutes' duration which may perhaps be what you want. I would work out only the main outline, leaving the rest to the maître de ballet.

This business with S. is just as unpleasant to me as it would be for you if d'Albert appeared on the scene. What is worse, S. is an intensely irritable, touchy and vindictive man; I must ask you therefore to treat the matter with extreme caution. Perhaps it would be best if you let him give you his outline sketches. They are, I am certain, sketches for fairly big ballets. If, contrary to my expectation, you like one of them, you might conceivably envisage it—but non-committally—for a later date. For the time being it does not seem to me advisable that you should devote your energy to a big ballet which has (qualitatively and quantitatively) such poor chances of performance, but rather to direct the flow of your imagination, filled as it obviously is with dances, into a *Divertissement*.

Then, by April, I should like to submit to you the light-hearted, operetta-like three-act sketch which closely approaches the world of Lucian.[1] Perhaps by that time you see enough clear water ahead of you again to set your beautiful craft afloat.

Sincerely as always, yours,

HOFMANNSTHAL

P.S. Let me know as soon as possible whether the piece appeals to you *as a whole*. In that case I would need a *few days to think over* the exact sequence of the individual scenes, but you could have it within a week.

[1] *Danae oder die Vernunftheirat.*

333

DIVERTISSEMENT

Duration thirty to forty minutes.

Without costume (i.e. modern dress, with the exception of one or two imaginary costumes).

No décor. Everything in front of a grey curtain, just like Schumann's *Carnaval*. (That makes the whole thing very mobile: one might form a touring company and send it on tour.)

Aim (according to the composer's wish): opportunity for real dances: pas de deux, pas de quatre and small dance ensembles, of gay as well as elegiac and grotesque character. The meaning which gives the whole piece its poetic unity: it is a representation of the inner world of the boy, of the very young man (about fifteen years of age), viz. the real world which still treats him badly, mortifies him etc., and blended into it the world of fantasy (of what he reads) which consoles him.

Characters:

The Boy (chief character)	The Young Girl,
The Young Man	her Admirer,
The Young Woman, her Husband,	

these are the characters of real life.

In addition, imaginary figures: Robinson and his man Friday, Schiller's Robbers (five or six grotesque dancers in black cloaks), Briseis, the fair slave of Achilles, and her fellow-slaves, a small band of attractive girls.

The action unfolds in a straightforward way in brief, sharply differentiated dances, like Schumann's *Carnaval*, roughly as follows:

The Boy alone. Robinson and Friday dance round him. But they can no longer captivate him.

The Boy and the Young Girl: she flirts with him but leaves him to fly into the arms of her twenty-year old admirer: valse à trois.

The Young Woman also flirts with him, but flirts at the same time with the Admirer of the Young Girl and lures him away from her. Solo dance of the jealous Husband.

The Husband comforts the Young Girl. The Boy witnesses these frightful, to him almost incomprehensible entanglements. In between his fantasy escapes to Schiller's Robbers and to the Iliad, to the beautiful Briseis.

The Robbers surround the Boy and carry him, released by death from the torment of love, across the stage on a bier: grotesque funeral march.

Scene of Briseis and her companions: elegiac, valse noble.

The individual scenes brief and sharply focused: each to constitute a separate musical item: some seven to nine *moments musicaux*, each lasting four to five minutes. The figures clearly characterized: the Boy —Pierrot; the Young Girl's friend—Harlequin; the Husband— Sganarelle.

Vienna, 8.3.20

My dear Friend,

Back from Berlin yesterday, sorry to hear that you also are ill. I hasten to ask you for a short line about your condition and to wish you and your wife a speedy recovery and early restoration to full health.

From Berlin I bring the good news that everything that has been done so far encourages hopes of a very good performance of *Fr. o. Sch.* for 28th March, with—following my energetic insistence—alternative casts. I have myself rehearsed hard, at the piano, seen the models of the stage designs, of the Dyer's Cottage and the Temple even the finished scenery on the stage, and am delighted at Aravantinos's achievement. He has imagination and taste, and above all a loyalty and respect for the author's intentions and the inherent requirements of the poetry, which are quite touching and hold out the promise that your intentions, in particular, will meet with a hitherto unrealized scenic interpretation. All the magic effects will be there, even the water and the collapse at the end of Act II. The sword and the shifting of the bed have been solved quite ingeniously and the best possible arrangements have been made for all the invisible voices on and off stage—so that we may expect a marked improvement over Roller who approached the piece with far too much resignation and gave up the 'magic tricks' from the start. The music alone can't do everything, and certainly not *this* kind of thing: one might as well write an oratorio and have done with the stage altogether! But *half* a stage is impossible because that cuts out the fantasy of the audience without fully satisfying the eye.

Wouldn't you like to come to Berlin with me for the final rehearsals on 22nd March? This time I am really trying to persuade you and get you to honour a changed Berlin for once with your presence and, I hope, your approval. Write to me or telephone me when I can see you.

With best regards, yours

RICHARD STRAUSS

Dear Dr. Strauss,

I am most grateful for the good report you have so kindly sent me about Berlin. Here in Vienna Roller of course failed me utterly over the magic contrivances. The fact is that he has no sense for the fantastic; I could not know this so clearly beforehand.

And in my case these magic effects are certainly not some super-added tinsel, but indispensable like joints of the whole piece. Let us hope the realization of these things on the Berlin stage will be as good as they seemed to you in the model.

For a number of reasons I should very much like to come to Berlin; quite apart from everything else, Reinhardt will be producing a Calderon translation of mine[1] at the end of March. But it is completely out of the question for me to travel to Berlin in a fortnight's time under present conditions. This harassing life in hotels and restaurants, the wretched food, the running around, rehearsals and so on—I could not stand it. A lingering influenza and rheumatism with constant slight fever for five weeks (still persisting) have exhausted me greatly; I am almost incapable even of reading, am suffering from constant nervous depression, and the slightest change of weather, a short letter like this or a short conversation, everything exhausts me unbelievably. Because chance had it that my wife should fall ill in town, we are separated and I am exceedingly glad of it. Being alone is in fact the only thing I can bear. And now in March I must be particularly careful: March is a critical month, in 1917, 1918, 1919 I fell ill in March, and I shall certainly eventually die in March, like my mother.

It is most kind of you to offer to come out here, but please don't think of it under any circumstances; the tram journey of one and three-quarter hours each way is torture and I do not enjoy visitors. I hope there is a chance of seeing you in town before the 22nd.

Sincerely yours,

HOFMANNSTHAL

My dear Friend,

Rosenkavalier is being done in Stockholm in April. *Salome* and *Rosenkavalier* are to be done in the summer in Buenos Aires; the latter

[1] *Dame Kobold.*

336

I think, also in Bologna. I'm going to Buenos Aires in August to prepare the ground if possible, for a Vienna Opera guest season there next summer—of which there seems to be some slight prospect—with our works, besides Wagner, forming the main part of the repertoire. (. . .) How are you? When can I see you? These are ghastly days and it takes a lot of energy to keep one's chin up. But it's got to be done if one's last ounce of creative vigour isn't to go down the drain. I'm working very hard, rehearsing and conducting like mad, orchestrating as well—only I shan't go to Berlin for the time being; anyway I've heard nothing from there, except that the theatres are said to be closed. So *Frau o. Sch.* will have to wait too. In Munich, according to Reichenberger's report, it is said to be doing very well.

Are you working? May I hope to get the promised material soon? Don't let things get you down. Best regards, yours very sincerely,

RICHARD STRAUSS

Vienna, 22.3.(1920)

Dear Dr. Strauss,

It was very kind of you to write and the letter did me good like everything personal I have had from you during these many years. I am most grateful. An advance on the proceeds from Buenos Aires I would not care for. To me, very much a middle-class person at bottom, there is something too unsound about the idea of an advance. I prefer the well-founded hope of future income to an advance. For the time being, in any case, I have a certain sum available in Switzerland, the proceeds from the sale of a picture. What you say about keeping up one's creative vigour is of course perfectly true. For that one needs to recover physically. At present I am in such a rotten state that even writing a letter like this exhausts me and every conversation brings out cold sweat on my forehead. Five weeks of neuralgia on top of influenza, fifty days of a creeping fever, sometimes worse, sometimes a little better, in between a slight bronchitis, all that takes it out of one.

Yet I am pretty tough and I am making a good come-back; all I need is recuperation, physical and moral.

I have come into town for a few days because not a ray of sunshine reaches our house out there (which faces North), a situation intolerable in the long run; soon, however, I must go back again with my wife, for here we are faced with other snags.

If only I had some half mechanical work like scoring, work which requires only half one's productive powers! That would be a real boon. Once more my grateful thánks!

Yours,

HOFMANNSTHAL

Rodaun, Friday (23rd or 30th April) 1920

Dear Dr. Strauss,

Although still very low and weak, I would feel I had failed you if I were to leave home without sending you what I promised. The success of our big, serious work in Berlin[1] gives me very great pleasure. I was really distressed at the time about Dresden. We are now presumably out of the wood in Germany and can turn to something lighter.

Danae[2] continues exactly the line *Rosenkavalier, Ariadne-Vorspiel, Bürger als Edelmann*. It asks for light, nimble-witted music, such as only you can write, and only at this stage in your life. The subject is early mythological antiquity, flippantly treated as a 'Milesian Tale' in Lucian's sense.

The more 'French' you are in your handling of this, the better; the German quintessence, the more profound and grave element will anyway be there at the core, just as in my case the lyrical core which veils the symbolical and metaphysical implications on a deeper level still. For costume please imagine antiquity à la Wiener Werkstätten (not Roller's gravity), or even better antiquity à la Poiret. I shall try to see you on Monday before I leave.

Very sincerely yours,

HOFMANNSTHAL

P.S. My fairy-tale, too, has a new impression of 5,000, which is good news.

[1] *Die Frau ohne Schatten*, first Berlin performance on 18th April 1920.

[2] *Danae oder die Vernunftheirat*. The scenario enclosed by Hofmannsthal with this letter was first published by Herbert Steiner in the periodical *Corona* in 1933, and edited in book form with the poet's notes by Willi Schuh (S. Fischer Verlag, Frankfurt a.M.). Strauss did not carry out the *Danae* plan. Not until 1936—by which time he had forgotten the scenario—was his interest in the subject aroused, when Willi Schuh submitted to him the *Corona* text, and the libretto was eventually prepared by Joseph Gregor (*Die Liebe der Danae*, a gay Mythology in three Acts, op. 83).

338

My dear Friend,

Now that *Rosenkavalier* has at last been produced here with the greatest possible success—on Saturday, 2nd October—as the final performance of the Stagione Bonetti (during which I have so far conducted six concerts here) under that excellent conductor Serafin, with Claudia Muzio as an exceedingly elegant and charming Marschallin and Ludikar as Ochs, it seems to me that the moment has come to let you have some interesting news from the 'colonies' (for 'countries' exist only in Europe). Scenically certainly the most beautiful city in the world with its combination of sea, mountains and tropical vegetation; in its fairy-tale magnificence I can liken Rio only to the 'Empire of the Eastern Isles', whither I believe myself transplanted every day when I gaze out over the bay from our roof terrace, or I look down at the lunar mountains from the magnificent view points which are reached by car along enchanting forest roads. I have often thought of you and wished you were here, so you could see your poetic vision become reality.— But when you've listed the charms of nature that's the lot. Artistic development at a primitive stage; the system of Italian *stagiones* presenting year after year the same ten operas (with only a different tenor) to a not very numerous public, which goes to the theatre chiefly for the sake of fashion, at a definite time of the year, and then always for the second acts, is beginning very slowly to arouse in a few educated minds a longing for some truly artistic activity with a changing repertoire— so that our plan to visit here with the Vienna Opera does not seem unhopeful, certainly not judging by what I have so far personally achieved with the President of the Republic and the Prefect of the City: to wit, probably a free passage from Trieste to Rio aboard a Brazilian steamer.

At the moment three parties are fighting for the control of the local theatre (for the next five years):

1. the impresario Mocchi, who has been the chief man here until now and who runs the Coliseo in Buenos Aires, where he staged *Salome* this year and likewise *Rosenkavalier* a few days ago as the two winners of his season—a very energetic, unscrupulous artistic *condottiere* who appears to have the best chances in Rio.

2. my very decent Bonetti, whose centre of gravity is in Buenos Aires in the Teatro Colon; and

339

3. a newly founded theatrical society headed by the richest people in Rio, who want to take over the theatre to free themselves from the tyranny of the impresarios and to have real art put on the stage.

It is with this third group that we're negotiating: if it wins, a visit by the Vienna Opera would seem to be assured. The decision is expected during the next few days: but in this *paese della tranquillità*—as my Italian orchestra clerk calls it—you never know!

Up to now we've negotiated very cautiously and briefly, and our Viennese have met with the greatest enthusiasm everywhere, from the President downwards.

But in a country where anything is promised and where real interest exists only in the Coffee Exchange, or at most in a King of the Belgians, it's still rather a long way to the signing of an official contract with the guarantees that we would require.

We're also working hard for Salzburg, distributing our propaganda leaflets to the ladies of the Salvation Army—so far without noticeable success. What's Salzburg to a Brazilian or, worse still, to a German living in Brazil?! There's one good thing in this kind of trip: one recovers one's full pride as a European and even feels nostalgic for hunger, fuel shortages and Bolshevism amidst all this material opulence! During the crossing I read all Goethe's literary essays: how far this marvellous spirit had brought us a hundred years ago! And where are we today? And yet!

I hope you are in good health and full of creative vigour; I am already looking forward, upon my return to Vienna about 12th Dec., to being allowed to enjoy the fine fruits of your productive summer! Is *Der Schwierige* finished? At any rate, our works still have a great future abroad! Italy is doing *Rosenkavalier* in Rome, Bologna, Turin. Madrid, too, is on the horizon. *Frau o. Sch.* is to come up in Milan next year. But please see to it that Schanzer translates it as literally as possible: *Rosenkavalier* contains some terrible howlers in this respect so that music and words frequently don't go together at all. All the very best, kind regards to your family and best wishes to yourself. Yours sincerely,

RICHARD STRAUSS

1921

Dear Dr. Strauss,

Although I hope to see you soon to discuss by word of mouth a number of important questions of mutual interest, I should like to settle a few points today in writing. Unfortunately we cannot come to tea tomorrow; I only got out here yesterday morning and too much travelling back and forth is exhausting. I shan't come back to town until Wednesday evening.

Enclosed is *Der Schwierige*, mainly as a personal expression of thanks for your kind interest. I hope the play will give you a pleasant hour. I should be glad if, towards Wildgans, you were to stress that your reaction is merely the impression of a member of the public.
(. . .)

I would, however, like to say this about the matter itself, so that you can employ your authority, which is obviously very considerable within the State theatres, to the best purpose. These are the facts: an Austrian, with an international reputation gained over a period of twenty-five years, submits for the first time in his life a dramatic work to the leading theatre of his native city for original performance, and does so under quite exceptional circumstances which secure for the play a definite cast (Bassermann in the leading part). In such a case a refusal would seem to me inconceivable even judging by common usage alone, unless the piece be immoral, downright unproducible or certain of failure. None of this arises here: it is a normal stage play, with normal prospects of success, perhaps rather better prospects than most new plays. If therefore the management were to depart from ordinary usage, there could be no explanation except mortal enmity on the part of the Director. But no such thing exists even remotely; on the contrary mutual relations have always been most friendly and his attitude to certain of my works is, I am sure of it, cordial. I am giving you these arguments since they are the arguments which represent the orthodox approach and which you, being at the moment yourself head of a big theatre, very properly adopt in any discussion. This orthodox approach is as valid in your attitude towards Pfitzner, for instance, as in my case here, though there is an additional difference between laboriously producing a Pfitzner opera with doubtful prospects and allowing Reinhardt and Bassermann to perform this comedy themselves with a visiting company.

341

Two more things which I forgot to mention when we saw each other recently. For Franckenstein an immense amount naturally hinges upon your decision about his opera,[1] and so he has asked me to talk to you about it. But what is the good of talking? I know that you are well disposed towards him, in every way. You realize also that he is in a very difficult situation. You will therefore decide as you can and must, but please let me have word what you think of it, in confidence. Finally this. Signor Francesco Alfano, Director of the Bologna Conservatoire, has chosen the extraordinary, circuitous route of sending a third person to me in order to ask you whether you will allow him to come to Vienna and play his opera to you. Please let me have a very brief reply to this and to the other question.

I have settled the publishing matter with Major Bischoff by giving my consent as you wished, and was at the same time able to offer him some advice concerning the artists to be approached. I look forward to seeing you soon and hope to hear about your conversation with K(err) (Berlin).

Very sincerely yours,

Papa is at work, so this letter is posted without signature.

CHRISTIANE HOFMANNSTHAL

Rodaun, Whit-Monday (16.5.1921)

Dear Dr. Strauss,

I am back, having come via Salzburg in order to see Reinhardt who instructed me, with very many kind regards, to talk to you at the earliest opportunity about *Der Bürger als Edelmann* and generally about *joint policy* concerning the tour. Agreement among those who belong together by position and ability is never more essential than in matters like these, especially after our depressing experiences of last winter. (It was these which made me long *to be alone* in Italy, and not 'bad nerves' as I wrongly said. Please forget our last conversation. My nerves are perfectly all right, my productive faculties are at my service, only external difficulties beset me, big ones, and these I must overcome, like every creative artist.)

I am always, and each time anew, pleased to see you. But we are spoilt; we have shared the best men can share: being united in creative

[1] Presumably *Li-tai-pe*.

production. Every hour we have spent together was connected with our joint work; the transition to ordinary social 'intercourse' would now be almost impossible. And I *wish* to remain united with the creative artist in you, in a serving, participating capacity, always. If the collaboration with Kerr were to materialize, I might dovetail myself into it in an assistant, advisory capacity (unnamed, even without Kerr's knowledge); nothing I would like more. Take me as I am: you have no better friend.

I often wonder about the equivocal, I would almost say still undecided, but in any case difficult fate of our last work.

Let us put all the blame for the 'difficulty' on me, all right; let everything be the fault of the libretto only—still the accounts don't seem to square perfectly. Difficult to understand? That is not true. All the foreigners understand it: the Italian correspondents, all the Italians, the French, Chantavoine, Ravel, Madame Hallier, all understand the libretto and express a special liking for it. (Therefore, in parenthesis, I would have high hopes of a production in Milan.) But one fault there may be. It is the text which makes the second act overladen, overweighted, strenuous. Yet, on the other hand, the first is so happy, the third so beautiful, the whole thing so beautifully invented, leading to moral good, homogeneous in conception and characters; the figures are so well rounded off: the Dyer, the Empress, the Children, the falcon. And this a *failure* as a libretto? Does an abortive opera libretto look like this? And does it not please wherever it is performed? This work, it is true, has to stand up to a lot: the reaction which, once every twenty years, ranges itself against great fame, against acknowledged greatness. Add to that the spirit of our age which is directed toward the excessive—which is, in the last resort, weak—whereas I seek what is universally human, what is morally strong, that which is quiet and simple in form. Now all this has been marshalled into carefully considered, methodical and uncommonly tough opposition by this man Bäcker or Bekker,[1] and is published where it must have the greatest effect.[2] Still I believe the work *will* live. But I say: I believe—in the case of *Ariadne* I say: I know.

What you have to thank me for more than anything else, perhaps the only thing you have to thank me for (since what ability can do must be taken for granted in a collaboration, and thanks are due only for what has been accomplished by dint of character), is that I did not lose my head over the apparent failure of *Ariadne*, but roused myself at once

[1] Paul Bekker.　　[2] *Frankfurter Zeitung*.

with alacrity and courage to the task of recasting it. Now *Der Bürger als Edelmann* will have to be taken up again and everything worked out as judiciously as possible, to shape it from the outset so that the subsequent transfer to the [Kleine] Redoute [in Vienna] is easy; that is Reinhardt's opinion, too.

I shall ring up Tuesday morning to find out how soon you can see me, preferably right away tomorrow afternoon: it's urgent!

Yours,

HOFMANNSTHAL

Rodaun, 17th May, 1921

My dear Friend,

Der Bürger als Edelmann contains sixteen acting parts, not counting the singers and dancers. The only suggestion for casting I can make is for the leading part (Hugo Thimig); for the rest, I have not sufficiently intimate knowledge of the Burgtheater personnel. Given my well-known awkward relations with the Burgtheater, my personal participation is in any case altogether out of the question. Reinhardt is willing to stage the piece as producer at Salzburg with the cast coming from here, but he absolutely refuses to have anything to do with organizing the enterprise. He lives there in a private capacity and has neither a company nor an office. It is the Vienna Opera which must undertake this performance. If the plan were to go through, it would be necessary to appoint an executive, viz. one of the younger Burgtheater producers to do the casting in constant touch with Reinhardt on the one hand and the treasurer on the other, and to deal with the contracts on that basis. This manager would have to be willing to subordinate himself to Reinhardt at Salzburg which, given Reinhardt's obliging manners, is obviously quite easy, but must be settled from the outset. If a suitable person were not to be found from within the Burgtheater, then I would suggest Geyer, the director of the Neue Wiener Bühne, one of the best and most reliable producers I know. But I cannot judge whether it would be possible to bring in an outsider.

My dear good friend, if this enterprise cannot be placed on a sound footing from here, you'd better keep off it altogether. You are leaving, and Schalk is going to Budapest; who then is to direct these things with the necessary authority?

344

One thing is definite: rather than make a mess of this, we had better *not* undertake it, but merely send the two existing operas to Salzburg. Nothing could be worse than to handle one's own things cavalierly— just remember Wagner and his unflagging perseverance whenever the quality of the production of his own works was at stake. If the necessary drive is wanting now, it is better to leave it alone.

If you call me (by telephone, through your servant), I shall be glad to come to town at any time, but you must call me; it is not I who want something from you; I am at your disposal.

Yours,

HOFMANNSTHAL

Salzburg, 23.7.(1921)

Dear Dr. Strauss,

I am still recovering from a serious attack of giddiness, and so will reply to your letter in a few days' time, from Aussee. Today only the news that a beginning has already been made between Lion and Karsavina's agents; there is hope.

Neither of the R(einhardt) brothers can give any news about the Vienna plans and prospects because negotiations between the Viennese owners and financial groups involving some Swiss interests, though progressing on the whole quite favourably, are being dragged out by endless cross-currents, and Reinhardt does not wish to come forward with questions, pressure or requests. They have themselves been without news for weeks.

Yours,

HOFMANNSTHAL

Neubeuern, 27.7.1921

Dear Dr. Strauss,

I understand your point of view perfectly. I knew nothing of posters of this kind. I agree with you entirely. (I am forwarding your letter to Reinhardt, for I cannot bear having to 'mediate' all the time between people and points of view; that becomes impossible in the long run.)

In June I worked like a cart-horse to bring about the Vienna company's guest performance at S(alzburg); at the last meeting Lion still assured me that the Opera would do it off its own bat, and this was the

345

last I heard of it! How easy it would have been to send at least musicians and dancers for *Der Bürger als Edelmann* to Salzburg; all the rest Reinhardt would willingly have taken upon himself. With a little bit of goodwill and energy it would have been so easy to do, and beautiful. But there is nothing but ill-will and sloth!

Yours,
HOFMANNSTHAL

Dear Dr. Strauss,   *Neubeuern am Inn, 2nd August, 1921*

Your very nice letter of July 16[1] has been forwarded via Aussee and has given me great pleasure. It is only due to this absurd heat, which makes one somewhat lazy and stupid—at least in the afternoons, and in the morning I am at work on my tragedy—that I did not reply at once. A ballet written by yourself![2] this is excellent news and I am sure it is good. You have the right feeling for it: a feeling, incidentally, in line with the traditional Bavarian gift for the Baroque theatre. The mythological ballets[3] which you showed me years ago were already good, if perhaps a little overladen; now, in your maturity, I am sure this one has turned out excellent. I am delighted with the news. Friendship between artists knows nothing finer than ungrudging joy in one another's productive work. I am immensely grateful for the way you have backed up *Der Schwierige*. By now I am getting appreciative, and occasionally even intelligent comments from many quarters. (But the fate on the present German stage of such half-romantic products— and everything Austrian is half, or at least a quarter romantic— continues to give rise to anxiety.)

To *Prometheus* and *Carnaval* I shall apply myself with all seriousness. Thank you for two such promising tasks. I have asked for the music of both to be sent to Aussee, where I have people who can play it to me decently. I take it that, in *Carnaval*, we shall have to stick to the figures of Harlequin and Pierrot? What is expected from me then, is to invent the action for the dances of these two figures. Am I right?

All good wishes and kind thoughts,   HOFMANNSTHAL

Hartung, a very intelligent chief producer from Darmstadt, told me recently that *Die Frau ohne Schatten* was holding its place in the

[1] Not extant.   [2] *Schlagobers.*   [3] *Kythere.*

346

Darmstadt repertory most successfully, and that it would do so everywhere provided it was put on with a proper appreciation for this most
valuable and difficult work, and at the right intervals of time.

Dear Dr. Strauss,   *Neubeuern, 11.8.1921*

Since you left the choice to me, I forwarded your letter to Reinhardt,
so that this matter should be cleared up and I am at last freed from
having to act as mediator and pour oil on troubled waters.

Reinhardt has now replied to me as enclosed.[1] As you see, this time
Reinhardt is the worm who, trodden on by everybody, begins to turn,
but of course in a manner thoroughly amiable towards you and me.

Sincerely yours,

HOFMANNSTHAL

My dear Friend,   *Garmisch, 19.8.1921*

I must tell you right away (. . .) not to count on any music from me for
the *Welttheater*. Not from ill-will, but simply from lack of time. Whom
do you want to entrust with the music? Perhaps Siegmund von
Hausegger (Munich); or I might direct your attention to a very gifted
young Spaniard, now a German, Philipp Jarnach, living at Polling
(Upper Bavaria), whose exceedingly gifted string quartet I heard the
other day.

Couldn't you do a little sounding out to find whether Mme
Karsavina and Novikoff might not be won for the Vienna Opera,
either outright, but with plenty of leave, or as guests for a few months?
That would give us a Potiphar's Wife straight away, and anything else
that the heart could desire: *Scheherazade, Antar, Petrushka, Carnaval.*
The full score[2] is finished: we're only waiting for you. I'm also sending
Lion down to Salzburg (from Grossgmain) to see if something can be
done with Mme Karsavina.

This is awful, not getting any news in writing from the Reinhardt
brothers: I must know what Reinhardt's plans are in Vienna.

With kindest regards, yours very sincerely,

RICHARD STRAUSS

[1] Not extant.   [2] *Couperin suite.*

1922

My dear Friend,

Many thanks for your friendly welcome. I'd like to see you soon: in the mornings I am always at the theatre (Raminger, Tel. 9176), in the afternoons mostly at home (Tel. 58109).

No objections to the Molière cut.

Mlle Cirul is going to dance to me at the Opera at 12 noon on Saturday. So far, Mme Gutheil is the one-eyed among the blind.

Looking forward to seeing you! Kindest regards, yours

RICHARD STRAUSS

Rodaun, Monday morning (20.3.1922)

Dear Dr. Strauss,

After a long peaceful stay at Aussee, I come back just in time to catch the whole bucket of iniquity which is nowadays habitually poured upon my head after each one of your successes. It strikes me as the height of disloyalty to drag me in, absent as I was,[1] along with the *maître de ballet*, the theatre tailor and the hairdresser, simply to possess myself of a little of the applause! Has it really never occurred to any of these gentlemen that in this sort of case I have been guided exclusively by the idea of doing you a service and of serving your art—and that all the detail, too (e.g. the Veronese style and the whole splendour and so on), had just the purpose of providing, in predetermined, definite conditions (Russian ballet, internationally comprehensible subject), the *canvas suitable* to your gifts (which have an affinity to high and late renaissance)? What a thankless *métier* in so ugly and dishonest a world!

In the Reinhardt affair I would neither like to press you, nor even to beg anything of you, although—or just because—his whole future as an artist in present circumstances literally depends on whether, in addition to his purely money-making activities abroad, he can take an *artistic* task in hand again somewhere, a *constructive* one (I mean, build up a new company). Now that his attitude to Berlin has in his own mind

---

[1] The Viennese première of *Josephslegende* took place on 18th March 1922 with Marie Gutheil-Schoder (Potiphar's Wife), Toni Birkmeyer (Joseph); producer: Heinrich Kröller; decor: Haas-Heye.

become hostile, he will and can do so nowhere within the German-speaking world except here. Therefore, after days of discussion with him, I will for the moment say only one thing: the argument that this is a minor affair to him, because it involves neither the Burgtheater nor a normal manager's position the whole year round, this argument is not valid, no more than it was valid against you in 1918 and 1919 when it was constantly put to me. What is essential for him—that I can vouch for—is to gain a foothold so as to transfer eventually his centre of operations to Vienna; he knows that the serious theatrical life here (outside the opera house) will be his *once he has gained a real foothold*, once his *activity* here has come to replace mere projects. It was just the same in your case; the parallel is striking.

For these reasons it would seem to me worth your while to do your utmost; had you but seen R(einhardt)'s agitation as he waits the whole day long for the evening telephone call from Vienna, you would realize that for him, too, the decision is one of the greatest significance, perhaps the last really significant and formative decision of his life. Breisky and Vetter are poor fear-ridden creatures. I believe you will have to fight it out with this (. . .) Wildgans, and that in the last resort (if it should still prove necessary) you can, by a conversation with Seipel, tip the scales of decision where the balance inclines a little, but not enough, in R(einhardt)'s favour.

I felt that I should say all this so as to leave nothing undone.

Sincerely yours,

HOFMANNSTHAL

P.S. (On the envelope): If you want to speak to me, you can reach me between 5 and 6 o'clock on the telephone at Hellmanns.

Tuesday morning (21.3.1922)

Dear Dr. Strauss,

What a great pleasure I had last night! A most lovely thing it is. What a feast for the eye—and the ear! My profound tribute to Haas-Heye—and to you for having chosen him. These are quite the most beautiful sets I have seen on the stage for years. (Roller's share is outstanding too.) Mme Gutheil exceeds all expectations (her listening, her walking, her handling of the chain!)—and Birkmeyer is simply perfect—as much the adolescent and the innocent as the future hero. This piece with this cast should be taken all round the world! What Kröller has accomplished as producer is most conspicuous and significant; the ballet proper naturally falls far short of the Russian performance, but the whole production is *greatly superior to it*, for the first time successfully realized as an entity. This has now effaced the effect of my own highly problematical passage, and the music, too, has made an altogether different impression on me here; the whole conception (I mean the Kessler-Nijinsky-Diaghilev realization of the individual ideas) turns out, after all, a beautiful and successful mixture of ballet and pantomime.

(. . .) And why on earth this never-ending denigration? I ask myself: is there anything better, or even as good in this genre?! If so, what? Where?—Have you sent Kessler a telegram (Berlin, Köthener Strasse 28)? Do it, he will be so pleased.—Now, for the first time, I look back with real satisfaction to that June morning in the Tuileries Gardens when the idea first came to me!

My dear friend, if ever you are under a little less pressure (perhaps such days may come), I would dearly like to read to you *Das Welttheater*, to you quite alone, at your home; it would give me pleasure and you would enjoy it too. Or would you perhaps prefer to read it for yourself? Yet, reading it aloud takes only one hour and a quarter and I would like it.

Now for *Helena* which, together with *Rosenkavalier* and *Ariadne*, is to become for me a third work certain of enduring for many years to come.

Sincerely yours,

HOFMANNSTHAL

Dear Dr. Strauss,

Rodaun, Easter Saturday (15.4.1922)

You can have me whenever you wish—I am always pleased when you call me. But you must remember this: I see your name so often billed as conductor, cannot fail to know how much else you do, not to speak of your social obligations—how then can I rouse myself to visit you, unless *I have something to bring you* as in years gone by? Of course our relationship is now less easy, for the very reason that it was once something so very special and rich in content. And then there is something else I would ask you—and your wife also—to bear in mind as far as we are concerned, and not to lose sight of: it would not be altogether correct to look upon us as living in Vienna. Our life, the modest hospitality which we offer and are so pleased to offer—but only out here!—all this has become, both in its economic aspects and in its mechanics, infinitely more difficult to give and to accept, for us (for we live nowadays, after all, like very humble little people whose aspirations cannot go beyond leading a reasonably *decent* and *honest* existence) as well as for our friends, since practically nobody has a car any longer. How can we expect anyone to undertake the tramway journey out here during the winter, except bachelors?

Yesterday however, on Good Friday, I did come to town to look you up and to ask whether you would like to see me sometime during the Easter days—only to be told that you are in the Prein district. I am delighted that the fine weather we are having now may give you a few agreeable days.

You do know, do you not, that I never forget any wish which you have expressed concerning a matter of art. Last summer I produced the outline of an action for *Carnaval*[1] and sent it to Schalk. It is quite slight and sketchy; all the poet can do here is to provide a framework for the *maître de ballet*. From what Haas-Heye has shown me, I see that my suggestions are being adopted. I have given thought more than once to *Die Ruinen von Athen*. This is both a difficult and at the same time most attractive task; I imagine a kind of ballet pantomime but with choruses, perhaps even with arias. It will have to be something which does not fly in the face of the original intention. To succeed in this would give me immense pleasure. I have a date to meet Alwin, perhaps together we may bring it off.

It is of incalculable importance to me that the Reinhardt matter is now finally settled. I know that he—and I—owe this in the first place to you. In the affairs of Salzburg, too, I feel the inestimable benefit of your good-will and your great influence at my side, and in this instance, too, it is your support for me which turns the scales. I am most grateful to you.

A conversation with Kapellmeister Stransky has brought *Die Frau ohne Schatten* very much back to my mind. To me, the finished works are not dead, but living cares and joys, like children. Then, and again during a recent conversation with Alwin, a new and possibly helpful idea struck me. What is wearying and oppressive is the second act, especially the periodic return to the Dyer's home. Here I have gone wrong. On the stage regular repetition is either *funny* or *tedious*. How do we find a way out? A really substantial cut is impossible, for word

[1] The performance of *Carnaval* with Schumann's music took place on 7th June 1922.

and music here have their firm structure. But what if we were to eliminate at least the monotony of the thrice recurring stage set by providing (say for a new production abroad) that three different corners of the Dyer's world (each time a small narrow section only of the set) are to be shown; for the first scene (Act II), a part of the chamber close to the door, let us say, for the third scene another with the cooking range, the fifth scene a different one again. The dyed cloth which is hung up there to dry makes it after all very easy to establish several quite distinct parts of the same large room or basement vault; the imagination of the scene painter would have to come to our aid here. The act which causes the weariness might perhaps gain immensely in this way, for I persist in my opinion—*confirmed as I am by so much appreciation from Frenchmen and Italians:* this is a work which could prove most effective and highly successful in the Latin countries.

With best regards, very sincerely yours,

HOFMANNSTHAL

Rodaun near Vienna, 25.5.(1922)

Dear Dr. Strauss,

After racking my brain for a while I have, I believe, arrived at a solution how to introduce fittingly and in good taste the *Geschöpfe des Prometheus* into the ballet spectacle *Die Ruinen von Athen*, so as to satisfy your wish to lengthen the duration of the whole thing. Taking the Wanderer or Stranger as an idealized German artist of those half-forgotten days and giving him the line: 'His soul yearning for the land of the Greeks' as a kind of motto, I present him as he meditates on the ruins of the past in the deserted market place of Athens and is lighted, like Goethe, by a Promethean, productive, creative spark (which he expresses in the aria with the horns). In short I turn him into Prometheus himself, surrounded by revived figures of the classic age who dance to the rhythm of the ballet music, until at the end we come to the vision of the Panathenaic procession (march and chorus) as the crowning climax. For this I envisage Mme Gutheil as the leader of the procession of the virgin priestesses, with all the other mimers in support. How I have made use of all the remaining beautiful passages from the *Ruinen* the enclosed scenario will show you. I would like to omit the overture, which is not very impressive, and to open instead with the chorus and a suitably modified text.

All good wishes to you both; have a good rest and come back refreshed. But do get us a good Donna Anna.

In warm friendship yours,

HOFMANNSTHAL

Karlsbad, 26.5.22

My dear Friend,

Many thanks for your fine draft[1] which represents a very happy solution of the idea I've had in mind. I would only ask you to consider: who is to represent the Wanderer-Goethe? An actor—or even—*horrible dictu*—a singer? Only Duhan or Oestvig would, at a pinch, be thinkable! If an actor—how would it be if an invisible contralto voice, perhaps stationed in the orchestra, were to sing a few Goethe-Beethoven songs while he is lost in his dreams? Do please get Alwin to play all the Beethoven songs for you. By the way, I once orchestrated *Wonne der Wehmut*.

As an overture, the one from *Prometheus* would be suitable: it could easily be used as music to a milling Greek crowd, with the curtain rising during its last third. Then the opening chorus you have mentioned, which could be positioned in front of the curtain, perhaps invisibly in the orchestra pit as in the *Flying Dutchman*. Could you please discuss the whole thing at once with Roller and Kröller, and bring along the completed plan for my final examination when you come to Salzburg, together with the full scores of *Ruinen* and *Prometheus* and the songs.

We are well: only rather bored, but apparently it's doing us good. With best regards from us to you all, yours sincerely,

RICHARD STRAUSS

Bad Aussee, 31.7.1922

Dear Dr. Strauss,

I am delighted you will be present at the première of the *Welttheater*[2] as my guest for once, after I, though as collaborator, have been so often the guest of your beautiful music. I recall your whole-hearted presence

[1] For *Die Ruinen von Athen*.

[2] The première of *Das Salzburger Grosse Welttheater* took place in the Kollegienkirche, Salzburg, on 12th August 1922.

at the first performance of *Jedermann* in Berlin; let us hope that this evening will not fall short of the other!

In the South Tyrol I began to feel much refreshed and have already completed two acts of a new comedy.[1] I saw few newspapers, but by good fortune I chanced upon the reports of the great success at Prague and of the Freiburg Festival. I am grateful to you for drawing my attention to Goethe's review of the Voss poems, for I took the volume with me and got much pleasure out of it. May I recommend to you, as a student of history, Ferrero's *Roman History*; I am just re-reading with admiration the middle volume (Caesar's death and the triumvirate with an entirely new interpretation of the figure of Mark Antony and his policy in the East). German edition in five volumes published by Julius Hoffmann, Stuttgart.

I am quite willing to do at once what remains to be done to the book of words for *Die Ruinen von Athen*, but Roller must first acquaint me with his solution of the decorative architectural problems on which the final shaping of the whole thing depends. For the theatre you have to work like cog-wheels, each turning the next.

Au revoir, therefore, and best regards, yours,

HOFMANNSTHAL

P.S. I am occupying myself in advance with the programme for next year's possible Festival. It would be charming to have *Der Bürger als Edelmann* there, but hardly, I think, by itself—coupled perhaps with one of the rarer Mozarts, not of course a buffo work, but a heroic one as a contrast. What about *La Clemenza di Tito*? In that case the *Bürger* would have to be done in Vienna first, perhaps in the spring under Reinhardt. The difficulty is as always the casting of the title part. When I approached Pallenberg recently (in connection with a new comedy), it turned out that, for all his attractive qualities, he has gradually become mercenary to an almost pathological degree and can only be secured if, acting in a big theatre, with an inferior company, he gets the major part of the receipts as well as a share in the author's royalties for which he invariably stipulates. We might ask him for Salzburg, but hardly for Vienna in the Kleine Redoute.

The dearth of comedians is grievous indeed. Waldau, who has just scored a very great success in *Dame Kobold*, would be a perfectly good possibility, but who knows whether Munich will let him go for any

[1] *Der Unbestechliche*.

354

length of time. We will have to consider this with Reinhardt before it is too late.

HOFMANNSTHAL

(. . .)

Garmisch, 29.8.22

My dear Friend,

In Hamburg I have just conducted *Ariadne*, superbly produced by Leopold Sachse, as well as *Josephslegende*, and also heard *Frau ohne Schatten*, which is very successful there, superbly done, especially on the musical side under Pollak. Wymetal's production a feeble compromise between Berlin and Vienna, without any ideas of his own. Hamburg is now very active in our interest; eight performances just recently in September, within three weeks. I have made my peace with Schalk, chiefly as a result of your and Roller's persuasion, and have received from him assurances which encourage me to look forward to more successful work than hitherto. What do you think of Prince Rohan and his Culture League? He said he'd so far been trying in vain to approach you! I have therefore only manifested non-committal sympathy with his intentions.

But now an urgent request: please get down to *Ruinen von Athen* in a hurry, together with Roller, so that I have the draft in my hands as soon as possible and can discuss the execution of the ballet part with Kröller on the basis of the music. I should like to bring the work out as early as the end of January. Would it be possible perhaps to use in the ballet the characters of Prometheus, Pandora, Achilles, etc., which are of such particular interest to Goethe?

I hope the enclosed review will amuse you as much as it did me.

From Fürstner I received the information that the Director of the 'Champs Elysées' has very little money at his disposal and is trying to build up a position through sensation. It would therefore be wise to show some caution where he is concerned. The post of President of the Salzburger Festspielgemeinde, which the good citizens of Salzburg want to offer me, I would rather decline. Surely it belongs more properly to Reinhardt, the master of Leopoldskron[1] and creator of the festival idea as such: the opera, though sponsored so much by the Salzburg people, is only a secondary thing. Don't you think so too?

With best regards, yours sincerely,

RICHARD STRAUSS

[1] Max Reinhardt owned Schloss Leopoldskron on the outskirts of Salzburg. (Translator.)

355

Dear Dr. Strauss,

Many thanks for your kind and pleasant letter and the good news; the part about Vienna was particularly welcome. As soon as Karpath hinted something of the kind I began to breathe freely again. Now that you have gained so fine and intelligent a victory over yourself, let me say this: You would have had the worst of it in any case; the real victim would have been this fine, unique institution, and that means the eventual sufferer you yourself—as a composer. For the Philistines (whether in the dress circle or in their public offices) dislike the serious, high and noble purpose which this institution still represents—and once it begins to totter they will do anything to bring it down.

Now for Salzburg: I wired you and will repeat again the *urgent* request: please accept this purely honorary position which involves no duties whatever (without of course vacating your place on the Artistic Council) and if by any chance you have already refused, please countermand the refusal. Please do this for mine and Reinhardt's sake, and so preserve this place for your and our activities; there is no other way if we are to continue our work there as artists. Never will these Philistines accept Reinhardt as president: they hate him, hate him three and four times over as a Jew, as lord of the castle, as artist, and as a solitary human being whom they cannot understand. Their attitude to me is unfriendly—for your own amusement just read the enclosed letter from a member of the governing body. I have donated a royalty of thirty millions and, without a word of thanks, without having seen any account even, I receive the cavalier proposal to put at the disposal of these gentlemen all subsequent royalties (*all rights!*).

Once again: do accept the chairmanship if you mean to preserve for me and Reinhardt (I speak also for him, *knowing how he feels*) this field of action which will be lost to us as soon as we get—in default—a chairman who is a 'Deutsch-nationaler' or some other boorish fathead; and, as your first action, do see to it that I am thanked decently for my in every respect unusual donation!

Since I now know where you are, I am sending you a copy of the *Welttheater* with a sincere dedication. With only a fragment before you, you once, in an unguarded moment, said something about a certain catholic dogmatism in it, which had troubled you. This is a misunderstanding, and you above all I should not like to miss as a receptive and comprehending spectator. True, there is a religious element in this work, just as there is in *Faust*—even a Christian one, for Christianity together with the classical tradition is the foundation of us all. But it is no more tied to Catholic dogma than *Jedermann*; indeed, in its final essence it is far freer still. (. . .). The core and substance is glorification of the element of the sublime within us, the freedom of the spirit, which is identical with the creative spark and a reflection of the supreme creator's splendour. This is what flashes through the Beggar, this is the 'most stupendous one among the gifts of heaven', and he who knows it, knows a feeling which scatters *all the burden of this life* before the wind like a grain of sand. By bestowing it for one moment upon my Beggar, I testify to my belief in something higher which stands above the struggle for power on this earth. This, alas, Mr. R. of Zürich cannot grasp, and so he takes for evasion, for compromise, what is in fact the answer on a higher level: the answer of the spirit to a world which has become impotent in the face of its 'practical' problems. Write me a word after reading it; your resistance is of interest to me and your agreement more important than that of sixty-six newspapers and coffee-houses (. . .).

I cannot go ahead with *Die Ruinen von Athen* until Roller tells me how he means to set it up architecturally. Please write and ask him to think it out, in general terms, sufficiently to put me right when I come to Vienna from September 16th to 19th. I will look into *Pandora* and so on. *Princesse de Babylone* I have ordered; with a light hand something light might perhaps be produced.

Yours,

HOFMANNSTHAL

Garmisch, 12.9.22

My dear Friend,

I was told in Salzburg that Reinhardt was deeply offended because the 'President' hadn't been offered to him. Since the post belongs to him by rights, I thought I should decline. But if you are certain that it is Reinhardt's wish also that I should accept the post and that R. can't be forced upon those Philistines anyhow, then I will gladly sacrifice myself.—Many thanks for the fine *Welttheater*, from which my wife declaims every evening, alternately imitating Thimig, Binder—and Mildenburg. However beautiful the idea of the sudden conversion of the Beggar may be poetically, to my dramatic feeling there is still a jarring crack intervening between the true dramatic solution (i.e. the completion of the destruction) and the Christian concept of sudden change of heart. This, of course, is the tragedy: that the Bolshevik is inwardly unfree, and so the salvation and liberation has something of the miraculous about it and strikes me as carried in from outside. Your Beggar doesn't act true to character right up to the end, but is at the critical moment illumined by Hofmannsthal. More about it when we meet!

I've already written to Roller about *Ruinen von Athen*. I had the impression that the architectural set-up was already fixed! I don't quite understand why you don't want, or are unable, to get down right away to devising the ballet interlude proper—the *Geschöpfe des Prometheus*. I would ask you urgently to take the matter up with Roller and Alwin in Vienna once more without delay and to send me the material as soon as you can, so that I can discuss the details with Kröller in Munich as soon as possible, especially the apportioning of the Beethoven music.

I've got the full score of *Ruinen* and *Geschöpfe des Pr.* here.

Where can one get Voltaire's *Princesse de B.* in German? I'm very curious about it; I feel like doing another *Rosenkavalier* just now! Couldn't you send me a copy?

With best regards, yours,

RICHARD STRAUSS

Bad Aussee, 21.9.1922

Dear Dr. Strauss,

Many thanks for your letter. Reinhardt will be as pleased as I am that you have taken on this position; he spoke of you more than once very warmly during the past few days in Vienna, from where I have just come back after two quite outstanding performances of *Clavigo* and *Dame Kobold*. The success is very great, the press with few exceptions excellent, only the cloud of a general theatre crisis hangs over the whole thing. Let us hope it will at least leave two enterprises unscathed: the Opera and Reinhardt's. The present head of the Burgtheater is behaving very decently towards Reinhardt, so this augurs quite well for the future. More about the 'Beggar' by word of mouth, with pleasure.

For today only this: you seem to me to take this figure and his symbolic experience more decidedly as personal individual experience than the unusual medium employed, here just as in *Jedermann*, will allow.

Princesse de Babylone I have unearthed in the Hofbibliothek. To my disappointment it is not a play, but one of those little 'philosophical novels'! You will presumably find it in the Insel Verlag *Voltaire* volume, well translated by Ernst Hardt. At present I have read about half of it and cannot see in the least how one might get a scenario out of it. But I have made a note of something else and early in the winter I shall try and see whether I cannot extract from it a scenario for a comic opera. Yes, a second *Rosenkavalier*—yet different. One can never relive anything. What I have in mind would have to be immersed in far more transparent music, and in another style, such as I had imagined it already for *Rosenkavalier*, e.g. for the treatment of the chorus in Act II; you yourself told me once that in retrospect you came round to it, but were not ripe for it at the time (1909). This means thoroughly in the manner of comedy, the conversational parts similar to *Rosenkavalier*, the rest approaching Auber rather, or *Don Pasquale*, or even *Ariadne*. I know you understand me, however awkwardly I express myself.

Now for the *Ruinen*. The discussions with Roller, which took several hours, proved very necessary after all, if only to find out what was to be the visual stage business of the big final festival (March and Chorus). 'Panathenaea', 'Eleusinian Mysteries', these after all, are nothing but words. The best of the Parthenon frieze: naked humans, horses, bulls, are out of the question on the stage. What would remain? An insipid procession of white-shirted figures, carrying humdrum emblems, the whole in the classicism of 1810. That would be intolerable. What is needed therefore is an occasion, festive and meaningful, which demands more than a mere procession. We have found it. The culmination of the Eleusinian Mysteries were 'nuptial rites', a ἱερός γάμος. I am sure an echo of this still lingers in the symbolic nuptials of Faust and Helena. Here is our chance. We mate the Wanderer, our German artist, with the virgin-bride Athene stripped of her armour and of her golden helmet. She is not to be a singer, but a beautiful actress: Mme Wohlgemuth. Two nuptial processions will move towards each other to the strains of this glorious music, cross each other's path, mingle with each other, separate again until finally they lead bride and bridegroom together—who disappear at the very end among jubilant rejoicings in a blaze of celestial light. This is another idea of mine in which I take some pride; the first was the linking up of the two Beethoven works through the figure of the poet as Prometheus/Pygmalion.

Now to the ballet centrepiece which is, as you say, Kröller's real task. Here, in my view and Roller's, everything is already definitely predetermined by the music. The visual content of this music cannot be anything but bucolic, shepherds and a vintners' festival (in the classicist taste of the closing rococo), with now and then some mocking fauns— quite plain in the music. If there is to be conflict, it must be of roving shepherds breaking in on the vintners as they take their ease with their girls, and carrying off the girls or nymphs. You may not know it perhaps, but Kröller has done something of this sort once before. It is familiar ground for him, therefore, which he will have to go over once more; the only difference is that this shepherds' play has now become merely an interlude in a serious and solemn work. I cannot see that individuals (Achilles, Pandora) would be much use at this point and with this music; it is, after all, in the whole context an attractive, but to our taste inadequate, vision of the classical age, and one which is anyway being pushed aside afterwards. Not this kind of thing, but something more solemn, more lofty, that's how I see the unity and mounting intensity of the whole piece.

A word about M. Hébertot. Of course, he is a man out for sensations. Coming from a German, this is damning comment. Since, however, he is the director of a theatre, the most beautiful theatre in Paris, but a seasonal one, run for tourists, wholly attuned to the sensational—what else should he be out for? He would be an ass. All depends on making it, with good taste, a civilized, discriminating, sensation. And for good taste, as well as a lavish, almost prodigal purse, I hear him commended by highly competent judges. Why should not *Rosenkavalier*—given the necessary financial backing—become such a sensation? No theatre could be further from chauvinism than his! By chance I have come across a Paris letter of Meier-Graefe's, written in 1922, in which he says: 'Hébertot has made the Théatre des Champs Elysées the apt tool of princely taste and equally high artistic aims . . .' This in any case should make one think twice, for Meier-Graefe is an independent judge, not in any way involved in the theatre world, and has taste.

Yours,

HOFMANNSTHAL

1923

Dear Dr. Strauss,

Throughout January I stayed very quietly out here and only came in to town occasionally for half a day. Now I have to go to Germany and will read my new comedy[1] to Pallenberg at Garmisch.[2]

Pray believe me that it is not indifference or, worse still, lack of inclination which prevents me from getting down to producing a suitable scenario (to find the scenario is the main thing, the rest comes by itself) for a new opera, of a lighter kind and with conversational touches here and there. On the contrary, my dear friend, I wish with all my heart to accomplish this. Once I have the thread, it would be an engaging and easy task, for I realize now better than ever what matters and would know how to weave the whole fabric finely and slenderly with few words. Strangely enough, in the old days a suitable subject used to occur to me so readily—today it is much harder. Were you to look, late in the evening, through my window, you would see me most assiduous and willing, turning over my Lucian, reading old stories by Stendhal and Musset, looking through Scribe libretti; humble and energetic goodwill must, I hope, be rewarded in the long run by the idea. Not that I lack ideas, but all of them belong to spoken drama. Scenarios and sketches of this kind are piling up in small heaps. (. . .).

Yours ever,

HOFMANNSTHAL

Dear Dr. Strauss,   *Hinteröhr, near Neubeuern am Inn, 27.2.1923*

My wife writes to me, deeply moved, about a performance of *Ariadne*; it must have been a great occasion. To this our joint work I am attached with heart and soul; this one, I know with assurance, will survive us by many years. My wife also tells me that you complained of never seeing me. In January I suffered for some time from influenza; then you were away and after that I was.

Besides, between two men like us there is nothing but our joint work and properly speaking no other common topic. I persist in musing over

[1] *Der Unbestechliche.*
[2] Pallenberg and his wife Fritzi Massary owned a house at Garmisch.

a graceful perhaps even slightly frivolous comedy with a good deal of *parlando*, placed in late antiquity, with some gay and pretty ritual, a festive occasion or something of the kind.

Nor has the process of pondering *Die Ruinen von Athen* been abandoned; if anything comes of it, it will be beautiful and must be done.

I shall, by the way, be in Vienna shortly, and would like to invite you and your family most cordially and well in advance to come to the first night of my new comedy (March 16).[1]

The final act of the tragedy *Der Turm* I have brought near to completion during my stay here.

Most sincerely yours,

HOFMANNSTHAL

Rodaun, Easter Sunday, 1st April, 1923

Dear Dr. Strauss,

Your wife has written me a very nice and amusing letter, most welcome since untroubled personal relations are obviously the prerequisite of our artistic collaboration. To invent for the little light opera[2] a pretty and ingenious short third act (which would take up immediately the end of Act II) is not a suggestion which scares me in the least; the only difficulty I can see in my task is to find the right style, and for that *Rosenkavalier* on the one hand, and *Ariadne* and *Der Bürger als Edelmann* on the other are my signposts. For the rest all such things need to be tackled with high spirits and a little impudence. What you told me recently of the unbridgeable gulf between your music, even at its lightest, and the common-or-garden operetta did not need saying at all—even to speak of the two in the same breath is to commit a wrong. For just such gradations and shades of specific gravity I have an unfailing instinct myself. In the same way I understand perfectly what you say of your inability to budge with regard to the orchestra. But you, in turn, must realize the difficulty of my position. In my mind, exactly as in yours, the creative impulse is now beginning to stir; but the mere anticipation of being vexed has a damping, dispiriting effect on it. Just as the thought of a mean and scruffy orchestra stifles all your zest, so it happens to me

---

[1] *Der Unbestechliche.* The première took place at the Raimund-Theater in Vienna on the date mentioned.

[2] *Die ägyptische Helena.*

as soon as I think of the performers. There is a lot you would still tolerate in this respect which fills me with disgust. When I see on the stage an actress like Fritzi Massary, whose intelligence, versatility, command of nuance fall in with the most profound of my own creative aspirations, and compare her in my thoughts with the opera singers, I feel myself torn from a banquet laid out with ambrosia for the Gods, to an ill-dressed meal in some filthy pot-house.

And now to think of all this in connection with such a light, gay, airy piece! Still, of course, the conception of the opera as such, a conception which actually craves for music, can attract and animate me, and so does the anticipation of your music and your pleasure. Although virtually unmusical, I am highly receptive to the beauty of music and especially to the complete—as yet quite inadequately appreciated—originality of style in which your *Bürger als Edelmann* is carried through.

I do not know when you are going to South America (will this be combined with your forthcoming Italian tour?) nor do I know whether you would find it desirable to take the first act with you on your journey, to play about with it a little. From my point of view it would be easier and preferable to give or send it to you, say, in August, for (even though all the main features of the action and the characters are fully worked out in my mind) I would be glad of a little time for thought and experiment in the matter of style.

Since the house out here is no longer quite so icy, we are wondering whether, if it suits you both, you and your wife would care to come to lunch or for the afternoon one of these days. I am sure someone will lend you a car; the Hellmanns, too, are no doubt at your disposal. Please arrange it as it best suits the pleasure and convenience of you both; that we would very much like to see you does not need saying.

Very sincerely yours,

HOFMANNSTHAL

Shall we perhaps bear next Sunday in mind, if the weather is good?

My dear Friend,   *Aboard the S/S Vestris, 12th July 1923*

You will be glad to hear that, after *Salome*, *Elektra* has now also had a tremendous success in Buenos Aires on 6th July. In a wretched season (the worst economic depression) my two operas were Mocchi's first box office successes, and so I hope that my works have now definitely

363

come to stay. Of course, *Rosenkavalier* (to be done again next season) and *Salome* were regulars even before: now, I hope, they'll be followed by *Ariadne* (also to be done shortly in Italy) and *Joseph*. After a wretched dress rehearsal, at which Mme Bland was a complete flop, also in her acting, I managed by a supreme effort to squeeze out a very respectable performance; at any rate it went down tremendously well and was enthusiastically praised by *Prensa* and *Nacion* (which had also carried very detailed previews, an example which the Viennese could well follow). I shall be in Garmisch on 15th September, without any work, and should like to find *Helena* (a delightful ballet in every act, please) waiting for me there! 'Get up, Kundry—to work!'

Yesterday a frightful gale; tomorrow with the Philharmonic Orchestra in Rio. My health is excellent, and the stay this time bearable! Hope you are in good spirits and productive vigour.

Best regards to you and your wife, yours sincerely,

RICHARD STRAUSS

Dakar, 8th Sept. (1923)

My dear Friend,

I am on my voyage home, in good health and high spirits. *Elektra*, with about ten performances, was a very great success. Next year they're doing *Rosenkavalier* again in Buenos Aires.

I hope to find *Helena* at Garmisch, preferably with entertaining ballet interludes; a few delightful elf or spirit choruses would also be most welcome. I have finished the full score of *Intermezzo* and would like to have some pleasant work to do at Garmisch during the autumn. Best of all, a second *Rosenkavalier*, without its mistakes and *longueurs*! You'll just *have to write that for me some day*: I haven't spoken my last word yet in that genre.

Something delicate, amusing and warm-hearted!

I'll be back home on the 16th and hope to have good news from you soon! With kindest regards, ever yours sincerely,

RICHARD STRAUSS

Bad Aussee, 14.9.(1923)

Dear Dr. Strauss,

Let me hope, as your letter from Buenos Aires leads me to expect, that you are now safely back at home, happily reunited with your family.

Now I can once more express to you yourself how warmly I share this pleasure and ask you at the same time to thank your wife for her particularly nice reply to our congratulations.

For a long time I have looked forward to presenting you with *Helena* in the course of this year when you enter upon your sixtieth and I my fiftieth year. Yet there is no certainty to be had where one depends on inspiration. When I told you the subject in April you expressed a very sound reaction: the first act is good and I like it—the rest still needs working out. Over and over again my mind has turned to this subject in propitious moments and now I have the whole piece worked out in my head. The second act is good, at least as good as the first, the third quite short; it leads to complete reconciliation amid a great feast. Yet, let me say at once that I am increasingly drawn towards combining the third act with the second. The third is the natural festive finale to the second act and gives the latter a quickening of tension; the feast, since it is at the same time full of emotional significance to the characters, would give the act an intrinsic goal towards which it gravitates, dynamically and psychologically. This would lead to the unusual form of two very rich acts of roughly equal length. The overall duration falls short of *Rosenkavalier* but exceeds *Ariadne*; what I have in mind is something like that of a Puccini opera.

You recall the chief characters of Act I: Aethra, the Egyptian sorceress and mistress of Poseidon, Helen, and Menelaus. The setting of the second act is an oasis in the desert adjoining Egypt to which the sorceress has carried off the rejuvenated couple for a short honeymoon, a beautiful spot to which neither the news of the Trojan war, which fills the whole of Europe, nor even the name of Helen has ever penetrated. Here two new characters make their appearance: the Sheikh of this oasis and his youngest son. Both fall in love with Helen. Merely as a suggestion and so as to illustrate my idea of the characters, I shall jot down a cast:

Helen—Jeritza.
Menelaus (most chivalrous and winning)—Oestvig (Tauber)?
Aethra—Schöne.
The old Sheikh—Duhan.
The young Sheikh—Jerger.

The style must be easy-flowing, on occasion as nearly conversational as the Vorspiel to *Ariadne*, sometimes coming close to the conversation scene in *Rosenkavalier*; never so heavy as in the opera in

365

Ariadne. There will, however, be plenty of opportunity for duets and trios. These *lyrical passages* will, unless I fail over my libretto, stand out clearly from the effortless and often psychologically subtle conversation. The more lightly, indeed light-heartedly you can handle this, the better it will be; there is, in any case, no German artist who does not become more heavy-handed over whatever he does than he ought to be.

Almost every day I add something valuable to the scenario.

Yours sincerely,

HOFMANNSTHAL

Bad Aussee, 22.9.(1923)

Dear Dr. Strauss,

Your kind letter of the 8th from Dakar is just to hand. In the meantime, however, I hope mine of Sept. 14 has reached you and a good reply is on its way to me!

I believe I know exactly what you mean by 'a second *Rosenkavalier*'. The action would have to be laid in Vienna around 1840 or so, something common-place, good-natured and gay at the same time. The action for *Rosenkavalier* came to me almost in my sleep—the second time it is always more difficult, for there could be nothing worse than trying to copy the earlier idea. Yet I believe, I feel that I shall get it one day. I have some notion of a plot.[1] It takes place among young people and ends in a multiple wedding. But I must develop it within myself, nurture it, foster it. The best way you can encourage and animate me is by getting to work on *Helena* with a rapid, easy hand. Tell yourself that you mean to handle it as if it were to be merely an operetta—it's bound to be by Richard Strauss in the end. Over *Die Frau ohne Schatten* we both became too heavy-handed. I am certain that some of your most beautiful music is in it—but remember for the few joint works which we shall still be allowed to do together that they must be, above all, good theatre. And very much for the ears of the ordinary people and for the voices, not of the most accomplished of singers, but of very many of them.

Goethe did not disdain writing a farce round the part of one 'Schnaps' brought into circulation by two sorry burlesques of some hack-writer; and Schiller, the severe, august Schiller, himself sketched a burlesque, whose central figure was to be the same Schnaps!

[1] *Arabella*, to some extent developed out of the characters in the story *Lucidor* (1910).

I hope and believe that *Helena* will give you greater pleasure, and will make headway more easily than you expect. I have given a great deal of thought to the texture of its style, to find the right, easy-going tone for the accompanied recitative, have endeavoured eagerly to recall the feeling of the most attractive passages from *Rosenkavalier* and from the *Ariadne* Vorspiel; yet in between there is ample scope for arias, everything is imagined as song, a style much lither than the *Ariadne* opera. The word operetta, if only one takes it in a pleasing, uncommon, earlier sense, covers it all. For dances and choruses we have plenty of room in the second act—and here I hope, with your advice, to build up a strikingly ingenious finale, not massive and artificial as in *Die Frau ohne Schatten*, but light and full of ideas, like fireworks throwing out bunches of flowers.

Your letter from Dakar asks for a chorus of elves; on the very same day I had reached the point in the first act where a truly romantic witchery in the style of Berlioz's *Queen Mab* is called for, where fleeting, chasing choruses of elves (but without, I am convinced, any male voices) could find a place. I enclose the passage so that your imagination can play about with it a bit, while in the meantime I continue writing my first act with high zest and not at all bad inspiration. Two scenes I will send you at the earliest possible moment. The incantation of the elves is the work of Sistre,[1] the Egyptian fairy and mistress of Poseidon, in the palace which provides the setting for the first Act. Menelaus, at the point where he seriously means to kill Helen, is to be lured away from her into the open; that is the point.

Looking forward to your letter and glad that we are once again in conversation in the only possible way, yours sincerely,

HOFMANNSTHAL

Dear Dr. Strauss,

I recall our whole talk with great pleasure. Everything you told me about your artistic aims in *Die Frau ohne Schatten* and in *Intermezzo* has very much enlightened me and I trust that all these works of ours, taken together, will eventually establish a new style and manner. In this way their *future*, too, will be assured. I hope to finish the first act

[1] i.e. Aethra.

367

shortly. The second, I seem to feel in advance, will be good and effective in construction, for I am impatient to make a start; if it were not so, if the construction were still in doubt, I would find myself diffident and loth to begin.

As you know, my position is always precarious; artistically on account of the present situation of the stage—and at this moment economically also. You, with your very great authority among people, can help me at every point without effort on your part. First of all immediately by seeing to it that the film project[1] comes off; the prospective returns from this are for you not unimportant, for me however more important still. The point is that you must get Rosenauer to report to you about the way the project is to be financed and about the people whom he means to interest in it, and that you make it, authoritatively, clear to Fürstner that you wish this plan to materialize. (Rösch apparently has nothing to do with it)—and then, please get hold of Goldstein and others to try and secure their goodwill and basic agreement to co-operate in raising the funds for the reconstruction of the [Salzburg] Felsenreitschule, so that the various sponsors can be assembled into a syndicate which will guarantee the 4000 million [Austrian] Schillings to be amortized within twenty years.

Yours sincerely,

HOFMANNSTHAL

Bad Aussee, 7.10.1923

Please, *my dear friend*, do not get impatient; I don't want to send you another fragment, but the whole remainder of the act. I am working very many hours each day and it is shaping very well; you will have it within a few days.

Please send me a line to say whether you were able to interest Goldstein in Salzburg.

Sincerely yours,

HOFMANNSTHAL

Bad Aussee, 14.10.1923

Dear Dr. Strauss,

Were you held up in Vienna and have you not yet returned to Garmisch? Have you sent me a line which has failed to reach me? I am quite at a loss.

[1] The *Rosenkavalier* film version.

On account of the possible financial returns for which nothing undue is demanded, I attach above all the greatest importance to the conversation with Rosenauer about the film project. My income last quarter from my (German) share in the operas, from German performances of my stage plays, and from all book sales totalled two and a quarter dollars!

At this moment, Pallenberg is acting *Der Unbestechliche* in Berlin every night; accounts are made up every four days and nonetheless the receipts of the steadily sold out theatre amount to practically nothing!— An unparalleled situation!—Act I is finished, and my wife will have completed copying the manuscript on the typewriter by today or tomorrow. As soon as I know you are back at Garmisch I will post it!

Sincerely yours,

HOFMANNSTHAL

Garmisch, 14.10.23

My dear Friend,

I'm back again and have already started sketching *Helena*; pieces such as the hymn-like 'Bei jener Nacht, der keuschen einzig einen' or the little duet 'Ich laufe und hole das Fläschchen!—Ich will nicht' etc., lend themselves particularly well to composition.

Everything that you have marked 'spoken' I should like—for the time being—to be really spoken. The so-called Mozartian *secco* recitative (with piano) is not, to my mind, a very happy art form, and I'm getting increasingly fond of dialogue between the musical numbers, which then seem all the fresher for it. To start with, the purely spoken word is better understood, and with a dialogue so realistic as the first scenes of Aethra the sung note would blur the characteristic intonation. I've also a feeling that in the solo scene between Helen and Aethra, which you read to me, a great deal would get across more effectively if it were only spoken, and longueurs would be avoided. *Vederemo!* In any event, please continue in that splendid style of the first few scenes and let me have the remainder of the act soon—if possible with an explicit scenario of Act II, so that I get the general idea. My stay in Vienna has advanced quite a few matters, and after a full hour's audience with that wonderful man Seipel I regard the artistic future of the Opera at any rate as safe.

With Goldstein I found much sympathy for your Salzburg project and have referred him to Direktor Stransky for detailed discussion. I've talked the film matter over with Rosenauer and recommended Fürstner to go ahead with it.

Ariadne is to be performed in Rome (Constanzi) in March, for the first time in Italian. Perhaps you'd get in touch with Schanzer, Rome, Via Volturno 34, about the translation, so it can progress under your constant supervision.

Finally, I wish you many more happy hours of work, so that the whole thing remains worthy of the magnificent beginning, and am impatiently awaiting your next instalments.

With best regards, ever yours,

RICHARD STRAUSS

My dear Friend,   *Bad Aussee, 16.10.(1923)*

Herewith in gratitude for your letter of October 14—the whole first act. Please add the pages you already have and read the whole thing through at leisure twice over: I hope you will enjoy it on second reading.

Whether the 'spoken' passages remain 'spoken' in the end, or whether they receive some very slight musical (orchestral) setting (like the dialogue in the *Ariadne* Vorspiel, which was, after all, also very realistic), does not worry me in the least one way or the other. What matters is that the work as a whole remains *light*. It is a heroic subject, but *treated as a comedy*: this fact must entirely determine the style, even where details of the libretto might seduce a man (but only a lesser man than you) to stray into 'music drama'. If that were to happen *all* would be lost. The elves are not the sweet fragile elves of Mendelssohn's *Midsummer Night's Dream*! They are evil creatures, importunate like flies, and aggressive. They do a lot at every point of this act to create the atmosphere of comedy. Something in their laughter or in their 'Yes, Yes, Yes, Yes!' ought to be diabolic and at the same time amusing. I rely on your inventiveness in this direction which never fails: I am thinking of the call of the falcon, and the cries of the little frying fishes. I have a distinct notion that there ought to be no male voices in the choruses of the elves. Perhaps there should not be *many* voices at all (how many were there for the calls of the little fishes?)

370

And the same for the Sea-Shell: let it sound really amusing and *mysterious*! When I mention 'gurgling' I have in mind the noise of water 'speaking' in a pipe. It is not absolutely vital that one should understand what it says; it might in fact be amusing if the Sea-Shell were to sound distorted like a voice on the telephone when one stands beside the receiver—if so the servant girl would have to repeat what it says.

If the set pieces like 'Ich laufe und hole das Fläschchen' and 'Bei jener Nacht' strike you as meeting the composer half-way, I know I have accomplished, in the treatment, what I had pictured to myself. Since there are so many such 'numbers' in the act (and since the beginning, compared with the rest, has spread itself rather) I suggest *leaving out* Aethra's little song (A–e–thra, always three syllables!) on the first page 'Das Mahl ist gerichtet'.[1] I would propose the following cuts: Page 1, Aethra: '—die keine ist und meiner spottet' (she rises), straight on to page 2, Serving Maid: 'Es scheint, dass sie sich zu einer Antwort herbeilässt'.

Is not the passage 'Bei jener Nacht' far too long? I would advise tentatively to reduce it to the following:

> Bei jener Nacht, der keuschen einzig einen,
> Die einmal kam, auf ewig uns zu einen;
> Und bei der heutigen wieder, da du kamest
> Mich jäh und zart aus allem Schrecknis nahmest:
> Bei ihr, die mich aufs neu Dir schenkt,
> Trink hier, wo meine Lippe sich getränkt![2]

Page 12, from Helen's decidedly over-long passage, please cut, without loss, the following three lines:

> Denn ich im Arme des anderen
> Zerdrückte in meinen Händen dein Herz
> Und du konntest mir nichts tun.[3]

On page 5 I should retain the short song-like exclamation of Aethra:

> Was wir sahen, da wir sehnten

only if it is justified by a very lively and attractive tune, and I would

[1] Strauss retained Aethra's little song, but left out the opening prose passage (up to 'und meiner spottet'). This is to be found only in the published book version: Mainzer Presse, Insel Verlag 1928.

[2] Strauss did not carry out the cut here proposed.

[3] This passage was cut in the opera even more severely than here suggested. Compare the published book.

suggest moving it in any case to the end of the spoken passage, *after* 'und ein wenig Gewalt über Wind und Wellen hat!'

Within the next few days I shall send you the opening scene of the second act and an outline of the action.

I shall get in touch with Schanzer. Many thanks for talking to Rosenauer and Goldstein—I am glad about your conversation with Seipel.

Sincerely yours,

HOFMANNSTHAL

P.S. My wife asks me to tender her apologies: the typewriter ribbon did not function properly when she copied out the enclosure.

Garmisch, 23.10.23

My dear Friend,

The end of Act I is very beautiful and I congratulate the two of us on this piece of poetry which is quite exceptionally suited to music. Whether the act isn't a trifle long I can't judge yet for certain. So far I've sketched out about a third: most of it virtually sets itself to music. You've again made great progress as a 'librettist'.

But more than ever I am in favour of purely spoken dialogue: partly entirely without music, partly melodramatic, partly punctuated only by short musical flourishes (e.g. the elfin choruses)—the grand finale would then start with Aethra's 'Am Hang des Atlas steht eine Burg'. That passages such as the first duet between Helen and Menelaus cannot be treated in light character and will go considerably beyond the Singspiel—that I'm afraid you'll have to reconcile yourself to. And I am fully aware that the transition from this pathos to purely spoken dialogue demands much artistic tact on the part of the composer and the actors. That the genre is possible is proved by *Fidelio, Oberon, Magic Flute, Freischütz*.

I even find it very attractive; it makes the audience particularly receptive for the musical numbers themselves, whereas no unbiased listener can avoid a considerable sense of fatigue during the third hour of *Don Giovanni, Figaro* or *Così fan tutte*. So please stick to the style you've started out with. It's excellent. And please send me a synopsis soon of Act II, so I can get an idea of the whole thing.

I hope to have basically sketched out the first act by the end of November. It's coming on unbelievably fast and is giving me no end of pleasure. But the work would be in vain if Act II were not to come off equally well or to contain the necessary climax.

Fürstner is now getting weekly accounts from the theatres and intends to negotiate about the film with Rosenauer at once.

I shall probably be in Vienna again for a few days next Monday. Perhaps Fürstner will come there too. My address until 13th Nov. is Garmisch; until 30th Nov. Meran, Obermais, Schloss Pienzenau, c/o Baron Kuh; then Vienna.

Many thanks again and best regards. Yours,

RICHARD STRAUSS

Spoken dialogue has moreover the advantage of greater intelligibility and quicker delivery.

Dear Dr. Strauss, *Bad Aussee, 1.11.1923*

Please do not get impatient or anxious. I am fully aware myself that the whole work is of *no use* if the second act were to fall short of the first, but I hope and believe that it will be good and that the whole thing will be good. It is happily conceived, the motifs (the psychological ones and the theatrical ones of Fairyland) go hand in hand. I am at work with great concentration and seriousness as well as cheerfully and with pleasure—that is, I am now at work again after the Föhn weather; sleepless nights, eternal headaches and nightmares made me literally ill for eight days. Of the three main parts (quasi exposition—centre piece—finale, analogous to the first act) I have begun the second and the first is already behind me. I am now on the very lively central piece which interweaves the outward and the psychological action; this is to be followed by a very grave scene between Helen and Menelaus (beginning of the finale)—but I find it quite impossible to give a *written* account now of all this lively and rich action (by word of mouth I might manage it if it has to be). You will get (before you leave for Meran) the first main part, and, in key words, the action right up to the end.

I am pleased with the praise you give me as librettist, and especially delighted with what is implied in the words 'A great deal sets itself to music'. This is what I aimed at and to this I apply myself, as to everything I do, earnestly and with constant endeavour—a rare phenomenon in our time which possesses no masters and so many bunglers.

All your preliminary remarks about the style of the music make good sense to me. A scene like the one between Menelaus and Helen must of course go far beyond the Singspiel. I am glad you mentioned two works of Weber's: both characters, but Menelaus above all, are bathed in a glow of fairy-tale chivalry such as Weber created so wonderfully. Any tenor who can *properly* personify Lohengrin—the *tenderly* heroic, truly chivalrous aspect of this character—will also make an excellent Menelaus.

There is still quite a lot I would like to say, but I close this letter to devote this quiet, peaceful November evening to another scene.

Sincerely yours,

HOFMANNSTHAL

P.S. The first act looks about as long as the first of *Rosenkavalier*, and even if it were longer by ten minutes no harm is done, for there are only two acts, and an over-all duration of some two-and-a-half to two-and-three-quarter hours, plus entr'acte, is just right. *Ariadne* is, as you will remember, too short for France, Italy, and so on.

Garmisch, 5.11.23

My dear Friend,

Many thanks for your letter of 1.11. Have got as far as the return of Menelaus and can seriously report that everything so far is wonderful. The duet and the falling-asleep scene I have, I think, brought off especially well. In Vienna I shall ask you to write me an additional twelve lines for the end of the duet: 'Mond und Meer, Erde und Nacht, helfet mir jetzt', in the same manner.

Likewise for Aethra, from 'Ich halte ihn hinweg mit Zaubereien', altogether some twenty-four lines which she can add in counterpoint towards the end of the duet. Otherwise everything is magnificent. I'm in Vienna from 7th to 9th Nov. From 15th Nov. Meran, Obermais, Schloss Pienzenau, till the 26th, then wholly in Vienna! May your cheerful creative atmosphere continue!

With best regards, yours

RICHARD STRAUSS

Dear Dr. Strauss,

A card like yours of the 5th naturally gives me great pleasure. It brings back to my mind most vividly the early days of our collaboration, when in the spring of 1909 you were working so cheerfully (but not more so than now) on *Rosenkavalier*. Although *Ariadne* turned out so beautifully in the end, the progress reports I received at that time were by no means equally good.

I for my part have entirely secluded myself to concentrate all my energy on the second act. I have already reached the finale, where Helen and Menelaus drain together the cup of remembrance sent to them by Poseidon (an antidote far more terrible than the harmless lotus drink of oblivion). I am straining all my mind and all my imagination to draw together all the motives (the psychological ones as well as those of the outward action) at the end into a powerful climax, but a clear and simple one.

In the composition you will now reach the scene between Aethra and Menelaus (pp. 22 to 29, for quite in accord with my own ideas, you have called page 29 the beginning of the finale). I find it hard to imagine this Aethra-Menelaus scene as a 'spoken' one, especially from page 26 onwards, say from 'ich trug niemand?' and so on. Here it is decidedly my idea that both characters should *sing*. (Presumably yours also.) But even earlier, on pages 22 to 25, I could perfectly well imagine Aethra's passages *spoken* (with musical frills) but hardly Menelaus's replies, e.g. 'Wie fass ich die Rede' or 'Wer hat gesehen, wer war Zeuge?' It might be quite an attractive idea to keep *her* replies very close to speech while *his*, as befits this heroic personality, are sung. I would like to draw your attention to a definite recurring rhythm in Menelaus' diction, used to depict his indignant wrath which remains at the same time always *chivalrous*. Take, for instance, the lines: 'Helena, merke zuletzt meine Rede!' Page 15, or: 'Bewahret mich rein, ihr oberen Götter, helfet, was sein muss, mir zu vollenden.' Page 14.

Then:

> Weib, welche Rede kommt Dir vom Munde?
> Sprich nicht von Paris und jenem Tage!
> Hüte Dich, Weib, dass ich Dich nicht strafe!
> Achte der Worte, bevor Du sie redest!

(on p. 28) all have the same nobly indignant rhythm highly characteristic of Menelaus.

A personal request: would it be a great trouble for you to bring with you to Vienna the book on the *Decline of the Ancient World*? I would so much like to read it but cannot at the moment afford to buy any books.

I am so late that I will not risk enclosing in this letter to Garmisch the first ten pages of the second act, but will post them tomorrow to Schloss Pienzenau.

Yours very sincerely,

HOFMANNSTHAL

P.S. Shall write the supplementary passages with pleasure in Vienna.

(from tomorrow onwards Neubeuern am Inn, Oberbayern)

Bad Aussee, 12.11.23

Dear Dr. Strauss,

I hope you have arrived safe and well.

Here now is the beginning of the second act.

The first scene between Menelaus and Helen is so to speak the overture. It discloses the new leading theme of the action: how *both* are compelled by their own nature to undo with their own hands the knot fastened by deceit. The outward action opens with the approach of the horsemen. It is brisk and rapid where that of the first act resembled a dream or fairy-tale. The desert wind dominates now instead of the damp moonlit night by the seaside. In my mind's eye I see the Sheikh sung by Duhan or by some other courtly baritone, like a good Telramund. I am not sure whether to think of Da-ud, who is quite young, as a very high baritone or as a tenor (like, say, David in *Meistersinger*) but he must not under any circumstances be sung by a woman. At Neubeuern I shall complete with extreme care the finale, for which I have already a detailed sketch.

Sincerely yours,

HOFMANNSTHAL

Neubeuern, 25.11.1923

Dear Dr. Strauss,

All you say in your letter[1] about the second act and about the requisite trend of the whole opera is perfectly correct.

The second act was completed a few days ago, but it does not altogether satisfy me in this sense and I shall have to revise it. The

[1] Not extant.

376

motives are right, the closing part (finale) I consider good, much can remain, but up to the beginning of the finale the treatment must become much more compact. Even the first scene (before the entrance of the Sheikh), which is already in your hands, will be changed in this sense.

On December 4th I shall be in Vienna.

Yours ever,

HOFMANNSTHAL

Vienna, 26.12.23

My dear Friend,

A happy New Year to you and your family! Three days of rest in bed have, I believe, now revealed to me the fundamental mistake of Act I as a drama to be set to music, from the second entrance of Menelaus to Aethra's tale. No matter how delicately it is all thought out and motivated by you on the psychological plane—if it can't be pure prose it would turn out an endless piece of dreary music. I believe Menelaus must burst on-stage and state clearly that he has murdered Paris *and* Helen.[1] Possibly, now that he is avenged at last, he wants to kill himself—Aethra stays his arm (the potion of oblivion perhaps later, immediately before Helen is roused) and now as quickly as possible, without any further retrospective narrative moments, forward to 'the spectre' and Aethra's tale: 'Am Hang des Atlas steht eine Burg.'

So that the act falls into the following scenes:

> Introduction and account of the storm.
> Scene of Helen and Menelaus.
> Spook and Menelaus's exit (perhaps Menelaus's growing confusion ought to be expressed more clearly here).
> Rejuvenation of Helen.
> Short dialogue Menelaus–Aethra.
> Finale.

When have you time to discuss this whole thorough revision and reduction to the most indispensable captions? I am at your disposal at any time.

With kindest regards, ever yours,

RICHARD STRAUSS

[1] Thus in the final version.

1924

Rodaun, Monday 7 p.m. (1924)[1]

Dear Dr. Strauss,

Herewith I send you the Menelaus-Aethra scene reduced to what is indispensable to the action. These sheets take the place of pages 22, 23, 24, 25, 26, 27, 28 of your manuscript. Here I make him drink for the first time; later, as if to make sure, he does so again immediately before he sees the transformed Helen. At the bottom of page 33, please add:

> Aethra: 'Noch einmal trinke aus meinem Becher
> und dann sieh hin, was Dir die Götter bereiten.'

A suggestion for a cut in the finale would be on page 31 down to Menelaus's exclamation: 'Furchtbares Weib!' This is a possible cut which would do no harm to the story. Equally on page 32, after Aethra's: 'Du wirst sie sehen, bereite Dich—', one could jump straight to page 33, Menelaus: 'Ich höre Becken, dumpf geschlagen', leaving out the intermediate links, though attractive in themselves, at the composer's discretion.

Finally on page 1, I am determined that, as soon as the harp has faded away, we should make Aethra enter impetuously to begin at once her song: 'Das Mahl ist gerichtet!'[2]

This prose passage is too slight, too close to operetta. Everything which is said in prose here becomes sufficiently clear later on and in this way (if we open with this little aria) we remain within the style which now emerges when one sees the opera as a whole; at the time I started writing I did not yet realize how much the second act was to step on to a higher lyrical plane. All those touches of comedy and conversation which still remain after the cuts are nonetheless of the greatest value; it is this combination which makes up the novelty of the genre and the delicate value of the work. In the meantime I have almost completed what is still missing from Act II (Menelaus asleep, Helen alone); it has, I believe, turned out very well.

I am writing this so that in any case you may have it before you as an *aide-memoire*; the actual manuscript I intend to bring you personally and hope to see you soon.

Very sincerely yours,

HOFMANNSTHAL

[1] Date uncertain.
[2] The introductory prose monologue was preserved in the book version.

Dear Dr. Strauss,

Manuscript in hand I have thought over what you recently said. There is of course no reason whatever why you should not introduce Aethra's incantation at an earlier point into the main scene (Helen–Menelaus) instead of leaving it exactly where it is in the text. The written word must establish everything consecutively, whereas the music is allowed a certain degree of simultaneity, of intermingling even. Your dramatic sense rightly demands that the spectator should *see* something as soon as the incantation starts. The curtain which is drawn across the rear of the chamber must therefore become a transparent veil here behind which a weird spook is afoot and from where now and then some pale green face emerges with glistening eyes, and then again some other animal figures. The whole scene however must remain throughout in the realm of the uncanny, of awe-inspiring sorcery. To achieve this we need a scene painter of vision and imagination; I dare say I shall find him and indeed that is not so very difficult, provided only I can count on your whole-hearted support. You will have to stand by my side with *all* your qualities and qualifications as opera composer, and you must subordinate your dramatic instinct to necessities of a different order. Without proper backing, my own authority on the operatic stage is too weak to assure that justice will be done to the whole work.

But even before then, in the purely creative work, the decisive task is yours. If the introduction of these elves suggests to the eye the slightest allusion to Mendelssohn's sweet and pretty Dance of the Elves, then the whole thing will degenerate hopelessly into triviality. Here the imagination of the painter, which is to lead the spectator, is in turn bound to receive its terms of reference from the music. Provided the singing and the interjections of the elves possess an intensely characteristic ring—the kind of thing you do better than anyone else, if they express the mocking, scoffing manner of night imps, the sneering hatred of man, the vampire aspect of these afrites—, then even the slightest hint provided by the painter will convey to the spectator all that matters, a peculiarly Southern, haunting nightmare of the witches' Sabbath; for in any case the spectator will seek to gather the essential meaning of this spook through the ear. Aware that all the scene painter can do is support, but not initiate, anything decisive, I have done my part in the manner in which I have put things in the text. All now depends on your charging with even greater, converging potency the manner in which these elfin voices express themselves in music. To my mind one should never hear too many of them, never more than one pair at a time, never a whole chorus.

Sincerely yours,

HOFMANNSTHAL

Rotterdam, 29th Jan. 1924

My very dear Friend,

I have deliberately not participated in any literary demonstration in honour of your fiftieth birthday[1] because I cannot escape the feeling that anything I could tell you in words would be banal in comparison with what, as the composer of your wonderful poetry, I have already said to you in music. It was your words which drew from me the finest music that I had to give: this knowledge must fill you with deep gratification. Let therefore Chrysothemis, the Marschallin, Ariadne, Zerbinetta, the Empress, and, not least, H.[2]—'admired much and much reproved'—join me in calling on you and thanking you for all you have dedicated to me out of your life's work, and kindled in me, and roused to life. That even our contemporaries are at last beginning to appreciate the magnitude and the beauty of the work you have been doing for me is proved by the sensational success which *Ariadne*— poetry and music—achieved in Amsterdam twice last week (in an exemplary rendering by our splendid Vienna company and Mengelberg's magnificent orchestra): may this give you special pleasure on your birthday. It was striking how quickly and with what humour the Dutch public—which admittedly has not been corrupted theatrically by any form of *verismo* and has been fed on nothing but the best music for the past twenty-five years—received the play in particular. I have never heard such loud, frequent and hearty laughter during the Vorspiel as here, and after Act I such a storm of applause broke loose as hardly after the fortieth performance in Vienna. I now have faith in the future of *Ariadne*—especially abroad. The performance is to be repeated shortly, together with *Rosenkavalier*, and the plan for the construction of a big German opera house in Amsterdam is taking more definite shape. Roller is to design the basic plan. For today then I am merely sending you my best wishes for good health and a long life full of

[1] 1st February 1924.   [2] Helen.

happy work and full of the joys which you are hoping for and deserve; what with our growing conquest of the 'hard currency countries' these, no doubt, will not be lacking much longer. Your kind letter reached me in Amsterdam and I am looking forward with pleasure to finding the finished work on my return to Vienna (12th February). This afternoon I am leaving direct for Rome, via Brussels, Milan.

Once I've settled in the Belvedere[1] no hard currency in the world is going to make me leave my botanical garden in the winter.

All the best then, and enjoy the festive day with the sense of humour needed for such 'milestones in one's life', and spare an occasional thought to your most loyal admirer,

RICHARD STRAUSS

Best regards to your family.

Rodaun, 14.2.1924

Dear Dr. Strauss,

Your letter was a good and kind one, and you feel the things exactly as I do myself. All this time I have gone on touching up the second act of *Helena*, thinning out some passages and pulling together others; I hope and believe that, as a specific text for music, as *opera*, it is the best I have ever done.

I am particularly gratified by the mounting suspense I have achieved, by the dramatic interplay of themes, and by the attractive and remarkable juxtaposition of the two acts; the idyllic fairy-tale-like first and the exciting second: water and fire.

You will get it, all done and finished within five or six days at the most. All I still lack are the last four lines (Menelaus–Helen *unisono*), and my wife is also well on with her copying. But do understand: I would much prefer not to send it to you, but to bring it and read it aloud again. This will, after all, take no more than twenty-five minutes at the outside and has its distinct advantages. So please spare me the time once more. It matters to me.

Another request: would you please get me a box for the *Ariadne* performance with Germaine Lubin, whether it is a full-dress affair or not, so that as host I can make the singer's husband, the poet Paul Géraldy, my guest; as a Viennese inviting the stranger, as co-author the

[1] Richard Strauss's Vienna house, into which he moved in October 1924, is situated on a plot belonging to the Belvedere complex of buildings.

foreign author. Please give instructions for this request of mine to be seen to. I will in that case of course *not* claim my two author's tickets.

Sincerely yours,

HOFMANNSTHAL

P.S. I was of course exceedingly pleased by the news of the success in Holland. *Ariadne* is, after all, my favourite among the children. Let us wish that *Helena* may come to rival her!

11.3.1924

Dear Dr. Strauss,

However modest my understanding of music, I am very well able to perceive whatever relates to the style of a work of art and for that reason I am delighted with what you have played to me.

To achieve stylistic homogeneity between the acts (as opposed to the very strong contrast of mood, and the contrast of pace which is almost like drowsiness compared to awakening—these contrasts are of course intentional), both Aethra's all-too-conventional prose passages which we marked must disappear from the first act. In my opinion this cut ought definitely to include the passages before the entrance of Helen, even though you have already set them to music. Everything Aethra says at this point can be spared; as *chatter* it detracts from the great and legitimate suspense of the occasion.

One word about the elves, if you will allow me; about the rest there is hardly anything to say. The exclamations, the jabber of the three elves need not necessarily all be understood; a great deal of it may pass for its musical attraction alone. It is, however, vital that the characteristic element should strongly preponderate over the graceful, and this is well within the reach of a master like you if you are determined to get it. They are evil, impudent, mocking spooks; only behind such a mask of sound can they fulfil their well-defined dramatic function. Only at a few isolated points, especially those right at the end of the act ('Wie—oder nicht?' and what follows), which are important to an understanding of the continuity of the story, and at a few specific earlier points, it would appear to me a very happy solution if single voices were to take the place of the chorus (which is, I take it, intended as a small chorus?) and if the treatment could possibly verge on the grotesque (so that, for instance, a deep female voice would attempt to speak like a basso, or again a man in falsetto or something like that). In this way that touch of the *sinister* would be gained which is paralleled later in the awakening in Act II. (. . .)

Sincerely ever yours,

HOFMANNSTHAL

15.3.1924

The tone of my letter, *my dear Dr. Strauss*, will have shown you that it was written without the slightest inkling of your anxieties.[1] After my second visit to you I was, on the contrary, under the impression that these anxious and troubled days lay behind you.

I would not like to leave unsaid at this moment how much, with all my heart, I share your anxieties. Yet what use is the sharing of troubles to him on whom they weigh! The burden is not lightened. That there may be, in the near future, a turn for the better—this is the confident hope, rather than the anxiety, which I would like to share with you soon.

We are making no inquiries, because to do so is a presumptuous annoyance.

I press your hand with all good and warm wishes.

Yours HOFMANNSTHAL

Vienna, 18.4.24

My dear Friend,

Congratulations again on the splendid success of *Der Schwierige*: I was extremely pleased about it. Shall I see you again before 15th May? Today only a request: could you return the books which Architekt Rosenauer handed on to you from me some time ago—French Theatre and Goldoni, Metastasio—to this address before your departure?

Happy Easter! Bubi is on the road to recovery. And best wishes from us to you all.

Yours sincerely,

RICHARD STRAUSS

[1] A serious illness of Strauss's son.

Dear Dr. Strauss,

Herewith the only trouble to which I for my part will put you in connection with the commission I have received for *Die Ruinen von Athen*. It is the monologue of the Stranger as he stands, at nightfall, at the foot of the Acropolis and before he begins his song (that aria with the horns). I find it quite unbearable to imagine this monologue unsustained by a single breath of music. It was always the intention to have some musical ground-work, however slight: just a soft touch of the strings here and there so that the spoken word should not hang in the air all too barely. Alwin would presumably be quite capable of providing these trifling chords; but since it is important that not even the most fastidious ear should be able to discover a discrepancy between this particle, however minute, and Beethoven's style, I naturally submit it to you with the request that you send your score direct to Turnau.[1]

This letter will reach you about the time of your birthday.[2] The past year was for you, I feel, a mixed one. Between festive occasions, annoyance, excitement, at one time anxiety even obtruded themselves upon you. May you be spared now the one as well as the other for years to come. The happiest occasion is a productive hour one spends alone—that *Helena* may not prove unsuited to give full scope to your creative faculty in a novel and attractive manner, this is my sole wish for you. Looking ahead, in this sense, to this significant anniversary, I have pulled myself together and spurred myself on and last year concentrated entirely on the execution of this piece of work, in order to demonstrate to you in this symbolic way that everything connecting us is dear, most dear to me, and that for my part I wish to see no end to this connection.

For it strikes me as something great and at the same time necessary in my life that, eighteen years ago, you approached me with your wishes and needs. There pre-existed within me something which enabled me to fulfil—within the limits of my gifts—these wishes and made this fulfilment in turn satisfy a most profound need of my own. Much of what I had produced in all the loneliness of youth, entirely for myself, hardly thinking of readers, were phantastic little operas and Singspiele—without music. Your wishes, subsequently, supplied a

---

[1] Richard Strauss fulfilled this request and provided some musical groundwork to the spoken monologue of the Stranger which is given in the postscript to this letter.

[2] Strauss's sixtieth birthday (11th June 1924).

purpose without restricting my freedom. Imbued with the idea, which growing insight has but served to confirm, that the individual can produce nothing of lasting value unless it be linked to tradition, I have learnt far more from what I was able to gather from the features of older, still living works of similar literature than from any 'demands of our time' which might seem to be in the air. As a result nothing of what I have done for you possessed at first sight any great appeal to our contemporaries and their spokesmen; what I had created was dismissed as nothing out of the ordinary, my humour was set aside as not humorous, my sentiment as not moving, my imagination as not imaginative. Everything was precisely not what, in the judgment of these oracles of wisdom and good taste, it should have tried to be. Invariably the essence has been missed, never did the marksman hit the mark—invariably it is the libretto which bears the full brunt of the scorn of all those who are for ever longing for beauty, but will die rather than see it. The only person who always recognized whatever there was, who received it with real joy, received it productively and translated it into higher reality, was you.

This is how you have rewarded me, as richly as any artist can reward another—the rest our works did for themselves and I believe that they, not all of them, but nearly all of them, with their inseparable fusion of poetry and music, will continue to live for some considerable time and will give pleasure to several generations. May the time ahead be a truly good one for you; this is a wish which includes, after all, the well-being of your whole family. May the house in the Belvedere unite you all happily.

I am today and always from the bottom of my heart your sincere and grateful friend.

HOFMANNSTHAL

Ruinen von Athen

Monologue of the German artist (Duhan). In the failing light of dusk the ancient crumbling statues seem to come alive among the decayed walls.

The Stranger: Hinauf zu Deiner Burg, meine Göttin! Empfängst Du mich mit dem ganzen Licht Deines Abends? Lässest mich mein Antlitz spiegeln in Deinem goldenen Schild, dass ich mir selber entschwinde und unverwelklich werde vor Dir wie einer von den Deinigen?

Oder soll ich an Deines Abends Schatten mich stillen, göttliche Herrin, der ich ein Kind des Abends bin und

zu später Stunde den heiligen Jugendpfad der Welt
betrete—einsam, scheu, wie die nachgeborene Waise,
demütig unterm Abendstern, dass er mir die Herrlichen
zusammenführe, die Götter der Erde, die der fühllos
spiegelnde Morgen mit rosigen Händen immer wieder
zerstückelt!

(Fade out background—the music opens the aria with the horns.)

Garmisch, 24.6.24

My very dear Friend,

I thank you from all my heart for your beautiful letter on my birthday:
I shall always treasure it as a most valuable document of our personal
and artistic relationship. I shall endeavour, by making *Helena* a particularly fine composition, to repay you for your renewed, precious co-
operation in my dramatic life's work. The melodrama for *Ruinen von
Athen* went to Turnau a week ago.

Today Oscar von Miller, the creator of the Deutsches Museum in
Munich, came to see me, and requested me to let them have the first
performance of *Ruinen von Athen* for the opening of the Deutsches
Museum on 8th May 1925.

Leaving aside Vienna's prior claim to this festival piece, the only
concession I could make to Herr von Miller was to ask you, as the
author responsible for the adaptation (I contributed merely the suggestion), that you would not allow any theatre other than Vienna to
perform the piece before 8th May 25, thereby reserving for the
Deutsches Museum in Munich the first performance in Germany. He
would, moreover, like us to dedicate the adaptation to the Deutsches
Museum. Would you agree to this? As some 5,000 visitors from all
over the globe will attend the opening, the newly revived piece would
thus become instantly known throughout the world. But to make sure
there is no unauthorized tampering with the piece in the meantime it
will probably be necessary for you to sign as the author—to safeguard
the copyright. Roller and Kröller would of course have to take an
active part in the Munich gala performance, for which no doubt ample
means are available, sufficient for the realization even of Roller's most
extravagant ideas. I have declared my readiness to conduct.

Maybe Fürstner will now decide to publish it: perhaps the Deutsches
Museum will even pay the printing costs (just occurred to me!).

386

In perpetual gratitude and with best wishes for a good, productive summer.

Yours very sincerely,

RICHARD STRAUSS

Rodaun, 1.7.(1924)

Dear Dr. Strauss,

Many thanks for your kind note. I do not consider it a good idea to have a reprint done of the music to the *Ruinen*;[1] nobody would buy it. Fürstner should, however, get my adaptation as well as your melo-drama passage copied, and later (after a success in Vienna) I shall appoint him agent for my performing rights. Compliance with Herr von Miller's request, if I am not to allow a performance by any German theatre before May 8, would in fact mean sacrificing the whole season; still, the advantages are great if Miller secures Roller and Kröller for me and if you will conduct! I shall, at any rate, make no promises anywhere before we meet again.

Yours ever,

HOFMANNSTHAL

Lenzerheide, Graubünden. Shortly at Bad Aussee, Obertressen
(end of July, 1924)

Dear Dr. Strauss,

It often occurs to me how much I would like to tell you this, that, or the other concerning *Helena*, just as it crosses my mind; how I would wish to draw attention to the relative importance of some idea or other underlying the libretto, of this or that theme—in all humility of course, in the way my remarks on earlier librettos have always obtained from you a ready hearing. But then it occurs to me also that I cannot even tell whether at the particular moment you are occupying yourself with this work or whether you are preoccupied with altogether different matters and affairs—and so I leave it. Not at such a moment would I wish my remarks to reach you, but only when your own creative activity has kindled your imagination to the subject.

I am given to understand that no decision has yet been taken whether the Théâtre des Champs Elysées is to do *Ariadne* or *Rosenkavalier*, that

[1] The piano score and book of *Die Ruinen von Athen* were nonetheless reprinted. There was in addition an anonymous introductory pamphlet, the text of which was written by Hofmannsthal himself.

Hébertot inclines towards *Rosenkavalier*, but that the final decision will of course be yours and that it is still open. May I, if this be the true state of affairs, venture to say something, of course in an equally humble, tentative manner? Since this concerns the debut of both works in Paris and since both works, as you can imagine, are equally dear to me, each in its own way, may I say then that just for Paris the prospects of *Ariadne* strike me as highly promising, those of *Rosenkavalier* more doubtful. I make this statement with the assurance of well-founded knowledge of social and theatrical history, unquestionably *greater* than Hébertot's, or of any ordinary man of the theatre. The French are persuaded that they have something of a monopoly of the *dix-huitième* (the period we call the rococo). *Ariadne*, this mixture of grand opera with Commedia dell' arte, in which both components, each in itself, are highly stylized exactly in the convention to which the French are accustomed, this combination is certain to score an impressive success in Paris as soon as decor and mise en scène are entrusted to a painter who has real command of the style of the 18th century—and there are several such in Paris. *Rosenkavalier*, on the other hand, is wholly Viennese, and not in the least Parisian 18th century; the *coarse* figure of Ochs, this whole half-bucolic atmosphere, this ending at the inn and so on, the style half-way between opera and operetta—all this does not suit me for Paris at all. The very feature which helped to secure the great success in London presents for Paris an obstacle, I am sure; I mean the fact that a burlesque figure of an 18th century country squire like Ochs is familiar to the English and that they feel at home with it (their plays and novels, from Falstaff down, are teeming with such characters).

All in all (and also taking into account the fact that Germaine Lubin will certainly make a good Ariadne by Parisian standards, whereas I am under the impression that she does not possess the verve nor the dramatic talent required for Octavian) the scales seem to me weighted so decisively in favour of *Ariadne* that, if it were for me to decide, I would not even hesitate to put up with the difficulty of finding some (possibly not Straussian) curtain-raiser. Quite conceivably, of course, the ultimate decision depends on other considerations; I have of necessity written without full knowledge of the facts.

A word from you to Aussee at any time would give me great pleasure, as everything from your hand always does.

Yours,

HOFMANNSTHAL

My dear Friend,

Entirely share your opinion about *Rosenkavalier* in Paris. In case of doubt, favour *Ariadne* like yourself. No further news from Hébertot to date; by the way, Fürstner is very much against the Champs Elysées.

I am making every possible effort to save *Ruinen von Athen* for Vienna, but there's a risk that it may all come to naught because of the incredibly petty chicanery of the Ministry of Finance.

Helena Act I ready in the draft, with a good final climax. I'm continually working on the piece and shall be open to and grateful for any observations or suggestions that happen to cross your mind.

From 11th August in Cortina (Hotel Savoy). Best regards, yours sincerely,

RICHARD STRAUSS

Bad Fusch, shortly Bad Aussee, Obertressen. 9.8.(1924)

Dear Dr. Strauss,

What I saw in a newspaper a few days ago makes me assume that the red-tape difficulties which held up *Die Ruinen* have been got over (presumably thanks to your intervention). I do hope it is not too late now to get the decor and the costumes ready in time!

Since you have given me permission so kindly, I shall, from time to time, send you remarks relative to individual passages in *Helena* as they occur to me. I have in mind only those passages which are of importance to the effect and the intelligibility. First of all for the elves in Act I. You were the first to point out that one must *see* them, and this I readily accept. But the following consideration is equally important: the elves are no longer fantastic, decorative ornament; they intervene, on the contrary, so decisively at a few points in the action that it is essential to grasp the actual words of this intervention, unless the whole meaning is to be lost. And it seems to me that at these few, but most *significant* points the relevant line of text, if it is to be understood as it *must* be understood, ought to be sung not by several but by a single voice alone; that means not always as in my libretto by 'the elves', but, at these few significant points by 'the first elf' (who would have to advance pertly to the very threshold of the lighted chamber and sing into it clearly). This applies above all to the first 'Wie—oder nicht?' (page 38, repeating Aethra's question with a mocking drawl).

For it is exactly this 'Wie oder nicht?' which introduces the link to the second act, to the new complications, the new tensions, after the whole thing seemed to have been happily resolved.

Of equal importance in this sense is the following passage on page 41:

(softly but maliciously)

Auf ewige Zeit?
Die teuren Seelen!
Auf ewige Zeit   (or perhaps addressing them
Das Beste verhehlen!   directly:
                            Ihr teuren Seelen!

Haha hahaha!
Das darf nicht sein!

The significant irony in this, which profoundly affects the meaning of the whole action, demands again beyond doubt the *single* voice, the 'first elf'. The 'Hahahaha! das darf nicht sein!' may afterwards very well be repeated by the whole cluster of elves which, given the particular dimensions of the whole opera, is not, I take it, likely to be a very *big* one? It would also seem to me fitting if the passage of page 16 (given by me to 'the elves')

Helena will ich wiedergewinnen!
Paris hier!
und sein Schwert!

were to be sung at first by a single elf, and one who apes a girl's voice; by a deep female voice or perhaps by a boy, but in any case in such a way as to bring out the spooky parodistical element, the mockery.

I cannot but hope very much that you will not abandon the idea of having the Helen-Aethra dialogue in Act II (pages 17–19) *spoken* and not sung as *Sprechgesang*. It is certain to prove a great relief to the ear; there is nowadays, among the whole of the younger generation, a violent reaction against the post-Wagnerian and to some extent even against the Wagnerian *Sprechgesang*! The return from the spoken word to heroic song (perhaps at the moment when Helen takes the little flask) will be one of those unexpected transitions in which your art has achieved rare mastery. Helen's monologue (page 1), the *cantilena* which you wanted, is thoroughly triumphant in expression: the woman, the great mistress, the goddess—a jubilant singing of Leda's daughter!

I attach great importance to the rhythm and expressiveness of the cabalistic song with which Helen accompanies the mixing of the magic potion (page 20). This is very much an incantation, rhythmically a most impressive, uncanny secret formula; especially the repeated: 'und noch und noch und nicht genug vom Zaubertrank Erinnerung!' cannot possibly sound too sombre and bewitched. I would look upon Aethra's interjections in between (never more than one line) as high-pitched outcries, like lightning breaking through dark clouds.

Forgive me if I overstep my bounds. It is only by granting my poetic imagination such licence to stray in the act of creation that I have been able, now and then, to produce something useful for your music. I may possibly send you some more comments soon.

Always yours sincerely,

HOFMANNSTHAL

Semmering, 22.9.24

My dear Friend,

I am now in Vienna till 1st October and would like to talk to you for a short hour or so! Would it be convenient if I came out to Rodaun one midday or afternoon towards the end of the week? Were you satisfied with *Ruinen*?[1] That stupid drivel of the press about the 'rather feeble' Beethoven! who can still crush that pack of scribes with his little finger!

I'm still furious beyond words at this impertinence!

Please let me know by telephone: 63079!

Kindest regards, ever yours,

RICHARD STRAUSS

Shall be back in Vienna for *Ariadne*!

Bad Aussee, 28.9.24

Dear Dr. Strauss,

Both the *Ruinen* and also the Gluck[2] struck me as most beautiful. The Gluck has in its favour compactness and *action*, the kind of thing that from the outset could not be carried into the *Ruinen*; the latter in turn

---

[1] The première took place on 20th September 1924 at the Vienna State Opera.
[2] The *Don Juan* ballet by Gluck.

contains some musical pieces of truly heavenly beauty. It seemed to me that the public both at the dress rehearsal and the premiere took to the whole programme with unreserved delight. I will not suppose that the spiteful twaddle mentioned in your postcard—I make a point of never reading any of the utterances of Herr K(orngold)—could falsify the success, or turn it, real and strong as it undoubtedly was, into the contrary and set the public against us, so that all the love and devotion which you, I, Kröller, and Roller have put into the thing would be wasted. I will not suppose so, but I am somewhat taken aback by finding no trace of the two pieces in the repertory issued yesterday for the next ten days. Please send me a word about this through Fräulein Raminger.

I could not possibly have stayed until the first,[1] however hard I found it to leave. The loss of fourteen working days at this time of the year I cannot make up for! When I asked Turnau in July, he told me in any case that *Der Bürger* presented no problems to him, neither the comedy nor the ceremonial, and that he did not need me. Today, however, I suddenly became apprehensive lest an individual like J.K(orngold), in his systematic campaign to undermine every single thing you do and so eventually to poison your existence in Vienna and drive you away, might easily turn the scale against a work so delicate and unusual as this Molière with your music. For this reason I have today sent to R. Auernheimer and to the editor of the *Neue Freie Presse* the urgent telegraphic request and advice that this premiere, *as a Burgtheater production*, concerns not only the music critic, but Auernheimer also. I have no doubt that, as a result, both critics, will write notices (as happened at the time of the Shakespeare production with the music by E. Korngold) and from this I expect a twofold gain. In the first place Auernheimer will report the success with good grace and respect. In the second place K(orngold) will thus be deprived of any chance of achieving his main object, which is to discredit, in his perfidious way, the whole piece through an attack on the libretto (not, at first sight, directed against you at all), and so to destroy its success in the theatre.

Ever most sincerely yours,

HOFMANNSTHAL

[1] The Vienna première of *Der Bürger als Edelmann* took place at the Redoutensaal, Vienna, 1st October 1924. The music was under the direction of Richard Strauss himself.

Dear Dr. Strauss,

I am really immensely pleased to hear of the excellent outcome of the Dresden performance.[1] I can honestly say that I was very much wondering, and a little concerned, how it would go and that I am now very glad about the success, not quite as if I had a share in it myself, but with the same sincerity and cordiality and pleasure. I foresee that without doubt this work, just by being what it is, a 'bourgeois comedy' (a very happy subtitle!), will give a lot of pleasure everywhere and will bring you every kind of gain. May it prove so!

What affects me especially in this matter is this: you have striven here for a new style (starting from what is suggested in the *Ariadne* Vorspiel and to some extent also of course from *Rosenkavalier*), and you have achieved what you wanted. That is very much. From your conversation fourteen months ago, as we walked up and down one evening at Ischl, I was able to gather very clearly what you had been trying to do, and today I know that it has been realized. This immediately gives me great confidence and hope for *Helena*, to which I am much attached. Although you will not be spared there the necessity of having to search once more for a new style (since one can never rest on one's laurels), certain features of what you have now done can in the future be relied upon as vested and indefeasible qualities. This is the real point of artistic development and in this sense one can speak of a master, indeed a master above all, learning and growing through what he has learnt. Among the features from which *Helena* will reap vast gain I count your wise and mature attitude towards the libretto which shows itself in the fact that every single word can be understood (this is stressed unanimously by all critics). This must be the result of your having learnt to achieve the desired effect with fewer means, a hall-mark of every masterly 'final' style.

This will, particularly in the case of *Helena*, be a powerful asset to the overall effect which emerges, after all, from the harmony of both arts—even if, in this union, the music be the dominant one. For I, too, have endeavoured to use words sparingly and effectively, and the few people to whom I have read the piece and who have given it encouragement and approval assure me that in this I have succeeded better than in any of the earlier librettos.

[1] Of *Intermezzo* (4th November 1924).

When I allow my thoughts to rove beyond *Helena* and try to absorb your wish that we might succeed once again in producing something like *Rosenkavalier* (but not a copy of it!), then *Intermezzo* (which I look forward to hearing at Dresden in December) provides the most exact cue for the line along which my imagination will have to travel, and is certain to give me definite stimulus and inspiration. The work I took in hand a few days ago will perhaps show you, on the other hand, better than anything else what I can do in my present state—fourteen years after *Rosenkavalier*—in the field towards which you wish to draw me. For last week I completed a tragedy in prose[1] on which I have been at work since 1920 and, in order to relax from the strain, I have picked out one of the most light-hearted and attractive of my subjects, a Viennese comedy[2] which I mean to put on the stage in the costume of the 1880's.

May I say this about the second act of *Helena*: Aethra's speech on page 23: 'Helena, ich lache' is there for one purpose only, namely to give you the words for a small trio. If you do not intend to use it for that purpose, it is *better* to leave out these nine lines of Aethra's, which are inserted in the dialogue between Helena and Altair.

I would prefer not to comment on the Vienna affair.[3] Since June 1923 I have foreseen this development and outcome as almost inevitable. It has always been connected with the fear that the future prospects of our works might thus be prejudiced in the very city where we both live. My only wish is that, among the various consequences which will flow from an eventual solution of this affair and in the status after the solution, it will be possible to avoid making such an unhappy result inevitable (what I have in mind is wholly hostile relations between the institution and yourself). This is a selfish wish, but we are so closely tied to each other that it is at the same time the one most plainly dictated by friendship towards you.

Yours ever,

HOFMANNSTHAL

P.S. Please tell your son with my regards that I will get your letters out in December and have them copied.[4]

[1] *Der Turm.*   [2] Later *Arabella.*
[3] Richard Strauss' resignation as Director of the Viennese State Opera.
[4] For the purpose of the first (and partial) publication of the Strauss-Hofmannsthal correspondence in 1925.

Dear Dr. Strauss,

Thank you very much for your kind letter of the 18th.[1] I can well understand what you say about the reasons for your resignation, and why you considered it appropriate just at this moment. I would only suggest that, since one can never foretell how things will develop (political events between 1918 and 1924 have shown that everything always turned out entirely, or at least to a large extent, differently from what one might have foretold), it would be desirable that your general relations with Vienna (including those with the authorities etc.) should remain *tolerable*. From my point of view, too, since I live here, it matters greatly, not in the financial sense but as a source of pleasure and satisfaction, that the operas should remain alive. That they cannot be thrown out of the repertory is quite plain, but between 'not throwing them out' and 'keeping them alive with love and care' there is a vast gulf. To me (who has a pretty shrewd idea of the way things go in this city) it seems more than doubtful that the situation will take in the near future a turn which would oblige Schalk to leave. Assuming, however, he remains for say another two years (I would almost be willing to bet on this), then of course it makes a huge difference whether your general relations with Vienna are those of lingering regret (on the part of the Vienna people), or whether antipathy has gained the day all round. Nor would I take it for altogether certain that Schalk's successor, sooner or later, will be a personality acceptable to you (and welcome to both of us). (. . .)

Finally, at the present precarious juncture of the German theatre, the importance of this city for the future prospects of our existing works (think of *Ariadne*) and for the first production of new ones cannot be underestimated, not least on account of the combination of factors like the orchestra, Roller's décor apparatus, and Kröller. I take a calm and detached view of things and do not expect or wish you to take any particular steps, but I do ask you in our common interest not to contribute to anything which might make the rift between Vienna and you unbridgeable. For the time being I would ask of you only one thing: certain quite fantastic figures about the salary which you have drawn are circulating among the Viennese public—deliberately launched by certain quarters. I have no doubt that they are false and that your pay was appropriate, indeed modest even. Do have this matter put straight

[1] Not extant.

by some paper which is well-disposed towards you, by quoting the true figures.

I hope that perhaps in February I may be able to comply with your and your wife's kind invitation for a visit. Of the plays, *Der Schwierige* will be posted to you at once (but have I not already sent you this piece, in 1922, with a dedication? I seem to remember!); then a little later the tragedy[1] as soon as a printed copy is to hand.

The other comedy[2] (acted by Pallenberg), being a slighter work which I may possibly revise once more, I have not committed to print for the time being. Since you are such a great and receptive friend of historical works, I would like to mention that I owe many valuable hours during the last few months to Ranke's *Weltgeschichte* and have learnt a great deal from it about the main currents of history (which in detail is often depressing).

I heard with pleasure from your son that the first act of *Helena* can be considered finished—in its first draft, I assume. I still continue to ponder frequently over details in this first act so as to bring about the necessary theatrical clarity. That the elves must become visible now and then was your most appropriate suggestion. In addition I have indicated to you certain passages of the elves where the words are essential to an understanding of the development of the action. The fact is that whenever I mentioned the elves I spoke of them always as a small chorus. I would nonetheless consider it extremely valuable if the various passages which I have repeatedly described as important in my letters could be sung by one elf (that means 'the first', 'the second', and perhaps 'the third' elf)—I picture the elves as male!—into the chamber through the open door.

I beg of you not to turn a deaf ear to these self-amendments of your librettist! What is at stake here is something decisive for the clarity and the dramatic effect of the whole work. There are great possibilities in the two acts of this romantic opera; this was confirmed to me on the few occasions when I read the text aloud to a few friends.

In order to clear the Sea-Shell entirely of all trace of obscurity, I have found the following device. The Sea-Shell (a trident star of immense size) lies on a stand in an alcove. Whenever the Sea-Shell is supposed to sing, a mermaid with green hair and bluish cheeks appears in the veiled and sparsely lit alcove behind, so that this vocal part comes

[1] *Der Turm.*
[2] *Der Unbestechliche.*

properly and clearly out of a human mouth. The shell after all has to provide the actual exposition.

Will look into my Wieland for Proteus. It is, however, quite possible that I have no gift for burlesque satire. Still, it would be wrong to make any such assumption from the outset.

Sincerely yours,

HOFMANNSTHAL

1925

Rodaun, 1.1.1925

Dear Dr. Strauss,

All best wishes for the New Year to you and yours. And good health, work, and happiness to you!

The letter I am about to write concerns the *Rosenkavalier* film project. I enclose Fürstner's letter to Fanto with our conditions and the rejoinder which Wiene, the director, has written on behalf of the film company to Fanto. This rejoinder contains in substance the ready acceptance of our conditions. As for the slight differences still outstanding, two gentlemen of the company will travel to Berlin as soon as we wish it, the sooner the better, and settle these points with Fürstner and Hofrat Rösch. (I do not doubt that this will be successful, because the company really means to go ahead.) Wiene is (next to Lubitsch) the only German film director who has acquired an international reputation and whose work is accepted in America.

It is my most seriously considered view that the prospects of the opera on the stage will not suffer in any way; on the contrary I would look upon the film, when it comes out, as a positive fillip and new impetus to the opera's success in the theatre. Why? Please have a look at my sketch for the film scenario or ask someone to read you a little of it. The whole thing is treated in the manner of a novel: it introduces the characters or, for those who know them, tells something new of these old acquaintances. Nowhere (not even in the final scene) are the events of the opera exactly repeated—*not in a single scene*. If the film appeals, it cannot but arouse great eagerness to see the now familiar characters in the *original* action on the stage, alive, speaking, singing. On this point Fürstner, I think, has mistaken ideas. He believes that the events to be transferred to the film screen will be identical with those in the opera—so as to compete with the latter; such a thing would, of course, be sheer madness. The same is true of the adaptation of the music. The opera contains a full three hours of music. It must therefore be easy (for an able musician of course) to extract from the material in the opera the themes he can weave into a musical arrangement which will accompany the film according to the sequence of the screen action. Naturally, all this must be done with good taste and skill; one cannot expect a miracle. And it can only whet the appetite for the opera. In this way, too, the project seems to imply value as advertisement rather than danger of competition.

Please let me have your decision in a few lines. If it is in the *affirmative*, then there is a certain amount of hurry about the affair. In that case the Berlin negotiations would have to be completed by the end of January. Wiene and I need three months for the preparations and by the end of April the actual production must begin; these people intend to invest what is for Europe a great deal of money, and they are sure they will get it back again with a substantial profit.

All good wishes from your

HOFMANNSTHAL

Garmisch, 29.1.25

My dear Friend,

My son tells me about the charming afternoon he spent with you: I too am hoping to see you again soon, perhaps in Munich on 7th May, for *Ruinen von Athen*? You understand now why I have turned my back on the Vienna State Opera: the annoyance with (. . .) Schalk was too much, the means for achieving anything worthwhile too little, and the offer of the Minister—who only wanted me as window-dressing and as a willing drudge for when he gets the post of 'Director General of the State Opera', said to have already been promised him when he resigns as Minister—unworthy of me.

Rid of this pointless burden, I am feeling extremely well, have just completed a piano concerto[1] and am gradually getting down to Act II of *Helena*. About the middle of February we're going to Spain, via Paris, and I'm hoping Granada will stimulate me for the Lord of the Desert.

[1] *Parergon zur Symphonia Domestica*, op. 73.

398

Fischer has sent me your *Collected Works*: many thanks for the lovely present in which your splendid shorter essays and prefaces interest me in particular.

The *Rosenkavalier* film all settled: very glad. The enclosed letter from Frankfurt will gratify you. *Frau ohne Schatten* still has a future—don't you worry. In Hamburg too it has again had a successful reception. Munich is now only waiting for a good cast: perhaps you might have a word with Franckenstein and get him to include this particularly suitable piece permanently in the repertoire of the festival.

In Salzburg I have joined the Honorary Board after being assured that you and Reinhardt are coming in on it again. Perhaps you could let me have some particulars about your and Reinhardt's intentions in Salzburg!

So much for now: I wish you good health and productive vigour and remain, with best regards from us to you all, always yours very sincerely,

RICHARD STRAUSS

Please write a few friendly lines, on your own behalf, to Krauss (Frankfurt) and Direktor Sachse (Hamburg)!

Rodaun near Vienna, 1.2.1925

Dear Dr. Strauss,

Your son and your daughter-in-law came to visit us here. She seems to be both intelligent and likeable, or rather: the feeling that one is face to face with an intelligent human being has a great share in the liking which one rapidly takes to her.

About the middle of February I shall leave for Paris, from there *via* Marseilles to Morocco. Before then I hope to go through the correspondence I have here and I will make the necessary cuts in my letters and by way of suggestion also in yours. I propose we collect for the time being the correspondence between 1908 and 1918; that will make a fairly stout and handy volume. The matter can be completed after my return and that will be the moment for negotiations with the publisher (Fischer or someone else). The obvious publication date for a book of this sort is about two months before Christmas. The division according to years, the running headlines, a few explanatory footnotes, all these things are self-evident. Naturally, in this case, there will not be anything in the nature of editorial work proper (the largely philological,

most laborious kind of thing), but if someone is to figure as *pro forma* 'editor', your son is of course the most acceptable to me.
(. . .)

My best regards to you as ever. Every good wish for the Spanish journey!

Yours,

HOFMANNSTHAL

Dear Dr. Strauss,

I assume that on your journey you are occupying yourself in your thoughts with the second act, and for this reason I want to say something which has troubled me for some time. It refers to the Helen-Aethra passage, halfway through the act, which you intended to have *spoken*, because you wished to steer clear of Wagnerian *Sprechgesang*. This (the 'steering-clear') I understand completely. The style such as I envisage it from your hints could obviously not stand this kind of *Sprechgesang*. But I am no less taken aback by the idea that this passage might actually be spoken by the two singers. Please do not cast to the winds the anxious warning of a layman and unassuming collaborator! I know you credit me, after all, with general artistic insight, with sensitivity in questions of style. Let these have their say. In the old-style opera, with its set numbers, we are used to the spoken word and can tolerate it, even if with slight reluctance. In that case however it must serve (according to the old tradition created by the Italians) to provide the dry bare bones of the action after the lyrical upsurge. It is most commonplace prose between the arias and the ensemble pieces. It is still treated in this way in *Fidelio*. The *Helena* scene is not of this kind. The mere fact that it is in verse makes it impossible to treat it as text to be spoken. (It was a grave fault of style in the German translation of *La Serva Padrona* at the Redoute to put the spoken passages into verse.) I plead here against the intention (such as I apprehend it) to have the words *spoken without accompaniment*. If, by any chance, it were to be your idea to have the passage *spoken* above the orchestra's continuous stream of sound and colour, this eventuality strikes me as more impossible still. Even the few words of the Empress in the last act,[1]

---

[1] Of *Die Frau ohne Schatten*.

spoken while the orchestra runs on, seem horrible to me and cut me through the ear right to the quick. Still—there, for that isolated and short passage, it may be excusable but not here, the less so since the words are to be clearly understood; for this is a turning point of the action!

What might be done here—forgive me for taking the liberty of hinting at something which pertains to the musical treatment—I believe I discovered recently when listening to *Falstaff*. Many dialogue passages in this opera are treated in a kind of recitative with the most transparent accompaniment imaginable, but still sung. One sentence, for instance, of one of the characters is musically phrased, but trips off the tongue without any accompaniment. The orchestra is entirely silent. The reply by his opposite number also begins without orchestra. Then there comes a brief splash of music from the orchestra and once more the sung conversation continues unaccompanied. I am having great trouble to explain something here which to you is of course as clear as a bell. But in this style (of which use is no doubt made in *Intermezzo* at several, perhaps at many points!) this awkward passage can surely be managed, and it is after all the only one which is awkward in this sense. Everything else in Act II is highly operatic.

I send you and your companions all the best wishes for the journey. In expressing my sincere regards to your son and your daughter-in-law I would like to mention the hope that before their departure from Garmisch they have carefully *locked away* the copies of my letters, so that not even by chance the eyes of an outsider may fall on them. So long as the letters have not been edited for publication, they remain highly confidential documents destined for your eyes alone; even an untoward chance might lead to a great deal of trouble!

Yours ever,

HOFMANNSTHAL

P.S. If the letters should not have been locked away, please ask your wife to lock them up!

Rodaun, 4.5.25

Dear Dr. Strauss,

What moved you to suggest publication of our correspondence was, if I understand it correctly, this: to make evident, on the one hand, the seriousness of our joint labours; to avail ourselves, on the other, of the

401

casual commentary provided by the letters to remedy the lack of understanding still shown for some of our works. And finally to kindle that response which, among Germans, often has to be provoked by means other than the direct ones.

It is true that, having looked into our mutual letters, I consider it possible in the overall result to achieve something of this kind. Yet I must say that certain of your letters make me highly apprehensive lest the manner in which these questions are treated on occasion might produce the very opposite effect, and harden this type of coolness and animosity, supplying it for ever with weapons from, so to speak, our own arsenal. I would like to draw your attention especially to the following discrepancy: In your letter of Dec. 13, 1913, you complain bitterly that the very originality of so distinctive and beautiful a work of art as *Ariadne* has been received with so little understanding. But now please have a look at your two letters of May 27 and July 19, 1911, both referring to *Ariadne* after the MS. had just reached you. You were not feeling quite yourself at that time, a passing physical depression, you had given up cigarette smoking, etc., in short *Ariadne* did not please you. You could not do anything with it at first, artistically; this you expressed in a charmingly sincere, entirely outspoken manner. You wrote in your letter of May 27, 'For the plot as such holds no interest— personally, I am not particularly interested by the whole thing'.

This criticism, whose point of departure is wholly unbridled realism —only from a *Cavalleria Rusticana* angle, which must be poles apart from the composer of *Salome* and *Elektra*, can the 'plot' of *Ariadne* appear uninteresting—this criticism, I say, might be quite amusing and striking as a piece of biography if it referred to an abortive libretto of mine which you had refused to compose. But the opposite was what happened. The very elements which you at first altogether refused to understand, even to consider in any way significant, subsequently impressed their force of formal design, the unusual style of the whole *Ariadne* upon your creative powers, and thus came about what is certainly, next to *Salome*, your most beautiful and distinctive work.

Since the Germans, however, confront every work of art unreceptively (an immutable truth this, proven a thousand times over in Goethe's case), and since they tend to dismiss it with the wholly misconceived epithet 'formal' to which they oppose a sentimental and spurious, and at the same time nebulous notion of 'soulful', a work of this kind is anyhow in a peculiarly awkward position (less so among foreigners, if I may remind you of the Amsterdam success of *Ariadne*). As soon as the German Philistines light, as *ipsissima verba magistri*, upon the following amusing sentence: 'Flourishes à la Rückert must do the trick where the action leaves me cold', you yourself, the creator of this incomparable opera, become the veritable spokesman of this chorus of the Philistines. What a madhouse! Alas I cannot even propose that we leave out the letters of May 27 and July 19 altogether. For it was just these two letters that touched off my replies which, if anything, may really have some elucidating and persuasive value. I am wondering therefore what could be done (you will come across a similar letter dealing in a similarly negative manner with *Die Frau ohne Schatten*). Well, I believe there is no harm in leaving out the letter of May 27; but that of July 19 is also most dangerous and a terrible weapon in the hands of Philistine criticism. What you say there in a mood of passing weariness about 'interpretation' in the action itself, of the 'symbolism that must leap out alive' and so on, of 'the explicitness needed by any theatrical work' (what the hell, since it was a theatrical work of a special kind, and today, after all, everybody understands it!)—to perpetuate all this in cold print, to stereotype your truly unjust, momentary criticism—forgive me, my polemics are directed against the old letter of July 1911—that seems to me undeniably rather absurd. I have therefore taken the liberty of suggesting by red pencil considerable cuts in this letter. And now I must urge you to see to it that work on this publication will not be rushed.

I view the whole enterprise with mixed feelings and I would regard the achievement of the above-mentioned purpose as the only positive thing about it. To me your letters, with their great spontaneity and impulsiveness, are a most dear, highly personal possession, but once they are brought body and soul before the alien frigid multitude, everything takes on a wholly different hue and one looks upon it oneself with other eyes. I must, above all, still ask you for the following: you use repeatedly the metaphor that I ought to spur, or urge on, my Pegasus etc. Taken out of the context of this intimate, quite unrestrained exchange of letters and printed, I would not care very much for this description of my method of 'poetizing'. Will you please therefore put your blue pencil through the various sentences appealing to Pegasus, or ask your son to do so.

Perhaps you will reconsider once more with your closest advisers, having the whole of our correspondence before you, whether on sober

403

scrutiny you feel that this publication promises to be a happy or a dubious venture. To everything we have done together I look back with pleasure, and I have therefore no hesitation in relying on your decision in this affair too.

Please forgive me for dictating this letter for once. The typist is my wife, who sends her best wishes.

Yours ever,

HOFMANNSTHAL

Garmisch, 1.6.1925

My dear Friend,

Back refreshed from taking the waters at Nauheim, I found your letters here: naturally, everything must come out of the letters that could serve as ammunition for stupidity and malice or provide fuel for fresh misunderstandings. Anyway, with whom could one seriously discuss the nature of artistic creation? At the most with Goethe, Schiller, Richard Wagner, and possibly with Nietzsche (whose *Birth of Tragedy* I am just re-reading with tremendous relish!). Hardly with Eckermann or Schopenhauer! And as for the rest of the mob which, even given goodwill, barely scratches the outermost epidermis of a work of art, let alone can see in the mystic darkness of the artist's workshop . . . I shall be in Vienna for a few days from 16th June, staying with the Grab's, Ring des 12. November 14, and hope to see you there or at Rodaun.

Until then with best regards, yours ever

RICHARD STRAUSS

With *Helena* I've been stuck for a long time at the entrance of Altair and can't make any progress. I want to give the whole thing the pure, sublimated style of Goethe's *Iphigenie*, and it is therefore particularly difficult to find, for this entrance of the sons of the desert, the kind of music that still sounds sufficiently characteristic to the ears of 1925 without degenerating into the so-called realism of *Salome* or even the eccentricities of today's modernists who hear only with (I don't want to insult the negroes) American ears.

Well, I suppose I'll get over this obstacle too!

Kindest regards from my family!

Dear Dr. Strauss,

I have just returned to your son the last bundle of letters. It is a moving experience to read them through like this. So many years—such devoted endeavour, ceaseless endeavour for the sake of detail, for minutiae often. May some of it live!

Your present struggles with *Helena* I understand very well, only too well. For each time it is the unity of style which is at stake. I hope, nonetheless, that our conversation at Rodaun has made you feel a little less tied down. Let the arrival of Altair be no more than the arrival of some strange prince, discard from it everything which seems to demand colour, and if the thunderous approach, the hasty coming of the horsemen, the rush of warriors and slaves reminds you of fantasia, discard that also. Let the whole approach be solemn like a march, as homogeneity of treatment requires it. (Twice in the course of our years you have come to such a deadlock before the entrance of a new character, until you almost abandoned the work: the first time before the arrival of Clytemnestra, the other time over Bacchus—strange that you should have forgotten this). As for the end, the action is handled in such a way that it could be set to music even in the style of Handel or Gluck. The feast which Altair prepares is the night of love with the beautiful woman—you must picture that wholly in the world of the Trojans, not in a 'modern' Islamic Orient. And if, by any chance, you should be troubled by the eunuch motif, though it is a theme as old as time and pertaining to the primordial, I would be ready to change it. Only let us have none of the cheap 'Orient' of present-day music. I have not introduced a single geographic conception which does not belong to ancient Greece! Atlas, Egypt, Lybia, they are all mentioned in Pindar and Aeschylus. The very fact that you wish to avoid such high colouring proves to me that this work can and will achieve something transcendental.

About the first act: I have a habit, when I read a play aloud to others, as I do now and then, of leaving out this or that passage from the opening scenes and I invariably find that this pays:

On page 2 the song of the Sea-Shell could be taken out and after the Serving Maid's: 'Es scheint, dass sie sich zu einer Antwort herbeilässt' we might have Aethra say immediately: 'Antworte mir ohne Um-schweife—wo ist Poseidon?'

On page 5 at the bottom the passage: 'Was wir sahen, was wir sehnten—unversehens uns ins Haus' might easily be left out.

From the great scene Helen–Menelaus, page 8, I would ask you, *if at all possible*, to cut Helen's exclamation: 'Menelaus!' The silent gesture is more effective here.

On pp. 8/9 one passage is very favourable. It is after Helen's: 'Trink hier, wo meine Lippen sich getränkt' straight on to page 9. Menelaus (stepping back): 'Ein Becher war . . .' (a great gain, this!).

Page 12. Helen: 'und ich verstehe auch den Umweg' etc., here, I remember, you have already done some pruning. That is necessary, for the passage is too long.

Page 29. Aethra's report which bothers you. It can, in any case, be cut by five lines, thus: 'Am Hang des Atlas steht eine Burg—mein Vater sass dort, ein gewaltiger König—zu uns ins Haus brachten sie schwebend deine Frau . . .' etc.

And then the elves. I consider it indispensable that you single out a 'first elf', which steals right up to the threshold of the chamber and from whose mouth we learn, *distinctly*, the few really vital things which affect the course of the action. Please do not make light of this proposal!

Page 32/3. Menelaus-Aethra. Cut on page 32:
Menelaus: 'Ich werde sie sehen'.
Aethra: 'Du wirst sie sehen, mit diesen Augen—'
Further cut (below).
Aethra: 'Was ficht dich an'
Menelaus: 'Was werde ich sehen
           Unseliger Mann   } Cut
           bereite dich'
and again:
Page 33 at the top, cut down to Menelaus: 'ich höre Becken . . .'
Page 34, Aethra's report, in a whisper only, I consider very happy.

On re-reading the whole, I cannot help finding it very beautiful and very operatic.

All good wishes in unchanging friendship, your

HOFMANNSTHAL

Garmisch, 22.7.1925

My dear Friend,

Many thanks for your so encouraging letter of 30th June. The first sketch of Act I has now been left untouched long enough for me to summon the necessary ruthlessness to make the various cuts you have proposed, and the need for which I have myself felt for some time.[1] You are meeting me half-way and your suggestions shall fall on fertile soil. Best regards in haste, yours ever,

RICHARD STRAUSS

Rodaun, 4.8.25

from Aug. 8 (until end of August) Salzburg, Hotel Österreichischer Hof

Dear Dr. Strauss

The Pantomimengesellschaft has made inquiries from me about turning the Till Eulenspiegel-Suite into a ballet. I have declared myself interested on principle, for I am very fond of this imaginative piece of music. Perhaps I can find an idea, a canvas on which the maître de ballet or the producer can continue to elaborate the detail. But please let me have a few lines through your son or your daughter-in-law telling me, just as they come into your head, the Eulenspiegel motifs (and their sequence) which you had in mind when writing the music. Perhaps there even exists a programme; if so please send it to me.

Since I am to look through the correspondence once more, please send it to Salzburg. I shall add the running headlines.

Many good wishes. In friendship your

HOFMANNSTHAL

(. . .)

Bad Aussee, 15.9.25

Dear Dr. Strauss,

As I read the galley proofs of the correspondence between 1907 and 1918, I see all these years going past, so much which the two of us have shared; it is amusing and makes one at the same time nostalgic. The kind words with which the editor refers to me in the Preface show me your own warm feelings towards me which have never changed throughout these many years, and that pleases me.

For the year 1909 rather too many letters were included which referred to details of *Rosenkavalier* and were pretty dry. My own interest cooled off here and this led me to realize that the reader, as

---

[1] Strauss carried out only some of the proposed cuts.

outsider, would be left quite cold; I have therefore marked several letters (most of them mine) which are to be left out. You can rely in this on my judgment; the volume can hold the interest and so enlighten the reader only if it never becomes dull.

Salzburg was a great success this year, above all socially. The public that came was thoroughly cosmopolitan, as it may have been at Bayreuth twenty or twenty-five years ago. Vienna was least well represented. It has always been one of my favourite ideas to arrange a performance of *Ariadne* at Salzburg before such a public, for *Ariadne* fits in like nothing else. I beg of you let *me*, without interference, work in my own way towards the realization of this plan which is most precious to me. Of course Mme Ivogün must be in the cast and everything of the very best, and there I can, for once, get up the decor as it should be, with a scene painter of my choice. In Vienna only some of it is good.

But who is to conduct the opera, so as to make it a pleasure for you, too? Walter would certainly like it, but you may not want him? Clemens Krauss perhaps? Given time to prepare the ground and to reconcile the various interests, which must be done with a light touch and with patience, I can get everything as I want it at Salzburg. What has already been achieved pleases me.

Yours ever,

HOFMANNSTHAL

7.10.1925

My dear Friend,

We have now given the Preface to the 'Correspondence' the enclosed amplified form, which I considered necessary to spare my son the imputation, on the part of ill-wishers, that he knows and recognizes only Wagner and Hofmannsthal. If this now has your *placet*, will you please inform the publisher that this Preface can now be printed. I am in Vienna from 16th to 20th October and hope to see you, provided you are back from Aussee by then.

With best regards, yours as ever,

RICHARD STRAUSS

408

My dear Friend,

Even the unpretentious preface struck me as very engaging; this new one, however, is perhaps better still.

Therefore: imprimatur.

I shall be here until the middle of November, working.

Many good wishes to you and your son.

And shall I get a little word about *Helena*?

For pity's sake! Loyally yours,

HOFMANNSTHAL

Bad Aussee, 17.11.25

Dear Dr. Strauss,

It made me very sad to get the obit card telling me of poor Rösch's premature death. I have thought of you warmly, for I believe you have lost in him your only close friend of many years standing.

What strange reading these proofs of our correspondence do make from my point of view. Ceaselessly they arrive, ever since the beginning of September, and have not quite come to an end yet; it will make a stout volume. They give a lot of trouble, for the MS. was by no means ready for the printer, the date order needed a lot of changing and some of it gave me quite a headache. Yet with what inexplicable feelings one reads such a thing oneself. (It is the first experience of this kind in my life; usually, of course, one puts it off until after one's death.) It is neither nostalgia, nor yearning for the past (for clearly it is not that one wants to re-live anything), not sadness, but not pleasure either: a wholly inexpressible feeling. How all this is strung together on the thread of time past: our first meeting, *Elektra*, *Rosenkavalier*, then *Ariadne*, *Die Frau ohne Schatten*, *Joseph*, the second *Ariadne*. It will be a strange sensation for you to take up the finished volume and see it all spread out before you. But I am quite unable to imagine what sort of an impression it can make on the public. Sometimes I fancy it must leave people entirely cold, must bore them even. At other times I think the opposite: that the rhythm of this unceasing effort and mutual stimulation cannot leave them cold. Well, we shall see how they take it.

Sincerely yours,

HOFMANNSTHAL

Dear Dr. Strauss,

I return to Vienna next Saturday or Sunday and hope to bring the completed second act. You are quite right with your remark that the first scene of Act II had a reflective element. This could not stand and I have not only carried out a thorough revision of this scene, but have expunged from the whole act all scenes which suffer from a similar trend. You speak of an action which must unfold without let-up, 'like *Elektra*'. Of course I take this 'like *Elektra*' only very figuratively. For the action of *Elektra* leads darkly and massively up to terrible murder, and how could that be reconciled with this ethereal, fairytale-like first act which barely touches upon the dark side and takes its origin from an almost comic intrigue? If *Elektra* might be compared to a taut chain of heavy, massive iron links, *Helena* is a festoon of interlaced lyrical wreaths. Yet in one sense the comparison holds good: in the second act of *Helena* the garland of flowers must be as taut as the iron chain in the other work. This is what I have endeavoured to achieve and stylistically it has had the result that not a single prose scene remains in Act II; the prose scenes, by interrupting the flow of the music, had a retarding effect.

How, in a proper comedy à la *Rosenkavalier*, as opposed to this lyrical-heroic subject, a mingling of prose and lyrical scenes might be possible *right up to the end*—that is a question which one would have to consider carefully, once one has the subject.

If it is still true that *Ariadne* is to be put on in Rome, please create an opportunity for me to make my influence felt, by letter, over the question of the mise-en-scène. How particularly important that is in the case of this opera Reinhardt endorsed when he told me that *Ariadne*, in the new Berlin version (where the decor was left to careless, indifferent hands), had made hardly any impression on him at all, whereas he has now heard the Vienna performance three times with delight.

Sincerely yours,

HOFMANNSTHAL

Vienna III, Jacquingasse 10 (about 10th Dec. 1925)

My dear Friend,

Arrived here at last and hope to see you soon! Today only the news that your beloved *Ariadne*, in a truly excellent performance, has scored an absolutely overwhelming success in Turin[1] and has, I think, in consequence conquered Italy for good. Right after the first act—which is always a little chancy in Italy—there was tumultuous shouting for me, during the opera itself there was applause after the first masked quintet and after Zerbinetta's aria, and there was universal enthusiasm. Training the operatic singers to be actors had given Dr. Erhardt a great deal of trouble, but in the end the Italians' native gift for play-acting triumphantly overcame all difficulties, and I believe that *Ariadne* has inaugurated a new theatrical era in Italy. A pity you weren't there!

In Berlin *Ariadne* is commanding full houses in Charlottenburg with Ivogün: three performances in one week, including a very good one at the State Opera. I think this will please you! I hope I shall soon be able to give you further details in person: do please let me know when you are coming to town!

With best regards from us to you all, yours most sincerely,

RICHARD STRAUSS

Rodaun, 19.12.1925

Dictated to my wife.

My dear Friend,

I must admit that your refusal to conduct the film in Dresden came quite unexpected and is a grave blow to me. I say: in Dresden, not in London, for as I shall explain lower down, I do not take the same view as far as London is concerned, and about the London premiere I shall venture to make a compromise proposal. But for now about Dresden only. After giving the matter careful thought myself, after thorough discussion with Dr. Wiene and after a prolonged telephone conversation with a member of the Gutmann staff, I can only say that I regret exceedingly your negative decision about Dresden. I cling to the hope that it may perhaps be tempered with 'blessed revocability', but if it were irrevocable, I foresee for you (and consequently also for me) (. . .) the loss of very considerable financial expectations. (. . .)

Sincerely yours,

HOFMANNSTHAL

[1] The first performance in Turin was on 1st December 1925.

1926

My dear Friend,

With cordial feelings towards you, I recently spent a quiet evening pondering some of those projects which we wish and hope to accomplish, a link between us more sensitive still than the things we have already done. Not long ago you wished to lead me once more to the world of Peregrinus Proteus and the like. Yet I feel, and I feel rather strongly, that I ought to gather together my roaming thoughts and productive day-dreams in a different field, yet one related to the *Rosenkavalier* subject: I mean in the bourgeois sphere, in the field of bourgeois comedy, in the costume of a fairly recent decade—in a plot, to describe it quite recklessly, of the Scribe kind: love, friendship, jealousy, intrigue—in a group built up of living, tangible figures to whom something happens as in *Rosenkavalier*—only of course different.

After that I took up my working copy of *Helena*, and went through the second act with due seriousness and severity, conscious of the librettist's responsibility. I cannot help saying that I found it beautiful and progressing irresistibly, as it ought to do, towards a solemn-conciliatory conclusion. The finale seems to open plainly on page 26, as the dead Da-ud is being carried on to the stage and Menelaus reappears.

I shall now look into some details.

Page 7, Helen's line: 'Wer gab so schönen Befehl?' might be left out —it interrupts Altair's address.

Page 8 at the bottom. The three lines:

'Eilig zusammengeraffte Gaben'—to 'deiner fruchtbaren Lippen' —had better be omitted, they are unimportant.

Page 16 suggested cut: Menelaus: 'Solche Blicke'—down to 'ob er die Gleiche wiederfindet' had better be cut. Helen's excitement links up these passages very well.

> Mit sehendem Aug
> erkenne mich wieder!
> Menelas! steh!—er ist dahin!
> und kehrt er zurück—etc.

Better if she accompanies his silent action, the choice of weapons and his exit, with her longing impatience; his sung interjections are psychologically too complicated.

412

Pages 17, 19. I cannot possibly conceive the vital Helen-Aethra scene (the turning point of the action) in speech alone, as you once had it in mind, for that would produce a hiatus. *Sprechgesang*, with most simple, most transparent accompaniment (so that every single word can be understood as if spoken, in the way the great composers have always employed it at certain points from Handel down to Verdi's *Falstaff*) strikes me as the proper form, with such slight digressions into actual song as are necessary to characterize these two well-contrasted women. (Aethra, I imagine, comes close to a coloratura soubrette, am I right?— while Helen at this point has a sombre, restrained note.)

Since even the slightest cut is of value here, I make the following proposals. Cut the line (page 18)

Versteh mich doch, Du Liebliche!

Also (page 18)

Helen: 'Dies ist'—
Aethra: 'Oh nicht den Duft davon
        solang ich Dir es wehren kann!'

Again (page 19)

Aethra: 'Gerettet, Liebste hat er Dich—
        und küsste Dich für unberührt.'

These cuts in a recitative scene are pure gain.

Page 23. Here the passages of Helen-Aethra ('Hüte Dich' and ... 'Helena, ich lache') have only the purpose of serving for a trio. If you do not mean to have one at this point, both passages would have to be left out and Altair goes straight on.

Page 35. Here everything urges forward to the conclusion. To be left out first of all: Menelaus: 'Warum zittert der da?' down to 'Lass mich der Toten und lebe'.

I wonder whether one should not perhaps also leave out, after page 35: Menelaus: 'Nicht netze die Lippen, mir ist er bestimmt' (which would have to remain) down to page 36, Helen: 'Bei jenem Trank...'[1] That would mean leaving out Menelaus's anxiety that, if Helena be a phantom, all the Greeks have died for a hallucination (although this is an important, profound idea), as well as the motif of the host of un-manned warriors which enters into it. Here it is a question of

---

[1] Of all the cuts suggested in this letter Strauss carried out only the last. The publication of *Die ägyptische Helena* in book form (Leipzig, 1928) contains the lines which were cut in the opera.

weighing the value of one solution against the other; only the composer can decide this. What I am afraid of is an over-excited kind of passage like the one the Empress has in the third act of *Die Frau ohne Schatten*, which is hardly song at all any longer; I am afraid of it if the overcharged expression makes it necessary to go beyond the limits of music.

With best regards yours

HOFMANNSTHAL

Rodaun, 10.2.1926

Dear Dr. Strauss,

This cut you suggest in Act II, the jump from page 8 at the bottom to page 12: 'Paris ist da! Paris aufs neu!' is bold and quite excellent. If you live in this way with the libretto and handle it on occasion with such freedom, real unity will come about. What is dramatically essential can be retrieved in a few lines.

> Menelaus: Paris ist da!
> Paris aufs neu!
> Altair (pointing at Menelaus, with equivocal affability):
> Dir zu Ehren stell ich ein Jagen jetzt an,
> Der Jagd zum Begleiter geb ich Da-ud,
> von meinen Söhnen den jüngsten!
> Menelaus: Frech und verwegen
> reckt er die Arme
> nach meiner Frau etc.

I consider this cut a great gain.

This morning I heard the following entirely trustworthy report: the authorities will not sign the contract with Wallerstein, because Turnau has submitted his application to the Council of Ministers, and to the new Minister of Finance an *exposé* in which he promises, if appointed, a saving of 17,000 million Austrian Schillings. It looks more than likely that they will take Turnau. This eventuality looks to me undesirable both for the Opera and for us, because it puts off the only satisfactory solution, Krauss-Wallerstein, and may even—given the close association of these two—make it impossible. Trust me and my conviction that in ability Turnau is nowhere within hailing distance of Wallerstein, and that we must back the better, not the lesser man, out of prudence and egoism. I would be very glad if you were to bring your influence to bear (through Ramek?) in favour of the combination Krauss-Wallerstein, before it is too late. Turnau's economy plan can only be stupidity or eye-wash. And a man with Turnau's physiognomy (trust my eyes!) is quite capable of striking a bargain even with Weingartner!

Turnau is backed by Achsel and Ramek. One would have to point out that he made a mess of things at Breslau, whereas Krauss showed distinct dictatorial capacity at F(rankfurt). This, in any case, is not the way to solve, but rather to confuse, the conductor issue.

The small but attractive picture gallery of the Akademie (Schiller-platz, second floor) is always open from 9 to 1 p.m. except Tuesdays.

Please take to heart my largely instinctive distaste for a T(urnau) regime under the aegis of Mme Achsel.

Yours,

HOFMANNSTHAL

Dear Dr. Strauss, *Rodaun, Monday, 15.3.1926*

I understand that you are back in Vienna and will therefore first of all rid myself of the enclosed manuscript. The author, Alfred Brust, Cranz in East Prussia (one of the most highly thought of among the younger German dramatists), asks me to transmit to you this play intended for music. Please let him have your decision, whatever it is, direct.

You mentioned that you would give me the pleasure of showing me the first act of *Helena*. That would be an immense pleasure for me. Would you feel like it sometime in the near future?

I could be with you on Wednesday at a quarter to five or on Thursday at half past four, or any day after Monday, possibly even this Friday (not quite so easy), or on Saturday, Sunday!

If you are in the mood, please let me know by telephone the day you would prefer.

Yours in friendship,

HOFMANNSTHAL

My dear Friend, *Vienna, 19.3.26*

Strangely enough I didn't receive your letter of the 15th until yesterday: forgive me, please, for not reacting to it before. I am going to Prague on Sunday, shall be back on Tuesday, and shall then be at your disposal any day you please. Just give me a ring: 98398.

In Berlin I conducted a magnificent *Rosenkavalier* and a totally sold-out *Frau ohne Schatten*. *Ariadne*, in a very pretty new production, had to be cancelled and is now being saved for Leo Blech. Also to be done in Stockholm next year.

(. . .)

Let me know then when you can come: I shall try as far as possible to be in good voice.

With kindest regards, yours in sincere friendship,

RICHARD STRAUSS

Chledowski: *Siena*, page 69:

Cleanliness was altogether on a low level in the cities. The story is told that the famous Italian troubadour Sordello had an affair with Cunizza, the daughter of Eccelines II, the tyrant of Verona; this lady bore the not exactly flattering epithet *magna meretrix*. In order to reach her chambers unseen he had to pass through an alley that was stiff with filth and refuse. So that he should not soil himself he was awaited at the appointed hour by a page of the beautiful lady, who would carry him across on his back. Eccelines, by the way, got wind of these meetings, disguised himself as his daughter's page, waited for Sordello and carried him across the alley. When he thereupon revealed himself the troubadour was petrified with fear, but for once the father tempered justice with mercy and merely forbade the minstrel to pursue such dirty business by such dirty paths. 'Abstineas accedere ad opus tam sordidum per locum tam sordidum!'

Surely an amusing incident for a comedy!

Rodaun, 27.3.26

Dear Dr. Strauss,

I am more delighted with this *Helena* music than, I believe, about any of your other compositions ever, and I feel I am right in this, even though I altogether lack the words to express myself properly. Yet, however inadequate my ear, I must have some sense for what matters in music, and this sense was most profoundly stirred by what I heard yesterday. (Certain people who possess a great deal of musical knowledge like, say, Korngold, must, on the other hand, lack this sense completely, for otherwise he would not misjudge these things so dismally on first hearing; for me it is just the first hearing that counts.) The after-glow of this music is wholly enchanting; everything so light and transparent, for all its high, noble seriousness. I am pleased beyond measure (. . .)

All good wishes to you.

In friendship yours,

HOFMANNSTHAL

Rodaun, 2nd May, 1926

My dear Frau Strauss,

May I beg you to remind your husband to send me (as soon as possible!) the names of one or two people (at least that *one* name in Vienna, but perhaps there is still somebody else somewhere!), to whom one can appeal for support for the decor of the Salzburg *Ariadne*. If I don't make good my promise to raise the means for the décor through friends, the whole thing (the Salzburg *Ariadne*) will probably fall through at the last moment, and that would be a great pity.

Yours obediently,

HOFMANNSTHAL

Garmisch, 4.5.26

My dear Friend,

I apologize—since Fürstner is still ill and not yet fit to negotiate—for having so far only acknowledged but not answered your kind letter containing the obliging offer. Today I can accompany my thanks for your understanding helpfulness by the news that the full score of Act I of *Helena* was finished on Labour Day and that I am off to Greece tomorrow to get a few beautiful tunes for Act II—even though my biographer, Herr Specht, considers it old-fashioned that nowadays I have *only* the ambition to 'make beautiful music'. Yes indeed: 'Der Esel ist ein dummes Tier, der Elefant kann nichts dafür!' My children tell me how beautiful *Cristinas Heimreise* was and that they spent some delightful hours at Rodaun.

I wish you a very good and productive summer and am, with kindest regards from us to you all, yours as ever,

RICHARD STRAUSS

Dear Dr. Strauss,

Thank you very much for your greetings from the Acropolis. There have been glowing accounts of your journey, and so I hope you are in good spirits.

With my idea of putting *Ariadne* on the Salzburg Festival repertory I have given myself quite a lot of anxiety and personal trouble. I do not regret it, however, for it was done for love of the work. Audiences in Western Europe have no chance of getting to know this opera; that is why I was so anxious to show it there for once. It is bound to help in the long run. The first difficulty I had to cope with was a question of principle. I myself had insisted that on principle works of living composers should not be included; there was bound to be constant pressure and demand for Pfitzner performances, not arising from enthusiasm for his work as an artist, but as a political demonstration for the 'national' composer. First of all therefore I had to establish *Ariadne* as an exception. The financial difficulties were greater still. *Ariadne* with a most carefully picked cast, with a conductor specially invited for the occasion (K) and the best available producer (W)[1], is *expensive*, so expensive that even fully booked a deficit for each night of ten to fifteen million Austrian Schillings must be reckoned with. We shall be able to cover this loss out of the surplus from *Jedermann*, for in any case the stage performances there must carry the opera, if we are to break even. If once we fail to do this, i.e. if the Festival ends with a deficit even once, we shall immediately lose control; political and business racketeers are only waiting for the chance to snatch this enterprise out of our hands.

In these circumstances it was quite inconceivable to burden the Festival budget with the absolutely essential decor, estimated at some 80–90 million Austrian Schillings; how could this sum be amortized if more, or repeated performances would but serve to increase the deficit? I saw only one way, and that was my promise to raise the sum through private donations—and in this I have actually *succeeded*, but only after a great deal of trouble.

Most sincerely yours,

HOFMANNSTHAL

---

[1] K=Clemens Krauss; W=Lothar Wallerstein.

My dear Friend,

Many thanks for your letter of the 9th; have just finished a triumphal Strauss week in Leipzig, with excellent performances of *Ariadne,* *Elektra, Rosenkavalier,* exemplarily rehearsed and, in part, magnificently conducted by Brecher.

My son is going to report to you about the Zsolnay business! Thank God Schneider is finished at last; he was a great pest. (. . .)

I highly approve of Schneiderhan's engagement—an excellent, very decent person: for the moment we shall just have to see he doesn't take any final decisions until he's heard me out in detail about the requirements of the Vienna Opera.

A re-engagement of (. . .) Weingartner, even as a guest conductor, would be a bad thing. I, at any rate, have no intention of expanding the Schalk-Weingartner duet into a trio. See what you can do behind the scenes, please, to prevent any further follies. The aim is still: Clemens Krauss as Director with two Chief Producers: Wallerstein and Turnau. I'm taking the waters here till 5th July and shall then be in Garmisch. Hope you have a good and productive summer. Best regards, yours

RICHARD STRAUSS

Dear Dr. Strauss,

I am really exceedingly pleased that now, while you are at work on the second act, this joyful creative mood has come over you as powerfully as you yourself have told me and as others report. This is indeed one of the greatest joys I have had for years.

Recently Dr. Eger passed through here to whom you had shown the manuscript of *Helena.* His comments to me were full of what was agreeable to hear and intelligent. I am glad he finds it so clear. He said that (in this libretto) I had fully achieved what was aimed at in *Die Frau ohne Schatten* (that is to give symbolic expression, in the characters and situations, to a secret of life). Let us hope he is right. About the curtain he said something which struck me as so convincing that it has not been out of my mind since. He said that at the end he had longed for Poseidon to appear and to embrace Aethra. And this for three reasons: (1) because the end, as it stands, possesses a certain stern grandeur and ignores entirely the gaily romantic aspect of the first act: (2) because Aethra ends up too empty-handed, indeed is left quite high and dry; (3) because the whole action has produced a kind of latent erotic tension which ought to be released sometime, otherwise the spectator will be left tense and dissatisfied. *All this is true.*

I am wondering whether it might not be possible to add such a moment of divine rejoicing between Aethra and Poseidon after Helen and Menelaus have galloped off. What I have in mind is not more than a minute and a half, that means a tiny final episode, analogous that would be—but in an altogether different style—to the reappearance of the little negro boy when he picks up the handkerchief in *Rosenkavalier*. Into a duet it must not, of course, develop (that would be to repeat Ariadne-Bacchus once more), nor can we possibly have a new tenor or baritone coming on to the stage; but a *young beautiful silent* Poseidon, a scream of Aethra's and a sinking on to the bed—enraptured and divine, divine and exalted beyond pain, beyond all the suffering of human kind.

I shall think it out carefully and will send you the draft within a few days. But I must completely saturate my imagination with it, each step and each gesture, exactly, so that it is just right.

Sincerely yours,

HOFMANNSTHAL

Dear Dr. Strauss,

Bad Aussee, 9.9.26

Here is the draft for the tiny addition which would certainly be a considerable gain for the end of Act II—a sensuous, lovely consummation after so much that is highly serious, a release after so much tension, in order to come back to the fairy-tale which envelops this high seriousness like a veil and thus to re-establish connection with the first act. Yet such is my respect for what your imagination may have devised for this curtain that I only dare to submit this little appendix in all humility.

Whether it will be possible to fit in such a sensuously lyrical addition depends presumably on the inherent fecundity of certain musical themes from earlier passages in both acts, which would have to be picked up again here; I am thinking of all the themes which refer to the sea, to waves, to playing fountains, to the rising waters and so on. For I do *not* imagine for a minute Poseidon stepping out of the sea on to the stage; this device is exploited once and for all with the stately entrance of Bacchus in *Ariadne*; no: he would have to stand there suddenly, as if raised by the surging waves of the sea. Perhaps your magic art will once again find a wonderful, brief water-music. This short scene follows immediately upon that between Helen and Menelaus. As soon as they mount their horses, the curtain of their tent, not the main curtain, falls. The audience can still hear the two riding off with their escort in blue armour, but this should not be, I feel that most strongly, a trotting like Wagner's, but rather like a gust of wind!—these are magic horses which move noiselessly. Then comes the rest, as enclosed.

Yours in friendship,

HOFMANNSTHAL

Helena II (conclusion)

Aethra's female attendants have drawn the tent curtain. Aethra steps out of the dark into the centre of the tent. Aethra (listless) (not too heavy, not too tragic, but in tone and gravity similar to the beginning of Act I)

> Ach—und ich?
> vergessen wieder!
> wieder allein!
> Armselige Zauberin!
> allen helfen
> Deine Künste—
> ausser Dir selber!
> Arme Aithra!

(she throws herself onto a couch, left, and buries her face in her arms). Waves surge up to the stage. A bluish light breaks through. Noiselessly a gap is opened in the centre of the curtain: Poseidon stands there in his cloak, holding the silver trident, raven hair, wholly beautiful. (A dancer.) The attendants move silently towards him from both sides. He drops the trident into the hands of the first attendant. He slips off the cloak from his shoulders and the second attendant catches it as it slides to the ground. The young god looks at Aethra who lies there tossing listlessly. The blue light fills the room, as if the scene had changed to the bottom of the sea. Poseidon takes three leaps towards Aethra and bends over her. Aethra flings herself round, stretches out her arms towards him, embraces him; her lips utter an ardent: 'Ah!' not a fierce cry, but like a dove, almost as if it were laughter. She draws him down, close to her.

Curtain

My dear Friend,

Just back from the Engadine I find—with thanks—your two interesting letters. The idea about Poseidon is decidedly very poetical—but for that reason not very happy theatrically, because it puts the main accent at the end of the play on a secondary character, because it makes scenic demands which do not as a rule come off, and above all because it would greatly weaken my intended grand final musical climax (at least for the general public, which is still rather necessary) and would therefore dangerously jeopardize the theatrical effect. The black boy at the end of that baroque comedy *Rosenkavalier* was after all a different thing, even though Verdi would certainly not have represented him musically either. Also, as you rightly feel, the similarity with Bacchus's entrance raises misgivings.

On the other hand I would gratefully welcome a personal appearance of the *Deus ex machina* to round off the antique drama and as a neat stylistic element—but certainly before the final duet of Helen and Menelaus, not after.

Wouldn't it be possible to have Poseidon appear with the Men in Armour, standing on a cliff above them, to have Aethra (who has now discharged her mission with respect to Helen) throw herself into his embrace, and to have them all, including the Men in Armour, swallowed up by the sea so that in the end only Helen, Menelaus with the child, and some servants with the horses are left behind; or else, instead of the spirits from the sea, have a ship appear in the background, which would take the reunited couple back to Sparta, and towards which, having concluded their final duet, they make their exit?

This final duet could (probably) contain twelve lines instead of its present four, in case the necessity arises of developing this concluding duet a little and leading it to a fine climax: please think it over!
(. . .)

In Holland the Vorspiel to *Ariadne* (and also in Paris) had a stronger theatrical effect than ever in Germany.

I shall be in Berlin during the second half of October, when I hope to get together with Fürstner to put the finishing touches on the contract: when I saw him in St. Moritz he seemed almost fully recovered. *Helena* is making progress!

With best regards, yours as ever,

RICHARD STRAUSS

Yes, that is so; the end must not be jeopardized and one should never attempt to imitate something unrepeatable like the last moments of *Rosenkavalier*. (And even those Verdi would not have expressed musically *in this way*, I do see that!) In that case, however, it is much better to leave it as it stands. What you propose, this *Deus ex machina* with surging waves and a ship, all that belongs to the apparatus of the fairy play for which our imagination today (as spectators above all) is no longer unsophisticated enough.

One more point: this *advancing* towards something by singers who, while they step backwards, must after all at the same time look forwards (towards the conductor) and sing forwards, this represents to me of all the fatuous final curtains in opera, the most fatuous. I know that Wagner has used it several times (in the *Ring*), but in this, great though his stagecraft was, I would decidedly not wish to follow him. If anything of that sort, I would still rather see them lined up and singing into the audience. Actually some of Verdi's final curtains are even scenically wonderful, that of *Aida* for instance. In *Ariadne* I tried to avoid this advancing backwards and kept the black ship off the stage, so that the couple are enveloped by the canopy where they stand (and this I still consider the most beautiful solution for the specific problem in *Ariadne*). For *Helena* the turning round of the horses is certainly the happiest conclusion; with a very definite instinct I cherish the hope that this *unisono* of the two will be relatively short, not endless like the Wagnerian finales. Afterwards, if the music should require it, the tent curtain can fall first to hide the inelegant moment of the actual mounting, and the main curtain could come down only afterwards—or the latter can come down at once, according to whether the music breaks off abruptly, or draws more slowly to a close. The final curtain must at the same time offer a beautiful scenic tableau and this will certainly be presented by the magnificently harnessed steeds standing in a magical play of spotlight such as a producer like Wallerstein can devise: the golden-haired child Hermione in the saddle, the escort in their shining blue armour around them. This will offer the eye and the ear so much that the fate of the *seconda donna* can well be left obscure. The knowledge that this work is making progress fills me with a glow of anticipation.

I, too, am having a very productive time.

Most sincerely yours,

HOFMANNSTHAL

Dear Dr. Strauss,

(. . .) I am wondering whether it would not be valuable for me to write to you, in good time, a letter about *Helena* similar to the one I wrote long ago about *Ariadne*, and to initiate a few people (of your and my choice) into the libretto, asking them to write about it?—let's say six months before the thing is staged (not immediately before). What do you think of this?

Most sincerely yours,

HOFMANNSTHAL

Rodaun, 12.12.1926

Dear Dr. Strauss,

Today I dipped into the volume of Verdi's letters. How many reminders of our own joint labours, I mean to say how many analogies. By chance I lighted first upon the passage where he says he has been looking for twenty years for the libretto of a buffo opera, and now, when he believes he has found it at last, everyone reminds him that Rossini had said forty years earlier that Verdi would never be able to produce a comic opera! How much the world remains the same everywhere and at all times! We had better luck, after all, with our buffo opera. (Better, too, in the end than Verdi with *Falstaff* which never achieved real popularity.) But I shall write you another light-hearted and gay libretto—I am sure of it.

I am more than curious to hear *Intermezzo*. Wallerstein, who is a really intelligent man, spoke to me with great discernment of the unique style of the work, and how this would have to be brought out, not through parody, but expressly through realism; it struck me as thoroughly convincing. That *Rosenkavalier* is to be done in Paris pleases me a lot. If only they don't botch it; I am told that, above all, they have not got a reasonable conductor. Well, *Rosenkavalier* has its own guardian angel, I feel.

I am glad to hear that affairs in Vienna are straightened out and, by and large, to your satisfaction, although I do not think you care very much about these things, or indeed about almost anything (apart from your productive work).

I have completed the stage version of *Der Turm*. The premiere will be in Berlin[1] next autumn, and probably in six or seven other cities the same night. In October I started another piece of work, again a serious one, but shall break it off for the time being and would like to do something very light in the meantime, a modern comedy, a kind of farce.[2]

Should you ever feel that you would like to see me, you must know that it will be a pleasure to me. I am in town for a day or two each week. (. . .)

Always most sincerely yours,

HOFMANNSTHAL

1927

Rodaun, 17.1.27

Dear Dr. Strauss,

It was with rather peculiar feelings that I was present at the premiere of a Strauss opera[3] in the position of 'librettist, without special duties *pro tem*' (but not 'retired'!). The warmth of the success and everything this warm reception was meant to convey (to you generally) gave me real pleasure. About the work itself I cannot yet say anything upon this first hearing, because the whole thing, style, approach and all, interested and preoccupied me too keenly—I lack as yet the right perspective. If I were asked I would not have the faintest idea where to place it among your other works. I was startled, too, by the high seriousness of the approach; I had imagined the whole thing far more like a comedy and the importance of the symphonic interludes not so weighty. Since I am not as clever as the critics, I must allow something so novel to reveal itself to me gradually and only after deliberation. As comedy, the penultimate scene, where the wife is alone with the servant girl, seemed to me particularly successful; as a serious scene the last one is perhaps especially fine; the style of the whole work I shall understand better once I have heard it a few more times. My predominant feeling

[1] The première of *Der Turm* took place not in Berlin, but at the Prinzregententheater, Munich, on 4th February 1928.

[2] *Lucidor*, at that time planned as a kind of Vaudeville.

[3] *Intermezzo*. The first Vienna performance took place on 15th January 1927.

was part nostalgia, part pleasure over all we have done together: a whole procession of years surging back with the music!

Very sincerely yours,

HOFMANNSTHAL

Dear Herr von Hofmannsthal,   *(Vienna) 22.1.27*

Many thanks for your last two kind letters. I can well imagine that *Intermezzo* surprised you on the stage. Harmless and insignificant as the incidents which prompted this piece may be, they nevertheless result, when all is said and done, in the most difficult psychological conflicts that can disturb the human heart.

And this is brought out only by the music. That you, as my old librettist, should have perceived this more keenly than many others who watch only superficially (not the audience, who always sense what is right and grasp what is true) has given me particular pleasure. I presume that the smoothly-flowing, the naturally-flowing dialogue has not escaped the poet Hofmannsthal either. I am sorry you couldn't come to us on Thursday and earnestly hope you will soon get better.

Yours very sincerely,

RICHARD STRAUSS

My dear Frau Strauss,   *Friday morning (?March or April 1927)*[1]

After an experience like last night's I feel the urge to tell you, who share Dr. Strauss's life so closely and so intimately, how warmly I participate in this great pleasure.

A beautiful, joyous and festive evening like this, achieved by the harmonious concurrence of all the factors, in a work conceived in so unique a style, is a gift of good fortune rare even in the life of so famous and recognized a creative artist. There are about this City a number of things which irritate us, but this we must rate most highly that, after sixty performances or so, the audience possessed the spontaneous impulse to burst out into such an unparalleled expression of joy and gratitude at the moment when Dr. Strauss stood alone on the stage.

For weeks it has been my and my wife's desire to visit you one afternoon—not without previous warning. The innocent cause of the

---

[1] The year and date of this letter are uncertain.

continual postponement am I, since I have been suffering for weeks from constant neuralgia, and at this particular moment we are having once again workmen in the house at Rodaun for urgent repairs, and my wife must keep an eye on them.

So it will have to be in the first few days of May; in the meantime I beg you kindly to accept the expression of constant and unalterable devotion and respect from your obedient HOFMANNSTHAL

Rodaun, 26.4.1927

Dear Doctor Strauss,

Fanto inquires whether I would be available for a discussion about *Helena* around May 1st. Of course I am; I would only ask for warning one or two days before, as I would like to spend a day in the Wachau, if possible.

Since I make a point of never inquiring of you, indeed not even asking myself how far a work on which you are engaged may have progressed towards completion, I was very much moved to gather from these signs that the time is now in sight when this opera will be put on the stage. I, too, would of course consider Dresden very attractive—if only because a world première in Vienna involves for me as librettist a very definite vexation: Korngold. (. . .) He has worked out for himself a regular system: to discredit each new work first of all by an attack directed against the libretto, while ostensibly paying homage to the composer. He knows perfectly well that so far as the stage and the theatre public are concerned, the damage is as good as done once the text has been written off as boring, obscure, unattractive or something like that. I should like to discuss with you shortly a question closely connected with this, so as to submit certain proposals to your judgment which is usually no less sound in matters of 'theatre policy' than in questions of stagecraft.

Most sincerely yours,

HOFMANNSTHAL

Rodaun, 6.5.1927

Dear Dr. Strauss,

I have now held my fire for forty-eight hours, have considered the matter in and out, and have slept on it again so as to avoid at all cost inflicting upon you a premature, perhaps unfounded objection, but the whole thing weighs on me more and more, and this morning it has even woken me out of my sleep—therefore I owe it to you and to our joint labours to express quite unequivocally my feelings which are utterly at odds with your idea of having Da-ud sung by a woman. And this although (in contrast to many other people) I am by no means fundamentally opposed to such a reversal of sexes in an artificial, figurative world like that of the theatre. I have, after all, in *Rosenkavalier*, created one of the greatest parts of this kind myself, but here in this work it strikes me as the worst mistake conceivable, indeed actually as dangerous to the whole effect. Why? Because the juxtaposition of the sexes is built into this whole action as a latent tension. Helen, the woman *par excellence*, is set against the men, against manhood as a whole. Is it not this that makes the situation of Menelaus so tragic that he wants to separate himself from this collectivity, from this promiscuity, as an individual, as the husband, as Helen's husband! This is the famous comic situation which has led me across the narrow line into tragedy! As soon as Helen makes her appearance anywhere, though her name be unknown, the male element in the world immediately gather for new conflicts, for another Trojan war. This is symbolized here in father and son who are both at once enamoured with this matchless woman. And now we are to have the son, this embodiment of all that is male and youthful, sung by a contralto! A woman to address this woman in this, this most ardent language of adolescence—no, here I am faced with the impossible! Fanto too was struck dumb by this idea. Please think it over!

Most sincerely yours,

HOFMANNSTHAL

P.S. Fanto says that you have a very young tenor: Fazzini. We have Patacky here. Elsewhere, too, we shall surely manage and anything would be better than this thoroughly confusing, alarming device.

Dear Dr. Strauss, *Rodaun, 16.5.1927*

I wrote to you, soon after our talk, of my grave misgivings if Da-ud were to be cast as a woman. Now I am beginning to suspect that this letter either did not reach you or that—contrary to all my intentions—it might have annoyed you. On the other hand I do not recall a single instance throughout these almost twenty years of our collaboration when artistic objections or suggestions of mine were received by you in any but a friendly, genial manner—even where I was wrong.

I have turned the thing over in my mind again and again, and always with the same result: the function of this figure within the context of the whole libretto is so pre-eminently a male one that a contralto voice here strikes me as downright impossible. Octavian is possible (or at least covered by Cherubino); Adriano was also, at a stretch, possible (perhaps more so around 1845 than today); Da-ud is impossible.

You did not tell me the other day that you were going to leave so soon, but now I hear that the whole family has already left, I presume for Nauheim. I hope you are well, and your wife recovering quickly and completely. The account of that recent, diabolic hoax[1] and of all that this poor woman had to go through has shocked me profoundly and every thought of it brings me close to her in my sympathy.

I hope to hear from you soon. Yours,

HOFMANNSTHAL

Dear Herr von Hofmannsthal, *Bad Nauheim, 22.5.27*

Of course you are right, but just think of the tenors at small opera houses! I know them.

I have now written Da-ud as a tenor, but am at the same time setting out an arrangement to indicate how the part can be sung, at a pinch, by a mezzo-soprano, e.g. Mlle Anday. With best regards, yours very sincerely,

RICHARD STRAUSS

Heard an excellent *Ariadne* in Frankfurt on Friday and am going there again tomorrow for *Elektra*. Krauss and Wallerstein splendid!

My dear Friend, *Garmisch, 16.6.27*

The other day I heard *Meistersinger* again—a tremendous work. Ever since I've been unable to shake off the urge to write a work of this type some day—unfortunately, needless to say, at a respectful distance. But nevertheless some really German piece, a play that is good theatre and at the same time a genuine document of German civilization. The best

[1] On 30th March the Strauss family had been thrown into anxiety by an anonymous telephone message according to which Richard Strauss had suffered a stroke at Dresden.

subject to serve as a background for this seems to me to lie in the age-old conflict between Romance art and German art—which would have to be personified, by analogy with the types of Walter, Sachs, Beckmesser, by three representatives of music and poetry, reflecting as it were three kinds of artists, say something like:

(1) the Italianized German bohemian,
(2) the artist who draws on both nationalities, the supreme representative of which is Mozart and the last modest one my humble self,
(3) the so-called Boche type (. . .)

This last one would have to be reduced *ad absurdum* in the end, à la Beckmesser, or else would have to be the disgraced and condemned villain of the piece.

Ideas for his villainy might be found perhaps in the telephone call inflicted on us the other day (when I was reported dead) or the following amusing incident that happened on board a ship which was carrying two Italian opera companies to the Argentine. Both of them were rehearsing the same Puccini opera (one lot in the fore of the ship and the others aft) and the question was which of them would get the opera fully rehearsed first. So one party bribed the ship's cook to mix poison into the food of the other prima donnas and tenors, and stole their piano scores and threw them overboard, until their impresario was left with one score which he put under his pillow and then nervously locked himself into his cabin. But this is only by the way! Two periods would be suitable as a setting for the above subject:

(a) the Minnesingers

(1) the utterly Italianized Ulrich von Liechtenstein on whom Gerhart Hauptmann is at present working, with an entertaining legend which starts in Venice and ends at a castle near Bozen. The South Tyrol would altogether be the obvious setting for this today.
(2) Walther von der Vogelweide (Mozart, H. Sachs).
(3) a German pedant.

Or (b) a milieu such as Mannheim about 1780, at the court of Karl Theodor of Bavaria, where the young Mozart gave a concert in 1777[1] and where German and Italian opera clashed for the first time.

[1] In the original: 1772.

430

Or else the court of August the Strong, whose mistress was the famous singer Faustina, the wife of the German composer Hasse who wrote Italian operas. I know that you will accept these suggestions in the right spirit. I have now ordered the following books from the State Library for private study:

Die Minnesänger, by Hagen.
Das deutsche Leben im Volkslied, by Rochus von Liliencron.
Fr. Walter: Geschichte des Theaters in Mannheim.
Mannheimer Geschichtsblätter
Geschichte der Dresdner Oper, by Fürstenau.
Die Faustina, by Urbani de Gheltof.

Perhaps you could browse a little in them too some time: it would be delightful if you could think of some entertaining story on the general subject mentioned—either 13th or 18th century.

Would you let your mind dwell on all this? Or maybe something else that's even better will occur to you: but it's got to be a 'Meistersinger No. III' (there can be no 'Second Meistersinger'—freely adapted from H. von Bülow who called me Richard III). I am in Bad Gastein (Hotel Astoria) from 15th July till the beginning of August; perhaps we could arrange a meeting there or in Salzburg and discuss this matter which is very close to my heart!

Helena will be ready in the autumn!

How are you?

With kindest regards, always very sincerely yours,

RICHARD STRAUSS

No reason why it shouldn't be a long five-hour opera with choruses and ballet! I have now time and leisure and feel there is still just about enough strength in me for a major opus such as this!

Dear Herr von Hofmannsthal,   *30.6.1927*

Now after *Helena* I should like to write a little one-act opera—either gay or sad—a kind of curtain-raiser for *Feuersnot*.

Haven't you got some attractive idea in stock for this sort of thing? The other day I read Turgenev's fine novel *Smoke*. Stripped of all accessory matter this story contains an operatic text. The conflict between Litvinov and the two women is exceedingly poetic and thoroughly dramatic—please read the piece again and tell me if you

431

think you can develop from it a short opera, of two acts at the most, some six or seven scenes, in telegram style.

I append a synopsis of scenes.

Act I:

Scene 1. Litvinov alone, explains his position in a few words, he meets Irina again for the first time (in her own surroundings, which would have to be put vigorously across the audience).

Scene 2. Again L. and I. Progress of their mutual relationship in the knowledge of Tatiana's impending arrival.

Scene 3. L. in doubt and torn by passion in his room. I.'s visit and their union. Curtain.

Act II:

Scene 1. Litv. and Tat. after her arrival.

Scene 2. Ir. and Lit. after she has received his critical letter.

Scene 3. Farewell from Tatiana.

Scene 4. Separation from Irina.

Scene 5. L.'s departure and I.'s collapse at the station. End.

Isn't this a good scenario?

Naturally, my opera could not be set in Russia: you can't set Russians to music any longer nowadays. Perhaps in Karlsbad at the time of the Emperor Ferdinand (with a little Court background), or in Kissingen under Ludwig I. of Bavaria. I find the conflict between the three people very moving and very interesting: it would attract me very much, except that the man would have to be stripped of his excessive bourgeois character.

Could he be made an ambassador or something like that?

From 15th July till 4th August I shall be in Bad Gastein (Hotel Astoria).

I have recommended Knappertsbusch to do *Bürger als Edelmann* with Waldau at the Residenztheater in Munich! Perhaps you could do a little prodding with Franckenstein, Waldau and the Munich drama director.

Josephslegende is to have its first Italian performance at the Scala in Milan on 28th March; I myself shall conduct!

With kindest regards, yours as ever

RICHARD STRAUSS

Dear Dr. Strauss,

The germ of an idea, a fable, any real joining together of a number of meaningful and significant characters into one piece which is suitable for a composer, that is a god-send, a great boon. I do not believe that this sort of thing can be spirited up by prodding and prompting, by reference to given human constellations, to certain epochs, or to a given type of subject; such an attempt would, I fear, be more likely to frighten it away. The great charm and conviction of *Meistersinger* (taken purely as a work of literature), the pre-eminence which lifts this work even above all the others which this unique man created, the key-stone of all this is not so very difficult to discern. There are of course a number of components, even an autobiographical one, which play their part, but the truly decisive element, which governs all the others, is Nuremberg. This city, which was still quite unspoilt in the eighteen-thirties offered not merely a mirror, but actually an example of the whole intellectual and spiritual life of the German middle class around 1500, this city world was one of the great decisive experiences of the romantics, from Tieck and Wackenroder's *Herzensergiessungen eines kunstliebenden Klosterbruders* (with the figure of Dürer in the back-ground) through Arnim and E. Th. A. Hoffmann down to Richard Wagner, the man who rounded off the romantic age. Wagner himself, after all, tells in his autobiography in unforgettable detail how much it was Nuremberg, to what great extent it was his discovery and per-ception of German life and manners in this city world which gave him the germ for *Meistersinger*. Even the night-time street brawl and the watchman who marks the transition to a tranquil mood have their place in this truly poetic personal experience. This is what gives the opera its indestructible truth: that it brings to life again a genuine, complete world which did exist—not like *Lohengrin* and *Tannhäuser* or even the *Ring* (*Tristan* is a different matter altogether) imaginary or excogitated worlds which have never existed anywhere. This is the so-to-speak Homeric element in *Meistersinger* which makes the opera akin to *Hermann und Dorothea* and *cum grano salis* even to *Faust* Part I and certainly to *Götz von Berlichingen*, this is what makes it so firm and solid and un-ageing. Nor is it difficult to trace the source of other components of this beautiful work. The intellectual situation of Hans Sachs, and at the same time the national, representative character of this figure Wagner owes to Goethe's wonderful interpretation of

433

Sachs in *Hans Sachsens poetische Sendung*. Read it; it is an inexhaustible treasure-mine. There, too, you will find the prototype of the two allegorical female figures in the prize song: the Muse as the humanistic aspect, and facing her the simple domesticity and sensuous element of the soul, embodied in a woman. You will discover, finally, that the fine intermingling of the world of the knight with the world of the burgher, the idea of bringing the young knight among the master craftsmen, is taken from E. Th. A. Hoffmann's beautiful story *Meister Martin der Küfer und seine Gesellen*. The remainder are autobiographical motifs: the ageing artist between desire and resignation; while the national pathos is the gift of a moment of great national enthusiasm (of the tangible growth of German unity). Even a picturesque detail like the Beckmesser-Hanslick equation is only possible, after all, because the institution of the 'marker' was already inherent in the given old setting. Something of this kind one cannot hope to imitate—at most one can look upon it, from the distance, as a model. The only reasonably successful opera where *Meistersinger* has been so used as a distant model is *Rosenkavalier*.

Just as in the former opera the Nuremberg of 1500 is the true vehicle of the whole thing, and that which gives life to the characters, in the latter it is the Vienna of Maria Theresa—a complete and real, and therefore convincing city world composed of a hundred living inter-relations, from Faninal to Ochs, from police constable and innkeeper to the great lady, from the palace through the backstairs world of the footmen to the peasant in the farmyard, etc., etc.

Ulrich von Liechtenstein is a figure which has always been repulsive to me; so far from attracting my imagination, he makes it bolt. I have no key to the medieval world in its decline. Maybe Hauptmann has and can find something useful for you in his head.

The 18th century with its princes and musicians, on the other hand, also strikes me as somewhat hackneyed and unattractive. My phantasy might find the atmosphere of a much less remote period a comedy atmosphere, more to its taste, say the eighteen-forties or fifties. But the germ of an idea, it all hinges on that!

I shall try to write a letter about *Helena* addressed to you, similar to the one I wrote at the time about *Ariadne*, a letter to *guide* people a little.

Sincerely yours,

HOFMANNSTHAL

434

Dear Dr. Strauss,

Do please send me the novel.[1] I cannot get hold of it. Many years ago it made a deep impression on me; the characters are still very much alive in my memory, and so is the atmosphere and the element of sombre, typically Russian despair in the character of Litvinov; only the actual plot escapes me. But how do you imagine it possible to transpose the figures in this particular constellation, these famous figures from one of the most famous of novels, all of them Russian to the marrow, all of them belonging so entirely to the sixties, so unforgettably typical of this *Russian* Baden-Baden of the sixties—how do you imagine it possible to transpose all this into another period, into a different setting? Litvinov between the two women is, after all, as well known as Raskolnikov. And everything in the conflict, as in the characters, is so sublimely Russian?! As it is, this slight action is completely dependent for its special quality, for its interest, for its mere existence on the characters in the novel.

If, therefore, one cannot or does not wish to set Russians to music, I do not think it would be any good taking one of the most famous of Russian 19th century novels as a subject. But I shall give it more thought, perhaps I may be able to guess or feel *what* it was that attracted you so much. I believe I can understand it. The simplicity and the strong lyrical element in the situations. *Vederemo.*

Yours,

HOFMANNSTHAL

Dear Herr von Hofmannsthal,

I didn't know Turgenev's beautiful novel was *all that* famous. You may be right: stripped of its Russian setting the subject would lose much of its charm, even though Litvinov is not quite so typically Russian as some Dostoyevsky characters and might crop up in any other country in the world.

I trust you do not mind if, from time to time, I try to knock at the door of your imagination and give you a rough idea of my wishes. Above all I should like to do a small lyrical one-act piece: a few sentimental scenes, but not so ripe-plum-soft as Schnitzler. How about a

[1] Turgenev's *Smoke.*

435

happily married artist: composer or poet, who suffers a passing weakness for a singer or actress after she has given an outstanding interpretation of his work: I am thinking of d'Albert, or Schillings, who immediately got married to the leading ladies of their new operas—or the Gerhart Hauptmann-Orska story—but the conflict to be solved in *my* way!

As I've said before, what I'd like best of all, time and again, would be to put myself to music—but unfortunately I can't put myself into poetry. I think therefore that you have not quite correctly understood my first suggestion. Your beautiful letter about *Meistersinger* gave me indeed much pleasure, but it failed to touch upon the very thing that I wanted to express in that work—no matter whether in the age of the Minnesingers or the baroque period of Karl Theodor of Mannheim—it was the autobiographical element that would have attracted me in particular: I myself ('the cosmopolitan'), between Puccini and Pfitzner, add three original female characters who tangle the threads of envy and jealousy even more, the whole thing in an attractive historical setting—I hope we shall discuss this yet in greater detail!

Wouldn't *Achill auf Skyros*[1] make a nice one-act play with ballet and women's choruses? There exists a Cherubini ballet on the subject.

I shall be in Bad Gastein (Hotel Astoria) from 15th July till 4th August and hope to have some news from you there, or else to meet you there or in Salzburg!

With best regards, yours

RICHARD STRAUSS

Rodaun, 16.7.1927

Dear Dr. Strauss,

I did not, as you assume, 'fail to understand' what it was (in your earlier letter to which I replied with my remarks about *Meistersinger*) you had at heart, this directly autobiographical element you want; I merely felt it more polite not to say that the fortuitous circumstances of an artist's life and a juxtaposition with his contemporaries offers me nothing to stimulate my imagination or appeal to me as a 'subject'. Instead I chose to suggest this indirectly by pointing out to you *what* it is that makes *Meistersinger* so captivating as a text for an

[1] At that time Hofmannsthal had already (anonymously) written a ballet scenario *Achilles auf Skyros*, which had been set to music by Egon Wellesz in 1925.

opera, and how little this has to do with the autobiographical theme which is quite unobtrusively woven into it. For certain poets a subject may emerge from autobiographical material (and this is due to the fact that intimate themes for this sort of thing lie hidden in us all), but of course never without highly artistic transmutation; *Tasso* is a case in point. Somebody else's biography can yield a subject only by virtue of an unusually remarkable train of striking events; the intimate associations which *his* (that is the 'other' person's) imagination alone connects with his life story are never enough. To speak quite crudely and plainly, the suggested juxtaposition (Strauss-Pfitzner-Puccini) offers me *nothing* as a subject, absolutely nothing—indeed it holds (even opposed to *Intermezzo*) a counter-indication as medical men say of certain treatment; namely that it would drag me into the odious field of the artists' drama. It is hard enough as it is to establish convincing characters which are real human beings; the dramatic work in which the characters must, on top of this, convince as artists is an odious form, and one which can come off tolerably only in the case of a self-portrait—like *Torquato Tasso*, which I have just mentioned, or Pfitzner's *Palestrina*. I personally can think of no subject which would appeal to me less than this.

'The whole thing in an attractive historical setting' you write; quite so, indeed, if only to establish this setting were not exactly the crux of the whole thing, and exceedingly difficult—*vide* my last letter. In the tragedy *Der Turm*, of which I have now completed the stage version, I have once again attempted to create such a setting, to imagine such a setting, a historical, supra-historical one—these are matters of immense difficulty and your mind has (necessarily) no perception whatever of the essence of *these* difficulties—you *cannot* understand them, it is quite out of the question. What was for Puccini's librettists (distinctly skilful and highly estimable as they were) the simple 'adoption' of a 'historical' milieu, *Tosca* or *Bohème*, this borrowing of such a setting from a novel or a piece by Sardou, by no means difficult (and at the same time quite permissible, perfectly legitimate), for me who is by nature obliged (by my nature, I say, not by some sort of pride) to produce something which is complete and rounded off—for me these are highly complicated, difficult tasks which can succeed only in very special circumstances.

To repeat therefore: such biographical themes contain nothing that could appeal to me, nothing that could set my imagination to work.

This strikes me as 'material' for your biographer, for the historian of music, but not for me. However pleased I am to see you, and to discuss with you anything, anywhere—this topic would be *barren*. Persuasion does not serve to stimulate my imagination; it makes it stubborn as a mule, and vicious.

The suggested one-act piece 'an artist who falls in love with an actress', that is everything—and nothing. I might as well rap out a rhythm on the table top with my knuckles and say: There you are, the theme for a symphony. True, even in the creaking of a cart wheel there may be a major theme, but only for the artist who already carries it within him.

More propitious is your idea of directing me to the Turgenev novel, with the suggestive words 'in telegram style'. One would have to find a way of *saying*, not of *concealing*, that it was this novel which prompted us. The trouble with the whole subject is that it bears so obviously the Russian stamp (that Russian, typically Turgenev urbanity) and that impress of the sixties! The costume of this period, it is true, would appeal to me greatly. Perhaps this suggestion does contain the germ of something one might be able to do after all!

Achill auf Skyros is also a pretty idea which occupied me years ago (with Nijinsky in mind). But I wonder whether there is any great pleasure to be had out of ballets? Do you find there is?

Sincerely yours,

HOFMANNSTHAL

Rodaun, 17.7.27

Dear Dr. Strauss,

You wrote to me last profoundly impressed by Turgenev's *Smoke*. This interests me very much. I can see exactly what you have in mind: an opera with very few characters, in telegram style—the figures linked together by a love story of a very simple kind. That is the best thing, though of course only for an opera. But remember: since you had just finished the novel, the characters were very much alive to you, like personal acquaintances. The problem is how to give them some sort of physiognomy on the stage, with a minimum of words? German audiences will not stomach figures almost devoid of distinctive features, as mere vehicles of a lyrical-sentimental mood. That is the difficulty.

438

Perhaps it can be solved by our remaining very close to the novel—this in any case would be essential and means not changing the scene. For the manner of treatment I would not be at a loss. But I have not got the book here and there is no one from whom I can borrow it. For this reason I asked you eight or ten days ago to send me the volume at once. Nothing has happened, however.

The day after tomorrow I shall go for some time to the South Tyrol, Mendel, Campiglio, and on 2nd August I shall be at the Österreichischer Hof, Salzburg. Would you see to it that I find the book there?

Sincerely yours,

HOFMANNSTHAL

Dear Herr von Hofmannsthal, 20.9.27

I read that you are working on a *Wiener Volkstheater*. Wouldn't that make an operatic text too some day, or a Singspiel with music (and a Punch and Judy show), or even a spoken popular play with musical interludes and ballet à la Molière?

I shall have finished the score of *Helena* in a week.[1] After much hesitation, rejecting, rewriting, altering and all the pleasant birth-pangs the conclusion has now turned out very beautiful, brilliant yet simple—in fact, I would now like the first performance to be given in Dresden on 23rd June instead of 1st October 28.[2] Dr. Reucker has wanted for some time to organize an annual Dresden Festival from late June to early July, to be supported to a very great extent by my works and to be based principally on the cosmopolitan public which seems to be in the habit of forgathering in Dresden just before the start of the summer holidays. For the inauguration of such a Festival he needs a particularly striking piece such as *Helena*, and confidently expects that between 23rd June and 4th July it will have passed through six, and by the beginning of October through twelve to fifteen, fully sold-out performances at increased prices even before the other theatres get down to the piece after the holidays and before Berlin launches the second première, say in October. It means that Dresden would advertise this Festival in honour of the fiftieth anniversary of its opera house throughout the world for a whole six months; the State of Saxony has already approved *unlimited* means for the decorative side of the production, which would

---

[1] The full score of *Die ägyptische Helena* was finished on 8th October 1927.

[2] The first performance of *Die ägyptische Helena* took place in Dresden on 6th June 1928.

be the case only on a much more limited scale for a run-of-the-mill repertory performance in October—in short, all these advantages so much outweigh the various misgivings which, in view of past theatrical usage, might arise (with Fürstner too) over such a summer première that I am determined to accept Reucker's proposition provided you have no objections yourself. Will you please send me a short telegram on this point.

The Strauss Week in Frankfurt, concluding with *Frau ohne Schatten* on 28th August, was a great success. Six full houses!

But now I have no work: completely cleaned out! So please: write some poetry. It may even be a 'second *Rosenkavalier*' if you can't think of anything better.

If the worst comes to the worst, a little stop-gap job—a one-act piece—to keep my hand in—oil to prevent the imagination from rusting up.

With kindest regards, always very sincerely yours,

RICHARD STRAUSS

Bad Aussee, 29th September, 1927

Your letter arrived unfortunately via Rodaun with delay

Dear Dr. Strauss,

I have written not a single letter for several weeks. I must do this occasionally in order to recuperate. For all that I am not forgetting your situation, your difficulty which is that, to produce your work, you depend on a libretto—how could I possibly forget? We have now been working together for twenty years—that must mean something in one's life.

But, my dear friend, it is also true that I have gradually become an older and more difficult person. Without an original idea I can do nothing, and such an idea is a god-send. Actually of course, I have ideas enough and at this very moment I am beset by the 'simultaneity' of a tragic subject and another for a comedy—but what is to be suitable for music must be something quite special. Three, no already four years ago when the long-hatched idea of representing Helen's return from Troy took on shape as a plot which, I felt, might yield an opera, it gave me wholly selfless, unmixed pleasure to think of you. Now this is another work finished and all the effort lies behind us.

440

The present moment, while I am in the grip of a productive mood almost too imperious for my nerves, is favourable and may perhaps yield some idea which will just tip the scales. You wrote once: 'in telegram style'—given a good subject this is a suggestive phrase. But I cannot just *dash something off* for you; the day when I could do this would be accursed, and your work would not prosper.

That of course is a good comedy plot: the 'interim-husband' who is wedded to a beautiful woman in name only but proceeds to insist on his rights. I believe such a substitute who lends himself to a nominal marriage is called a 'hullah' in Arabic, and under this title somebody once made a German play of it. But there was also some twenty or twenty-five years ago an immensely successful French farce with a Parisian setting and an aristocratic nincompoop as the nominal husband, with a title which I cannot recollect—and the subject has also been used several times in operettas.

My anxious concern for you is such that in the summer I tried to talk Beer-Hofmann most seriously into unearthing from his store of material and scenarios something that might be suitable for music; but he maintained he had nothing. That there should not be in the whole of Germany a single person in whose pen one could have sufficient confidence!

The following will amuse you: a Munich personality has pursued me for the past two years saying that I must make an opera for Pfitzner, that I am the only one, *exactly* what he wants and so on, and has tried for all he is worth to bring about a meeting at Salzburg. I replied politely, but very firmly that I cannot spare the time for a meeting and that, if I did have an idea for an opera, I would write it for you. But please do *not* repeat this.

My dear friend: the premiere in Dresden at the end of June, as the centre piece of a festival, this strikes me as an altogether excellent scheme; the date, the occasion, all this is excellent and I am delighted with it— (. . .). But, my dear Dr. Strauss, I am a little anxious, especially about the decor. Of this you shall hear more one of these days. Today only this (. . .). I understand (from apparently reliable sources) that Mme Jeritza, who is after all the person *born* for the part, will this year be back by the end of March, and pines for a *new* part. It would be madness, would it not, if we did not try our utmost to get her?

Yours,

HOFMANNSTHAL

441

Dear Dr. Strauss,

I am profoundly concerned. Yesterday I thought about it the whole evening and now I see what (I hope) may be a possibility, if you will have a little patience.

Two years ago I occupied myself with a comedy, made notes and drafted a scenario, and then I put this work aside again. It was called: *The Cabby as Count (Der Fiaker als Graf).* (Please keep the title to yourself.) It was quite attractive as a subject, but in the end I found there was not enough to it if it was to be done in contemporary dress. The whole situation of the piece was still entirely true in my youth (so long as the court and the aristocracy meant everything in Vienna); today it would have to be switched back in point of time: I did think of the eighteen-eighties, or even of the eighteen-sixties. I was turning it over in my mind and as I did so another subject, a serious one, took hold of me and so I put the sketch into my drawer with all the rest. Last night it occurred to me that this comedy might perhaps be done for music, with the text in a light vein, largely in telegram style.

The first act—as far as I recollect—will do; the second will be particularly suitable: it takes place in a ballroom and offers enchanting possibilities. The third act I can no longer remember very clearly. Now yesterday it occurred to me for the first time that the whole thing had a touch of *Rosenkavalier* about it, a most attractive woman as the central figure, surrounded by men, mostly young ones, a few episodes, too— no sort of outward likeness or similarity to *Rosenkavalier*, but an innate affinity. But I cannot possibly give you, or even tell you any of it before January. To begin with I shall have to get my notes forwarded from Rodaun, where they are buried somewhere, and then the scenario for a light opera (in the *Rosenkavalier* style, but lighter still, still more French, if one can say that—still further removed from Wagner) will have to gain substance in my mind. If the scenario pleases you, and if it pleases me too, getting the first act on to paper will be no great feat, for the style in which the libretto is to be done is already shaping in my imagination, and you know how important it is to be able to picture to oneself the first line (or the first few bars). Therefore, if you can muster enough patience, I take hope!

Sincerely yours,

HOFMANNSTHAL

P.S. I have no news at all how Fanto is getting on. In this case the whole business (the decor) makes me thoroughly apprehensive. Whether the Marschallin's bed-chamber, or the dining-room in the conductor's house look a little bit better or a little bit worse makes not the slightest difference to an opera like *Rosenkavalier* or *Intermezzo*. But this fairy-tale of classical antiquity, where everything depends on ingenuity and ideas, where one must be aware of no more than a very faint hint of the Greek style, this requires gifts of a quite unusual order. You never let me have any say in the matter by asking me, before you approached Fanto, whether I wished to entrust him with this. Well, obviously one cannot take it away from him, but if he were not yet well enough, or perhaps had to take care of himself, in that case there are two artists who are definitely worth considering: not in any circumstances Roller, who is completely at a loss when faced with anything of this fantastic kind, but Aravantinos and Strnad.

At Salzburg I notice time and again how much the decor matters to the international section of the public—please do not underestimate this! The story about the Vienna Volkstheater is a mistake. The reference was to performances of my *Salzburger Welttheater* in Vienna.

Very sincerely yours,

HOFMANNSTHAL

Garmisch, 3.10.1927

My dear Friend,

Many thanks for your two highly promising letters! Of course I'll wait —I'm not in *that* much of a hurry! As for Jeritza, who is of course the only one, I have written to Schneiderhan and asked him to negotiate. When you get to Vienna please talk to him about it!

Fanto is still at Arosa: I've written him the enclosed letter. Don't you think we ought to wait and see what designs he submits to us? There's always time enough to reject them when I am in Dresden at the end of November. Couldn't you come to Dresden too for a day for that purpose? I don't feel sufficiently competent to make the final decision on this point.

Helena will be ready in the next few days!

With best regards and kindest wishes for pleasant autumnal work, yours very sincerely,

RICHARD STRAUSS

443

You couldn't wish for a finer recognition than Pfitzner's application for a libretto! That outweighs a hundred unfavourable reviews! It pleases me more than anything!

Bad Aussee, 13.10.27

Dear Dr. Strauss,

You will forgive me for dictating to my wife, since I am a little tired after my work. I should like to say one or two things about the matter of the decor for the Dresden performance of *Helena*. If, by the way, I can manage to square it somehow with my work, I shall come to Dresden for a day while you are there. If not, the designs would have to be sent to me here, and I should comment on them in detail and with complete frankness. This, after all, is a matter exclusively within my competence, much more so in this case than in any other, because it requires a fairly high degree of a particular kind of background knowledge as well as of imagination to decide upon decor for which one cannot draw on any historical models whatever. Some time ago I drew Fanto's attention to a certain work of Bakst's, so that he might to some extent, with perfect freedom, of course, be guided by that. His illness has probably made this impossible, for the book is very bulky and only to be had in public libraries. Well, we shall see.

It is of course, on principle, quite a good thing for you to insist that special funds shall be made available for this performance; it is a good thing, quite apart from everything else, since it may possibly enable us to procure Mme Jeritza. But to get this quite straight between you and me, *Helena* is not the kind of opera where the decor depends in the first place on money, like say *Boris Godunov* or *Turandot*. The stage is never, after all, crowded with performers, except perhaps for the final ten minutes, and even then the effect depends much more on cleverly designed costumes and on the lighting, than on costly materials; what we need for the whole thing is flair and rather more subtlety and ingenuity than one gets in the average spectacular opera. The first set, where the element of magic must not by any means be gaudy, but elegant, a little Parisian (but I am thinking of the Parisian couturiers' salons, not of the Opera there), will, if it is to be of any use at all, have to be done with real wit by the designer who must, at the same time, be able to manage his lighting very cleverly. Pomp will be no good there, only talent.

444

As for the costumes, especially those of Helen and Aethra, the subtlety must consist in their not simply being dull antique trappings, but approaching modern evening dress in some surprising way. I take it from *Vogue* that this winter a lot of such glittering gold and silver materials will be worn again. This kind of thing will have to make up Aethra's wardrobe. Perhaps Fanto has a real flair for this sort of thing. In any case one can easily put the idea in his mind. He is, after all, both amiable and malleable. What it comes to is that we shall have to do our very best on every point, and I unreservedly endorse the proposition that over our next premiere we ought to take special care and trouble.

With sincere regards, yours ever,

HOFMANNSTHAL

Garmisch, 15.10.27

My dear Friend,

Naturally you are to have the sole right of decision on the decor and the costumes of *Helena*: that's why I asked you to come to Dresden. Meanwhile, especially in view of Dr. Reucker's mentality, I considered it wise to assure myself, as far as possible, that the necessary means are in fact available. But now that I have your letter I would advise you all the same to get in touch again with Professor Fanto (Arosa) and brief him in greater detail on all that you have told me about your wishes. If you wait till Dresden, and he then shows you things that don't suit you, precious time will have been lost. But I believe that Fanto has more taste, and even sophisticated taste, than the rest of the theatrical costumiers—he is also well up on ancient China— and I have the greatest hopes of him provided you deal with him thoroughly.

Schneiderhan informs me that Mme Jeritza is in principle prepared to create Helen and adds the hope that the first performance will therefore have to be in Vienna, if only because Dresden, under the rules of the Deutscher Bühnenverein, is not allowed nor able to pay her fee. That a first performance in Vienna is as good as out of the question I have already explained to Schneiderhan at some length. Nevertheless I have threatened Reucker with it, and Fürstner as a result is now negotiating with the Bühnenverein and with Reucker. Which do you consider the lesser evil?

(1) Dresden without Jeritza (if it just can't be managed)

(2) or Vienna with Jeritza?

I should prefer the former: Dresden with Mme Schenker-Angerer in June, Vienna with Jeritza in September, and afterwards Mme Schenker when she has created the part in Dresden.

I am colossally curious about your announced *Fiaker als Graf* and should be grateful if at any time you could reveal to me a few more details about it—perhaps in Dresden?

I am conducting *Frau ohne Schatten* in Stuttgart on 23rd October and likewise in Dresden on 4th December!

With kindest regards, yours as ever

RICHARD STRAUSS

The rest of the Dresden week contains: *Rosenkavalier* on 27th November, *Elektra* on 29th November!

Garmisch, 25.10.27

My dear Friend,

From the enclosed letter you will see that the Dresden-Jeritza plan is encountering insuperable difficulties.

In Stuttgart, where last Sunday I conducted a *Frau ohne Schatten* which was as brilliant musically as it was dismal in stage design (the cursed war is almost everywhere to blame for the decor of this 'spectacular opera' and we can only hope for a better future), Reucker came to see me and proposed that excellent singer Rethberg as Helen for the first performance. She sang a magnificent Empress at the time, is now the great star in New York, next to Jeritza, and is about to enter into a similar relationship to Dresden as Jeritza to Vienna. Since I believe there is no chance now of getting Jeritza I have definitely decided for Rethberg, whose somewhat bourgeois appearance has 'greatly improved' in America; she is not so tall as Mme Jeritza, and will therefore go better with the short Taucher as Menelaus; she enjoys a great international reputation and is today generally considered the best German singer with the most magnificent voice and an accomplished singing technique. She intends to call on me during the next few days so as to convince me personally of her 'sophisticated' appearance—I don't believe we'll find anything better in the circumstances. Moreover, she is a native of Dresden and can continue to sing the part in the autumn.

446

Jeritza, if she really wants to, can then create the part in Vienna in September and alternate with Rethberg in New York.

I hope you agree. Best regards, yours sincerely,

RICHARD STRAUSS

Dear Dr. Strauss, (*Bad Aussee, 27.10.1927*)

I am utterly struck dumb by your letter. How am I to reconcile all this? You want me to write something new for you, and yet at the same time you inflict on me what I consider more loathsome than anything else that could happen. It looks as if, although we have known each other for so long and mean well by each other, you had not the least idea what it is in our collaboration that gives me pleasure and what has the opposite effect. I do not think there is anyone who knows me so little.

I remember perfectly the energy with which, sixteen years ago in Dresden, you opposed, jointly with me, an impossible actor for Ochs. Yet that actor could not have killed *Rosenkavalier*, whereas *Helena* with a graceless Helen is simply ruined. This opera, of that I am well aware, is not a dead certainty; but it has very real chances of complete, genuine success on the stage, provided the histrionic elements go hand in hand with the musical ones. It is not the face of the actress that matters; a very pretty doll might make a wretched Helen. Nor does it matter whether Mme Rethberg has now got a better dressmaker and looks 'more sophisticated' (what goes for sophisticated among theatrical people in Germany is in any case something awful), but everything depends on the magic of acting and movement, that means on a specifically feminine talent for the theatre. Mme Rethberg may sing like a nightingale, I understand nothing about that; what I do know is that she is worse than mediocre as an actress and this will ruin Helen, completely ruin her (it would not ruin Isolde, for her part can be done through the voice alone and with a certain acquired 'style', whereas the usual opera style will not do for acting a single scene of *Helena*). How could it be said from Fürstner's letter that the thing is impossible? All it shows is that one must handle her cleverly and subtly. And if Jeritza is not to be had, then there is still someone else, I mean Mme Schenker who combines an increasingly beautiful voice with real ability as an actress.

But of course one must not simply be out for what is most easy and convenient. In art nothing worthwhile is ever achieved without inconvenience.

447

I hope nothing is finally settled yet and since a certain amount of annoyance is inevitably associated with the theatre, I shall put up with this incident as one such intermezzo.

Sincerely yours,

HOFMANNSTHAL

Garmisch, 27.10.1927

Dear Herr von Hofmannsthal,

Your telegram[1] gave me quite a fright: but I fear the Jeritza business is hopeless. If you read again carefully Fürstner's very cautiously phrased letter you will realize, as I have done, that Jeritza will not and cannot sing in Dresden, and probably not even in Vienna which has meanwhile acceded to the convention of the Bühnenverein. Last summer in Berlin she demanded 12,000 Mark per night; because of the objections of the Bühnenverein the guest performance did not come off. If she were now to sing in Dresden for a *mere* 6,000 M (Schneiderhan wrote me that she last demanded 1,500 dollars in Vienna and got approximately that much) Berlin would be up in arms! Now Reucker, in accordance with the rules of the Bühnenverein, is offering her 1,000 M (a sum with which even people like Bohnen and Lehmann content themselves nowadays) plus 200 M per rehearsal: how is that to come to anything like 6,000 M? No, it's impossible; and (since you write: better Dresden without Jeritza than a first performance with Jeritza in Vienna—and you are quite right) we shall simply have to do without Jeritza! In which case Mme Rethberg is still the best we've got: superior to Mme Schenker in maturity, beauty of voice and singing technique— you only know her, just as I do, from the time before she went to America, and—according to Reucker—she is said to have altered greatly to her advantage and to have become prettier and more sophisticated. She enjoys a great international reputation and, lastly, she is a native of Dresden whom one can accept even if she is not everything one would wish a Helen to be. From what I have heard lately about Jeritza I'm not at all sure that, apart from appearance and stage talent, she too would not leave a good many other wishes unfulfilled.

And if I now persevere in lengthy negotiations and nothing comes of it in the end we shall be falling between two stools because Mme

---

[1] Not extant.

Rethberg, if she is to be available in June, must cancel a South American tour at once. Inviting a guest singer for a premiere in Dresden has always in the past involved so much unpleasantness that the chance of having a singer for once who is acceptable to the Dresden public and is engaged at their Opera outweighs many a lesser evil. In *Frau ohne Schatten* in Dresden, Rethberg as the Empress was the only one that was up to the requirements.

Anyway, I shall be seeing her myself in a few days and if she seems quite irreconcilable with your intentions I shall still be able to back out. I fear we shall see a good many non-Helens yet and hope the piece will prevail, just as in its time *Salome* prevailed in spite of Auntie Wittich.

Nevertheless I shall ask Reucker to make inquiries of Jeritza, so that nothing is left undone.

Kindest regards, yours,

RICHARD STRAUSS

Bad Aussee, 28.10.27 (Friday)

Dear Dr. Strauss,

I fear my letter yesterday was somewhat brusque and vehement. Forgive me, but this is after all truly a matter of life and death. I am not primarily a dramatist like Schiller or Sardou; if I were, you would be out of the wood (or perhaps I might never have taken it into my head to write for music and we might never have come together!). Still, *Helena* is not devoid of dramatic invention, though dependent on acting, and not mere singing! This question of beauty is neither here nor there; what is unbearable is the drabness of such a person's colourless performance, her nonentity as an actress. This sort of thing will do for some provincial first night but not for the world première on which everything depends. On top of it, the tenor may also quite possibly be a very weak actor, tenors usually are; he alone will not ruin the opera, but given a Helen insipidly acted whose gestures are flat and possibly graceless (. . .), what can conceivably come of this but a flop courteously disguised by an 'ovation' for the great composer, such as Hauptmann has received at every première for the past twenty years.

And if at least it had been a proposal of Seebach's which you have accepted, but Reucker (. . .). Three times I have re-read Fürstner's letter—and cannot see the slightest reason for throwing up the sponge! Why didn't that man Schneiderhan negotiate with Jeritza on precise terms?! No one even knows yet how much she would ask *in this particular case*! For all I care let her sing twice and Rethberg twice, surely that could be managed with travelling expenses and allowances, and from her point of view this appearance in Dresden would represent a kind of dress rehearsal for Vienna requiring no extra study.

How can one give in so easily in so *vital* a matter! Just remember what a fight Wagner used to put up for this sort of thing, for the *performers*, for the suitability of a singer as an actress. Are you really so indifferent to the fate of your works on the stage?

We have made all kinds of experiments together; the first *Ariadne* was an experiment, so was *Der Bürger als Edelmann—Intermezzo* also was one, and one which did not *entirely* come off—*Helena*, however, is no experiment, but a solid opera, with solid chances of success, unless one throws them away!

By now even that producer, Erhardt, makes me anxious. Is he really a good producer? I always say so on your authority. But that *Frau ohne Schatten* at Stuttgart, where you described the mise en scène as dismal—was not that his production? Please let me have a word about this.

At Reinhardt's request I shall have to go to Berlin tomorrow for three days (Hotel Esplanade): I shall be there until the evening of the third and then back here again. This is about some American affair of great financial importance to me, so I must interrupt my work for a few days. Next Friday I shall be back here again. I will go to see Fürstner and consider his letter a model of sense and prudence.

Sincerely yours,

HOFMANNSTHAL

Garmisch, 28.10.1927

My dear Friend,

Of course I am still after Mme Jeritza and have postponed the next decision until 8th November, when Reucker and Mme Rethberg intend to visit me here. Probably Fürstner and A. Wolff, the Director of the Deutscher Bühnenverein, will be coming here too for this conference!

But I'm afraid the fee problem won't be soluble: the gap between 1,000 and 6,000 M is too wide.

I shall in the end have to take the line of asking Mme Jeritza outright if she would sing in Dresden *for nothing*. But I doubt whether the publicity will seem to her worth the sacrifice. If therefore Jeritza is out, there arises the second, and almost more difficult, question: Rethberg, the renowned, with her wonderful voice, or Schenker of the beautiful appearance, but a beginner with a weak middle range? I shan't be able to make up my mind till December, when I have heard her a few more times, whether really to trust her with Helen!

And by then the much sought-after Rethberg may well be no longer available and we shall have fallen between three stools! What are we to do?

The time of setting your wonderful poetry to music was so marvellous—and now all this ghastly trouble is starting again!

With kindest regards, yours as ever,

RICHARD STRAUSS

Garmisch, 29.10.27

Dear Herr von Hofmannsthal,

Just received your letter of the 27th! But why do you always turn so poisonous the moment artistic questions have to be discussed in a business-like manner and you don't share my opinion? To accuse me immediately of not understanding you is neither polite nor just. If I may say so, I think I understood you a good deal sooner than many other people: otherwise I wouldn't have put your books to music against the advice of the 'most competent' people—among whom theatre managers and critics are as a rule included, *though not by me.* After this little retort let us consider the matter closed: let me assure you again that nothing has yet been settled about Helen and that I have even sent your telegram to Reucker with an emphatic note that I still insist on Mme Jeritza and that our planned conference in Garmisch on 8th November (Reucker, Fürstner, A. Wolff) must first discuss the way in which Mme Jeritza might be approached. As for Mme Schenker-Angerer, unfortunately she is still rather an unwritten page: she is beautiful to look at but her acting skill for a part of this nature is by no means proved—I must see her for myself in Vienna in December before making a final decision. I hope we'll meet before then in Dresden, between 27th November and 4th December.

In the meantime I'll do my best to get Mme Jeritza.

With best regards, yours as ever,

RICHARD STRAUSS

Dear Herr von Hofmannsthal,

Your letter of the 28th is no longer so grim as the earlier ones: but you are still doing me an injustice if you think me indifferent to the fate of my operas on the stage! Why else am I constantly travelling about among big and small theatres, to keep an eye on things both good and bad?

The Stuttgart décor was cheap post-war work: even Erhardt couldn't do anything about it. He is a good producer but no genius (. . .). It will certainly be necessary for you to keep a sharp eye on him and to arrive at the setting rehearsals in Dresden in good time yourself. I have asked Fürstner, provided you wish him to do so, to arrange a meeting in Berlin between yourself, A. Wolff and if possible Reucker, and I should be grateful if you could then press our request for Jeritza as energetically as possible! It may well be that I have grown a little weary from wriggling through perpetual compromise and the invariably enforced renunciation of the most important artistic demands. That our operas (even if you are no Schiller and I no Richard Wagner) have now survived on the repertoire for over twenty years is an indication, at least, that there isn't anything better. After all, my operas (even *Salome* and *Rosenkavalier*) at first had but slight success and a terrible press. The success of *Elektra* and *Ariadne* has been growing steadily for the past four years; and the late fruits *Frau ohne Schatten* and *Intermezzo* will also find recognition one day, if only for their artistic qualities—I believe that your comparison with Gerhart Hauptmann's latest works does not apply here.

Therefore, please be very firm about Jeritza: your suggestion about Rethberg as an alternative cast seems to me entirely acceptable, provided this great prima donna will have it!

With kindest regards, yours as ever,

RICHARD STRAUSS

Bad Aussee, Saturday (29.10.27). (Not leaving for Berlin until tomorrow)

Dear Dr. Strauss,

Your kind, patient and intelligent letter just to hand. Indeed I had no notion that Jeritza receives (or has hitherto received) such an immense fee in Vienna.

Everything you say: the need for a singer acceptable to the Dresden public, for a singer who will carry on with the part and so forth, all that is perfectly true. But it is not the crux of the matter! No, the crux is the complete, the unqualified success of the première, and that does not, alas, turn upon the music (otherwise your most successful opera would be *Die Frau ohne Schatten* whose score is described as a veritable miracle, and there would be no *Euryanthe* and no *Così Fan Tutte*), it turns upon—the theatre, the dramatic overall impression on the stage! I am a poet, but not a man of the theatre, you are not primarily a dramatist either (but somewhere between this and a symphonist), or else you would have redeemed *my* blunders on occasion and would not have written yourself a libretto like that for *Intermezzo* which consists of static tableaux rather than compelling, even if commonplace *action*.

You remind me that *Salome* triumphed with a poor actress. True, but then *Salome*, in all its splendid impetuous novelty, was the irresistible upsurge and triumph of a *new* composer. And Salome as a character needs no acting at all, she is *carried* by the action. Helen, on the other hand, must be acted, that is the whole difference! Still, I do see all the arguments in your letter. And what about Erhardt? A great deal, a very great deal could be achieved with the help of Gutheil's coaching. It is astonishing what she made of Germaine Lubin, astonishing what she got out of that plump L. (in the part of Donna Anna). Could Gutheil by any chance be fitted into the production side (for a few weeks) under Erhardt's overall responsibility? In that case I for my part would spare no trouble to make Gutheil *thoroughly* familiar with the part.

Perhaps, if only Rethberg is able and willing to learn, that might be our salvation. Please think it over.

Sincerely yours,

HOFMANNSTHAL

Garmisch, 2.11.27

Dear Herr von Hofmannsthal,

In spite of all idiotic reviews I still believe that *Frau ohne Schatten* is not only a fine piece of poetry but also an operatic libretto of great theatrical effectiveness. Indeed there are already some people who actually 'understand it'.

That the present is generally a bad age for art and that the public who can afford a seat in the opera today is stupid and uneducated—surely that's not our fault! Gutheil side by side with Erhardt would be rather difficult, but we could try and have the Helen in question undergo some preliminary drilling by Gutheil in Vienna!

For the moment, please help me get Jeritza for Dresden!

With kindest regards, yours,

RICHARD STRAUSS

My dear Friend, *Bad Aussee, 13.11.27*

Please forgive my outburst; I am really sometimes very vehement, even more so than I show. Yet one thing I never meant to imply, the very idea never entered my head, that you do not know me *as an artist*— what I said referred not to our relation between artist and artist, but from man to man—but in any case I ask you now to expunge the whole thing from your memory.

My goodwill towards you, as artist to artist, is truly unlimited. You will gather this from what I am now going to tell you and what will, I hope, give you a little pleasure. Although I am *wholly* engrossed in a new dramatic piece of work, I have sent for the notes to *Der Fiaker als Graf* and for the sketches of several other comedies besides. *Der Fiaker als Graf* was intended as a spoken play, depending entirely on its dialogue; the action, in so far as one can speak of action at all, was too flimsy for an opera. But I have been able to combine several features of this cabbies' world with elements from another projected comedy and hope (I may still find myself mistaken, but I hope!) to have invented the scenario for a three-act comic opera,[1] indeed almost an operetta (I would describe *Rosenkavalier* as an operetta too!) which in gaiety does not fall short of *Fledermaus*, is kindred to *Rosenkavalier*, without any self-repetition, and contains five or six very lively parts, above all a very strong second act and a third which does not in any way fall off. Over all this tumult I have entirely failed to express to you how warmly we share the good news of the arrival of the grandson.[2]

I am most impatient to learn how the Dresden affair has been settled. I left poor Fürstner in much distress and anxiety.

Very sincerely yours,

HOFMANNSTHAL

[1] *Arabella.* [2] Richard, born 1st November 1927.

454

Dear Dr. Strauss,

I hope you received the letter in which I asked you kindly to forgive my outbursts and to expunge them from your memory. I know I am given, on occasion to impetuous vehemence, especially during creative periods like the present when I find myself in a state of something akin to exaltation—but I would never dream of meaning to hurt you!

The characters of this new comedy for music are cutting their capers under my very nose, almost too obtrusively. The spirits which I summoned for your sake now refuse to leave me alone. The comedy might turn out better than *Rosenkavalier*. The figures have taken very distinct shape in my mind and offer excellent contrasts. The two girls (sopranos) could develop into magnificent (singing) parts. They stand to each other roughly in the same relation—as characters—as Carmen and Micaela (one extremely dazzling, the other very meek and gentle). As lovers a high tenor and a baritone. This latter is the most remarkable character in the piece, from a semi-alien world (Croatia), half buffo and yet a grand fellow capable of deep feelings, wild and gentle, almost daemonic, a part for—well, for whom? For Chaliapin, for Baklanov, conceivably for Bohnen, for Bender ten years ago, but *not* for Mayr, not in any circumstances, if only so as not to carry any similarity to Ochs into this figure! Perhaps I shall be able to offer you once more, as I did seventeen years ago, something which lends itself to easy-flowing, happy creative labour. I haven't any idea yet what was finally decided about Dresden. When are you coming to Vienna?

Very sincerely yours,

HOFMANNTSHAL

Vienna, 5.12.27

Dear Dr. Strauss,

I have written several times to say how sorry I am for certain outbursts in my letters a little while ago, but this expression of my regret was always sent to Garmisch while, as I now discover, you never were anywhere near there. So let me repeat it once more!

As soon as you have had a little while to settle down, I shall be delighted to tell you the story of the comic opera or musical comedy with which we are going to challenge *Rosenkavalier*. We cannot of course expect our work, neither words nor music, to soar to the heights of the light opera now said to be coming from the pen of Erich Wolfgang [Korngold]! But then it is no use asking for the moon.

This letter has two enclosures: one refers to a passage in the *Helena* libretto, and if I hear no more from you in the matter, I shall assume that my proposal is accepted by you.

(. . .)

Sincerely yours,

HOFMANNSTHAL

Helena Act 1

The fact that you have made Menelaus repeat some words of Helen's has led to a situation which would strike students of ancient Greece as nonsensical. But it is very easy to correct. This is it: Menelaus and Helen are appealing here not to the same, but to opposing and mutually hostile groups of deities. Helen, who is a demon, invokes the ancient demons of nature: earth and night, moon and sea, so that these wholly amoral forces of nature may lend her their magic. Menelaus, on the other hand, the husband, calls upon the higher, the Olympian gods as guardians of right and *mores*. If Menelaus, too, is made to sing: 'Earth and night, moon and sea, assist me now' (knowing full well that these are the allies of ever-deceitful womanhood, not of a man who claims his rights), the whole thing is turned upside down. I therefore suggest: Menelaus: 'Erde und Nacht, Mond und Meer weichet hinweg!' After that the two can still, if need be, sing *unisono*: 'Erde und Nacht, Mond and Meer!' since each will attach the opposite meaning to the words. Then we have once more, quite accurately, Menelaus's appeal to the higher gods and Helen's invocation of the nether, dark ones.

Now they both sing together again: 'Erde und Nacht, Mond und Meer'. Helen's last line is: 'Helfet mir jetzt' [Assist me now]. And Menelaus: 'Weichet hinweg!' [Depart from hence]. I have corrected the libretto in this sense. If this slight correction is acceptable to you, please make sure it is entered in the score, too.[1]

Since the contrast between the daemonic element of Helen and the human-moral one of Menelaus is so to speak the hinge upon which the whole opera turns, the acceptance of this correction is naturally a matter of great consequence to me.

[1] This correction was taken over by Strauss.

456

Dear Herr von Hofmannsthal,

Many thanks for your letters. I hear you were with the Russians in the Director's Box. Why didn't you come and see me? I thought you were still ill.

Reucker is here today: the question of the first performance is now to be finally settled. After no end of annoyance and weeks of negotiations the situation is now as follows:

6th June: Dresden with Rethberg.

11th June: Vienna with Jeritza.

Why it had to be like this I can only explain to you in person.

When are you coming to town?

Why don't you please simply ring up (98398) and invite yourself for lunch (1.15) or tea (4.30)?

> With best regards, yours,
>
> RICHARD STRAUSS

There are also a few text points (Elves) to be discussed!

Vienna, 18.12.1927

Dear Herr von Hofmannsthal,

The lively subject[1] which you related to me the day before yesterday does not seem to have assumed such a definite shape as to make it impossible to 'release' a few suggestions or utter a few misgivings which have arisen in me on comparing it with *Rosenkavalier*. So far as I can pass any considered judgment after no more than a cursory acquaintance with your draft, it seems to me that you are again making the mistake that led you, as the loving author, to overestimate the theatrical effect of Ochs von Lerchenau. However well this figure is equipped by the poet, and however much it is bound to interest us artists—we are not the public! And strangely enough, to that public Ochs is not only a matter of indifference, uninteresting, or boring, but to the Italian audience downright repulsive and distasteful in the extreme. The character which, after the initial victories of the misunderstood waltz, ensured final victory for *Rosenkavalier* is the Marschallin: her meditations about time, the passage about the clocks, the

---

[1] The reference is to an earlier version of Act 1 which is printed, together with the somewhat later Arabella-Matteo scene (see p. 504) in Hofmannsthal's *Gesammelte Werke*, (*Lustspiele IV*, pp. 437 ff.).

parting—and this is what seems to me to be lacking in the new subject. Your Croatian (even if enacted by a guest *Pagliacci* baritone such as Chaliapin) wouldn't draw a hundred people into the theatre—I'm trying to put myself in the position of the audience for whom, after all, we are doing the play-acting! The new piece, so far as I can judge at this stage, lacks a genuinely interesting female character. The two daughters don't seem to me to fill the bill sufficiently.

Could the mother be made into such a figure—without becoming a sister of the Marschallin? How does the mother directly intervene in the plot in your present draft? Could she be one of those mothers-in-law who are themselves in love with their sons-in-law and jealous of their daughters? You did say she was still young? Could there have been something between the Croatian and herself at an earlier date? *Or else could she be so much like her daughter that the Croatian, going by the picture, takes her for the daughter at their first meeting?* And the things that might result! In short—I'm sure you'll know what I mean—I should like to inject into the subject a few more serious psychological conflicts that would raise it above the ordinary comedy entanglements and make the participation of music really necessary. Perhaps these are present already and I simply can't see them yet—but perhaps these hurried hints will induce you to reflect how your piece could be raised even further above the level of *Fledermaus* and *Bettelstudent* than it is already by the mere fact that it is treated by Hofmannsthal instead of by Genée. If you are troubled about the structure of the piece as a whole and if the subject matter cannot well be accommodated in three separate acts, why don't you choose the looser, dissolved form of *Intermezzo*, perhaps just for the exposition scene of Act I? Do please let me know every week which day you will be in town and when and how you can be reached at the Stallburggasse—so that the time I spend in Vienna can be utilized for our joint works to a greater degree than hitherto. I am more or less certain to be found at home every afternoon between 2 and 3 : telephone 98398. What's your idea about the costumes for *Helena* in Paris? Would you like to take the necessary steps now? I met Messrs. Ungar and Grünbaum by chance yesterday, at the Director-General's office.

Ought Fürstner to start negotiations through his Paris representative?

With kindest regards, yours,

RICHARD STRAUSS

Dear Herr Hofmannsthal, *Vienna, 21.12.1927*

Fürstner is impatiently waiting for your corrections to the libretto of *Helena*. When these are finalized I shall want to revise my piano score accordingly, the first act of which is to go to New York as soon as possible. As quick as you can, please! I have before me, from the Hofbibliothek, four splendid volumes of South Slav folk-songs and dances[1] from which not only a colossal ballet could be knocked together for our second act, but which might even yield the most enchanting songs for our Croatian, possibly with highly characteristic *original words*! Am very anxious to hear more particulars from you about our new piece, of which I know so far only the rough outlines. I am meanwhile doing exercises in Croatian costume! When shall I see you? With best regards, yours,

RICHARD STRAUSS

Dear Dr. Strauss, *Rodaun 22.12.1927*

Forgive the dictation. In order to discuss your reflections on our comic opera, I must write at some length; otherwise one cannot understand one another.

Your sense of the theatre and of life is completely right. The central figure must be a woman, and not the baritone nor, for that matter, the bass-buffo. I never intended anything else. My very first bundle of notes already bears the altogether provisional title *Arabella oder der Fiakerball*. I have misled you by speaking so warmly of the figure of the baritone, the Croatian country gentleman who interests me as a picturesque and in several ways promising character; consequently you mistook him for the leading figure. In truth he is not, any more than Ochs is in *Rosenkavalier*, but just like Ochs this Mandryka is the character who, by his very entrance, by his arrival from the country in an alien world, sets the action going. And I must have misled you further by speaking of Chaliapin; Chaliapin would be the ideal man for the part, but who knows whether he would ever have been willing to sing it, just because it is by no means an altogether dominating, central figure.

[1] Franja S. Kuhač, *Južno-slovjenske narodne popievke* (Südslawische Volkslieder, gesammelt, in Stimmen gesetzt und mit Klavierbegleitung herausgegeben). Agram, K. Albrecht, 1878–82. It was from this collection that Strauss took the two South Slav folk melodies which underlie the duet of the sisters in Act I ('Aber der Richtige') and the love duet Arabella-Mandryka in Act II ('Und Du wirst mein Gebieter sein').

Enough, therefore, of that. The main character is a female one: Arabella, the elder of the two sisters, of whom I said that she contrasts with the younger, the blonde one like, say, Carmen with Micaela. This time she is not a woman, but a young girl, a thoroughly mature, wide awake young girl conscious of her strength and of the hazards she runs, completely mistress of the situation—in other words rather like a very young woman and an entirely modern character. She is in fact the type of young female who appeals nowadays; it is the job of a good tailor not to copy the old fashion but to help create the new. Such intelligent and self-assured young girls are Bernard Shaw's best figures; his St. Joan is one of them.

After Electra and the Marschallin, Ariadne, the Dyer's wife and Helen you will have to take it on trust that, once I have placed a female figure in the centre of my action, I shall be able to endow her with the distinctive qualities which make her the focal point of interest. What makes a focal figure is neither quantity of text, nor even by themselves the traits of character which one may give her, but above all the place she has in the action. The Marschallin (almost a small part if measured by bulk alone) is a perfect example. After the Dresden première the *Berliner Tageblatt* critic (since it is invariably the prerogative of the critics to give sententious utterance to the worst nonsense) expressed his regret that the poet had so clumsily reduced to episodic scale the only lovable and attractive character in the whole piece! Whereas in fact the Marschallin with her few scenes is so much alive that every single further word put into her mouth would be wholly superfluous. Coming now to Arabella, all the characters, and the whole action revolve round her. She is the idol of her parents, beloved by Matteo, the tenor (by no means a small part, but a very pretty, proper beau); the younger sister is her humble rival, the counts are her admirers. She is the Queen of the big ball and of the whole piece, and, as in a fairy-tale, she marries the rich stranger in the end. But what she is like and who she is, only the action can tell. That cannot be put down in black and white any more than the flight of a bird.

The mother is definitely still a young and very pretty woman, and I had already thought of her as a little bit in love with her daughter's admirers herself. She is a gay and original figure, very necessary to the whole action and by no means an altogether insignificant part. But to involve her in serious scenes of love and resignation, to make of her a sort of sham Marschallin, to introduce a kind of 'quotation' of the

Marschallin's fate—no, for God's sake not that; that really would be a damaging improvement.

You see, my friend, in a well and soundly conceived dramatic plan certain motifs have their place and their interplay makes up the charm of the whole piece. But everything that is not in keeping with it does harm. Let us assume for example that someone, having heard the scenario of *Rosenkavalier* roughly described, had said: but it lacks a real man, a tenor. You have a boy and a buffo, but what you need is a tenor, a beau who is in love with the Marschallin and jealous of the boy. That sounds quite plausible, doesn't it? And yet today, when you have the action of *Rosenkavalier* before you as a living, integrated entity, just try and discover where you might insert this sentimental tenor scene? It is an entity, whose complete animated world can only gain life as it is shaped by the poet, because in a good stage text characters and action are wholly one. The behaviour of the protagonists in each situation, and the situation itself are after all governed by the 'being thus and no other' of every character. In narrative prose, on the other hand, one is always obliged to tear action and characters apart. Just imagine someone had to give you an exact description of the final scene of the first act of *Rosenkavalier* while you have no notion what kind of beings the Marschallin and the boy are. What would be left of the narrative? Therefore I beg of you do not ask me for anything 'more detailed' while I am happily and fondly engaged in the task of creating these details in my imagination. You must have a little confidence after so many works, tolerably successful on the whole (despite certain short-comings in *Die Frau ohne Schatten*).

You touch upon the idea of a looser structure in place of the rigid one; a series of scenes rather than three acts. This form is at the moment rather fashionable, presumably owing to the cinema. I do not much care for it and believe that anything done in this manner will date much sooner than works which adhere to a more severe structure: *Meistersinger, Figaro, Carmen* and *Rosenkavalier*. The looser form is suitable for one of two things: either for tense, exciting action with violent, strong effects impetuously swept along from scene to scene; that is the form of the good film, which now fascinates all bad dramatists. Or again for biography, like Massenet's *Manon Lescaut* (taken from a novel, the prototype of an epic rather than dramatic story) or like what you attempted to do in *Intermezzo*, more character sketch than drama. *Wozzek* is between the two, half psychological study, half crime story.

461

A comedy in this form is quite impossible. What makes the charm of a comedy like *Rosenkavalier* (which I do not mean to imitate but certainly to emulate in its good points), that special *brio* which, for seventeen years now, has never and nowhere failed, is the concentration of colourful contrasts and incidents in each separate act. Just look at the second act: intense expectation, ceremonious solemnity, small talk, buffo scenes, lyrical moments, scandal and confusion, complacency again, one thing arising out of the other. How could a series of disjointed tableaux ever produce comparable serene contentment? It is the symphonist in your breast—ever at war with the dramatist—who hankers after this form. But this time I wish to ally myself wholly to the light-hearted dramatist with whom I produced *Rosenkavalier*, and speaking for an unsophisticated theatre audience, I want to see something happening on the stage all the time, as in every good opera. All that music-making with the curtain down is hateful to me and with me, I assure you, to many thousands of less nimble-witted theatre-goers, however beautiful these individual concert-pieces, or 'interludes', may be.

Therefore again and for the third time: trust your old, but still quite sprightly librettist! I visualize this action with more relish, and more confidence, than any of our other plots for music. I see it as a shipwright visualizes a soundly constructed vessel whose draught, ballast and canvas are properly balanced. The wind which must swell the sails is your music. But even assuming (which God forbid!) that you were to blow only at half strength, the vessel, if she is well-built and trim, ought still to ride easily.

I was in town for twenty-four hours, but all one's time gets swallowed up by family, tailor, dentist, lawyer, etc. Most willingly would I visit you in the near future, but please don't ask me to tell you much at this stage. I have to be terribly careful not to spoil my own fun in the whole thing and that might easily happen at the present stage.

I do not see any objections to Fürstner's opening negotiations for *Helena* in Paris in the near future. Lubin as Helen and study with Gutheil should be essential conditions.

I have received a letter from Fürstner (copy of one addressed to you) concerning the preliminary terms. The fifth (presence of the Berlin press in Vienna) hardly looks very practicable; I take this rather as a courtesy of yours towards Vienna. It is in fact much more important and useful to draw international critics here rather than the arrogant Berliners.

This man Reucker strikes me as a trimmer in all directions, and on the pretext that Gutheil would not obtain leave from here (of course she will get it!) he now tries to wriggle out of the awkward situation *vis-à-vis* Erhardt. You will have to be after him like a devil. This is vital!

I would, on the other hand, implore you not on any account to go beyond preliminary inquiries on the question of the costumes. For God's sake make no promises and do not let yourself be talked into anything, otherwise you will once again get involved in an inferno of unnecessary bother. What can look splendid in a Paris review, where the costumes are all and the décor usually nothing but a bare framework, may be utterly impossible in an opera. This whole costume question can anyway be dealt with only by Schneiderhan or Schalk or myself approaching Strnad. Strnad is an extremely touchy person: he has had an immense vogue for the past two years and is overwhelmed with commissions from Berlin, Paris, Holland and God knows where. We need him badly here, for the costumes must not spoil the whole effect. The question ought to be tackled as a sort of collaboration between him and someone gifted more in the tailoring direction.

I have dealt with all this in writing, although I am rather tired, so as to enable you, my dear friend, to look at these things—involving, as they do, important questions of principle—in your own good time, and to have them conveniently before you. I have this moment found your note among today's letters and hasten to add my reply. Naturally I am delighted to hear of your little preliminary exercise. Given the masterly assurance with which you subject such alien material to your own interpretation, slight nuances of this kind in colour and rhythm can greatly benefit this particular figure, but of course only this particular figure, that Croatian gentleman. And I do in fact intend to make him strike up now and then a line or half a verse from some of his native folk-songs and have for this purpose already marked an abundance of such passages in a big collection of Slav folk-songs. I cannot, on the other hand, provide you with these passages yet, however much I should like to, for I cannot possibly foretell how many, and which of them, I can unobtrusively introduce, and this must be done with immense tact. It would be appalling if this figure were to become a music-box for Croat folk-tunes, in the way Schubert steps out of the action all the time in that magnificent *Dreimäderlhaus* to treat the audience to a Schubert song! Your reference to a ballet, or indeed to

463

a 'colossal ballet' founded on a South Slav air has somewhat horrified me. For heaven's sake! Here I shall have to make a firm stand, for it is exactly the decisive point that everything must be authentic, the authentic Vienna of 1860, just as *Rosenkavalier* owes some part of its success to the fact that it is throughout the authentic Vienna of 1740. Therefore: we are at the Vienna Cabbies' Ball and on such an occasion there can be no more question of a Croatian dance than of a Persian or an Indian one.

At a Court Ball one might find a perfectly good excuse for a csardas or a kolo or a mazurka, but not, for goodness sake, at the Cabbies' Ball, that would jar intolerably. By now I have come to regret my premature description which has led your phantasy, busy and active as it is, along the wrong track. If these things please you so much, I don't mind making you a ballet later on out of some Serb ballad material. But for the Cabbies' Ball itself, that ought not to give you any trouble whatever. The action of the comedy which is highly concentrated and lively, takes place at the front of the stage; up-stage one descends into the ballroom and for my own part I rather thought of the ball as more or less invisible, only of course the characters join the dancers now and then and return again. I felt that to a master like you this hint of a ball in the background would be welcome, this touch of the ballroom atmosphere, and at the same time of an animated, pulsating crowd, this flash of a dance rhythm now and then, while the foreground is entirely given over to *parlando* and to a sentimental-lyrical mood. The kind of dances people would in fact have danced around 1860 were waltzes, waltzes above all, then fast polkas and at the end a jaunty can-can. But this does not concern us in the least, and the action will certainly *not* lead up to such a finale *à la* Offenbach. That is not my line at all and I don't even know whether the can-can is your kind of affair.

Once again most sincerely yours,

HOFMANNSTHAL

Rodaun, 25.12.(1927)

Dear Dr. Strauss,

A letter like the one in which you raised all sorts of doubts and queries always has the virtue that it forces me to think over with care how much there is to the various points.

464

I do not fall blindly in love with a subject, so much is plain; or else why would I have in my desk some twenty and more dramatic sketches, half or wholly finished, and eventually rejected scenarios and why would I hesitate so long before bringing anything on to the stage? I am more inclined to be hypercritical towards my own ideas—Reinhardt often accuses me of this. But this particular plot really has a very great deal to recommend itself and—when I recollect how downcast and tongue-tied I felt after your letter last October—I consider it a stroke of great good fortune that I have lighted upon it, i.e. that a number of ideas have grouped themselves together in my imagination to form this complete and living entity. One of the chief motifs, that of the younger sister whose love for an admirer of the older one grows in proportion to the increasingly unkind treatment he receives from the latter, until finally, to console the unhappy lover, she grants him an assignation—in the name of her sister, in a completely dark room, speaking only in a whisper—this motif has been in my mind for some fifteen years.[1] I told Reinhardt of it years before the war and with his very sure instinct he said that it would make a happy motif for a *musical* comedy, because it contains so much sentiment. But as the main plot it would, by itself, be too thin. Then there occurred to me, in a flash, a distinct, very pregnant situation for Arabella. She is a mature and beautiful girl who has probed too deeply into certain aspects of life, a little seared by cynicism and resignation, she is ready to enter into an arid *mariage de convenance* (with a man who never appears on the stage at all). For this girl the most unlikely suitor now turns up out of the blue. And the same flash of imagination revealed to me the figure of this suitor: a most picturesque personality composed of many attractive qualities (and what is more a *singing* figure). So what was before the main motif receded into the background and from now on functions merely to motivate the action and as an element of suspense (and very happily at that; as suspense which is resolved only in the third act). Not until then, and when the essential characters began to combine and contrast effortlessly and manifestly in groups, not until then did I feel really happy about the whole thing, and this feeling has gained strength in the past ten days while I organized the first act in great detail. It is an act which holds much movement, gaiety and sentimentality (the sentiment I have, not

---

[1] *Lucidor, Figuren zu einer ungeschriebenen Komödie,* was published by Hofmannsthal as early as 1910 in *Neue Freie Presse* and later in book form. It was included in the collected edition of his works of 1924.

without skill, brought in at the end), and at the same time provides a real exposition, i.e. arouses interest for what is to come, introduces all the characters, and strikes me as the best first act I have ever written, not excluding the first act of *Der Schwierige*, which is also not altogether bad, but in a wholly different manner.

Very sincerely yours,

HOFMANNSTHAL

Vienna, 31.12.27

Dear Herr von Hofmannsthal,

There now: I've again set a stage direction to music in *Helena*.[1] But since it has turned out a pretty vocal phase:

I want to ask if, instead of 'schon in halben Schlaf hinein'[2], you couldn't write some other suitable words to the music so I don't have to cut out the tune.

With the best wishes for the New Year and kindest regards from us all. Yours very sincerely,

RICHARD STRAUSS

1928

Rodaun, 7.1.(1928)

Dear Dr. Strauss,

Please forgive delay in writing. I was for four days with the Chilstons in Styria where I felt very well and did not fail to occupy myself, in very much the right mood, with the first act of the comic opera.

Obviously we must save Helen's passage, if it has turned into a beautiful phrase for the voice, and I think we can do it by simply preserving it as it stands 'schon in halben Schlaf hinein', for if I were to

---

[1] As in Act I of *Rosenkavalier* the words 'diskret vertraulich'.
[2] 'Drowsy and overcome by sleep.'

try and provide different words, the poetry might possibly be 1 per cent better, but the musical fit 50 per cent worse!

I am sorry to have missed *Ariadne*, as I am told on all sides that it was a wonderful performance. Opinion on Mme Schenker as the Composer is very divided. How much I would like to know, between ourselves, what you thought of her. Pondering the Vienna performance of *Helena*, I am beset by grave doubts in case Jeritza were to refuse finally. We are left in that case with Schenker, a beginner whose voice is apparently not without blemish, nor wholly safe in all positions—and with her alone! Should we not in that case try after all to conciliate L(ehmann)—as an actress she is certainly not what we want, not by a long chalk, but of course the voice too means a great deal. I confess I am rather anxious about the whole matter. Jeritza's reply telegram is almost due.

Sincerely yours,

HOFMANNSTHAL

To put your mind at ease!

Vienna, 9.1.1928

Dear Herr von Hofmannsthal,

Mme L(ehmann) is already fully pacified: she is singing *Intermezzo* on Wednesday and is only waiting for Jeritza's refusal to take over Helen at once. She is today still preferable to Mme Schenker who, I am afraid, will never quite outgrow a certain amateurishness as a singer. She looks very fresh and youthful and has a pleasant talent. But Lehmann is now right at the top, both in singing and in acting. *Ariadne* was excellent.

Of course: Jeritza is irreplaceable in her appearance! No reply from her yet!

With best regards, yours,

RICHARD STRAUSS

Vienna, 12.1.1928

Dear Herr von Hofmannsthal,

Roller asked me yesterday who was 'going to do *Helena*'. I replied evasively that you hadn't discussed the decor with me yet! He believes you are 'angry with him'. The time has certainly come to settle this important question! Don't you want to inform Messrs. Schneiderhan and Roller of your definitive wishes soon? I asked Mme L(ehmann) today whether, even if Jeritza still accepts, she wouldn't like to sing the part in turn with her. She didn't say No, provided matters could be so arranged—perhaps by way of two premières—that she is not regarded as a second cast.

Do let me know when you are in town!

With best regards, yours,

RICHARD STRAUSS

Dear Herr von Hofmannsthal,   *Vienna, 13.1.1928*

I have here another set of galleys of the libretto, with my corrections marked in, but think it needs looking through by you once more, if only for the punctuation!

In Act I is it: 'ein Luftgebild, ein *luftig* Gespenst' or '*lustig* Gespenst'?

In Act I the names of the three sisters are: Salome, *Elissa*, Aethra; in Act II they are: Salome, Morgana, Aethra. Am I to send the libretto to you at the Stallburggasse?

Best regards, yours,

RICHARD STRAUSS

Dear Dr. Strauss,   *Rodaun, 15.1.(1928)*

Shall look into everything carefully and will send it to Fürstner. I am seeing Roller on Wednesday. For the title I prefer the *simplest* wording: Opera in two Acts.

Best wishes yours,

HOFMANNSTHAL

P.S. On page 30 Aethra sings: 'Menelaus, do you recollect the day three times three years *and a year* ago?'

You have left out the underlined words, but that makes nine instead of ten years and I fear the more educated section of the audience *knows* that the Trojan war lasted for ten years.

Is there anything that can still be done about this?

It is no very grave matter since one can always assume that the war took some nine or ten years.

On page 34 she sings accurately: 'three times three years and a year ago', so all is well there!

Dear Dr. Strauss,

Today I only want to tell you how delighted and moved I am with your *Helena* music. How incredibly beautiful this is, how grand, and often new in style; it really gives me immense pleasure. It is akin to *Ariadne*, and also to the best passages in *Die Frau ohne Schatten*, but excels them in homogeneity.

Alwin, obliging as always, has played to me the first, and large parts of the second act; I was quite enraptured with delight. I congratulate you and myself.

I am having many and, I hope, useful talks with Erhardt, Fanto, Mme Gutheil, Wallerstein, Roller.

The troubles over Jeritza seem to me part and parcel of that whole prima donna business. I don't think this is the kind of part anyone would refuse.

Ever in friendship, yours,

HOFMANNSTHAL

Rodaun, 2.4.1928

Dear Dr. Strauss,

I hope that Milan was pleasant and not too strenuous, that you are well and that you will quickly succeed in smoothing down Jeritza's touchiness, so that no time is lost for the study of the part. With such a magnificent part, what more can she want!

Several people in Vienna and Berlin have suggested to me repeatedly that I should once again, and in good time, write something which will guide audiences (and above all the critics) to some understanding of *Helena's* modern classical world—something like that letter concerning *Ariadne* many years ago. I have now done this, but the form I have chosen is not an imaginary letter again, but an imaginary conversation between the two of us, in which I tell you the action and add a few remarks.

I hope, indeed I am sure that I am not making you say anything in this little conversation which you might not, in fact, actually have said.

Wallerstein and Roller are working quite harmoniously, and along what I consider the right lines, exactly half way between the classical and the modern, between comedy and fairy-tale.

Sincerely yours,

HOFMANNSTHAL

P.S. You will find the above-mentioned prose piece in the Easter supplement of *Vossische Zeitung* and in *Neue Freie Presse*.[1]

Rodaun, Wednesday 4.4.28

Dear Dr. Strauss,

The additional passage will appear in *Neue Freie Presse* according to your wish. I have sent the same passage to Berlin by express letter, but fear it may arrive too late. If, as is unlikely, the Berlin version (*Vossische Zeitung*) should fall into Mme Jeritza's hands and if the absence of the passage should attract her attention, one would have to say (quite truthfully) that the editor there asked me, in view of the limited space available in the Easter issue, for permission to make a number of small cuts!

I am incessantly occupied, in mind but also on paper, with our comedy. The course of baths is rather tiring me, but on the off-days I feel particularly active. I believe the comedy will be light, full of movement, and gay, and the parts very good.

Very sincerely yours,

HOFMANNSTHAL

Vienna, 9.4.1928

My dear Friend,

Your *Helena* essay is excellent in every respect, needs greatest possible circulation, and must certainly be published once more by the biggest local daily, the *Dresdner Neueste Nachrichten* (Wolff), before the Dresden première. One thing only: I should have liked—for the reading public at large—to see the beautiful 'potion of remembrance' stressed a little

---

[1] Appeared in the newspapers mentioned on 8th April 1928.

more. Otherwise impeccable. May I visit you at Rodaun on Wednesday afternoon 4.30? If this is convenient no reply is needed!

Is it too soon to hear a little of *Arabella*, perhaps?

I am going to Chemnitz on the 18th, to Berlin on the 22nd (on the 30th: third opening performance of the rebuilt State Opera: *Rosenkavalier*). From 1st to 20th May I shall be in Karlsbad, and only after 21st May back here for the final rehearsals for *Helena*!

With best wishes for Easter, yours,

RICHARD STRAUSS

Rodaun 17.4.1928

Dear Dr. Strauss,

Please send me a few words about the Jeritza affair, how you liked her voice in *Salome* and what you have decided; I am absolutely in the dark. I am working on the comic opera, and naturally anxious for news and disquieted by this affair. I have the firm hope that I may be able to read you the first act before you leave for Karlsbad and that you can take it with you there.

Sincerely yours,

HOFMANNSTHAL

Berlin, 25.4.1928. Heerstrasse 100

Dear Herr von Hofmannsthal,

Fürstner shares my opinion that your fine Easter article has appeared too soon and has therefore failed in its purpose of instructing the press, unless it appears once more, immediately prior to the first performance, and in such a form that every one of those malicious blockheads *must* have read it: say, in the Sunday issue (3rd June) of the *Dresdner Neueste Nachrichten*, or perhaps in some other way. What would you say to prefacing the libretto with that fine passage about the potion of oblivion from the Fourth Book of the *Odyssey*, as a quasi-motto? From all that I hear from the mouths of laymen and the snouts of producers your various 'potions' will be marked down as faults—in which case it would be an excellent thing to tell that mob where the original potion first occurs. Couldn't you marshal a few more ancient sources, proving that the love potion in *Tristan*, and the potion of oblivion in Act I and

471

that of remembrance in Act III of *Götterdämmerung* are not inventions of R. Wagner? I regard this as tremendously important in your interest![1]

All theatres have lately adopted, as a substitute for reading the libretto, the objectionable practice of giving a synopsis of the plot in their playbills which have developed into programme booklets. (Can't be prevented as the law stands.) Fürstner has already asked you—in vain—for such a short synopsis of the two acts of *Helena* (each act separately)! I consider it imperative that you should fall in with his request before every single drama director of every opera house doles out such a synopsis on his own misunderstanding. Fürstner would supply this synopsis of yours together with the printed music! Do please let me convince you that everything ought to be done now to meet all malicious or uninformed misinterpretations of your poetry from the very outset, before they take root in those boneheads for decades to come—as with *Frau ohne Schatten*.

Am conducting *Ariadne* today, *Elektra* on Friday, and *Rosenkavalier* on Monday in the newly reopened State Opera!

Shall be in Karlsbad (Hotel Pupp) on 1st May. Shall I get the first act by then—soon?

With kindest regards, yours as ever,

RICHARD STRAUSS

(Rodaun) 30.4.1928

Dear Dr. Strauss,

I have done my utmost to give you the little pleasure of finding the first act of the comic opera where you now are; a fairly productive mood has come to my aid and so you will get the MS. within a few days. This act is at least as lively and animated as any act in *Rosenkavalier* and the characters are established with at least as much life. Fürstner never told me that he wants a synopsis even for Germany. I shall write him one at once. So this time I am told that my explanatory article has appeared too *soon*! (. . .) Why does Fürstner not order a dozen copies from Vienna and send them personally to the most important critics! I shall *draft him the model* of a courteous and non-committal covering

---

[1] Hofmannsthal did not comply with this request, but arranged for the *Helena* essay to be republished, with minor alterations and cuts, in the Berlin theatrical periodical *Schallkiste* (June 1928) and in the *Insel-Almanach* for 1929.

letter which he can enclose. Since the critics don't arrive until the 4th or 5th, no one is likely to see the *Dresdner Zeitung* of June 3rd!

And what is all this about the *potions*? I am utterly at a loss to understand. After all Wagner did not, for heaven's sake, *invent* these potions! One (in the *Ring*) comes from the Edda, the other from the Tristan legend. In sagas and myths these potions are a *standing* institution, in the Indian sagas *ages before* Homer, in the Celtic ones, the Teutonic, everywhere! Are these people really such Hottentots?! Surely one must presuppose some sort of education. But there is in any case another way out, namely that you summon one of these critics (Kralik, for instance, or someone in Dresden, five or six days before the première) to come and see you, and touch upon this point in conversation, saying: surely your colleagues cannot be so illiterate as to need reminding that this happens in the Fourth Book of the *Odyssey*, and so on. This sort of thing is more effective than a motto; for (a) nobody looks at a motto, or those who do ignore it, and (b) to put there 'Homer' smacks at once of school, museum, philology and does much more harm than good.

It is not without some anxiety that I am sending something so important as the first act of the comic opera to Karlsbad of all places. I remember that the cure makes you nervous and irritable. Please, if you feel that way, it would be better not to look at the act, for over such a gay and attractive piece we must not get a repetition of what I shall never be able to forget: how you let me send you *Ariadne* at the very moment when the effort to stop smoking had set you at odds with everything for several weeks!

Sincerely yours,

HOFMANNSTHAL

P.S. I had no possibility of placing an article as long as the *Helena* one anywhere except in a Christmas or Easter supplement. Later on in the year the daily papers have no space for such a thing.

Rodaun 2.5.(1928)

Dear Dr. Strauss,

Here is Act I, I hope it reaches you in good health and spirits—the comedy cannot do without that. Deducting the cuts (please do not remove the paper stuck over them, they really are unimportant passages) the act runs to about 500 full lines. The first act of *Rosen-kavalier* has about 620.

Most sincerely yours,

HOFMANNSTHAL

Dear Herr von Hofmannsthal, *(Karlsbad), 3.5.1928*

Many thanks for your letter. I have already sent the necessary information to Fürstner and suggested that he should have special reprints
made of your Easter article in the *Neue Freie Presse*—provided this is
permitted and you've no objections—and enclose them with the libretti
for the reviewers. I have moreover informed him that you would
yourself write and send him the synopsis required by the theatres. Perhaps you could include a gentle hint that for all real poetry and also for
operatic texts of a superior standard an ordinary synopsis is meaningless
and unnecessary. After all, what is the so-called external framework of
Tristan? Meaningful is only what Wagner put into it. The most important thing would be to get the people, as in the case of *Tristan*, to study
your text properly; the synopsis should stimulate the people to read
the text rather than save them the trouble. How would it be if (as I did
for *Intermezzo*, on the musical and stylistic aspects) you wrote a real
preface to the libretto, to include (in addition to the synopsis already
mentioned) some fundamental observations on the nature and form of
an operatic text, the difference between recited drama and poetry
written for music: i.a. the remark that, apart from the person about to
compose it, no one can possibly judge a serious, poetically valuable
operatic text until he has heard it with the music. Also your remarks
about the potions must be included! If only you knew how much
nonsense I have already had to listen to about those potions and the
'obscure, incomprehensible' text. We two still cannot quite realize the
extent of present-day ignorance. Moreover, these ignorant barbarians
are still full of malice towards the successful authors of *Rosenkavalier*.
Just think of those entertaining and stinging prefaces Bernard Shaw has
written for his plays: and he remains relatively unmolested by those
gentry.[1]

Besides, prefaces are greatly in fashion nowadays. (. . .) Anything
that can be done by way of enlightenment must be done before

---

[1] Hofmannsthal confined himself to adding a synopsis to the libretto.

474

6th June. *Intermezzo* in particular showed the big-shots among the critics less ready to tackle the music than on other occasions. Above all, a preface distracts their attention from the piece itself—so they write less about it and concentrate more on the preface! And the less nonsense they scribble about the thing itself, the better! To expect them to understand it would be too much in any case!—

I have just received *Arabella*, have already read it attentively three times and find the first act[1] on the whole splendid. The characters are very good and three-dimensional, the 'land-owner' particularly attractive and original. So far only Arabella strikes me as rather vague in outline and her short dialogues with the three Counts as rather insignificant and ordinary (for Hofmannsthal). But the end of the act strikes me as not happy. To my mind it would have to conclude definitely with a solo voice, an aria, a lyrical outpouring from Arabella. The present curtain is quite pretty, but not effective enough for an opera. Cosima Wagner once told me: 'The main thing is the curtains!' Above all, I should now like to know the further development of the plot and the other two act endings! Couldn't you, in story-telling fashion, dictate the skeleton of the further action, in so far as you have already planned it, and send it to me so that I could gain some slight idea of the whole? I should be most grateful! I shall be in Vienna again from 21st to 28th May and perhaps we could then still have a profitable conference in person! In any case, my warmest congratulations on what you have already done; I'm having high hopes of the remainder! Perhaps you might reflect that, apart from the misunderstood waltz, the success of *Rosenkavalier* was in the entry of the Rose Bearer, the end of Act I, and the trio!

With kindest regards, yours most delightedly, gratefully and very sincerely,

RICHARD STRAUSS

Karlsbad, 6.5.1928

My dear Friend,

With reference to my last letter I would suggest that you prepare, first, a synopsis for Fürstner, which he can supply to the theatres for their programme booklets before the drama directors concerned start doling

---

[1] The reference is to the first version of Act I of *Arabella*, published by W. Schuh in *Die Neue Rundschau*, S. Fischer Verlag, Frankfurt a.M., Vol. 65, 1954.

out some nonsense or other. Second, a genuine, extensive preface to the libretto along the lines I've already sketched out to you, with a full list of all the sources (which, according to Karpath, the press people like to have before them in black and white instead of having to hunt them up laboriously), and also the essential parts of your article in the *N. Fr. Pr.* which, by the way, good old Karpath again found 'rather obscure'. The same Karpath also volunteered to write a 'popular' synopsis of *Helena* for the Vienna programme booklet, instead of Gregor, but I am declining his offer. Instead I propose to write an interview[1] for him myself, in which there will be room for a good many things that I've got on my chest, and also for the 'potions' about which Karpath had no more of a clue than, presumably, most of his colleagues! Do you agree with all this? I believe it's our job to wrest as many weapons as possible from these people's hands from the start. The other day I saw the sketches for the Dresden decor—on the whole rather nice. Do you want the Sea-Shell there to stand on a tripod, as stipulated (only it does look a bit like a gramophone!) or built into a column as in Vienna? There's still time for either! Will you write to Fanto about it yourself?

I have thought a great deal about *Arabella* and have come to the conclusion that the first part of Act I, as far as the land-owner's scene (incl.), is well planned, but from then onwards the line somehow snaps and the thing rather falls to pieces.

Surely the culmination of the act, after the subdued opening, is the moment when Waldner says to his wife: 'Er hat ums Mädel angehalten.'

At that moment, or after the passage:

> *Adelaide:* 'Der Graf Mandryka—hat um dich angehalten, meine Tochter'

there would have to be a definite caesura, a lyrical halt, perhaps a longish quintet: Waldner, Adelaide, Arabella, Zdenka, Matteo—the last two, standing a little apart, might at this point get through part of their later dialogues (think of the quartet in Act IV of *Rigoletto*).

This quintet would have to be cut short by Arabella's statement: 'Papa, heute nachmittag bin ich nicht frei'—from that moment onward the characters must gradually fade away until only Zdenka and Matteo are left, and to end with we'd have Arabella's aria which I've

[1] This *Helena* interview is quoted in *Betrachtungen und Erinnerungen* by Richard Strauss, Zürich 1949.

476

already asked for, as an effective conclusion of the act (a pretty example is Katharina's aria in the last act of Goetz's *Widerspenstige*).

As I've said, the architecture of the last seven pages is not good, lacks musical line, dialogue too confused, bound to compose badly, and almost impossible to forge together into an integrated musical shape. Do please reflect how this could be improved by rearrangement until we are able to confer on 22nd May.

With best regards, yours,

RICHARD STRAUSS

Karlsbad, 9.5.28

My dear Friend,

I am studying Act I zealously every day and am trying hard to discover what it lacks for being set to music. I believe the mistake lies in the fact that its structure is not sufficiently integrated and that the various important motives are scattered about piecemeal and often only *en passant*, thereby presenting serious obstacles to a continuous musical line. Thus, for instance, I don't like Zdenka and Matteo having three scenes instead of covering all that they've got to say to each other in two longish scenes, or again the theme of Zdenka, when she is to reveal herself as a girl, having 'something dangerous' about her being treated so desultorily and almost as a side-issue, as well as a good many other points which, to my mind, require working over by you once more before they can take musical shape successfully.

Again I can only refer you to Act I of *Lohengrin*, or Act I of *Jungfrau von Orleans*, whose plan, taken *cum grano salis*, very nearly fits *Arabella*.

Scene 1: subdued mood of Waldner's impending ruin (with a brief, rather lively interruption by the three cabbies), maintained until the scene with Mandryka.

Scene 2: gleam of fresh hope following the land-owner's announcement: as the lyrical climax the quintet I've already asked for, with Waldner providing the underlying bass (perhaps by reading out his bills, with interruptions of 'Teschek, bedien Dich'), the middle voice Adelaide with her hysterical outbursts about the fortune-teller's prophecies and repeatedly crying out lottery numbers—as a counterpoise in the background Zdenka and Matteo in passionate dialogue, and soaring above all this the tune of Arabella (in the manner of the Marschallin in Act III: 'Heut oder morgen oder den übernächsten Tag'—).

When the quintet has been cut short by Arabella's announcement: a drifting apart of the various elements, exits of Waldner and his wife with somewhat longer characteristic lines, Arabella's desperate decision to take up with the building contractor, then the scene Matteo-Zdenka, and finally, as already requested, the great aria of Arabella who so far in this act (which rather favours her sister) has had decidedly less than her fair share.

General layout therefore:

. Scene 1: depression.

Scene 2 (Mandryka): gay and lively, concluding hopefully with the quintet.

Scene 3: despair, passion, leading up to the psychological conflicts of the subsequent acts.

I don't know if I am making myself clear to you; I only know that the structure so far is not sufficiently integrated, the line not sufficiently continuous, and that many important motives are hinted at only cursorily and woven in too sporadically, and that a good deal ought to be given more precise shape and clearer utterance. For a spoken comedy the present form would no doubt be adequate; but for an opera, where so much text is invariably lost, the outline is too delicate. I shall be making the necessary notes before I go back to Vienna on 20th May, so that we can get down straight away to some useful verbal work: in the meantime I hope you will not be angry with me for being so critical again. But when all's said and done it's I who have to compose it all, and I want to make a good job of it. With kindest regards, yours,

RICHARD STRAUSS

I'm hoping confidently that you'll be attending the final *Helena* rehearsals with me in Dresden, starting Tuesday after Whitsun. Most important!

(*Karlsbad*) *13.5.28*

My dear Friend,

In reading your fine synopsis I am trying to put myself in the position of the layman, the Philistine, the obtuse, vindictive critic—and would like to submit the following doubts.

478

Aren't the lines that I've underscored going to be a handle for the ill-wishers: the remark that in the second act the same thing happens as in the first? Wouldn't it be better to suppress those two lines altogether, and instead emphasize rather more the change in Menelaus and the progress of the psychological development? And also mention the death of Da-ud?

My wife, from the point of view of the lay reader, asks that the preface be broken up into more paragraphs, since such long pages without paragraphs are 'hard on the eyes'. I have indicated the paragraphs and also written to Fürstner asking him not to print the synopses until he has received from you the final version—that is, if you are at all disposed to make any further changes.

As for *Arabella*, I still consider the characters excellent, and the exposition thrilling and promising—only the form of the act is not sufficiently finished, too scattered and not pulled together firmly enough for the musical treatment of the individual motives.

Are you disposed to go over this act once more with these points in mind? It seems to me to have been left rather sketchy and in some rather prosaic turns of phrase to be not quite up to the high level of Hofmannsthal diction!

Don't be angry! Best regards, yours always very sincerely,

RICHARD STRAUSS

Rodaun, June 15, 28

Written under the impact of the third hearing at Vienna.

My dear Friend,

I *beg* of you to ask Alwin and Wallerstein to come and see you tomorrow or the next day, in any case before you leave (otherwise the chance is lost!) and straighten out the end of Act I, with those elves. Left and right two or three elves each, or even more, should creep up right to the front of the stage (that fits in with the importunate inquisitive nature of elves), and they must sing the final passages (preferably already the 'wie, oder nicht?') towards the spectators, otherwise the curtain loses its point and becomes *blunt*. That would be a pity.

Further: the Menelaus scene, the true exposition of the opera, so charming, so strong and so effective in Dresden is ruined here. (a) One cannot hear a single word of what the Sea-Shell says, indeed one hardly

479

hears that anyone is singing at all. An undefined sound mingles with the orchestra, the audience (I watched the boxes and the dress circle through the glasses) loses interest and concentration—people say to themselves: this is *unimportant*. (In Dresden it was the exact opposite!)

The trouble is (b) that the Serving Maid is also *most* difficult to understand. This is the result of her positioning. She must come up stage and stand *vis-à-vis* the Sea-Shell and farther away from Aethra, so that (as in Dresden) she sings with full voice *towards* Aethra what she has gathered from the Sea-Shell. The singer of the Sea-Shell, on the other hand, *must be placed elsewhere*, possibly right up behind the curtains, *singing forward* through a concealed hole.

Has this woman Kittel any voice at all? This exposition is one of my better ideas; in Dresden it was shown that it can stand and be *effective*. Here, alas, it is one of the weakest, dullest moments of the act! Already a witticism goes round the audience: the Sea-Shell is omniscient, but of what she knows, nothing is vouchsafed. I did not interfere at the rehearsals because I felt this to be a matter for the musicians alone; but still—it is my duty to tell the truth. So please straighten this out.

Most sincerely yours,

HOFMANNSTHAL

Leopoldskron (Salzburg), 21st June, 1928; shortly Rodaun

Dear Dr. Strauss,

I have most carefully reconsidered Act I on the basis of the notes made during our Rodaun conversation. I shall recast the final scenes, beginning at page 25 (ensemble with Arabella's voice soaring above it and so on) within the next few days, as soon as I get back to Rodaun. Such re-shaping requires considerable concentration so that in the new form everything appears natural and unforced.

You need not hesitate, on the other hand, to base your productive musings on the existing text up to page 25, with *one* alteration: you rightly pointed out that three encounters between Zdenka and Matteo are too many. Very well then: nothing is lost if the second one disappears. Please insert in your copy: p. 11: Matteo (in uniform with cap and sword and carrying his gloves, enters centre quietly): 'Die drei schon wieder!' (exits at once), then cut Matteo's passage lower down on

p. 11. Further cut Adelaide: 'Herr Leutnant, kommen Sie doch zu uns!' (p. 11) and everything on page 14 from Zdenka, by Matteo's side, down to: Matteo (withdraws). Adelaide will be a *very* good acting and singing part. She will get longer and rewarding passages in II and III. I would rather not make any changes in Act I other than those after page 24.

I do believe that the style of the whole thing is well suited to yield something new. I consider it my chief obligation towards you that nothing I do should in style resemble too closely anything already done. But please do jot down a few of the passages which you consider careless in phrasing!

(Hofmannsthal's signature lacking)[1]

Garmisch, 24.6.1928

My dear Friend,

On your daughter's marriage[2] my family and I send you, Frau Gerty and the young couple our warmest congratulations! I've received your letter from Salzburg. Did you discuss our new work with Reinhardt? Has he no amusing ideas for the production? So far I still miss in *Arabella* a string of scenically effective highlights, such as are contained in *Helena* and particularly in *Rosenkavalier*. Think of the levee, of the long, exceedingly affecting closing scene of Act I, the superb presentation of the rose, the waltz at the close of Act II, the trio in Act III. In short: the essentially pictorial, mimically convincing element that is so necessary in a libretto where over a third of the words are almost invariably lost and where even the best dialogue remains on the whole uninteresting to the general public. I've seen it again now with *Helena*, although I made every effort to present the poet's text in the greatest possible relief. The first act of *Arabella* in its present form, attractive though it is in itself, is not sufficiently sparkling as an operatic text. Whether it can pass as an exposition (without any very great immediate effect) will depend on Acts II and III. The ending with the two subsidiary characters is not good in any case.

Please send me Act II as soon as possible, either in its entirety or clear sketches of the last two acts so that I can get a better idea of the whole thing.

[1] Perhaps another sheet is missing from this letter.
[2] Christiane von Hofmannsthal married the indologist Heinrich Zimmer (1890–1943).

At present I can't really do very much with that somewhat disjointed first act, especially as the title part is still rather sketchily treated.

Above all, Arabella is certainly not yet—a part.

Don't be angry if, especially after that excellent *Helena*, I am getting more and more exacting.

With best regards, yours very sincerely,

RICHARD STRAUSS

Rodaun, 27th June, 28

Dear Dr. Strauss,

How could there be any question of being angry! In the first place I am, as you once said of yourself, 'immune to offence in matters of art', and then, what is more, your doubts and reflections are after all perfectly justified, justified both in the demand (a) for mimically convincing situations and (b) for good parts! These are fundamental truths.

But please do not rush me, *everything* that is any good comes to me only through concentration. I depend on *ideas*, even for *small* things on which the essence often hangs. Thus the levee, the presentation of the rose; these were in the overall conception of the work seemingly small things—but of great significance.

All in all: I have great confidence in this subject, more almost than in any of the earlier ones. Therefore it must be possible to turn it into something good, something animated, something which surges forward in pace and emotional appeal. For all this I shall have your requirements before me as an iron law.

Give me now a few days to think the whole thing over with care and to write for you a lively account of the action in Acts II and III.

This time I have from the outset, even in the original conception, looked upon Act I as purely expositional, in complete contrast to *Rosenkavalier* where Act I is practically a piece in itself, while in Act II the true central figure, the Marschallin, does not appear at all (what a mistake, theoretically speaking!) and Act III struck many people as 'pieced together'! I remember Arthur Schnitzler telling me of his apprehension that the comedy was *falling off* from I to II to III.

And *your* objection that there was nothing 'funny' in it, nothing to make one laugh—your fear lest Ochs fall short of Lortzing's characters!

And yet! *One must never cease to be on one's guard!* I must therefore be on mine, especially over the figure of Arabella, as an opera part. Zdenka is a good part, Matteo too, Waldner and Adelaide are good, clear-cut, happy characters, and Mandryka with his Slav ballads, dance songs and folk-songs will prove a novel and *very strong* part—it is Arabella, therefore! This much is already agreed between us, that she gets the curtain of the first act, first in a subdued mood, then abrupt. Therefore *coraggio e pazienza*!

I also had the idea of reading this act to Reinhardt, and of describing to him the others; and I shall certainly do so still, as soon as possible! But at Leopoldskron there was not a moment to spare, work on this film scenario[1] swallowed up all our energy and time late into the night. I ought to explain that he asked for my help over this and that, as an exception, I agreed to do so. It is a piece of work which will be done and decided within a few weeks. If the result is negative, I shall have wasted a fortnight; if, on the other hand, it succeeds, I shall never be troubled with it again and shall be paid on the spot a sum of money which will enable me to build Christiane's house at Heidelberg. As a father you will understand that I could not turn this down.

Very sincerely yours,

HOFMANNSTHAL

P.S. Why don't you please write down a few of the passages which struck you as careless in phrasing; it will *not* hurt me *in the least*; on the contrary it interests me!

P.S. I have just gone through Act I again most critically and have sketched out the ensemble with Arabella's voice soaring above it (page 25ff.). Also the curtain—Arabella concluding her letter, sad for a moment, then closing abruptly.

Yes, the danger to be avoided is this: I must not come too close to spoken comedy!

May I make a suggestion?! Why don't you occupy yourself a little with the ballad-like passage of Mandryka's, beginning at the bottom of p. 20! 'Kommen meine Verwalter, was ist's mit unserm Herrn? . . .' as if these were the words for a song. Perhaps in this way this highly important figure will begin to take on style and shape!

---

[1] The film project, which never materialized, was based on a religious subject.

My dear Friend,

Many thanks for your fine letter: I find we understand each other better every year. A pity such good, continuous progress towards perfection must come to an end some day and that others must start again from the beginning. Your accurate grasp of what I still want to put into the new subject gives me the assurance that you will hit on the right thing (i.e. that which, as a musician, I still *think I need!*)—though possibly, during composition, it may turn out that I don't need it after all. Take as much time over it as you like—I've got patience and—following your excellent advice—am at present concentrating on Mandryka who, after all, is the one who determines the tone of the whole piece and must fix its style.

I'll wait, therefore! With best regards, yours

RICHARD STRAUSS

Helena in Dresden also full houses right to the end.

Dear Dr. Strauss,

You can imagine that your doubts have made me think twice, too, and that I came near putting aside what I had begun—at the risk of not finding, perhaps for years, anything that seems to me suitable for music. All this time I have been preoccupied almost exclusively with our comic opera, and the result is that I am getting fonder and fonder of subject and characters and have the greatest confidence in the whole thing—the complete confidence that, in a somewhat different style, it can vie with *Rosenkavalier*.

You will receive tomorrow or the following day the completely recast end of the first act (the figure of Arabella given revealing prominence, a point of repose, the ensemble, all in accordance with your so well-founded wishes) and a detailed and clear description of the action in Acts II and III.

I have also in the meantime read Act I to several people in whose judgment about dramatic construction I have confidence (not all of them librettists, but including Max Mell whose stage sense is excellent), and have told them the rest asking for utmost severity and frankness. The result was *unreservedly* positive. The subject was considered more

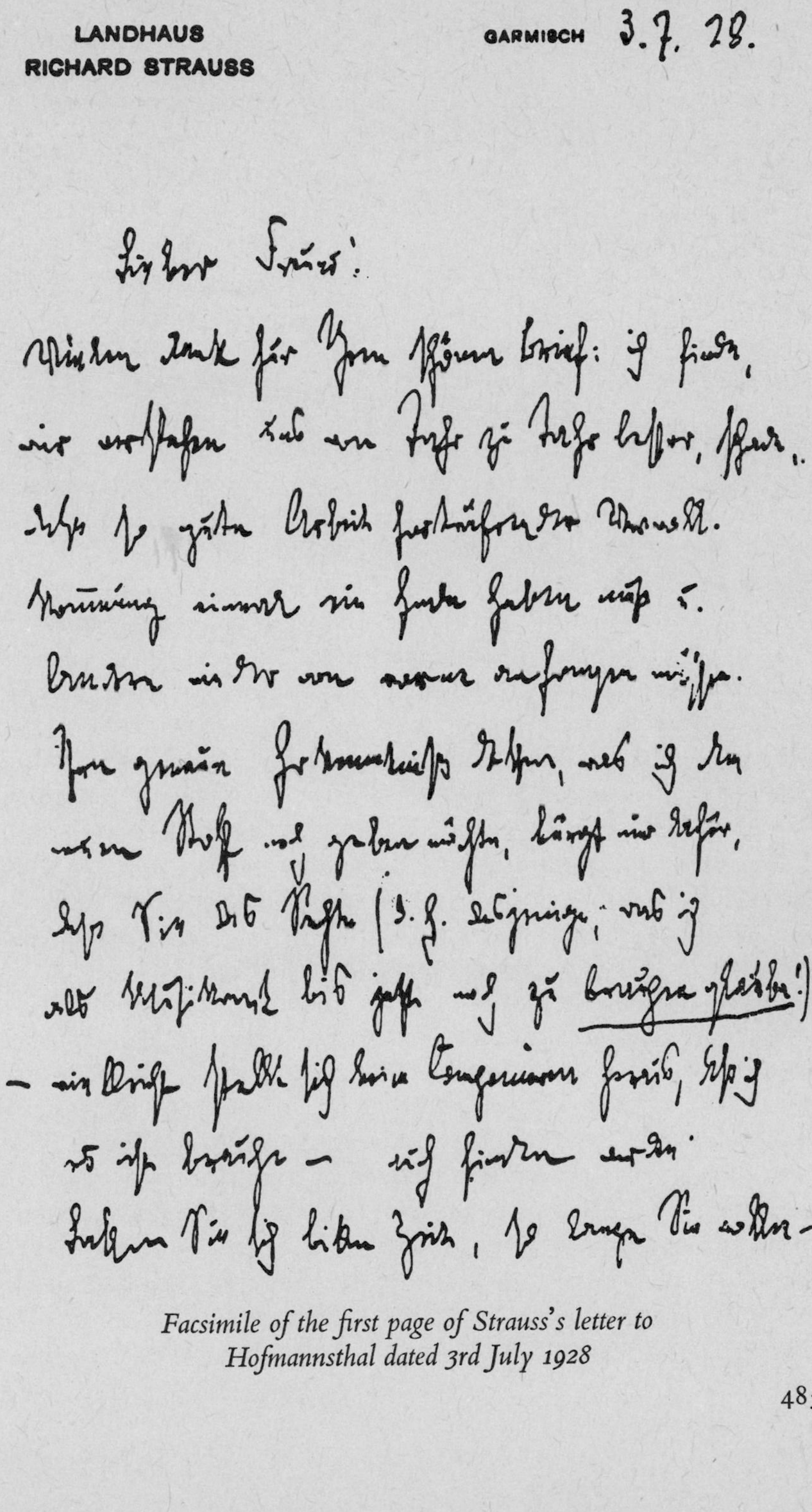
LANDHAUS
RICHARD STRAUSS

GARMISCH 3.7.28.

Lieber Freund!

Vielen Dank für Ihren schönen Brief: ich finde,
wir verstehen uns von Brief zu Brief besser,

Facsimile of the first page of Strauss's letter to Hofmannsthal dated 3rd July 1928

attractive, more homogeneous and better constructed than *Rosen-kavalier*, the characters animated, engaging and all of them novel (in fact in all theatrical literature I do not know any figures like these two girls, like Mandryka, like Waldner and Adelaide)—compared with them the character and situation of the Marschallin are conventional. The unhackneyed period of the sixties which is 'due' for revival, the choice of this period was welcomed also by Roller and Wallerstein as particularly happy. In short I note *not a single* negative point in all these verdicts which I have solicited.

But the decision must of course rest with what you feel. A few words about the language. For me the actual creative work of the poet consists in finding for the figures their distinct diction. Manner of speaking, change of tone, rise and fall of diction, these are my means of establishing the character of living figures and to convey their different social standing; even much of what is implied *between* the characters and can hardly be communicated outright. Take, for instance, the gap dividing Octavian from the boorish Ochs, or Sophie's silly-bourgeois, stilted and artificial behaviour and so on and so on. This is a matter to which I invariably give the same great care. You are in error when you write that at some point or other the diction does not reach 'H.v.H.'s usual high level'. Everything requires exactly the same degree of concentration, whether a line for Aethra or one for Waldner, and the line: 'Leopold, i zahl, i geh' is in essence neither more difficult nor more easy to light upon than: 'Gewogene Lüfte, führt uns zurück!'

What is vital is to find the right atmosphere for the whole thing, a certain general atmosphere in which the whole piece lives. In *Helena*, for instance, this is somewhere between the elegant and the solemn (and infinitely far from the sombre massive note of *Elektra*, but very different also from the elegiac tone of *Ariadne*). The atmosphere of *Arabella*, again, differs greatly from that of *Rosenkavalier*. In both cases it is Vienna, but what a difference between them—a whole century! Vienna under Maria Theresa—and the Vienna of 1866! By means of the (incidentally quite imaginary) idiom, I steeped the Vienna of the 18th century in an atmosphere at the same time pompous and cosy—the atmosphere of *Arabella*, quite close to our own time as it is, is more ordinary, less glamorous, more vulgar. The three Counts in frivolous pursuit of all skirts, Waldner that cashiered cavalry captain and his whole shady milieu, these figures are tainted by vulgarity, tangled up with a rather vulgar and dubious Vienna—it is this background which sets off the courageous and self-reliant Arabella and the touchingly impulsive Zdenka. For Mandryka above all this pleasure-seeking, frivolous Vienna, where everybody lives on tick, is the foil; he is steeped in his world of unspoilt villages, his oak forests untouched by axe, his ancient folk-songs. With him the wide open spaces of the vast half-Slav Austria enter Viennese comedy and carry into it a breath of fresh, totally different air; that is why I was so delighted when, with your sure artistic instinct, you saw the figure of Mandryka as the key to the whole piece.

Adelaide will also be a very good and very attractive *part*. She must still be very pretty—I am thinking of Mme Olszewska.

I enclose a letter from Franz Werfel[1] in which he repeats once more, late the same night, what he had told me earlier.

Very sincerely yours,

HOFMANNSTHAL

P.S. The slight oddities of language in Mandryka's speeches, when he says 'der Donau' or 'hineingeschlossen wurde', are of course intentional characterization.

Garmisch, 20.7.1928

My dear Friend,

Many thanks for your letter of the 13th (with Werfel's gratifying note) and its valuable remarks about the style of *Arabella*—even though it hasn't made the somewhat rotten setting of Vienna in 1866 any more palatable to me. To keep up this style throughout three acts a man would almost need the levity and the talent of the composer of *Fledermaus*. True, in *Rosenkavalier* I managed a few corrupt episodes for Ochs von Lerchenau, but whether I shall now be able to feign dissolute naïveté for three whole acts has yet to be seen. The true dramatist, of course, ought to be able to do it—but will I have the patience?

Now to the libretto itself, which I received with many thanks the day before yesterday and which I have already mugged up thoroughly. The first impression was excellent: I was blinded by the good structure and the sure architecture! On more intensive reflection, however, a sense of disappointment crept over me, which slowly but surely concentrated on the character of Arabella. Today at last the penny dropped, and I believe I know for certain what this character, the most important

[1] Not extant.

487

of all, lacks. In short: she is not sufficiently interesting and almost unattractive (which surely was not your intention). But where's the snag?

Let me analyse: she flirts with the three Counts, superficially, without any particular affection. That she gets embittered by the knowledge that none of the three can marry her is too self-evident to interest the audience. That out of this bitterness and realization of her position she is even willing to marry the unattractive building contractor is understandable, but again not interesting. The suddenly emerging passion for Mandryka, however, loses much of its true value since he is in any event a better match than the contractor. A new motive must therefore be found that would lend this new interest in Mandryka (quite apart from the financial advantages such a marriage would offer) a truly moral significance. This is possible only if Arabella has been in love before and made her *renunciation* before her new attachment to Mandryka. Therefore I propose that she should really love Matteo and would have been prepared to marry him if he were not such a poor devil. As it is, one can't get over the impression that she doesn't want him for the simple reason that he hasn't got a bean. This means that right at the beginning of Act I Arabella and Matteo must have things out: in the course of this conversation she declares her love for him but also makes it clear that he must give up all hopes of marrying her because she feels obliged to save her family by contracting a rich marriage.

This conversation would have to be conducted in such a way that he ends up by nursing the hope that she might after all, as an end of her girlhood—just as she is spending a gay evening dancing with the three Counts—*grant him that assignation* which her sister eventually enjoys in her place. A farewell letter which he asks of her as a remembrance might fan that hope: her sister substitutes this letter.

It would greatly enhance the character of Matteo if both sisters were to be in love with him, and, above all, that splendid scene in Act III between Arabella and Matteo would gain considerably in seriousness and significance if Matteo, at Mandryka's entrance, could hurl at her: 'But you love me: *you admitted it to me yourself.*'

How much more beautiful would be Arabella's explanation: 'Yes, I did love him, but I renounced my love before I met you, Mandryka. I am innocent of the misdemeanour of which he now accuses me: I come into your arms pure, with sincere love.' Whereupon Mandryka (against a protesting Matteo): 'I believe you; these eyes cannot lie.'

And now Zdenka bursts in, explanation, end.

How do you like that? I know you'll be horrified at first, because my suggestion knocks half your opera into a heap. But Acts II and III, thank God, are still only drafts. And once you've accepted my ideas the alteration won't give you too much trouble. As it stands, the figure of Matteo is too insignificant; a really serious psychological conflict occurs only in the supporting character of Zdenka, whereas the principal character of Arabella is altogether too flat and psychologically too insignificant.

I do hope that—once you can view it from a little distance, which is of course more difficult for you at the beginning—you'll agree with me. I believe the whole thing would be much more interesting psychologically than it is now, when Arabella's affairs are developing in a rather humdrum and matter-of-course manner. May this letter find you at a propitious hour and with willing ears. Meanwhile, many thanks and best regards, yours always very sincerely,

RICHARD STRAUSS

Garmisch, 23.7.1928

My dear Friend,

How useful it is to have a concise sketch, the bare skeleton, stripped of all accessories! So far you had always told me the action in person, when one is all too easily enchanted by the lovely things that are revealed (which is apparently what happened to Werfel if he was honest)—and after that I always got the finished product, where the weaknesses are even more carefully concealed by luxuriant poetical ornament. But faced with this pure 'outline' one feels bolder and is the more encouraged to voice merciless criticism as a great deal, or so it seems, can still be saved and not too much work has as yet been done on it. This polite preamble is designed to propitiate you for the news that I have still a good deal to find fault with—to wit, the two principal characters and Act II, which is devoid of all real conflict and has definitely not been fully thought out by you with an eye to the ultimate consequences inherent in the subject. It is absolutely uninteresting to have Mandryka—uncritically enraptured by the photograph from the start—agree in advance with everything that Arabella does or demands in Act II, and to have him declare unhesitatingly in Act III: 'These eyes cannot lie.' That would positively make him a hero out of a Marlitt novelette!

489

And then Arabella: does she really do anything particularly exciting? She doesn't love Matteo from the start; as for her flirtation with the three Counts, who display no particular personality in any way, I think you probably overrate its poetical effect. That she should easily switch from the building contractor to that wealthy paragon of virtue, Mandryka, is as natural as it is uninteresting. And then: does anything else happen between the two? Nothing at all. That she still wants to dance a little on her last evening, with his permission—why, that happens in the best families! A real conflict exists only in the subsidiary plot between Matteo and Zdenka, and only for a single moment in Act III is this tied up with the principal characters—in the scene with Matteo, which now becomes doubly unattractive owing to the fact that poor Arabella is dragged in quite innocently and that, moreover, no complications are to be expected anyhow in view of Mandryka's almost imbecile good-naturedness. Also I am getting less and less keen on that drink of pure water! Just think: we are being accused already that there's nothing but drinking in *Helena*: but there at least it was a case of interesting magic potions! The joke 'Hofmannsthal must have got water on the brain' is too cheap to be passed over by a single 'witty' journalist. The gipsy with the fiddle, too, has already been worked pretty hard by Ferdinand Bonn and reeks strongly of Lehar.

Don't be angry with me for my merciless slaughtering: but my feeling that the subject lacks a proper conflict is steadily growing stronger.

But what's to be done about it? I've already explained in my last letter that the effect of Mandryka's 'To be loved at first sight' is heightened and the Matteo scene gains in power if Arabella has really loved Matteo and given him up 'by force of circumstances'. Now I have had the following further ideas: In the course of Act II, and later, Mandryka's naïve faith in Arabella must be thoroughly shaken. For that purpose, to begin with, the leave-taking scene with the Counts must not be too innocent—and Mandryka must subsequently overhear Zdenka and Matteo making their assignation and must *hear* that the key in question is that to Arabella's room. Thereupon outburst of jealousy by Mandryka who, in a kind of despair, hurls himself into the vortex of the Viennese ball and, under the influence of the champagne, now has a real love scene—possibly with Fiaker-Milli. While then in Act III, in the scene with Matteo, Arabella appears seriously guilty and is yet totally innocent, Mandryka feels himself to be disloyal and guilty—even if pardonably so, since he was swept away by emotions of jealousy and love, which amid the temptations of a ball of that kind easily confuse their object. Think of the famous scene in *Wahlverwandtschaften*! Waldner and Adelaide are standing wholly aloof from the action in Acts II and III; i.e. they disappear almost entirely except for the scene between Adelaide and Mandryka. 'She is charmed by his chivalry.' When? Surely, he has had no opportunity yet for proving any real chivalry. 'She has her happy hour.' Again I ask: When?

How would it be if the three Counts whom unfortunately you have, so far, treated very monotonously and in a niggardly manner, and who have no individual features whatever—if these Counts, amiably but irrevocably dismissed by Arabella, were now to conspire, partly for revenge and partly for the fun of it (the champagne having gone to their heads), to make a pass at the mother since the daughter has been denied them?

Since you expressly state that Adelaide is still young and pretty (about 40), this ballroom flirtation with one of the Counts (but not the one whom Arabella kisses on the forehead), which starts as a joke, might develop into something a little more serious (even on both sides) and might likewise end in a kiss. This would indeed be a 'happy hour' for the poor mother, something she, too, feels 'guilty' about in Act III.

The first scene, when during Arabella's conversation with Mandryka the three Counts ask for their dances, might perhaps be dropped for the sake of brevity. Waldner, on the other hand, who's got some money again after a long time, could for his part have a little gambling adventure or an amorous one—if only by being drawn into the crazy whirlpool by a jealous and desperate Mandryka—so that by the end of Act II, following the above-mentioned love scene between Mandryka and Fiaker-Milli, everybody feels more or less guilty. Even Mandryka has for the moment almost forgotten the incident of the key to Arabella's room and only when he gets her note does he come to his senses and feels convinced that it is in *this* way that Arabella wants 'to bid farewell to her girlhood' by an assignation with Matteo. Therefore the theme of the real betrothal with the drink of water (if indeed you want to keep this somewhat childish symbolism rather than replace it with something a little stronger) must be mentioned much earlier, so that it can now have the effect of a bombshell as Adelaide realizes what is happening: 'For God's sake, she is gone; we must hurry home—the betrothal!'

Mandryka sobered, desperate: the betrothal—the drink of pure water—*who is to serve it, and to whom is it to be served?*

Thus Act III opens with the whole lot of them being or feeling more or less guilty, and the only person who seems really compromised emerges entirely pure from this whole confusion in Act III.

This will of course be a little reminiscent of the pretty third act of *Wildschütz* which culminates in the charming quartet 'Unschuldig sind wir alle, alle, alle!' But that doesn't matter! Mandryka, the virtuous hero out of a Marlitt novelette, has by then also had his knuckles rapped a little by the gay city of Vienna, and the pretty, virtuous Arabella has truly become the engaging ideal character that you had in mind. And so, not without a last little test (in having something to forgive her future spouse even at the moment of her betrothal) she climbs into her provincial matrimonial bed.—This, more or less, is all that I personally think can be squeezed out of the subject and I don't think I've mentioned anything that isn't in the subject. This way, at least, it would be good theatre.

But you are the poet! You'll probably think of something even better and more original; if so, these lines were intended merely to stimulate you to exploit all the psychological and dramatic possibilities of the promising scenario to a greater extent than you have done so far! As it stands it is flat, and Arabella, the principal character, isn't getting all the highlights she needs in order to be really captivating.

In writing I don't suppose we'll get much further than we are now —it seems to me that we've reached the same point as, at the time, with Act II of *Rosenkavalier*.—You then trusted my dramatic instinct to give the action its decisive impulse—you admit yourself that you approach the ultimate dramatic consequences with invariable hesitation —and I believe we have here another case in point. Act I is good (except for the relationship between Arabella and Matteo, provided you are disposed to accept my suggestion) and could pass as a mere exposition.

But Act II must be invested with conflicts and tensions, of which it is now entirely devoid—the whole thing is a mere lyrical gurgling— so that a real explosion in Act III is felt as a satisfactory solution.

Wouldn't you like to come here for a few days so that we can discuss it all at leisure and you don't give yourself any unnecessary work which, in the end, may still not lead to the result I am hoping for? We are here definitely until 15th August and after that shall probably go to the Engadine. Pontresina, Hotel Saratz.

With best regards, yours very sincerely,

RICHARD STRAUSS

My dear friend,

To anticipate one thing: your proposal concerning the relation between Arabella and Matteo does not grate upon me nor does it prey on my mind. I find it very good, for it gives the whole thing up to the decisive scene at the beginning of the third act additional suspense which is most welcome. In fact, I have just discovered that in the first, very earliest note of the middle of last October this very development is already hinted at in these words: 'Affection for the lieutenant on the part of the elder sister also suppressed by her.' If I abandoned this idea later, I did so presumably out of a desire to simplify as much as possible. Yet I consider it a gain to take it up again. The place for the Matteo-Arabella scene is obviously at the beginning of the first act, during the conversation between Zdenka and Matteo; Arabella enters, gets rid of her little sister by a hint—and remains alone with Matteo. I have her exact attitude before me in every detail; she speaks of her affection for him as something which she has overcome, but grief and love must still throb through her words and one must realize that he feels love vibrating in them more than the resolve towards resignation. This wistful scene will then also act as a foil to the scene with the three Counts, and Arabella's flirting with Lamoral out of despair will derive from it a slight nuance of the forbidden fruit. The end of the act (the letter scene) I would leave as it now stands (do you agree?), but even this will gain appeal from the fact that the sacrificed lover is present during the writing of the letter.

Thus I have every reason to be grateful to you for your suggestion. I shall work out this small but by no means easy scene at the earliest propitious moment.

As for your doubts of a more general kind, even these I understand completely: the reference to *Fledermaus* and its composer illustrates quite distinctly what you have in mind.—Still, I should hate to let go of this subject at any price! Twenty years' experience has taught me to recognize what a happy chance it is if a subject offers itself like this one, with animated, attractive figures, with a clear and unfaltering action, divided into the correct, traditional three acts. The unanimous approval, too, of such different people upon hearing the action told (Werfel's letter was not even the most enthusiastic) comes as an excellent, altogether unusual, omen; and is it not remarkable that I am receiving delighted letters of congratulation from total strangers in various

493

German cities at the mere hint of the story which must have appeared —apparently through Karpath—in some newspaper or other? An architecturally well-constructed scenario is after all the only almost unfailing guarantee of success on the stage, and in this respect I could have prepared the ground for you far more thoroughly than in *Helena* where, especially in the transcendental and subtle second act, you had to do a great deal of hard work to make it theatrically convincing.

I understand perfectly what you mean by the atmosphere going somewhat against your grain. But I am not the librettist of *Fledermaus*, but of *Rosenkavalier* which means that this half-naïve, disreputable element which pervades the whole Frenchified Viennoiserie of *Fledermaus* can in my case never be anything but backcloth for contrast. Arabella, and Mandryka who steps into this atmosphere as a complete outsider (and a particularly operatic guest), and Matteo and Zdenka as well—all this is reality imbued with life in its serious aspect, and it stands out from the backcloth represented by that other element. You have command of the means to bring this out, as is proved not only by the figure of Ochs, but also by Faninal and the whole third act of *Rosenkavalier*, in the *Ariadne Vorspiel* and in some passages in *Intermezzo*.

As in every one of these librettos, there is an implied appeal for, an indication of, some definite style. You yourself have authorized me to do what I am endeavouring to indicate, to elaborate in *Arabella*. During a certain conversation touching retrospectively upon *Rosenkavalier* and upon this very question of style, you told me yourself that today you would write different music for quite a few passages in *Rosenkavalier*, especially in the second act, but that you were *at that time* not yet at the point of your development where you could enter successfully upon objectives which would, in a certain sense, bring you closer to the old operetta (a description which I would give for instance to *Don Pasquale*). (Let us say those choral passages after the Ochs-Octavian duel, which were meant to be in the style of an operetta.)

Let me now try and say something in all modesty. One of the strong points of your judgment about my writing and one reason why I always take this judgment most seriously is that you are an artist but a clear case of a non-poet, of a non-librettist; free, for this reason, in the most naïve way from all the literary prejudices, preferences, fashions and so on of our time. I, in turn, am a non-musician and a stranger to musical tastes and education, but at the same time almost frighteningly free from ephemeral judgments, scales of value etc. My appreciation of music might almost be called barbaric, but still, with great attentiveness and with the sensitivity of the artist, I listen and try to get right inside all music presented to my ears by an orchestra, by a piano or by a gramophone, whether Beethoven or Lehár, a scene by Verdi or one of yours, gipsy music or *L'Après-Midi d'un Faune*. And somehow, in my barbaric manner, I do know what it is all about; I am open to all that is creative and have always, even amid the clamour of enthusiasts and sycophants, refused to countenance what is heterogeneous, hybrid and vague aspiration rather than solid achievement, as in Gustav Mahler's music, for instance.

After this introduction I would venture to say the following, ashamed of my incapacity to express myself in even remotely accurate musical terms, yet sure that you will understand me and will receive indulgently and not altogether without receptivity what may perhaps sound absurd. As I try to think and feel with the public, with our contemporaries, for whom we are, after all, creating these things, I have a very good inkling (yet how far beyond the grasp of my barbaric means of articulation!) of what they would long for, of what would pluck from their joy-craving minds a storm of delight, *far* beyond the joy which *Rosenkavalier* affords and presents for them. Not that I mean to say you should write like Lehár! You answered that once and for all years ago when you said to your wife in a Berlin restaurant: 'Like him I can't write, for in a few bars of mine there is more music than in a whole Lehár operetta.' But this being understood, thoroughly understood (and it implies that these are two wholly incommensurate artistic levels of musical creation), there still remains something which I can perhaps adumbrate in the following clumsy terms: if only it were possible, as a move towards a new style of expression—undertaken not with declining power, but out of more mature artistic insight—to reach a 'less-of-music', to reach a point where the lead, the melody would be given rather more to the voice, where the orchestra would accompany (at least over lengthy passages) and would be subordinated to the singers (not with regard to volume, but in the distribution of 'the lead'), and not, as in a symphony, have all to itself. If this could be done, operetta might be made to yield up to this type of work its magic ring which conquers so completely the souls of an audience! And here, when I speak of operetta, I mean once again Auber and Boieldieu, Donizetti and all the rest rolled in one.

I am not so foolish as to imagine it feasible to *resuscitate* simpler and more unsophisticated forms of art. That is dilettantism, trifling à la Wolf-Ferrari, etc. No—but if it were possible to escape, half way, or even two thirds, from that German *professorial* concept of music, that something, that 'too-muchness' in German music which made Piccini say of Gluck: *puzza di musica*—it reeks of music. Oh, if only it were possible for the master, in the mature assurance of his power, somehow to leap over his own shadow, his German 19th century shadow, his time-bound prejudices (even that word is already too clumsy, for this is the subtlest of the subtle), if that were possible, perhaps then the gain would indeed be magical, so enchanting that all the Korngolds and Beckmessers would start off by calling it treason, monstrosity, bankruptcy, fraud, impudence—and these would be names of honour to accompany our child on its way across the world amid the cheers of the public.

Forgive these digressions. Nine parts may be ignorance, barbarism, misinterpretation of the rules of art, failure to see essentials and so on, but one part is intuitive knowledge of a highly developed artistic sensitivity derived from the spirit of time and nation.

Yours,

HOFMANNSTHAL

Garmisch, 26.7.1928

My dear Friend,

Many thanks for your interesting letter: I only hope that you will receive no less favourably my letter of two days ago and my request for a reshaping of the relationship between Arabella and Matteo. Don't be afraid of the thing getting too long or too complicated: length didn't do *Rosenkavalier* any harm, and the main point is that the piece should become more colourful, entertaining and thrilling than it is now when everything is moving along all too smoothly, with no real or even only apparent conflict. Whether you accept my suggestions or not is irrelevant. I hope that your poet's imagination will yield something better and more original than occurred to me, seeing that I had to stick to the given characters, situations and motives.

I can only say, quite frankly and honestly: so far I am still looking in vain for the decisive 'ideas', but I feel sure that they will come to you if you think over and go over the whole thing again from the start, with an eye to its ultimate dramatic possibilities and consequences. It would be a terrible pity if this attractive subject were to get stuck at its very beginning and, in particular, if that charming figure of Arabella were not to become what you intend her to be.

I know that my brutal demands will impose on you great sacrifices, possibly renunciations, and certainly a great deal of fresh work—but I believe it's got to be.—

As for your fundamental warnings concerning the musical matter, I understand you entirely. What's more, you're quite right! But you forget that ever since *Intermezzo* I have been pursuing the goal you suggest with unflinching persistence, and that in the case of *Arabella* I shall try even more to leap over my own shadow. But for all that a German can never become an Italian—even Goethe and Mozart knew that!

Please put my mind at ease soon—if possible by a telegram—as to how you've received my last letter and whether you think we can reach agreement along the road I've set out on.

I am anxiously awaiting your news. With best regards, yours always very sincerely,

RICHARD STRAUSS

Rodaun, 1.8.(1928) evening

Dear Dr. Strauss,

Forgive me for not telegraphing sooner than yesterday. I was away for three days, then I found your letters but, you see, I had to think the matter over. And for the past four or five days we have had sultry oppressive Foehn weather which is most unpropitious to the imagination and makes the mind sluggish and incapable of creatively coherent thinking. It is not least this weather, especially aggravating as it is to me, which prevents me from giving final shape to the already fully thought-out scene between Matteo and Arabella which, with its blend of love and resignation, needs a particularly tender hand.

As for your new ideas and suggestions, even the mist of these *Foehn* days does not prevent me from seeing clearly enough that you are right on the main point and that the action must still be made to yield another twist, nor do I see in this any risk that the second act may become too long; while the culminating scene of Act III will gain further from such a complication. The *how* will be my preoccupation during the next few days, but once the goal is clear, the road to it is never far to seek. If not everything, quite a lot of what you propose already suggests this road; the trick is to make the characters emerge from these new complications still more living, but nowhere coarsened.

A visit to you for twenty-four hours could certainly be arranged shortly before August 20th. But I feel this exchange of letters gets us further than a conversation. Conversation easily tends to lead from one thing to another, one touches on too much and eventually becomes tired etc., impatient—while an exchange of ideas by letter always gives one, between receipt and despatch of a letter, the time to think everything over with care and to reduce it to essentials. There is, after all, no misunderstanding which would have to be voiced and solved; we understand each other perfectly.

I am closing my letter for today in view of increasing migraine. I have had all the relevant points typed out and as soon as the weather relieves me of this undue strain, I would like to see what is to prevent us from surpassing *Rosenkavalier* with this subject both in action and structure.

Very sincerely yours,

HOFMANNSTHAL

P.S. Of what you call the 'Marlitt novelette' aspect of the character of Mandryka, this great simplicity of outline in the manner of the fairy-tale or folk-song, I am quite aware and I am sure it is good—but this is not to deny that more action can, and perhaps ought to be given to this figure also.

(*Garmisch*) *2.8.1928*

My dear Friend,

Many thanks for your obliging telegram which has delighted and greatly reassured me. I shall wait therefore, and hope for a northerly wind!

Will it annoy or confuse you if, from my unsorted, sometimes more and sometimes less tasteful 'treasury of dramatic ideas', I hurl at you a few more rather questionable motives, on a hit-or-miss basis?

But I can't help myself: our Arabella is so far innocence personified and the man Mandryka as white as a lily. There must be conflicts, guilt on both sides—the theme of the bridegroom who, in spite of his

498

love for his bride, slips up just before the wedding is, as far as I am aware, fairly new.

How would this be: have the contractor (a broadly comic character) also appear in Act III with claims on Arabella? He has meanwhile received Arabella's letter from Elis[1] (Matteo: So that's the letter I'd been hoping for!) and Mandryka can reproach her at least for encouraging the contractor even while she was aware that he had asked Waldner for her hand.

And again, couldn't Fiaker-Milli also come chasing after Mandryka in Act III? With claims? So that Arabella, *seemingly* guilty in many respects but in fact the only one who is innocent, would have quite a goodish bit to forgive her dear Mandryka. For this kind of gesture—to shape it attractively and tastefully—you've got just the right delicate touch!

For what you lack—the thickening of the plot and riotously comical situations—I should like to inject you with a little Scribe and Sardou, at the risk of you berating me as an old-fashioned trashmonger!

A year ago I asked you for a grand cultural tableau à la *Meistersinger*. If I can't have that, then at least a little Scribe, Sardou, or even Lortzing in Hofmannsthal garb!

Don't be angry with me for wantonly goading you: but it has always been beneficial in the past—also when you did me the same service!

Best regards, yours,

RICHARD STRAUSS

Rodaun, 5.8.28

I am by no means annoyed by your letters and suggestions, *my dear Dr. Strauss*; they are on the contrary of real service to me, and it is after all perfectly true that from time to time I can do very well with an injection of Scribe and Sardou. I have, on the other hand, the gift— which these two never possessed—of kindling in the characters a breath of life. Sardou's plays have been summed up as 'life through movement' —and against this the naturalists have pitted their motto 'movement through life'. The true aim of course is to combine the two, as Shakespeare did and the Spaniards, Molière, and Lessing, too, in his few imperishable stage works. Now your new proposal to involve Mandryka and through him Arabella much more gravely than hitherto in

---

[1] A friend of Arabella's, mentioned in the original version of Act I.

the critical Matteo-Zdenka affair by making him jealous, is quite excellent, and the incidental gain is considerable, for in this way Mandryka ceases to be quite so guileless (but turns on occasion rather wild and savage, without however losing his essential character as a noble-minded and unsophisticated fellow). The idea that in Act III all turn out to be more guilty than the gravely incriminated Arabella, this evolves beautifully and rightly out of the whole action and the gain is, *in toto*, very great. Fiaker-Milli will come in as if naturally required by this phase of the action, and if you will just leave it to me, the second act will progress towards a turbulent curtain, by which time one is really afraid of Mandryka and an unhappy end until, after extreme suspense, everything is beautifully and happily resolved in the big *quid pro quo* of the third act.

For the detail now: how to extract all this from the given characters in a lively and natural manner? how to draw Adelaide and Waldner into this conflict effectively (without the need for such involved subsidiary devices as a flirtation of the Counts with the mother, since such a scene would be branded from the outset with the stigma of 'subsidiary scene' and makes the interest of the audience flag at once)? For all this you must give me a free hand, your confidence and *time*, time above all, well into the autumn, always my most propitious season. Every detail will have to flow naturally from the life of the characters, for only thus is the life-like, breathing quality kindled which has kept *Rosenkavalier* fresh for some twenty years now and will no doubt do so for another thirty to fifty. Over this piece I have rushed myself a little all along, for your sake. By the end of October I did not have anything; then the characters presented themselves to me and the atmosphere of the whole piece; right at the beginning of winter you wanted to be told the story; right at the outset of your Karlsbad stay you wished to have the finished first act before you—very well; but now, when it is to unfold itself to become a true *tableau*, now I must not be rushed any longer. Calculating reason may move at a trot, but the imagination gets footsore and is left behind; it will do no more than amble along.

Whether for instance the building contractor will fit into the whole scheme (as a rule it is not a good idea to introduce a new character in the third act and 'broadly comic' might at this stage easily look coarse and retarding), all that sort of thing must await the actual writing. The richest pattern results not from an accumulation of characters, but from showing the given characters in their manifold relations with each other and, as you rightly say, from squeezing everything possible out of the subject. In this respect you have helped me to leap somewhat over my own shadow, which is inclined to content itself with using the characters statically instead of exploiting their full potentialities in action—but now the worst is behind us, what was too soft is gaining strength, what was too lax is being tightened up and that which was always good, the structure, gains and does not lose.

Now, if you agree, we shall proceed as follows. Within the very next few days I shall write for you the scene between Arabella and Matteo; that completes the first act, and will, I hope, with the prospect of an increasingly animated action in the following acts, give pleasure.

And then I shall pick my very best days for the second (and third), so that the whole thing is really of one cast; the characters wholly natural at every stage and each twist of the action spontaneously and clearly arising out of the characters. Given all this, a tableau will in the end emerge by itself and perhaps even something of a picture of social history—at least as far as in me lies. *Rosenkavalier*, baldly told, is also no better than a puppet show, and the last act pretty thin, and yet the whole thing has a life of its own.

If another motif were to force itself upon you which emerges palpably from the subject, please let me know; I shall receive it as willingly and as gladly as I have received the earlier ones.

Yours,

HOFMANNSTHAL

But not too many new combinations, otherwise we shall have a room all cluttered up! Each motif must have space enough to unfold itself in terms of character, that is Shakespeare's wonderful secret.

If you dislike the fiddling gipsy at the end of Act III, I shall readily leave him out. But in the whole context the three figures as the personal suite of a rich gentleman from the Balkans are good: the dragoon, the gipsy and the Jew—and they will come in very useful in the wild finale of Act II.

I can't see for the life of me why the magic potions in *Helena* should now prevent me from introducing the presentation of as much as a glass of water. Nor do I think that I shall be able to find anything better and at the same time equally simple for the quiet lyrical close of Act III, neither in my imagination nor in any collection of Slav popular customs. For it must, after all, be something that can happen in the village and can be copied quite fittingly on the staircase of a hotel. If on the other hand one takes something more complicated, it may easily look forced, intentional and almost theatrical if staged by Arabella at midnight. Instead of any ceremony at this point, one could of course have the still outstanding engagement kiss. Yet this simple ceremony of carrying the filled glass down the stairs, has immense mimic advantages. A kiss she cannot *carry towards him*, she would simply have to walk up to him and give him the kiss; the other implies the most bridal gesture in its chastest form, and it can be followed by the kiss which thus gains solemnity, something that raises it out of the ordinary; from this final moment after such a lot of fracas I expect much.

Garmisch, 8.8.28

My dear Friend,

I am delighted that you have received my humble suggestions in such an obliging spirit and would ask only one thing of you: please take your time over it and don't even trouble to send me the Matteo-Arabella scene in Act I. I am already reconciled to not embarking on the job until the whole thing is absolutely ready.

The main thing is that the subject must be fully exploited and the best possible yield squeezed out of it. That requires time and leisure. For the moment I have written enough operas, and a rest will do my imagination good: I shall therefore wait till the autumn—I'll wait till Easter, I'll wait as long as you like.

As for my suggestions, which you have so kindly received—needless to say, you deal with them as you please!

The glass of water, if it is indeed a Slav ceremony, must of course remain. I'll even settle for the fiddling gipsy if it doesn't turn out too sentimental and operetta-like. On the other hand, I very much like the Galician half-Jew, a character I hadn't heard of before, to whom I'd like to allot a somewhat bigger part (for a tenor buffo). He might be used as a spy in the intrigue of Act II.

Permit me now to set out for you the following plan for Act II:

At the beginning no dance music: only the various entrances (without chorus, without Fiaker-Milli), only Waldner, Adelaide (possibly with Arabella's three Counts), Mandryka. Arabella's first encounter with Mandryka—of which I don't like Arabella's alarm and sudden anxiety to leave: it strikes me as a bit trivial.

Conversation Arabella-Mandryka, betrothal, as far as Arabella: 'Jetzt geben Sie mich eine Stunde frei', etc.—At this point I would start the waltz in the orchestra and let it run on (as at the end of Act II of *Fledermaus*), and into this continuous waltz I should now like to fit:

Arabella's leave-taking scene with the three Counts, the scene Matteo-Zdenka (overheard at first by the half-Jew?), and possibly a passing flirtation between Adelaide and one of the Counts—

all of these as separate ensembles, quintets, sextets, as in Act II of *Zar und Zimmermann* where negotiations go on at two separate tables—in short, something like:

Arabella with the three Counts—on the other side Mandryka with his three servants; or Arabella with the three Counts—on the other side Mandryka, Waldner, Adelaide. After this perhaps Matteo-Zdenka—and on the other side Mandryka with his three servants.

Next Mandryka's outburst of despair, at the same time frenzied climax of the ball, entrance of Fiaker-Milli amidst homage, now perhaps Mandryka's Slav song, equivocal, a blend of love, jealousy, desperate gaiety; exit Arabella with the whole ensemble, end of the waltz.

Mandryka left alone, desperate; Arabella's note, confirmation of her unfaithfulness—scene between Fiaker-Milli and Mandryka, abruptly cut off at its climax (kiss) by Adelaide and Waldner: 'Where's Arabella?' 'Gone? We must go home', the betrothal, the glass of water—sudden awakening of Mandryka: home! Arabella! Tragic end!

No more dancing! No noisy crowds! No ensemble! Wouldn't this be a better plan? This would also avoid any similarity with Act II of *Fledermaus*, quite apart from the fact that I should never hit on such a rousing waltz as that genius Johann of sacred memory.

The waltz as a climax in the middle of Act II definitely makes a better curve!

During this above-mentioned *continuous* waltz there could very easily be a perpetual coming and going of the different characters and groups at one side or the other, in the manner of Act II of Gounod's *Faust*, when in the garden scene Marguerite and Faust, Mephisto and Martha keep appearing and disappearing all the time. In such a continuous waltz, which can be elegiac at one moment (Arabella and the three Counts), passionate (Matteo and Zdenka), burlesque (Mandryka with his Jew), or swirling (Fiaker-Milli with the entire ball ensemble), any kind of conversation (no matter how motley) can easily be fitted in!

The act would open with a ceremonial beginning, turn tenderly amorous, in the middle the great waltz as the climax, then passion and despair, and an abrupt end as a thrilling transition to the development and denouements of Act III.

Would this shape suit you?

But now I'll definitely leave you in peace. All good wishes: I'll *wait* —and remain, yours very sincerely,

RICHARD STRAUSS

Rodaun, 11.8.28

Dear Dr. Strauss,

Here is the Arabella-Matteo scene.[1] With not inconsiderable effort, I have been able, I hope, to integrate the characters, the tone and style of the whole, and the required lyrical content. I believe the figure of Arabella is now firmly and clearly established; the contrast with this painful scene now puts the flirtation with the three Counts into the proper light, and the curtain, her prayer-like monologue as she writes the letter, makes quite a different impact. An important dramatic cue is gained for the scene in the second act when Zdenka brings the letter with the key; Matteo must long for that 'final' letter, because it will once more bring him kind words, and he must fear it even more, because it is likely to be the last farewell. Thus he shrinks from Zdenka, and she has to run after him and force the letter on him. This incident is so striking that Mandryka, who is no eavesdropper, finds himself intrigued by these strange goings-on and in stepping forward overhears the words: 'It is the key to Arabella's room.'

I hope this act is now in order, but I would very much like to have this confirmed by you. From the 17th onwards I shall be in Salzburg, Österreichischer Hof. I could, if it seems necessary, meet you somewhere half-way in Upper Bavaria for discussion, not on the 18th, but on the 19th. Otherwise we shall meet early in October, for the Munich *Helena*.[2] But please do not keep me waiting long for news.

Yours ever,

HOFMANNSTHAL

[1] Not used in the opera. Printed in Hofmannsthal's *Gesammelte Werke* (*Lustspiele IV*, pp. 440–44).

[2] The Munich première of *Die ägyptische Helena* took place on 8th October 1928.

My dear Friend,

The Arabella-Matteo scene, to hand yesterday, is very good! *Vivant sequentes!* With kindest regards, yours,

RICHARD STRAUSS

28th August till 10th September Pontresina (Hotel Saratz); 17th and 18th August in Munich (Jahreszeiten), leaving for Zermatt on the 19th.

Please discuss our *Arabella* with Reinhardt! And for God's sake he is not to revive that damned operetta with Marischka, but had better do classical tragedy jointly with the Burgtheater, comic opera with the Vienna Opera, and ballet at the Theater an der Wien. (My old plan!)

Rodaun, 13.8.28

Dear Dr. Strauss,

Thank you very much indeed for your kind, amiable letter. I find this detailed epistolary conversation about the scenario of the comic opera quite excellent, since in this way I am for once in touch with the wishes of the musician before I actually get down to work. Surely only the devil's own luck can stop this comic opera from turning out *better* than *Rosenkavalier*, more homogeneous in style and words and music, really fitting like a glove. Your line of development for Act II convinces me at first sight; these three parts: first a quiet conventional one, then the colourful spirited centre part in which the waltz carries all and connects all, and finally the sharply contrasting conclusion—you cannot direct my imagination into any more welcome channels—and during the propitious autumn months I shall get down to it with every goodwill and all my energy. If you don't wish to put pen to paper before you have the whole complete thing before you—very well; but I in turn do not wish to start on the second act (on which everything depends) until I am sure that the first as it now stands satisfies you in all essentials as an exposition. I am always easily convinced by your criticism and if you should want further changes, I shall enter into your ideas and make changes—but before I tackle the other acts, I want to have firm ground under my feet.

To give Jankel a little more elbow room will be a pleasure. But as for the notion that *he* should play the spy on Matteo and Zdenka, I have dropped that again on account of the all-too-obvious resemblance to the intriguers and their calling for Ochs in *Rosenkavalier* Act II. (Both scenes, moreover, occur at the same point, in the middle of the second act.) I would rather, therefore, have Mandryka himself overhear the conversation and then let him give orders to Jankel to keep an eye on Arabella, in case she should leave the ball. I can already foresee that there will be further good use for Jankel in Acts II and III.

Will you now add the new sheets to your copy and seek to define your reaction to the first act as a whole, so that you can approve it or, as the case may be, subject it to further criticism.

Sincerely yours,

HOFMANNSTHAL

After the 17th Salzburg, Österreichischer Hof.

Bad Aussee, 14.9.28

Dear Dr. Strauss,

If only you could look through the little window between the branches of an old apple-tree into my tiny room, I feel sure you would be rather touched by the sight of your faithful librettist, your recent letters spread out before him, turning over by the light of a desk lamp the libretto of *Zar und Zimmermann*. Some triteness notwithstanding, there is quite a lot to be learnt from it, as there is from every good stage work that was once alive and has remained so for decades.

The demands and requests for the second act formulated in your last letter have impressed themselves upon me, as they convinced me from the outset. This triple division, the conventional opening, the lengthy middle part entirely carried by the waltz and interspersed with many fluctuating incidents, the exciting and ominous close—all this is excellent and it is a real blessing to me to feel so immediately what the composer wants and needs. I like to think that, provided these wishes can be faithfully and happily fulfilled, the second act and the third ought to excel in dramatic execution any one act of *Rosenkavalier*.

Of details I should like to mention only one. That Arabella is taken aback at the sight of Mandryka, for fear of experiencing yet another disappointment with this very man—this whole feature strikes me as arising naturally out of the character of this young girl who has already arrived at a danger point, and I would give it up only with reluctance. Yet you call this feature 'a bit trivial'. That surprises me, and even on reconsidering it I remain surprised. Nor do I recall its having been used in any other well-known comedy, novel or libretto and thus perhaps trivialized on that account. Something of the kind however must have been in your mind. Please let me have a word about it.

I am most willing to give a little prominence in the second act to Jankel the Jew. Only not as the one who overhears the Matteo-Zdenka scene, because otherwise this eavesdropping on someone else's behalf once again right in the very middle of Act II would look like an unpleasant and unnecessary reminiscence of Valzacchi, and this is just the kind of thing the critics seize upon.

In reliance on your ever-ready indulgence I would like to use the Lortzing libretto as an excuse to take up again, and for the last time, certain highly tentative and amateurish ideas which I communicated to you in July. Then you replied: the one thing you cannot expect or demand is that a German should ever become an Italian; even Mozart was unable to do that. But Italian *versus* German—is that the true antithesis? There can be nothing more German, nothing more genuinely old-time German than Lortzing; and yet just here I meet again most strikingly the element from which—if *mutatis mutandis* it could somehow be revived—such an immense benefit might be gained, particularly for comic opera. How am I to find the right word for it? On reading one of these libretti, on recalling one or another of Lortzing's operas which I have heard, I feel, though a downright layman, how the whole character of this Peter, of van Bett, of Maria, lies in the voice and how the orchestra merely accompanies (and that is what happens, I imagine, also in the *Ariadne Vorspiel*). In *Rosenkavalier*, on the other hand, and even in *Intermezzo* (am I mistaken? am I wrong?) the life of the whole thing is centered on the orchestra and the voice is only woven into it, emerging sometimes and submerged again, but is never—unless my impressions deceive me—wholly sovereign, never *takes the lead*. (I am here speaking only of comic opera, for the style of *Helena* belongs somewhere else, and *Salome* and *Elektra* somewhere quite different again.)

To my mind it is not just a matter of Italian sweetness in the handling of the voice, not even of louder or less loud, of more or less polyphony; I mean a conscious decision on the part of the composer to entrust *the decisive role* to the voices, as it is done, for instance, in *Freischütz*.

I know very well what is meant by historical development in music. But then that leads straight to Pfitzner and Schreker; while the secret of individual creation lies in fact just in this: that the individual does undergo certain reversals, certain spirals of development such as we see in present-day trends in painting and architecture too. Enough and already too much! Forgive me! The outsider expresses everything crudely, as if it were possible to turn the vessel about by ninety degrees; the master knows how hard it is to alter course even very slightly against the current, and 'against the current' is only a pale metaphor for the inherent complexities and compulsions to which the creative artist is chained by his destiny. Therefore once again please forgive me!

Yours,

HOFMANNSTHAL

Nuremberg, 29th Sept. 1928

My dear Friend,

I have just arrived from two rehearsals in Munich.[1] *Helena* promises to be very beautiful there—the whole cast a very good lower-first class. Knappertsbusch is doing his stuff excellently. The decor seems to me very nice; except that I had to make some representations about Pasetti's costumes: they are partly too heavy, too genuinely Grecian, too many long cloth garments. Aethra in particular is a broad lady of medium height who looked impossible in that long garment. The three serving maids in Act II likewise walk about like nuns. Helen looked more like Brünnhilde. I hope Pasetti is going to consider my wishes, but since unfortunately I am going to Berlin tomorrow and won't be back in Munich till I arrive there straight for the première on 8th October it would be highly desirable if you could go to Munich as soon as possible, some time this week, to attend the daily rehearsals. The dress rehearsal is on 6th October.

I have drawn Pasetti's attention to your wish to lend the costumes a certain Parisian flavour and, above all, to have Aethra and the three serving maids wear short dresses. Only when she was rehearsing again in her own modern clothes did Aethra look good and move about naturally; I have therefore asked for her costume to be adapted to this modern style. I believe it is very important in the interests of the piece that it should have your personal supervision and advice. One other

[1] The Munich première of *Die ägyptische Helena* took place on 8th October 1928.

thing: the chief electrician and the producer will meet your wish and have *Helena* acted with the house lights half up. Naturally, the stage lighting will have to be adjusted accordingly, for which again your advice would be desirable.

So that the audience should not only have an opportunity to look into the libretto on the night, but should get used to the idea of arming themselves with copies for the performance, I hit on the idea of having several music lovers send a letter to the Editor of the *Neueste Nachrichten*, publicly putting this request to the theatre management. I sent for Dr. von Pander, the critic, and discussed the matter with him, and in the end he made the sound suggestion that it would be best if you yourself wrote a pleasant, possibly slightly humorous, article on those lines for the *Münchner Neueste Nachrichten*, perhaps under the headline 'The Blacked-Out Poet', on the evils of a totally darkened auditorium and with a *cri-de-cœur*: What's the use of the poet putting beautiful ideas into beautiful words if nobody reads them and if only part of them can be caught from the stage? That it is cheap and insulting to call the poet confused and obscure if one hasn't had a chance of acquainting oneself with his work. You could say: my honest composer takes immense pains to have my words clearly articulated and to make his orchestration as transparent as possible, but an opera just isn't a play, and with eyes and ears in an opera so fully engaged in many directions the poet may very easily get a raw deal. Hence his request: if anyone goes as far as to buy a ticket for the opera, couldn't he add another Mark for a copy of the libretto—so that afterwards his strictures on the poet will at least be confined to what he thinks justified and not just spring from ignorance of the work.

From Berlin[1] I hear very good news: in particular Maria Müller as Helen and Laubenthal as Menelaus promise to be very good. Tietjen is very proud of having solved all technical stage problems, and Schoder is fighting with energy and fanaticism, and it seems victoriously, against the opposition of obstinate producers.

Hope to see you in Munich. With best regards, yours always very sincerely,

RICHARD STRAUSS

Berlin address: Heerstrasse 100.

[1] The Berlin première took place on 5th October 1928.

Dear Dr. Strauss,

Back from Munich and stimulated by the delightful meetings with you and with our joint work, I immediately tackled the second act of *Arabella* and have written down the proposal scene with delight and zest, and with as much talent as I can muster. That accomplished, I am now turning all my attention and imagination to the writing of the middle part, to those numerous alternating encounters in twos, in threes and in fours, which will—always adhering to your clear and ingenious suggestions—be woven more or less into the continuous waltz all through, and which must serve the progress of the story, must help to establish the characters in action, and must produce a certain scintillating atmosphere, broadly comic now and then, and then again sentimental. It has, for instance, become possible to introduce into this sketch quite spontaneously several moments of 'song' for Adelaide which help to bring out this part gracefully as that of a woman still young and loving who all-too-suddenly finds herself in the position of mother-in-law, but who can also still easily attract admirers (like that Count Dominik); and this will help to make the part palatable to a singer like Mme Olszewska. All this, with so little room for development, requires not only goodwill and a happy frame of mind, but also a certain amount of luck. Therefore do think of me with special regard during these days! I feel that this act offers much more by way of steadily moving action and mounting suspense than the corresponding act of *Rosenkavalier*.

Your wife has raised the question in how far one is entitled to expect something of a popular success with a comic opera of this kind. That sort of question cannot of course be answered with any certainty. I cannot give any guarantee of success and you have never asked me for any such thing, least of all in the case of *Rosenkavalier* where you wrote: 'Naturally, it will be said that this is *not* the "long-awaited" German comic opera!' But what one can do at any rate is to try and increase the chances of popular success and that has been done in this case, I believe, through choice of subject, milieu and characters. Anything mythical or heroical makes a modern audience uneasy, anything sombre and grand (which, moreover, tends to conjure up associations with the *Ring*) terrifies them to the marrow of their bones; but give them a hotel lounge, a ballroom, betrothal, officers, cabbies, tradesmen and waiters, and they know where they are.

And then we need not forget altogether the example of our own, by no means short-lived and highly successful work. If for almost twenty years I have summoned up sufficient intelligence and strength of character not to desire any repetition of this work, and have patiently waited for a similar inspiration (with a very dissimilar plot), then I do feel I am entitled now to count on a little confidence from you (and from those closest to you). Just consider at this point one plain fact. By now the repertory contains only *few* light-hearted works, and that accounts for the immense success with the public of the libretto of a light opera musically so weak as *Jonny*.[1] The whole of Lortzing, Boieldieu, Auber, Cherubini, Donizetti is faded, after all, and the repertory consists almost exclusively of heavy, solemn stuff, most of it with a sombre ending.

What prevented *Intermezzo* from achieving popular success can also, I think, be attributed to the libretto—for it is after all the libretto which settles the matter *on the stage*. *Intermezzo* offers a character sketch rather than a plot; such action as there is, the episode with the young Baron, is at once deprived of its effect and suspense by the fact that the librettist has trivialized this young man's character. From the very outset one feels that this figure is to be taken as merely episodic; thus the dramatic effect it was to achieve is lost. One feels no anxiety for the woman; how could a woman with so much drive be seriously threatened by so shadowy a fellow; not a soul in the whole theatre feels any alarm on her behalf, nobody is seriously worried for the husband, we are not swept away by these happenings and so they remain for us a picture, a symphony! To say this is not to imply any scepticism towards this animated musical comedy which is so rich in characters and contrasts.

And so Good-night! Sincerely yours,

HOFMANNSTHAL

Garmisch, 1st November 1928

My dear Friend Hofmannsthal,

Many thanks for the glad tidings that you've got down to Act II with zest: I'm most eager to see how it turns out.

I think you are still judging *Intermezzo* a little unfairly. The fact that the critics and the public don't understand what it is meant to be and what it is ought not to speak against it in our eyes. Of course it has little 'action'; on the contrary, the action is trivialized from the outset (as you

---

[1] *Jonny spielt auf* by Ernst Křenek.

quite rightly observe of the figure of the Baron) and treated ironically. But then, what are these so-called dramatic plots? They've remained the same for two thousand years: murder and destruction, the intrigue of mean minds against the hero, betrothal after overcoming obstacles, or separation—surely all this is not very interesting and has, moreover, been seen Heaven knows how many times before. On the other hand— as Goethe said when he advised everybody to write their memoirs— each individual is unique in his way and will never occur again. And that is why I consider an attractive and consistent character portrait as in *Intermezzo* more interesting than any so-called plot. Some day per- haps some people with more highly developed stage sense will share my taste and appreciate *Intermezzo* more than today's cinema generation.

And this brings me to the slight anxiety that I still feel over *Arabella*: the characters are not interesting, they're all a bit like the old-fashioned theatre, and so far I've been unable (spoiled as I am by my Christine and also by Helen) to warm to any of them in particular. For the same reason I still haven't been able to make a start with the music and shall have to wait till the whole thing lies finished before me if I am to get into that first act. I therefore wish you much creative vigour and hope that perhaps there'll be something beautiful for me to hear around Christmas in Vienna.

The Hamburg performance of *Helena* was likewise excellent, con- ducted with much verve by Pollak, produced by L. Sachse with great skill and with conscientiousness *vis-à-vis* the poet, had a tumultuous success and only in part the usual silly press. One of these otherwise good-natured kaffirs: (. . .) assured me, after sympathizing with me over the *Helena* text which 'weighs down my music', that in spite of everything he now (after ten years) understands the libretto of *Frau ohne Schatten*! *Ecco*!

In Munich too, full houses so far!

With best regards from us to you all, yours,

RICHARD STRAUSS

My dear Friend, *Garmisch, 7.11.28*

After a long interval I've had a good look again at the first act of *Arabella*, and have even tried to compose some of the beginning—but the thing doesn't even begin to come to music and, to be perfectly frank, the

512

characters don't interest me in the least: neither the Croatian, that wealthy and noble companion piece to the poor and dissolute Ochs, nor above all the principal character Arabella who does not experience the slightest psychological conflict throughout the three acts. Consider it quite dispassionately: in the first act, coolly smiling, she dismisses one admirer whom she cannot marry because he lacks money; she has a last flirtation with the three Counts who, in their turn, cannot marry her; she decides to marry a building contractor whom we don't even know and who interests us even less—and then immediately in Act II— 'at first sight'—she turns to the much wealthier and certainly more presentable Mandryka. And this, properly speaking, is the end of the plot proper. All that follows is a rather forcible tie-up with a subsidiary plot (Zdenka-Matteo) which is the only real conflict of the evening and which leaves the sister Zdenka the only character in the play of more than moderate interest.

The parents are of little interest; Mandryka with his hangers-on is going to be written off as an inversion of Ochs with his satellites; the three Counts, the cabbies' ball, all is weaker and more conventional than in *Rosenkavalier* unless you yet succeed in turning Arabella into a really interesting figure like our dear Marschallin who, when all's said and done, carries *Rosenkavalier*—even perhaps at the cost of Act III having a *tragic* ending. Now don't get alarmed! Yes indeed, why not tragic, in whichever form you like, a simple renunciation on her part or on his. As it stands today the end is also rather flat—Matteo comforts himself with the sister, everybody gives their tearful blessings and nobody sees anything extraordinary in it; the relationship Arabella-Mandryka, after quite a short-lived cloud which not even a single soul in the audience will regard as serious, is restored to where it was at the beginning of Act II—this lack of consistency of a conflict cannot be offset even by the loveliest poetical raspberry syrup which poet and musician may yet pour into that 'glass of water'. As you see, I am trying to learn a little arrogance and malice from the gentlemen who criticized *Helena*, although I flatter myself (since the eyes of love see more clearly still than the eyes of hatred and envy) that in my criticism of *Arabella* I am not as wide of the mark as the newspapers were in connection with the *Helena* libretto, which I shall always defend to my last drop of blood and which I simply won't allow to be criticized at all: for it is a downright masterpiece! The last Sunday performance in Munich was totally sold out.

Now don't be angry with me: consider my scruples and pangs of conscience sympathetically (I can tell exactly when I have to force myself to a new subject, when the characters don't 'suit' me and fail to assume melodic shape in me)—perhaps you will still hit on some intensification of the dramatic content. After all, it doesn't have to be a comedy, especially as by now it doesn't really contain anything funny or witty and everything tends to gravitate towards tragi-comedy. Please reflect carefully whether the whole subject (in spite of the cabbies' ball) is not really tragic. How would it be if that temperamental Mandryka, the moment Arabella is presented to him as unfaithful were to shoot himself and if Arabella then offered the 'glass of water' to the dying man? What about it? What about it? It doesn't have to be a 'comic opera'!

Many kind regards, yours ever,

RICHARD STRAUSS

Bad Aussee, 16.11.28

My dear Friend,

Your letter of 7th November reached me with a little delay, for I was in Vienna for two days and after that I continued at once and with very great zest writing the third act without even looking at the mail, so that quite intentionally I read your letter only yesterday.

One must look at the matter quite soberly. I have written the second and the third act (practically) with great pleasure and believe that much, indeed even most of what you hint at in the words: 'it does not after all have to be funny', 'it may, if need be, come close to tragi-comedy' and so on, is actually given effect there, simply because it is inherent in the subject. Now, however, please do not give yourself any further concern over the first act, in which there will undoubtedly have to be certain changes, such as for instance Arabella's attitude during her meeting with Matteo, which is somewhat misleading. From the beginning of December onwards I shall be in Vienna and will expect you. Then we shall read Acts II and III together and make our decision quite soberly.

The few, but widely different people to whom I have shown the MS find it excellent, and I myself am after all old and sceptical enough to be able to distinguish what people say out of politeness from what has really amused and interested them, but all this is of secondary importance. Nor does it matter in the last resort that I fail altogether to see the slightest resemblance between the alarming and tense end of the second act and *Fledermaus*, or between the very virile and awe-inspiring Mandryka and the Falstaffian Ochs. In short, nothing matters except the one thing on which this whole collaboration is based: your reaction to the libretto. On this point we shall have to come to a very sober and clear decision after you have heard the whole thing, for sober clarity and not muddle-headedness is the true climate of artistic creation.

Most sincerely yours,

HOFMANNSTHAL

If a protracted illness of Mme Schenker's has caused, as I assume, the prolonged gap at Vienna, a press notice to that effect should be issued to scotch wrong notions among the public.

Garmisch, 19.11.28

My dear Friend,

I have today received your letter of the 16th and will do as you wish. From 2nd to 20th December I shall be in Berlin W., Rauchstrasse 16, c/o Frau Geheimrat Deutsch, and shall be conducting, among other things, *Rosenkavalier, Elektra, Frau ohne Schatten, Helena*.

On 1st December I shall be in Dresden for the 19th (gala) performance of *Helena*. Tietjen reports from Berlin also 'increasing box-office returns for *Helena*'. It seems therefore that even the Berlin critics couldn't kill the piece. As a verse for the album of those fine gentlemen I have found the following epigram by good old Reinhold Lenz:

About the *obscurities* in Klopstock and others!
> *Schmecker(!)*: Ich bitte, gebt mir Licht,
> Herr ich versteh Euch nicht.
> *Reply*: Sobald *Ihr* mich versteht,
> Herr, bin ich ein schlechter Poet.

A Hamburg critic commiserated with me for having my 'marvellous music' weighed down by your 'incomprehensible text'. When I retorted that surely *Helena* was easier to understand than *Frau ohne Schatten*, he replied: '*Oh, but I understand* Frau ohne Schatten *quite well now!*'

Well, I hope he doesn't need ten years for *Helena*!

It takes a lot of patience to be a serious German author! About the gap in the Vienna performances of *Helena* I was on to Schneiderhan a fortnight ago and have now written again to Karpath along your lines. (. . .)

I'll be back in Vienna then about 25th December and am looking forward to enjoyable co-operation with you.

Yours always very sincerely,

RICHARD STRAUSS

(Hofmannsthal to Strauss; from a copy which lacks address and signature)

(*Bad Aussee*) *19.11.1928*

A few days ago I looked at the last Vienna box office accounts. They include three *Helena* nights. Receipts for one of them were very poor, only 4,500. There must be some reason for this. The other two takings are quite good, about 8,000, but still fall considerably short of two *Rosenkavalier* performances included in the same accounts and even (which surprises me) of a performance of *Ariadne*. That speaks for itself: after the enormous success of the June performances there can be only one unimpeachable explanation: the production, such as it has now turned out to be, with a tenor who has no reputation in Vienna and is now on loan from Leipzig, with a mediocre utility Helen and with a conductor who (whatever pains he may take over his job) is the least appreciated of all, well it makes an altogether lack-lustre production. And yet in Vienna the 'how' is at least as important as the 'what'. Even *Rosenkavalier* could have been killed in the beginning with such singers. All our works consolidate their position in due course, but this is all the more reason why at the start our policy should be one of extreme caution. I assume Schalk was determined to escape at any price the odium of having failed to put on *Helena* over a prolonged period. But it would have been a thousand times wiser to do exactly that, with your consent; to take it off, if need be, for four months and to announce in advance a resumption or continuance of the performances at a definite date with the cast it deserves. At a theatre which relies on runs such a thing would be the end, but at a repertory theatre, at a great opera house, by no means. Only one thing can undo us there, and that is if it gets about that the performance of the opera is uninspired.

(No signature)

Dear Dr. Strauss,

Enclosed some lines from a very intelligent person. Wassermann's judgment, too, was quite as enthusiastically positive as Werfel's at the time, and he intended to put it on paper in some form, but I stopped him from doing this, since all this sort of thing is irrelevant and the only person competent to judge the libretto is he who has to set it to music. Still, I am glad to have heard something pleasant about it, because I was becoming quite unsure whether I had not perhaps lost all self-criticism.

Getting your letter at that particular moment, right in the middle of my work, was really a little hard, even if one has entirely accepted your excellent motto: 'Immune to offence in matters of art.' Yet, on thinking it over again and on realizing that under so jaundiced an eye no story would stand any chance of passing muster (not even the *Rosenkavalier* libretto: the one engaging character, the Marschallin, disappears for an act and a half and is only dragged in with difficulty at the end; the buffo a garrulous and repulsive fellow; the third act most artificially tacked on to the second by means of that letter; the opening of the third act well below the general level, lapsing towards operetta and so on)—I cannot help wondering whether, wholly against your will, indeed quite subconsciously, something may not have happened which sometimes occurs also in marriage after fifteen years or so and which leaves both partners entirely helpless: I mean a getting tired and cool, so that suddenly my whole palette, my way of drawing characters and the kind of characters I draw, in short my—obviously limited—individual characteristics which, over so long a period, proved attractive and so to speak complementary to you, have suddenly become unpalatable and uninteresting. Such a phenomenon, too, one would have to face quite soberly and calmly and act on, but not of course before you know this new work as a whole, that is after December 25. Otherwise, if the consistency and animation of the whole piece, the completeness of the characters appeals to you, as it appeals to others, if therefore we have something firm to build on, in that case I would endeavour to carry out several, even fairly far-reaching changes in the expositional act, of which I shall now mention a few, though not all. Mandryka, whom I consider one of my best and most original characters, has really no resemblance to Ochs, none whatever. But so as to avoid even all superficial analogy, I would get rid of his retinue and leave him with only a single valet. I would give more sparkle to the entrance of the three Counts by a little ceremony (which, however, still remains to be found), a sort of short *entrée de ballet*. The triad of Counts definitely must be retained, for that is the only way of symbolizing that Arabella has given herself up to 'flirtation' in general, without any serious implications. But I might conceivably in the first as well as in the second act (at the leave-taking) throw only one of the Counts into relief, and treat the other two as mere subsidiary parts. That would make *the one* into a stronger figure and give greater psychological interest to Arabella's attitude towards him. Still further alterations might prove possible, but if I am to raise the right spirits and impulse to make them (which is the *sine qua non*), you would have to arrive at, and express, a positive attitude towards the whole work. And that is not after all, something which depends *in any way whatever* on your goodwill.

Very sincerely yours,

HOFMANNSTHAL

Bad Aussee, 19.11.(1928)

Please allow me to dictate to my wife a few words about *Helena* as postscript. Your loyal attitude wherever criticism assails my share [in our works] in a particularly silly fashion always moves me deeply and I am glad that you have found the pretty little lines by R. Lenz to cheer you. There is something very peculiar about German intellectualism. Everything that rises above the ordinary has always had to face heavy odds in this allegedly most intellectual of countries (a description which is accurate enough in other respects). There is a book *Goethe and his Contemporaries* which is positively appalling and as late as thirty years after Goethe's death a famous professor of aesthetics, Friedrich Theodor Vischer, concocted a bulky pamphlet, entitled *Faust Part III* which maintains that the second part of Goethe's poem is a jumble of incomprehensible rubbish. Therefore let us forget about these 'mediators between creative artists and the public'. I do not doubt that *Helena* will firmly establish itself in the theatre in spite of these scribblers, just as *Ariadne* has done, but more quickly. True, to have written decent stuff over many years and not just to have been born last year so as to produce now some long-awaited world-shaking novelty—this discredits one with the critics, but with the public at large one enjoys immense credit on that very account (. . .)

My dear Friend,

I should be very sorry if my criticism were to mar your pleasure in your fine work! That isn't the intention at all. But I believe that I *must* tell you everything that passes through my mind. But since I don't know Acts II and III the figure of Arabella still seems to me a little insipid and devoid of conflict, and more like a character from a novel than from a play!

But as I said: I'll wait—hopefully. Of the other thing that you fear I am not so far conscious at all.

Reports from Stettin, Lübeck, Nuremberg, Magdeburg speak of very gratifying successes of *Helena*. On Tuesday next I'm conducting it in Nuremberg.

You're quite right about Vienna. Neither Schwarz nor Leuer, who is utterly unpopular in Vienna, is possible in the long run.

I wrote off to Schalk immediately (informing Schneiderhan at the same time) and asked him to give *Helena* a rest, with convincing explanation to the press, until such time as a first-rate cast can be found. You know that Mme Lehmann has perfidiously let me down; the other Helen *du premier ordre* is singing in America; that leaves only Mme Schenker who won't dare tackle the part just yet.

A hopeless business!

> With kindest regards, yours very sincerely,

> RICHARD STRAUSS

I am just reading Richard Wagner's *Oper und Drama* again: a marvellous book, as topical as it was eighty years ago, and still as misunderstood and unknown!

But for the likes of us a consolation and an encouragement; please re-read it!

Bad Aussee, 23.11.28

Dear Dr. Strauss,

Forgive me if, having written already a great deal today, I dictate to my wife a short answer to your kind letter, in which I may be able to give you information of practical value. As chance will have it I have met someone, a person belonging to an entirely different milieu but connected with Mme Lehmann, and in this round-about way I have heard something which is probably the true explanation of Lehmann's attitude and why she is frightened of so beautiful and inviting a part. It relates to certain real or imaginary risks in the vocalization which make her fear for her voice which is indeed at present perhaps the most beautiful and least strained in Europe. She is said to have in mind a few, not many passages that could be dealt with by what is called 'rephrasing'. To ask you to do that, however, requires too much courage and for this reason it is said she prefers to refuse the part outright.

I pass this on to you for what it is worth. For the time being the line you have taken is the only dignified and correct one; in the long run, however, her singing would be the only effective way to keep this beautiful opera going. You will readily understand how very much this must mean to me. This is, after all, the city where I live and where these works, by regular, enjoyable performances, give me so much happiness and ever-renewed relaxation. The successful performances in German cities and abroad are by comparison no good to me. *Au revoir*, with the most sincere good wishes from your faithful,

HOFMANNSTHAL

Rodaun, 28.11.28

Dear Dr. Strauss,

After an hour and a half's conversation with Alwin, who is really a very good fellow, I recognize that I have taken the wrong attitude over the *Helena* business at Vienna and must correct what I said. My indiscreet information concerning Mme Lehmann was obviously inaccurate; the point is not a few high notes or anything like that; the reason why she does not want to sing the part is resentment over Jeritza. For three weeks Alwin has exerted all his great tenacity (to the point of self-abasement, as he himself says) in an all-out effort to win her over. Some personal influence, too, is apparently being brought to bear on her (a very self-willed singing teacher who is just studying Isolde with her); in short there is obviously no hope, I would not say for ever, but in any case for the immediate future; and what matters to us is exactly the right short-term policy, since after April Mme Jeritza will presumably sing the part a few times and from the autumn onwards Mme Schenker and Graarud, with Mme Gerhardt as Aethra, will be available, and that will be a real cast.

It looks impossible to bring out Schenker in this part before the autumn. She is not very strong and still a beginner. Last autumn she studied Iphigenia, after that another part I cannot recall, and now, at Schalk's suggestion, she is in the middle of studying Octavian. Her strength is obviously limited, her nervous resistance also; if one drives her, she escapes into illness and then we are worse off than ever.

That leaves the possibility of keeping the opera off the bill, off the bill throughout all the months of your Vienna engagement right down to April! After my conversation with Alwin I have given this gap an hour's hard thought and it strikes me—given the kind of public we have nowadays—as nothing short of murder of a wholly living and lively creature. That *one* really poor house we had was a Monday, too soon after the previous performance, and after that there was another performance with almost 3,000 and it must be admitted that (Alwin quoted the figures) in its first year, *Rosenkavalier* did not have very good box offices either. Now Alwin's proposal is as follows: he will *not conduct this opera any more at all*. Then you are to conduct at least two performances. One with Vera Schwarz, Schubert and Mme Schenker, since her Aethra has had very good notices; then another with Vera Schwarz, Schubert and Mme Gerhardt to introduce this new Aethra. But at least these two performances; if to very good houses (as seems to me probable) then one or two more. After that comes Mme Jeritza, and that makes about eight performances for this opera during the present season—then comes the announcement of the resumption in the autumn.

This seems to me no more than *right*. In my last letter, starting from false premises, I took a different view and that I withdraw now. I put this forward in all modesty and merely as a suggestion, but one arrived at after conscientious consideration.

Even the fact that there will be no performance in December and none until your return ought to be explained in the press.

Very sincerely yours,

HOFMANNSTHAL

Salzburg, 4.12.(1928) (tomorrow back at Rodaun)

My dear Friend,

I have had a long talk with Schalk and feel it would be best to leave it at what he suggests and what you have sanctioned by telegram, even if

521

it does not wholly coincide with my proposals. That means *one Helena* performance without you early in December, the next one on December 30 under your baton with Schubert whose type of voice (after the recent *Tristan*) Schalk described as—in the circumstances—very appropriate. As an actor he is certainly very good.

What you wanted has now happened and Schalk is no longer Director. The very brusque manner which Schneiderhan saw fit to adopt in this occasion must go as much against your grain as against mine, simply out of a sense of solidarity among artists against the excesses of officials. What matters now above all is that you should be proved right and not I (I should vastly prefer to have been mistaken!) and that the new era will turn out better and not worse—for this admirable institution and for our works.

Sincerely yours,

HOFMANNSTHAL

Rodaun, 24.12.28

Dear Dr. Strauss,

Let me wish you and the various generations of your family a happy Christmas. I hope you are satisfied with the final solution of the Opera affair; it convinces me more than the earlier one, for this man[1] has had to deal with the theatre all his life, while the other one always struck me as interested not in the theatre, but only in his own person. May I urge you now at once (i.e. to be effective already at the performance on December 30th) to send *one word* to Schalk, by word of mouth, by telephone or as you wish, to see to it that the house-lights are a quarter up so that one can still read the libretto, as in Munich and Berlin. This opera cannot possibly make a real impression so long as nobody has any idea what is being said on the stage. With such a handicap from the outset the *Ring* itself would never have been understood and would never have become popular. Even a librettist cannot function under *impossible* conditions.

Oertel writes that in his view the opera is gradually beginning to gain 'a firm foothold' on the German stage. It looks as if the public needed four to six weeks in every city to shake off the humbug drummed into them by the critics and to form their own judgment. But in this

[1] Clemens Krauss.

process one must help them and that can be done by enabling them to follow the action in the libretto.

I shall be at Rodaun on 25th and 26th where my wife's family will be our guests, especially on the 26th. From the 27th to the 29th I expect to be in town. (I cannot travel backwards and forwards too much, because I have no chauffeur in the winter.)

The comic opera I have not touched since it was finished, but I have repeatedly thought about it. If we were to find ourselves in agreement over Acts II and III, one might consider making further substantial changes in Act I, perhaps even in the *attitude* of Arabella. I would concentrate the *three* Counts into one in the first act as well as in the leave-taking scene, for that makes this single figure more significant and Arabella's attitude towards him more interesting. I do, however, intend to keep that whole triad of noble admirers on the stage, because in this case three are less than one—because three admirers compromise her less than one serious one. What I shall do is to make two of them merely shadows, mute or almost so, and only one (Elemer) a real lover.

Yet all this is of secondary importance and what matters first of all is the piece as a whole. I should very much like to come to you and read you the two acts one afternoon when you are not conducting in the evening.

Always sincerely yours,

HOFMANNSTHAL

Wien III, Jacquingasse 10 (December 1928)

My dear Friend,

Many thanks for your kind wishes which we reciprocate most warmly.

Provided you are in town till Saturday my wife and I would be very pleased if you could have lunch with us on Saturday, 29th, 1.30 p.m. Before or afterwards I would then ask you to read *Arabella* to me: I am, of course, most anxious to hear it.

Please confirm briefly: Telephone U 18398.

With kindest regards, yours

RICHARD STRAUSS

1929

Dear Dr. Strauss,   *Rodaun, 1.1.1929, evening*

At the outset of this new year I am really delighted to know that you
liked the two acts and to find that I was not mistaken in my subject.
I shall do my utmost to make the first act—as far as one can with an
expositional act—no less brisk and light than the two subsequent ones.

Unfortunately I failed to ask you the other day whether you have
already been able to arrange the half-lighting in the theatre for *Helena*!
I definitely count on that, for it just won't do without.

Very sincerely yours,

HOFMANNSTHAL

My dear Friend,   *Rodaun, 27.1.1929*

Please do me the following personal favour. Will you write on a
visiting card or a small slip of paper a few words to the Munich picture
dealer Böhler introducing Sebastian Isepp, painter, whom you can
describe as a good friend of your friend H.v.H. Isepp (a painter and an
excellent picture restorer) is in fact a dear friend of mine. The matter
relates to a certain credit balance which I have in the German art trade
arising out of some earlier transaction; I have asked Isepp, who is going
to Munich, to look and see whether B(öhler's) might have something
suitable. I thank you in advance.

Now I shall say goodbye to you for a few weeks, and wish you and
all your family health and happiness. I hope to return with (*inter alia*)
the new first act.

What a charming Zdenka Mme Schenker-Angerer leads one to
expect after her performance the other day!

Yours in old friendship,

HOFMANNSTHAL

Munich, Hotel Vier Jahreszeiten, Monday, 25th March 29

Dear Dr. Strauss,

I hope to return to Vienna within a few days. But my hope that I
might be able to bring you the new version of the first act has, alas, not

materialized. This time of year (February/March) is never very good for me; this year I started by dragging a kind of gastric influenza around with me for weeks, and then I was in bed here with a slight bronchitis and only got rid of my temperature yesterday.

I know exactly what the first act ought to be like to serve as an attractive exposition for Acts II and III which you have now seen; I also know how it must be shaped so as to lend itself readily to composition. Therefore you may set your mind at rest about this.

In your suggestions and conversations with me you have touched upon several heroic-mythical subjects; the Semiramis myth, I remember, and also the story of the Danaides who murder their husbands, with the exception of one who saves hers. These are all magnificent subjects but, my dear friend, I doubt whether today I could find in myself the right key for such a thing; indeed I am almost completely convinced I could not. In my case all these questions are subject to some law which I can neither wholly understand nor escape. I made my *debut* with verse drama and have gone over entirely to prose, whether I wanted to or not. The tone and style of what I might be able to write for music have come to me, as a kind of modest inspiration, from one work to the next. The present half-serious, half-gay piece was the latest such inspiration. If I had to imagine anything new beyond that, however vaguely, it would most likely be something with few words and an unusual plot. A psychological framework and altogether modern—the sort of thing the theatre, too, seems to demand. For the high-flown tone and for the manner in which our opera singers produce the heroic stuff (where obviously the style of the *Ring* holds impregnable sway) I have neither the inclination nor the courage. Perhaps someone younger can do it!

In friendship yours,

HOFMANNSTHAL

Rodaun, 7th May 1929

My dear friend,

I am very glad to learn from your son that you are beginning to feel better. I, too, am on the point of regaining my strength, after two-and-a-half truly miserable months. Over this comic opera we have got ourselves into an awkward spot for the first time in our lives. You see, it might be true that at the outset I get enamoured with a subject and that this deceives and blinds me to its weaknesses, but such an error cannot persist throughout two whole years with its numerous critical and dispirited moods. I remain firm: this new subject contains lively and lovable figures full of contrasts (and in this respect does not fall short of *Rosenkavalier*) and it knits these figures together in an action which is unexpected from turn to turn, exciting right up to the end and far superior, in this, to the earlier work. I am, moreover, inclined to believe that when I read you Acts II and III last winter, your response was quite positive and that the acts moved you. (Always assuming a successful transformation of Act I.) In the meantime, however, a cooler attitude has come to prevail with you again. I ask myself whether once again the idea of the effect, on others and on the public, may have entered into it. (Or is it perhaps that someone, anyone, has expressed negative comment to you?) There is always something tricky about these outside judgments. I implore that handful of people to whom I have shown the MS. to tell me the truth and tell them what matters is the truth and not politeness, and yet all seem genuinely enchanted.

And who is competent to judge? As soon as Act I is done, I shall read it to Reinhardt, but however firm my faith in his judgment on spoken drama, I am not so sure over a libretto.

Recently I told Arthur Schnitzler that I might shortly ask him for his opinion on this piece of work. His answer was: 'My dear friend, in these things one cannot be too careful. Years ago when you read *Rosenkavalier* to me, I did not care for the third act at all. I thoroughly disliked this lapse into farce. I would unquestionably have advised the composer against this work, until the final act were wholly redone, and by doing so I might have spoilt all Strauss's and your pleasure in the work which I have now enjoyed twelve or fifteen times!' And as a matter of fact it is you alone who must take the blame for that 'lapse into farce'. You wrote to me incessantly, letter after letter, saying that there was nothing in it to make one laugh, that in a comic opera one ought to laugh and so on, and yet I believe to this day that the third act without this trend would have become far more beautiful still. *Ergo*: One can't tell about anything.

In the rewriting of Act I I have now done everything goodwill, reason and thought can do. The whole piece is a tidy sunny flower bed, but rain is needed now so that the seeds can germinate. What is still left to be done can be done in ten days, but days which bring with them a productive atmosphere, such as came to my aid last autumn for Acts II and III. Therefore I am grateful to you indeed for not setting me any time limit—yet the mere thought that you are waiting preys somewhat on my mind. If only I knew you supplied with interim work of some kind! Then I would not fail to avail myself of the first *Föhn* wind to launch our little craft, moored as it is at the quayside. But the actual task you have set me, to establish the central figure in action and to throw her into stronger relief so that subsequent events should gain a grip on our hearts, this requires inspiration to dovetail the various themes in Act I. All the rest can do with fewer words. You would rather, I gather, cut the flirtation between the mother and Dominik. That I shall do with pleasure![1] Your letters of last summer seemed to ask for something of this kind and there was certainly nothing impossible about it, since the woman is still young; but I willingly give it up.

At this stage of my life I cannot hold out to you or to myself any prospect for a new subject of a somewhat heroic character; I would not be able to strike the key of erotic transport which such a theme demands if it is to be suitable for an opera. And the public too—it is a mysterious thing like all changes in the spirit of the time—has lost the capacity for taking it.

Next Monday I am going to Florence for twelve or fourteen days only and shall make excursions from there. Since that climate suits me very well, I expect much from it, not least for our purpose. By the beginning of June I shall be back here again. I hope by that time you will have fully recovered.

Mme (Schenker-)Angerer as Octavian was really quite enchanting and will improve still further with every performance. Taken as a whole (singing, acting, appearance) this is certainly the first wholly satisfactory performer for the part the opera has ever had. Surely it would be mad to take not her, but some indifferent utility singer like S(chwarz) (whose value, *qua* utility, I do appreciate) to Salzburg, where so many foreigners (and people from the provinces) have their first chance of hearing as perfect a performance as is possible! Letters always reach me *via* Rodaun.

Always sincerely yours,

HOFMANNSTHAL

[1] Some part of this was nonetheless preserved in the musical score.

My dear Friend,

Paul Bekker cables me from Wiesbaden: enthusiastic reception of *Helena*.

Of course Schenker-Angerer should sing in Salzburg: it doesn't depend on me, however. I think Wallerstein has already got his eye on the trio Lehmann, Schenker, Kern.

My health is getting better daily: I'm staying here for another fortnight, then *via* Venice (25th to 27th May, Hotel Britannia) to Aachen and Berlin (1st to 12th June). Then Karlsbad. I shan't therefore get back to Garmisch and to my work before 5th July. So you've got plenty of time for the first act. And if it takes even longer I'll still wait patiently.

A break will do me good, too.

You are quite right: operatic texts can only be judged by the person who's got to set them to music. So don't go about asking any more people but write your poetry! Besides, it was your idea that in this instance I should ask others about *Arabella*. In the past I never asked anybody but simply put to music whatever appealed to me. The public has always been a matter of indifference to me. And a good thing too!

By the way, who's the author of that incredible article in the *Wiener Journal* the other day: Sketch for *Arabella*? Can't you forbid those people to write about *Arabella* before it is even ready?

Have a good rest in Florence and may your work prosper. Could a little more lyricism be fitted into *Arabella*? The *aria*, after all, is the soul of opera. And there's a marked lack of that. *Separate numbers with recitatives in between*. That's what opera was, is and remains. In Act I a great contemplative solo scene for Arabella! I've mentioned this before in a letter.

Best of luck and kindest regards also from my wife!

Yours very sincerely,

RICHARD STRAUSS

Rodaun, 12.5.(1929)

Dear Dr. Strauss,

I learnt only from your letter that this newspaper printed something about *Arabella*. I have no contact whatever with this particular paper (whose attitude towards me is anything but friendly), so that I would not even know how to stop anything there: I know nobody. If one wanted to find out from whom they got this (to me it is a mystery), C.C.[1] would be the man. You are perfectly right in everything you say.

Tomorrow I am leaving for a fortnight in Florence, and shall be there for about ten days (Hotel Porta Rossa).

Delighted to hear of your recovery.

Very sincerely,

HOFMANNSTHAL

Karlsbad, 15.6.1929

My dear Friend,

Have arrived here in good shape and am now really impatient for Act I. Couldn't the enclosed *feuilleton*[2] be turned into an entertaining satyr play to go with *Helena*? For Mme Massary? One act with three or four changes of scene? Small orchestra? Regina, an operetta star, into whose mouth a few amusing couplets could be put? What do you think of it?

Best regards, yours very sincerely,

RICHARD STRAUSS

Rodaun, 20 June 1929

Dear Dr. Strauss,

I believe there must be some invisible link between us. Exactly three days ago, that means before your letter reached me, I got out the file with the *Arabella* notes and after spending three mornings with them the characters have come thoroughly alive for me again. I hope I shall now be able to get the first act done.

I have once again and most seriously thought over your remarks and wishes. To establish Arabella as the central figure needs something more than focusing all the action and all the talk of the other characters on her—she herself must put herself across strongly in the chief scene of the act. I have thought long how to manage this. It must be one of the important scenes with a man in it, not with the elegiac Matteo with whom she has already finished, but with her latest, the object of her

[1] Camillo Castiglione.   [2] Enclosure not extant.

last flirtation before the right man turns up (Mandryka)—with one of the three Counts. For this purpose I am giving prominence to Elemer, while the other two remain as they are. This strong (lyrical) scene in Act I will help to lay the main emphasis on Elemer's leave-taking when it comes to the threefold parting in Act II, and as Elemer gains personality, so the whole scene will gain in meaning.

Taking all in all, you must not expect (and you have already accepted this) in the expositional act the accelerated tempo of the second or the concision and impact of the third, which I am almost inclined to consider the best I have ever done for the stage (in contrast to the weakish third act of *Rosenkavalier*). But I shall do my utmost to achieve greater consistency of mood (the earlier version offended against this principle) and to provide proper and effective exposition of characters and action, so as to engage the sympathies of the audience. From the very start of Act II, then, everything moves from surprise to surprise towards the final curtain. I am in any case much fitter now than I was two months ago.

All the best wishes,

HOFMANNSTHAL

P.S. That little thing is pretty as a story, but how could you make it plausible to an audience on the stage that a wife fails to recognize her former husband—or at least that he *thinks* she does not?

Karlsbad, 29.6.1929

My dear Friend,

Many thanks for your kind letter of the 20th. Your new intentions about Act I seem to me excellent. It is most important that Arabella should be put into rather more relief even in the first act. Couldn't the Count who in Act II flirts with the mother be brought into closer relations with Adelaide even in Act I—in such a way that he already fluctuates a little between mother and daughter, so that the relevant passage in Act II doesn't come too unexpectedly?—

I also think that the first few words exchanged between Arabella and Mandryka at the beginning of Act II must be changed. Arabella's question: 'What brings you here?' strikes me as somewhat naïve. Well, I'm full of anticipation! I shall be in Garmisch on 5th July. I've made quite a good recovery, but after the boundless boredom of all those cures I am charged with energy. I am returning *Der Rächer* to you: I believe a pretty little one-act conversation piece could be made of it. I don't share your doubts! We've seen more improbable things on the stage before! Just think of *Così fan tutte*!

With best regards, yours as ever,

RICHARD STRAUSS

Dear Dr. Strauss,   *Rodaun, 30.6.29*

Every morning I sit in my summer-house with my notes to recast the first act, and I am making progress, though slowly. For the past nine days we have had the kind of weather most unbearable to my constitution and above all to my imagination: low pressure, very humid thundery atmosphere, cool one minute and close the next. I have almost constantly a kind of migraine and a head as large as a barrel and filled, so it seems, with straw. During the better hours I can just manage to work out in my mind exactly what I want to do, but not to give the dialogue real life and existence; I cannot rise to that. One good week, or even only four days would be enough to write the whole thing straight down; as it is I must be patient and ask you to be the same. There would be no point in going to the Semmering, for up there the weather is no better, only colder, and it is the low pressure and excessively humid air which so gravely reduces my ability to think as well as my powers of imagination. I hope to have better news for you soon. My younger son has, thank heaven, safely returned *via* China and Singapore; in the autumn he will go to California again.

Very sincerely yours,

HOFMANNSTHAL

Dear Dr. Strauss,   *Rodaun, 2nd July 1929*

Our letters have crossed. The close, thundery, unsettling weather which interferes with my work continues (this hyper-sensitivity of mine to atmospheric conditions is not, by the way, an acquisition of oncoming age, but of old standing, inherited from my mother), but I am making progress nonetheless and all that is missing from the part to be rewritten (the new material will make up three quarters of the first act) is only one more scene.

531

My purpose in the revision has been twofold: (1) to place the character of Arabella more definitely in the centre, to throw her into every possible relief, but with soft, not harsh outlines; (2) to eliminate from the first version of the act that string of so many scenes of varying tempo, varying purpose and varying mood which proved unacceptable to the composer. I am now treating the scenes in such a way that from the outset everything is wholly centered on Arabella and her engagement (Fortune-teller and Adelaide, Matteo and Zdenka), then comes Arabella's entrance and two big scenes for her, one with her sister (referring to Matteo), the other with Elemer (to whom she is far more gracious than to Matteo and to whom she holds out the prospect of a decision on the night of the ball). These scenes dominated by Arabella fill two-thirds of the act. Then comes the scene between Adelaide and Waldner (distress of the family, Waldner's letters to old comrades), then Waldner (alone for a minute), Mandryka and Waldner, after that only one lightning scene between Zdenka and Matteo to create the necessary suspense over the letter for Act II.

First, therefore, Arabella dominates musically the whole mood of the act; then after a brief transition to Mandryka there follows his visit.

After much self-criticism, reflection and quiet thought, taking it all in all, the exposition of Mandryka as he pays his visit strikes me as attractive and original, and this whole character as so novel, so much of one piece and so complete that it can stand up to the best in *Rosenkavalier*, I mean the figure as a whole, from the first word to the last at the end of Act III: both a magnificent *part*, and yet a part for a *singer*.

One more word about the beginning of the Arabella-Mandryka scene in Act II, about the way Arabella opens the conversation with the words: '...What brings you here?'—You deprecate this turn of phrase as naïve. It would actually not be too difficult to substitute some other opening for this conversation, but I would like to defend the present one strongly to you. It is, as it stands, the result of much thought, i.e. of thinking with the figures and in their situation, and coming from Arabella, it is anything but naïve. Mandryka has for weeks been deeply in love with her picture; a meeting at the hotel has made a strong, a striking impression on her (Act I, new); her father, what is more, has naturally told her that this gentleman has arrived from the furthest corner of Slavonia expressly in order to marry her. Both are very nervous. (Beginning of the act, when Mandryka practically crushes Waldner's hand, and when Arabella for a moment is on the point of fainting with excitement.) Now they are face to face, alone. Arabella is in the stronger position, for she knows how he feels towards her— he has not the slightest notion how she will receive him and his suit. He stands before her, elegant, strong, heavy—and visibly ill at ease. She possesses the greater self-control, and since she is also the lady and there- fore the superior of the two, it is up to her to open the conversation. He has pleased her from the outset and so she is eager to hear him confess his love. But to begin, say, with the words: 'I am told you want to marry me!'—that would be most unladylike. Therefore, just because she knows perfectly well that he has come to Vienna and to the Ball for her sake alone, she asks this question, not naïvely, but most deliberately and a little *coquettishly*: 'And what brings you here?—for you don't look like a habitué of the ball-room, but rather like a solid country squire accustomed to solitude.' This question throws him into some slight confusion, but sets him going nonetheless. The poet (librettist) had to aim at bringing the two figures as rapidly as possible, and in a psychologically convincing, not operatically trivial manner, to the point where they express their love for each other, where they actually sing. I fancy I have succeeded in doing this naturally and attractively by mixing retarding phrases and motives ('delayers') with the desire of both to speak of love as soon as possible (that means to become lyrical), and I consider this passage of three and a half pages one of the best I have ever done as a librettist. But here as everywhere else I do not wish to persuade, but to convince you.

Very sincerely yours,

HOFMANNSTHAL

P.S. I am dropping the scene of the three Counts as cabbies. It does not yield a great deal, might be difficult, if not almost impossible to under- stand outside Vienna, and there is not space enough to give the three Counts individual character.

Garmisch, 6.7.1929

My dear Friend,

Back here since Friday, received your beautiful letter of the 2nd and agree with the general plan of Act I, as explained by you, with one exception: Arabella must at all costs conclude the first act with a longish aria, soliloquy, contemplation, if only for dramatic reasons:

> 1st curtain: Arabella
> 2nd curtain: Mandryka
> 3rd curtain: Arabella-Mandryka

Contents of the soliloquy something like this: she sits down to write a farewell letter to Matteo, interspersed with recollections of her scene with Elemer, of her first encounter with Mandryka—comparisons, vacillation, etc. This, I think, is enough material for such a soliloquy, always particularly effective in an opera because it gives the audience the necessary rest after pure dialogue scenes, the composer an important opportunity of spreading himself lyrically, and the singer a chance to *sing* by herself for a little while.

The Arabella curtain as it was before was also much too short and abrupt. In a three-act opera the first curtain, in particular, must be very effective.

I am therefore asking you urgently to arrange the whole act in such a manner that it moves with a compulsive inevitability towards this lyrical solo scene of Arabella (after the brief 'lightning' scene Zdenka-Matteo).

I hope the heavens will grant you the necessary weather! I am waiting impatiently. Best regards, yours,

RICHARD STRAUSS

Rodaun, 10.7.29

Dear Dr. Strauss,

Such a quiet, contemplative close had been my objective, but I was uncertain whether this would be what you want. Your letter, therefore, took a load off my mind.

I have done my best, especially in the scene between the two sisters, to provide transitions from the dialogue into the lyrical mood at several points—for Arabella alone, as well as for the two sisters together. What else I have tried to do I have told you in my last letter.

With best wishes your

HOFMANNSTHAL

534

Facsimile of Hofmannsthal's last letter to Strauss
dated 10th July 1929

(Telegram)[1]

First act excellent. Many thanks and congratulations. Sincerely

RICHARD STRAUSS

---

[1] This telegram was never opened by Hofmannsthal. It arrived at Rodaun on 15th July 1929, the day of the funeral of his son Franz. The poet died on the same day of a stroke.

APPENDIX

LETTER OF CONDOLENCE FROM RICHARD STRAUSS
TO FRAU VON HOFMANNSTHAL

Garmisch, 16.7.29

Dear Frau von Hofmannsthal,

After yesterday's terrible news of the death of your unfortunate son[1] now this frightful blow[2] to yourself, to your children, to me, and the entire world of art. I still cannot comprehend it or lend words to my grief. It is too terrible!

This genius, this great poet, this sensitive collaborator, this kind friend, this unique talent! No musician ever found such a helper and supporter.—No one will ever replace him for me or the world of music! Posterity will set up to him a monument that is worthy of him and which he has always possessed in my heart—ineffaceable gratitude in the heart of his truest friend will be the feeling that I shall preserve for him in admiration to the end of my days. The wonderful libretto which he sent me so shortly before his tragic end, and for which in my supreme happiness I was only able to thank him in a brief telegram, will remain a last glorious page in the work of this noble, pure, high-minded man. I am profoundly shocked, and moreover still indisposed, so that I cannot even see my unforgettable friend to his last rest. We have not even been able so far to learn the date and time of the interment. My son and Alice are hurrying to Vienna! If they manage to arrive in time they will represent my wife and me at the bier of him whom I shall never forget. Pauline joins me in conveying to you her sincerest participation in your grief! To you and the children all good wishes in profoundest sympathy,

Yours, most deeply moved,

RICHARD STRAUSS

---

[1] Franz von Hofmannsthal had put an end to his life on 13th July.

[2] Hugo von Hofmannsthal died at Rodaun on 15th July, immediately before setting out for his son's funeral.

MAIN GROUP OF LETTERS COVERING EACH OPERA

ELEKTRA
March 1906–August 1908 (pages 2–22)

DER ROSENKAVALIER
February 1909–September 1910 (pages 26–69)

ARIADNE AUF NAXOS I
March 1911–September 1912 (pages 75–139)

JOSEPHSLEGENDE
June–July 1912 (pages 134–141). September–December 1912 (pages 142–150).
July 1913 (page 173). September–October 1913 (pages 174–178)

DIE FRAU OHNE SCHATTEN
March–May 1911 (pages 76–86). September 1912 (pages 141–142). January–
March 1913 (pages 153–162). June 1913 (pages 166–172). December 1913 (pages
179–184). January 1914 (pages 187–189). April 1914 (pages 191–193). July 1914
(pages 200–210). October 1914 (pages 211–212). January 1915 (page 213).
March–September 1915 (pages 217–236). July–August 1916 (pages 254–261).
April 1922 (page 351)

ARIADNE AUF NAXOS II
December 1912 (page 152). January 1913 (pages 152–153). June 1913 (pages 169–
172). April–May 1916 (pages 241–250)

DER BÜRGER ALS EDELMANN
May–October 1917 (pages 266–295). December 1917 (pages 296–298)

DIE RUINEN VON ATHEN
April–May 1922 (pages 351–353). August–September 1922 (pages 355–360).
June–July 1924 (pages 384–389)

DIE ÄGYPTISCHE HELENA
September–December 1923 (pages 364–377). February–March 1924 (pages 381–
383). August 1924 (pages 389–391). November 1924 (pages 393–397). February
1925 (page 400). June–July 1925 (pages 404–407). December 1925 (page 410).
January–May 1926 (pages 412–417). August–September 1926 (pages 419–424).
May 1927 (pages 427–429). September 1927 (pages 439–441). December 1927
(pages 456–466). January 1928 (pages 466–469)

ARABELLA
October–December 1927 (pages 442–466). April 1928–July 1929 (pages 470–536)

THE JOINT WORKS OF RICHARD STRAUSS AND HUGO
VON HOFMANNSTHAL WITH ORIGINAL OPERATIC CASTS

ELEKTRA

Tragedy in one Act by Hugo von Hofmannsthal
Music by Richard Strauss, opus 58
Première: Königliches Opernhaus, Dresden, 25th January 1909
Conductor: Ernst von Schuch
Production: Georg Toller
Decor: Emil Rieck. Costumes: Leonhard Fanto

Clytemnestra	Ernestine Schumann-Heink
Electra	Annie Krull
Chrysothemis	Margarethe Siems
Aegisthus	Johannes Sembach
Orestes	Carl Perron
Guardian of Orestes	Julius Puttlitz
The Confidante	Gertrud Sachse
Train-Bearer	Elisabeth Boehm-van Eudert
A Young Servant	Fritz Soot
An Old Servant	Franz Nebuschka
The Overseer of the Serving Maids	Riza Eibenschütz
	Franciska Bender-Schäfer
	Magdalena Seebe
Five Serving Maids	Irma Tervani
	Anna Zoder
	Minnie Nast

DER ROSENKAVALIER

Comedy for Music in three Acts by Hugo von Hofmannsthal
Music by Richard Strauss, opus 59
Première: Königliches Opernhaus, Dresden, 26th January 1911
Conductor: Ernst von Schuch
Production: Georg Toller
Decor and Costumes: Alfred Roller

The Marschallin	Margarethe Siems
Baron Ochs von Lerchenau	Carl Perron
Octavian	Eva von der Osten
Faninal	Karl Scheidemantel
Sophie	Minnie Nast
Marianne Leitmetzerin, the Duenna	Riza Eibenschütz
Valzacchi	Hans Rüdiger
Annina	Erna Freund
The Marschallin's Major-Domo	Anton Erl
Faninal's Major-Domo	Fritz Soot
Notary Public	Ludwig Ermold
Inn-Keeper	Josef Pauli
Singer	Fritz Soot

ARIADNE AUF NAXOS

Opera in one Act by Hugo von Hofmannsthal
Music by Richard Strauss, opus 60
To be performed after Molière's *Bourgeois Gentilhomme*
Première: Königliches Hoftheater (Smaller House), Stuttgart,
25th October 1912
Conductor: Richard Strauss
Responsible for the Production: Max Reinhardt
Decor and Costumes: Ernst Stern

PLAY:		
	Jourdain	Victor Arnold
	His Wife	Rosa Bertens
	Dorimène	Else Heims
	Dorante	Alfred Abel
	Nicoline	Kamilla Eibenschütz
	Music Master	Jakob Tiedtke
	Composer	Josef Danegger
	Journeyman Tailor } *Scullion* }	Grete Wiesenthal

OPERA:		
	Ariadne	Mizzi Jeritza
	Bacchus	Hermann Jadlowker
	Naiad	M. Junker-Burchardt
	Dryad	Lilly Hoffman-Onegin
	Echo	Erna Ellmenreich
	Zerbinetta	Margarethe Siems
	Harlekin	Albin Swoboda
	Scaramuccio	Georg Meader
	Truffaldin	Reinhold Fritz
	Brighella	Franz Schwerdt

KANTATE

Poem by Hugo von Hofmannsthal
Music (for male choir) by Richard Strauss
(For Count Niklaus von Seebach on the occasion of his twentieth
anniversary as Director General of the Royal Saxon Court Theatres.)
Set to music 22nd February 1914

JOSEPHSLEGENDE

Scenario by Count Harry Kessler and Hugo von Hofmannsthal
Music by Richard Strauss, opus 63
Première: Opéra, Paris, 14th May 1914
Conductor: Richard Strauss
Mise-en-Scène: José-Maria Sert. Costumes: Léon Bakst
Choreography: Michel Fokine

Potiphar's Wife	Marie Kussnetzoff
Joseph	Léonide Massine

ARIADNE AUF NAXOS

Revised Version
Opera in one Act and Vorspiel, by Hugo von Hofmannsthal
Music by Richard Strauss, opus 60
Première: Operntheater, Vienna, 4th October 1916
Conductor: Franz Schalk
Production: Wilhelm von Wymetal

VORSPIEL:
Major-Domo	August Stoll
Music Master	Hans Duhan
Composer	Lotte Lehmann
Tenor	Béla von Környey
Zerbinetta	Selma Kurz
Primadonna	Maria Jeritza
Harlekin	Herr Neuber
Scaramuccio	Hermann Gallos
Truffaldin	Julius Betetto
Brighella	Herr Nemeth

OPERA:
Ariadne	Maria Jeritza
Bacchus	Béla von Környey
Naiad	Charlotte Dahmen
Dryad	Hermine Kittel
Echo	Carola Jovanovic
Zerbinetta	Selma Kurz
Harlekin	Hans Duhan
Scaramuccio	Hermann Gallos
Truffaldin	Julius Betetto
Brighella	Georg Maikl

DER BÜRGER ALS EDELMANN

Comedy with Dances, by Molière
Freely adapted for the Stage in three Acts
Music by Richard Strauss
Première: Deutsches Theater, Berlin, 9th April 1918
Conductor: Richard Strauss
Production: Max Reinhardt
Stage Sets: Ernst Stern

Jourdain	Max Pallenberg
Lucille	Helene Thimig
Cleonte	Wanka
Dorante	Riemann
Mascarille	Bergen
Dorimène	Else Heims
Nicole	Kupfer
Covielle	Hermann Thimig

DIE FRAU OHNE SCHATTEN

Opera in three Acts by Hugo von Hofmannsthal
Music by Richard Strauss, opus 65
Première: Operntheater, Vienna, 10th October 1919
Conductor: Franz Schalk
Production: Hans Breuer
Decor: Alfred Roller

The Emperor	Karl Aagard-Oestvig
The Empress	Maria Jeritza
The Nurse	Lucie Weidt
Messenger of the Spirit World	Josef von Manovarda
Apparition of the Young Man	Sybilla Blei
Voice of the Falcon	Felicie Mihacsek
Barak	Richard Mayr
His Wife	Lotte Lehmann
The One-Eyed	Viktor Madin
The One-Armed	Julius Betetto
The Hunchback	Anton Arnold

DIE RUINEN VON ATHEN

Festive Spectacle with Dances and Choruses
Music incorporating parts of the Ballet *Die Geschöpfe des Prometheus*
by Ludwig van Beethoven
Newly adapted by Hugo von Hofmannsthal and Richard Strauss
Première: Operntheater, Vienna, 20th September 1924
Conductor: Richard Strauss. Choreography: Heinrich Kröller
Production: Josef Turnau. Stage Set: Alfred Roller

The old Greek Woman	Carola Jovanovic
The elder Daughter	Luise Helletsgruber
The younger Daughter	Paula Hentke
The old Greek Man	Josef von Manowarda
The Stranger	Alfred Jerger
Pallas Athene	Käte Loitelsberger

THE ROSENKAVALIER FILM

Film Script by Hugo von Hofmannsthal
Music by Richard Strauss
Première: Opernhaus, Dresden, 10th January 1926
Conductor: Richard Strauss
Director: Robert Wiene
Sets and Costumes: Alfred Roller, Stefan Wessely, Hans Rouc
Photography: Hans Theyer, Hans Androschin, Ludwig Schaschek
Production Manager: Karl Ehrlich
Chief Organizer: Theodor Bachrich
A Robert Wiene Production by Pan-Film A.G., Vienna

542

The Field Marshal	Paul Hartmann
The Marschallin	Huguette Duflos
Octavian	Jaque Catelain
Baron Ochs von Lerchenau	Michael Bohnen
Faninal	Carl Forest
Sophie	Elly Felicie Berger

DIE ÄGYPTISCHE HELENA

Opera in two Acts by Hugo von Hofmannsthal
Music by Richard Strauss, opus 75
Première: Opernhaus, Dresden, 6th June 1928
Conductor: Fritz Busch
Production: Otto Erhardt
Artistic Adviser to Producer and Singers: Marie Gutheil-Schoder
Stage Sets: Leonhard Fanto

Helen	Elisabeth Rethberg
Menelaus	Kurt Taucher
Aethra	Maria Rajdl
Altair	Friedrich Plaschke
Da-ud	Guglielmo Fazzini
Hermione	Annaliese Petrich
The Sea-Shell	Helene Jung

ARABELLA

Lyrical Comedy in three Acts by Hugo von Hofmannsthal
Music by Richard Strauss, opus 79
Première: Opernhaus, Dresden, 1st July 1933
Conductor: Clemens Krauss
Production: Josef Gielen
Artistic Adviser to Producer and Singers: Eva Plaschke von der Osten
Decor: Leonhard Fanto and Johannes Rothenberger
Costumes: Leonhard Fanto

Count Waldner	Friedrich Plaschke
Adelaide	Camilla Kallab
Arabella	Viorica Ursuleac
Zdenka	Margit Bokor
Mandryka	Alfred Jerger
Matteo	Martin Kremer
Count Elemer	Karl Albrecht Streib
Count Dominik	Kurt Böhme
Count Lamoral	Arno Schellenberg
Fiaker Milli	Ellice Illiard
A Fortune Teller	Jessyka Koettrik
Welko	Robert Büssel
Djura	Rudolf Schmalnauer
Jankel	Horst Falke
A Waiter	Ludwig Eybisch

INDEX

engraver whose realistic work cast invaluable light on the manners of the seventeenth century, 101

Carmen (Bizet), 211, 461

Carmi, Maria, Italian stage and screen actress; trained with Reinhardt and appeared in his production of *The Miracle* and *Josephslegende* in London, 195, 200n.

Cassirer, Paul, Berlin art dealer and publisher, 319, 329

Cavalleria Rusticana (Mascagni), 402

Chaliapin, Feodor (1873–1938), Russian bass; sang in all the world's leading opera houses; considered the greatest interpreter of Boris Godunov, 455, 458, 459

Chamberlain, Houston Stewart (1855–1927), English writer who married Wagner's daughter Eva and lived at Bayreuth, 154

Chantavoine, Jean (1877–1952), French writer and critic; general secretary of the Paris Conservatoire from 1923; 343

Cherubini, Luigi (1760–1842), Italian composer who settled in Paris; his greatest works are probably *The Water Carrier (Les Deux Journées)* and *Medée*, 436, 511

Clemenza di Tito, La (Mozart), 354

Corinth, Lovis (1858–1925), painter; designed frontispiece and headpiece for *Elektra*, 319

Cortolezis, Fritz (1878–1934), German conductor; active at Munich, 1907–11, Karlsruhe, 1913–24, and Breslau, 1925–28; brought by Beecham to London for Strauss and Wagner performances, 1911; 71, 73

Così fan tutte (Mozart), 210, 261, 372, 453, 531

Dante Alighieri (1265–1321), Italian poet; episodes in his *Divina Commedia* have furnished libretti for a number of composers, 186

da Ponte, Lorenzo (1749–1838), Italian librettist, who provided Mozart with most of his libretti; also an operatic impresario and teacher in America from 1805; 15, 29, 155

Degenfeld, Countess Ottonie von, friend of Hofmannsthal, 101

Destinn, Emmy (1878–1930), Czech soprano, Kammersängerin; appeared in London and New York as well as all over Germany. First Berlin Diemut in

Feuersnot, and chosen by Strauss to sing title-role in the Berlin and Paris premières of *Salome*, 115, 117, 118

Diaghilev, Serge (1872–1929), Russian impresario; creator and director of the Ballet Russe, and of the Russian opera seasons in Paris and London before the first war, 122, 134, 136, 139, 140–1, 161, 164, 176, 177, 183–4, 185, 186, 189, 193, 350

Diebold, Bernhard (1886–1945), Swiss writer and theatre critic of *Frankfurter Zeitung*, 324n.

Dillmann, Alexander (1878–1951), German music critic centred on Munich, 160, 238

Domino Noir, Le (Auber), 262, 263

Don Giovanni (Mozart), 24, 321, 372

Don Pasquale (Donizetti), 359, 494

Donizetti, Gaetano (1797–1848), Italian composer, whose prodigious output included more than sixty operas of which the most famous are *Lucia di Lammermoor* and *Don Pasquale*, 495, 511

Droescher, Georg (1854–1944), actor, author and producer; stage director of the Berlin Opera, 1902–15; 315, 317, 319, 321, 325, 328

Duel, Le (Hérold), 82, 87

Duhan, Hans (b. 1890), Austrian baritone, Kammersänger; member of the Vienna Opera 1914–48; since then producer and teacher; created the role of the Music Master in the second version of *Ariadne auf Naxos*, 1916; 353, 365, 376, 385

Duse, Eleanora (1859–1924), Italian actress, generally considered one of the greatest of all time, 121

Eckermann, Johann Peter (1792–1854), German writer who assisted Goethe in the preparation of the final edition of his works, 404

Ecorcheville, Jules (1872–1915), French writer and musicologist, pupil of César Franck, 135

Eden, Irene, German coloratura soprano; member of the Mannheim Opera, 1916–24, Berlin, 1924–44, first as singer, then assistant producer; a famous Zerbinetta, 265

Eger, Paul (1882–1947), Austrian theatre manager; director Berlin State Theatre, 1926–33, Prague, 1933–38; Lucerne, 1942–47; 299, 300, 419

Erb, Karl (1877–1958), German tenor, Kammersänger; member of the

Stuttgart Opera, 1910–13, and Munich, 1913–25; husband of Maria Ivogün, 1921–31; 117, 186

Erhardt, Otto (b. 1888), German producer, active Stuttgart, 1920–27, Dresden, 1927–32, where he produced the première of *Ägyptische Helena*, 1928, Salzburg, Covent Garden, and since 1938 Buenos Aires; author of a Strauss biography (1950), 411, 450, 452, 453, 454, 469

Euryanthe (Weber), 453

Eysoldt, Gertrud (1870–1955), German actress at the Deutsches Theater, Berlin, 4

Falstaff (Verdi), 47, 401, 413, 424

Fanto, Leonhard, German scenic designer of the Dresden Opera during the Busch régime; painted several portraits of Strauss, 397, 427, 428, 443, 444–5, 469, 476

Farrar, Geraldine (b. 1882), American soprano; Berlin Opera, 1901–6, Metropolitan, New York, 1906–22; 27, 84, 85

Fassbender, Zdenka (1879–1954), Czech soprano, Kammersängerin; member of the Munich Opera 1906–19; sang Herodias, Electra, Marschallin, the Nurse (*Frau ohne Schatten*) in Munich; also heard as Electra in London; wife of the conductor Mottl, 59, 190

Faust (Gounod), 503

Fay, Maud (b. 1883), American soprano; member of the Munich Opera, 1906–17; sang Diemut in the Munich, Berlin and London premières of *Guntram*; and was also the first Munich Composer in *Ariadne*, 186

Ferrari, Gaudenzio (1484–1546), Italian painter, 163

Ferrero, Guglielmo (1871–1942), Italian historian, 354

Fidelio (Beethoven), 24, 260, 372

Fischer, Samuel (1859–1934), German publisher based on Berlin, 6–7, 9, 238–9, 399

Fledermaus, Die (J. Strauss), 454, 458, 493, 494, 503, 515

Flotow, Friedrich von (1812–83), German composer; his most famous opera is *Martha*, 243

Flying Dutchman, The (Wagner), 353

Fokine, Michel (1880–1942), Russian dancer and choreographer, 176, 177, 318, 321

Forest, Karl, actor, 298

Fra Diavolo (Auber), 100

Fragonard, Honoré (1732–1806), French painter, well represented in the Louvre, 134

Franckenstein, Clemens von (1875–1942), German composer and manager; director of the Munich Opera, 1912–18 and 1924–34; early friend of Hofmannsthal, 51, 142, 158, 159, 165, 175, 178, 183, 186, 187, 210, 211, 232–4, 247, 332, 342, 399, 432

Freischütz, Der (Weber), 74, 372, 507

Freksa, Friedrich (b. 1882), writer; married Margarete Beutler, 185

Fried, Oskar (1871–1941), German conductor and composer; for a time at the Deutsches Theater, Berlin; left Germany for Russia in 1934, 106, 110, 113, 325

Frischauer, Paul (b. 1898), Austrian critic active in Vienna, 195

Fuchs, Anton von (1849–1925), German bass-baritone, Kammersänger; member of the Munich Opera from 1873; later producer there, 74, 165, 166

Fürstner, Adolph (1833–1908), German publisher; founded firm in Berlin, 1868, then in 1872 acquired the catalogue of the Dresden firm of C. F. Meser which included several operas by Wagner; the first publisher of Richard Strauss, 22

Fürstner, Otto (b. 1886), son of above who succeeded to his father's business; forced to leave Germany in 1933, but eventually won back the German rights to the original editions of the firm, 32, 61, 70, 104, 118, 124, 127, 128, 131, 145, 153, 156, 159, 179, 215, 217, 238–9, 267, 273–4, 289, 290, 302, 320, 328, 329, 332, 355, 368, 370, 373, 386, 387, 389, 397, 417, 422, 440, 445, 447, 448, 449–52, 454, 458–9, 462, 471, 472, 474, 475, 479

Garden, Mary (b. 1877), Scottish soprano; the first Mélisande; member and later director of Chicago Opera; famous Salome, New York, 1909; 27, 84

Genée, Richard (1823–95), German composer and librettist; wrote libretti for Johann Strauss, Suppé and Millöcker, 458

Géraldy, Paul (b. 1885), French poet and playwright, 381

Gerhardt, Marie (b. 1890), Austrian soprano; member of the Vienna Opera 1923–38, a famous Zerbinetta, 520, 521

Gerhäuser, Emil (1868–1917), German tenor and producer; member of Munich

Kemp, Barbara (1886–1959), German soprano, Kammersängerin; member of the Berlin Opera, 1914–32; married (1923) to the composer Max von Schillings; first Berlin interpreter of Färbarin in *Die Frau ohne Schatten*, 328

Kern, Adele (b. 1907), Austrian soprano, Kammersängerin; member of the Vienna Opera, 1929–35, and of the Munich Opera, 1937–43; a famous Zerbinetta and Sophie, she sang the latter role in London 1933, 528

Kerr, Alfred (1867–1948), German writer and critic of *Berliner Tageblatt*; wrote libretto for Strauss's *Peregrinus Proteus*, 182, 342, 343

Kessler, Count Harry von (1868–1937), German diplomat and director of the Cranach-Presse, Weimar, 27, 134, 136, 139, 140, 141, 150, 170, 172, 173, 175, 177, 193, 194, 196–7, 198, 200, 217, 265, 350

Kittel, Hermine, Austrian soprano, Kammersängerin; member of the Vienna Opera, 1901–31, 480

Kiurina, Berta (1888–1933), Austrian soprano, Kammersängerin; member of the Vienna Opera, 1905–21 and 1926–27; sang Diemut in the 1922 revival of *Feuersnot* under the composer; wife of Hubert Leuer, 70, 322

Klatte, Wilhelm (1870–1930), German critic and writer; studied with Strauss and wrote several essays and monographs about him, 264

Knappertsbusch, Hans (b. 1888), German conductor; musical director, Munich Opera, 1922–36, Vienna Opera, 1936–50; one of the great Strauss and Wagner conductors of the day; conducted *Salome* at Covent Garden, 1937, 432, 508

Knüpfer, Paul (1866–1920), German bass, Kammersänger; member of Berlin Opera, 1898–1920; appeared at Covent Garden, 1904–14, and was the first London Baron Ochs, 265

Kokoschka, Oscar (b. 1886), Austrian painter and designer, 325–6, 327, 328

Korngold, Julius (1860–1945), Austrian critic; critic of *Neue Freie Presse*; lived in America from 1938 until his death, 315, 392, 416, 427

Korngold, Erich Wolfgang (1897–1957), Austrian composer, son of above; his most popular opera was *Die tote Stadt*, 226, 227, 317, 392, 456

Kralik, Heinrich (b. 1887), Viennese music critic; adviser to Austrian Radio, 473

Krauss, Clemens (1893–1954), Austrian conductor; director Frankfurt Opera, 1924–29, Vienna Opera, 1929–35, Munich Opera, 1937–42; a close friend of Strauss, and conducted premières of *Arabella* (1933), *Friedenstag* (1938), *Capriccio* for which he wrote the libretto (1942), and *Die Liebe der Danae* (1952); husband of the soprano Viorica Ursuleac, 399, 408, 414–15, 418–19, 429, 522

Krebs, Carl (1857–1937), music historian and critic, 157

Křenek, Ernst (b. 1900), Austrian composer; famous for his jazz opera *Jonny spielt auf*, 244, 511n.

Kroller, Heinrich (1880–1930), German dancer and choreographer; Ballet Master Munich Opera, and Vienna Opera, 1923–30; choreographer of Strauss's *Schlagobers*, 348n., 350, 353, 355, 358, 360, 386, 387, 392, 395

Krüger, Emmy (b. 1886), German soprano; first Octavian in Zürich; also sang in Munich and Vienna, 243

Kruszelnicka, Salomea (1875–1953), Polish soprano who made most of her career in Italy; first Italian Electra and a famous Salome, 29

Kufferath, Maurice (1852–1919), Belgian cellist and writer on music; for a period director of La Monnaie, Brussels; great propagandist for works of Wagner in Belgium, 190

Kurz, Selma (1875–1933), Austrian soprano, Kammersängerin; brought by Mahler to Vienna 1899, where she remained until 1927; first Zerbinetta of the second version of *Ariadne auf Naxos* (1916), 82, 83, 264, 297

Kussnetzoff, Marie (better known as Maria Kusnetzova) (b. 1880), Russian soprano, trained as a dancer, and so created Potiphar's Wife in *Josephslegende*, Paris, 1914; sang in opera London and Chicago, 195, 205

Laubenthal, Rudolf (b. 1890), German tenor; member of the Berlin Opera and also sang in London and New York; first Berlin and New York Menelas in *Ägyptische Helena*, 509

Lehár, Franz (1870 – 1948), Austrian operetta composer; famous for The

and librettist; some of his texts were set as operas sixty or seventy times, 383

Meyerbeer, Giacomo (1791–1864), German composer, whose operas enjoyed a great vogue last century; the most famous are probably *Les Huguenots* and *L'Africaine*, 243, 331

Mignon (Thomas), 211

Mikado, The (Sullivan), 68

Mildenburg, Anna: *see* Bahr-Mildenburg, Anna

Miller, Oskar von (1855–1934), German engineer; founder of the Deutsches Museum in Munich, 386, 387

Mona Lisa (Schillings), 234

Montenuovo, Alfred Prince von (1854–1927), for many years Lord Chamberlain of the Austrian Emperor, Franz Joseph, 52, 189

Mottl, Felix (1856–1911), Austrian conductor and composer; conductor of Munich Opera, 1903–11, director from 1907; appeared in London, New York, and Bayreuth; married the soprano Zdenka Fassbender, 71, 72–73

Mozart, Wolfgang Amadeus (1756–91), Austrian composer, 25, 88, 149, 243, 308, 331, 430, 497

Müller, Maria (1898–1958), Austrian soprano, Kammersängerin; member of the Berlin Opera, 1926–33; sang in London, New York, and Bayreuth, 509

Muzio, Claudia (1889–1936), Italian soprano; member of the New York Metropolitan 1916–22 and 1933–34; created Giorgetta in Puccini's *Il Tabarro*, and considered one of the greatest Violettas in *La Traviata*, 339

Nedbal, Oscar (1874–1930), Czech composer and conductor; for a period conductor of the Vienna Volksoper, 226

Nietzsche, Friedrich (1844–1900), German philosopher and poet; wrote much about Wagner, 179, 404

Nijinsky, Vaslav (1890–1950), Russian dancer; member of Diaghilev's Ballet Russe; considered by many the greatest male dancer of all time, 121, 134, 140, 141, 150, 151, 176, 350, 438

Novikoff, Laurent (1888–1956), Russian dancer, teacher and choreographer; member of Diaghilev's company; partner of Pavlova for many years, 347

Nozze de Figaro, Le (Mozart), 15, 25, 46, 76, 100, 152, 261, 372, 461

Oberon (Weber), 372

Oertel, Johannes, manager of the firm of Adolph Fürstner; later set up his own publishing house in Berlin, 159, 254, 298, 522

Oestvig, Karl Aagard (b. 1889), Norwegian tenor; member of the Vienna Opera 1919–26; created the role of the Emperor in *Die Frau ohne Schatten* (1919), and a famous interpreter of Bacchus in *Ariadne auf Naxos*; married the soprano Maria Rajdl, 265, 327, 353, 365

Offenbach, Jacques (1819–1880), German, later French composer of operas and operettas, most famous being *Les Contes d'Hoffmann* and *Orphée aux Enfers*, 68, 250, 251–2, 258

Olszewska, Maria (b. 1892), German mezzo-soprano, Kammersängerin; member of the Vienna Opera since 1923; a famous Octavian; sang regularly at Covent Garden between the wars, 487, 510

Orlik, Emil (1870–1932), painter and etcher, 267

Orphée aux Enfers (Offenbach), 250

Osten, Eva von der (1881–1936), German soprano, Kammersängerin; member of the Dresden Opera for many years; created Octavian in *Rosenkavalier* both in Dresden and London; married the baritone Friedrich Plaschke, 296

Paalen, Bella (b. 1881), Austrian contralto; member of the Vienna Opera, 1907–37; often sang Herodias in *Salome* in Vienna; now living in New York, 53

Pagliacci (Leoncavallo), 458

Palestrina (Pfitzner), 437

Palladio, Andrea (1518–80), Italian architect who greatly influenced Inigo Jones, 150

Pallenberg, Max (1877–1934), comic actor, worked originally with Reinhardt; married to Fritzi Massary, 287, 297, 298, 299, 300, 301, 304, 305, 354, 361, 369, 396

Pander, Oscar von (b. 1883), music critic of *Münchner Neueste Nachrichten*, 509

Parsifal (Wagner), 180, 197

Part du Diable, La (Auber), 262, 263

Pasetti, Leo (1882–1937), stage designer of the Munich Opera; married the soprano Elisabeth Ohms, 508

Patacky, Koloman von (b. 1896), Hungarian tenor; member of the Vienna Opera, 1926–38; 428

Pavlova, Anna (1885–1931), Russian

dancer: one-time member of Diaghilev's Ballet Russe, later managed and danced with her own company, 177

Perron, Karl (1858–1928), German bass, Kammersänger; member of the Dresden Opera for many years and the first Baron Ochs (1911), 71, 72, 107

Petzel-Perard, Luise, German soprano; member of the Munich Opera for many years; sang Chrysothemis in London, 1910; 178

Pfitzner, Hans (1869–1949), German composer and conductor; director of Strasbourg Opera, 1910–16; his most famous opera is *Palestrina*, 304, 341, 418, 436, 437, 441, 444, 507

Piccini, Niccolò (1728–1800), Italian composer whose works were staged in Paris at the same time as Gluck's and caused the famous Gluck-Piccini feud, 496

Pini-Corsi, Antonio (1859–1918), Italian bass-baritone, chosen by Verdi to create Ford in *Falstaff*; sang regularly in London and New York, 72

Placci, Carlo (b. 1861), Italian author and journalist, 75, 161, 163, 164

Pollak, Egon (1879–1933), Czech conductor; director Frankfurt Opera, 1912–17, Hamburg, 1917–32; also appeared in London and New York; conducted many Strauss performances; collapsed and died while conducting *Fidelio* in Prague, 1933; 355, 512

Puccini, Giacomo (1858–1924), Italian composer; renowned for his *Bohème*, *Tosca*, *Butterfly* and *Turandot*, 331, 365, 436, 437

Putlitz, Baron von, Intendant of the Stuttgart Opera at the time of the production of *Ariadne auf Naxos*, 117, 118, 134, 145, 146

Ramek, Rudolf (1881–1941), Austrian Federal Chancellor, 1924–26; 415

Raminger, Frau, secretary of the Vienna Opera, 392

Ravel, Maurice (1875–1937), French composer; his two operas are *L'Heure Espagnole* and *L'Enfant et les Sortilèges*, 343

Reichenberger, Hugo (1873–1935), conductor of the Vienna Opera, 1908–35; 188, 189, 337

Reinhardt, Edmund (d. 1929), brother of Max Reinhardt, 111, 112, 113, 266, 345, 347

Reinhardt, Max (1873–1943), theatre manager and producer, 25, 71, 72, 81, 82, 83, 85, 86, 89, 102, 103, 105–6, 108, 110–18, 123–4, 127, 128, 131, 133, 137, 145, 146, 156, 157, 168, 172, 176, 187–8, 211, 248, 252, 259, 269, 274–6, 281, 286, 287, 288, 290–1, 292, 294, 296, 300–1, 302, 304, 316, 320, 326, 327, 330, 331, 336, 341, 342, 344–7, 348–9, 351, 354, 355, 356–8, 399, 420, 450, 465, 481, 483, 505, 526

Rembrandt (van Rijn) (1606–69), Dutch artist, 6

Rethberg, Elisabeth (b. 1894), German soprano; member of the Dresden Opera, 1915–22, Metropolitan New York, 1922–42; created title-role in *Ägyptische Helena* (Dresden 1928); appeared frequently in London, sang the Marschallin at Covent Garden, 1936; 446–7, 448–9, 450–1, 452, 453, 457

Reucker, Alfred (1868–1958), German manager; director Zürich Stadttheater, 1901–21, and of the Dresden Opera, 1921–33; 439–40, 445, 446, 448–52, 457, 463

Rigoletto (Verdi), 87, 476

Ring des Nibelungen, Der (Wagner), 321, 423, 433, 472, 473, 522, 525

Ripon, Marchioness of (Lady de Grey), friend and patron of Diaghilev; her husband was one of the directors of Covent Garden Opera before the first war, and she exercised an enormous influence at the opera house, 176

Rohan, Prince Karl Anton von (b. 1898), Austrian writer; in 1922 founded Cultural League; editor of *Europäischer Revue*; librettist of Ravel's *L'Heure Espagnole*, 355

Rolland, Romain (1866–1944), French writer and musicologist, 265

Roller, Alfred (1864–1935), Austrian designer and artist; worked with Mahler in Vienna and was chief designer of the Opera there 1903–9 and 1918–35; designed scenery and costumes for the first *Rosenkavalier* (1911), and *Die Frau ohne Schatten* (1919), 24, 31, 40, 42, 53, 54, 59, 69, 70, 71, 75, 89, 124, 126, 173, 197, 221, 224, 240, 314, 315, 316, 318–22, 323, 325–9, 331, 335, 336, 349, 353, 354, 355, 357–8, 359, 360, 380, 386, 387, 392, 395, 443, 467–8, 469, 470, 486

Rösch, Friedrich (1862–1925), German composer; with Hans Sommer and Strauss organized the 'Genossenschaft deutscher Tonsetzer' (dissolved 1937), 368, 397, 409

Rosenauer, Michael, architect; designer of Strauss's Vienna house, Jacquingasse 10, 368, 369, 370, 372, 373, 383

Rossini, Giacomo (1792–1868), prolific Italian operatic composer, remembered for his *Il Barbiere di Siviglia*, *La Cenerentola* and other works, 424

Rubinstein, Ida (b. *c.* 1880), Russian dancer, choreographer, teacher, etc.; member of Diaghilev's Ballet Russe, formed her own company, 1928–35; 177, 189

Rückert, Friedrich (1788–1866), German poet and oriental scholar; many of his poems have been set to music by composers of lieder, including Strauss, 5–6, 85

Sachs, Hans (1494–1576), the shoemaker poet of Nuremberg, immortalized by Wagner in his opera *Die Meistersinger*, 430, 433

Sachse, Leopold (1890–1961), German producer; director of opera houses at Münster, Halle, and Hamburg, the latter 1922–23; left Germany 1933, and worked at Metropolitan, New York, 1935–43; 295, 355, 512

Salten, Felix (1869–1945), Austrian writer, 65, 67

Sanden, Aline (b. 1880), German soprano, Kammersängerin; member of the Leipzig and Munich Operas, 243

Sardou, Victorien (1831–1908), French playwright; his *Tosca* and *Fedora* were turned into operas, 7, 437, 449, 499

Schalk, Franz (1863–1931), Austrian conductor; conducted at the Vienna Opera from 1900; director from 1918, with Strauss as co-director 1919–24; sole director 1924–31; conducted first *Die Frau ohne Schatten*, 71, 72, 90, 120, 188, 189, 224, 245, 288, 289, 300, 311, 312–13, 314–16, 317, 318, 321, 323, 325, 327, 328, 344, 351, 355, 395, 398, 419, 463, 516, 519, 521–2

Schanzer, Ottone (b. 1877), writer and government official in Rome; translated *Elektra*, *Rosenkavalier*, *Ariadne auf Naxos* and *Ägyptische Helena* into Italian, 14, 61, 266, 340, 370, 372

Schenker-Angerer, Margit: see Angerer-Schenker, Margit

Schiller, Friedrich (1759–1805), German poet; many musicians have turned to his works for inspiration, 85, 366, 404, 449

Schillings, Max von (1868–1933), German composer and conductor; general music director Stuttgart, 1908–18, Berlin State Opera, 1919–25; married the soprano Barbara Kemp, 117, 118, 132, 144, 145, 234, 327, 328, 436

Schinkel, Karl Friedrich (1781–1841), German architect and painter; his designs for *Die Zauberflöte* are very famous, 321

Schmidt, Franz (1874–1939), Austrian composer; a pupil of Bruckner; director of the Vienna Academy of Music, 1925–27, and of the Hochschule für Musik, 1927–31; his most famous opera is *Notre Dame*, 193

Schmidt, Leopold (1860–1927), German writer and critic; critic of *Berliner Tageblatt* from 1897; wrote guides to Strauss's *Salome* and *Ariadne*, 135, 136, 137, 195

Schneiderhan, Franz, general director of the Austrian State Theatres, 419, 443, 445, 448, 449, 463, 468, 516, 522

Schnitzler, Arthur (1862–1931), Austrian novelist and playwright, 47, 158, 159, 160, 180, 181, 248, 298, 299, 482, 526

Schoder, Marie: see Gutheil-Schoder, Marie

Schöne, Lotte (b. 1898), Austrian soprano; member of the Vienna Opera, 1917–25, also Berlin, Salzburg and London; a famous Mozart singer, 365

Schopenhauer, Arthur (1788–1860), German 'pessimist' philosopher, 404

Schreker, Franz (1878–1934), Austrian composer, whose first of many operas, *Der ferne Klang* (1912), made a deep impression, 507

Schubert, Franz (1797–1828), Austrian composer, 463

Schubert, Richard, Austrian tenor; member of the Vienna Opera, 1920–29, but continued to make appearances there until 1937; 521, 522

Schuch, Ernst von (1846–1914), Austrian conductor; court conductor of the Dresden Opera from 1872, musical director there, 1882–1914; conducted first performances of *Feuersnot*, *Salome*, *Elektra* and *Der Rosenkavalier*, 71, 296

Schumann, Robert (1810–56), German composer; wrote one opera, *Genoveva*, 334, 351n.

Schwarz, Vera (b. 1889), German soprano; member of the Vienna Opera 1924–29;

sang Octavian at Salzburg; appeared at Glyndebourne, 1938; now teaches in New York, 519, 521, 527

Scribe, Eugène (1791–1861), French playwright and librettist, who provided countless libretti for Meyerbeer, Halévy and other composers, 29, 248, 361, 412, 499

Seebach, Count Nikolaus von (1854–1930), director of the Dresden Opera, 1894–1919; 10, 59, 60, 64, 66, 68, 78, 115, 190n., 212, 220, 449

Seipel, Ignaz (1876–1932), Austrian Federal Chancellor, 1922–24 and 1926–29; Minister of Foreign Affairs, 1930; 349, 369, 372

Serafin, Tullio (b. 1878), Italian conductor who has enjoyed a world-wide career; conducted many world premières and first Italian performances of works by foreign composers including *Rosenkavalier*, *Elektra*, and *Feuersnot* at La Scala; has recently returned to Covent Garden, 339

Shakespeare, William (1564–1616), English poet and playwright, 97, 499, 501

Shaw, George Bernard (1856–1950), Irish author and playwright, who, as Corno di Bassetto, and then under his own name, wrote musical criticism between 1890 and 1894; championed Strauss's *Elektra*, 460, 474

Siems, Margarethe (1879–1952), German soprano, Kammersängerin; member of the Dresden Opera 1908–22; created Chrysothemis, Marschallin and Zerbinetta; the first London Marschallin, 1913; 110, 296

Slevogt, Max (1868–1932), German painter and designer; notable for his lithographs and woodcuts, 319, 329

Sonnambula, La (Bellini), 82

Sonzogno, Milan music publishing house, founded in 1874 by Edoardo Sonzogno (1836–1920), who inherited a printing works and bookshop from his father; he inaugurated a series of international contests for new operas, in 1883; 32, 77

Specht, Richard (1870–1932), Austrian writer and critic; in 1909 founded *Der Merker*, which he edited until 1919; wrote a two-volume work on Strauss (1921), 417

Speidel, Albert von (1858–1912), director of Munich Opera 1905–12; 112, 113, 142

Stanislavsky, Konstantin (1863–1938), Russian actor, producer and teacher, 176

Steiner, Franz (b. 1880), Austrian singer; Strauss gave many song recitals with him, 280

Steiner, Herbert, publisher of Hofmannsthal's collected works, 338n.

Steinrück, Albert (1872–1929), actor, 165, 186

Stern, Ernst, stage designer of the Deutsches Theater, Berlin, 115, 116, 117, 119, 123–4, 125–6, 127, 128, 139, 298

Sternheim, Carl (1879–1938), dramatist and writer, 122, 125

Stransky, Joseph (1872–1936), Czech conductor who resigned from his position at the Hamburg Opera to devote himself to the concert hall; succeeded Mahler as conductor of New York Philharmonic, 1911; 351, 370

Strassmeyer, Leopold, Viennese comic actor, 298

Strauss, Alice (*née* von Grab), Richard Strauss's daughter-in-law, 399

Strauss, Franz ('Bubi') (b. 1897), Richard Strauss's son, 240, 255, 256, 259, 267, 272, 276, 281, 297, 300–1, 314, 383, 394, 396, 398, 399, 400, 403, 405, 408, 419, 525

Strauss, Josephine (*née* Pschorr) (1838–1900), Richard Strauss's mother, 56

Strauss, Richard (b. 1927), elder grandson of the composer, 454

Strauss, Johann (1825–99), Austrian composer of waltzes and operettas, 180

Strindberg, August (1849–1912), Swedish writer and dramatist, 143

Strnad, Oscar (d. 1935), Austrian architect and stage designer; responsible for the décor of *Ariadne auf Naxos* in Vienna (1916), 443, 463

Sylvester, Julius, Austro-German state notary; from November 1918 until March 1919, administered the public treasury in Vienna, 317

Tales of Hoffmann (Offenbach), 211

Tannhäuser (Wagner), 98, 433

Tauber, Richard (1892–1948), Austrian tenor, Kammersänger; member of the Dresden Opera, 1913–25, and of the Vienna Opera, 1926–38; sang in opera in London, 1938–39; 365

Taucher, Kurt (1885–1954), German tenor; member of the Dresden Opera 1928–34; first Menelaus in *Ägyptische Helena*, 446

Tetrazzini, Luisa (1871–1940), Italian